THE UNHEAVENLY CHORUS

THE
UNHEAVENLY CHORUS

Unequal Political Voice and the Broken Promise of American Democracy

KAY LEHMAN SCHLOZMAN
SIDNEY VERBA
HENRY E. BRADY

Princeton University Press
Princeton and Oxford

Published by Princeton University Press,
41 William Street, Princeton, New Jersey 08540
In the United Kingdom: Princeton University Press,
6 Oxford Street, Woodstock, Oxfordshire OX20 1TW
press.princeton.edu

Library of Congress Cataloging-in-Publication Data

Schlozman, Kay Lehman, 1946–
    The unheavenly chorus : unequal political voice and the broken promise of
American democracy / Kay Lehman Schlozman, Sidney Verba, Henry E. Brady.
      p.   cm.
    Includes index.
    ISBN 978-0-691-15484-8 (hardcover : alk. paper)
    1. Political participation—United States.   2. Equality—United States.
3. Pressure groups—United States.   4. Democracy—United States.   I. Verba,
Sidney.   II. Brady, Henry E.   III. Title.
JK1764.S365   2012
323′.0420973—dc23   2012001822

British Library Cataloging-in-Publication Data is available

This book has been composed in Minion Pro with Quadraat
display by Princeton Editorial Associates Inc., Scottsdale, Arizona

Printed on acid-free paper. ∞

Printed in the United States of America

10 9 8 7 6 5 4 3 2 1

To our many students, then and now—

with whom we feel a deep connection;

to whom we hope we have given a richer understanding

of democratic equality;

from whom we know we have learned.

The flaw in the pluralist heaven is that the heavenly chorus sings with a strong upper-class accent.

E. E. Schattschneider, *The Semisovereign People*

No government is legitimate if it does not show equal concern for the fate of those citizens over whom it claims dominion.

Ronald Dworkin, *Sovereign Virtue:*
The Theory and Practice of Equality

When you are in the legislature, it can be hard to distinguish the loud from the many.

Maggie Wood Hassan, former state senator, New Hampshire

If you're not at the table, you're on the menu.

Washington adage

"What are you complaining about? It's a level playing field."

CONTENTS

FIGURES

TABLES

PREFACE

Just as we were in the late stages of finishing a draft of the manuscript for this volume, the satirical newspaper, *The Onion*, announced that the American people had hired Jack Weldon, a heavy-hitting Washington lobbyist from Patton Boggs, to help to represent their concerns before Congress:

> Known among Beltway insiders for his ability to sway public policy on behalf of massive corporations such as Johnson & Johnson, Monsanto, and AT&T, Weldon, 53, is expected to use his vast network of political connections to give his new client a voice in the legislative process.
>
> Weldon is reportedly charging the American people $795 an hour.
>
> "Unlike R. J. Reynolds, Pfizer, or Bank of America, the U.S. populace lacks the access to public officials required to further its legislative goals," a statement from the nation read in part. "Jack Weldon gives us that access."
>
> "His daily presence in the Capitol will ensure the American people finally get a seat at the table," the statement continued. "And it will allow him to advance our message that everyone, including Americans, deserves to be represented in Washington." . . .
>
> The 310-million-member group said it will rely on Weldon's considerable clout to ensure its concerns are taken into account when Congress addresses issues such as education, immigration, national security, health care, transportation, the economy, affordable college tuition, infrastructure, jobs, equal rights, taxes, Social Security, the environment, housing, the national debt, agriculture, energy, alter-

native energy, nutrition, imports, exports, foreign relations, the arts, and crime.[1]

The deeply troubling issue underlying this humorous spoof—a concern about whether ordinary Americans have a voice in the politics of their democracy—is the same one that brought us to write this book. For some time, economists have been using systematic data to demonstrate convincingly the extent of the inequalities of income and wealth in the United States—most recently in an authoritative study by the nonpartisan Congressional Budget Office.[2] We have undertaken a parallel project for the political arena: to use systematic evidence of several kinds to measure and analyze inequalities of political voice or, to echo our title, to listen carefully to the chorus of American political activists to determine whether it sings with an upper-class accent.

In September 2011, some months after this unsettling satire appeared, we were putting the final touches on the manuscript when concern about inequality—which, despite increasing attention and debate among elites, had gained little political traction within the public—was suddenly dramatized by populist protest on the left. The unstructured and leaderless Occupy movement spread quickly from Wall Street not just to San Francisco and Seattle but to Omaha, Dallas, Miami, and Cheyenne. Although its objectives seem somewhat inchoate, a dominant theme in its anticorporate, egalitarian rhetoric is the gap between rich and poor. However, a subsidiary goal, achieving political voice for the politically silent, is expressed in hand-lettered signs with the following messages: "You have the right to remain silent, but I wouldn't recommend it." "I can't afford a lobbyist. I am in the 99%." "I am so angry, I made a sign." At this point, we cannot predict whether the Occupy protest will be sustained after the first blizzard of 2011, much less whether it will have a political impact. Still, like the Tea Party—in many respects its counterpart on the opposite side of the political spectrum—Occupy Wall Street demonstrates the frustrations of ordinary people who think that nobody in a position of power is listening.

---

1. *The Onion*, October 6, 2010. Reprinted with permission of THE ONION. Copyright © 2011, by ONION, INC. www.theonion.com.

2. Congress of the United States, Congressional Budget Office, "Trends in the Distribution of Household Income between 1979 and 2007" (October 2011), http://www.cbo.gov/ftpdocs/124xx/doc12485/10-25-HouseholdIncome.pdf (accessed November 9, 2011).

Why Another Book?

A decade and a half ago, the three of us published a hefty tome on the subject of inequalities in political activity.[3] *Voice and Equality* described the extent to which the preferences and interests of citizens are represented unequally through the political activity of individuals and analyzed the origins of participatory inequalities. The core of *Voice and Equality* was a series of statistical analyses explaining why some people get involved in politics and others remain quiescent. A subsidiary theme was to delineate the consequences of what we had found for political voice: that is, to explore the implications for the cacophony of political expression from citizens of the way that the process of political participation works and to assess the extent to which political input is representative of the citizenry as a whole.

Why, one might ask, have we now written another book on inequalities of political voice? In publishing *Voice and Equality*, we exhausted ourselves—and probably our readers—but not the subject, one we found endlessly fascinating and considered to be critical to democratic governance in the United States. We recognized that, while we had written a lot, we had not said our last word.

Jointly and severally, we continued to work on aspects of citizen participation, eventually deciding that *Voice and Equality* needed a sequel, one that would not be *V and E Redux* in either substance or form. We knew from the outset that we wanted to extend our earlier analysis of the problem of inequalities in political voice in several directions: to investigate inequalities of political voice that result not only from the participation of individuals but also from the multiple activities of the organizations that are involved in politics; to understand whether inequalities of political voice persist over time and, if so, to discover the origins of that persistence; to assess whether it is possible to break the pattern by which inequalities of political voice are associated with inequalities in education and income; and to investigate how the possibilities for political participation on the Internet fit into the picture.

Furthermore, the follow-up volume would be very different from *Voice and Equality* in terms of its sources. Rather than taking a single rich data set and analyzing it to a fare-thee-well, we would explore more widely in a variety topics and sources, drawing from existing literatures and data as well as archival materials. Moreover, we took an oath: "Read our lips. No new data."

---

3. Sidney Verba, Kay Lehman Schlozman, and Henry E. Brady, *Voice and Equality: Civic Voluntarism and American Politics* (Cambridge, MA: Harvard University Press, 1995).

However, our pledge to resist the opportunity to gather new data turned out to be—to paraphrase Calvin Trillin—about as realistic as asking the customs official to ignore the little plastic envelopes with white powder in them.

Readers of what is to come will recognize that we have sought to fulfill our original aims. Our explorations have ranged widely, delving into, among many other things, what state constitutions have to say about equality, what economists have to say about increasing concentration of income, and what reformers have to say about the possibilities for breaking the links between participation and socio-economic status. While none of our sources is as rich in coverage of matters relevant to the nature and origins of individual participation as our own 1990 Citizen Participation Study, whenever possible we have exploited surveys that contain information about citizens' political involvements. Nevertheless, we rapidly learned that our intellectual agenda would require—surprise!—the collection of new data. We could find no publicly available data that permitted investigation of how the possibilities for online political activity have altered the mix of voices in the political chorus. We were fortunate to have been able to work with Lee Rainie and Scott Keeter of the Pew Internet and American Life Project to design a survey to collect information about citizens' Internet use and their political activity both off and on the Internet.

Analyses of citizen political activity, including our own, have ordinarily focused on the unequal voice of individual citizens. However, political voice in the United States emanates not only from individuals but also from organized interests, many of which—for example, corporations, think tanks, and universities—do not have members in the usual sense. If we were to be able to say anything systematic about the consequences for the accent of collective political voice of political input from the organizations active in politics, we would have to start from scratch. Working incrementally as we uncovered various Web and library sources that would permit us to add information about the organizations active in Washington politics, the interests they represent, their histories, and the activities they undertake to influence public outcomes, we eventually constructed a database encompassing more than thirty-five thousand organizations.

As the possibilities for analysis of the data about organized interests in politics expanded, we toyed with the possibility of writing two books: one about individual participation that would extend the themes in our earlier book and a second about organizations in politics. The further we went, the more we recognized the convergence between what we were finding out about individuals and what we were finding about organizations, and the clearer it became that dealing with the topics together was a natural. So we compromised and wrote one book treating two subjects as part of a single story—a book that is probably as long as the two books together would have been.

By culling evidence from diverse sources rather than relying on a single survey, we may be sacrificing coherence, but we are, we hope, rectifying an earlier error. Decades ago, two of us were working on an article based on a Gallup survey from the 1930s. Ericka Verba—then a high school student deeply immersed in a U.S. history course, now a tenured professor herself—asked us a series of questions: Had we considered this? Were we including that? Not infrequently, we responded that we could not treat a particular pertinent matter because it had not been covered in the survey on which we were relying. Finally her puzzled expression vanished and she remarked, "Oh, I get it! This isn't an article about a subject. It's an article about a survey." We hope that this time we have written a book about a subject.

Description and Explanation

Voice and Equality contained both description and causal explanation based on the in-depth analysis of a single comprehensive survey. The heart of that work, however, was an analysis of the origins of political participation, the multiple factors that predispose some people to take part in politics and others to be less active. Some emphasis was placed on the depiction of the various forms of participation and their implications for representative political voice, but these were secondary themes.

In the chapters that follow, we reverse the relative weight of description and explanation. We engage in explanatory analysis when, for example, we delineate the alternate paths by which political participation is handed down from one generation to the next or the process of rational prospecting by which those who seek to mobilize others to become involved in politics find the targets of their requests for political action. Still, description of the shape of input to public officials from politically active citizens and organizations is front and center.

Description is not very fashionable in political science these days, but we make no apology for our emphasis on detailed systematic description that relies on large data sets and, sometimes, multivariate analysis.[4] There are two reasons for our emphasis on description. First, many important scientific

---

4. On the importance of description and the characteristics of useful description, see, among others: Gary King, Robert O. Keohane, and Sidney Verba, *Designing Social Inquiry:*

questions are, in fact, primarily descriptive ones, and good description is needed for good science. Second, considering such normative questions about democracy as "Who should be represented in a democracy?" or "Is equal expression of political voice among citizens necessary for democracy?" requires, first, that we ascertain the empirical answers to such questions as "Who is represented?" or "Who expresses political voice?" In terms of the metaphor of our title, we cannot characterize the chorus as "unheavenly" if we do not know whether it does, indeed, sing with an upper-class accent.

The case for in-depth description to hone questions about representation seems persuasive to us. The case for description as a scientific enterprise may appear more controversial. Yet consider the fact that all the following crucial scientific projects involve systematic description: observing the basic characteristics of all astronomical objects in the sky, identifying all the physical elements, mapping the human genome, cataloging the diversity of species, describing the characteristics of DNA, inventorying human languages, and undertaking a census or a survey of human populations. These examples leave no doubt about the importance of description for science.

Moreover, in some cases scientific description leads immediately to insights about causal structures and processes, as in Watson and Crick's famous aside in their paper on the double helix structure of DNA: "It has not escaped our notice that the specific pairing we have postulated immediately suggests a possible copying mechanism for the genetic material."[5] In other cases, centuries of description and discovery require substantial systematization before they can be useful, as in Mendeleev's nineteenth-century development of the periodic table of the elements. Once described, this table immediately suggested unknown properties of elements in the same columns of the table.[6] In still other cases, such as that of the Human Genome Project, description lays a foundation for systematic thinking about the topic by providing a set of useful concepts and a map of the relevant terrain.

In political science, path-breaking descriptive research has focused on inventorying the forms of democracy, characterizing the American ethos,

---

Scientific Inference in Qualitative Research (Princeton, NJ: Princeton University Press, 1994), chap. 2; David Collier, Jason Seawright, and Gerardo L. Munch, "The Quest for Standards," in *Rethinking Social Inquiry: Diverse Tools, Shared Standards,* ed. Henry E. Brady and David Collier (Lanham, MD: Rowman and Littlefield, 2004), pp. 21–50.

5. James D. Watson and Francis Crick, "Molecular Structure of Deoxyribose Nucleic Acid," *Nature* 171, no. 4356 (1953): 737.

6. Eric R. Scerri, *The Periodic Table: Its Story and Its Significance* (Oxford, England: Oxford University Press, 2007).

describing public opinion on tolerance and other issues, delving into the nature of belief systems in mass publics, describing the jobs of members of Congress, and many other topics.[7] These efforts reach beyond anecdote and narrative by invariably taking the following systematic scientific steps:

- Careful delineation of the universe of interest and the use of reproducible methods for sampling or inventorying it[8]

- Development of scientific categories and concepts and their measurement based on the best available scientific understanding[9]

- Use of these categories and concepts to provide a systematic picture of the phenomena under scrutiny[10]

We have taken these steps in this book. We describe with some care what we mean by *political voice*. We develop categories for individual political par-

---

7. In the examples cited here, we do not want to imply that these works were exclusively descriptive but rather that they had a substantial descriptive component. On inventorying the forms of democracy, see Arend Lijphart, *Patterns of Democracy: Government Forms and Performance in Thirty-six Countries* (New Haven, CT: Yale University Press, 1999). On characterizing the American ethos, see Herbert McClosky and John Zaller, *The American Ethos: Public Attitudes toward Capitalism and Democracy* (Cambridge, MA: Harvard University Press, 1984). On describing public opinion on tolerance and other issues, see Samuel Stouffer, *Communism, Conformity, and Civil Liberties* (New York: Doubleday, 1955); John L. Sullivan, James Piereson, and George E. Marcus, *Political Tolerance and American Democracy* (Chicago: University of Chicago Press, 1982); Herbert McClosky and Alida Brill, *Dimensions of Tolerance* (New York: Russell Sage Foundation, 1983); William Mayer, *The Changing American Mind: How and Why American Public Opinion Changed between 1960 and 1988* (Ann Arbor, MI: University of Michigan Press, 1992); Byron E. Shafer and William J. M. Claggett, *The Two Majorities: The Issue Context of Modern American Politics* (Baltimore: Johns Hopkins University Press, 1995). A vast literature on the topic of delving into the nature of belief systems in mass publics followed from Philip Converse, "The Nature of Belief Systems in Mass Publics," in *Ideology and Discontent*, ed. David Apter (New York: Free Press, 1964). On describing the jobs of members of Congress, see Richard Fenno, *Congressmen in Committees* (Boston: Little, Brown, 1973).

8. This step requires a definition of the "universe" of interest—for example, what is meant by a "democracy," a "celestial object," or "political voice." The two preeminent methods for sampling are random sampling and taking a census, but carefully defined purposive samples can also be useful.

9. In astronomy this step might involve the separate identification of planets, stars, and galaxies and other celestial objects. In political science, it might entail the description of democracies in terms of an "parliamentary-presidential" dimension and a "federal-unitary" dimension or the measurement of tolerance based on the civil liberties accorded one's least liked group.

10. By simply providing a systematic picture of belief systems among the American public, Philip Converse was able to transform our understanding of public opinion.

ticipation and lobbying and use these categories to produce a systematic picture of the expression of political voice. The result, we hope, is a synoptic view of who does and does not have voice in American politics.

A Brief Apology

Although this book moves in many directions, its diverse parts are connected by common themes. As we were editing, we recognized that often part of the context required for the introduction of new material is a point made previously—sometimes more than once. We considered making once and for all such critical points as these: that the single best predictor of making a political contribution is family income; that those who are well educated have multiple characteristics—for example, high levels of work-based civic skills and political interest—that predispose them to be politically active; and that the vast majority of organizations active on Washington politics are not membership associations of individuals. However, because we know from our own habits that many readers will read chapters selectively or assign individual chapters to students, we retained the repetition so that each of the chapters would function more easily on a stand-alone basis. To readers who stick with us from beginning to end—bless you!—our apologies for what we know to be a certain amount of repetition.

ACKNOWLEDGMENTS

All scholarly projects, especially ones as sprawling as this one, incur many debts. In our case, the number of our debts reflects the particular history of our inquiry. Because our project was less ambitious at the outset and grew organically to its present scope, we never applied for any outside funding and never ran a research shop. Instead, each time one of us had an idea for additional data collection or needed assistance with some project-related task, we would draw on resources from our universities to hire superb undergraduates and graduate students to help us out. We are grateful to our home institutions, Boston College, Harvard University, and the University of California, Berkeley, not only for having made research support available to us but, more importantly, for having provided such a hospitable environment in which to do our work as teachers and scholars. In its early phase, the project also benefited from institutional support provided by the Russell Sage Foundation to the Survey Research Center (now the Institute for the Study of Societal Issues) at Berkeley. We also thank Shirley Gee of Boston College, Lilia Halperin of Harvard University, and Lyn Civitello, Eva Seto, and Cathy Beemer at Berkeley for logistical support of many kinds. Robert Herbstzuber and Robert McColgin at Boston College and Roy Guyton at Harvard kept our machines running when Bill Gates threatened to make things difficult. With great skill and good cheer, Emily Ware at Harvard and Megan Landin at Berkeley assisted in myriad ways with manuscript preparation.

Working on this research with terrific students, who in many cases have taken on a role as extended family, has been a special pleasure. Without them, we would have been working on this project even longer, we would have made many more mistakes, and we would have had much less fun. It has been especially gratifying to work with a large number of undergraduates, all of whom have moved on to other things including, in several cases, graduate study in political science: Will Bacic, Patrick Behrer, Ageliki Christopher, Anthony Coppola, Spencer Cross, Lauren Daniel, Joshua Darr, Sarah Debbink, Lauren Escher, John Gattman, Gail Harmon, Caitlyn Jones, Lora Krsulich, Jeremy Landau, Kate Letourneau, Miriam Mansury, Timothy Mooney, Rafael Munoz, Taylor Norton, Janice Pardue, Michael Parker, Robert Porter, Nathaniel Probert, Veronica Roberts, Amanda Rothschild, James Sasso, Julia Schlozman, Ganesh Sitaraman, Dorothy Smith, Kathryn Smith, Emily Thorson, Clay Tousey, Jill Weidner, and Greta Weissner. We are also appreciative of research assistance from a number of graduate students who helped in many ways: Jeremy Bailey, John Barry, Shilo Brooks, Elizabeth Dionne, Glen Feder, Dan Geary, Heitor Gouvea, Randall Hendrickson, Courtney Kaminski, Katie Marcot, and Maria McCollester.

Lee Drutman, Sam Lampert, Karthick Ramakrishnan, and Martin Steinwand were all deeply involved in developing the Washington Representatives data; Janna King and Tony Hill worked on organizing and checking the data and otherwise helped in many ways; and Douglas Spencer worked tirelessly to recheck the data analysis and create an archive file so that future generations of graduate students could second-guess us. Laurel Elms and Samantha Luks, who are coauthors of sections of Chapters 6 and 9, produced the Roper data. Sounmen Hong and Daniel Nadler, who are coauthors of a section of Chapter 16, were responsible for the background digging and data analysis for the postscript to that chapter. Because we were often feeling our way, input from all of them was essential to shaping our project. We thank them for their labors, their brains, and their commitment.

Traci Burch, Nancy Burns, Jennifer Erkulwater, Philip Jones, and Shauna Shames, all of whom started working on this project as graduate students, some of them in the distant past, made contributions of such magnitude that they became coauthors. The presence of their names in the table of contents attests to the significance of those contributions and to our gratitude for their collaboration.

Lee Rainie and Scott Keeter of the Pew Internet and American Life Project responded to our suggestion that it would be useful to have survey data that would permit us to compare political activity on the Internet with its offline counterpart. We enjoyed our collaboration with them and with Aaron Smith and are very grateful for the Pew survey that allowed us to investigate the contours of participatory inequalities in the digital age.

Valerie Sheridan, the editor of the *Washington Representatives* directory at Columbia Books, was unfailingly helpful in answering our questions about how she assembles the directory that is the source of our organized-interest database.

Two of us were privileged to have been part of the American Political Science Association's Task Force on Inequality and American Democracy under the leadership of Lawrence Jacobs and Theda Skocpol. The exhilarating discussions at Task Force meetings pushed us to think more critically about the issues we examine here. Several members of the Task Force have subsequently published first-rate books about aspects of political and economic inequality. We hope that ours is worthy to stand beside them.

It is well known that "It is better to have your friends criticize you in draft than to have your enemies trash you in print." We were fortunate that the Mindich Foundation sponsored a one-day conference at Harvard at which we received comments on the draft manuscript from a remarkable group of scholars and friends (mostly both). We are grateful to Larry Bartels, Jeff Berry, Traci Burch, Andrea Campbell, Jennifer Erkulwater, Archon Fung, Bill Galston, Dave Hopkins, Vince Hutchings, Phil Jones, Ken Kersch, Jenny Mansbridge, Shep Melnick, Tom Sander, Danny Schlozman, Shauna Shames, Peter Skerry, and Graham Wilson, who read carefully and commented insightfully. We are equally appreciative of the thoughtful and thorough readings from Frank Baumgartner, Andrew McFarland, Dara Strolovitch, and John Tierney.

We are indebted to Chuck Myers and his team at Princeton University Press—Julia Livingston and Terri O'Prey, and Peter Strupp of Princeton Editorial Associates—for having been helpful in so many ways great and small as the manuscript made its way into print. We are especially grateful to Chuck—who gained our deep respect by actually reading *Voice and Equality* in order to make sure that we had something new to say—for becoming engaged with the substance of our argument in a way that we had never experienced with an academic editor.

We thank our family and friends—Cookie and the late Malcolm Kates, Peter Kates and Laura Linda McCann, Ed Blumenstock and Belle Huang, Nancy Adler and Arnie Milstein, and Frank and Prue Beidler—who, by providing the generous hospitality that facilitated a bicoastal research collaboration—made travel more fun.

As always, we owe a profound debt to Stanley, Cynthia, and Patricia—who have been with us for a total of 131 years—for being supportive and patient, for understanding what this work means to us, and, most importantly, for being our life-long partners.

As we were winding down, one of us came across a reference to the motto of the British Royal Society: *Nullius in Verba*. Not being well versed in Latin, another assumed the phrase meant "Don't believe what Verba says." A quick trip to the Web site of the Royal Society revealed that "The Royal Society's motto 'Nullius in verba' roughly translates as 'take nobody's word for it.' It is an expression of the determination of Fellows to withstand the domination of authority and to verify all statements by an appeal to facts determined by experiment."[1] We hope that we have been true to this aspiration.

KLS

SV

HEB

We have drawn in various places on the following previously published works:

Henry E. Brady, Kay Lehman Schlozman, and Sidney Verba, "Prospecting for Participants: Rational Expectations and the Recruitment of Political Activists," *American Political Science Review* 93 (1999): 153–168.

Kay Lehman Schlozman, Sidney Verba, and Henry E. Brady, "Civic Participation and the Equality Problem," in *Civic Engagement in American Democracy*, ed. Theda Skocpol and Morris Fiorina (Washington, DC: Brookings Institution, 1999), chap. 12.

Sidney Verba, Nancy Burns, and Kay Lehman Schlozman, "Unequal at the Starting Line: Creating Participatory Inequalities across Generations and among Groups," *American Sociologist* 34 (2003): 45–69. Used with kind permission from Springer Science+Business Media B.V.

Sidney Verba, "Would the Dream of Political Equality Turn out to Be a Nightmare?" *Perspectives on Politics* 1 (2003): 663–679.

Sidney Verba, Kay Lehman Schlozman, and Henry E. Brady, "Political Equality: What Do We Know about It?" in *Social Inequality*, ed. Kathryn Neckerman (New York: Russell Sage Foundation, 2004), chap. 16. © 2004 Russell Sage Foundation, 112 East 64th Street, New York, NY 10065. Reproduced with permission.

Sidney Verba, Kay Lehman Schlozman, and Nancy Burns, "Family Ties: Understanding the Intergenerational Transmission of Participation," in *The Social Logic of Politics*, ed. Alan Zuckerman (Philadelphia: Temple University Press, 2005).

1. http://royalsociety.org/about-us/history/ (accessed October 21, 2010). In the spirit of the Royal Society's advice that one should verify all statements, we have prepared a guide to the data we have used with directions as to how to obtain access to the data files used and code for the descriptions and analyses we present so that readers can replicate our analyses and move beyond them. See www.press.princeton.edu/unheavenlychorus.

Kay Lehman Schlozman and Traci Burch, "Political Voice in an Age of Inequality," in *America at Risk: Threats to Self-Government in an Age of Uncertainty*, ed. Robert Faulkner and Susan Shell (Ann Arbor: University of Michigan Press, 2009), chap. 7. Copyright © University of Michigan Press.

Kay Lehman Schlozman, "Who Sings in the Heavenly Chorus? The Shape of the Organized Interest System," in *The Oxford Handbook of American Political Parties and Interest Groups*, ed. L. Sandy Maisel and Jeffrey M. Berry (Oxford, England: Oxford University Press, 2010), chap. 22. Used by permission of Oxford University Press.

Kay Lehman Schlozman, "Political Participation," in *Encyclopedia of Political Science*, ed. George Thomas Kurian (Washington, DC: CQ Press, 2010). Copyright © CQ Press, a division of SAGE Publications Inc.

Kay Lehman Schlozman, "Creative Participation: Concluding Thoughts from the Land of the Boston Tea Party," in *Creative Participation: Responsibility-Taking in the Political World*, ed. Michele Micheletti and Andrew McFarland (Boulder, CO: Paradigm, 2010), chap. 10. Used courtesy of Paradigm Publishers.

Kay Lehman Schlozman, Sidney Verba, and Henry E. Brady, "Weapon of the Strong? Participatory Inequality and the Internet," *Perspectives on Politics* 8 (2010): 487–510.

Kay Lehman Schlozman, "Public Interest Groups," in *CQ Guide to Interest Groups and Lobbying in the United States*, ed. Burdett A. Loomis, Peter L. Francia, and Dara Z. Strolovitch (Washington, DC: CQ Press, 2011), chap. 19. Copyright © CQ Press, a division of SAGE Publications Inc.

Kay Lehman Schlozman, Sidney Verba, and Henry E. Brady, "Who Speaks: Citizen Political Voice on the Internet Commons," *Daedalus* 140 (2011): 121–139.

Kay Lehman Schlozman, "Counting the Voices in the Heavenly Chorus: Pressure Participants in Washington Politics," in *The Scale of Interest Organization in Democratic Politics: Data and Research Methods,* ed. Darren Halpin and Grant Jordan (Basingstoke, England: Palgrave, 2011). Reproduced with the permission of Palgrave Macmillan.

THE UNHEAVENLY CHORUS

1

Introduction:
Democracy and Political Voice

American politicians have long claimed to speak for those who have no voice. Sounding a theme with an enduring pedigree in American politics, Richard Nixon famously appealed to "the great silent majority of my fellow Americans"—whom he contrasted with the "vocal minority" protesting the war in Vietnam. More than a century before, Andrew Jackson had lamented a situation in which "the laws undertake to add . . . artificial distinctions, to grant titles, gratuities, and exclusive privileges, to make the rich richer and the potent more powerful" and justified his veto of Bank of the United States in the name of "the humble members of society—the farmers, mechanics, and laborers—who have neither the time nor the means of securing like favors to themselves." Similarly, William Jennings Bryan exalted "the farmer who goes forth in the morning and toils all day, begins in the spring and toils all summer, and the miners who go a thousand feet into the earth" and claimed that "We come to speak for this broader class." Later on, in a time of "grave emergency," candidate Franklin D. Roosevelt urged the nation not to neglect "the forgotten, the unorganized."[1]

1. The sources of the quoted material are as follows: Richard M. Nixon, "President Richard M. Nixon Rallies 'The Silent Majority' to support the War in Vietnam" (November 3, 1969), in *Lend Me Your Ears: Great Speeches in History*, selected and introduced by William Safire (New York: W. W. Norton, 1992), pp. 839, 838; Andrew Jackson, "Veto Message Regarding the Bank of the United States" (July 10, 1832), http://avalon.law.yale.edu/19th_century/ajveto01.asp (accessed March 6, 2011); William Jennings Bryan, "Democratic Candidate William Jennings Bryan Delivers His 'Cross of Gold' Speech" (July 9, 1896), in *Lend Me Your Ears*, selected by Safire, p. 769; Franklin D. Roosevelt, "The Forgotten Man" (April 7, 1932), http://newdeal.feri.org/speeches/1932c.htm (accessed March 6, 2011).

Who are the silent for whom the politicians claim to speak? Who are the articulate, even the clamorous, who speak for themselves? Is it a problem for American democracy that some have no voice and others speak loudly and clearly? And when the voices from citizens and organizations come together, does the "heavenly chorus," in E. E. Schattschneider's memorable phrase, sing "with a strong upper-class accent"?[2]

Political Voice in American Democracy

Among the requirements for a functioning democracy are mechanisms for the free expression of political voice so that members of the public can communicate information about their experiences, needs, and preferences and hold public officials accountable for their conduct in office. Citizens in American democracy who wish to have an impact on politics have a variety of options for exercising political voice by acting on their own, with others, or in formal organizations. Working individually or collectively, they can communicate their concerns and opinions to policy makers in order to have a direct effect on public policy, or they can attempt to affect policy indirectly by influencing electoral outcomes. They can donate their time or their money. They can use conventional techniques or protest tactics. They can work locally or nationally. They can even have political input as the unintended by-product when, for reasons entirely outside politics, they affiliate with an organization or institution that is politically active.

This book is concerned not simply with political voice but with equality of political voice in American democracy. While it matters for democracy that there be ample opportunities for the free expression of political voice and sufficiently high levels of participation across various political acts, the distribution of that participation across individuals and organizations is also significant. Citizens are not equally likely to undertake actions to let public officials know what they want or need, political activists are not representative of the citizenry at large, and a particularly acute form of participatory distortion results from the fact that those who are disadvantaged by low levels of income and education are less likely to participate in politics.

We examine inequalities of political voice—in the participation of Americans as individuals and in the activities of organizations that represent their

2. E. E. Schattschneider, *The Semisovereign People: A Realist's View of Democracy in America* (New York: Holt, Rinehart, and Winston, 1960), p. 35.

interests—from a variety of perspectives. Among other topics, we consider how active and inactive individuals differ in their educations and incomes, their ages, and their preferences, needs, and priorities for government action; how inequalities of political voice are passed along across generations and how they have changed in an era of increasing economic inequality; how the possibilities for amplifying political voice by devoting more time or money to politics alter our expectations about the convergence of parties and candidates at the median voter; how inequalities of political voice among individuals are reinforced by the multiple forms of political involvement by organizations active in Washington politics; how the processes of recruitment by which friends, workmates, neighbors, and fellow organization and church members who ask one another to take part politically affect the socioeconomic stratification of political voice; how the possibilities for political participation on the Internet affect the extent to which political voice underrepresents both younger citizens and those who are disadvantaged in terms of socio-economic status; and whether various procedural political reforms hold the potential to alleviate participatory inequalities. Although this book relies, in the main, on the analysis of relevant evidence about individuals and organized interests, we place the subject in the broader context of, on the one hand, the American political tradition and, on the other, the contemporary increase in economic inequality.

Equal Political Voice and Democratic Accountability

Why does political voice matter in a democracy? Whether the medium is the participation of individuals or the activity of organizations, political voice performs two democratic functions: communicating information and providing incentives to policy makers. That is, through political voice, citizens inform policy makers about their interests and preferences and place pressure on them to respond positively to what they have heard.

Political acts vary in their information-carrying capacity. The vote is a blunt instrument of communication, conveying a voter's decision to support a particular candidate but, in the absence of an exit poll or other type of election follow-up, nothing about why the choice was made. In contrast, a letter from an individual to a government official or a statement made at a community meeting can carry a lot of information, especially if it is trenchant and compelling. Similarly, communications from organizations—in such forms as advertisements, congressional testimony, research reports, or amicus briefs

—can convey detailed information. Organizations are particularly likely to be in a position to provide expert information that is useful in the formulation of policy.

Political acts also vary in the extent to which they give policy makers an incentive to heed the messages conveyed. When political input includes valued resources—whether votes, campaign contributions, campaign work, political intelligence, favors, or information germane to the making of policy—politicians may feel pressure not to ignore the accompanying messages. The member of Congress who is drafting a piece of legislation, the mayor who wants to pacify a restive group that has been staging regular protests, the state legislator who seeks votes and political support in anticipation of a run for governor, and the agency regulator who needs cooperation to ensure regulatory compliance all have incentives to pay attention to activist publics.

The Level and Distribution of Political Voice

Recent political science inquiries into political voice place the spotlight on the amount or level of citizen involvement. Has political participation been declining and, if so, why?[3] What are the implications for democratic governance of the erosion in political engagement? In the discussion of this important issue, what matters about the condition of civil life is the overall level of voluntary involvement rather than its uneven distribution across society. As we shall discuss from a number of perspectives in Chapter 4, the level of participation has consequences for democracy. Citizen voice emanating from a limited number of activists might lack the legitimacy of the activity of a larger group—as witnessed by the unacceptability of using surveys to gather Census data. Similarly, the significant educative and community-building functions of political activity can be achieved only if participation is sufficiently widespread.

Nevertheless, our concern is the equality of political voice rather than the amount of political voice. While it matters for democracy that there be ample

3. On the theme of changing levels of turnout and participation, see, among others, Ruy A. Teixeira, *The Disappearing American Voter* (Washington, DC: Brookings Institution, 1992); Steven J. Rosenstone and John Mark Hansen, *Mobilization, Participation, and Democracy in America* (New York: MacMillan, 1993); Robert D. Putnam, *Bowling Alone: The Collapse and Revival of American Community* (New York: Simon and Schuster, 2000); Martin P. Wattenberg, *Where Have All the Voters Gone?* (Cambridge, MA: Harvard University Press, 2002); and Stephen Macedo et al., *Democracy at Risk: How Political Choices Undermine Citizen Participation and What We Can Do about It* (Washington, DC: Brookings Institution, 2005).

opportunities for the free expression of political voice and sufficiently high levels of participation across various political acts, the distribution of that participation across individuals and groups is also significant. Equal political voice does not require universal or even a very high level of activity; it requires only representative activity. Just as a few thousand responding to a carefully selected random-sample survey can yield a fairly accurate snapshot of public attitudes, a relatively small but representative set of activists might satisfy the requisites for equal voice. Thus the conditions for political equality would be fulfilled if, across political issues, the total volume of activity were representative, containing proportionate input from those with politically relevant characteristics—which include such attributes as income, race or ethnicity, religion, gender, sexual orientation, age, veteran status, health, or immigrant status; attitudes on political matters ranging from school prayer to taxes to environmental preservation to U.S. policy in the Middle East; or such policy-relevant circumstances as reliance on government benefits or employment in an industry that is regulated by the government or a firm that has a government as a customer. However, the individuals and organizations that are active in American politics are anything but representative. In particular, those who are not affluent and well educated are less likely to take part politically and are even less likely to be represented by the activity of organized interests.

Equal Voice—Equal Consideration

One of the hallmarks of democracy is that the concerns and interests of each citizen be given equal consideration in the process of making decisions that are binding on a political community. Robert Dahl explains the case for political equality on the basis of "the moral judgment that all human beings are of equal intrinsic worth . . . and that the good or interests of each person must be given equal consideration. . . . [Furthermore, that] among adults no persons are so definitely better qualified than others to govern that they should be entrusted with complete and final authority over the government of the state."[4] Thus, our concern is with equality of voice, the input side, and not with equality of response, the output side. Equal voice does not imply equal responsiveness or equal outcomes. Because politics involves conflict among those with differing preferences and clashing interests, it is inevitable

---

4. Robert A. Dahl, *On Political Equality* (New Haven, CT: Yale University Press, 2006), p. 4.

that political outcomes will not leave all contenders equally satisfied. Yet it is possible for everyone to be heard and their views considered on an equal basis.

Nevertheless, as we shall demonstrate over and over in the pages that follow, the disparities in political voice across various segments of society are so substantial and so persistent as to preclude equal consideration. Public officials cannot consider voices they do not hear, and it is more difficult to pay attention to voices that speak softly. If some stakeholders express themselves weakly and others say nothing at all, there is little or nothing for policy makers to consider. As Lindblom and Woodhouse comment: "If poorer, less educated minorities participate less, their judgments about what problems deserve government's attention will attain less than proportionate weight in the process of partisan mutual adjustment."[5] Of course public officials have other mechanisms besides participatory input from individuals and organizations for learning what is on the minds of citizens. They can, for example, consult polls or follow the media. And the influences on policy include many additional factors—ranging from an incumbent's values and ideology to partisan pressures to a desire to take a political career up a notch—other than policy makers' perceptions of what the public wants and needs. Still, if votes, campaign contributions, e-mails, lobbying contacts, comments on proposed agency regulations, or amicus briefs come from an unrepresentative set of individuals and organizations, government policy is likely to reflect more fully the preferences and needs of the active part of the public.

Unequal Voice: A Persistent American Problem

Unequal political voice is a persistent feature of American politics. As an illustration, Figure 1.1 presents data from surveys in the United States across half a century. The surveys contain similar questions about a variety of modes of participation beyond voting. They make clear that socio-economic stratification of political activity has been present in American politics for a long time.[6] We can see that in each of the surveys, the average amount of political

---

5. Charles E. Lindblom and Edward J. Woodhouse, *The Policy Making Process*, 3rd ed. (Englewood Cliffs, NJ: Prentice Hall, 1993), p. 111.

6. The data are drawn from the following studies: 1959—Gabriel Almond and Sidney Verba, *The Civic Culture* (Princeton, NJ: Princeton University Press, 1963); 1967—Sidney Verba and

activity rises steeply across five quintiles of socio-economic status (SES).[7] Furthermore, the association between socio-economic status and political voice presumably dates back much further than the half century for which we have data.

We shall explore the theme of persistence from several perspectives in later chapters. Using panel data, we demonstrate that, even when characteristics associated with political participation are taken into account, individuals who are politically active at one time are more likely to take part politically in the future. Using cross-sectional surveys collected over several decades, we show the continuity over time of the characteristics of participant publics. And, using recall data, we establish that individuals are more likely to be politically active if their parents were, and we seek to explain why.

From the perspective of democratic equality, the finding that the same individuals are more likely, over time, to be politically active might not be cause for concern. We have argued that what matters is not that the expression of political voice be universal but that it be representative. When it comes to equal political voice, much more important than the tendency for the same individual citizens and organizations to be persistently active is the remarkable continuity in the *kinds* of individuals and organizations that express political voice. Across several decades, there has been a great deal of stability in the distribution of the kinds of individuals and organized interests

---

Norman H. Nie, *Participation in America* (New York: Harper and Row, 1972); 1990— Sidney Verba, Kay Lehman Schlozman, and Henry E. Brady, *Voice and Equality: Civic Voluntarism in American Politics* (Cambridge, MA: Harvard University Press, 1995); 2008—August Tracking 2008 Survey of the Pew Internet and American Life Project. The data for 1967, 1990, and 2008 are based on the same five measures of activity: working in a political campaign, contributing to a candidate or campaign, contacting a government official, belonging to a political organization, and working with others on a community issue. The data from 1960 are based on a somewhat different set of activities: acting to influence a local policy, acting to influence a national policy, taking part in a campaign, belonging to a party organization, and belonging to a nonpolitical organization that takes political stands. Because our purpose is to illustrate continuity of stratification, what counts is the similarity in the upward slope of the lines.

7. Our principal focus is on inequality of political voice on the basis of socio-economic status, a term we use interchangeably with *social class* and often identify by its abbreviation, SES. As a term in the social sciences, *social class* has accrued complex meanings, but it invariably refers to one's position in the social and economic hierarchy. The measure of socio-economic status used throughout our analyses is, in fact, quite straightforward: a combination of the respondent's level of educational attainment and family income. For details on the construction of our measure of SES and SES quintiles, see Chapter 5.

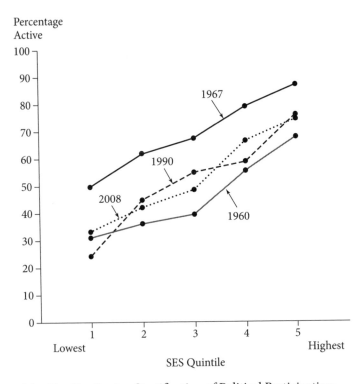

Figure 1.1 The Continuing Stratification of Political Participation: Political Activity by SES Quintile, 1960, 1967, 1990, 2008

Sources: 1960—Civic Culture Study; 1967—Political Participation in America; 1990—Citizen Participation Study; 2008—Pew Internet and American Life Survey.

Note: The figure shows for SES quintiles the percentage engaging in at least one political act other than voting. The data for 1967, 1990, and 2008 are based on the same five measures of activity: working in a political campaign, contributing to a candidate or campaign, contacting a government official, belonging to a political organization, and working with others on a community issue. The data for 1960 are based on a somewhat different set of activities, although ones that closely parallel those used in the other studies.

represented in politics. Such findings converge with the message conveyed by the data in Figure 1.1 with respect to the long-term structuring of political voice by socio-economic status and underscore that inequalities of political voice are deeply embedded in American politics. Although public issues and citizen concerns may come and go, the affluent and well educated are consistently overrepresented.

Individual and Collective Political Voice

Implicit in the concept of equal political voice is equality among individuals. In the vast political science literature concerned with public opinion and political participation, the individual is the main actor in the democratic system. However, while the voice of a single individual is usually fairly weak, when collectivities of individuals are coordinated within organizations, they can be a more potent force. Political voice in America is often the voice of organized interests. Organizations frequently speak loudly and clearly on political matters.

The political participation of members of the public and the activities of organized interests are often studied separately from one another with different frameworks and methods. When it comes to inequalities of political voice, however, they are two aspects of the same issue. Essential to our inquiry is that we construe political voice in terms of both the activity of individual citizens and the efforts of the thousands of organized interests. A large section of what is to come is dedicated to understanding the kinds of interests and concerns that achieve political voice through the varied forms of collective advocacy. We consider politically active organizations of many kinds: membership associations like unions, professional associations, and citizens groups that have individuals as members; trade associations that unite firms in an industry; state and local governments; and organizations like corporations, hospitals, and even universities—which, following Robert Salisbury, we designate as "institutions"—that have no members at all.[8]

In considering political voice through organizational activity, we ask the same questions about political organizations that we ask about individual citizens: What interests do they represent through what kinds of activity, and how equal or unequal is that representation? The results for organized interests parallel the findings for individuals and show the extent and durability of political inequality in America.

Who Is Speaking When an Organization Speaks?

When an individual speaks in politics, there is no ambiguity as to who is being represented by the message. The voice is that of the individual. When

---

8. Robert H. Salisbury, "Interest Representation: The Dominance of Institutions," *American Political Science Review* 78 (1984): 64–76. As a matter of fact, among political organizations, even membership associations are less likely to have individuals as members than to be made up of institutions.

organizations serve as the conduits for giving voice to citizen interests, however, complex questions of representation invariably arise. Robert Michels originally posed the issue of the ambiguity of organizational representation in membership groups in his discussion of the "Iron Law of Oligarchy."[9] Membership associations are assumed to communicate the interests of their members. But whose interests? Those of management? The board? The staff? The rank and file? And which ones among the rank and file? The old or the young? The most privileged or the least? This problem is even knottier for the vast majority of politically active organizations that are not membership associations composed of individuals. It is even more difficult to discern for whom an organization speaks when it is composed of institutions rather than individuals or when it has no members at all. Which of the various stakeholders are being represented when a corporation or a museum speaks in politics? In short, an organization may have a powerful voice in politics, but it may not be clear whose voice it is.

Defining Political Voice

We understand political voice as any activity undertaken by individuals and organizations "that has the intent or effect of influencing government action—either directly by affecting the making or implementation of public policy or indirectly by influencing the selection of people who make those policies."[10] Although this understanding encompasses many forms of activity in multiple venues, in recent years there has been considerable interest in an even more capacious understanding of what constitutes political participation.[11] In particular, arguments are made that two important forms of civic

9. Robert Michels, *Political Parties: A Sociological Study of the Oligarchical Tendencies of Modern Democracy*, trans. Eden and Cedar Paul (New York: Dover, 1959).

10. Verba, Schlozman, and Brady, *Voice and Equality*, p. 38.

11. For discussion of the limitations of conventional definitions of participation and references, see Pippa Norris, *Democratic Phoenix: Reinventing Political Activism* (Cambridge, MA: Cambridge University Press, 2002), pp. xii, 190 ff.; Dietlind Stolle and Marc Hooghe, "Review Article: Inaccurate, Exceptional, One-Sided or Irrelevant? The Debate about the Alleged Decline of Social Capital and Civic Engagement in Western Societies," *British Journal of Political Science* 35 (2004): 154; Cliff Zukin, Scott Keeter, Molly Andolina, Krista Jenkins, and Michael X. Delli Carpini, *A New Engagement? Political Participation, Civic Life, and the Changing American Citizen* (Oxford, England: Oxford University Press, 2006), pp. 5–10; and Lawrence R. Jacobs, Fay Lomax Cook, and Michael X. Delli Carpini, *Talking Together: Public Deliberation and Political Participation in America* (Chicago: University of Chicago Press, 2009), p. 153. For a different perspective, see Ben Berger, "Political Theory, Political Science,

involvement should be brought under the conceptual umbrella of our understanding of political participation. The first includes many ways of engaging in civic life that bypass the usual institutions of politics and government and seek the public good without appeal to government intervention. Scholars have introduced several terms—among them, "creative participation," "civic innovation," "postmodern participation," "lifestyle politics," "individualized collective action," and "DIY [do-it-yourself] engagement"—to capture these forms of involvement, to which we, for convenience's sake, shall refer as creative participation.[12] The other includes a variety of ways—called "discursive participation" in a recent study—in which citizens talk and deliberate about public life.[13]

Creative participation includes a somewhat idiosyncratic set of actions that seek social change without involving public authorities. Some prominent examples are anti-sweatshop campaigns, protests against the World Trade Organization, and the most common form of creative participation, political consumerism—buying, or refusing to buy, products with the objective of achieving a public good.

Although there is ample historical precedent—for example, the Boston Tea Party, nineteenth-century utopian communities, and the brief movement to get women out of their corsets and into bloomers—for efforts to seek public outcomes without appeal to government, significant recent economic, technological, and social developments would lead us to expect an upsurge of creative participation in recent years. For one thing, creative participation may be the only option when there is no governmental entity with the wherewithal or inclination to confront a particular problem. The proliferation of transnational economic and political institutions—in particular, multinational corporations and the World Trade Organization—imply that there may be no single governing authority with jurisdiction over a matter that activists seek to have addressed. In addition, technological developments make it fea-

---

and the End of Civic Engagement," *Perspectives on Politics* 7 (2009): 335–350. Berger argues that the term *civic engagement* has been stretched to accommodate "almost anything that citizens might happen to do together or alone" and argues that "politics loses all meaning if anything and everything can fall within its purview."

12. For examples and discussion of "creative participation," see Michele Micheletti and Andrew McFarland, eds., *Creative Participation: Responsibility-Taking in the Political World* (Boulder, CO: Paradigm, 2010), and Andrew S. McFarland, *Boycotts and Dixie Chicks: Creative Participation at Home and Abroad* (Boulder, CO: Paradigm, 2011).

13. See Jacobs, Cook, and Delli Carpini, *Talking Together*, pp. 23–24, 35–36.

sible to communicate with large numbers of people at great distance. Digital media can be used to assemble on short notice large groups of people who are connected by weak ties for some kind of goal-oriented action. Moreover, civic innovation articulates with the distinctive values and preferences of twenty- and thirty-somethings that would predispose them to postmodern modes of voluntarism. A number of observers have commented on the extent to which post-Boomer cohorts gravitate toward voluntary support of direct delivery of services rather than political activity in the name of policy change; prefer to eschew traditional political intermediaries, most notably parties and interest groups; and favor participatory forms that are anchored in non-hierarchical and informal networks and therefore permit greater spontaneity and individual autonomy.[14]

A second form of engagement that is sometimes classified along with political participation includes several forms of discussion about politics and public issues.[15] Such discussions can take place in person, on the phone, or over the Internet; they can be informal and spontaneous or can occur in structured meetings, often organized by a religious, social, civic, political, or government groups; they can involve exchange of views or self-conscious attempts to persuade.[16] Obviously, this is an important set of activities.

14. Variations on these themes can be found in many places. See, for example, W. Lance Bennett, "The UnCivic Culture: Communication, Identity, and the Rise of Lifestyle Politics," *PS: Political Science and Politics* 31 (1998): 745; Paul Kennedy, "Selling Virtue: Political and Economic Contradictions of Green/Ethical Marketing in the United Kingdom," in *Politics, Products, and Markets: Exploring Political Consumerism Past and Present,* ed. Michele Micheletti, Andreas Follesdal, and Dietlind Stolle (New Brunswick, NJ: Transaction, 2006), pp. 24–25; Stolle and Hooghe, "Review Article," p. 159; and Zukin et al., *A New Engagement?* chap. 4.

15. Although there is an extensive literature—much of it theoretical and philosophical—about deliberative democracy, investigations about how ordinary citizens engage in discussions about politics are less common. For a systematic survey-based study of political discussions, see Jacobs, Cook, and Delli Carpini, *Talking Together.* Other empirical studies of political discussion include William A. Gamson, *Talking Politics* (Cambridge, England: Cambridge University Press, 1992); Stephen E. Bennett, Bonnie Fisher, and David Resnick, "Political Conversations in the United States: Who Talks to Whom, Why and Why Not," *American Review of Politics* 16 (1995): 277–298; Verba, Schlozman, and Brady, *Voice and Equality,* pp. 362–364; Nina Eliasoph, *Avoiding Politics: How Americans Produce Apathy in Everyday Life* (Cambridge, England: Cambridge University Press, 1998); Stephen E. Bennett, Richard S. Flickinger, and Staci L. Rhine, "Political Talk over Here, over There, over Time," *British Journal of Political Science* 30 (2000): 99–119; Katherine Cramer Walsh, *Talking about Politics* (Chicago: University of Chicago Press, 2004); and Andrew J. Perrin, *Citizen Speak* (Chicago: University of Chicago Press, 2006).

16. We have adapted our understanding of the varieties of political discussion from the questions asked by Jacobs, Cook, and Delli Carpini in *Talking Together,* chap. 2.

According to a recent survey, 68 percent of respondents reported taking part in political conversations in person or on the phone, a figure that is comparable to the share indicating having gone to the polls.[17] Besides, political discussions may foster political interest or clarify thinking about political matters and thus facilitate future participatory acts.

In short, by focusing on actions directed at government, our definition of political voice excludes acts of creative participation, and in focusing on doing not talking, our definition excludes political discussion. However, we should make clear that the boundaries between these two important forms of engagement and our more conventional understanding of political participation are quite porous. Moreover, data presented in Chapter 5 show that these alternative forms of civic involvement are characterized by the same kind of social class stratification typical of acts falling under our definition of political voice.

Measuring Inequalities of Political Voice

The empirical analysis to come investigates inequalities of political voice from many angles. However, because there are so many avenues for the expression of political voice, there is no simple way to measure degrees of inequality with precision. The individual acts that convey political voice have no single metric of input, thus making it difficult to make comparisons across acts. These acts differ with regard to their capacity to convey information to policy makers and to exert pressure on them to respond to what they hear.[18] They also vary in the extent to which their volume can be multiplied. Political arrangements like the selection of the president by the Electoral College and political disputes over the drawing of electoral districts to gain partisan advantage or to ensure the election of candidates with particular racial characteristics to the contrary, among particular political acts, voting would seem to pose the fewest obstacles to measuring equal political voice. In contrast to votes, the quantity of other forms of political activity can be increased as the time and resources of the activist allow. Thus the measurement of political voice requires that we consider not just how many people are active and whether they are a representative set but also how much they do. These con-

---

17. Jacobs, Cook, and Delli Carpini, *Talking Together*, p. 37. For information on the national telephone survey that forms the basis of their analysis, see pp. 24–25.

18. On these distinctions among participatory acts, see Verba and Nie, *Participation in America*, chap. 3; and Verba, Schlozman, and Brady, *Voice and Equality*, pp. 44–46.

siderations loom especially large when it comes to political money: even in the extremely unlikely circumstance that all eligible voters made some kind of political contribution, the high variation in the size of the donations would preclude anything resembling political equality when it comes to the financing of campaigns and other political causes.

That the acts that carry political voice vary with respect to their volume and the form taken by their input means that it is difficult to sum across them to assess the relative weight of different bundles of activities. That is, how many hours of volunteering at the phone bank at campaign headquarters is the equivalent of a $5,000 check? How many e-mails from constituents equal a large protest? How can these participatory acts be added up to produce a number that can be compared across individuals? For these reasons, we shall consider particular political acts as well as composite indexes of participation.

The data in Figure 1.2 illustrate the implications for inequalities of political voice of the way that certain political acts can be expanded in volume. As in Figure 1.1, the respondents in the 1990 Citizen Participation Survey are divided into equal socio-economic quintiles. Figure 1.2 shows for each of three forms of political input—voting, giving time to politics, and making contributions to campaigns and other political causes—the proportion coming from the various quintiles. There is substantial variation in the concentration of activity across the three modes of political expression. Comparing the highest and lowest SES quintiles, the top quintile is responsible for 1.8 times the number of votes, more than 2.6 times the number of hours, and 76 times the number of dollars of the lowest quintile.

When we move from the political voice of individuals to that emanating from political organizations, we do not obviate any of these difficulties. Nevertheless, for all the limitations in our ability to measure political voice with precision, the differences we find across individuals, aggregations of individuals, and organizations are sufficiently striking that there can be no doubt about the existence and persistence of real inequalities of political voice in America.

Fostering Activity: The Origins of Political Voice

The political voice expressed by individuals, aggregates of individuals, and organizations reflects a variety of factors that operate to boost or depress political activity. Some of these factors—most importantly, the rights that inhere in citizenship—place most members of the political community on an

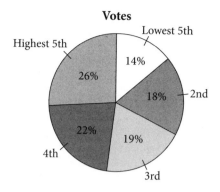

Votes

Lowest 5th 14%
2nd 18%
3rd 19%
4th 22%
Highest 5th 26%

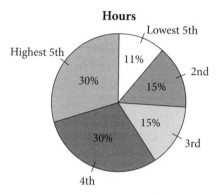

Hours

Lowest 5th 11%
2nd 15%
3rd 15%
4th 30%
Highest 5th 30%

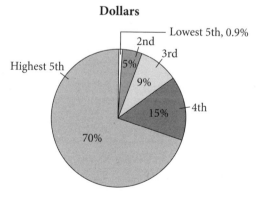

Dollars

Lowest 5th, 0.9%
2nd 5%
3rd 9%
4th 15%
Highest 5th 70%

Figure 1.2 Distribution of Political Inputs: Percentage of Activity from SES Quintiles, 1990

Source: Citizen Participation Study (1990).

Note: Inputs are percentage of votes, percentage of hours given to politics, and percentage of dollars given to politics.

equal footing. However, most of them—the motivation to take part and the resources so to do, as well as the connection to networks that foster activity— are unequally distributed and contribute to inequalities of political voice. The more unequal the distribution of the factors that foster participation across politically relevant groups, the more unequal is political voice.

The Basic Requisite: The Right to Participate

The clearest and most basic requisite for equal political voice is the right to express that voice. For most forms of political activity, the right to take part is very widely dispersed. As applied to the states through judicial interpretation of the Fourteenth Amendment, the basic participatory rights of the First Amendment—freedom of speech and press, the rights of assembly and petition—are generally available to all within the borders of the United States, regardless of citizenship status.[19] In fact, within limits, such rights may be available to noncitizens, even those who do not reside in the United States. The op-ed pages of major newspapers often feature opinion pieces by foreign commentators. Although their communications might not be heeded or even answered, non-Americans are free to get in touch with American public officials. Aware of the worldwide repercussions of American electoral outcomes, foreign visitors have been known to take part in presidential campaigns while visiting the United States. Nevertheless, although making campaign contributions has been interpreted as a form of protected speech by the Supreme Court, foreigners are not permitted to donate to federal campaigns.

The right to take part in particular ways is limited to some citizen members of the relevant political community. For example, residents of one town are not free to vote in the elections of an adjoining town. They may not even be free to attend town meetings in a neighboring community even though an issue on the agenda—say, a pending decision to close the bridge that spans the river—might have an impact on them. As is well known, important categories of citizens—including those without property, African Americans, and women—have been excluded from the franchise in the past.[20] In fact,

---

19. Illegal aliens have been deported when their illegal status was discovered through their political speech. In *Reno* v. *American-Arab Anti-Discrimination Committee*, 525 U.S. 471 (1999), the Supreme Court affirmed their right to speak out but did not overturn their deportation, arguing that they were deported for their illegal residential status, not for their speech.

20. Alexander Keyssar, *The Right to Vote: The Contested History of Democracy in the United States*, 2nd ed. (New York: Basic Books, 2009).

when Virginia Minor sued the Missouri voting registrar who denied her application to register under the Privileges and Immunities clause of the Fourteenth Amendment, the Supreme Court ruled unanimously in 1875 that, although Minor was a citizen, the franchise is not necessarily a right protected from state infringement.[21] Although racial, gender, and economic barriers to the vote have fallen after a long and bumpy journey, there are, even today, categories of citizens who are denied the vote. Children—whose First Amendment rights are also circumscribed—are the most obvious example of citizens who lack access to the ballot.[22] Another category is convicted felons.[23] All but two states have some restrictions on the voting rights of felons, and a number disenfranchise them even after they are no longer under the supervision of the criminal justice system. Nevertheless, for all the qualifications that are applied to the universality of the right to take part politically, political rights and liberties have the effect of acting as an equalizing force with respect to political voice.

The political rights of organizations are not as broad as the rights of individuals. Organizations have free speech rights for communicating on public issues, but such rights may be constricted when it comes to partisan participation in elections. Nonprofits with 501(c)3 tax status are restricted in the amount of lobbying they are permitted to undertake without losing the tax deductibility of donations made to them. As we discuss in Chapter 17, the right of corporations and other organizations to make campaign contributions is currently being contested in the courts, and the Supreme Court has ruled to permit greater freedom for such involvement.

The equal right to act does not inevitably lead to equal political voice. It functions as a form of political equality of opportunity, a necessary but not a sufficient condition for political action. We focus on the participatory inequalities flowing from disparities in the factors that shape the activity levels of rights-bearing individuals. Among the factors that foster political activity are the motivation to take part; resources that provide the capacity to act, such as knowledge and skills, money, and time; and location in the

---

21. *Minor v. Happersett*, 88 U.S. (21 Wall) 627 (1875).

22. On the First Amendment rights of minors, see, for example, John W. Johnson, *The Struggle for Student Rights* (Lawrence: University Press of Kansas, 1997), and Erwin Chemerinsky, "Students Do Leave Their First Amendment Rights at the Schoolhouse Gates: What's Left of Tinker?" *Drake Law Review* 48 (1999–2000): 527–546.

23. For a summary of state restrictions on felon voting, see Jeff Manza and Christopher Uggen, *Locked Out* (New York: Oxford University Press, 2006), p. 247.

social networks that serve to stimulate activity and to mediate requests for participation.[24]

Motivation

Not all who have the right to participate do so. Voting turnout among eligible voters is lower in the United States than in most democracies, and the proportion of the population that takes part in other ways—by working in campaigns, taking part in protests, and so forth—is much lower than the proportion that goes to the polls. Often the catalyst for the expression of political voice is the motivation to do so.[25] A series of psychological orientations to politics predispose some individuals to participate politically. Among them are an interest in political matters, a belief that they could make a difference politically, and a sense that it is a civic obligation to vote and to be otherwise actively engaged in the political process. When an intense concern about an issue is coupled to a perception that politics is connected to individuals' preferences and needs, citizen activity is more likely to ensue.

We ordinarily consider such motivations with respect to an individual's propensity to express political voice. However, they are also germane to organizations with potential interests in politics. Although studies of organized interests in politics tend to focus on organizations that are politically active and exclude organizations outside politics, there are many examples of organizations that self-consciously eschew political involvement even though they are well endowed with the necessary resources, only to decide later that the benefits from political activity outweigh the costs. Samuel Gompers's reluctance to bring organized labor into politics is a famous historical example. Less widely known is the process of learning by which many corporations have come to appreciate the remarkable return on investment that accrues to political activity.[26]

---

24. These are the factors specified in the Civic Voluntarism Model presented in Verba, Schlozman, and Brady, *Voice and Equality*.

25. Hahrie Han, in *Moved to Action: Motivation, Participation, and Inequality in American Politics* (Stanford, CA: Stanford University Press, 2009), makes the point that less is known about the way that motivations function in fostering participation and argues that deep issue commitments can overcome resource deficits in stimulating political activity among the resource disadvantaged.

26. For example, at one time high-tech firms such as Microsoft and Google had little involvement in political matters, but they now devote major resources to lobbying. On political learning by corporations, see Lee Drutman, "The Business of America Is Lobbying" (PhD Dissertation, University of California, Berkeley, 2010).

Resources: Knowledge and Skills,
Money, and Time

Motivation, especially strong motivation, fosters political activity, but those who command such resources as knowledge and skills, money, and time are much more likely to be able to act on that motivation.

Knowledge and Skills. Those who have a deep reservoir of knowledge and skills are less likely to feel daunted about taking part and more likely to be effective as participants. They are more likely to know how to participate—to be able to figure out, for example, the location of their polling place or who in town hall can help with a missed garbage pick-up or when the crucial zoning board meeting is to take place or how to contact their representative in Congress about a pressing matter. They are more likely to understand politics and public issues and thus to be able to connect their preferences to their participation—for example, to identify which candidates deserve their votes or campaign support or to find the political organization associated with a cherished cause. And they are more likely to be effective when they take part—to be able to organize a demonstration that attracts favorable media attention, to inspire campaign workers and deploy their talents efficiently, to make a compelling presentation or write a convincing letter, and, most importantly, to know when it is the right time to act.

Political skills and information are perhaps even more important for the effective expression of political voice by organized interests. Just as individuals communicate information about their preferences or their needs and circumstances, so do organizations. In particular, they can use their resources to convey information from policy experts, information that is often highly valued by policy makers. As we shall show when we turn to the role of interest organizations in the communication of political voice, lobbyists use information and political expertise to gain access to policy makers and to influence their decisions. The effectiveness of organized interests depends on many factors, among them the number and quality of their lobbyists.

Money. Mark Hanna is said to have remarked more than a century ago: "There are two things that are important in politics. The first is money, and I can't remember the second." We might not go quite as far as did Hanna—many factors do matter in politics—but money certainly deserves a place of honor among the factors that facilitate political activity. While individuals use money to make contributions to electoral campaigns and to political organizations and causes, organizations use financial resources for many political purposes—for example, to staff an office, hire lobbyists and other experts, make donations to political action committees, or engage in independent spending in elections.

We have already seen in Figure 1.2 the way that forms of input based on dollars amplify the possibilities for inequality of political voice. As a medium of participatory input, money has some special characteristics. In contrast to time, there is no ceiling on income and wealth, and individuals are much more unequal when it comes to money than when it comes to time. Comparing the best and worst off with respect to extra dollars and extra hours, the most affluent person is relatively much better off than the most leisured one. Although there are obvious limits on the amount of time that an individual can devote to political activity, bank accounts have no such upper bound. Besides, money not used today can be banked for later use. Time cannot.

Individual activity in making financial donations is, not unexpectedly, highly stratified, with a substantial gap between the affluent and the less well off. In fact, while a number of factors, ranging from civic skills to interest in politics, are associated with such participatory acts as working in a campaign, attending a local community meeting, or contacting a public official, only one factor, family income, strongly predicts the size of the contributions made to political campaigns and causes. Money is an even more critical resource for organized interests. Because they can convert cash into staff and expert assistance, organizations are able to use their financial resources to expand political activity, with the consequence that organizations vary even more than individuals in the volume of their political activity.

For several reasons, including the strength of First Amendment protections, the United States tends to allow more freedom in using market resources to influence political outcomes than do other countries. Because financial resources are so unevenly distributed and because differences in income hew to the fault lines of important political conflicts, political money raises the dilemma of how to reconcile inequalities of market resources with the desire to establish a level playing field for democracy. Thus money is unusual among political resources as the one for which free use is regulated. We are not limited in using our spare time to work as many hours in a campaign or to attend as many protests as we like. We are not restricted in exploiting a talent with words as we dispatch zinger e-mails to public officials. However, as we shall discuss at several points in the coming chapters, in politics we are not free to spend as much as we wish in whatever ways we wish. Some of the restrictions on how money is used in politics—for example, the proscription on bribing voters or public officials—are not controversial. Others—in particular, limitations on campaign contributions—have been attacked as unconstitutional infringements on free speech.

Time. In contrast to money, time is the political resource on which there is an upper bound. Because no one has more than twenty-four hours in a day, we are much less unequal with respect to leisure time than with respect to money. Besides, compared to inequalities in income, inequalities in spare time are much less likely to adhere to the boundaries of politically relevant categories—not only socio-economic status but also race, ethnicity, and gender. Instead, the availability of extra time is structured by such life circumstances as paid work and the presence of children, especially young ones, in the household.[27] What is more, the likelihood of taking part politically is not affected by the amount of available spare time.[28] Thus it seems that "If you want something done in politics, ask a busy person. If you want a political contribution, don't ask a poor one."

Location in Social Networks

Location in supportive social networks is yet another factor that can function to catalyze political participation. Whether groups of family and friends or networks located in such nonpolitical settings as schools, workplaces, voluntary associations, or religious institutions, the social networks in which individuals are embedded foster or inhibit political activity. In such settings people are exposed to informal conversations about politics, to information about political issues and developments and opportunities for political involvement, and to requests—from other individuals or from the institution itself—to take part politically. As we shall see, extensive and supportive networks accentuate socio-economic inequalities in participation. These inequalities are further amplified by the differential extent to which various categories of individuals are represented by organized interests.

The Pervasive and Durable Role of Socio-economic Status

The factors that foster political participation are not independent of one another. Those who have the skills and information to take part are more likely to want to do so. Reciprocally, those with a concern about politics are

27. See Nancy Burns, Kay Lehman Schlozman, and Sidney Verba, *The Private Roots of Public Action* (Cambridge, MA: Harvard University Press, 2001), pp. 184–185.

28. Verba, Schlozman, and Brady, *Voice and Equality*, chap. 12. However, the availability of leisure time is related to *how much time* is given to politics among those who are active.

predisposed to make efforts to learn the relevant skills of influence. Similarly, as we shall see in Chapter 15, those who are embedded in social networks are more likely to be asked to take political action and to get involved politically. Moreover, those who have the capacity to participate effectively—those who are able to write a big check to a campaign or to make a coherent statement at a school board meeting—are more likely to be the targets of such requests. Thus the processes that foster political voice also create unequal political voice.

At the root of these self-reinforcing processes is socio-economic status. Those who are well educated are likely to have a stockpile of a variety of other participatory factors: for example, to have the kinds of jobs that inculcate civic skills and generate high incomes; to be politically interested, knowledgeable, and efficacious; and to be connected to the networks through which requests for political activity are mediated. When we embarked on this project, we did not anticipate the extent to which we would uncover, under every intellectual rock we excavated, the deeply embedded and durable character of socio-economic inequalities in political voice. Inequalities of political voice are found in every cross-sectional analysis, and they are linked to such politically relevant circumstances as living in dilapidated housing, being without health insurance, needing Pell Grants, and suffering such problems of basic human need as having to cut back spending on groceries. They persist over time and are passed on across generations. The same biases pertain to political voice expressed through organized interests—a fact that, over time, has consistently led to overrepresentation of the concerns and needs of business and other resource-endowed publics. In short, however we look at the issue and however we analyze our wide-ranging data, SES always seems to return to the center of our understanding. Inside this fox of a big book with its many parts beats the heart of a hedgehog.

Breaking the Persistence of Political Inequality

The pervasiveness of inequalities of political voice leads us to investigate the possibilities for ameliorating the political underrepresentation of the young and the disadvantaged. What, if anything, might be done? We approach this question from three different perspectives. We consider first the possibility of reducing inequality through political mobilization. The history of social movements provides vivid examples—the labor movement and the civil rights movement come to mind—in which disadvantaged groups overcame the participatory hurdle rooted in social and economic structures and were brought into politics as effective voices for political and social change. We look next at the new and constantly expanding possibilities for political participation on the Internet. Does the Internet bring into politics not just new people but new kinds of people—in particular, younger people and those from lower on the SES hierarchy—thus equalizing political voice? Finally, we review a variety of procedural changes and public policies that might equalize activity. To give away our conclusion prematurely, those expecting a silver bullet are likely to be disappointed.

Other Bases of the Inequality of Political Voice

Our analysis of data about individuals emphasizes socio-economic status—and, to a lesser extent, age—at the expense of other major distinctions that are fundamental to politics: not only demographic characteristics like race or ethnicity, gender, and religion but also ideology and party.[29] Still, our concern with inequalities of political voice extends to any politically relevant attribute—that is, to any characteristic that might become a source of conflict in politics.

One explanation for the limitation of focus in this context is simply that we could not cover everything in a project of already substantial scope. A more substantive justification for our emphasis on SES is that it is not only a significant distinction for politics but also, as we have just seen, an important causal factor in the explanation of individual differences in political activity. Income and education are strongly associated with political participation.

In a multivariate analysis, disparities in participation among non-Latino whites, African Americans, and Latinos or between men and women can be largely or fully understood in terms of differences in characteristics that have

29. We have dealt with participatory stratification based on race and gender in other writings. On race, ethnicity, and political activity, see Sidney Verba, Kay Lehman Schlozman, Henry Brady, and Norman H. Nie, "Race, Ethnicity, and Political Resources: Participation in the United States," *British Journal of Political Science* 23 (1993): 453–497, and "Race, Ethnicity and Participation," in *Counting by Race*, ed. Paul E. Peterson (Princeton, NJ: Princeton University Press, 1995). On gender, see Burns, Schlozman, and Verba, *Private Roots of Public Action*, as well as Kay Lehman Schlozman, Nancy Burns, and Sidney Verba, "Gender and the Pathways to Participation: The Role of Resources," *Journal of Politics* 56 (1994): 963–990; Kay Lehman Schlozman, Nancy Burns, Sidney Verba, and Jesse Donahue, "Gender and Citizen Activity: Is There a Different Voice?" *American Journal of Political Science* 39 (1995), 267–293; Sidney Verba, Nancy Burns, and Kay Lehman Schlozman, "Knowing and Caring about Politics: Gender and Political Engagement," *Journal of Politics* 59 (1997): 1051–1072; Nancy Burns, Kay Lehman Schlozman, and Sidney Verba, "The Public Consequences of Private Inequality: Family Life and Citizen Participation," *American Political Science Review* 91 (1997), 373–389; and Kay Lehman Schlozman, Nancy Burns, and Sidney Verba, "What Happened at Work Today? A Multi-Stage Model of Gender, Employment, and Political Participation," *Journal of Politics* 61 (1999): 29–54.

their roots in socio-economic status. That socio-economic status is behind the attributes that explain racial or ethnic and gender differences in political participation does not, however, justify the conclusion that these differences are all about SES and that race—or ethnicity or gender—is irrelevant. Just because we can use SES to explain disparities in political voice between groups differentiated on the basis of such characteristics as race, ethnicity, or gender does not reduce the substantive political significance of these characteristics. As long as there are politically relevant issues associated with policies that have a differential impact on men and women or on Latinos, African Americans, and non-Latino whites, it matters for politics that public officials hear disproportionately from members of some groups. More generally, inequalities of political voice among persons with politically relevant characteristics are consequential even if those characteristics are not themselves causally related to the group differences in political participation.

Furthermore, it is not exactly a coincidence that persons of color and women command fewer of the SES-based resources for political activity than do non-Latino whites or men. Indeed, these gaps in socio-economic status are intimately connected to the structures that sustain social and economic distinctions on the basis of race or ethnicity and gender in America. For these reasons, even though they are not central to our SES-based analysis of inequalities of political voice, it is essential not to dismiss inequalities of political voice rooted in other bases of political conflict.

A Note on Data

To pursue these multiple themes we draw on evidence from a number of sources ranging from the U.S. Census to the constitutions of the states. However, we rely principally on data from four sources:

- The Citizen Participation Study. Although the data from this 1990 survey are now two decades old, this survey contains the most comprehensive set of measures of individual participatory acts, the factors that facilitate participation, and the institutional contexts of adult life—work, nonpolitical organizations, and religious institutions.[30]

30. We designed and conducted the Citizen Participation Study in conjunction with Norman H. Nie. It forms the basis for the analysis in Verba, Schlozman, and Brady, *Voice and Equality*.

- American National Election Studies (ANES). Although the ANES focus on forms of individual participation associated with elections and only occasionally include items about nonelectoral forms of activity, the invaluable ongoing portrait of the American electorate they provide has a time series that dates back more than half a century as well as several panels in which respondents were re-interviewed in successive surveys. Electoral participation follows a zigzag pattern, spiking in years with presidential elections and falling off in the congressional elections two years later; therefore, unless otherwise noted, we use only the data from the surveys conducted in presidential years.

- Pew Internet and American Life Project–August Tracking 2008. This survey, which replicated some of the questions on the Citizen Participation Study, included items about Internet use as well as political engagement and activity both on the Internet and offline.[31]

- Washington Representatives Study. We have assembled the most extensive and comprehensive database to date of organizations active in Washington politics. The more than 35,000 organizations in the database include all the organizations listed in the 1981, 1991, 2001, and 2006 editions of the *Washington Representatives* directory —along with additional organizations listed in archival sources as having been politically active by, for example, testifying in Congress or filing an amicus brief.[32] For each organization, we coded infor-mation on its history, the kinds of interests on behalf of which it advocates, and the activities it undertakes in the quest for policy influence.

Our practice throughout is to use the most recent available data set that allows us to answer the intellectual questions we are posing and, whenever possible, to use other data sets to check our results. Because the Citizen Par-ticipation Study contained such rich measures, it often permits more complex —if cross-sectional and possibly dated—analysis. When we use that survey, we do so because we could not find a more recent data set containing appro-priate measures.

31. We were fortunate to have been able to work with Lee Rainie and Scott Keeter of the Pew Internet and American Life Project in the design of this survey.

32. *Washington Representatives,* ed. Valerie Stevens (Washington, DC: Columbia Books).

What Comes Next

Unequal political voice, the subject of this book, is a major problem in American democracy. Despite the prominence of equality among American values, political voice is more unequal in the United States than in most comparable affluent industrialized democracies. It is manifest in the political participation of individuals and the political activity of organizations. It is rooted in social and economic inequalities and produces participant publics that are unrepresentative of the nation as a whole. It is a persistent problem, reproduced over time and across generations. It is a violation of basic ideals of American democracy. And, sadly, it is hard to change.

Let us provide a road map to the chapters to come. Part I (Chapters 2–4) provides additional background for our inquiry, placing the question of inequality of political voice in context and reflecting on the complicated relationship between, on the one hand, the commitment to political equality among citizens and, on the other, American individualism and the deep-seated public belief in the American Dream of equality of opportunity. We examine the debates about equality at the writing of the Constitution, debates with relevance today, as well as what state constitutions have to say about equality and what public opinion polls tell us about citizen attitudes. We also survey the economic environment of growing economic inequalities and weakening labor unions. We consider dilemmas of democratic governance, asking whether we really would want a condition of equality of political voice and whether fundamental liberties are in tension with equality of political voice.

Part II (Chapters 5–9) considers inequalities of political voice among individuals from several perspectives. In particular, we focus on the persistence of political participation, including how inequalities of political voice are passed along from one generation to the next and how they have changed over the past several decades. In addition, we investigate how participatory habits vary over the life cycle and seek to explain the deficit in activity of younger adults. Moreover, we use our findings to rethink two predictions about democracy derived from the Downsian model: that parties and candidates will converge at the point of the median voter and that voters lower on the scale will direct redistributive policies at the resources commanded by those higher up.

Part III (Chapters 10–14) looks at many of the same questions with respect to the organizations that become involved in Washington politics. We devote attention to considering the kinds of interests that are represented by the thousands of organizations in the Washington pressure system and how the distribution of organizations has changed over time. Furthermore, we show how those myriad interests are represented through different forms of advocacy—for example, lobbying, testifying in congressional hearings, or making campaign contributions.

Part IV (Chapters 15–17) inquires whether it is possible to break the pattern of inequality of political voice through the processes of mobilization into politics by which people ask their neighbors, workmates, and fellow organization and church members to get involved in politics; as a result of the possibilities for enhanced political participation over the Internet; or through the introduction of procedural reforms.

PART I

Thinking about Inequality and Political Voice

2

The (Ambivalent) Tradition
of Equality in America

All men are created equal.
  Declaration of Independence, 1776

All men are born free and equal.
  Constitution of Massachusetts, 1780

I believe in the equality of man.
  Thomas Paine, *The Age of Reason*, 1794

During my stay in the United States, nothing struck me more forcibly
than the general equality of condition among the people. I readily
discovered the prodigious influence which this primary fact exercises on
the whole course of society.
  Alexis de Tocqueville, *Democracy in America*, 1835

All men and women are created equal.
  Declaration of Sentiments, Seneca Falls, 1848

. . . a new nation, conceived in liberty, and dedicated to the proposition
that all men are created equal.
  Abraham Lincoln, Gettysburg Address, 1863

In respect of civil rights, all citizens are equal before the law. The humblest
is the peer of the most powerful.
  John Marshall Harlan, Dissenting opinion, *Plessy v. Ferguson*, 1896

Although many Americans attribute them to the Constitution, the ringing
words of the Declaration of Independence, "All men are created equal," occupy
a singular place in our collective heritage. Since the colonists chafed under the
rule of the British king, a commitment to equality has formed a thread in
American political discourse. One student of American exceptionalism underlines the significance of egalitarianism in the American ethos clearly:

There have been many attempts to distill the essence of American political thought into a list of themes. Huntington, for instance, says that

the content of what he calls "the American Creed" includes constitutionalism, individualism, liberalism, democracy, and egalitarianism. Lipset notes in one book that the most important of American values are equality and achievement; in another he observes, "The American creed can be subsumed in four words: antistatism, individualism, populism, and egalitarianism." . . . I will start with two aspects of American political thought, individualism and equality, because these two categories tend to include a lot of the other ideas that scholars have identified as significant parts of American political thought.[1]

Nevertheless, perhaps uniquely among the values on which democracies rest, equality is a complicated and puzzling concept.

To locate the distinctive underpinnings of the American democratic tradition, students of political thought look to a variety of sources—not just to philosophical writings but to Supreme Court opinions, political speeches, even novels. In this chapter we draw evidence from several sources—the debates occasioned by the drafting and ratification of the federal constitution, Supreme Court decisions, the fifty constitutions of the separate states, and public opinion as measured in surveys over the past several decades—to consider the place of equality, in all its complexity, in the American civic culture. In considering American understandings of equality in this chapter, we expand our focus beyond our central emphasis on equality of political voice to encompass the multiple aspects of the concept of equality. We are fully aware, of course, that a single chapter hardly does justice to a subject to which volumes have been devoted. Still, our brief look at these sources provides a context of normative debate in which to understand the empirical evidence that forms the bulk of this work and suggests that, while Americans are egalitarians, they are somewhat ambivalent egalitarians. As J. R. Pole, the foremost historian of equality in America, put it, "Many Americans have positively rejected ideas of equality, and those who did the rejecting have often made the rules by which the others had to live."[2]

Because the terrain of equality is so complicated, what may appear to be confusion or ambivalence is often actually nuance.[3] One immediate distinc-

---

1. John W. Kingdon, *America the Unusual* (New York: St. Martin's, 1999), pp. 25–26. Internal references have not been included.

2. J. R. Pole, *The Pursuit of Equality in American History*, rev. ed. (Berkeley: University of California Press, 1993), pp. xi–xii.

3. An interesting discussion of some of these complexities is found in Douglas Rae, *Equalities* (Cambridge, MA: Harvard University Press, 1981).

tion is the familiar one between inequalities of *result* and inequalities of *opportunity;* that is, the distinction between, on one hand, unequal rewards at the end of the race and, on the other, a circumstance in which differences in background place some contestants at a disadvantage from the very starting line. Furthermore, when it comes to inequalities of condition, there is variation in the size of the gaps between the best and worst off. For example, as we shall see in Chapter 3, in the United States economic inequalities were more pronounced on the eve of World War I than they were after World War II; today, they are more pronounced in the United States than in Canada, France, and Spain—not to mention Sweden. Analogously, over time and across societies, there is variation in the extent to which opportunities are unequal and inequalities are passed on from one generation to the next. Even in systems in which equality of opportunity is valued, having well-educated, affluent parents confers advantage, though not a guarantee, which raises the paradox that extreme inequalities of result, even if they result from genuine meritocracy, may be inconsistent with equality of opportunity in the next generation.[4]

Questions about equality become more complicated when we engage the question "Inequality with respect to what?" Societies distribute many kinds of valued rewards. Among the multiple dimensions of potential hierarchy, the three discussed by Max Weber—economic wherewithal, social respect, and political power—seem especially fundamental.[5] The extent to which economic, social, and political dominance are coterminous, a matter of serious controversy among students of social stratification, varies across time and place. In the United States, there is obviously a great deal of overlap among class, status, and power, especially in some of the more traditional areas of the country. Still, these are separate dimensions: those who enjoy social respect—whether because of their achievements in such areas as science, medicine, or the arts or because their forebears arrived on the *Mayflower*—do not necessarily wield political power; those who have served as speaker of the U.S. House, while undeniably powerful, have not necessarily been wealthy; and, although the ranks of the socially prestigious have been more permeable to wealth in the United States than in Europe, the doors of the

4. A satirical consideration of this dilemma is contained in Michael Young, *The Rise of the Meritocracy* (Baltimore: Penguin Books, 1958).

5. See Max Weber, "Class, Status, Party," in *From Max Weber: Essays in Sociology*, trans. and ed. H. M. Gerth and C. Wright Mills (New York: Oxford University Press, 1946 [1921]), chap. 7.

most exclusive country club may not be open to the newly rich, especially if they do not have the "right" ethnic background.

That the economy is the domain for the allocation of income and wealth and the polity the domain for power is obvious. However, there are economic, political, and social asymmetries in a variety of domains—not just in the economy and the polity but at home, in church, in school, and in the community. We know, for example, that not all members of a household have an equal say in decision making or an equal claim on its financial resources. We are all familiar with "office politics" and aware that bosses not only earn more than workers but also wield power over them. Besides, in some workplaces—academic departments are a notable example—disparities in professional prestige loom as large as disparities in income.

Another set of considerations derives from the alternative principles of distributive justice that might underlie inequalities of wealth, power, or respect.[6] Departures from strict equality among individuals might represent allocations made on any of a number of bases: differences in need; in willingness to work hard; in talents, skills, and training; in results obtained; in ascriptive traits.

The use of ascriptive traits to define who is entitled to enjoy economic, social, and political rewards poses a particular challenge to the American tradition of liberal individualism. Neither slaves nor married women could own property in the early nineteenth century in the United States, and both groups were excluded from the right to exercise political power. Still excluded are aliens, whether legal or illegal, and children. Even when ascription is not explicitly invoked as a distributive principle, inequalities among individuals may cumulate to create inequalities among groups defined by race, ethnicity, gender, or age.

The U.S. Constitution: Political Equality at the Founding

While the colonial constitutions included preambles asserting equality of rights and the egalitarian spirit expressed in the Declaration of Independence was an important force animating the American Revolution, the men who met at Philadelphia to write the constitution that continues to govern us were

---

6. For a lucid discussion and helpful citations, see Jennifer L. Hochschild, *What's Fair? American Beliefs about Distributive Justice* (Cambridge, MA: Harvard University Press, 1981), chap. 3.

not uniformly committed to equality.[7] With Shays's Rebellion and the threat of civil disorder in the background, some were concerned to protect the new government from the "temporary errors and delusions" of the people. In fact, the constitution they produced has remarkably little to say about equality. The clauses proscribing the granting of titles of nobility by either the national government or the governments of the states (Article I, Sections 9 and 10) and prohibiting the imposition of religious tests as a qualification for public office (Article VI) provide limited guarantees against particularly conspicuous forms of inequality. However, it was not until after the Civil War, when the Fourteenth Amendment was added forbidding any state to "deny to any person within its jurisdiction the equal protection of the laws," that serious deference to citizen equality was inserted into the U.S. Constitution.[8]

Although the constitution that emerged in 1787, even as amended a few years later by the addition of the Bill of Rights, gives little indication of concern about equality, lively debate at the time about the franchise engaged matters of political equality that are close to the heart of our concern with equality of political voice. The debate, which was carried on at an enviably

7. Among the many accounts of the Founding, we draw, in particular, on Gordon S. Wood, *The Creation of the American Republic: 1776–1787* (New York, W. W. Norton, 1972), and Sean Wilentz, *The Rise of American Democracy: Jefferson to Lincoln* (New York: W. W. Norton, 2005), as well as on Pole, *The Pursuit of Equality.* An especially useful guide to the arguments made in the debate over the franchise in the early years of the republic is contained in Alexander Keyssar, *The Right to Vote: The Contested History of Democracy in the United States* (New York: Basic Books, 2000), pp. 8–21.

8. Even then the application of the Equal Protection Clause was quite spotty. The literature on the Fourteenth Amendment is extensive. See, for example, Judith A. Baer, *Equality under the Constitution: Reclaiming the Fourteenth Amendment* (Ithaca, NY: Cornell University Press, 1983); Ronald Dworkin, *A Matter of Principle* (Cambridge, MA: Harvard University Press, 1985), chaps. 14–16; William E. Nelson, *The Fourteenth Amendment: From Political Principle to Judicial Doctrine* (Cambridge, MA: Harvard University Press, 1988); Catherine A. MacKinnon, "Reflections on Sex Equality under Law," *Yale Law Journal* 100 (1991): 1281–1328; H. N. Hirsch, *A Theory of Liberty: The Constitution and Minorities* (New York: Routledge, 1992); David A. J. Richards, *Conscience and the Constitution: History, Theory, and Law of the Reconstruction Amendments* (Princeton, NJ: Princeton University Press, 1993); Andrew Koppelman, *Antidiscrimination Law and Social Equality* (New Haven, CT: Yale University Press, 1996); Earl M. Maltz, *The Fourteenth Amendment and the Law of the Constitution* (Durham, NC: Carolina Academic Press, 2003); Jack M. Balkin and Reva B. Siegel, "The American Civil Rights Tradition—Anticlassification or Antisubordination?" *University of Miami Law Review* 58 (2004): 9–33; Michael J. Klarman, *From Jim Crow to Civil Rights: The Supreme Court and the Struggle for Racial Equality* (Oxford, England: Oxford University Press, 2004); and Reva B. Siegel, "Equality Talk: Antisubordination and Anti-classification Values in Constitutional Struggles over Brown," *Harvard Law Review* 117 (2004): 1470–1547.

high level of discourse, raised issues that have reverberated throughout American history. While the specific controversies change over time, the opposing perspectives on the wisdom of the democratic experiment show remarkable resilience.

Clearly, the vote is only one aspect of equal political voice. At this point, we focus exclusively on the franchise because who should have the right to vote was the subject of such explicit discussion at the time of the Founding. Moreover, of the various modes for the expression of political voice, conflicts surrounding the regulation of the franchise have arisen with regularity since then. In contrast to the right to vote, the rights to the expression of political voice protected in the First Amendment's guarantees concerning "freedom of speech, or of the press; or the right of the people peaceably to assemble, and to petition the government for a redress of grievances" are extended to all. Even noncitizens fall under this amendment's protections. Of course, in remarking upon the presumptive universal applicability of the First Amendment, we do not mean to overlook the number and intensity of ongoing conflicts surrounding its guarantees, the historical exclusion of slaves from its protective umbrella, or the restrictions on the First Amendment rights of, for example, minors and prisoners. Still, it is worth noting that, of all forms of expressing political voice, the vote is the one for which the question of *who* is permitted to take part has been most consistently contested.

The discussion about whether the franchise should be restricted to property owners or should be extended more widely among adult white males took place within a context of broad consensus rejecting monarchy or systems of hereditary privilege. Furthermore, in the controversy about the right to vote, there was never any question that individuals' votes should count equally. That is, although districts of unequal size—most notably, the states as represented in the U.S. Senate—meant that votes would have unequal weight, there was no suggestion that particularly deserving individuals should have more than one vote. Also consensual, though obviously less egalitarian, was the implicit agreement that women and slaves could not qualify for the franchise. Beyond these consensual understandings, there was sharp disagreement on how far the right to participate ought to be extended. At stake was difference of opinion about the capacities of ordinary citizens for self-rule. On one side were those who believed in the innate equality of humans and argued that sovereignty must be in the hands of the citizenry to avoid oligarchical domination and that only broad-based participation would fulfill the democratic promise and avoid the dominance of the wealthy and the established. On the other were those who deemed the mass of citizens ignorant and unqualified to rule, maintaining that widespread participation would be a danger to democracy and result in mob rule and that governance should be in the hands of the educated and established few. Such skeptics emphasized the role of the ownership of private property in ensuring that voters have a stake in society and sufficient independence to render political judgments on their own. Thus, where the former group saw widespread participation as a defense against autocracy, the latter saw it as an invitation to autocracy.

At one end of the spectrum were those like Tom Paine, who placed ultimate sovereignty in the people and believed that their collective wisdom would protect against oligarchical domination by the rich. At the Constitutional Convention, Benjamin Franklin argued in favor of a broad franchise across social groups and opposed any property qualification for voting on the principle that each citizen should have an equal right to shape the acts of the government: "The important ends of Civil Society, and the personal Securities of Life and Liberty, these remain the same in every Member of the society; and the poorest continues to have an equal Claim to them with the most opulent."[9] Convinced that the mass of citizens was competent to vote, he considered them to be a bulwark against the greed and autocracy of the wealthy. Concerned that their virtuous behavior would only be diminished if they were not empowered to vote, he commented at the Constitutional Convention that "it is of great consequence that we should not depress the virtue and spirit of our common people."[10]

At the other end of the spectrum were those like Gouverneur Morris and Alexander Hamilton, who profoundly distrusted the mass of citizens as ignorant, uncontrollable, likely to destroy liberty and confiscate property. Such conservatives favored a government of the wise, rich, and propertied—in Hamilton's words, a government that would "consist almost entirely of proprietors of land, of merchants, and of men of the learned professions."[11] According to Morris, should the poor have votes, "they will sell them to the rich who will be able to buy them."[12]

9. Benjamin Franklin, "Queries and Remarks Respecting Alterations in the Constitution of Pennsylvania," in *The Founders' Constitution*, ed. Philip Kurland and Ralph Lerner (Chicago: University of Chicago Press, 1987), vol. 1, chap. 12, document 25.

10. James Madison, *The Debates in the Federal Convention of 1787*, Tuesday, August 7, at http://www.constitution.org/dfc/dfc_0807.htm (accessed January 13, 2010).

11. Alexander Hamilton, "The Federalist No. 36," in *The Federalist*, ed. Edward Mead Earl (New York: Modern Library, n.d.), p. 216.

12. Jonathan Elliot, *Debates on the Adoption of the Federal Constitution in the Convention Held at Philadelphia in 1787* (Philadelphia: J. B. Lippincott, Taylor & Maury, 1866), p. 395, quoted in Wilentz, *The Rise of American Democracy*, p. 33.

Dubious about both the capacities of ordinary citizens and the motives of elites, John Adams emphasized the link between property and the virtues of competence and independence: "Men . . . who are wholly destitute of property, are also too little acquainted with public affairs to form a right judgment, and too dependent on other men to have a will of their own."[13] Skeptical of wide popular participation, he accepted the inevitability of conflict between rich and poor and argued for using the institutions of representative government to check the conflict:

> The controversy between the rich and the poor, the laborious and the idle, the learned and the ignorant, distinctions as old as the creation . . . will continue, and rivalries will spring out of them. These parties will be represented in the legislature, and must be balanced, or one will oppress the other. . . .
>
> Let us adopt it as a certain principle, that they ought not to be prevented, but directed to virtue, and then stimulated and encouraged by generous applause and honorable rewards. And from these premises let the conclusion be, as it ought to be, that an effectual control be provided in the constitution, to check their excesses and balance their weights.[14]

Ever sober, James Madison occupied a middle ground. At the Convention he sounded a cautious note about the twin dangers of universal and restricted suffrage: "The right to suffrage is a fundamental Article in republican Constitutions. The regulation of it is, at the same time, a delicate task. . . . Allow the right exclusively to property, and rights of persons may be oppressed. . . . Extend it to all, and the rights of property . . . may be overruled by a majority without property." And he asks: "In a just & a free Government, therefore, the rights both of property & of persons ought to be effectually guarded. Will the former be in the case of universal & free suffrage? Will the latter be so in a case of a suffrage confined to the holders of property?"[15] Later, in *The Federalist*, Madison offered a strong defense of broad citizen participation: "Who are

13. "John Adams to James Sullivan," in *The Founders' Constitution*, vol. 1, chap. 13, document 10.

14. John Adams, "Discourses on Davila," in *The Portable John Adams*, ed. John Patrick Diggins (New York: Penguin Books, 2004), pp. 386, 392.

15. James Madison, *The Records of the Federal Convention of 1787*, ed. Max Farand (New Haven, CT: Yale University Press, 1966), 3, 450–452.

to be the electors of the federal representatives? Not the rich, more than the poor; not the learned, more than the ignorant; not the haughty heirs of distinguished names, more than the humble sons of obscurity and unpropitious fortune. The electors are to be the great body of the people of the United States."[16]

In Madison's understanding, the government established by the Constitution solved the dilemma of popular control. An extended republic in which factions counter one another limits the possibility of majority tyranny. In addition, the division of governing powers between the central and state governments and the checks and balances within the central government would protect against both "the cabals of a few" and "the confusion of a multitude." Furthermore, in a republic popularly elected representatives can "refine and enlarge" the preferences of the people. Madison maintained that the governing arrangements under the proposed constitution would serve to "secure the public good and private rights against the danger of such a [majority] faction, and at the same time to preserve the spirit and the form of popular government" in the face of "the mischiefs of faction," the danger posed by "a number of citizens, whether amounting to a majority or a minority of the whole, who are united and actuated by some common impulse or passion, or of interest, adverse to the rights of other citizens, or to the permanent and aggregate interests on the community."[17] Later on, after experiencing several decades of government under the Constitution, Madison became much less concerned about the problem of majority faction and more congenial to majority rule.[18]

Continuing Debates about the Franchise: Literacy Tests and Poll Taxes

The federal constitution left the determination of eligibility for the franchise to the states, with the result that controversies surrounding voter eligibility have been a leitmotif of American political history. What is notable from the perspective of our concern with the place of equality in the firmament of

---

16. James Madison, "The Federalist No. 57," in *The Federalist*, ed. Earl, p. 371.

17. All quotations in this paragraph are taken from one of the most notable pieces of writing about American democracy, James Madison, "The Federalist No. 10," in *The Federalist*, ed. Earl, pp. 53–62.

18. See Robert A. Dahl, *How Democratic Is the American Constitution?* 2nd ed. (New Haven, CT: Yale University Press, 2003), pp. 34–37.

American political ideals is the extent to which the discourse surrounding such conflicts—for example, the controversies over literacy tests and poll taxes—echoes the rhetoric of the disputes at the time of the Founding.

The underlying logic behind literacy tests is that the right to participate in governing should be limited to those who are sufficiently informed to do so wisely. The corollary is that literacy, in particular literacy in English, is an appropriate measure of citizen competence. However, from the outset, the purpose of literacy testing was not only—or, perhaps, not even—to raise the overall standard for the electorate but rather to raise barriers to the franchise against former slaves, immigrants, and the "ignorant vote."[19]

In ruling on literacy tests, the Supreme Court reflected understandings that informed the discussion surrounding the franchise at the time of the Founding—accepting the premise that the ability to read was legitimately linked to the capacity to vote intelligently and therefore that a literacy test was not on its face an illegal means of protecting the democratic process. As late as 1959, Justice William O. Douglas echoed this approach when he wrote for a unanimous court upholding a literacy test: "Certainly we cannot condemn [a literacy test] on its face as a device unrelated to the desire of North Carolina to raise the standards for people of all races who cast the ballot."[20] Six years later, the Court discerned clear evidence that the purpose of literacy tests was to deny blacks the right to vote and rejected a Louisiana law making the ability to interpret a constitutional provision a requirement for voting. Speaking for a unanimous court, Justice Hugo Black highlighted the use of a skill requirement as a guise for blocking some citizens from the franchise: "This is not a test, but a trap, sufficient to stop even the most brilliant man on the way to the voting booth. The cherished right of people in a country like ours to vote cannot be obliterated by the use of laws like this, which leave the voting fate of a citizen to the passing whim or impulse of an individual

19. On literacy tests, see Keyssar, *The Right to Vote*, pp. 105–116, 141–146, and Table A.13. For accounts of the history of the black franchise during the late nineteenth century, see, for instance, V. O. Key Jr., *Southern Politics in State and Nation* (New York: Alfred Knopf, 1949); J. Morgan Kousser, *The Shaping of Southern Politics: Suffrage Restriction and the Establishment of the One-Party South, 1880–1910* (New Haven, CT: Yale University Press, 1974); Michael Perman, *Struggle for Mastery: Disenfranchisement in the South, 1888–1908* (Chapel Hill, NC: University of North Carolina Press, 2001); Richard M. Vallely, *The Two Reconstructions: The Struggle for Black Disenfranchisement* (Chicago: University of Chicago Press, 2004); and Klarman, *From Jim Crow to Civil Rights*.

20. *Lassiter* v. *Northhampton County Board of Elections*, 360 U.S. 45 (1959).

registrar."[21] Literacy tests were finally eliminated by congressional action in a 1970 amendment to the Voting Rights Act.[22]

The debate surrounding poll taxes had a similar character. Behind the widespread property requirements imposed as a condition of the franchise in the early years of the republic was the belief that those who did not own property would lack the independence of judgment and the stake in society necessary for responsible citizenship. In the early decades of the nineteenth century, property requirements were dropped in state after state, and new states joining the union enfranchised white males without regard to property ownership. Still, even after the Civil War, some states imposed material requirements as a condition for the franchise. Some of these provisions reflected the understanding that participation in democratic governance should be restricted to those who have a stake in the outcome. Like literacy tests, poll taxes had consequences for the class and, especially, the racial composition of electorates. In fact, at the same time that Massachusetts, Rhode Island, and Delaware were repealing poll taxes imposed earlier in the century, most of the states of the former Confederacy were imposing new poll taxes, usually with explicit discriminatory intent.[23]

The issue of the poll tax was resolved for federal elections by the passage in 1964 of the Twenty-Fourth Amendment, which bars poll taxes in federal elections. In 1966 the Supreme Court extended the ban to state elections, ruling that poll taxes could not be used in any elections.[24] In their minority opinion, Justices John Marshall Harlan and Potter Stewart justified a monetary requirement—in this case, a small one—for the right to participate in an

---

21. *Louisiana* v. *United States*, 380 U.S. 145 (1965).

22. The Voting Rights Act of 1965, as amended several times thereafter, was remarkably successful in increasing black registration in the South. In 1965, before the passage of the act, black registration in the southern states stood at 35.5 percent. In Mississippi, the registration rate was 6.7 percent. By 1967 the figure had risen above 50 percent; by 1992 it had reached 66.7 percent, nearly identical to the rate in the North. Richard L. Engstrom, "The Voting Rights Act: Disenfranchisement, Dilution, and Alternative Election Systems," *PS: Political Science and Politics* 27 (1994): 685–688, and James E. Alt, "The Impact of the Voting Rights Act on Black and White Registration in the South," in *Quiet Revolution in the South*, ed. Chandler Davidson and Bernard Grofman (Princeton, NJ: Princeton University Press, 1994).

23. On poll taxes, see Keyssar, *The Right to Vote*, pp. 130, 228–229, 236–237, 250, 259, and Table A.10. Klarman, in *From Jim Crow to Civil Rights*, p. 142, points out that, after three southern states, North Carolina, Louisiana, and Florida, abolished their poll taxes, the number of black voters did not increase appreciably.

24. *Harper* v. *Virginia Board of Elections,* 383 U.S. 663 (1966).

election. They pointed to the history of such taxes both before and after the Constitutional Convention and invoked earlier arguments to defend the rationality of the poll tax: "It is also arguable . . . that people with some property have a deeper stake in community affairs and are, consequently, more responsible, more educated, more knowledgeable, more worthy of confidence than those without means, and that the community and nation would be better managed if the franchise were limited to such citizens." Writing for the majority, Justice Douglas struck a more egalitarian note: "We conclude that a state violates the Equal Protection clause of the Fourteenth Amendment whenever it makes the affluence of the voter or the payment of any fee an electoral standard. Voter qualifications have no relation to wealth."[25]

Constitutional Equality and Constitutional Voice in the States

While the U.S. Constitution makes few nods in the direction of equality, the constitutions of the states show much more deference to equality as a democratic value. Curiously, students of political thought have not paid much attention to the constitutions of the states, which for many reasons offer a rich source for systematic study. There are fifty of them—a large enough number to provide diversity and a small enough number to be read in their entirety. The oldest, that of Massachusetts, had its two hundredth birthday a generation ago. The newest—Georgia's 1983 constitution, its tenth—is barely an adult. They address matters, ranging from education to marriage to the rights of crime victims, that are not covered in the federal constitution. They are constantly being revised. Indeed, 233 state constitutional conventions were held between 1776 and 2005,[26] and many more constitutional alterations have been incorporated as the result of legislation or ballot propositions. In

---

25. The poll tax issue illustrates the multiplicity of goals involved in political rights cases in another way. The tax had a differential effect on the basis of income as well as race and thus had a greater impact on poor whites than on affluent whites. In the South, objections to the tax were raised by those supporting equal access for poor whites (though not poor blacks). The issue existed in the North as well. As Keyssar (*The Right to Vote*, pp. 89–90) points out, the poll tax was common in some northern states in the late nineteenth and early twentieth centuries. In the North, the issue of partisanship and winning elections was added. The poll tax was supported by Republicans who wanted to reduce Democratic voting among the poor in northern cities.

26. John J. Dinan, *The American Constitutional Tradition* (Lawrence: University Press of Kansas, 2006), pp. 7–11.

this section we consider what the state constitutions say about our concerns, democratic equality and political voice.

A commitment to equality is very much in evidence in the constitutions of the states. Article I of the oldest operative constitution on the planet, Massachusetts's 1780 constitution, begins "All men are born free and equal." In contrast to the federal constitution, which contains no such language, the constitutions of a majority of states contain a general statement—usually as part of an enumeration of rights—proclaiming the essential equality among persons.[27] Most of these statements show a debt to the language of the Declaration of Independence, a debt occasionally so substantial as to border on plagiarism. In its emphasis on rights and in its addition of "property" to the trio of "life, liberty, and the pursuit of happiness," the following, from Idaho's 1890 constitution, is typical of many state constitutional statements: "All men are by nature free and equal, and have certain inalienable rights, among which are enjoying and defending life and liberty; acquiring, possessing and protecting property; pursuing happiness and securing safety."[28] Such general statements are less important for the legal guarantees they confer than as evidence of the significance of equality among political virtues in America.

These general assertions of human equality are not a recent addition to our political discourse, the rhetorical flourish of an era that has been characterized as celebrating both rights and equality. Indeed, all but ten of the thirty-one state constitutions in a collection compiled in 1853[29] contain such a general proclamation of rights-based equality, often in precisely the form in which it presently appears. Yet from the perspective of the twenty-first century, it is revealing to note the limits to the egalitarian embrace of these pre–Civil War constitutions. Slave states were much less likely than free states to include a constitutional nod to equality.[30] Of those that did, only Virginia included "all men" under the umbrella. The others restricted the egalitarian

---

27. See Appendix A. In March 2006, each of the fifty state constitutions was accessed on the Internet, usually on the Web site of the state government. In a few of the cases listed in Appendix A, a state constitution contains a universal guarantee of rights without the use of the word *equal*.

28. Article 1, Section 1. For examples involving almost verbatim quotation from the Declaration, see Article 1, Section 2, of the Constitution of the State of North Carolina and Article 1, Section 1, of the Constitution of the State of Indiana.

29. *The Constitutions of the Several States of the Union and the United States* (New York: A. S. Barnes, 1853).

30. Seven of the ten states whose constitutions lacked a general guarantee of equality in 1853 were slave states.

promise to "all freemen." These relics of the era of slavery were, in one way or another, expunged during the process of widespread rewriting of state constitutions that followed the Civil War.[31]

Moreover, as in the Declaration of Independence, every single one of these nineteenth-century egalitarian references extended only to "men." Although it might be assumed that such statements represent a generic use of the masculine to refer to all people, it is worth noting that nearly all these pre–Civil War constitutions included some kind of gender-neutral reference, such as that in a preamble that begins, as does the U.S. Constitution, "We, the people . . ." or a declaration that "all power is inherent in [resides in, derives from, etc.] the people."[32] Moreover, other rights guarantees were usually expressed in gender-neutral language. The Constitution of Arkansas promised that "the people should be secure in their persons," Illinois's that "no person shall be imprisoned for debt," Connecticut's that "every citizen has a right to bear arms." Six of these mid-nineteenth-century constitutions eventually replaced their gender-exclusive language.[33] Among contemporary state constitutions, the general statements about equality are split just about evenly between those that refer to "men" and those that use the encompassing language of "persons," "people," "individuals," or "men and women."

In the aftermath of the addition of the Fourteenth Amendment to the U.S. Constitution, a majority of states have added to their constitutions some kind of guarantee of equal protection that echoes that of the Fourteenth Amendment.[34] A number of states supplement an unadorned equal protection clause with an enumeration of bases of mandated equal treatment. These statements

31. Texas's solution was to add a space to produce the following: "All free men, when they form a social compact, have equal rights." Mississippi dropped its general statement on equality. Alabama, Arkansas, Florida, and Kentucky eliminated the reference to "freemen" either by omitting the "free" or by substituting another statement entirely. On nineteenth-century southern state constitutions and the efforts to rewrite them during Reconstruction, see G. Alan Tarr, *Understanding State Constitutions* (Princeton, NJ: Princeton University Press, 1998), pp. 128–132.

32. Of the thirty-one constitutions from 1853, only three (those of Georgia, Michigan, and North Carolina) include no such reference to "the people."

33. These states are California, Indiana, Iowa, Maine, New Jersey, and Vermont.

34. See Appendix A. Only five states—Colorado, Minnesota, Mississippi, Oklahoma, and Tennessee—have neither a general statement about the natural equality of persons nor an equal protection clause in their constitutions. In a few cases, the clauses coded in Appendix A as providing equal protection are more oblique. The following, from the Constitution of Idaho (Article I, Section 2), is an example: "All political power is inherent in the people. Government is instituted for their equal protection and benefit."

vary in several ways. Although race and religion are most commonly cited as bases of proscribed discrimination, nearly half the state constitutions contain some version of the defeated federal Equal Rights Amendment providing for equal treatment on the basis of sex. Other listed characteristics include dimensions as disparate as national origin, physical handicap, and political ideas. Ordinarily, these clauses provide for equal treatment by the state. However, a few—like a particularly comprehensive example from the Montana Constitution—constrain private institutions as well. As specified in Article II, Section 4, of the Constitution of Montana: "No person shall be denied the equal protection of the laws. Neither the state nor any person, firm, corporation, or institution shall discriminate against any person in the exercise of his civil or political rights on account of race, color, sex, culture, social origin or condition, or political or religious ideas."

Unlike the general statements of equality among persons, which are significant as indicators of the deference paid to equality as a democratic value, these equal protection clauses confer legal rights. When a state constitutional equal protection clause is coupled with a list of dimensions for which discrimination in public action is impermissible, the legal potential is multiplied. It has been left to the courts to specify what legal distinctions are unacceptable under the Equal Protection Clause of the Fourteenth Amendment of the federal constitution. By indicating the grounds for nondiscrimination, the explicit lists in the state constitutions contain the possibility in some cases—for example, disability—for protection beyond that afforded by the Fourteenth Amendment Equal Protection Clause.[35]

In addition to such guarantees of equal protection are two egalitarian provisions that derive from the federal constitution.[36] The first is a narrower, and older, guarantee of nondiscrimination, the prohibition against religious tests. Following the example of the U.S. Constitution, a majority of state constitutions proscribe religious tests for some or all of a variety of civic privileges and responsibilities—most commonly, holding public office, but also serving on a jury, serving as a witness, or casting an electoral ballot. The other is the ban on titles of nobility. Just over a third of the state constitutions contain a clause that disallows titles and other forms of hereditary privileges or honors.

35. On the extent to which the bills of rights in state constitutions confer rights not available in the federal constitution and the movement to take advantage of those guarantees, see the discussion and references in Tarr, *Understanding State Constitutions*, pp. 160–170.
36. See Appendix A.

By way of qualification, we should make clear that the state constitutions have not always been used in the name of egalitarian objectives. Most obviously, the state constitutions have historically been mobilized to buttress profoundly antiegalitarian ends related to race, particularly in the antebellum and Jim Crow South. Much more recently, after Massachusetts legalized gay marriage on the basis of its state constitution, a majority of states added provisions outlawing gay marriage to their state constitutions. Still, taken together, the state constitutions pay much greater deference to the norm of equality than does the federal constitution.

State Constitutions and the People's Voice

The state constitutions also underline the role of the people in governing.[37] Every one of the state constitutions contains, usually very near the beginning, an assertion of popular sovereignty similar to this one from Wyoming: "All power is inherent in the people, and all free governments are founded on their authority."[38] Occasionally, as in the case of Illinois, the statement is framed in the language of the Declaration of Independence, reminding us that "governments are instituted among men, deriving their just powers from the consent of the governed."[39] These universal statements serve as an affirmation that all political authority in the republic derives ultimately from the people.

Moreover, every one of the state constitutions includes a discussion of elections and a clause guaranteeing the right to vote to citizens of the United States who have resided in the state for some minimal period of time. These constitutional guarantees of the franchise are fortified by a variety of further measures, such as mandates to the legislature to provide for absentee ballots and stipulations that those who are out of the state serving in the military shall not be disenfranchised. The state constitutions also may list grounds for disenfranchisement, including treason, insanity, and, most commonly, conviction of a felony. With the exception of Maine and Vermont, all states deny the franchise to those convicted of a felony—at least while incarcerated.[40] Just

37. G. Alan Tarr argues that state constitutions have been explicitly anti-Madisonian in giving the people a more central role in governing than they are given in the federal constitution. See "For the People: Direct Democracy in the State Constitutional Tradition," in *Democracy: How Direct?* ed. Elliott Abrams (Lanham, MD: Rowman and Littlefield, 2002), chap. 6.

38. Constitution of Wyoming, Article I, Section 1.

39. Constitution of Illinois, Article I, Section 1.

40. In fourteen states (Alabama, Arizona, Delaware, Florida, Iowa, Kentucky, Maryland, Mississippi, Nebraska, Nevada, Tennessee, Virginia, Washington, and Wyoming) the dis-

about all of these states include a clause disenfranchising felons in their constitutions. Only a few of them accomplish this end by statute.[41]

The state constitutions make other provisions for the exercise of the people's voice to public officials. The right to petition for redress of grievances —a right also protected in the Bill of Rights—is nearly universal. In addition, about a third of the state constitutions provide for a right—one especially germane to our concerns—that has no federal counterpart, the right to instruct their representatives.

A majority of the state constitutions not only make explicit a republican role for the people in choosing and informing public officials but also provide for direct democracy in the form of the initiative and/or referendum.[42] Both the initiative and the referendum process transform voters into policy makers.[43] The constitutions of twenty-seven states provide for some form of direct democracy.[44] With a few exceptions, these arrangements are a legacy of the Populist and Progressive movements: the first was South Dakota's in 1898.[45] They are much more common west of the Mississippi than east. With the exception of Hawaii, all of the Rocky Mountain and Pacific states have provision for some form of initiative or referendum.

---

enfranchisement extends, for some or all felons, beyond the period of probation or imprisonment and parole. For a summary of state restrictions on felon voting, see Jeff Manza and Christopher Uggen, *Locked Out* (New York: Oxford University Press, 2006), p. 247.

41. See Appendix A. Connecticut, New Hampshire, New Jersey, New York, Oklahoma, and Pennsylvania disenfranchise felons by statute rather than constitutional provision. Indiana's constitution (Article II, Section 8) empowers the legislature "to deprive of the right of suffrage, and to render ineligible, any person convicted of an infamous crime."

42. On state constitutional provisions for initiative and referendum and the debates at state constitutional conventions about direct democracy, see Dinan, *American State Constitutional Tradition*, chap. 3.

43. In the former, members of the electorate present petitions for measures that will be placed on the ballot to be approved or rejected by voters. In the latter, measures already enacted by the legislature are placed on the ballot for voter ratification or rejection. For elaboration of these and other variants, see Elisabeth R. Gerber, *The Populist Paradox* (Princeton, NJ: Princeton University Press, 1999), p. 15.

44. See Appendix A. The list of states that make constitutional provision for direct democracy was compiled by checking state constitutions against lists contained in M. Dane Waters, *Initiative and Referendum Almanac* (Durham, NC: Carolina Academic Press, 2003), and on the Web site of the Initiative and Referendum Institute, http://www.iandrinstitute. org/ (accessed April 5, 2006).

45. It is interesting to note that several states with strong Progressive traditions—most notably, Minnesota and Wisconsin—are not among the states providing for initiative or referendum.

A bare majority of the state constitutions recognize political equality in yet another way by including provisions outlining a political punishment for a conviction for political bribery. Although political bribery is condemned in democracies, as we shall discuss in Chapter 10, the underlying logic as to why bribery corrupts the political process is often left implicit. Whether it is targeted at voters or public officials, a bribe violates democratic norms by substituting an exchange of market resources for the political equality of citizens. The states that incorporate a clause about bribery into their constitutions include both states with reputations for corruption and states with clean government traditions.[46] More importantly, state constitutional provisions vary in whether they focus on the bribery of voters, which has the effect of corrupting the electoral process; on the bribery of public officials, which has the effect of corrupting the policy process; or on both. Furthermore, they vary with respect to the political penalty for a bribery conviction—ranging from a fine to, in the case of a public official, permanent exclusion from public office. For all the diversity in these provisions, that half the state constitutions contain political sanctions for bribery is evidence of an implicit commitment to political equality.

State Constitutions and Social Citizenship

In a famous passage, British sociologist T. H. Marshall distinguishes among three forms of citizenship:

> I shall call these three parts, or elements, civil, political and social. The civil element is composed of the rights necessary for individual freedom —liberty of the person, freedom of speech, thought and faith, the right to own property and to conclude valid contracts, and the right to justice. The last is of a different order from the others, because it is the right to defend and assert all one's rights on terms of equality with others and by due process of law. This shows us that the institutions most directly associated with civil rights are the courts of justice. By the political element I mean the right to participate in the exercise of political power, as a member of a body invested with political authority or as an elector of the members of such a body. The corresponding institutions are parliament and councils of local government. By the social element I mean the whole range from the right to a modicum of eco-

---

46. See Appendix A.

nomic welfare and security to the right to share to the full in the social heritage and to live the life of a civilized being according to the standards prevailing in society. The institutions most closely connected with it are the educational system and the social services.[47]

We have seen how much deference state constitutions pay to what Marshall calls civil and political citizenship. When it comes to social citizenship, a topic on which the federal constitution is completely silent, the guarantees are much more mixed. On one hand, education—which is critically related to the resources and psychological orientations needed for political voice and which is traditionally a state rather than a federal concern—receives extensive recognition in the state constitutions. On the other, state constitutions do not evidence a parallel sense of public responsibility for the economic well-being and security of citizens.

Free and compulsory public education came early to the United States; most state constitutions devote a separate article to education, and every state constitution says something about it. In their provisions about education, two-thirds of the state constitutions specify that the schools shall be free or shall not charge tuition.[48] A few even specify that students are not expected to pay for textbooks. In their discussions of education, many of the state constitutions also include general words about the salutary effects of the diffusion of knowledge.

Surveys of citizens have demonstrated over and over that those who are well educated are likely to hold attitudes that are supportive of democracy and to take part politically. From the perspective of our concerns, it is interesting that state constitutions often make connections between education and the protection of democratic rights and governance. Minnesota's is typical: "The stability of a republican form of government depending mainly upon the intelligence of the people, it is the duty of the legislature to establish a general and uniform system of public schools."[49] This observation has a long pedigree in American state constitutionalism. The following phrase,

---

47. T. H. Marshall, *Class, Citizenship, and Social Development* (Garden City, NY: Doubleday, Anchor Books, 1965 [1947]), pp. 78–79.

48. See Appendix A.

49. Constitution of Minnesota, Article XIII, Section 1. The following state constitutions also contain language linking education to democratic governance: Arkansas, California, Idaho, Indiana, Maine, Massachusetts, Michigan, Minnesota, Missouri, New Hampshire, North Carolina, North Dakota, Rhode Island, and Texas.

excerpted from the section of Massachusetts's 1780 constitution, demonstrates that American constitution writers recognized the association between education and democracy a century and a half before it was documented by students of political behavior: "Wisdom and knowledge, as well as virtue, diffused generally among the body of the people, being necessary for the preservation of their rights and liberties. . . ."[50]

Because inequalities in educational finance resulting from property tax–based school funding have spawned lawsuits in so many states, it is sometimes assumed that the state constitutions promise educational equality to all. However, free schooling is not the same as equal education. In fact, state constitutional guarantees of educational equality are quite limited. A clause like Louisiana's promising that "the goal of the public educational system is to provide . . . every individual . . . an equal opportunity to develop to his full potential" is the rare exception.[51] Additional egalitarian concerns are, however, manifest in the education provisions of several state constitutions. For example, a few state constitutions contain clauses that proscribe discrimination in education on the basis of such characteristics as race, ethnicity, or sex.[52] A few constitutions mention disabled students—either mandating separate schools for their instruction or providing educational guarantees to the disabled.

50. Constitution of Massachusetts, Chapter V, Section II.

51. Constitution of Louisiana, Article VIII, Preamble. The Constitution of Montana (Article X, Section 1) states: "It is the goal of the people to establish a system of education which will develop the educational potential of each person." On the issue of school finance reform, see Jennifer Hochschild and Natan Scovronick, *The American Dream and the Public Schools* (New York: Oxford University Press, 2003), chap. 3. Hochschild and Scovronick argue (p. 65) that early school finance cases sought equality on the basis of the equal protection clauses of, first, the federal and, later, the state constitutions. More recent cases have sought educational adequacy, not educational equality.

52. Sometimes, a particular group is singled out for protection: New Mexico's constitution (Article XII, Section 10) provides: "Children of Spanish descent . . . shall never be denied the right and privilege of admission and attendance in the public schools or other educational institutions of the state, and they shall never be classed in separate schools." Taking a different approach—one of cultural recognition rather than nondiscrimination—Montana "recognizes the distinct and unique cultural heritage of the American Indians and is committed in its educational goals to the preservation of their cultural integrity" in its constitution (Article X, Section 1). In contrast is the 1901 Constitution of Alabama, which provides (Article XIV, Section 256): "Separate schools shall be provided for white and colored children, and no child of either race shall be permitted to attend a school of the other race." This provision has subsequently been superseded. However, because amendments to the Alabama constitution are collected at the end of the document rather than being interwoven, this provision is still present. Its existence may be one reason that there is agitation for the writing of a new Alabama constitution.

In contrast to the universal state constitutional concern with education is the relative silence when it comes to other aspects of social rights.[53] Twenty state constitutions contain some mention of matters concerning the protection of workers or the well-being of various needy publics. However, these provisions are striking for their diversity—covering a large number of subjects and a number of groups. No specific provision appears in more than eight state constitutions. Moreover, in contrast to the state constitutional provisions regarding the establishment of schools, these provisions tend to be permissive rather than mandatory. That is, the legislature *may* enact policies to assist a specified group but is not required to do so. Thus in most cases, when state constitutions broach certain issues associated with social rights— and the majority do not even do so—they are likely not to confer rights.

In various ways workplace matters are germane to inequalities of political voice, and the constitutions of sixteen states confer some kind of protections on workers. They cover a range of subjects, including the eight-hour day, workers' compensation, unemployment compensation, the minimum wage, and child labor. It is interesting to note that the most common state constitutional provision regarding workers, contained in the constitutions of eight states, is the right of workers not to be excluded from employment because they are not labor union members, a right that some other states protect by statute. This provision is, of course, controversial—establishing a right that, according to some, is fundamental for workers but, according to others, does not protect workers at all. In contrast, two states bestow constitutional protection on the opposite right, the right of workers to organize.[54]

Eleven states refer to some form of assistance to particular needy groups. These constitutional provisions are notable for the diversity of groups referenced—the disabled, the infirm, veterans, or, most commonly, the elderly. The most encompassing statement of state responsibility for public welfare appears in the Constitution of New York: "The aid, care and support of the needy are public concerns and shall be provided by the state and by such of its subdivisions, and in such manner and by such means, as the legislature shall from time to time determine."[55] This provision goes further than any other in a state constitution in affirming a public responsibility for the well-

53. On state constitutional protections for social rights, see Dinan, *American State Constitutional Tradition*, chap. 6.

54. Workers' right to organize—but not a right to work without joining a union—is recognized in Article 23 of the Universal Declaration of Human Rights.

55. Article XVII, Section 1.

being of those in need. Still, by leaving the determination to the legislature, it falls far short of the guarantee contained in the Universal Declaration of Human Rights, adopted by the United Nations General Assembly in 1948: "Everyone has the right to a standard of living adequate for the health and well-being of himself and of his family, including food, clothing, housing and medical care and necessary social services, and the right to security in the event of unemployment, sickness, disability, widowhood, old age or other lack of livelihood in circumstances beyond his control."[56] This provision of the Universal Declaration of Human Rights highlights the distinctive character of the egalitarian commitments that emerge from the state constitutions. On one hand, as foundational statements the state constitutions show much greater deference to democratic equality than does the federal constitution. On the other, that egalitarian spirit is suffused with liberal individualism and extends to equal rights and to supports for equal political and economic opportunity rather than to equality of economic condition.

How Do Americans View Equality?

In many ways, public opinion data about Americans' views of equality echo the lessons that emerged from our consideration of the state constitutions.[57] Surveys of the public show that equality is a fundamental democratic value to Americans. They are deeply committed to equality among citizens, and, when asked about public life in America, concern with equality figures importantly in their discourse. Nonetheless, as readily as "equality talk" comes to Americans, the embrace of equality does not always take precedence over competing values. Both belief in equality and support for acceptable inequalities are embedded in the American tradition.

That Americans are selective rather than thoroughgoing egalitarians has led to the inference that Americans are confused and inconsistent about equality.[58] Surely students of public opinion in America make a convincing

---

56. Article XXV, Section 1.

57. This discussion differs somewhat in its coverage and emphases from an earlier piece of which two of us were coauthors. See Kay Lehman Schlozman, Benjamin I. Page, Sidney Verba, and Morris P. Fiorina, "Inequalities of Political Voice," in *Inequality and American Democracy*, ed. Lawrence R. Jacobs and Theda Skocpol (New York: Russell Sage Foundation, 2005), pp. 20–28.

58. The way that egalitarian commitments are reconciled with competing democratic values has been conceptualized in various ways. Stanley Feldman and John Zaller, in "The Political Culture of Ambivalence: Responses to the Welfare State," *American Journal of Political*

case that Americans' attitudes are not always deeply informed and are sometimes illogical and contradictory. The literature on attitudes toward inequality—whether reporting the results of public opinion surveys or in-depth interviews—provides plenty of examples of individual and collective attitudes that are inconsistent when juxtaposed with one another, of assessments that are at variance with objective realities and that do not change with greater exposure to information, and of support for general statements that evaporates in the face of specific circumstances.[59]

Part of the reason for the seeming contradictions derives from the complexity of the concept of equality itself. Still, when differences among socially desired rewards, among domains of human life, among principles of distributive justice, and so on are taken into account, what might be considered inconsistent positions could be construed as reasonable responses that seek to balance a commitment to equality with other cherished values. Is the person who considers the following to be fair demonstrating mere ideological incoherence or a reasonable approach to acceptable inequalities?

That the electoral ballots cast by the scientists and the custodians who work at the National Institutes of Health should have equal weight but that their salaries should reflect the differences in their skills and training?

That grades awarded in elementary school might reflect how hard students work but that only the size of the orders, not the effort expended in generating them, should govern the commissions earned by members of a company's sales force?

Science 36 (1992): 268, cite Lloyd A. Free and Hadley Cantril, *The Political Beliefs of Americans: A Study of Public Opinion* (New York: Simon and Schuster, 1968), p. 37, who discussed the "schizoid combination of operational liberalism with ideological conservatism." In a similar formulation, Benjamin I. Page and Lawrence I. Jacobs, in *Class War? What Americans Really Think about Economic Inequality* (Chicago: University of Chicago Press, 2009), p. xi, maintain that "most Americans are *both* philosophically conservative and operationally liberal." See also Hochschild, *What's Fair?* pp. 229–237.

59. See, for example, Larry Bartels, *Unequal Democracy: The Political Economy of the New Gilded Age* (Princeton, NJ: Princeton University Press, 2008), esp. chaps. 5–7. On the basis of their specially commissioned 2007 survey, Page and Jacobs, in *Class War?*, cite several instances of public confusion—with respect, for example, to the earnings of workers in different occupations and the impact of different kinds of taxes.

That, with a few exceptions such as the insane, all adults should be eligible for jury service without regard to their educational attainment but that judges should be recruited from the ranks of the most able lawyers?

That a family that believes in treating children equally might respond to need by making greater resources available for the care and education of their child with Down syndrome or to ascription by giving greater freedom and responsibility to their teenager than to their toddler?

That differentials in compensation between CEOs and production workers in the United States—which are, on average, nearly three times higher than in Japan or Germany—are excessive but that CEOs should earn more than production employees?[60]

These examples make clear that characterizing an individual's attitudes with respect to equality is likely to be complicated enough and that characterizing the public's attitudes is likely to be even more perplexing. In order to make comparisons over time, across domains, and among societies, we would ideally like both to have longitudinal survey data asking about attitudes toward economic, political, and social inequalities in a number of developed democracies and to supplement the results of surveys with studies that involve in-depth interviews. Alas, the available information does not approach the ideal. Questions are asked in various formats. Although there are several interesting new surveys that researchers have put to good use, these surveys, like the cross-national batteries, cover only economic inequalities and do not ask about political inequalities. Also, the time series are somewhat spotty.

Although the data are far from perfect, the results of surveys and earlier work based on in-depth interviews converge on several broad generalizations. First, American egalitarianism is tempered by a strong strain of liberal individualism. Jennifer Hochschild summarizes one of the main themes running through in-depth interviews about views of "What's fair?" in terms of

---

60. Cross-national data about the ratio of average CEO and production worker pay are taken from Lars Osberg and Timothy Smeeding, "'Fair' Inequality? Attitudes towards Pay Differentials: The United States in Comparative Perspective," *American Sociological Review* (2006) 70: 464, Table 4.

the "strength of Anglo-American liberal political theory in ordinary people's distributive judgments. Respondents' distinctions between private and public, their individualistic view of the world, their perception of capitalism as the natural economic order, their beliefs that economic fairness differs from political and personal justice are all fundamental liberal tenets."[61] What is more, Americans believe in the existence of opportunity and—in contrast to many cultures, for example, the aristocracies of ancien régime Europe, in which work is disdained—respect work and are convinced that those who work hard can get ahead.

Consistent with the liberal individualism in which American egalitarianism is embedded, both public opinion data and in-depth interviews show that Americans are much more egalitarian with respect to political life than with respect to economic life. Americans are much more likely to believe in the equal dignity of persons and in equal legal and political rights than in equal economic rewards.

Public attitudes regarding these matters are hardly uniform, and such political orientations as party identification or thinking of oneself as a liberal or a conservative tend to be better predictors than demographic characteristics of attitudes toward equality.[62] Although the similarities among groups defined by their class or race are quite striking when it comes to these matters, there are differences that bear mention. Overall, blacks are more likely to espouse egalitarian positions than whites, and support for egalitarian principles and policies tends to be inversely related to education and income. A typical pattern shows agreement among demographic groups with respect to the direction of opinion but differentiation among groups with respect to the strength of opinion. For example, in a battery of items about equal opportunity and equal rights in the 2008 American National Election Study, fully 88 percent of whites and 95 percent of blacks agreed with the statement "Our society should do whatever is necessary to make sure that everyone has an equal opportunity to succeed." However, 59 percent of whites, as opposed to 81 percent of blacks, agreed strongly. Analogously, when respondents were

61. Hochschild, *What's Fair?* p. 233. A similar assessment is made by James R. Kluegel and Eliot Smith, *Beliefs about Equality* (Hawthorne, NY: Aldine de Gruyter, 1986), p. 11: "American culture contains a stable, widely held set of beliefs involving the availability of opportunity, individualistic explanations for achievement, and acceptance of unequal distributions of rewards."

62. See Bartels, *Unequal Democracy*, chap. 5, and Leslie McCall and Lane Kenworthy, "Americans' Social Policy Preferences in the Era of Rising Inequality," *Perspectives on Politics* 7 (2009): 459–484.

divided into five groups on the basis of socio-economic status (a combination of education and income), 48 percent of those in the highest group agreed strongly, in contrast to 70 percent in the lowest group.

Political Equality

Maria Pulaski, who earns her living cleaning houses, "insists that her rich employers are not '*better* than me. Because they're rich, they probably *think* they're better than me. But I think I'm just as equal as they are.'"[63] This assertion illustrates the respect in which Americans are unambiguously egalitarian: their belief in the inherent dignity and worth of every human being and in the equal political and economic rights of all. Unfortunately, such attitudes are rarely probed in surveys. However, in two surveys conducted during the 1970s, substantial majorities agreed that "teaching people that some kinds of people are better than others goes against the American idea of equality" (74 percent), that "teaching children that all people are really equal recognizes that all people are equally worthy and deserve equal treatment" (78 percent), and that "most of the people who are poor and needy could contribute something valuable to society if given the chance" (78 percent).[64] Even when these general statements were made more specific, by a margin of more than two to one, Americans opted for equality of respect: 64 percent agreed that "a person who holds a position of great responsibility, such as a doctor, judge, or elected official should be treated the same as anyone else," and only 29 percent that such a person "is entitled to be treated with special respect."[65]

In short, Americans have internalized the sentiments of the Declaration of Independence. Indeed, so widely dispersed is this opinion that an item about whether "all men are created equal" contained in early surveys elicited so little disagreement that it was dropped. It was asked again in 1958, a time when Jim Crow still ruled the South. When asked whether "the Declaration of Independence was right, only half right, or not right at all when it stated that 'all men are created equal,'" fully 67 percent of southern whites deemed

---

63. Hochschild, *What's Fair?* p. 113. Emphasis in the original.

64. Herbert McClosky and John Zaller, *The American Ethos: Public Attitudes towards Capitalism and Democracy* (Cambridge, MA: Harvard University Press, 1984), p. 66. Those who responded "Don't know" or were unwilling to choose between the options offered are included in the denominator. With those responses eliminated, the figures are 87 percent, 88 percent, and 92 percent, respectively.

65. McClosky and Zaller, *American Ethos*, p. 66.

the egalitarian statement to be right and only 6 percent considered it "not right at all."[66]

The political corollary to this egalitarian commitment to equal human worth is that we are equal as citizens—not only that citizens enjoy equal rights but also that they should have equal influence over public officials. According to the part-time secretary whom Hochschild interviewed at length, "'All men have the same basic rights. God didn't love one person more than another just 'cause he made one Hungarian and one Polish.'"[67] Nearly all of Hochschild's subjects expressed such views. Surveys have rarely covered this aspect of political equality. When Americans were asked in 1942 whether "it would be a good idea if we had titles like Lord, Duke, and Sir in this country the way they have in England," a whopping 98 percent said, "No," and absolutely no one said, "Yes."[68]

Nonetheless, Americans have a long history of tempering such egalitarian views with discriminatory attitudes and treatment. They have long espoused points of view that make invidious distinctions on the basis of race, ethnicity, religion, and gender and have acted on those opinions by denying basic political, economic, and social rights on such ascriptive bases. At least when it comes to attitudes, the second half of the twentieth century witnessed substantial change in an egalitarian direction. For example, in 1944 only 45 percent of those polled agreed that "Negroes should have as good a chance as white people to get any kind of job." By 1963, 85 percent of respondents chose the nondiscriminatory option. In 1972 nearly all respondents, 97 percent, agreed, so after that the question was not asked. Analogously, the expressed willingness of whites to vote for black candidates rose from 37 percent in 1958 to 52 percent in 1967 to 78 percent in 1978 to 95 percent in 1997.[69] Similarly, the proportions indicating that they would vote for a woman for presi-

---

66. McClosky and Zaller, *American Ethos*, p. 65. With those who had no opinion eliminated, the figures are 74 percent and 7 percent, respectively.

67. Hochschild, *What's Fair?* p. 157.

68. McClosky and Zaller, *American Ethos*, p. 74.

69. Howard Schuman, Charlotte Steeh, Lawrence Bobo, and Maria Krysan, *Racial Attitudes in America*, rev. ed. (Cambridge, MA: Harvard University Press, 1997), pp. 104–114. The authors point out (pp. 137–139) that there is less support for government efforts to enforce equal rights and implement equal rights policy than there is for the abstract principle of equal rights. However, with the exception of support for implementation of school integration, which has declined, support for government enforcement of equal rights policy has also increased over the period. Benjamin I. Page and Robert Y. Shapiro report similar findings in *The Rational Public* (Chicago: University of Chicago Press, 1992), pp. 68–75.

dent, approve of a woman "earning money in business or industry" even if she had "a husband capable of supporting her," or favor giving "women an equal role with men in running business, industry, and government" rose over the same period.[70]

Another aspect of Americans' political egalitarianism demonstrates that, over time, the issues raised in debates over the suffrage at the time of the Founding have been unambiguously resolved in the public mind in favor of support for equal citizen influence on government.[71] When asked whether "every citizen should have an equal chance to influence government policy," an overwhelming 95 percent of respondents agreed and a mere 5 percent disagreed. Similarly, 91 percent agreed that "everyone should have an equal right to hold public office today," and only 8 percent dissented. In addition, fully 91 percent rejected the suggestion that they would "like to see a dictatorship established in this country," and only 3 percent replied that it would be a "good idea."[72] When survey questions made explicit the varying capacities of citizens for self-government, support for equal citizenship eroded somewhat. Still, compared to some of the views expressed at the time of the Founding, support for political equality among contemporary citizens remains substantial. When asked, "Who should be allowed to vote?" 69 percent of respondents said, "All adult citizens, regardless of how ignorant they may be," and 10 percent indicated that "only people who know something about the issues" should be permitted to go to the polls.[73]

70. Page and Shapiro, *Rational Public*, pp. 100–104.

71. From a somewhat different perspective, Sidney Verba and Gary R. Orren also characterize Americans as more committed to equality in the political than in the economic domain in *Equality in America: The View from the Top* (Cambridge, MA: Harvard University Press, 1985), esp. chaps. 9–10. Verba and Orren surveyed leaders from a variety of sectors—business, labor, the media, the political parties, and so on—and found them to be egalitarians when it comes to political influence but not when it comes to economic rewards. However, while these elites were in agreement about the desirability of equality of political influence among important groups, they were in complete disagreement on which groups actually have more political influence: "Each group thinks that it is deprived of influence and its adversaries are advantaged. As a result, the general consensus has little equalizing potential. If any contending group were in a position to do so, it might try to equalize the distribution of influence. But if it did so according to its own perceptions of reality it would only make the situation more unequal from the perspective of other groups. Business would reduce the influence of labor, making things more equal from its perspective and much less from labor's. Labor would return the favor" (p. 242). Note that, because the groups in question are of very different sizes, equal political influence among groups would produce unequal influence among individuals.

72. McClosky and Zaller, *American Ethos*, p. 74.

73. McClosky and Zaller, *American Ethos*, p. 75. Of those who were willing to make a choice, 77 percent selected the egalitarian option. This item was included in a survey con-

Americans' commitment to equal political influence does not necessarily imply that they put ordinary citizens on an equal footing with duly constituted political elites. That is, Americans' political egalitarianism does not extend to a populist belief that the opinion of the majority of ordinary citizens should necessarily prevail over the considered judgment of public officials. When asked, "How much influence do you think the views of the majority of Americans *should* have on the decisions of elected and government officials in Washington?" fully 68 percent of those surveyed responded, "A great deal," and another 26 percent said, "A fair amount." However, when the issue was posed as a pair of alternatives, this overwhelming consensus crumbled. When forced to choose, 42 percent said that "elected and government officials should use their knowledge and judgment to make decisions about what is the best policy to pursue even if this goes against what the majority of the public wants"; 54 percent responded that "elected and government officials should follow what the majority of the public wants, even if it goes against the officials' knowledge and judgment." When the question received additional qualification, the commitment to majoritarian democracy eroded somewhat further. When respondents were questioned after being told, "At times in the past, the majority of Americans have held positions later judged to be wrong, such as their support of racial segregation of blacks and whites," 40 percent indicated that they thought that "officials in Washington should do what the majority wants because the majority is usually right," while 51 percent replied that "officials [should] rely on their knowledge and judgment when they think the majority is wrong."[74]

Economic Equality

In complicated ways Americans' overall commitment to equality when it comes to politics spills over into economics. For the past quarter century, a

---

ducted in 1978–1979. Other questions about literacy qualifications for the vote asked in 1958 and 1965 elicited somewhat lower levels of support, but in no case did majority opinion favor denying the right to vote to voters "even if they can't do so intelligently."

74. These data are taken from the results of a survey conducted early in 2001 in collaboration with the Henry J. Kaiser Family Foundation and reported in *Public Perspective*, July–August 2001, pp. 10–24. McClosky and Zaller, in *American Ethos*, pp. 78–79, present data from their 1978–1979 study showing the same ambivalence. Americans are overwhelmingly likely to say that "elections are one of the best ways to keep elected officials on their toes" and that "elected officials would badly misuse their power if they weren't watched and guided by the voters." Yet there is no consensus on whether most voters have the ability to "use their vote[s] wisely," to "know what's best for them," and to "pick their own leaders wisely."

majority of Americans have agreed that "money and wealth in this country should be more evenly distributed among a larger percentage of the people" and rejected the alternative that the "distribution of money and wealth in this country today is fair."[75] Furthermore, in 2007, 72 percent of respondents—including 56 percent of Republicans—agreed that "differences in income in America are too large."[76]

Nevertheless, Americans are most definitely not economic egalitarians.[77] In contrast to their embrace of equality of political influence is their willingness to condone inequalities in economic rewards. The rejection of economic equality rests on a foundation of supportive beliefs. One aspect of those beliefs is a strong consensus on what might be called "capitalist values"—even among those for whom free markets work less well.[78] While Americans sometimes assume the universality of their high regard for work, many societies have disdained work in favor of a life of prayer or luxury. In contrast, as Tocqueville pointed out, Americans consider work to be virtuous. Indeed, a substantial majority of Americans, 77 percent, indicated that they "sometimes feel that laziness is almost like a sin."[79] Moreover, there is a strong consensus on the value of free enterprise, private property, and competition and a reciprocal hostility to government ownership of industry.

A second aspect of the foundation for the endorsement of economic inequality is the belief in American Dream of equal opportunity—an aspect of the American ethos that functions to bridge the potentially antagonistic commitments to equality and liberal capitalism. An overwhelming 95 percent of those polled agreed that "everyone should have equal opportunities to get ahead."[80] Not only do Americans believe that equality of opportunity should exist, they believe that equality of opportunity does exist. Over the second half of the twentieth century, pollsters periodically posed questions in various forms about whether those who work hard have opportunities for

75. Page and Jacobs, *Class War?* p. 41. See also McCall and Kenworthy, "Americans' Social Policy Preferences," pp. 459–463. Bartels, in *Unequal Democracy*, p. 146, points out that the public assessments of economic inequality do not seem to be driven by changes in the actual level of economic inequality.

76. Page and Jacobs, *Class War?* p. 44.

77. Verba and Orren, in *Equality in America*, chaps. 8–10, come to the same conclusion in their study of attitudes toward inequality among elites drawn from various sectors.

78. Bartels, *Unequal Democracy*, p. 149.

79. Data from a 1958 poll contained in McClosky and Zaller, *American Ethos*, p. 108. This paragraph is based on the evidence and argument the authors present in chap. 4.

80. Data cited by Page and Jacobs, *Class War?* p. 57.

success. Over and over, opinion has come down squarely on the side of opportunity: 76 percent of those polled—and 70 percent of low-income respondents—agreed in 2007 that "it's still possible to start out poor in this country, work hard, and become rich."[81] When asked to rate the importance of a long series of factors for "getting ahead in life," Americans placed gumption and industry at the top of the list. The percentages rating the following factors as "essential" or "very important" for getting ahead were as follows: ambition, 90 percent; hard work, 88; having a good education, 87; natural ability, 52; knowing the right people, 43; coming from a wealthy family, 18; being born a man or a woman, 17.[82] Nevertheless, in response to a question probing possible inequalities of opportunity on the basis of class, a substantial majority, 83 percent, indicated that "compared to the average person, people who grew up in rich families" have a "better" or "much better" chance of getting ahead.[83]

Against the background of belief in capitalism, hard work, and opportunity, it is hardly surprising that Americans do not import their political egalitarianism to the economy. When asked whether "it would be a good thing if all people received the same amount of money no matter what jobs they do," only a handful of respondents, 7 percent, agreed or agreed strongly.[84] When alternatives are posed as to how income should be distributed—equally or on the basis of need, hard work, or ability—Americans always favor the latter two over the former two. Fully 78 percent of respondents indicated that "under a fair economic system . . . people with more ability would earn higher salaries" and only 7 percent that "all people would earn about the same." When asked in another survey, "Which would be fairer?" 71 percent said "to pay people wages according to how hard they work" and only 6 percent "to pay people wages according to their economic needs." In fact, 85 percent of Americans believe that "giving everybody about the same income regardless of the type of work they do . . . would destroy the desire to work hard and do a better job." Only 5 percent deem such an arrangement to be "a

81. Page and Jacobs, *Class War?* p. 51. Everett Carll Ladd and Karlyn H. Bowman present the responses to seven different questions asked in surveys between 1952 and 1997 in *Attitudes toward Economic Inequality* (Washington, DC: AEI Press, 1998), pp. 54–55.

82. 1992 data from the National Opinion Research Center (NORC) presented in Ladd and Bowman, *Attitudes toward Economic Inequality*, pp. 30–31.

83. The data are from an Illinois survey conducted in 1980 and reported in Kluegel and Smith, *Beliefs about Inequality*, p. 49.

84. Data from their 1980 Illinois survey reported by Kluegel and Smith in *Beliefs about Inequality*, p. 112. Note that only 1 percent of respondents agreed "strongly."

fairer way to distribute the country's wealth than the present system."[85] When the attitudes of groups defined by race or social class are considered, not unexpectedly, whites and respondents of higher socio-economic status are more likely to espouse inequalities in economic outcomes than are blacks and those of more limited education and income. Still, what is striking is much less the magnitude of the group differences than the extent to which there is agreement on the existence of opportunity and the legitimacy of economic inequalities.[86]

This configuration of opinions leads to a circumstance of much wider support for government efforts that would promote equality of opportunity than for government efforts to establish equality of economic results. In fact, when the alternatives were posed in a 1993 survey—promoting "equal opportunity for all, that is allowing everyone to compete for jobs and wealth on a fair and even basis" as against promoting "equal outcomes, that is ensuring that everyone has a decent standard of living and that there are only small differences in wealth and income between the top and the bottom in society"— respondents opted 84 percent to 12 percent for the former.[87]

Although Americans recognize that inequality has grown, their opinions about a variety of policies that would narrow inequalities of economic outcomes by either squeezing the top or elevating the bottom are complicated and ambivalent. Overall, they reject the notion that it is the government's responsibility to narrow the income gap between the best and the worst off.[88] In surveys conducted since the New Deal, they have rejected strongly the suggestion that there should be a limit on what either individuals or companies can earn. In 1994, only 22 percent endorsed "a top limit on incomes so that no one can earn more than $1,000,000 a year."[89] Yet when asked about earnings in a series of specific occupations, Americans did not simply endorse the status quo. More than 60 percent of respondents indicated that certain

85. Data from surveys conducted during the 1970s reported in McClosky and Zaller, *American Ethos*, p. 84. Kluegel and Smith, in *Beliefs about Inequality*, pp. 112–114, show similar results derived from other surveys. Interestingly, survey researchers have not probed the trade-off between hard work and ability—that is, how economic rewards should be allocated between an industrious employee of low skills and an indolent but highly trained one.

86. See Kluegel and Smith, *Beliefs about Inequality*, pp. 129–134, 295–297.

87. NORC data presented in Ladd and Bowman, *Attitudes toward Economic Inequality*, p. 33.

88. Page and Jacobs, *Class War?* p. 54.

89. Ladd and Bowman present the responses to ten questions asked in surveys between 1939 and 1994 in *Attitudes toward Economic Inequality*, p. 108.

types of workers (teachers, lower-level white-collar workers, and nonunion-ized factory workers) earn too little and other types of workers (entertainers, professional athletes, owners and executives of large corporations, physi-cians, and government officials) earn too much. With respect to poverty, opinion was not monolithic but leaned in the direction of holding the poor themselves, rather than the system, responsible for their need and, by a mar-gin of more than two to one, suggested that "to improve their conditions, the poor . . . should help themselves" rather than "receiv[ing] special government help."[90]

Attitudes toward welfare are especially complex, combining, on one hand, skepticism about government assistance to the poor and, on the other, a gen-uine desire to help those in need. For example, in 2007, 80 percent of all respondents—and 72 percent of Republicans—favored having their "own tax dollars . . . used to help pay for . . . retraining programs for people whose jobs have been eliminated."[91] In general, the inclination to assist the poor pre-vails over the distaste for government help to the needy when the poor are deserving—that is, when their poverty results from circumstances beyond their immediate control and they strive to overcome their situations and when programs on their behalf discourage dependence and are not charac-terized by abuse, fraud, or waste.[92] The American aversion to welfare presents less of a dilemma for conservatives, who are less likely to espouse egalitarian principles, than for liberals, for whom such principles may be in tension with economic individualism.[93]

In a parallel to what emerged from the state constitutions, no such ambiv-alence emerges from the surveys with respect to support for education, which

---

90. Data and conclusions in the last portion of this paragraph are drawn from McClosky and Zaller, *American Ethos*, pp. 92, 120, and 125, and Kluegel and Smith, *Beliefs about In-equality*, pp. 78, 122, and 165.

91. Page and Jacobs, *Class War?* p. 62.

92. On public opinion and government assistance to the poor, see Fay Lomax Cook and Edith J. Barrett, *Support for the American Welfare State* (New York: Columbia University Press, 1992); and Hugh Heclo, "Poverty Politics," in *Confronting Poverty*, ed. Sheldon H. Dan-ziger, Gary Sandefur, and Daniel H. Weinberg (Cambridge, MA: Harvard University Press, 1994), pp. 396–437. Both of these works predate the reform of the welfare system in 1996 and the substitution of Temporary Assistance for Needy Families for Aid to Families with Depen-dent Children. In spite of the policy change and the change in opinion that preceded it, the generalizations in this paragraph probably remain apt. For an analysis emphasizing the changes in opinion that preceded welfare reform, see Steven M. Teles, *Whose Welfare?* (Law-rence: University Press of Kansas, 1996), chap. 3.

93. Feldman and Zaller, "The Political Culture of Ambivalence," p. 273.

is viewed as key to establishing equality of opportunity. At least as measured by a battery of items in a 2007 survey, Americans are willing to invest heavily in education: 87 percent agreed that "government should spend whatever is necessary to ensure that all children have really good public schools they can go to" and 70 percent that "spending tax money to provide a college education for those who can't afford it is a good idea."[94]

Although Americans pay universal homage to the principle of equality of opportunity, they have long been skeptical about a second policy with implications for inequalities of opportunity, inheritance taxes that limit what can be handed on from one generation to the next. Considerably before the movement to kill the "death tax" had gathered visibility and momentum, ordinary Americans—the overwhelming majority of whom would never be required to pay it—supported the repeal of the estate tax. According to Larry Bartels, public opposition to estate taxes—which cannot be explained by an elite-level effort to generate grassroots anger and which is resistant to greater information—is anchored in "the sanctity of private property" and "deeply held views about family, work, and economic opportunity."[95]

American Attitudes in Cross-National Perspective

Cross-national surveys, which focus almost exclusively on economic rather than political or social inequality, place American attitudes in perspective. When we consider evidence about the opinions about inequality of citizens in other advanced democracies, much of what we have already observed with respect to Americans' attitudes continues to obtain. Like Americans, citizens elsewhere invoke multiple and shifting principles of distributive justice—in ways that are often not fully rational, consistent, or respectful of abstract distinctions but that are usually relatively sensible. The authors of one cross-national study summarized it as follows:

> Our results point toward respondents articulating established attitudes to distributive justice, although rather broad ones; namely, those of equality of outcome, justified inequalities, and need. These general ori-

---

94. Page and Jacobs, *Class War?* pp. 58–59. McClosky and Zaller, in *American Ethos*, pp. 83 and 91, and McCall and Kenworthy, in "Americans' Social Policy Preferences," pp. 467–468, report similar findings from earlier surveys.

95. Bartels, *Unequal Democracy*, pp. 215, 216. On public opinion and the estate tax, see also Michael J. Graetz and Ian Shapiro, *Death by a Thousand Cuts: The Fight over Taxing Inherited Wealth* (Princeton, NJ: Princeton University Press, 2005), chap. 12.

entations gloss the more nuanced philosophical distinctions between, for example, entitlement, merit, and the need for incentives, as different ways in which inequalities might be justified. But there seems little doubt that ordinary people deploy multiple criteria in making justice judgments, giving prominence to considerations of need in the allocation of scarce health care and housing; recognizing that inequalities in wealth and income may be justified on grounds of merit, entitlement, or incentives; and making separate judgments with respect to a guaranteed minimum standard of living and some restrictions on the maximum income available to any one individual.[96]

In addition, surveys show that there is a popular consensus in all societies against radical equality of incomes. Furthermore, across societies there is rough congruence in the hierarchy of relative compensation among occupations.[97] Moreover, social group differences in attitudes toward economic inequality tend to be similar across societies.[98]

Despite these similarities among advanced democracies, the United States stands at one end of a continuum with respect to each of the tendencies outlined in the preceding section.[99] Compared with citizens of other advanced democracies, Americans tend to be the most likely to be committed to "capitalist values."[100] They are the most likely to believe that hard work should and will be rewarded, to think that in their country there are equal opportunities

96. Adam Swift, Gordon Marshall, Carole Burgoyne, and David Routh, "Distributive Justice: Does It Matter What the People Think?" in *Social Justice and Political Change: Public Opinion in Capitalist and Post-Communist States*, ed. James R. Kluegel, David S. Mason, and James R. Wegener (New York: Aldine de Gruyter, 1995), pp. 34–35.

97. Jonathan Kelley and M.D.R. Evans, "The Legitimation of Inequality: Occupational Earnings in Nine Nations," *American Journal of Sociology* 99 (1993): 95, 97.

98. James R. Kluegel and Masaru Miyano, "Justice Beliefs and Support for the Welfare State in Advanced Capitalism," in *Social Justice*, ed. Kluegel, Mason, and Wegener, p. 90.

99. In *Attitudes toward Economic Inequality*, pp. 118–123, Ladd and Bowman present the responses to twenty different questions asked in three different surveys in ten countries during the early 1990s. (None of the questions was asked in every country. The plurality were asked in eight of the ten countries.) For twelve of the twenty items, respondents in the United States were the least egalitarian (or the most oriented to opportunity and hard work). For half the remainder, American respondents were in second place. On none of the items were American respondents below third place.

100. David S. Mason, in "Justice, Socialism, and Participation in the Postcommunist States," in *Social Justice*, ed. Kluegel, Mason, and Wegener, pp. 60–61, show that Americans scored lowest of respondents from thirteen countries on a scale indicating support for socialist principles.

to get ahead, and to consider the poor to be responsible for their circumstances.[101] Furthermore, Americans are more comfortable with unequal economic results than are their counterparts in other advanced democracies: more likely to consider pay differentials to be fair and, when asked what workers in a series of occupations do and should make, willing to countenance a wider spread in the compensation of workers with high and low pay.[102] In addition, they are the least likely to be supportive of government efforts to address economic inequalities by redistributing income, providing

101. Duane F. Alwin, Galin Gornev, and Ludmila Khakhulina, "Comparative Referential Structures, System Legitimacy, and Justice Sentiments," in *Social Justice*, ed. Kluegel, Mason, and Wegener, pp. 121, 125; Giacomo Corneo and Hans Peter Grüner, "Individual Preferences for Political Redistribution," *Journal of Public Economics* 83 (2002): 90; Alberto Alesina and George-Marios Angeletos, "Fairness and Redistribution" *American Economic Review* 95 (2005): 913; Edward L. Glaeser, "Inequality," *Oxford Handbook of Political Economy*, ed. D. Fullerton, and Barry Weingast (New York: Oxford University Press, 2006), chap. 34.

102. Kelley and Evans, "Legitimation of Inequality," pp. 95, 100, 112; Stefan Svallfors, "Worlds of Welfare and Attitudes to Redistribution: A Comparison of Eight Western Nations," *European Sociological Review* 13 (1997): 289–290; and David L. Weakliem, Robert Andersen, and Anthony F. Heath, "By Popular Demand: The Effect of Public Opinion on Income Inequality," *Comparative Sociology* 4 (2005): 267–268. Addressing this issue, Osberg and Smeeding, in "'Fair' Inequality?" assert (p. 456) that "the key point is that the United States is *not* a clear outlier when one compares mean responses across nations" (emphasis in the original). It is not altogether clear how to square this assertion and the data analysis in this sophisticated paper with the common wisdom. Several points are worth noting. First, the pattern Osberg and Smeeding describe is a complicated one involving polarization of attitudes with respect to income redistribution and shifting patterns over time such that those at the top have become relatively less willing to tolerate economic inequalities while those at the bottom have become more so. In addition, they are using data from the 1999 International Social Survey Program (ISSP). Other researchers cited in this section have used earlier versions of the ISSP or data from the International Social Justice Survey or the World Values Survey. Moreover, the United States looks more like an outlier when the comparison countries include advanced democracies only. When a larger number of countries is included in the analysis, the United States looks less distinctive.

Another point concerns the meaning of national data based on items asking whether income differences are too large or whether the government should be doing more to reduce income differences in that particular country. Answers in the United States frequently do not look very different from those in Norway or Sweden. However, the Norwegians and Swedes start at such a different baseline with respect to the actual distribution of income and to government efforts to redistribute income and aid those who are less well off that equivalent preferences for additional redistribution mask real differences between Americans, on the one hand, and Norwegians or Swedes, on the other, with respect to a desired level of inequality of economic outcomes. On this point, see Sidney Verba and Steven Kelman, Gary R. Orren, Ichiro Miyake, Joji Watanuki, Ikuo Kabashima, and G. Donald Ferree Jr., *Elites and the Idea of Equality* (Cambridge, MA: Harvard University Press, 1987), p. 128; and F. John Mehrtens III, "Three Words of Public Opinion? Values, Variation, and the Effect on Social Policy," *International Journal of Public Opinion* 16 (2004): 125–129.

a minimum income and standard of living to the needy, making sure that those who need jobs can get them, or limiting the amount of wealth that can be passed along to the next generation.[103] In an analysis based on the 2004 International Social Survey Project, Ursula Dallinger reports that the United States ranks highest among 23 nations in terms of the proportion of respondents who reject the view that the government should reduce income inequality, a striking result in light of the fact that the United States ranks quite high in income inequality.[104]

Americans—The Ambivalent Egalitarians

Our brief consideration of the extent to which the constitutions that govern Americans and surveys of public attitudes show evidence of egalitarian commitments demonstrates at best an ambivalent egalitarianism. The federal constitution had remarkably little to say about equality until the Equal Protection Clause of the Fourteenth Amendment was added after the Civil War. Although the state constitutions have been used in certain circumstances in the service of inegalitarian ends, taken together, the state constitutions show much more deference to the value of equality both in their rhetoric and in the extent to which they contain substantive egalitarian protections. That

---

Another qualification is suggested by Kelley and Evans, who point out (pp. 112–114) that, when national differences in the distribution of occupations are taken into account, Americans look less distinctive when it comes to preferred wage differentials. This point helps us to understand that Americans' level of comfort with inequalities in compensation may reflect social structural differences rather than a culture uniquely congenial to capitalism. Still, it is important to recognize the significance of the descriptive finding that Americans are willing to accept larger income differences than those in other advanced democracies.

103. Kluegel and Miyano, "Justice Beliefs and Support for the Welfare State," pp. 89–90; Alwin, Gornev, and Khakhulina, "Comparative Referential Structures," pp. 124–125; Svallfors, "Worlds of Welfare," pp. 288–289; and Corneo and Grüner, "Individual Preferences for Political Redistribution," pp. 89, 102.

104. Ursula Dallinger, "Public Support for Redistribution: What Explains Cross-National Differences," *Journal of European Social Policy* 20 (2010): 333–345. Similarly, data collected between 1998 and 2001 about 27 countries surveyed as part of the International Social Survey Program show that with respect to several measures of the existence of opportunity and the government's responsibility for reducing differences in income, opinion in the United States is consistently far from the median in the direction of belief that rewards are apportioned on the basis of talent, effort, and skills. See Julia B. Isaacs, "International Comparisons of Economic Mobility," in *Getting Ahead or Losing Ground: Economic Mobility in America*, ed. Julia B. Isaacs, Isabel V. Sawhill, and Ron Haskins (Washington, DC: Brookings Institution and Pew Mobility Project, 2008), p. 37.

said, no state constitution approaches the kinds of egalitarian provisions set forth in the Universal Declaration of Human Rights. Even so, it is clear that the state constitutions reflect that the controversy in the early years of the republic over the extent to which participation in democratic governance should be restricted has, more or less, been settled. While that conflict reverberates in such contemporary matters as the dispute over felon disenfranchisement, the contemporary state constitutions contain important guarantees of the political equality of adult citizens.

With respect to citizen attitudes toward inequality, the preferences expressed in surveys reflect the complexities of what is contained in the state constitutions. Americans invoke a variety of criteria of fairness, not always fully consistently, in considering matters of distributive justice. Their genuine belief in the words of the Declaration of Independence still leaves space for a broad zone of acceptable inequalities. Overall, they are much more likely to subscribe to an egalitarian point of view in society and politics than in economics. They are committed to the fundamental equality among persons and to equal citizenship—equal political rights and equal political influence for all. When it comes to economic outcomes, their egalitarianism extends to equal opportunity for all but expects unequal rewards to accrue to the hardworking and talented. Yet within the boundaries of these broad generalizations we found ample evidence of ambivalence. For example, to establish genuine equality of opportunity requires a modicum of equality of condition among the young. However, Americans are skeptical about empowering the government to take a number of actions—including limiting the inheritance of great wealth—that might facilitate the creation of equality of opportunity among members of the next generation.

More germane to our concern with equal political voice, the strong preference for equal political influence among ordinary citizens coexists with ambivalence about whether the dictates of equal political influence require duly chosen political elites to respond to the will of the majority or only to listen equally carefully to all before exercising independent judgment. In either case, it is clear that equal political voice is required. Whether the model of democracy is a populist one in which political elites respond automatically to citizen preferences or a representative one in which political elites draw on their own expertise and judgment in responding to expressions of preference from citizens, equal political voice is a prerequisite for political equality.

3

The Context:
Growing Economic Inequality
and Weakening Unions

The context in which contemporary political inequalities are embedded includes two significant trends over the past generation: increasing economic inequality and decreasing labor union membership and strength. These two trends are probably related to one another, although there are different interpretations as to just how. While both tendencies are evident in other developed democracies, they are especially pronounced in the United States. Both have consequences not only for economic outcomes but also for inequalities of political voice. While their economic implications surely outweigh their political ones, they constitute an essential part of the backdrop for our consideration of political voice. In this chapter we draw on scholarship in several fields to present a brief overview of the growth in economic inequality and the erosion in union strength. Throughout, we anchor our understanding of contemporary circumstances in longitudinal and cross-national data in order to make comparisons across time and space.

In two fundamental ways, class inequalities underlie our inquiry into both the roots and the consequences of inequalities of political voice. First, inequalities of political participation are grounded in disparities in income, occupation, and especially education. As we shall demonstrate over and over, social class has multiple consequences for differences in individual and collective political participation. Second, inequalities on the basis of class shape the content of political conflict. That is, class differences are an important source of political division. Although the list of contentious political issues in contemporary America is long and varied, there can be no doubt that matters associated with differences in income and material well-being are critically important in generating political conflict.[1]

Of the two trends that we treat in this chapter, which many observers consider to be interrelated, the increase in economic inequality is an especially significant part of the context for our inquiry.[2] We write during a period when the United States has not yet pulled out of a recession of a severity not witnessed since the 1930s. While the pain associated with this economic dislocation is unambiguous, the longer-term consequences are much less certain. Even though the burden of an economic downturn falls much more heavily on those on the lower rungs of the economic ladder, recessions have sometimes had the short-run impact of ameliorating economic inequality. In the recession after the turn of the millennium, the combination of a plunging stock market, falling dividends, and sinking home prices temporarily diminished economic inequalities.[3] Although some journalistic accounts suggested that the same pattern may be manifest in the current recession, systematic data through 2009 are less clear as to whether the current recession will diminish inequality over the longer run.[4]

1. See, for example, Mark D. Brewer, *Split: Class and Cultural Divides in American Politics* (Washington, DC: CQ Press, 2007); Larry M. Bartels, *Unequal Democracy* (Princeton, NJ: Princeton University Press, 2008); and Jeffrey M. Stonecash, "Class in American Politics," in *New Directions in American Politics*, ed. Jeffrey M. Stonecash (New York: Routledge, 2010), chap. 7.

2. Investigating the matters under consideration here—in particular, doing so cross-nationally—presents a variety of difficulties, implying the need for caution in interpreting results. For elaboration of the concerns, see the studies cited later. Nevertheless, with respect to many themes, especially the extensiveness of economic inequalities in the United States and their exacerbation in recent decades, there is consensus among studies.

3. Edward N. Wolff, in *Poverty and Income Distribution*, 2nd ed. (Chichester, England: Wiley Blackwell, 2009), p. 12, makes the point that recent trends constitute a reversal of the traditional pattern, in which inequality increases during periods of recession and decreases during periods of economic growth.

4. See David Leonhardt and Geraldine Fabrikant, "After 30-Year Run, Rise of the Super-Rich Hits a Sobering Wall," *New York Times*, August 21, 2009; Arloc Sherman and Chad Stone, "Income Gaps between Very Rich and Everyone Else More than Tripled in Last Three Decades, New Data Show," Center on Budget and Policy Priorities, Washington, DC, June 25, 2010, http://www.cbpp.org/files/6-25-10inc.pdf (accessed February 24, 2011); and Economic Policy Institute, "Low-, Middle-, and High-Income Growth, 1947–2009," and "2007 Most Unequal of Any Year Barring One—1928," in *The State of Working America* (Washington, DC: Economic Policy Institute, 2011), http://www.stateofworkingamerica.org/charts/view/137 and http://www.stateofworkingamerica.org/charts/view/155 (accessed February 24, 2011).

Increasing Economic Inequality

It is widely acknowledged that, by a variety of metrics, economic rewards have become more unequally distributed over the past generation.[5] Fortunately, we have information going back to the time of the passage of the constitutional amendment authorizing the federal income tax in 1913 about household income: that is, the income of households from a variety of sources including, most importantly, the earnings of household members as well as government transfers such as Social Security, dividends, rents, and so on. Although many households encompass members who are not related to one another as family, household income is also referred to as "family income."

The story of the changing share of pretax national income commanded by the top 10 percent and the top 1 percent of American households since 1913 is by now familiar. Between the two world wars there was variation, but no long-term trend, in the share of income commanded by these well-off groups. Then, during World War II, it decreased markedly, remaining relatively stable until the 1970s, when, once again, it began to climb fairly steadily.[6] After

5. On the growth of economic inequality, see Sheldon Danziger and Peter Gottschalk, eds., *Uneven Tides: Rising Inequality in America* (New York: Russell Sage Foundation, 1993); Peter Gottschalk, "Inequality, Income Growth, and Mobility: The Basic Facts," *Journal of Economic Perspectives* 11 (1997): 21–40; Richard B. Freeman, *When Earnings Diverge: Causes, Consequences, and Cure for the New Inequality in the United States* (Washington, DC: National Policy Association, 1997); Frank Levy, *The New Dollars and Dreams: American Incomes and Economic Change* (New York: Russell Sage Foundation, 1998); Edward N. Wolff, *Top Heavy* (New York: New Press, 2002); Thomas Piketty and Emmanuel Saez, "Income Inequality in the United States, 1913–1998," *Quarterly Journal of Economics* 118 (2003): 1–39; Gary Burtless and Christopher Jencks, "American Inequality and Its Consequences," in *Agenda for the Nation*, ed. Henry J. Aaron, James M Lindsay, and Pietro S. Nivola (Washington, DC: Brookings Institution, 2003), chap. 3; Lane Kenworthy, *Egalitarian Capitalism* (New York: Russell Sage Foundation, 2004); Lars Osberg, Timothy M. Smeeding, and Jonathan Schwabish, "Income Distribution and Public Social Expenditures," and Howard Rosenthal, "Politics, Public Policy, and Inequality: A Look Back at the Twentieth Century," in *Social Inequality*, ed. Kathryn M. Neckerman (New York: Russell Sage Foundation, 2004), chaps. 22 and 23; Lawrence Mishel, Jared Bernstein, and Heidi Shierholz, *The State of Working America, 2008/2009* (Ithaca, NY: Cornell University Press, ILR Press, 2009); Ron Haskins and Isabel Sawhill, *Creating an Opportunity Society* (Washington, DC: Brookings Institution, 2009), chaps. 2–3; and Arloc Sherman, "Income Gaps Hit Record Levels in 2006, New Data Show," Center on Budget and Policy Priorities, Washington, DC, April 17, 2009, http://www.cbpp.org/cms/index .cfm?fa=view&id=2789 (accessed December 29, 2009). Wolff, *Poverty and Income Distribution*, chap. 1, provides a succinct summary of the issues discussed here. Other chapters provide extensive analysis, data, and bibliographical references.

6. Using Internal Revenue Service data, Piketty and Saez describe this pattern in "Income Inequality," pp. 7–11. They define *income* as market income but exclude capital gains. Updated

decreasing somewhat with the end of the stock market bubble of the late 1990s, by 2007 income inequality had reached a level surpassed in only one year since 1913—1928.[7]

Table 3.1, which presents data about what happened between 1979 and 2007, shows a reversal of the pattern that obtained during the preceding generation. Between World War II and the mid-1970s, the most affluent households lagged behind the vast majority of households below the top tenth with respect to income benefits from gains in productivity and increases in national income. Afterward, those benefits accrued disproportionately to the households in the highest income decile.[8] Because these data, the most recent available at this writing, stop short of the recession that began in 2008, there may have been some amelioration of these trends.

Nonetheless, the pattern is quite striking. As measured in constant dollars, the average after-tax household income for those at the bottom of the economic ladder—and for the middle-class households in the middle three-fifths —grew quite modestly over the period from 1979 to 2007. In contrast, household incomes for those in the top fifth increased substantially: the *growth* in household income of those in the highest fifth was larger than the *average 2007 income* of those in the fourth quintile on the economic ladder and more than five times the income of those in the lowest fifth.[9] Even more notable is the extent to which this growth was concentrated in the top 1 percent of households, whose average household incomes nearly quadrupled in real terms over the period. The result of these changes is that the *share* of total household income accruing to the top quintile grew by more than a fifth, from 42.4 percent to 52.5 percent, and the shares of each of the bottom four-fifths diminished. In fact, this redistribution benefited only an extremely narrow slice of households: only the top 10 percent saw their share of after-tax

---

data can be found at http://elsa.berkeley.edu/~saez/TabFig2004prel.xls (accessed September 23, 2010).

7. Economic Policy Institute, "2007 most unequal of any year barring one."

8. See Avi Feller and Chad Stone, "Top 1 Percent of Americans Reaped Two-Thirds of Income Gains in Last Economic Expansion," Center on Budget and Policy Priorities, Washington, DC: September 9, 2009, http://www.cbpp.org/files/9-9-09pov.pdf (accessed December 29, 2009).

9. It is interesting to note the difference between the patterns for the earlier and later periods in these data. From 1979 to 1993, real after-tax household incomes actually decreased for the bottom two groups and grew quite sluggishly for the third and fourth quintiles. Only in the top fifth was income growth more or less steady throughout the period.

Table 3.1   Growing Economic Inequality:
After-Tax Household Income by Income Group, 1979–2007

Income Group	Average After-Tax Income (2007 Dollars)			Share of After-Tax Income (Percent)		
	1979	1993	2007	1979	1993	2007
Lowest Fifth	$15,300	$14,900	$17,700	6.8%	5.3%	4.9%
Second Fifth	$31,000	$30,600	$38,000	12.3%	10.9%	9.4%
Middle Fifth	$44,100	$45,100	$55,300	16.5%	16.0%	14.1%
Fourth Fifth	$57,700	$62,200	$77,700	22.3%	22.1%	20.0%
Highest Fifth	$101,700	$124,600	$198,300	42.4%	46.8%	52.5%
Top 10 Percent	$128,700	$165,200	$289,300	27.6%	31.7%	38.7%
Top 5 Percent	$169,600	$225,100	$404,500	18.1%	21.8%	29.3%
Top 1 Percent	$348,600	$529,400	$1,319,700	7.5%	10.0%	17.1%

Source: Congressional Budget Office, "Average Federal Tax Rates and Income, by Income Category (1979–2007)," June 2010, http://www.cbo.gov/publications/collections/collections.cfm? collect=13 (accessed February 24, 2011).

income grow; at the apex, the share of household income attributable to the highest 1 percent more than doubled, from 7.5 to 17.1 percent.

Discussions of increasing economic inequality tend to focus attention on the extent to which the rich have become richer. A trend less often noticed is the fact that the poor have gotten poorer.[10] After decreasing for a number of years during the 1960s, the poverty rate leveled off and has varied within a relatively narrow range since then. The relative stability of the poverty rate, which separates families into groups of poor and nonpoor, obscures what has happened below the poverty line. The late 1970s and early 1980s witnessed a sharp rise in two poverty measures: the proportion of poor families with household incomes less than half the poverty line and the "poverty gap"— that is, the average difference, measured in constant dollars, between the poverty threshold and the incomes of poor families. Since then, these two poverty indexes have continued to rise—though less consistently and more

10. Discussion in this paragraph is based upon the argument and data presented in Mishel, Bernstein, and Shierholz, *The State of Working America, 2008/2009*, pp. 306–309.

slowly. Thus the long-term pattern is one of deeper poverty among poor households.

Earnings

The story about earnings and wealth parallels that for household income. For most households, the principal source of income is earnings, that is, wages and salaries derived from paid work. Wage and price controls during World War II resulted in substantial wage compression, especially among high-wage earners. Surprisingly, when the controls were lifted, the share of wages commanded by top earners did not immediately bounce back to prewar levels. However, in the 1970s it began to increase steadily before skyrocketing in the late 1980s and late 1990s. Although much has been made of the increasing returns to education, what is striking is the extent to which the fruits of sustained economic and productivity growth in recent decades have accrued so disproportionately to those at the very, very top and not to low- and middle-wage workers or even to workers who have college diplomas or advanced degrees. Between 1972 and 2001, the wage and salary income of Americans at the 90th percentile grew 34 percent. The analogous figures for those at the 99th percentile, the 99.9th percentile, and the 99.99th percentile are 87 percent, 181 percent, and 497 percent, respectively.[11] Between 1970 and 1999, the average compensation of the top one hundred CEOs, as reported in the annual surveys in *Forbes*, was multiplied roughly thirty times.[12] These developments have been fueled, at least in part, by the restructuring of executive pay, in particular the inclusion of stock options in compensation packages.[13]

Meanwhile, wage growth was very modest lower down on the wage scale.[14] As shown in Table 3.2, in the three decades between 1979 and 2009, workers in the lowest decile actually lost ground in terms of real wages, and improvements in real wages for all but those in the top two deciles were quite limited.

11. Data from a paper by Ian Dew-Becker and Robert Gordon, "Where Did the Productivity Growth Go?" *Brookings Papers on Economic Activity* 36 (2005): 67–127, cited by Paul Krugman in "Graduates Versus Oligarchs," *New York Times*, February 27, 2006.

12. Piketty and Saez, "Income Inequality," pp. 29–33.

13. See, for example, Julie Creswell, "Pay Packages Allow Executives to Jump Ship with Less Risk," *New York Times*, December 29, 2006, and Eric Dash, "Compensation Experts Offer Ways to Help Curb Executive Salaries," *New York Times*, December 30, 2006.

14. This paragraph is based on the data presented in Mishel, Bernstein, and Shierholz, *The State of Working America, 2008/2009*, chap. 3, pp. 125 and 134, Tables 3.1 and 3.5, and "Wages at the High end Are Growing Faster: Change in Real Hourly Wages by Wage Percentile, 1973–2009," in *The State of Working America* (Washington, DC: Economic Policy Institute, 2011), http://www.stateofworkingamerica.org/charts/view/15 (accessed February 24, 2011).

Table 3.2   Change in Hourly Wages by Wage Percentile,
1979–2009 (2009 Dollars)

	Wage Percentile					
	10	20	50	80	90	95
Increase in Wages	$–.08	$ .55	$1.46	$4.82	$9.17	$13.49
Percentage Increase	–1.1%	5.9%	10.1%	20.8%	32.3%	39.0%

Source: Calculated from data presented in "Wages at the High End Are Growing Faster: Change in Real Hourly Wages by Wage Percentile, 1973–2009," in *The State of Working America* (Washington, DC: Economic Policy Institute, 2011), http://www.stateofworkingamerica.org/charts/view/15 (accessed February 24, 2011).

The data in Table 3.2 obscure the extent to which the pattern varied over the period. The years from 1979 to 1989 were especially unkind to lower-wage workers: all of those below the sixth decile lost earning power in real terms, and the wages of those in the lowest tenth lost nearly 15 percent of their real value. In contrast, between 1995 and 2000, wages grew in real terms for all groups, and the rate of growth of wages for the lowest 20 percent was higher than for the top 5 percent. Nevertheless, even then, productivity gains far outstripped wage increases.

At the same time, the safety net provided by the private welfare state has been frayed in terms of both the proportion of workers whose employers provide such benefits as health insurance and pensions and the generosity of the benefits if provided.[15] Along with such widely recognized developments as the sharp rise in copays for health insurance and the replacement of defined-benefit pensions with defined-contribution retirement plans are such less visible developments as the diminution in the share of workers who qualify for unemployment compensation if they lose their jobs.

Wealth

The pattern of substantial, and increasing, inequality also obtains for wealth: that is, the assets held by a household—for example, housing, consumer dura-

15. On the erosion of the private welfare state, see Michael B. Katz, *The Price of Citizenship: Redefining the American Welfare State* (New York: Henry Holt, 2001), chaps. 6–8, and Jacob S. Hacker, *The Great Risk Shift: The Assault on American Jobs, Families, Health Care, and Retirement and How You Can Fight Back* (Oxford, England: Oxford University Press, 2006).

bles such as cars, or businesses, savings, or investments—minus any out-standing mortgage or consumer debt. Wealth—especially financial wealth like equities, bank deposits, or bonds—has always been more unevenly divided than either earnings or household income. Over the period since 1983, the bottom four-fifths of households have never had as much as 20 percent of net worth or as much as 10 percent of financial wealth. In 2004, the top 1 percent commanded fully 34 percent of net worth and 42 percent of financial worth.[16] An important aspect to the unequal division of wealth is the racial divide.[17] Black households command much less wealth than white households, and racial inequalities in wealth are much more pronounced than analogous in-equalities in income or wages. Compared to whites, blacks are more likely to have zero or negative net worth and much less likely to hold various kinds of assets, especially financial assets. They are also less likely to be homeowners and, if homeowners, twice as likely as white homeowners to hold subprime mortgages.

With respect to changes over time, the pattern for concentration of wealth has affinities to what we have seen for earnings and household income. The share of wealth owned by the top 1 percent grew during the 1920s to a peak in 1929 before falling during the Depression and continuing to decline during and after World War II. Concentration of wealth reached a low point in the mid-1970s and then began to increase, reaching, by the late 1990s, levels not equaled since 1929.[18]

The United States in Comparative Perspective

While it is well known that the distribution of income is especially unequal in less affluent countries, it is instructive to compare the United States to other affluent democracies.[19] For a variety of reasons, making cross-national

---

16. Mishel, Bernstein, and Shierholz, *The State of Working America, 2008/2009*, pp. 263–270.

17. Mishel, Bernstein, and Shierholz, *The State of Working America, 2008/2009*, pp. 271–272, 281–282, 294.

18. Kevin Phillips, *Wealth and Democracy* (New York: Broadway Books, 2002), pp. 122–123. See also Wolff, *Poverty and Income Distribution*, pp. 150–159.

19. This section draws on arguments and data in Burtless and Jencks, "American Inequal-ity," and in Timothy M. Smeeding, "Public Policy, Economic Inequality, and Poverty: The United States in Comparative Perspective," *Social Science Quarterly* 86 (2005), 955–983. Of the countries Smeeding discusses, only Russia and Mexico have higher levels of income inequality than does the United States. Burtless and Jencks cover a variety of issues and have

comparisons is difficult. For one thing, it is not clear whether cross-national differences in the financing of health care, housing, and higher education yield a circumstance such that the level of inequality in disposable income in the United States is overstated or understated by current data.[20] Therefore, we must be circumspect in interpreting the findings.

To summarize briefly, when it comes to hourly wages, inequalities in the United States are quite substantial in comparative perspective. As we have mentioned, well-paid executives and professionals in America are very well paid indeed. At the bottom of the hierarchy, compensation for low-skilled work is quite stingy, a circumstance not helped by the fact that the minimum wage was not raised for an entire decade between 1997 and 2007, by which time its purchasing power had diminished to its lowest point in more than half a century, an era of substantial economic growth.[21]

Although hourly wages are comparatively unequal in the United States, the United States is, perhaps surprisingly, not an outlier when it comes to the distribution of market incomes—that is, household incomes before taxes and transfers. One study using Gini coefficients for market incomes in thirteen countries of the Organisation for Economic Co-operation and Development (OECD) places the United States, along with the United Kingdom and Australia, in the middle of the pack, with market incomes more unequal than in Switzerland, Finland, Canada, the Netherlands, Germany, and Sweden, and less unequal than in France, Russia, Belgium or Mexico.[22] The explanations for the seeming contradiction between highly unequal wages and relatively equal pretax, pretransfer incomes are complex. However, several factors—including high rates of labor market participation, long working hours, and low rates of unemployment in the United States—contribute to this outcome.[23] That is, compared to their counterparts in other wealthy democracies, Americans are more likely to be in the work-force, they work longer hours and take shorter vacations, and, although the

---

an especially helpful discussion of how the seeming contradiction between highly unequal wages and relatively equal pretax, pretransfer incomes can be resolved by taking into account high rates of labor market participation, long working hours, and low rates of unemployment in the United States.

20. Burtless and Jencks, "American Inequality," p. 75.

21. Jared Bernstein and Isaac Shapiro, "Nine Years of Neglect: Federal Minimum Wage Remains Unchanged for Ninth Straight Year," Center on Budget and Policy Priorities, Washington, DC, August 31, 2006, http://www.cbpp.org/8-31-06mw.htm (accessed August 10, 2007).

22. Smeeding, "Public Policy, Economic Inequality, and Poverty," pp. 971–973.

23. See Burtless and Jencks, "American Inequality," pp. 77–79.

current recession may reverse the generalization, they are less likely to be unemployed.

Still, while the level of inequality in pretax and pretransfer American income is not notably high, government benefits are not particularly generous, and taxes are not especially redistributive in the United States. The result is that cross-national studies concur in finding a higher level of inequality in disposable income in the United States than in other developed democracies. In the United States, taxation and government benefits diminish inequalities in market incomes less than in any of the thirteen OECD countries mentioned earlier except for Russia and Mexico. Public policies in America have an effect such that net disposable income—that is, income after taxes and transfers have had a redistributive impact—is more unequally distributed in the United States than in any of the affluent nations on the list.[24] A few specific comparisons are instructive. As measured by Gini coefficients, Sweden and the United States are more or less on a par with respect to inequalities in market incomes. However, after taxes and benefits, these inequalities are reduced much more substantially in Sweden than in the United States. The pattern is different for Belgium, which has a Gini coefficient for market incomes that is considerably higher than that of the United States, higher in fact than that of any of the nations listed except for Mexico. However, taxes and transfers operate so powerfully to redistribute income in Belgium that the Gini coefficient for net disposable income in Belgium is very close to Sweden's.

Overall, the redistributive impact of government interventions is not related to the extent of inequalities in market income. The evidence confirms

---

24. Smeeding, "Public Policy, Economic Inequality, and Poverty," Figure 8, p. 972, provides the following data:

Country	Market Income Gini	Disposable Income Gini
Finland	40	24
Netherlands	42	25
Germany	43	25
Sweden	44	25
Belgium	50	26
France	49	29
Switzerland	39	30
Canada	41	30
Australia	45	31
United Kingdom	45	34
United States	45	37
Russia	49	43
Mexico	53	49

neither of two plausible hypotheses: nations with especially pronounced inequalities in market incomes are not systematically more likely to reduce
them through taxes and benefits, nor are nations with more egalitarian distributions of market incomes particularly likely to reduce these inequalities
further through government action.

While there is no single pattern that obtains for all wealthy democracies,
cross-national data show a general trend over the last generation toward
greater income inequality.[25] Data for ten affluent democracies between 1977
and 2000 show that in no nation except the United Kingdom has the increase
in income inequality been as pronounced as it has been in the United States.
However, the United Kingdom began the period with a relatively egalitarian
income distribution and, after sharp increases in income inequality during
the 1980s that leveled off during the 1990s, ended up toward the middle of the
group of nations. In contrast, the United States started the period with the
least egalitarian income distribution. Its income inequality increased fairly
steadily throughout the period, leaving the United States with by far the most
inegalitarian income distribution by 2000.[26]

Does American Affluence Compensate?

Two arguments are sometimes made that blunt concerns about the level of
income inequality in the United States. The first is that the high level of affluence in America—as measured, say, by per capita gross domestic product—
implies a higher, if unequal, standard of living for all. However, according to
one comparative study, "Low-paid workers in the United States—the most
productive economy in the world—have markedly lower living standards
than low-paid workers in other advanced economies."[27] According to another

25. This paragraph is based on data presented by Smeeding, "Public Policy, Economic
Inequality, and Poverty," pp. 961–963.

26. According to Freeman in *When Earnings Diverge*, p. 15, during the 1980s and early
1990s, inequality rose more in the United States than in every nation in a group of sixteen
countries except for New Zealand. In a recent book, Richardson and Pickett argue that many
other adverse social outcomes—ranging from high levels of obesity to high levels of violence
to reduced life expectancy—accompany high levels of economic inequality. See Richard
Richardson and Kate Pickett, *The Spirit Level: Why Greater Equality Makes Societies Stronger*
(New York: Bloomsbury Press, 2009).

27. Freeman, *When Earnings Diverge*, p. 19. Smeeding, in "Public Policy, Economic Inequality, and Poverty," warns of the difficulties in making such comparisons across nations.
Thus we urge caution in drawing conclusions. Nonetheless, the patterns reported in this
paragraph emerge in a number of studies.

study, in 1979 American manufacturing production workers earned more per hour than their counterparts in a group of nineteen OECD countries. By 2006 their relative compensation had fallen to the point that they were in the middle of the pack, eleventh on a list of twenty.[28] The contention that affluence in America compensates for income inequality in America is also called into question by 2005 data comparing household incomes in twelve countries.[29] For the United States and eleven other countries, figures are given showing the household incomes of the richest 10 percent and the poorest 10 percent of households *relative to the median for the United States*. Even though the median income is quite high in the United States and the top decile of American households have much higher incomes than their counterparts in all the other countries on the list, those at the bottom of the economic ladder are not necessarily better off in terms of absolute income than are the poor elsewhere. In fact, the households in the poorest decile in the Netherlands, Germany, Sweden, Finland, Austria, the United Kingdom, Australia, and France have higher incomes—but those in Canada and Japan slightly lower incomes—than their American counterparts.[30] In short, in spite of American affluence, the poor in America are not particularly well off economically.

What about the American Dream?

The second argument suggesting that income inequality is less problematic in the American context focuses on the opportunities for success available in America. In what is said to have been the first definition of the American Dream, James Truslow Adams observed: "There has been also the *American Dream*, that dream of a land in which life could be better and richer and full

28. Mishel, Bernstein, and Shierholz, *The State of Working America, 2008/2009*, pp. 377–378. Comparisons are in terms of purchasing power parity exchange rates, which are designed to "reflect the ability of the compensation levels in each country to guarantee a specific standard of living" (p. 378).

29. Mishel, Bernstein, and Shierholz, *The State of Working America, 2008/2009*, p. 382, Figure 8E. Smeeding, "Public Policy, Economic Inequality, and Poverty," Figure 2, shows a similar overall pattern but a somewhat different ranking for particular countries on his list of eight developed countries. He finds that the real purchasing power of those in the poorest tenth of the population in the United States is, in fact, below the average for that stratum in Canada, Belgium, the Netherlands, and Germany; a shade higher than Sweden and Finland; and higher than in the United Kingdom.

30. Countries are listed in decreasing order of the incomes of households in the poorest tenth. Ireland is tied with the United States with respect to the incomes of the households in the poorest decile.

for every man, with opportunity for each according to his ability or achievement."[31] Adams's definition has two components, both of which have been incorporated into the understanding of what it means to live the American Dream. The first emphasizes that life gets better—in particular, improvements in standard of living in absolute terms over the life cycle or across generations, regardless of whether the improvement involves a relative as well as an absolute rise.[32] As suggested by a variety of data already discussed, sluggish wage growth over much of the period since the mid-1970s implies that achieving this version of the American Dream has become harder for middle- and lower-income Americans. Over the life cycle, earnings tend to increase with age as workers gain experience and seniority. Someone who was thirty in 1946 could expect a real increase in annual family income of 107.9 percent by the time of his or her fiftieth birthday two decades later. In 1976, however, a thirty-year-old could expect family income to rise only 57 percent in the next twenty years.[33]

American standards of living have improved, of course. Several factors account for the improvements. One of them is the smaller families in the post–Baby Boom era. Because a given income is apportioned among fewer people, smaller numbers of children have the effect of raising household living standards.[34] Another development is greater workforce commitment— more family members working more hours at more jobs. Especially significant is the increased workforce participation of married women. The median household income for married couples in which the wife is in the labor force is substantially higher than that for married couples in which the wife is at home—a gap that has grown over the last generation.[35] Another way that

31. James Truslow Adams, *The Epic of America* (Boston: Little, Brown, 1931), p. 404, emphasis in the original. The two components of the American Dream specified by Adams correspond roughly to the distinction made between absolute and relative mobility.

32. The two versions of the American Dream discussed in this section reflect the distinction made by James Truslow Adams.

33. The figures are for real median family income growth between ages thirty and fifty and are taken from Mishel, Bernstein, and Shierholz, *The State of Working America, 2008/ 2009*, p. 102.

34. See, for example, Julia B. Isaacs, "Economic Mobility of Families across Generations," in *Getting Ahead or Losing Ground: Economic Mobility in America*, ed. Julia B. Isaacs, Isabel V. Sawhill, and Ron Haskins (Washington, DC: Brookings Institution and Economic Mobility Project, 2008), chap. 1. However, by proliferating households with only a single wage earner, lower marriage rates have the opposite effect.

35. Wolff, *Poverty and Income Distribution*, p. 513. Wolff also points out (p. 3) that the rapid rise in the share of married women in the workforce that took place in the 1970s and 1980s has slowed markedly since then—with a concomitant impact on growth in real living standards.

families have financed a higher standard of living has been by increasing their debt. From 1949 to 2005, household indebtedness as a percentage of disposable income rose from 33.2 percent to 133.8 percent.[36]

The second aspect of the American Dream posits that opportunities for success, while differential, are available to the talented and industrious, irrespective of initial circumstances of disadvantage. In Chapter 2 we saw that, more than citizens in other developed democracies, Americans are willing to accept economic inequalities if unequal rewards reflect individual capacities and perseverance rather than family background or a previous condition of privilege and if the able and hardworking thus have opportunities to rise above modest beginnings. Nevertheless, rags-to-riches—and riches-to-rags—stories, however newsworthy, are exceptional, and, over time, most people stay quite close to the economic stratum in which they started out.[37]

Furthermore, we are not all equal at the starting point, and recent research shows considerable correspondence in the economic deserts of successive generations.[38] Affluent, well-educated parents are able to transmit their eco-

36. Ron Haskins, "Wealth and Economic Mobility," in *Getting Ahead or Losing Ground*, ed. Isaacs, Sawhill, and Haskins, p. 51.

37. Gregory Acs and Seth Zimmerman, "U.S. Intragenerational Economic Mobility from 1984 to 2004," Economic Mobility Project, Washington, DC, October 2008, http://www .urban.org/UploadedPDF/1001226_intragenerational_economic_mobility.pdf (accessed December 31, 2009). Over a ten-year period, those in the highest income quintile have roughly a 50-50 chance of remaining in that quintile or moving into a lower one, and those in the lowest quintile have roughly a 50-50 chance of remaining in that quintile or moving into a higher one, rates of mobility that were unchanged for the two decades under consideration. Acs and Zimmerman read their data as showing considerable evidence of mobility. However, because most of those who move out of the highest or lowest income quintile end up in the adjacent quintile, these data can also be interpreted as indicating more limited mobility.

38. On these themes see, for example, P. M. Blau and O. D. Duncan, *The American Occupational Structure* (New York: Wiley, 1967); Rita M. Hauser and David L. Featherman, *The Process of Stratification* (New York: Academic Press,1977); Michael Hout, "More Universalism, Less Structural Mobility," *American Journal of Sociology* 93 (1988): 1358–1400; Harry B. G. Ganzeboom, Donald J. Treiman, and Wout C. Ultee, "Comparative Intergenerational Stratification Research," *Annual Review of Sociology* 17 (1991): 284; Gary Solon, "Intergenerational Income Mobility in the United States," *American Economic Review* 82 (1992): 393–408; Daniel P. McMurrer and Isabel Sawhill, *Getting Ahead: Economic and Social Mobility in America* (Washington, DC: Urban Institute Press,1998); Burtless and Jencks, "American Inequality"; Michael Hout, "How Inequality May Affect Intergenerational Mobility," in *Social Inequality*, ed. Neckerman, chap. 26; Samuel Bowles, Herbert Gintis, and Melissa Osborne Groves, "Introduction," Bhashkar Mazumder, "The Apple Falls Even Closer to the Tree than We Thought: New and Revised Estimates of the Intergenerational Inheritance of Earnings," chap. 2, and David Harding, Christopher Jencks, Leonard M. Lopoo, and Susan M. Mayer, "The Changing Effect of Family Background on the Incomes of American Adults," chap. 3, in

nomic status through several mechanisms: they use their income to invest in their children's health, education, and development; they create a home environment that cultivates attitudes, interests, habits, and personality traits that are helpful in the marketplace; and they make direct bequests of useful resources, including family wealth and personal contacts. In short, those who are savvy enough to have chosen affluent, well-educated parents are much more likely to end up affluent and well educated themselves.[39] Later on, in Chapter 7, we shall treat a parallel—though less often studied—aspect of intergenerational transmission, the extent to which participatory habits are passed on from parents to their offspring. We find that having well-educated and affluent parents confers an advantage not only in occupational success but also in political voice.

Equal Opportunity and Education

The contemporary version of the American Dream places considerable emphasis on the possibilities for advancement through educational opportunity.[40] In light of the central role played by educational attainment in the achievement of economic success, the educational advantage enjoyed by the offspring of affluent parents is quite striking. They are more likely to graduate from high school; to continue their education thereafter; to attend a four-year institution of higher education, especially a selective one; and to graduate if they matriculate.[41] Comparing students from the top and bottom income

---

Unequal Chances: Family Background and Economic Success, ed. Samuel Bowles, Herbert Gintis, and Melissa Osborne Groves (Princeton, NJ: Princeton University Press, 2005), chap. 3; and the essays in *Getting Ahead or Losing Ground*, ed. Isaacs, Sawhill, and Haskins.

39. Isaacs, in "Economic Mobility of Families," pp. 19–21, describes a phenomenon of regression to the mean such that, in spite of the strong association between the incomes of successive generations, it is those whose parents were in the top income group whose offspring are most likely to experience downward mobility and those whose parents were in the bottom income group whose offspring are most likely to experience upward mobility.

40. As Ron Haskins, in "Education and Economic Mobility," in *Getting Ahead or Losing Ground*, ed. Isaacs, Sawhill, and Haskins, p. 91, put it, "Most Americans believe that the road to achieving the American Dream passes through the schoolhouse door." Haskins presents data about most of the themes discussed briefly here and makes clear that, while educational attainment and economic success are strongly related, the nation's educational institutions have relatively modest effects in establishing equal opportunity.

41. This paragraph draws on the arguments and data in Robert Haveman and Timothy Smeeding, "The Role of Higher Education in Social Mobility," *Future of Children* 16 (2006): 125–150, and Jennifer Engle and Colleen O'Brien, "Demography Is Not Destiny," Pell Institute, Washington, DC, n.d., http://www.pellinstitute.org/files/files-demography_is_not_destiny .pdf (accessed January 3, 2010).

deciles, one study found that 98 percent of the students from the top income decile, as opposed to 57 percent of students from the bottom income decile, graduated from high school; 78 percent of the former, but only 20 percent of the latter, attended college; and 49 percent of the students from the high-income families, in contrast to 6 percent of the students from low-income families, graduated from college.[42] Data about the composition of the entering classes at various kinds of institutions of higher education tell a similar story. Of the students entering community colleges in 1988, 22 percent came from families in the lowest socio-economic quartile and 21 percent from families in the highest quartile. In contrast, of those matriculating in the most selective colleges, 3 percent were recruited from the lowest quartile and 74 percent from the highest.[43]

Children from affluent and well-educated families bring many advantages to the acquisition of higher education. The "ability, motivation, and preparedness" that are sought by college admissions offices and that predispose a student to be successful in college "are all linked to the economic position of the children's families. Children from well-to-do families tend, on average, to have more of all three traits; children from disadvantaged families, to have less."[44] Not only do those from affluent families benefit from all the factors we mentioned earlier but they enjoy additional advantages that are specific to educational attainment. They are likely to have attended high-quality elementary and secondary schools and to have taken the kinds of rigorous courses that are associated with admission to and performance in college. Their parents are more likely to be able to help them to negotiate the college search and admissions process. They are less likely to need financial aid to meet the increasing costs of higher education or to need remedial courses and services when they matriculate.

It is interesting to note the extent to which the children of parents of high socio-economic status (SES) retain an advantage even when a rough measure

---

42. Data about the educational attainment of the 1966–1970 birth cohort from the Michigan Panel Study of Income Dynamics are taken from an unpublished paper by Robert Haveman and Kathryn Wilson, "Economic Inequality in College Access, Matriculation, and Graduation," cited in Haveman and Smeeding, "The Role of Higher Education," p. 132. The income deciles are based on family-size-adjusted income.

43. Data from the National Education Longitudinal Study of 1988 are taken from Anthony P. Carnevale and Stephen J. Rose, "Socioeconomic Status, Race/Ethnicity, and Selective College Admissions," in *America's Untapped Resource: Low-Income Students in Higher Education*, ed. Richard D. Kahlenberg (New York: Century Foundation Press, 2004), cited in Haveman and Smeeding, "The Role of Higher Education," p. 131.

44. Haveman and Smeeding, "The Role of Higher Education," p. 129.

of academic ability is taken into account. Of the eighth-graders who were high scorers on a mathematics assessment test, 74 percent of those from high-SES backgrounds—but only 29 percent of those from low-SES backgrounds—had graduated from college twelve years later. Among the low scorers on the mathematics assessment, the eventual college graduation rates were 30 percent and 3 percent for the high-SES and low-SES students, respectively.[45]

All these considerations cast doubt on the extent to which America provides avenues of upward mobility to the talented and hardworking regardless of their origins. Making comparisons among nations can help us to put into perspective the extent to which the present circumstance constitutes a compromise of the promise of the American Dream. It is difficult to make such comparisons with respect to the availability of opportunities to get ahead even among developed democracies, and the various studies are not in complete agreement as to the rank order. However, it seems that, contrary to the expectation in the United States and abroad, the United States is not notable for high rates of class and occupational mobility across generations.[46] One factor that may depress rates of upward mobility in the United States relative to other developed countries is the way that growing economic inequality widens the distance between economic groups.[47]

Changing Opportunities in America

When it comes to change over the last generation, it is too early to discern the impact of increasing economic inequality on the prospects for mobility of the next generation, and there is no definitive answer as to how these processes have been altered in an era of growing economic inequality in the United States. As for the recent past, there is disagreement as to whether,

45. Mary Ann Fox, Brooke A. Connolly, and Thomas D. Snyder, *Youth Indicators 2005: Trends in the Well-Being of American Youth*, U.S. Department of Education, National Center for Educational Statistics (Washington, DC: U.S. Government Printing Office, 2005), Table 21, p. 50. High and low scorers are in the highest and lowest quartiles, respectively. The composite measure of SES includes parents' education and occupation(s) and family income.

46. See the data and discussions of literature in Miles Corak, "Do Poor Children Become Poor Adults? Lessons from a Cross Country Comparison of Generational Earnings Mobility," IZA Discussion Paper No. 1993 (Bonn: Institute for the Study of Labor, 2006); Hout, "How Inequality May Affect Mobility," pp. 971–976; Julia B. Isaacs," International Comparisons of Economic Mobility," in *Getting Ahead or Losing Ground*, ed. Isaacs, Sawhill, and Haskins, chap. 3; as well as the essays in Miles Corak, ed., *Generational Income Mobility in North America and Europe* (Cambridge, England: Cambridge University Press, 2004); Harding et al., "Changing Effect of Family Background," p. 133.

47. This point is made by Mishel, Bernstein, and Shierholz in *The State of Working America, 2008/2009*, pp. 108–109.

after rates of class mobility increased during the 1960s, they have leveled off or whether they have in fact reversed.[48]

Nevertheless, there is strong evidence that, over the last generation, the well off have increased their capacity to bequeath educational advantage to their offspring. One study comparing high school graduates from the classes of 1980 and 1982, on the one hand, and 1992, on the other, shows a growing advantage of affluent students in access to higher education. The post-secondary profile of students from the lowest income quartile barely changed over the period: the proportion pursuing any further education rose, from 57 percent to 60 percent, and the proportion attending four-year colleges actually fell very slightly, from 29 to 28 percent. In contrast, the educational prospects of the students from the highest income quartile were enhanced visibly. In that affluent group, 81 percent of the 1980 and 1982 graduates fur-thered their education, and 55 percent attended four-year colleges; for 1992 graduates from the top income quartile, 90 percent continued their educa-tions further, and 66 percent went to four-year colleges.[49] Data over the three-decade period from 1970 to 2002 show that the proportion in the top income quartile who had acquired a bachelor's degree by age twenty-four rose from 40 to 51 percent. Over the same period, the proportion of twenty-four-year-olds in the lowest income quartile with a bachelor's degree re-mained stable, at 6 percent.[50]

Among the sources of the widening educational gap in younger genera-tions is the increasing cost of higher education. In a variety of ways, meeting the costs of a four-year college education has become increasingly financially difficult for all but the most affluent students. At the same time that tuition at both public and private institutions has been increasing more quickly than most economic indicators, the value of Pell Grants, the most substantial form of federal tuition assistance for low-income students, has fallen. In addition, more financial aid is coming in the form of loans rather than grants. More-over, an increasing share of financial aid from the federal government is not

48. See Harding et al., "Changing Effect of Family Background," as well as the discussion of various studies in Isabel V. Sawhill, "Trends in Intergeneration Mobility," in *Getting Ahead or Losing Ground*, ed. Isaacs, Sawhill, and Haskins, chap. 2.

49. David T. Ellwood and Thomas J. Kane, "Who Is Getting a College Education: Family Background and the Growing Gaps in Enrollment," in *Securing the Future*, ed. Sheldon Dan-ziger and Jane Waldfogel (New York: Russell Sage Foundation, 2000), p. 286, Table 10.1.

50. Thomas G. Mortenson, "Policy Imperatives, Policy Choices, and Policy Conse-quences," paper presented to the New England Regional Assembly of the College Board, Bos-ton, MA, February 6, 2005, p. 61.

need based; in a parallel development, colleges and universities are awarding an increasing portion of their aid on the basis of merit—whether athletic or academic—rather than need.[51] The bottom line is that, in an era when a college education has become almost essential for upward mobility, lower-income students have increasingly been priced out of the market.

A Note on the Decline of Union Membership

Another aspect of the economic context that is germane to our concerns is the erosion of union membership and strength. Later on, in Chapter 11, we consider the kinds of organizations that are active in American politics and see that—other than unions, which are very active in national politics—there are very, very few organizations that advocate on behalf of the economic interests of workers who are not professionals or managers. Moreover, with other factors taken into account, union members are more likely to take part politically. Because of the consequences of the decline of union membership for political voice, in this section we look briefly at this decline and the multiple factors that have been adduced to explain it.

The unionized share of the workforce actually peaked in the 1950s, but the past three decades have witnessed especially pronounced erosion in the proportion of workers who are union members and the slightly higher proportion who are covered by union contracts. It is notable that, even as the size of the workforce expanded substantially, the absolute number of union members declined by nearly four million over the period. In 1981, 21.4 percent of all wage and salary workers were members of unions; by 2010, the figure had dropped to 11.9 percent.[52]

The decrease in union ranks has been sustained entirely by workers in the private sector. While the share of public-sector workers who are union members fluctuated within a very narrow range and ended the period at a slightly higher level, 36.2 percent, than it had been at the beginning, the proportion of private-sector workers who were union members decreased steadily, from

51. Haveman and Smeeding, in "The Role of Higher Education," pp. 137–140, provide an overview of studies demonstrating that "trends in family income, tuition, and financial aid policy have adversely affected those students least able to afford postsecondary schooling" (p. 137).

52. Data taken from the Union Membership and Coverage Database constructed by Barry Hirsch and David Macpherson, http://www.unionstats.com/ (accessed February 24, 2011). See also Steven Greenhouse, "Sharp Decline in Union Members in '06," *New York Times*, January 26, 2007.

18.7 percent in 1981 to 6.9 percent in 2010. In the private sector, the decline among workers in manufacturing—traditionally a heavily unionized sector—has been particularly steep. While workers in manufacturing are still somewhat more likely to be union members than are other private-sector workers, the gap has narrowed very substantially.[53] Construction work, another traditionally heavily unionized sector, suffered especially heavy union losses: from the mid-1970s to the mid-1990s, the share of construction workers in unions dropped by half and the dollar volume built by union workers from 80 percent to 30 percent.[54]

When taken together with the changes in the composition of the American workforce due to such factors as immigration and women's increased workforce commitment, the consequence of such differential rates in the decline of union membership across various occupations and economic sectors is that the character of the unionized workforce has been altered significantly.[55] The joint impact of the shrinking share of the workforce employed in manufacturing and the plummeting share of union members among manufacturing workers has produced a circumstance such that manufacturing workers are currently a much smaller share of union members than in the past—falling from nearly a third in 1983 to just over a tenth in 2008. Moreover, the proportion of workers in manufacturing is higher in the workforce as a whole than among union members. In contrast, while the share of the workforce employed in the public sector fell ever so slightly over the quarter-century period, from 17.6 percent to 16.5 percent, the share among union members rose sharply, from 34.4 percent to 48.9 percent.

The increasing dominance of public-sector workers among union members has consequences for the gender and educational composition of the unionized workforce. Among union members in 2008, 38.4 percent of the men, compared to 61.5 percent of the women, were employed in the public sector. While women are still a smaller share of union members than of all employees, their traditional underrepresentation among union members has been ameliorated in recent decades. Furthermore, in absolute and relative terms, the educational level of the unionized workforce has risen. In 1983,

53. See John Schmitt and Kris Warner, "The Changing Face of Labor, 1983–2008," Center for Economic and Policy Research, Washington, DC, November 2009, pp. 17–18.

54. Nelson Lichenstein, *State of the Union* (Princeton, NJ: Princeton University Press, 2002), p. 230.

55. The conclusions in this paragraph are drawn from Schmitt and Warner, "The Changing Face of Labor," Table 1, p. 7, et passim.

union members were slightly less well educated than the overall workforce. By 2008 that pattern had been reversed, and the unionized workforce was slightly better educated than the workforce as a whole. When it comes to education, union members show a significant gender gap: among union members, nearly half of the women, 49.4 percent—compared to just over a quarter of the men, 27.7 percent—had at least a college degree. Reflecting changes in the population as a whole, with respect to race and ethnicity, the unionized workforce, which has always more or less mirrored the composition of the workforce, now has a smaller share of whites, and a correspondingly larger share of Latinos and Asian Americans, than in the past. Taken together, these trends imply that white males, once a majority—and, in countless pictures of union leaders, the face of the union movement—no longer predominate among union members.

Explaining the Labor Union Decline

What explains the steep decline in the share of American workers who are union members? A number of factors have been adduced to account for this trend, among them structural changes in the American economy, miscalculations by the unions themselves, increased aggressiveness by employers in opposing union drives, antiunion changes in public policy, and diminished support for unionization among workers.[56] While in agreement that a combination of these factors is responsible for the outcome, scholars differ in the assessment of their relative weight and meaning.

This trend in the United States is a long-term one. Although, as mentioned, the share of unionized workers peaked in the 1950s and has fallen since then, a number of seeds were planted earlier.[57] Especially important was the passage in 1947 of the employer-friendly Taft-Hartley Act, which outlawed a number of labor practices and permitted states to pass "right-to-work" laws outlawing the union shop. Although attempts have periodically been made to alter or repeal it, Taft-Hartley remains in place today. Further-

---

56. For a succinct discussion and bibliographical references, see Richard B. Freeman, *America Works: The Exceptional U.S. Market* (New York: Russell Sage Foundation, 2007), chap. 5. See also Michael Goldfield, *The Decline of Organized Labor in the United States* (Chicago: University of Chicago Press, 1987); Richard B. Freeman and Lawrence Katz, "Rising Wage Inequality: The United States vs. Other Advanced Countries," in *Working under Different Rules*, ed. Richard B. Freeman (New York: Russell Sage Foundation, 1994); and Jacob S. Hacker and Paul Pierson, *Winner-Take-All Politics* (New York: Simon and Schuster, 2010), pp. 56–61.

57. On these factors, see Lichenstein, *State of the Union*, chaps. 3–4.

more, according to labor historians, the expulsion of the Left with the Cold War proved divisive and deprived unions, if not of large numbers of members, of dedicated and enthusiastic organizers. Moreover, firm-centered rather than industrywide bargaining decentralized labor and provided an advantage to management. Later on, during the Carter administration, the Democratically controlled Congress handed organized labor two legislative defeats with the failure of legislation providing for common situs picketing in 1977 and, more importantly, labor law reform in 1978.[58]

Both the rate at which unions won representation elections and the pro-union share of the vote in such elections fell steadily after 1940 before leveling off in the mid-1970s.[59] In addition, the number of accusations of unfair labor practices against employers has steadily increased. Furthermore, in the aftermath of a successful union election, workers have had increasing difficulty in actually negotiating a first contract.

In the context of these long-term trends, the 1980s were pivotal. During the early 1980s, the probability that a pro-union worker would be fired during a union election campaign spiked sharply to a level not equaled at any time during the period between 1951 and 2005, and the number of union elections plummeted. Also relevant were political developments in the early years of the Reagan administration. In the summer of 1981, Reagan dismissed striking air traffic controllers and replaced them with nonunion employees, an occurrence that has been interpreted as a turning point in labor history after which employers have felt free to replace striking workers. In addition, as their five-year terms expired, Carter's appointees to the National Labor Relations Board (NLRB) were replaced by Reagan's. An especially important part of the process was the appointment as chair of Donald Dotson, a steadfast union opponent who, in contrast to his predecessors, was not a labor relations professional. The meaning of these developments in explaining the erosion of union density is, however, contested territory.

One aspect of the decline in union density that is often overlooked is that, over the last generation, erosion in the proportion of the workforce that is

58. See Hacker and Pierson, *Winner-Take-All Politics*, pp. 127–132.

59. Discussion in this paragraph is based on Henry S. Farber and Bruce Western, "Ronald Reagan and the Politics of Declining Union Organization," *British Journal of Industrial Relations* 40 (2002): 385–401, and John Schmitt and Ben Zipperer, "Dropping the Ax: Illegal Firings during Union Election Campaigns," Center for Economic and Policy Research, Washington, DC, January 2007, available at www.cepr.net (accessed September 23, 2010).

unionized has been common across industrial democracies. In a group of twenty advanced democracies, the proportion of unionized workers diminished between 1979 and the late 1990s in fourteen of them.[60] Still, even if the United States is hardly alone in the erosion of union density, it is worth noting that the United States has, in comparative terms, very low levels of union membership. Moreover, the same configuration of factors may not explain this widely shared trend in all the nations where it is manifest. In fact, there seems to be agreement among observers that employers in the United States are more likely than their counterparts elsewhere to resist attempts by workers to unionize.

This historical and cross-national evidence suggests that several of the factors cited are indeed helpful in understanding why the share of the workforce that is unionized has diminished so substantially. Structural factors—the comparatively rapid growth of employment in job categories and economic sectors that have traditionally had a low proportion of union members—have had an impact, but the consequences of changes in the distribution of jobs are not the whole story.[61]

With respect to the role of unions in contributing to their own weakening, there is evidence that the leadership of the American Federation of Labor and Congress of Industrial Organizations (AFL-CIO)—including Lane Kirkland and, especially, George Meany—did not devote sufficient attention or resources to organizing. In a 1972 interview, Meany remarked, "Why should we worry about organizing groups of people who do not want to be organized? . . . Frankly, I used to worry about the membership, about the size of the membership. But quite a few years ago, I just stopped worrying about it."[62] In 1995 an insurgent group challenged the established labor leadership,

60. Robert J. Flanagan, "Has Management Strangled U.S. Unions?" *Journal of Labor Research* 26 (2005): 35, Table 1. Of the nations on the list, only France has a lower share of its workforce unionized. Nevertheless, despite relatively low levels of union membership in France, the overwhelming share of French workers are covered by union contracts. See Mishel, Bernstein, and Shierholz, *The State of Working America, 2008/2009*, p. 375. Of the thirteen countries about which Mishel, Bernstein, and Shierholz present data, union coverage is lowest in the United States.

61. Chris Riddell and W. Craig Riddell, in "Changing Patterns of Unionization: The North American Experience, 1984–1998," in *Unions in the 21st Century*, ed. Anil Verma and Thomas A. Kochan (London: Palgrave Macmillan, 2004), p. 160, estimate that approximately 20 percent of the decline was the result of structural factors.

62. Quoted in Lichtenstein, *State of the Union*, p. 247.

and John Sweeney was chosen to head the AFL-CIO with the explicit goal of strengthening organizing efforts. In 2005 a coalition of several large unions left the AFL-CIO with, once again, the intention of focusing on organizing. Nevertheless, at this point the union base has fallen so far that the resources needed to turn the tide may simply not be available.[63]

In terms of both tone and tactics, businesses—aided by consultants who specialize in "union prevention"—have become substantially more hostile to union-organizing drives. According to one description, activity deemed legal by the NLRB can range from forbidding unions to approach or meet with workers on company property to having supervisors conduct individual meetings with workers at which antiunion messages are delivered.[64] Moreover, during a union election campaign, a union organizer or activist has a not insubstantial probability of being fired, a probability that rose substantially during the early 1980s and again just after the turn of the twenty-first century.[65] Although it is illegal under the National Labor Relations Act to discharge a worker who is active in a union-organizing effort, the NLRB can order only minimal penalties: payment of back pay to the worker minus any earnings after the worker was fired. In 1990 the average back pay award was $2,946.[66]

The capacity of management to act aggressively against unions has been facilitated by changes made under Reagan at the NLRB.[67] The NLRB has no

63. Freeman, *America Works*, pp. 76–82.

64. Freeman, *America Works*, p. 80. We find persuasive the evidence presented by Freeman and many others that increased antiunion activity by management is part of the explanation for the erosion of union density. Nevertheless, we should make clear that there is some disagreement over the point. See Flanagan, "Has Management Strangled U.S. Unions?" pp. 44–50; and Kenneth McLennan, "What Do Unions Do? A Management Perspective," in *What Do Unions Do?: A Twenty-Year Perspective*, ed. James T. Bennett and Bruce E. Kaufman (New Brunswick, NJ: Transaction Publishers, 2007), pp. 580–582.

65. See the findings and references in Schmitt and Zipperer, "Dropping the Ax."

66. Figure from the 1994 Dunlop Commission report cited in Schmitt and Zipperer, "Dropping the Ax," p. 3. According the Bureau of Labor Statistics CPI (Consumer Price Index) Inflation Calculator, in 2009 dollars the figure would be $4,820—still a nominal sum under the circumstances.

67. On the NLRB under Reagan, see Paul Alan Levy, "The Unidimensional Perspective of the Reagan Labor Board," *Rutgers Law Journal* 16 (1985): 269–390; Terry Moe, "Interests, Institutions, and Positive Theory: The Politics of the NLRB," *Studies in American Political Development* 2 (1987): 266–271; and James A. Gross, *Broken Promise: The Subversion of U.S. Labor Relations Policy, 1947–1994* (Philadelphia: Temple University Press, 1995), chap. 13. Farber and Western, in "Ronald Reagan and the Politics of Declining Union Organization," use the fact that the decline in the number of union representation elections began before the strike of the Professional Air Traffic Controllers Organization (PATCO) and the ascension of the Reagan majority on the NLRB as evidence that an antiunion climate rather than public

rule-making capacity but proceeds, instead, by conducting hearings and making decisions in particular cases with the result that policy is made by accretion. According to one analysis, it was, ironically, the absence of rule-making authority that permitted the NLRB to have such a substantial impact on labor policy during the early years of the Reagan administration. Freed from such administrative requirements as notice and comment procedures that slowed Reagan-era policy changes by other agencies with rule-making powers, the NLRB was able to weaken worker protections under the National Labor Relations Act by overturning worker-friendly precedents, many of them long standing, through a series of decisions in carefully selected cases. At the same time, whether by accident or design, the number of decisions in cases of unfair labor practices dwindled, and the backlog of unresolved cases expanded to the largest number in history.[68]

The latest chapter in the ongoing story of the attrition of union membership and political power continues to unfold. During the 2008 presidential campaign, Barack Obama promised to support the Employee Free Choice Act, which would have had the effect of diminishing the attrition in union membership. However, the bill died in a heavily Democratic Congress, a testament to the political weakness of organized labor.[69] The Republican tide in the 2010 elections shifted partisan control of many governors' mansions and state legislatures. Bolstered by friendly state legislatures, Republican governors in a number of states sought to deal with revenue shortfall by cutting the medical benefits and pensions of unionized public employees and, more fundamentally, targeting their collective bargaining rights. Not surprisingly, these moves have generated partisan conflict and, in some states, public protest. Although a February 2011 Pew survey in Wisconsin showed considerable support for the public employee unions, at this point, it is not clear whether the particular configuration of fiscal emergency and Republican Party strength will succeed in hobbling state and local public employee unions.[70]

---

policy was responsible for the fall in the number of union elections. It is difficult to read accounts of the NLRB under Dotson and come away with doubts about the independent effect of NLRB actions in tilting the playing field in the direction of management and making it more difficult for unions to organize.

68. Gross, *Broken Promise*, p. 253.

69. Hacker and Pierson, *Winner-Take-All Politics*, pp. 278–279.

70. See, for example, Steven Greenhouse, "Strained States Turning to Laws to Curb Labor Unions," *New York Times*, January 3, 2011; Steven Greenhouse, "A Watershed Moment for Public-Sector Unions," *New York Times*, February 11, 2011; and Kris Maher and Amy Merrick, "Bills Try to Curb Reach of Unions," *Wall Street Journal*, May 9, 2011. The public opinion data

As for the possibility that union attrition reflects changes in the preferences of workers themselves, there is no consensus whether lack of interest by workers in becoming union members plays a role. Some observers interpret the continuing slide in the number of union elections as a revealed preference indicating workers' desire to avoid union membership, an interpretation that is questioned on the reasonable ground that hostile tactics by management have so raised the stakes that unions are forced to exercise great caution in choosing to undertake a representation election. In contrast, others cite surveys indicating that many workers would be receptive to joining a union.[71] In rejoinder, these survey results are questioned on the also reasonable ground that there is frequently a gap between what respondents say when canned questions are posed by pollsters and what respondents do when the chips are down.[72]

Conclusion

This chapter has reviewed a great deal of evidence about two complex trends that form a critical part of the background for our analysis of inequalities of political voice: the increase in economic inequality and the decrease in union membership. With respect to the former, this brief overview has made clear the extent to which economic deserts in the United States are not only unequally distributed but are more unequally distributed now than at any time in several generations. Considering the data in cross-national rather than historical perspective underlines the extent of inequality in America. Although market incomes are not especially unequally distributed in the United States, after-tax family income is distributed more unequally than in other affluent democracies—an outcome that reflects, at least in part, the limited redistributive impact of taxes and government benefits in the United States.

What we have seen undermines several clichés about economic life in America. For one, it is often argued that a rising economic tide lifts all boats.

---

were reported in "More Side with Wisconsin Unions than Governor" on February 28, 2011, on the Web site of the Pew Research Center for People and the Press, http://people-press .org/2011/02/28/more-side-with-wisconsin-unions-than-governor/ (accessed June 8, 2011).

71. See Richard B. Freeman and Joel Rogers, *What Workers Want*, updated ed. (New York: Russell Sage Foundation, 1999), esp. chaps. 4 and 7.

72. Once again we can contrast the arguments made by Freeman in *America Works*, pp. 82–86, and Flanagan in "Has Management Strangled U.S. Unions?" pp. 42–44.

However, the impressive levels of prosperity over the past quarter century have lifted the yachts but left the dinghies still grounded. Moreover, it is argued that, even though income is unequally distributed, American affluence implies that low-income workers are better off in absolute terms in America than they are elsewhere. However, the evidence from separate studies shows that, on the contrary, workers and poor people are worse off in America than are many of their European counterparts. Finally, in spite of the American Dream of equality of opportunity, well-educated, affluent parents are ordinarily able to pass their high status along to their children. Compared to the situation in other affluent democracies, rates of upward mobility in the United States are not especially high. While it is not clear whether the possibilities for those of modest origins to become successful have diminished in an era of increasing economic inequality, there is strong evidence that the class-based intergenerational gap in educational attainment has widened. That is, while those who have the good fortune to have high-income parents are increasingly likely to graduate from college, or even to attain an advanced degree, those who hail from families of limited means have increased their educational attainment only very modestly. In sum, the United States has never been the domain where all are created equal, and it is less so in the early twenty-first century than in the not-so-distant past.

When it comes to the erosion in union membership and the transformation of the character of the unionized workforce, a development with implications for political voice to which we shall return periodically, it seems that any fair-minded explanation stands on its head the truism that victory has a hundred fathers but defeat is an orphan: a combination of factors is required to account for the attrition in the share of the American workforce that is unionized. The decline of unions has resulted from the preferences and actions of most, or perhaps all, the major stakeholders—union leadership, employers, public officials, and workers.

Although the precise nature of the causal links is debated, it is not coincidental that the increase in economic inequality and the weakening of unions have occurred at the same time. Both have roots, at least in part, in government policies and the actions of policy makers, and both have implications for what and from whom public officials hear. We shall be reminded of these developments as we proceed with our multifaceted analysis of inequalities of political voice.

4

Equal Voice and the
Dilemmas of Democracy

Underlying our analysis of inequalities of political voice is the premise that equal consideration of the interests and preferences of all citizens is an important component of democratic governance. Equal consideration depends on equal political voice. Those who express political voice—by voting or otherwise taking part in politics—are able to inform the government of their needs and preferences and to pressure public officials to pay attention; they are therefore in a better position to protect their interests. As we shall demonstrate over and over, the United States deviates from the ideal of equal voice. But is equal political voice—or, more realistically, more nearly equal voice than is currently the case—a desirable goal?

Before we begin our long journey into an empirical analysis of equal voice, we need to pause for a brief consideration of whether it is a goal worth pursuing.[1] One of the frustrations of democratic governance is how frequently

1. Our understanding of why we care about political participation and political equality has been shaped by a number of scholarly discussions. Among them are Jane J. Mansbridge, *Beyond Adversary Democracy* (New York: Basic Books, 1983), chap. 17; Geraint Parry, George Moyser, and Neil Day, *Political Participation and Democracy in Britain* (Cambridge, England: Cambridge University Press, 1992), chap. 1; Robert D. Putnam, *Making Democracy Work* (Princeton, NJ: Princeton University Press, 1993); Amartya Sen, *Inequality Reexamined* (Oxford, England: Oxford University Press, 1995); Michael Schudson, *The Good Citizen: A History of American Civic Life* (New York: Free Press, 1998); Mark E. Warren, *Democracy and Association* (Princeton, NJ: Princeton University Press, 2001); Robert D. Putnam, *Bowling Alone: The Collapse and Revival of American Community* (New York: Simon and Schuster, 2000); Theda Skocpol, *Diminished Democracy* (Norman: University of Oklahoma Press, 2003); Stephen Macedo et al., *Democracy at Risk* (Washington, DC: Brookings Institution,

the multiple values underlying democracy come into conflict one with another. To assume up front that equality of political voice is an objective to be sought may obscure the extent to which it may clash with other values such as free speech and liberty, effective and efficient policy, respect for minority rights, or deference to the opinions of those with a particular stake, deep wisdom, or demonstrated expertise. Equal voice is a valued end in a democracy but far from the only one.

As we have discussed, these issues date back to the earliest days of the republic and remain matters of contention today. They were debated intensely at the Constitutional Convention. Opponents of equal voting rights for all at the Convention were concerned that giving the vote to the lower orders would have negative consequences: that the masses would use the vote to destroy liberty and to support policies that were ineffective and harmful. Even those who, like James Madison, supported widespread suffrage were concerned about domination by a tyrannical majority or a mischievous faction. That most adult citizens should be full members of the political community with access to the franchise is no longer contested. Still, to achieve more nearly equal political voice would, in practice, mean amplifying the voices of younger, less affluent, and less educated citizens—with multiple, and not uniformly desirable, consequences for democratic functioning. In Chapter 17 we return to the issue of the trade-offs implicit in attempts to ameliorate inequalities of political voice. There we consider such concrete matters as the conflicting claims of the integrity of the electoral process and promotion of equal voice implicit in the controversy over requiring voters to present photo identification at the polling place or the competing goals of encouraging free speech and diminishing unequal voice underlying the conflict over restricting direct campaign spending by corporations and unions.

Clear-headed thinking about such debates and the larger normative considerations behind them requires an understanding of the empirical realities, the objective of the analyses presented in the remainder of this volume. Of course we cannot do justice to issues about which volumes have been written, but we want to sketch quickly some of the dilemmas in balancing equal political voice with other democratic values.

2005); Robert A. Dahl, *On Political Equality* (New Haven, CT: Yale University Press, 2006); and Diana C. Mutz, *Hearing the Other Side* (Cambridge, England: Cambridge University Press, 2006).

In Support of Equal Voice

There are numerous reasons to rank equality of political voice high among the alternative democratic values. Some of them speak to the beneficial consequences of political participation; others partake of a concern with political equality. Although our primary concern is facilitating equal protection of interests, there are a number of additional reasons for favoring political equality as a democratic goal. Let us survey them briefly.

Promoting Equal Protection of Interests

Our concern for equal political voice is rooted in the desire for equal consideration of the preferences and interests of all citizens. As George Bernard Shaw said, "Do not do unto others as you would that they should do unto you. Their tastes may not be the same."[2] The recognition that people have different goals and desires is essential to democracy. To the extent that democracy implies equal consideration of the differing needs and preferences of all citizens, the possibilities for equal consideration are enhanced when political voice is equal. Those who express political voice are able to inform the government of their opinions, needs, and experiences, to give public officials incentives to pay attention to what they hear and thus to protect their interests. Of the various positive consequences that ensue from equal political voice, equal protection of interests is central to our inquiry. The relationship of equal political voice to equal protection of interests goes to the heart of our concerns.

Ensuring Full Membership in the Polity

The ability of an individual to express political views is constitutive of membership in the polity. It confers a sense of selfhood, agency, and belonging. Put another way, facile dismissals of the significance of voting often point to the experience of African Americans in the South or blacks in South Africa to argue that achieving the right to vote hardly guarantees the solution to the problems faced by disadvantaged groups. However, what is essential to democracy is not necessarily that democratic rule solves all problems or produces the best policies—whatever that means. Rather, it is fundamental to the nature of democracy that democratic rule confers an important and valued status on its members: the status of citizens, who have the equal right and

---

2. George Bernard Shaw, "Maxims for Revolutionists: The Golden Rule," in *Man and Superman* (Baltimore: Penguin Books, 1960), p. 257.

ability to control their own lives and the fate of the community by taking part in collective decisions. This status is not only a means to some other end but also a valuable status per se. Those who dismiss the importance of the right to vote probably already have that right.

Judith Shklar discusses the way that those who are denied the "marks of civic dignity feel dishonored, not just powerless and poor. . . . The struggle for citizenship in America has, therefore, been overwhelmingly a demand for inclusion in the polity, an effort to break down excluding barriers to recognition, rather than an aspiration to civic participation as a deeply involving activity."[3]

Developing Democratic Individuals

Political participation is also educational. In the process of taking part, not only do activists become better informed about politics but they also develop individual capacities—independence, competence, respect for others, the willingness to take responsibility, the ability to assess the interests of self and community.[4]

Building a Democratic Community

In addition, the educational effects of civic participation are valued not just for their meaning for the individual but for their consequences for community and democracy. The heirs to Tocqueville who make this argument stress several themes.[5] They point to the kinds of democratic orientations and skills that are fostered when people work together voluntarily: social trust, norms of reciprocity and cooperation, and the capacity to transcend narrow points of view and conceptualize the common good. Thus, when there is a vigorous sector of voluntary involvement and political engagement, it becomes easier for communities, and democratic nations, to engage in joint activity and to

3. Judith N. Shklar, *American Citizenship: A Quest for Inclusion* (Cambridge, MA: Harvard University Press, 1991), p. 3.

4. See, for example, Peter Bachrach, *The Theory of Democratic Elitism: A Critique* (Boston: Little, Brown, 1967); Carol Pateman, *Participation and Democratic Theory* (Cambridge, England: Cambridge University Press, 1970); and Geraint Parry, "The Idea of Political Participation," in *Participation in Politics*, ed. Geraint Parry (Totowa, NJ: Rowman and Littlefield, 1972), chap. 1.

5. This perspective clearly draws from the concept of social capital in James S. Coleman, "Social Capital in the Creation of Human Capital," *American Journal of Sociology* 94 (1988): 95–120. For a rare empirical test of this hypothesis, see John Brehm and Wendy Rahn, "Individual-Level Evidence for the Causes and Consequences of Social Capital," *American Journal of Political Science* 41 (1997): 999–1023.

produce public goods.[6] Communities characterized by high levels of voluntary activity are in many ways better places to live: the schools are better, crime rates are lower, tax evasion is less common.[7] Moreover, a vital arena of voluntary activity between individual and state protects citizens from overweening state power and preserves freedom. Because these processes involve horizontal connections, they imply the engagement of equals.

Conferring Legitimacy

Legitimating democratic rule is among the most important reasons for wanting equal voice in a democracy. The struggle for political control inevitably produces winners and losers. Democratic governments depend on voluntary acquiescence: obedience to laws without constant coercion, acceptance of election outcomes by the losing side, and so on. Why do losers accept the results of elections or contests over policy? One answer is that, even though the losers may dislike the outcome, they will be more likely to accept it as legitimate if they believe that the rules of democratic procedure have been followed and if they believe those rules to be fair. Process justifies outcomes.[8] The losers are also more likely to deem such outcomes acceptable if they feel that they have been given a fair hearing, with no individual or group given more voice in that decision than any other. Legitimacy thus depends on a belief in the fairness of political processes, which, in turn, depends on the equality of political voice. The process of decision making—free, honest, and open to all—legitimizes outcomes even among the losers. For this reason, Rawls highlights the need for an "overlapping consensus" on political process—freedom to speak and to act—in pluralist societies where there is no agreement on the conception of the good.[9] Equality of political voice fos-

---

6. Many commentators point out that the inevitable result of collective action is not necessarily the fostering of community and democracy. Some groups—for example, militias—hardly promote democratic values. Moreover, organizations of like-minded individuals beget conflict as well as cooperation. See, for example, the arguments and references found in Michael W. Foley and Bob Edwards, "Escape from Politics? Social Theory and the Social Capital Debate," and Sheri Berman, "Civil Society and Political Institutionalization," *American Behavioral Scientist* 40 (1997): 550–561 and 562–574, respectively.

7. Putnam, *Bowling Alone*, Section IV.

8. On the issue of the consent of the losers, see Christopher J. Anderson, Andre Blais, and Shawn Bowler, eds., *Losers Consent: Elections and Democratic Legitimacy* (Oxford, England: Oxford University Press, 2005).

9. In *The Theory of Justice* (Cambridge, MA: Harvard University Press, 1971), John Rawls started in an imagined world of rational people in a contrived state of ignorance as to who they are and where they fit into society, and thus do not have conflicting preferences. But

ters the peaceful reconciliation of conflicts that inevitably exist among those with different political preferences or ideologies. If some category of citizens is relatively quiescent and receives less consideration in the policy-making process, its members are less likely to consider the result legitimate. As Robert Post puts it: "In a modern democracy . . . citizens are free to engage in public discourse to make the state responsive to their ideas and values, in the hope that even if the state acts in ways inconsistent with those ideas and values, citizens can nevertheless maintain their identification with the state."[10]

Although there is clearer empirical support for some of these contentions than for others, all of them are plausible and thus lend weight to the desirability of equal political voice. We should make clear that some of the reasons for wanting equal citizen participation rest more heavily on the participation part of the term and others on the equality part. The community-building and legitimacy-enhancing aspects of political participation would seem to depend on the *level* of activity—that is, on how many people take part. In contrast, the equal protection of interests depends more on *who* participates— that is, on the representativeness of those who participate.

Equal Voice: The Dark Side

Could the expansion of the chorus that would accompany an effort to equalize political voice endanger the democratic process? Concerns about this issue were expressed frequently at the time of the Founding. Madison expressed apprehension about those "particular moments in public affairs when the people, stimulated by some irregular passion . . . or misled by the artful misrepresentations of interested men, may call for measures which they them-

---

later, in *Political Liberalism* (New York: Cambridge University Press, 1993), he addressed the inevitability of conflicting values and preferences and found the solution to peaceful decision making in agreement on a free-standing, overlapping consensus on a democratic process that involves tolerating alternative doctrines. Given the inevitable plurality of competing doctrines subscribed to by citizens in a democracy, this overlapping consensus is needed, as Rawls notes and as many democratic theorists have noted before, to maintain a stable democracy. Some theorists of deliberative democracy might try to avoid differences in preferences for outcomes by open discussion through which people would come to an enlightened consensus. One need not be cynical, however, to believe open discussion will not remove all disagreements about policies or personnel.

10. Robert Post, "Democracy and Equality," *Annals of the American Academy of Political and Social Science* 603 (2006): 28.

selves will afterwards be the most ready to lament and condemn."[11] Reflecting similar concerns about the lower orders, Alexander Hamilton argued: "The republican principle . . . does not require an unqualified complaisance to every sudden breeze of passion, or to every transient impulse which the people may receive from the arts of men."[12] Distrust of the public is no longer as acute as it once was, but there is still reason for skepticism about the capacities of ordinary citizens. Beginning with Samuel Stouffer's 1955 investigation, studies over an extended period have found that socio-economic status—in particular, its education component—is a significant predictor of support for civil liberties, democratic procedure, and political tolerance. Regardless of their ideological predispositions or policy preferences, the well educated are less intolerant of alternative views and less inclined to compromise the liberties of those with whom they disagree.[13] This observation is supported by our own analyses demonstrating that the same participatory processes that lead to the overrepresentation of those with high levels of income and education among activists also result in participant publics that are more tolerant of deviant points of view.[14] From this perspective, the relative quiescence of the disadvantaged concomitant to political inequality is supportive of democracy and democratic liberty.

Equal Voice, Majority Tyranny, and "Minorities Rule"

A related concern is that promoting equal voice would also lead to majority tyranny. That democratic procedures ordinarily provide for the majority to prevail raises no concerns about majority tyranny when the losers in the

---

11. James Madison, "The Federalist No. 63," in *The Federalist: Alexander Hamilton, John Jay, and James Madison,* ed. Robert Scigliano (New York: Modern Library, 2000), pp. 403–404.

12. Alexander Hamilton, "The Federalist No. 71," in *The Federalist,* ed. Scigliano, p. 458.

13. Samuel Stouffer, *Communism, Conformity, and Civil Liberties* (New York: Doubleday, 1955). Among the many replications that come to the same conclusion about the role of education, see John L. Sullivan, James Pierson, and George E. Marcus, *Political Tolerance and American Democracy* (Chicago: University of Chicago Press, 1982), chaps. 5, 7, and 8; Herbert McClosky and Alida Brill, *Dimensions of Tolerance* (New York: Russell Sage Foundation, 1983), chap. 6 (with Dennis Chong); and Larry Bobo and Charles C. Licari, "Education and Political Tolerance," *Public Opinion Quarterly* 553 (1989): 285–308. For a recent work on some of the puzzles associated with political tolerance, see James Gibson, "Enigmas of Intolerance: Fifty Years after Stouffer's *Communism, Conformity, and Civil Liberties,*" *Perspectives on Politics* 4 (2006): 21–34.

14. Sidney Verba, Kay Lehman Schlozman, and Henry E. Brady, *Voice and Equality* (Cambridge, MA: Harvard University Press, 1995), pp. 500–506.

minority are not deeply invested in the outcome. However, if the losing minority has strong and intensely held views, majority rule may be more problematic—particularly if the triumphant majority compromises the basic rights of the minority or if the losing minority is defeated over and over on issue after issue. A circumstance in which a relatively indifferent majority on one side is opposed by an intense but smaller public on the other obtains for many issues in American politics. This pattern characterizes controversies as diverse as handgun control, consumer product safety regulation, and community conflicts over the siting of facilities like sewage treatment plants or, even, new schools.

How should a minority that cares deeply—especially a group that constitutes a more or less permanent minority—be treated in a democracy? Can equal voice be harmonized with deference to views that are intensely held? As Madison observed in "Federalist No. 10": "Measures are too often decided, not according to the rules of justice and the rights of the minor party, but by the superior force of an interested and overbearing majority."[15] In fact, Madison makes clear later in the essay that the structure of the American government was established to ensure that majority factions do not prevail.

To ignore the fact that some people care deeply about a particular issue while the large and politically quiescent majority are more or less indifferent would seem unreasonable. Yet to allow an intense and active minority to prevail over and over again has other risks. The history of American political contestation demonstrates—and the data in Chapters 11 and 14 about the organizations active in American politics confirm—that majority tyranny is not the only danger and that an intense minority often carries the day in policy controversies, a circumstance that has sometimes been dubbed "minorities rule." Indeed, later in life Madison expressed concern about the need for ordinary citizens to have a voice in politics and demonstrated greater congeniality to majority rule.[16]

Political Equality vs. Effective Governance

By jeopardizing effective government that can make decisions that serve the community and the nation in the long run, equal voice for all citizens might

---

15. Madison, "Federalist No. 10," in *The Federalist*, ed. Scigliano, p. 54. On Madisonian democracy, see Robert A. Dahl, *A Preface to Democratic Theory: Expanded Edition* (Chicago: University of Chicago Press, 2006), chap. 1.

16. See the discussion of Madison in Robert A. Dahl, *How Democratic Is the American Constitution?* (New Haven, CT: Yale University Press, 2002), 33–37.

pose a threat to another requisite of democracy. There is a natural tension between effective government from above and democratic control from below. Governing depends on expertise, on the capacity to understand and judge potential policies, and on the ability to make complex policy decisions that balance the needs and preferences of many actors. Yet the diverse members of the public have widely varied preferences and needs; their attention to and knowledge of policy issues is limited, making them ill equipped to judge among alternative policies.[17] Equal voice for all—regardless of educational level, interest in and knowledge about politics, or relevant experience—might lead to government that is less effective, efficient, and far-sighted.

In brief, because those who currently speak less loudly in politics are also less likely to be committed to civil liberties, tolerant of dissenting views, and competent as citizens, reducing inequality of political voice might imply negative outcomes for democracy.

Representative Government: The Madisonian Solution

The American response to this tension is well known: representative government. Citizens elect representatives who can, in Madison's terms, "refine and enlarge" the preferences of the public. Representative democracy moves decisions away from the direct control of the citizens and into the hands of representatives who use their own judgment and expertise. These representatives would be more likely to be committed to democracy, in Hamilton's words more "likely to possess the information and discernment requisite"[18] for governing than would the citizenry at large—especially compared to those of more limited education, who would figure more importantly in the chorus if political voice were less unequal. Under such leadership, politics would be more open and tolerant, and policy would be more effective. Democratic govern-

---

17. There is an extensive literature on this subject. See, for example, Michael X. Delli Carpini and Scott Keeter, *What Americans Know about Politics and Why It Matters* (New Haven, CT: Yale University Press, 1996). See also W. Russell Neuman, *The Paradox of Mass Politics: Knowledge and Opinion in the American Electorate* (Cambridge, MA: Harvard University Press, 1986); Stephen E. Bennett, "'Know-Nothings' Revisited: The Meaning of Political Ignorance Today," *Social Science* Quarterly 69 (1988): 476–490; Philip E. Converse, "Popular Representation and the Distribution of Information," in *Information and Democratic Processes,* ed. John A. Ferejohn and James H. Kuklinski (Urbana: University of Illinois Press, 1990), pp. 369–388; and Vincent Price and John Zaller, "Who Gets the News? Alternative Measures of News Reception and Their Implications for Research," *Public Opinion Quarterly* 57 (1993): 133–164.

18. Alexander Hamilton, "The Federalist No. 68," in *The Federalist*, ed. Scigliano, p. 435.

ment would be protected from the irresponsible masses so feared by many at the Constitutional Convention—and, to a lesser extent, by some commentators today. Representatives are expected to act on the basis of their enlightened knowledge and wisdom, on their deeper moral commitment to democracy and its long-term health. Representative government thus ameliorates many democratic mischiefs: policy based on expertise would mitigate citizen incompetence; elected elites who are more committed to civil liberties would bolster support for the democratic process; the intermediation of representatives would reduce the danger of tyranny by a majority faction that squashes minority rights or by minority factions uninterested in the common good.[19] More than two centuries later, American democracy remains based on representative government.

What is the role of political voice—and equal voice—in a democracy based on representative democracy? Although they may act as trustees more capable of producing effective and efficient policy for the benefit of the people than the people can produce for themselves, representatives still seem to need to hear the views of the populace if they are to be effective trustees. As Edmund Burke—well known as a proponent of representative government that gives a great deal of autonomy to representatives to use their own judgment in making policy—put it, a representative ought to maintain "the closest correspondence, and the most unreserved communication with his constituents. Their wishes ought to have great weight with him; their opinion, high respect; their business, unremitted attention."[20]

In their introduction to the policy-making process, Charles E. Lindblom and Edward J. Woodhouse apply this Burkean understanding to the process. They make clear that policy making depends on policy makers having an understanding of how citizens view their problems and information about

19. We realize that the description of the representative is somewhat idealized. The citizenry may not be well informed and committed to the common good, but a variety of historical incidents—ranging from bribery to sex scandals to McCarthyism—suggest that representatives may not always be paragons of virtue either.

20. Edmund Burke, *The Works of the Right Honourable Edmund Burke* (London: Henry G. Bohn, 1854), vol. 1, pp. 446. For examples of the ways in which representatives seek information about citizen preferences in retrospective voting regimes, see John W. Kingdon, *Congressmen's Voting Decisions* (New York: Harper and Row, 1981); Dennis Thompson, "Representatives in the Welfare State," in *Democracy and the Welfare State*, ed. Amy Gutmann (Princeton, NJ: Princeton University Press, 1988), chap. 6; and James A. Stimson, Michael B. Mackuen, and Robert S. Erikson, "Dynamic Representation," *American Political Science Review* 89 (1995): 543–565.

the performance of existing programs, and therefore that systematically unequal information can undermine the making of what Lindblom and Woodhouse call "intelligent" policy:

> Political inequality obviously reduces the extent to which policy mak-
> ing can be fully democratic. Not quite so apparent is that inequality
> interferes also with the *intelligence* of democracy. If government func-
> tionaries are to focus their attention on important social problems, the
> broader policy-making process needs to help them see and conceptual-
> ize those problems. . . . When some important problems are not force-
> fully called to attention, then all of us are deprived of the opportunity
> to deliberate about them, deprived of the opportunity to reappraise our
> own judgments of what issues most deserve scarce time, attention, and
> funding.
>
> When potentially relevant participation is undermined or shut out by
> systematic biases differentially empowering certain social groups or
> ideas, less intelligence can be brought influentially to bear.
>
> If intelligent, democratic policy making requires mutual adjustment
> among those concerned with a problem, what is required for a working
> majority of those people to reach a well-probed, reasoned judgment on
> how to proceed? Among other helpful contributions to that cause will
> be having in circulation a diverse set of ideas on the subject in ques-
> tion. Great diversity will help prevent careless, grossly simplistic, pre-
> mature agreement on policies that do not offer much prospect of
> ameliorating the problem.[21]

Thus elected representatives are expected to be more knowledgeable about
policy, less self-interested, and more elevated in their civic commitments
than the citizenry. They act as trustees of the public good, serving the public
with enlightened values and exercising their own judgment in appraising the
long-term interests of the polity, whether or not constituents themselves
would make the same assessment. After all, the Madisonian representational
ideal is the *refinement* of citizen voice, not its *reflection*. Still, as Lindblom

---

21. Charles E. Lindblom and Edward J. Woodhouse, *The Policy-Making Process*, 3rd ed.
(Englewood Cliffs, NJ: Prentice Hall, 1993), pp. 111, 141, 147–148, emphasis in original.

and Woodhouse make clear, even under this construction of democracy, political voice—indeed, equal political voice—has an important place. Even when public officials rely on their own judgment or expertise rather than citizens' opinions, the political voice of citizens performs an essential function by communicating information about their actual circumstances and needs. Whether elected representatives rely on greater expertise or deeper wisdom, they need to understand what ordinary people are experiencing. If that information comes from an unrepresentative set of voices, ensuing policies will fulfill neither the democratic requirement of giving equal consideration to the needs and preferences of all nor the trustee task of serving the public based on the representatives' own determination of what ought to be done. Equal voice retains a critical role even in a trustee-run government.

A somewhat different view of representation is propounded by Joseph Schumpeter in his classic *Capitalism, Socialism, and Democracy*.[22] Though the book was written seventy years ago, it is relevant to more recent considerations of representation including social choice theory and retrospective voting.[23] The first task of the citizenry in theories of representative democracy is to elect officeholders. Schumpeter's more restricted interpretation of the role of the citizenry makes this the primary—indeed the only—purpose of elections. Given the limited capacities of the public and the need for expertise in policy making, citizen participation should begin and end with electoral participation. Citizens elect leaders from the choices offered them and then leave the more expert elites free to rule.

By focusing on votes as the means of expression of citizen voice, this elitist version of democracy does have a democratic basis. Voters leave political matters alone until the next election, at which point they can engage in retrospective evaluation of the performance of elected officials. Because they must be mindful of the next election, when they will be forced to compete for votes, political leaders cannot ignore the public. Citizens judge the performance of the incumbents after the fact. Thus they do not need to understand

22. Joseph Schumpeter, *Capitalism, Socialism, and Democracy* (New York: Harper & Brothers, 1942).

23. See William H. Riker, *Liberalism against Populism: A Confrontation between the Theory of Democracy and the Theory of Social Choice* (San Francisco, CA: W. H. Freeman, 1982), chap. 10. Schumpeter bases his preference of a limited role for the citizens on their incompetence. Riker comes to a similar conclusion as to the desirability of a limited voice for citizens in a social choice analysis of the likely inconsistency and incoherence of election systems in terms of the policies they would espouse. See also Morris P. Fiorina, *Retrospective Voting in American National Elections* (New Haven, CT: Yale University Press, 1981).

the complexity of policy; they need to understand only whether they are satisfied with the performance of the incumbents in office. Each citizen answers the question that he or she can answer better than anyone else: "Are you better off now than you were at the last election?" Although citizens are expected to be quiet between elections, their preferences and needs will not be ignored, because incumbents and candidates look toward the next election and anticipate what they must do to win it.[24]

In some sense, it is easier to achieve equal voice under Schumpeter's constricted view of citizen voice. Ironically, equal treatment—including equal consideration—may be most easily attained when the preferences and interests of the public, both those who are noisy and those who are quiet, are treated by being *equally ignored*.[25]

The retrospective voting approach, indeed, does seem to entail equal political voice; each citizen is limited to one vote and is therefore equal in the voting booth. However, voting is equal only if all citizens vote or if voters are representative of all citizens, which is, of course, not the case. Voters are, for many reasons, not representative of the public at large. However, as an approach to achieving equal voice, the major flaw in an understanding that confines the role of citizens to the exercise of the franchise is that it overlooks the many other avenues for citizen expression between and during elections. Elections are basic to democracy and crucial for other kinds of political voice, but, as we have stressed, voting is only one of the ways in which citizens take part in politics. There are many others, many of which are more amenable to the communication of precise messages, more expandable in the volume of activity an individual is able to generate, and more stratified in the socio-economic status of those who are active.

Unequal voice is especially pronounced in the arena of organized interest politics. Obviously, organized interests—whether labor unions, professional associations, trade associations, or universities—do not vote, but they are

24. For additional perspective on these issues, see Jane Mansbridge, "Rethinking Representation," *American Political Science Review* 97 (2003): 515–528. Mansbridge differentiates between "anticipatory representation," which is based on retrospective judgments on the part of citizens and anticipatory actions on the part of the representatives, and "promissory representation," which combines forward-looking judgments by voters followed by responses by elected officials.

25. As Green Bay Packers defensive tackle Henry Jordan is said to have commented about the way Coach Vince Lombardi dealt with members of the team: "He treats us all the same—like dogs!" Quoted in Jerry Kramer, "Winning Wasn't Everything," *New York Times*, February 5, 2011.

deeply engaged in the political process through their electoral activity and through their direct expressions on policy matters. Input from organizations provides information that is important in making policy. However, that information comes from a highly stratified set of sources.

In sum, by emphasizing the governing authority of elected officials who are expected to bring wisdom and expertise to the job of governing, different constructions of representative government—whether Madisonian, Burkean, Schumpeterian, or based on retrospective voting—help to protect democratic policy making from the excesses of a mass public that may be mercurial, intolerant, and ignorant. However, none of the versions of representative government either obviates the need for information from a representative group of citizens about their problems and experiences or resolves the dilemma created by the fact that the most information-rich forms of political activity by individuals and organizations provide information that is skewed sharply in the direction of the affluent and well educated.

Equal Voice through Direct Democracy?

Because government by referendum partakes of the principle underlying democratic elections—one person, one vote—direct democracy would seem to guarantee equal voice and equal consideration. Leaving aside the complicated matter of the kinds of policies that are made as the result of referendums, such an approach would seem a foolproof way of solving the equality problem.[26] However, as is so often the case when it comes to democratic governance, what seems to be clear at the outset rapidly becomes cloudy. Referendums offer the potential for equality of voice, but in reality, referendum participation is affected by the full set of processes that produce the class stratification characteristic of voting and other political activities. Unless a referendum is tied to a regular election, voting turnout is likely to be low and

26. On the place of referendums in democracy, see, for example, David B. Magleby, *Direct Legislation: Voting on Ballot Propositions in the United States* (Baltimore: Johns Hopkins University Press, 1984); Elizabeth R. Gerber, *The Populist Paradox: Interest Group Influence and the Promise of Direct Democracy* (Princeton, NJ: Princeton University Press, 1999); Matthew Mendelsohn and Andrew Parkin, eds., *Referendum Democracy: Citizens, Elites, and Deliberation in Referendum Campaigns* (Basingstoke, England: Palgrave, 2001), Introduction; and John G. Matsusaka, *For the Many or the Few: The Initiative, Public Policy, and American Democracy* (Chicago, IL: University of Chicago Press, 2004). The election of instructed delegates to public office is a form of direct democracy, with public preferences directing policy. Referendums are widespread in American states; instructed delegates are not.

therefore more skewed in the direction of the well educated and affluent. Furthermore, referendum campaigns provide many opportunities for activists to multiply their influence by giving time or money to promote the desired outcome. Besides, organized interests frequently play a major role in referendum campaigns, introducing further possibilities for unequal voice.[27] Thus direct democracy does not bypass the ordinary stratified processes of policy making in America but rather operates within the more general political process replicating its patterns of stratification.

Equal Political Voice in Deliberative Democracy

Many students of democracy have called for deliberative democracy in which political decisions emerge from reasoned discussion among citizens and between citizens and governmental decision makers.[28] In the ideal deliberative setting, participation goes beyond the expression of preferences to the expression of reasons and justifications for the preferences and includes openness to the reasoning of others. In contrast to representative democracy, deliberation puts greater demands on citizens to understand issues and to give reasons for their preferences. Equality of political voice in a deliberative setting would entail equal access to the public discourse and equal capability to take a full and effective part in the discussion. In light of the substantial disparities among individuals in the capacities to articulate opinions and in political knowledge and interest, deliberative settings would seem an unlikely

27. In *First National Bank of Boston v. Bellotti*, 435 U.S. 765 (1978), the Supreme Court ruled that the First Amendment protects the right of corporations to make contributions in contests over ballot propositions, widening the opportunities for the use of financial resources to influence referendum outcomes.

28. There is a substantial literature on deliberative democracy, much of it engaged with matters of democratic theory. A few works include Jane J. Mansbridge, *Beyond Adversary Democracy* (New York: Basic Books, 1983); Benjamin Barber, *Strong Democracy* (Berkeley: University of California Press, 1984); James Fishkin, *Democracy and Deliberation: New Directions for Democratic Reform* (New Haven, CT: Yale University Press, 1991); James Bohman and William Rehg, eds., *Deliberative Democracy* (Cambridge, MA: MIT Press, 1997); Jon Elster, *Deliberative Democracy* (Cambridge, England: Cambridge University Press, 1998); Stephen Macedo, ed., *Deliberative Politics: Essays on Democracy and Disagreement* (New York: Oxford University Press, 1999); James Fishkin and Peter Laslett, *Debating Deliberative Democracy* (Malden, MA: Blackwell, 2003); Amy Gutmann and Dennis Thompson, *Why Deliberative Democracy?* (Princeton, NJ: Princeton University Press, 2004); Shawn Rosenberg, ed., *Deliberation, Participation, and Democracy: Can the People Govern?* (New York: Palgrave Macmillan, 2007); and John Gastil, *Political Communication and Deliberation* (Thousand Oaks, CA: Sage, 2008).

venue for equality of political voice. Indeed, a recent inquiry shows a strong upward tilt in the direction of well-educated and affluent participants that characterizes discourse among those who take part in political deliberation.[29] While there are compelling arguments to be made on behalf of deliberative democracy, the achievement of equal political voice is unlikely to be among them.

Liberty and Equality

We have made clear that one line of objection to political equality is that equal voice—including from those parts of the public that are ill-informed, intolerant, and changeable—might produce policies having analogous defects. Another arises from the concern that efforts to reduce inequalities of political voice would jeopardize liberty and would thus, to echo Madison, constitute a remedy "worse than the disease."[30] Any inventory of the values underlying American democracy would place at the top of the list equality and liberty—two values that are often understood to be in conflict.

Essential to the complex relationship between liberty and equality of political voice is the fact that the expression of political voice is voluntary. Some people go to the polls; others stay home. Activity beyond the vote—speaking up, making political contributions, petitioning, protesting, working in the community—is also voluntary. Unlike voting, for which there is mandated equality, with each vote counting the same, these activities can be pursued at different levels: many hours of political work or a little; a large contribution or a small one; a long, compelling letter or a brief one supplied by a voluntary association and forwarded to a public official.

Because individuals can choose whether and how to express political voice, inequalities of political voice ensue from the fact that some do not want to take part—even if they thereby forgo the chance to communicate their preferences and interests or to enjoy other benefits of political activity, such as the sense of community that comes from joining with others to promote a cause. Perhaps they feel no civic or political commitments. They may be too busy with work and family to go to a community meeting, or they may prefer sports to politics.

29. Lawrence R. Jacobs, Fay Lomax Cook, and Michael X. Delli Carpini, *Talking Together: Public Deliberation and Political Participation in America* (Chicago: University of Chicago Press, 2009), chap. 6.

30. Madison, "The Federalist No. 10," p. 54.

Chapter 17 discusses a number of political reforms and social changes that would have the effect of equalizing political voice. Among the more prominent suggestions for reducing inequalities are some that take aim at the voluntary character of political voice and therefore potentially compromise our liberties. They do so either by placing a ceiling on activity, and thus limiting the freedom to do as much as one wishes to exercise political voice, or by putting a floor under political activity, and thus limiting the freedom *not* to act.

When we discussed the paths to political activity in Chapter 1, we pointed to several resources that facilitate political participation, among them time, skills, and money. The liberty to use time or skills in the expression of political voice is essentially unconstrained by any government policy. No ceiling is imposed on our freedom to talk and write, to work for political candidates or causes, to organize protests and so on as much and as effectively as our skills and leisure permit. Money is another matter. For more than a century, there have been political battles over the regulation of the free use of money in pursuit of political objectives—especially with respect to campaign finance. As we discuss in Chapter 17, part of the controversy centers on the question of whether money is speech and thus enjoys the same First Amendment protections as other forms of political expression. Compared to other democracies, the United States is more open to the free use of economic resources for the purpose of political influence.

An alternative policy to promote political equality involves a floor rather than a ceiling and threatens political liberty by making political activity mandatory rather than voluntary. More than two dozen countries require eligible voters to go to the polls. Those who do not turn out may be fined. Mandatory voting has the effect of equalizing turnout across social groups. In spite of the fact that other democracies mandate electoral turnout, in a nation uneasy with mandates, there seems to be no active debate about or much evidence of support for a requirement that voters go to the polls.

Unequal Capabilities and the Exercise of Liberty

That political activity is voluntary implies that unequal political voice derives from differences in the motivation to be active. However, inequalities of political voice also reflect differences in the resources of education, income, knowledge, skills, and social ties that foster political participation, a theme we raised in Chapter 1 that will recur with regularity in Part II. These endowments are not randomly distributed but instead hew to the fault lines of socio-economic hierarchy. Bringing into the conversation the role of resources in generating political participation suggests that political inactivity may not be genuinely voluntary and that positing a zero-sum relationship between political liberty and political equality may be too simplistic.

Amartya Sen argues that equality and liberty are not necessarily opposed to one another but must be seen as part of a more complex relationship. Sen applies his argument to various forms of freedom: political, economic, and social. The freedom to express political voice by voting or engaging in other activities, as well as many other freedoms, depends on an individual's capabilities—capabilities that depend, in turn, on education, economic status, and social support. If these capabilities are unequally available, freedoms cannot be exercised.[31] The argument is a rich and complex one, but it is, at its center, directly related to our analysis of the origins of inequalities of political voice. Even if individuals have the right to act, they need other requisites to take advantage of that right. The motivation to act may not be sufficient. It may need to be coupled to resources and, perhaps, to supportive social circumstances. The factors that foster activity are highly stratified, and the stratification derives in large part from an economic system that is grounded in the free market with its attendant inequalities in income and education.

Libertarians may consider policy interventions to make political voice less unequal to be threats to liberty. However, the absence of the capability to be active is itself a limitation on freedom. Therefore, another way to think about the relationship between liberty and equality is that attempts to ameliorate inequalities in citizen activity—which, as we shall indicate, may unfortunately be difficult—might foster equality and liberty at the same time.

Conclusion

That we have written a long book about equality of political voice makes clear that we deem it an important value in a democracy. Equal political voice would have many payoffs for democracy: promoting equal protection of interests, conferring on all a sense of full membership in the community, nurtur-

31. See Amartya Sen, *Inequality Reexamined* (Cambridge, MA: Harvard University Press, 1992),as well as *Development as Freedom* (New York: Knopf, 1999). Lindblom and Woodhouse, in *Policy-Making Process*, make a similar point when they note (p. 194) "the axiom that democracy requires not simply responsiveness to citizens, but an equal distribution among them of capacities for exerting influence."

ing the democratic capacities of individuals, cultivating norms of social trust and reciprocity that shore up democratic communities, and endowing policies with greater legitimacy. That said, we have also made clear in this chapter that trade-offs among important values are built into democracy. With respect to equal voice, there are two sets of trade-offs that go in quite different directions. On one hand is the concern that, if political voice were more nearly equal, members of the public who are too ill-informed, mercurial, and intolerant to get involved in politics would press for policy outcomes that were ill advised, responsive to short-run considerations and lukewarm majorities, and insufficiently protective of the rights of others. On the other hand is the concern that measures designed to reduce inequalities of political voice would jeopardize essential liberties, either by forcing the quiescent to go to the polls when they would not otherwise or by constraining superactivists from spending as much as they would like on political candidates and causes.

In each case, however, the trade-offs are more complex than they seem at the outset. For all the limitations of the capacities of citizens, especially those who are not involved in politics, they can attest to their own experiences; therefore, they possess information that those who govern—who may command greater wisdom and substantive expertise—would be well advised to take into account. Thus ameliorating inequalities of political voice might improve policy outcomes, not threaten them. Regarding the risk to liberty from efforts to diminish political inequality, we have also discussed the problem that those who lack certain capacities that foster political participation are in no position to exercise the liberties that accompany citizenship. Under the circumstances, the apparent conflict between liberty and equality is made more complex, and reductions in inequality could result in enhanced liberty.

These dilemmas of democracy to the contrary, the empirical analyses that occupy our attention for the remainder of our inquiry demonstrate that inequalities of political voice are powerful and enduring, deeply rooted in socioeconomic disparities and resistant to change. Whatever station is assigned to political equality in the hierarchy of democratic values, we demonstrate that it would be a difficult circumstance to achieve.

PART II

Inequality of Political Voice and Individual Participation

5

Does Unequal
Political Voice Matter?

Beginning with this chapter, we switch gears and begin a multifaceted empirical exploration of the meaning of inequalities of political voice in American democracy. We tackle the problem of what the government hears from a variety of perspectives—considering, for example, the political voice of individuals and organizations, political voice offline and via the Internet, and the implications for political voice of processes of political mobilization and procedural reforms. In the context of growing inequality in the economic sphere, we consider whether inequalities of political voice have been increasing in a parallel fashion, as well as whether they are handed on across generations and whether they are transformed over the life cycle. As we proceed, we shall refer to the many issues we have already discussed.

Our data about inequalities of political voice focus on the input side. While we concentrate on one side of the equation only, our intellectual project acquires greater significance to the extent that messages sent have some impact and policy makers heed the voices emanating from the public. In this chapter we address the issue of governmental response in order to reassure readers, as well as ourselves, that our journey is worthwhile. We draw on previous research—including research we conducted ourselves—in order to assess whether inequalities of political voice make a difference; that is, we examine not whether the loudest voices always prevail but whether the messages expressed by citizens and organizations are noted and given serious consideration.

To introduce our discussion of whether political voice matters, we can suggest three conditions under which inequalities of political voice would *not* make a difference. If any of the following obtains, we could conclude that unequal political voice would have no impact on policy outputs. First, if citizens and organizations expressing political voice through their participation are representative of the preferences, needs, and priorities of those who are quiescent, there is no reason for concern about unequal political activity. The messages communicated would be the same ones that policy makers would hear in greater volume if everyone were equally active. Second, even if political voice is not representative, unequal political participation would not matter if decision makers ignore what they are hearing from activist individuals and organizations and do whatever they want. Third, even if political voice is unrepresentative and public officials are responding to what is being communicated, unequal political participation would have no further consequences if decision makers were aware of the distortions in political voice and sought to engage in a kind of affirmative action—learning about the opinions of the silent and attempting to respond equally to all regardless of whether they take part politically.

In this chapter we investigate each of these conditions for individuals; that is, we ask whether the active voices are representative, whether they elicit a response from policy makers, and whether public officials seek to compensate for inequalities of voice by learning about and responding to the quiescent. Later on, in Chapter 10, we shall raise the first two issues with respect to the political voice of organized interests: Whom do they represent, and what effect do they have? Just to relieve any tension as to how the plot will unfold, we can reveal that the evidence indicates unambiguously that neither active individuals nor active organizations represent all politically relevant segments of society equally. Furthermore, activity by both citizens and organized interests makes a difference for public policy, and, if anything, public officials are disproportionately responsive to the affluent and well-educated members of their constituencies. Thus political voice in America is not equal in what it communicates about the preferences and concerns of the public, and the response of the government is not equal across all citizens.

Is Citizen Political Voice Representative?

To assess whether active and inactive citizens differ in politically relevant ways requires comparing the preferences, needs, and concerns of political participants with the preferences, needs, and concerns of those who do not take part.[1] Scholars have taken different approaches to measuring the "unobservable" concerns and preferences held in silence—often by disadvantaged individuals and groups. Studies of disadvantaged communities have documented the issues they face and make clear that the absence of political voice does not imply that the politically inactive have no preferences or concerns. The more common method is to use surveys to solicit the views of those who do not take part politically. Surveys of randomly selected individuals can record the preferences and concerns of inactive citizens who, although they do not volunteer their views via public participation, express those views to interviewers and thus can reveal the issues—often matters that are not even on the political agenda—about which those who do not take part would like to see action from policy makers.[2] Comparing those who

1. At one time, a vigorous debate in political science relevant to the meaning of political voice and political silence focused on "issues and nonissues" and engaged the question of whether it is possible to know the preferences and interests of inactive citizens. The debate raised the question of the extent to which the issues on the public agenda reflect the policy concerns of "silent" citizens. Because many problems remain unarticulated and other issues of equal or greater importance are not on the table, the set of issues before the public is only a selection of the matters about which citizens are concerned. Other scholars pointed out in rejoinder that, if no one raises them, the issues that never make it to the political agenda are "nonissues" that do not need to be—and, in fact, cannot be—studied. The reply to this point made clear that sometimes those issues do not make it to the agenda not because nobody tried to raise them but because positive action was taken to squelch them. Actions undertaken to keep issues from being resolved by democratic political processes—which range from procedural maneuvers to ensure that there is no political forum in which to locate them to threats and intimidation—can, on the contrary, be studied using the same techniques that are applicable to ordinary decision-making processes. Among the works in this debate are Peter Bachrach and Morton S. Baratz, "Two Faces of Power," *American Political Science Review* 56 (1962): 947–952; Peter Bachrach and Morton S. Baratz, "Decisions and Nondecisions: An Analytical Framework," *American Political Science Review* 57 (1963): 632–642; Nelson W. Polsby, *Community Power and Political Theory* (New Haven, CT: Yale University Press, 1963); Richard M. Merelman, "The Neo-elitist Critique of Community Power," *American Political Science Review* 62 (1968): 451–460; and Raymond E. Wolfinger, "Nondecisions and the Study of Local Politics," and Frederick W. Frey, "Comment on Issues and Nonissues in the Study of Power," *American Political Science Review* 65 (1971): 1063–1080 and 1081–1101, respectively.

2. The sample survey is not the perfect instrument for capturing the views of the disadvantaged. Surveys often undersample lower-status respondents and always omit the incarcerated, thus reproducing in a less pronounced fashion the same biases that we find for political participation. See John Gaventa, *Power and Powerlessness: Quiescence and Rebellion in an Appalachian Valley* (Urbana: University of Illinois Press, 1980); Jennifer L. Hochschild, *What's Fair? American Beliefs about Distributive Justice* (Cambridge, MA: Harvard University Press, 1981), pp. 15–22; and Adam Berinsky, *Silent Voices: Public Opinion and Political Participation in America* (Princeton, NJ: Princeton University Press, 2004). For examples of studies conducted in other nations, see Louis Dumont, *Homo Hierarchicus: An Essay on the Caste*

express voice through political activity with those who do not allows us to understand the issues that are salient to the politically quiescent.[3]

The Concerns of Actives and Inactives: Voters and Nonvoters

For several reasons, the literature on the policy response to political voice focuses on voters—rather than on those who undertake other political acts that can communicate more detailed messages or can be expanded in volume beyond the mandated equality implicit in the principle of one person, one vote. For one thing, we have better longitudinal data about the characteristics and political commitments of voters than about other kinds of political participants. Furthermore, election-based survey data make it possible to link voters to candidates on the ballot in a way that is not always possible for activists like protesters or contactors. In addition, the outcomes—if not the influence of a single vote—are, except in rare instances, clear and known to the public.

With respect to our concern with equality of voice, voting is the act for which there is mandated equality: each voter is allowed only one vote. Nevertheless, political voice communicated by voting is, of course, unequal in that even presidential elections have far less than full turnout. Thus we can compare those who express political voice by voting with those who do not.

Are there politically significant differences between voters and nonvoters? In a key book on citizen activity, *Who Votes?*, Raymond Wolfinger and Steven Rosenstone conclude that those differences may matter less than we might imagine. They consider the relationship between citizen policy preferences and voting and report finding little or no difference in policy preferences between voters and all citizens as revealed by answers to a series of forced-choice policy questions in the 1972 American National Election Study.[4] Work following that of Wolfinger and Rosenstone has found similar patterns of quite marginal differences between voters and nonvoters in their responses

---

System, trans. Mark Sainsbury (Chicago: University of Chicago Press, 1970), and James C. Scott, *Weapons of the Weak: Everyday Forms of Peasant Resistance* (New Haven, CT: Yale University Press, 1985).

3. This matter is a central concern in our earlier work, Sidney Verba, Kay Lehman Schlozman, and Henry E. Brady, *Voice and Equality* (Cambridge, MA: Harvard University Press, 1995).

4. Raymond E. Wolfinger and Steven J. Rosenstone, *Who Votes?* (New Haven, CT: Yale University Press, 1980), chap. 6.

to survey questions on policy matters.[5] Still, the position that voters and non-voters are essentially similar has been challenged. In an analysis using American National Election Studies data from 1972 until 2004, Jan Leighley and Jonathan Nagler find a strong tendency for voters to differ from nonvoters in their policy positions, especially in relation to class-based economic issues. The pattern is weakest in the data from 2004, but even those data—supported by a parallel study conducted using the Annenberg National Election Study— show a similar pattern of difference between nonvoters and voters, with the former taking more liberal positions.[6]

Beyond Voting—Beyond Attitudes Expressed in Surveys

In our earlier work we argued that the question of whether voters and non-voters are different has been posed too narrowly.[7] In order to understand the representativeness of citizen input, it is necessary to expand the analysis in

5. See Stephen Earl Bennett and David Resnick, "The Implications of Non-voting for Democracy in the United States," *American Journal of Political Science* 34 (1990): 771–802. Verba, Schlozman, and Brady, in *Voice and Equality*, pp. 204–205, also replicated the Wolfinger and Rosenstone analysis in their 1990 Citizen Participation Survey and confirmed their finding with respect to voting turnout and policy positions. Highton and Wolfinger repeated the earlier analysis in later work and found confirmation for the earlier finding. See Benjamin Highton and Raymond E. Wolfinger, "The Political Implications of Higher Turnout," *British Journal of Political Science* 31 (2001): 179–192. They also looked at the demographic characteristics of nonvoters (for example, age, income, education, and race or ethnicity) and found (p. 191) "that no single characteristic is shared by a majority of those who did not vote in 1992 or 1996; the 'party of non-voters' is rather diverse." In a surprising omission that seems germane to the intellectual question they raised, they do not compare the distributions of voters and nonvoters with respect to demographic characteristics. Although they were surely correct that the set of citizens who do not go to the polls is diverse, the "party of non-voters" is not representative of the electorate as a whole.

There have also been follow-up studies asking whether differential turnout rates across citizens with various characteristics have an impact on election outcomes: because Democrats tend to be, on average, somewhat lower in socio-economic status, would Democratic candidates benefit from increased turnout? The results have been mixed, but studies have tended to find that a change in turnout would not likely change an election outcome. In "What If Everyone Voted in Presidential Elections?" paper delivered at the Annual Meeting of the American Political Science Association, Philadelphia, August 2006, Jack Citrin, Eric Schickler, and John Sides considered a number of presidential and senate elections and found that, even if turnout had been universal, it is unlikely that election outcomes would have differed.

6. Jan Leighley and Jonathan Nagler, "Who Votes Now? And Does It Matter?" paper delivered at the Annual Meeting of the Midwest Political Science Association, Chicago, April 2007.

7. The discussion in this section draws on Verba, Schlozman, and Brady, *Voice and Equality*, chap. 7.

two fundamental ways. First, it is important to take a broader view of politically relevant attributes, encompassing not only the policy positions expressed by voters and nonvoters in response to survey questions but also policy-relevant individual circumstances and the actual content of participatory input. Those who express political voice through political participation, including voting, can be distinguished from the politically silent in ways that are of great political significance. Even if they are similar in their attitudes, activists are distinctive in other more significant ways: in their personal circumstances and dependence on government benefits, in their priorities for government action, and in what they say when they get involved. Second, we can expand our focus by looking beyond voting to employ a broader view of political activity—moving beyond the most common political act, voting, to acts that can convey more precise messages to policy makers and that can be multiplied beyond the enforced equality of ballots.

Socio-economic Status and Political Participation

Knowing that political participation is distributed unequally does not, however, necessarily mean that activist publics are unrepresentative. Nevertheless, those who take part in politics are distinctive in many ways that are germane to politics. To begin with, those who are politically active differ from the less active in their social circumstances, circumstances that are relevant to policy issues in politics.

As we and numerous other scholars have demonstrated, those who are higher in the hierarchy of socio-economic status (SES) are more likely to be active—more likely both to vote and to undertake other political acts.[8] In

---

8. See Verba, Schlozman, and Brady, *Voice and Equality*, chaps. 7 and 9–12, for a discussion of socio-economic stratification, its extent, and its origins. Numerous works support the significant stratifying role of SES and its two components, education and income. See, for example, Gabriel Almond and Sidney Verba, *The Civic Culture* (Princeton, NJ: Princeton University Press, 1963); Lester Milbrath, *Political Participation* (Chicago: Rand McNally, 1965); Raymond E. Wolfinger and Steven J. Rosenstone, *Who Votes?* (New Haven, CT: Yale University Press, 1980); Steven J. Rosenstone and John Mark Hansen, *Mobilization, Participation, and Democracy in America* (New York: MacMillan, 1993); Norman Nie, Jane Junn, and Kenneth Stehlik-Barry, *Education and Democratic Citizenship in America* (Chicago: University of Chicago Press, 1996); Larry M. Bartels, *Unequal Democracy: The Political Economy of the New Gilded Age* (New York and Princeton, NJ: Russell Sage Foundation and Princeton University Press, 2008). For a dissent from the consensus on the impact of education on political participation, see Cindy D. Kam and Carl L. Palmer, "Reconsidering the Effects of Education on Political Participation," *Journal of Politics* 70 (2008): 612–631. For a critique of this work, see John Henderson and Sara Chatfield, "Who Matches? Propensity Scores and Bias in the Causal Effects of Education on Participation," *Journal of Politics* 73 (2011): 646–658.

Figure 5.1 we have used data from the 2008 survey of the Pew Internet and American Life Project to show the relationship between political participation and a measure of socio-economic status constructed by ranking respondents in terms of the sum of their educational attainment and family income and dividing them into five equal groups, or quintiles.[9] The top line shows the percentage of respondents in each SES group who reported having engaged in two or more of the five acts in the participation scale. The other lines show the data for the five individual acts: contacting a government official, working with fellow citizens to solve a community problem, making a political contribution, attending a protest, and working for a political party or candidate. Figure 5.1 makes clear that, with the single exception of attending a protest, political activity rises with socio-economic status.[10] Although

9. The SES measure is constructed to give equal weight to family income and the respondent's educational attainment. (We use this pair of measures because they are available in nearly every survey. Some surveys do not ask about the educational attainment of other family members, and some do not ask about the respondent's income. Moreover, it is hard to combine the educational attainment of all members of a family.) The SES measure was also constructed to create five quintiles containing equal numbers of people. Because family income and educational attainment are typically reported in "categories," we had to find a way to convert these categories into quintiles. We proceeded as follows. First, we identified everyone for whom we had both income and educational information. Second, we scored the income and educational categories with ascending integer numbers (one, two, three, four, etc.). Third, for each measure we added a small random number to these integers so that each person had a distinctive score and could be assigned an integer-numbered ranking arranged in ascending order. These ranking numbers went from one to the total number of respondents for whom we had both income and educational information. Then we added together the two ranking scores for each person to obtain a final rank. Finally, we divided these ranks into the lowest fifth, the second-lowest fifth, and so forth until five quintiles were constructed. We broke ties with random numbers. This method yields results that depend on the random numbers assigned to each case, but it has the advantage of randomness. Furthermore, in some methodological checks we found that our basic results were very robust with respect to different assignments of random numbers.

10. The unambiguous evidence of the stratification of political activity by socio-economic status raises the same question that is debated in the literature on voting: To what extent do the active and inactive differ in their political attitudes, at least as measured by answers to surveys? Stuart Soroka and Christopher Wlezien, in "On the Limits to Inequality in Representation," *PS: Political Science and Politics* 48 (2008): 319–327, look at a number of issue questions asked in the General Social Survey and find a surprising similarity in policy positions across income groups. With the exception of welfare spending—which is, as they point out, a not insignificant exception—the proportion of citizens in the top tercile of income who support government spending is similar to the proportion in the bottom tercile. Wlezien and Soroka make a similar point in "Inequality in Policy Responsiveness?" in *Who Gets Represented?* ed. Peter K. Enns and Christopher Wlezien (New York: Russell Sage Foundation, 2011), chap. 10. In contrast, Martin Gilens calls into question the finding that there are few

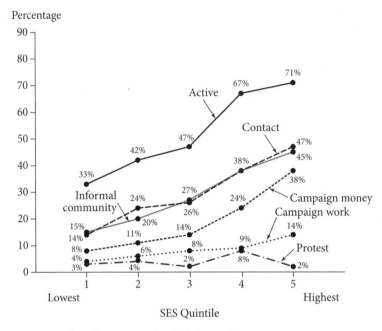

Figure 5.1   Political Activities by SES Quintile

Source: Pew Internet and American Life Survey (2008).

Note: Percent active means engaged in 2 or more of 5 acts: contacting a government official, working with fellow citizens to solve a community problem, making a political contribution, attending a protest, or working for a political party or candidate.

there is no consistent relationship between attending a protest and social class, the fact that there is so little variation across the SES quintiles for an act that is often characterized as the "weapon of the weak" is itself noteworthy.[11]

In light of the extent to which, as we saw in Chapter 3, economic gains have in recent years been accruing disproportionately to those at the very

policy differences between rich and poor. On the basis of examination of the most extensive sample of survey questions reviewed by any research on this subject, he finds substantial difference across income groups and concludes that "preferences across income groups do differ by significant amounts on a large range of issues." See Martin Gilens, "Preference Gaps and Inequality in Representation," *PS: Political Science and Politics* 42 (2009): 340.

11. Data from the 1990 Citizen Participation Study show an overall pattern of stratification similar to that for 2008. However, for 1990 the data for protest show an upward tilt. There were relatively few protesters in that survey, but those in the top quintile of SES were, in fact, five times as likely to protest as those in the bottom quintile (10 percent vs. 2 percent).

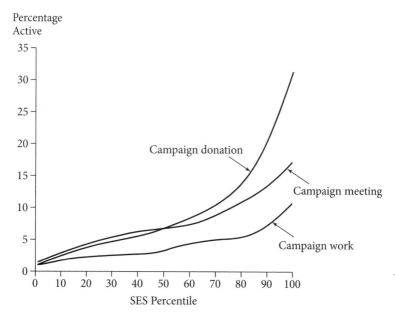

Figure 5.2   Active in Campaigns—Donating, Attending Meetings, and Working by SES Percentile

Source: American National Election Studies (ANES) (1952–2008).

Note: For this analysis the ANES presidential surveys from 1952 to 2008 were pooled and the final results were smoothed using a LOESS smooth of 30 percent.

top, we were interested to look more closely at the participation of those in the highest quintile.[12] In order to obtain enough data to consider smaller slices of the SES hierarchy, we combined the nearly 23,000 respondents to all quadrennial American National Election Studies between 1952 and 2008 and divided them into SES percentiles. Figure 5.2 presents data about the proportion in each of these socio-economic groups that engaged in three campaign acts: donating money to a party or campaign, working for a party or candidate, and attending campaign meetings or rallies.[13]

As expected, the share who engage in each of the three activities climbs with SES, especially among those in the upper third of the SES hierarchy.

12. We are grateful to Andrea Campbell for this suggestion.

13. The SES groups were constructed using the same technique described earlier in the chapter but dividing the respondents into percentiles rather than quintiles. The curves were smoothed using LOESS.

What is striking, however, is the pattern for contributing money. In the lowest percentiles, contributing money is rarer than attending a campaign meeting or rally and even working for a candidate or campaign. The line for giving money crosses both of the other two lines and then skyrockets upward into the upper-SES ranges. By the 90th percentile, only 7 percent reported working for a campaign, about 13 percent going to campaign rallies or meetings, and more than 20 percent donating money. In the highest percentiles, less than 12 percent indicated working in a campaign, about 18 percent attending a campaign rally or meeting. In contrast, more than 30 percent reported having made a contribution. Because the members of this upper-SES group are in a position not only to make campaign donations but also to give more generously when they do, these data reinforce our understanding of the extent to which making campaign contributions places the affluent in a position to amplify their political voices.

Economic Need and Unequal Political Voice

We can take a politician's-eye view by considering groups defined not by their socio-economic status but by their political participation. The left-hand two columns of numbers in Table 5.1 present data from the 2008 American National Election Study about attitudes toward national health care. In this case, voters and nonvoters do differ somewhat in their opinions as measured in a survey: those who are completely politically inactive are more favorable to universal health care than are voters. What is especially striking is that, in contrast to inactives, voters, and campaign workers, all of whom lean in the direction of support for universal health care, campaign contributors were more opposed than favorable. The differences among participant groups in their actual experiences are even more notable. The other two columns show the proportion of the various activity groups lacking health care coverage and living (according to the assessment of interviewers) in dilapidated dwellings or neighborhoods. When it comes to the indexes of need, the inactives are much more likely—and the campaign contributors much less likely—than the other groups to report being without health coverage or to have been classified by interviewers as living in problematic dwellings or neighborhoods.

Thus, with respect to experiences that are relevant for government policy, the voters to whom politicians are ultimately responsible and the campaign workers and contributors to whom candidates are exposed and, presumably, beholden differ substantially from the inactives, who are less visible. The distinctiveness of campaign contributors with respect to such experiences is noteworthy. Observers of elections have commented that the need for candi-

Table 5.1   Are Activists Typical? Health and Housing

	Universal Health Care[a]		Percentage with No Health Insurance[b]	Percentage with Housing or Neighborhood Problems[c]
	Percentage Who			
	Favor	Oppose		
Inactives[d]	59%	24%	27%	28%
All Respondents	51%	36%	17%	19%
Voters	48%	40%	14%	16%
Campaign Workers	51%	37%	16%	19%
Campaign Contributors	44%	47%	7%	12%

Source: American National Election Study (2008).

[a] A random half of the sample was asked: "Do you favor, oppose, or neither favor nor oppose the U.S. government paying for all necessary medical care for all Americans?"

[b] Respondents were asked: "Do you presently have any kind of health insurance?

[c] Indicates, as noted by the interviewer, a dwelling or neighborhood characterized by any of the following problems: missing roofing, boarded windows, broken windows, missing siding, torn screens, doors off hinges, peeling paint, broken siding, unkempt yard, or litter and trash (buildings); boarded houses, graffiti, abandoned cars, demolished houses, trash in road, or trash next to buildings (neighborhood).

[d] Did not vote, work in a campaign, or contribute to a candidate or party.

dates to raise vast sums of money in order to make a credible run for office implies that they spend more and more time rubbing elbows with wealthy donors rather than interacting with constituents, with the consequence that they are more likely to encounter the rarified concerns and experiences of the affluent and less likely to come into contact with those who face such basic problems as needing health care and shelter.[14]

The same pattern emerges in Table 5.2, which presents similar data from the 1990 Citizen Participation Study. Respondents were asked whether they had been forced to do any of the following to make ends meet: put off medical or dental treatment, delay paying the rent or making house payments, cut

14. On this point, see Mark C. Alexander, "*Citizens United* and Equality Forgotten," in *Money, Politics, and the Constitution*, ed. Monica Youn (New York: Century Foundation Press, 2011), pp. 161–163.

Table 5.2   Are Activists Typical? Cutting Back to Make Ends Meet
and Receipt of Means-Tested Benefits

	Percentage Who	
	Cut Back in Order to Make Ends Meet[a]	Received Means-Tested Benefits[b]
Inactives	59%	17%
All Respondents	46%	9%
Voters	40%	6%
Campaign Workers	40%	5%
Campaign Contributors	35%	2%

Source: Citizen Participation Study (1990).

[a] Did any of the following in order to make ends meet: put off medical or dental treatment, delayed paying the rent or making house payments, cut back on the amount or quality of food, or worked extra hours or took an extra job.
[b] Indicated that they or any family member in the household received food stamps, Aid to Families with Dependent Children, housing subsidies, or Medicaid.

back on the amount or quality of food, or work extra hours or take an extra job. They were also asked whether they or any member of their immediate family living with them received any of the following: housing subsidies, Medicaid, or the means-tested government benefits then known as food stamps and AFDC (Aid to Families with Dependent Children). The campaign contributors are, once again, distinctive in having been much less likely than voters, or especially those who undertook no activity at all, to have reported cutting back on essential expenses or receiving means-tested government benefits. These data make clear that those whose political quiescence renders them less visible have very different life experiences than the people whom candidates encounter at campaign fund-raisers.

Data from the Citizen Participation Study allow us to go one step further and show the consequences of disparities in activity for the messages about government programs sent to public officials by people with an obvious stake in those programs. Those who indicated in the 1990 survey that they or an immediate family member received some form of government benefit were asked follow-up questions about political activity *in relation to that program*.[15]

15. For each program for which respondents indicated that either they or a family member in their household were beneficiaries, respondents were asked whether, in the past five

Table 5.3   Political Activity in Relation to Benefit Programs
by Recipients of Government Benefits

Political Activity Related to a Government Benefit[a]	Percentage Who Receive Income Benefits		Percentage Who Receive Medical Benefits	
	AFDC[b]	Social Security[c]	Medicaid[b]	Medicare[c]
Vote	10%	25%	10%	26%
Campaign Contribution	0%	6%	0%	5%
Contact Public Official	6%	7%	3%	6%
Organization Member	2%	24%	4%	22%
N	(109)	(546)	(123)	(423)

Source: Citizen Participation Study (1990).

[a] Respondents who indicated that they or any family member in the household received a particular government benefit were asked whether they had, in the past five years, taken into account the position of a candidate in relation to the program in question in deciding how to vote, made a campaign contribution with the program in mind, contacted an official to complain about the program, or belonged to an organization concerned about the program.
[b] Means tested: AFDC (Aid to Families with Dependent Children) and Medicaid.
[c] Not means tested: Social Security and Medicare.

Table 5.3 presents data about political activity by beneficiaries of four federal programs: two programs that provide income support, AFDC and Social Security, and two that provide medical care, Medicaid and Medicare.[16] In each category, the first provides assistance to the indigent and is means tested, and the second provides assistance to the elderly and is not means tested.

Beneficiaries of all these programs clearly have incentives to be politically active in their defense. However, aspects of the politics and implementation of means-tested programs give those who benefit from them particular reason to take part politically. For one thing, in terms of policy, means-tested programs are politically vulnerable and more easily cut than their non-means-

years, they had taken into account the position of a candidate in relation to the program in question in deciding how to vote, had made a campaign contribution with the program in mind, had contacted an official to complain about the program, or had belonged to an organization concerned about the program.
16. The data in Table 5.3 are taken from Verba, Schlozman, and Brady, *Voice and Equality*, Figure 7.12, p. 218.

tested counterparts.[17] In addition, as indicated in the following official descriptions of the eligibility requirements for Medicare and Medicaid, the rules governing means-tested benefit programs are more complex, and eligibility is usually more discretionary:

> General Medicare coverage (Part A) is generally provided automatically, and free of premiums, to persons 65 or over who are eligible for Social Security or Railroad Retirement benefits, whether they have claimed these monthly benefits or not. . . . All citizens . . . age 65 or over . . . are eligible to enroll in Part B on a voluntary basis. Almost all . . . choose to enroll.

In contrast,

> Medicaid does not provide medical assistance for all poor persons. . . . Even for very poor persons unless they are in one of the groups designated below. Low income is only one test for Medicaid eligibility within those groups.[18]

The document goes on to list twenty specific eligibility requirements, nine of the federal government and eleven of state governments. The upshot is that means-tested programs also usually involve more difficult and uncertain relations with program administrators.[19] Thus individuals seeking or receiving means-tested benefits have reasons to be politically active, and often incentives to contact public officials.

17. See Douglas M. Imig, *Poverty and Power: The Political Representation of Poor Americans* (Lincoln: University of Nebraska Press, 1996), p. 16.

18. Barbara S. Klees, Christian J. Wolfe, and Catherine A. Curtis, "Brief Summaries of Medicare & Medicaid Title XVIII and Title XIX of The Social Security Act as of November 1, 2009," Office of the Actuary Centers for Medicare and Medicaid Services, Department of Health and Human Services, Washington, DC, pp. 7–8 and 18, https://www.cms.gov/Medicare ProgramRatesStats/downloads/MedicareMedicaidSummaries2009.pdf (accessed October 22, 2010).

19. Joe Soss interviewed beneficiaries of AFDC and Social Security Disability Insurance (SSDI). Compared with SSDI, AFDC is seen as more "supervisory, disciplined, and discretionary." SSDI clients "tend to find the [Social Security Administration] reasonably responsive and rarely find themselves on the receiving end of a summons or threat. . . . In contrast, clients who participate in the AFDC program are far more likely to develop perceptions of the welfare agency that emphasize a lack of responsiveness and even a degree of hostility." Joe Soss, *Unwanted Claims: The Politics of Participation in the U.S. Welfare System* (Ann Arbor: University of Michigan Press, 2000) pp. 191–192.

Nevertheless, as shown in Table 5.3, in each case the beneficiaries of programs that are not means tested were more active than their counterparts in means-tested programs. For some forms of activity, the differences are quite small; for others, the disparities are substantial. While relatively few program beneficiaries made campaign contributions in relation to the program, it is striking, if hardly surprising, that not a single beneficiary of a means-tested benefit did so. The data on contacting public officials are interesting. While overall levels of contacting about these programs were quite low and there was virtually no difference between AFDC and Social Security recipients, Medicare recipients were more likely than Medicaid recipients to contact an official about their benefits. Presumably reflecting the role of the AARP, the massive membership association that acts as the political advocate for those who are fifty and over, the disparities with respect to joining an organization concerned about the program are especially noteworthy. In summary, among recipients of non-means-tested benefits, 44 percent undertook at least one political activity in relation to that benefit; among recipients of means-tested benefits only 18 percent did so. Unless activity by individuals and organizations has no consequence for policy, an issue we take up later in this chapter, it is striking whose interests are represented.[20]

Furthermore, in spite of the fact that inactive citizens do not differ substantially from activists in their responses when survey researchers choose the issues, when it comes to what political activists *actually say* when they take part, members of various underrepresented groups have distinctive par-

---

For other assessments that contrast the two kinds of programs, see, among others, Frances Fox Piven and Richard A. Cloward, *Regulating the Poor: The Functions of Public Welfare* (New York: Vintage, 1993); Sheldon H. Danziger and Daniel H. Weinberg, "The Historical Record: Trends in Family Income, Inequality, and Poverty," in *Confronting Poverty: Prescriptions for Change*, ed. Sheldon Danziger, Gary Sandefur, and Daniel Weinberg (Cambridge, MA: Harvard University Press, 1994), chap. 2; Mark R. Rank, *Living on the Edge: The Realities of Welfare in America* (New York: Columbia University Press, 1994); Linda Gordon, *Pitied but Not Entitled: Single Mothers and the History of Welfare* (New York: Free Press, 1994); Joel F. Handler, *The Poverty of Welfare Reform* (New Haven, CT: Yale University Press, 1995); John Karl Scholz and Kara Levine, "The Evolution of Income Support Policy in Recent Decades," in *Understanding Poverty*, ed. Sheldon H. Danziger and Robert Haveman (New York and Cambridge, MA: Russell Sage Foundation and Harvard University Press, 2002), chap. 6; Robert A. Moffitt, ed., *Means-Tested Transfer Programs in the United States* (Chicago: University of Chicago Press, 2003); and John Karl Scholz, Robert Moffitt, and Benjamin Cowan, "Trends in Income Support," in *Changing Poverty, Changing Policies*, ed. Maria Cancian and Sheldon Danziger (New York: Russell Sage Foundation, 2009), chap. 8.

20. We discuss the matter of who is represented by organized interest groups in Chapter 11.

ticipatory agendas. When asked in the 1990 survey about the issues and problems that animated their political activity, those who engaged in the kinds of participatory acts that permit the communication of explicit messages to policy makers—for example, contacting, protesting, or serving as a volunteer on a local board—mentioned a wide variety of issues, ranging from the environment to schools to taxes to the need to get the garbage collected.[21] However, compared with those who are more advantaged, those who had limited income and education were considerably more likely—and those who received means-tested government benefits were even more likely—to discuss issues of basic human need (that is, matters involving poverty, jobs, health, housing, and the like) in association with their participation. However, because the disadvantaged were so inactive, public officials actually heard *less* about these matters from the disadvantaged than from more advantaged activists.

Moreover, it is not simply that members of various groups talked about different issues when they took part, they also conveyed different messages. When those disadvantaged by low levels of education and income sent messages about policy issues concerning matters of basic human need, they were much more likely to be discussing policy issues that were germane to their own lives rather than abstract matters. Furthermore, they inevitably urged greater government attention to these concerns. The more numerous messages on these subjects sent by advantaged activists were much more mixed with respect to whether they advocated greater government efforts on behalf of basic human needs. In short, when we consider what policy makers actually hear, the stratification of political voice would seem to have potential political consequences.

In sum, when it comes to socio-economic disadvantage, political voice is not representative of all citizens. Evidence drawn from our own work and that of others makes clear that the observation that nonvoters are not distinctive in their policy views as expressed in surveys is important but incomplete. When we consider forms of political participation beyond the vote—activities that can send more precise messages and that can be multiplied in volume—the advantaged are more active and the disadvantaged less so. Furthermore, those with a presumable stake in policy outcomes, as measured by their reliance on means-tested government programs or their demonstrated economic need, are especially likely to be inactive. In addition, when we con-

21. The discussion in this paragraph is drawn from Verba, Schlozman, and Brady, *Voice and Equality*, pp. 84–91. To the best of our knowledge, no national survey subsequent to the 1990 Citizen Participation Study has asked activists open-ended questions about the issues and concerns behind their participation.

sider their participatory priorities we see that advantaged and disadvantaged activists cite different issues and concerns as being associated with their participation—suggesting that, if participants were more representative of the public, policy makers would be exposed to a different set of messages. The result is that the advantaged give more voice to their preferences and make their circumstances more visible than do the disadvantaged—a theme that we shall investigate from many perspectives throughout this volume.

Is Local Politics More Hospitable?

Although decisions made in Washington have profound consequences for our lives, local politics is in many ways closer to ordinary citizens. Many of the most important public services, ranging from schools to garbage collection, are under the control of local authorities. Depending on the size of the community and the nature of its politics, we may know local officials personally and encounter them in our daily lives. We wondered whether local politics might be more hospitable to those who do not enjoy high levels of income or education, thus ameliorating the social class structuring of citizen participation.

The data in Figure 5.3 lend some credence to this conjecture but tell a slightly complicated story.[22] The top two lines in Figure 5.3 show a pattern well known to students of voting: across all five SES quintiles, the proportion claiming that they had voted in all or most president elections is higher than the proportion claiming that they had voted in all or most local elections. Thus even though local politics may be closer to ordinary citizens, local elections do not receive the sustained attention of presidential elections, with the result that turnout is lower. With respect to SES bias, while the tendency to go to the polls rises steadily across the SES quintiles for both kinds of elections, the gap between the upper and lower SES groups is more pronounced for presidential elections than for local elections. The bottom two lines, which reflect the data about five acts other than voting for which activists indicated whether they took part at the national or local level, show a pattern that is in certain ways the reverse. In this case, a higher proportion engaged

22. We use the 1990 Citizen Participation Study, which allows us to differentiate local from national activity in a way that is unusual. Not only did that survey ask separately about voting in presidential and local elections but it also allows us to distinguish local from national activity with respect to five acts: working in a campaign; contributing to a campaign; contacting a public official; taking part in a protest, march, or demonstration; and being affiliated with an organization that takes stands in politics.

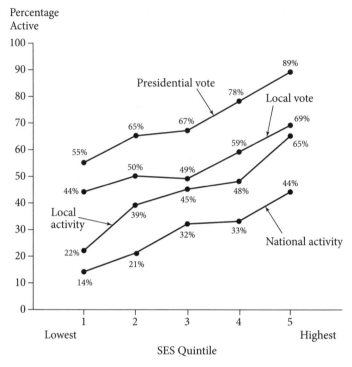

Figure 5.3   Voting and Active beyond the Vote in Local and National Politics by SES Quintile

Source: Citizen Participation Study (1990).

Note: The figure shows the percentage who voted in all or most local or presidential elections and the percentage who engaged in 1 or more of 6 political activities (working in a campaign, making a campaign contribution, being affiliated with an organization that takes stands in politics, attending a protest, contacting an elected official, or contacting a non-elected official) at the local or national level.

in at least one of the political acts at the local level. However, the social class gradient for local activity is sharper than for national activity.

In sum, the evidence that local politics provides an arena that reduces that SES structuring of political voice is mixed. Across all five SES groups, voting turnout is higher in national than in local elections, but so is the extent to which turnout is structured by socio-economic status. For participatory acts other than voting, local and national political activity more or less switch places: the members of each of the SES quintiles are more likely to report local activity than national activity in modes of participation other than voting, but, compared to national participation, local participation is more stratified by social class. Of course, for both the overall pattern is the strong association between political activity and socio-economic status.

What If We Construe Civic Involvement More Broadly?

In the introduction we mentioned two other important categories of civic involvement—the various ways that citizens seek the public good without appeal to government intervention and the various ways that they talk and deliberate about public life—that are sometimes classified as modes of political activity, and we discussed why we do not bring them under the conceptual umbrella of our understanding of political participation. Because the manifestations of such participation are so widely disparate and idiosyncratic, the former, which is sometimes referred to as "creative" or "postmodern participation," is difficult to measure. To the extent that surveys ask about civic involvements that seek social change without engaging governmental institutions or policy, they usually ask about political consumerism—that is, buying, or refusing to buy, products with the objective of achieving a public good. The latter form of civic involvement—which a recent study called "discursive participation"—is usually measured in terms of frequency of political discussion.

Although we believe that our decision to exclude these forms of civic involvement from our understanding of political voice is appropriate for our intellectual concerns, it is interesting to note that they are characterized by the same social class structuring as the explicitly political forms of participation at the center of our inquiry. Figure 5.4 shows for five SES groups the proportion who engage in four acts of civic engagement. Two of them, making a campaign donation and contacting a public official, repeat data from Figure 5.1 and fall under the rubric of our definition of political voice; the other two, boycotting a product to express one's position on an issue or cause and engaging in political discussion, do not. For all four forms of activity, the propensity to take part rises with socio-economic status.[23] Thus, a more ex-

---

23. The data about discussing politics were generated by combining two items from the August Tracking 2008 survey sponsored by the Pew Internet and American Life Project. Respondents were asked how often they discussed politics and public affairs with others, first "on the Internet—by e-mail or instant message, or on a social networking site, or in an online chat," and second, "in person, by phone, or in a letter." The data on boycotting are taken from the 2002 Citizenship, Involvement, Democracy (CID) Survey. Respondents were presented with a list of actions they might have taken, preceded by this question: "Over the past 5 years

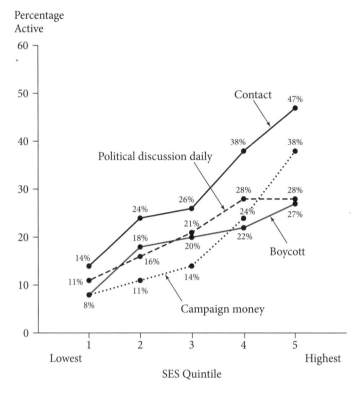

Figure 5.4   Political Voice and Political Engagement by SES Quintile: Percentage Contributing Money and Contacting Government Compared with Discussing Politics and Boycotting

Sources: Campaign money, discussion, contact—Pew Internet and Life Project (2008); boycott—Citizenship, Involvement, Democracy (CID) Survey (2005).

pansive definition of what constitutes political participation does not change the generalization that activity is strongly associated with socio-economic status.[24]

---

have you done any of the following [actions] to express your opinion about an issue or your support for a cause: Boycotting a product . . . ?"

Compared to the probability of engaging in the other three acts, that of engaging in political discussion rises more steeply, from the lowest through the middle SES quintile, and then levels off slightly for the upper two quintiles. For the other three acts, the slope is shallower at the bottom and steeper at the top.

24. Jan Teorell, Paul Sum, and Mette Tobiasen, in "Participation and Political Equality: An Assessment of Large-Scale Democracy," in *Citizenship and Involvement in European*

Social Class and Participatory Inequalities
on the Basis of Race or Gender

Historically, American politics has involved contestation along a number of fault lines—on the basis of not only economic concerns but also such divisions as region, religion, and moral commitments. Participant publics are also unrepresentative with respect to a variety of characteristics that are relevant to such political conflicts—perhaps most important, gender and race or ethnicity. Traditionally, men have been, on average, somewhat more politically active than women and non-Hispanic whites somewhat more active than African Americans and, especially, Latinos.

At least when it comes to participatory differences among groups based on race or ethnicity or on gender, social class is an important part of the story. Although the education gap has now closed, until very recently, women lagged behind men with respect to both education and income.[25] Furthermore, compared to non-Hispanic whites, African Americans and Latinos are disadvantaged in educational attainment and income. Once education and income are taken into account, gender and racial or ethnic differences in political activity diminish substantially—often to the point of statistical insignificance. The corollary is that, just as it does in the population as a whole, socioeconomic status structures political activity within subgroups based on gender or on race or ethnicity. The data in Figures 5.5 and 5.6 show, for men and women and for non-Hispanic whites, blacks, and Latinos, the propor-

---

Democracies, ed. Jan W. van Deth, José Ramón Montero, and Anders Westholm (London: Routledge, 2007), pp. 392–398, find a relationship between education and political consumerism for European democracies.

25. Among younger cohorts, women's educational attainment surpasses men's, with the result that women are now, in the aggregate, more likely than men to have graduated from college and to have graduate degrees. See U.S. Census Bureau, "Educational Attainment in the United States: 2010—Detailed Tables," http://www.census.gov/hhes/socdemo/education/data/cps/2010/tables.html (accessed June 28, 2011).

By focusing separately on race or ethnicity, on one hand, and gender, on the other, we do not mean to overlook the matter of gender differences within racial or ethnic groups or of racial and ethnic differences within gender groups, an issue sometimes called "intersectionality." For extended treatment of intersectionality with regard to political participation, see Nancy Burns, Kay Lehman Schlozman, and Sidney Verba, *The Private Roots of Public Action* (Cambridge, MA: Harvard University Press, 2001), chap. 11.

One important intersectional matter involves the extent to which high rates of incarceration of young males of color in recent decades imply that survey data on political participation may overestimate the rates of activity of Latino and, especially, African American males in their twenties and thirties.

tion in each of the five SES quintiles who engaged in at least two activities on a seven-act scale of political participation. The association between socio-economic status and participation appears in each of these groups. At any level of socio-economic status, the differences between groups based on gender or on race or ethnicity are small in magnitude.

That inequalities of political participation on the basis of gender or race or ethnicity derive from group differences in education and income—disparities that are hardly mere coincidence but are instead rooted in group differences in socially structured experiences—does not vitiate their implications for political voice. Whatever their origins, there are inequalities of political voice between women and men and among Latinos, Africans, and Anglo whites. Thus participant publics are unrepresentative in yet another way that is germane to politics—not only on the basis of class but also on the basis of gender and race or ethnicity.

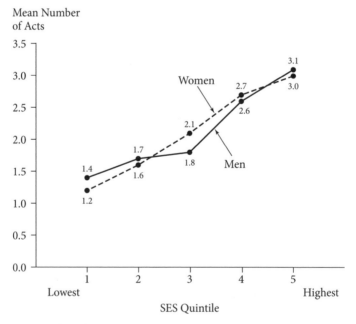

Figure 5.5   Political Activity by Gender and SES Quintile: Mean Number of Acts on a Seven-Act Scale

Source: Pew Internet and American Life Survey (2008).

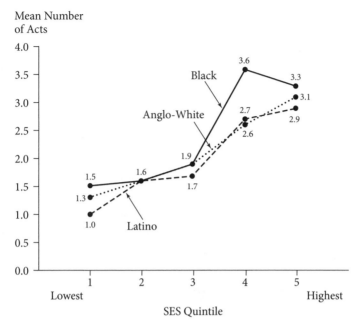

Figure 5.6   Political Activity for Blacks, Latinos, and Anglo Whites by SES Quintile: Mean Number of Acts on a Seven-Act Scale

Source: Pew Internet and American Life Survey (2008).

Governmental Response: Does Voice Make a Difference?

It is hard for public officials to take into account preferences and needs of which they are unaware. However, inequalities of political voice have forward consequences only if policy makers pay attention to what they hear. Determining whether political voice influences public policy makers—which requires linking the explicit and implicit messages sent by the public through their activity to the actions of governmental decision makers—presents difficulties at every step in the process.

Consider the messages sent. We have already made clear that the different kinds of political participation vary in their capacity to carry specific information about public preferences. Elected officials may or may not know what was on the minds of either the voters who cast ballots for them or the campaign workers who made calls on their behalf. In contrast, protesters can send strong, if general, messages about the policy matters that concern them—indicating their displeasure with the failure to take action, for example, to curb racial profiling by the police, to ameliorate global warming, or to stop illegal immigration. Those who send letters or e-mails can communicate in much more detail their preferences for providing particular services to special-needs children in the schools, loosening the regulation of a specified financial instrument, covering certain forms of in-home care under Medicare, or fixing the light at the end of the street.

What is more, as we have discussed, aggregating expressions of opinion that vary in both their quantity and their intensity and that lack a common metric of measurement presents further difficulties. How do we compare the quantity of political voice expressed by millions of votes, thousands of dollars in campaign contributions, hundreds of hours volunteered in a campaign, or dozens of letters? Besides, those millions of votes represent an equivalent number of voters. Thousands of dollars in campaign contributions represent a much smaller number of donors, who have made contributions of quite disparate sizes. Another dilemma is how to take into account that some of these activists care a great deal and others have preferences that are less intense.

The other side of the equation, governmental response, is even more complex. Consistent with the truism "If you want to know what a policy is all about, don't look at the title of the bill, look at the details," it is difficult to assess whether the policy output matches the citizen input. Even if the weight of political messages coming from the public tilts strongly in one direction, it may be complicated to establish links between general public predispositions and the detailed policies that ensue—between, for instance, overall public sentiment in favor of lower taxes and the precise provisions contained in a tax law that runs more than a thousand pages. In addition, policy makers gain information about public attitudes and priorities from many sources other than participation by citizens—among them organized interests, the media, public opinion polls, party leaders, other public officials, and notables outside politics. With multiple sources of information and multiple sources of pressure, public officials have incentives to interpret what they hear in ways that are congenial to their own political views, politically expedient, or consistent with budgetary constraints or legal requirements. Under the circumstances, it may be impossible to gauge which of many forces—among them the voice of the public—is having a decisive impact on a policy maker's actions.

In addition, congruence between expressed public preferences and the actions of public officials is not necessarily proof that the latter are responding to the former. In fact, the causality might run in the reverse direction, with the public preferences shaped by those of the policy makers.[26] Or a similarity might reflect the impact of some other factor. Or there may be no simple way to determine how close to the public's position is to that of the representative.[27]

The Research on Public Input and Governmental Response

Despite the difficulty of making such connections, there is research on the connection of citizen input and government response. Following the initial pioneering work of Warren Miller and Donald Stokes, a number of studies have found congruence between the views of the public and government policy.[28] Using national opinion samples on many issues over a long time span,

---

26. The literature on this subject is vast, and reviewing it is well beyond our current task. A classic and still highly relevant analysis of the difficulty of connecting the public and elected officials is Christopher H. Achen, "Measuring Representation," *American Journal of Political Science* 22 (1978): 475–510. For examples of literature arguing that the causality runs from governing officials to the public—with any congruence of the positions of the citizenry and the legislators deriving from the influence of the latter on the former—see John Zaller, *The Nature and Origins of Mass Opinion* (Cambridge, England: Cambridge University Press, 1992), and Lawrence R. Jacobs and Robert Y. Shapiro, *Politicians Don't Pander: Political Manipulation and the Loss of Democratic Responsiveness* (Chicago, IL: University of Chicago Press, 2000).

27. An additional difficulty in connecting citizen input to policy output is the complexity of governmental institutions. The results might differ if one were looking at federal, state, or local connections between citizens and legislators. Furthermore, citizen input might be directed to Congress, but the legislative output may be aimed at particular districts. See Paul S. Martin, "Voting's Rewards: Voter Turnout, Attentive Publics, and Congressional Allocation of Federal Money," *American Journal of Political Science* 47 (2003): 110–127, for an example of the relationship between voting on the targeted allocation of funds to electoral districts and high turnout.

28. See Warren E. Miller and Donald E. Stokes, "Constituency Influence in Congress," *American Political Science Review* 57 (1963): 45–56. Other works include Kim Quaile Hill and Patricia A. Hurley, "Mass Participation, Electoral Competitiveness, and Issue–Attitude Agreement between Congressmen and Their Constituents," *British Journal of Political Science* 9 (1979): 507–551, which shows that issue agreement between majority-party constituents and elected representatives increases the higher the level of participation in a district. In "Patterns of Representation: Dynamics of Public Preferences and Policy," *Journal of Politics* 66 (2004): 1–24, Christopher Wlezien shows a connection within various issue areas. See also Alan D. Monroe, "Public Opinion and Public Policy: 1980–1993," *Public Opinion Quarterly* 62 (1998): 6–28, which also finds that the salience of an issue does lead to greater consistency between the public and elites, and Lawrence R. Jacobs, *The Health of Nations: Public Opinion and the Making of American and British Health Policy* (Ithaca, NY: Cornell University Press, 1993), pp. 21–22, which discusses the way that the growing capacity to "influence and track public opinion directly affected the motivations and behavior of state actors . . . involved a shift from a preoccupation with secrecy and seclusion to a recognition of public opinion as a critical influence on government decision making."

Benjamin Page and Robert Shapiro find general congruence between citizen preferences and government policy. Furthermore, Robert Erikson, Michael MacKuen, and James Stimson show a dynamic connection between public views and policy shifts such that, as opinion changes, governmental response changes in the same direction.[29] The mechanism connecting public opinion to governing officials is not always specified, but the links are clear.

Our major concern, however, is not with the overall connection between public attitudes and government actions but with the differential responsiveness of public officials that reflects the unequal political voice of citizens. Although research on this subject is limited, it provides evidence that public officials do heed what they hear from citizen activists—who tend, as we have seen, to be more advantaged—and thus that policy responds to their particular preferences and needs. For example, Kim Hill, Jan Leighley, and Angela Hinton-Andersson provide evidence that the greater the class bias in voter turnout across the states of the United States, the less generous are state welfare policies. Interestingly, they also show that it is the underrepresentation of the poor rather than the overrepresentation of the more affluent that plays the larger role.[30]

Moving beyond voting to encompass other forms of political voice, in a quite different kind of study Andrea Campbell investigated a reciprocal relationship in which citizen activity influenced national policy on Social Security, which, in turn, created conditions that facilitated increased participation.[31] It is difficult to prove the impact on government policy of the spikes in

---

29. See Benjamin I. Page and Robert Y. Shapiro, *The Rational Public: Fifty Years of Trends in Americans' Policy Preferences* (Chicago: University of Chicago Press, 1992), and Robert S. Erikson, Michael B. MacKuen, James A. Stimson, *The Macro Polity* (Cambridge, England: Cambridge University Press, 2002).

30. Kim Quaile Hill, Jan E. Leighley, and Angela Hinton-Andersson, "Lower-Class Mobilization and Policy Linkage in the U.S. States," *American Journal of Political Science* 39 (1995): 75–86. See also Kim Quaile Hill and Jan E. Leighley, "The Policy Consequences of Class Bias in State Electorates," *American Journal of Political Science* 36: (1992): 351–365. Using data about changes in turnout from a sample of local communities and assuming that declining turnout implies increased turnout inequality, Trounstein and Hajnal argue that "changes in voter turnout are closely linked to policy outcomes at the local level. As turnout declines, cities are less and less likely to spend money on programs that might aid the poor. In contrast, as turnout declines, spending on infrastructure, downtown development, and other key business interests substantially increases. In other words, when turnout goes down, those who vote less regularly appear to lose out in American democracy." Jessica Trounstine and Zoltan Hajnal, "Low Voter Turnout Does Matter: Spending Priorities in Local Politics," paper delivered at the Annual Meeting of the Midwest Political Science Association, Chicago, Illinois, April 2008.

31. Andrea Louise Campbell, *How Policies Make Citizens: Senior Political Activism and the American Welfare State* (Princeton, NJ: Princeton University Press, 2003).

participation among seniors that follow quickly on policy initiatives with implications for their interests. However, Campbell marshals persuasive evidence to show how members of Congress responded to pressure from the elderly with policy concessions in the case of the repeal of the Medicare Catastrophic Act. While many factors impinge on voting decisions in Congress, it seems likely that, in this case, communications from seniors were among them.

In a 1967 study across sixty-four American communities, Verba and Nie measured citizen and elite community priorities. They compared the agendas of ordinary citizens with the agendas of community governing elites in order to estimate the impact of citizen political activity in the community on the concurrence between what the public, on one hand, and the political elites, on the other, considered to be community priorities. They found that, where citizens were more active, there was stronger agreement between the public and the political leaders on the most important issues facing the community. More significant was the fact that the agreement was significantly greater between activist citizens and community leaders than it was between less active citizens and the leaders. Verba and Nie tested to see if the concurrence between activists and leaders is due to the political activity or—because both leaders and activists enjoy, on average, higher social status—to the similarity of activists and leaders in socio-economic characteristics. Although they do not claim a causal relationship and were not able to establish that activity begets concurrence or vice versa, they did demonstrate that activity rather than social similarity plays a more important role in the agreement between citizens and elites. The study is significant for our discussion in several ways: in going beyond voting as the measure of citizen activity to a measure of a range of citizen activities; in using the community as the unit, thus making possible a close comparison of citizen views and elite responsiveness; and in measuring agreement in terms of the desired agenda for community action, a major issue in the policy-making process.[32]

A more limited but very interesting study involved a field experiment conducted in conjunction with two citizens groups in the context of a grassroots lobbying campaign advocating for the passage of a smoke-free workplace bill in the New Hampshire legislature. Randomly selected members of the legislature were part of a treatment group that received e-mails from activists supporting passage. Legislators in the control group were not contacted.

---

32. Sidney Verba and Norman H. Nie, *Participation in America: Political Democracy and Social Equality* (New York: Harper and Row, 1972), pp. 301–308 and chaps. 17 and 18.

Multivariate analysis showed that the e-mails had a significant impact on legislative votes.[33]

Do Public Officials Engage in Compensatory Responsiveness?

Consistent with this evidence about the impact of political voice, in his study of the responsiveness of U.S. senators to the views of their constituents, Larry Bartels finds some evidence for the impact of income differences in contacting senators—as well as more substantial, if indirect, evidence for the impact of income differences in campaign contributions—on patterns of voting by senators.[34]

The central conclusion of Bartels's study is relevant to the third condition that we specified with respect to our concerns about the consequences for American democracy of participatory inequalities: the possibility that policy makers compensate for the fact that they hear so much less from the disadvantaged by engaging in a kind of affirmative action in order to respond to the politically quiescent. Bartels demonstrates unambiguously that senators do not seem to seek out and respond to information about the preferences and needs of lower-income constituents. On the contrary, they seem to ignore their lower-income constituents while voting in concert with the views of their upper-income constituents—a pattern that is especially pronounced when it comes to an economic matter like raising the minimum wage.[35] He concludes that "senators consistently appear to pay *no* attention to the views of millions of their constituents in the bottom third of the income distribution[, which] must be profoundly troubling to anyone who accepts Dahl's stipulation that 'a key characteristic of democracy is the continued responsiveness of the government to the preferences of its citizens, considered as political equals.'"[36]

---

33. Daniel E. Bergan, "Does Grassroots Lobbying Work? A Field Experiment Measuring the Effects of an E-Mail Lobbying Campaign on Legislative Behavior," *American Politics Research* 37 (2009): 327–352.

34. Larry M. Bartels, *Unequal Democracy: The Political Economy of the New Gilded Age* (New York and Princeton, NJ: Russell Sage Foundation and Princeton University Press, 2008), pp. 275–282.

35. Bartels, *Unequal Democracy*, pp. 262–264. In "How Poorly Are the Poor Represented in the U.S. Senate?" in *Who Gets Represented?*, ed. Enns and Wlezien, chap. 8, Yosef Bhatti and Robert S. Erikson raise methodological concerns about Bartels's approach but conclude (p. 241): "Our reinvestigation is not directly contradictory to Bartels's findings."

36. Bartels, *Unequal Democracy*, p. 282. Emphasis in the original.

On the basis of a large-scale study of nearly 2,000 survey questions on proposed policy changes between 1981 and 2002, Martin Gilens reaches a parallel conclusion—finding that policy change reflects the policy preferences of the most affluent and not at all the preferences of the poor.[37] He comments, "The vast discrepancy I find in government responsiveness to citizens with different incomes stands in stark contrast to the ideal of political equality that Americans hold dear. Although perfect political equality is an unrealistic goal, representational biases of this magnitude call into question the very democratic character of our society."[38] In a follow-up, he focuses on particular clusters of issues and shows that the overall finding obtains with varying strength across policy domains but is, in fact, weakest for social welfare policy—including such matters as welfare reform, Social Security reform, Medicare spending, and employer health care mandates.[39] He explains this perhaps surprising finding in terms of the presence of strong interest groups—including, for example, pharmaceutical manufacturers and the AARP—in this domain. Elizabeth Rigby and Gerald C. Wright consider policy responsiveness at the state level and find somewhat different patterns for rich and poor states and for economic and social policies. They show that, especially in poorer states, economic policy outcomes are more responsive to the opinions of middle- and upper-income constituents than to the preferences of the poor.[40]

In an essay demonstrating the methodological issues behind the sometimes conflicting results with respect to the matter of differential policy re-

37. The studies just cited focus on disparities in representation based on income. A similar pattern seems to obtain for race and ethnicity. Using state-level data, John D. Griffin and Brian Newman, in *Minority Report: Evaluating Political Equality in America* (Chicago: University of Chicago Press, 2008), pp. 195–196 et passim, analyze the inequality in governmental responses to whites, African Americans, and Latinos. They find patterns of differential response between whites and both of the minority groups. The roll-call votes of senators and representatives are closer to the views of their white constituents than to those of their African American or Latino constituents.

38. Martin Gilens, "Inequality and Democratic Responsiveness," *Public Opinion Quarterly* 69 (2005): 778.

39. Martin Gilens, "Policy Consequences or Representational Inequality," in *Who Gets Represented?* ed. Enns and Wlezien, chap. 9.

40. Elizabeth Rigby and Gerald C. Wright, "Whose Statehouse Democracy? Policy Responsiveness to Poor versus Rich Constituents in Poor versus Rich States," in *Who Gets Represented?* ed. Enns and Wlezien, chap. 7. In an analogous result, James N. Druckman and Lawrence R. Jacobs, in "Segmented Representation: The Reagan White House and Disproportionate Responsiveness," in *Who Gets Represented?* ed. Enns and Wlezien, chap. 6, find that Reagan-era economic policy was disproportionately responsive to the preferences of higher-income Americans.

sponsiveness, James A. Stimson queries: "Is representation pretty much equal? Or do some Americans—often richer Americans—command more than their fair share of attention in the policy process? No one asserts a third alternative, like the antiunion rhetoric of an earlier era, that the poor command more attention than they proportionally deserve."[41] In short, there is no evidence at all that policy makers are making special compensatory efforts to learn about and respond to the concerns of disadvantaged citizens. If anything, the opposite is the case.

Conclusion

At the outset we outlined three conditions, any one of which would override concerns about the fact that not all Americans are equally likely to take part politically. If political voice, even though not universal, were representative; if public officials were not responsive to what they hear through the medium of citizen participation; or if they made special efforts to learn about and respond to the preferences and needs of the politically inactive, inequality of political voice would not pose a challenge to democratic governance. In fact, none of these three conditions is met. Although surveys show that voters and nonvoters do not differ substantially in their policy views as measured by responses to questions on surveys, when we consider forms of political participation other than voting and consider such politically relevant characteristics as economic need, receipt of means-tested government benefits, and the content of participatory messages, we find that political voice is unrepresentative in important ways. Furthermore, although for many reasons it is difficult to connect citizen input to policy response, evidence shows that public officials pay attention to what they hear through the medium of citizen participation. Finally, policy makers do not attempt to compensate for the fact that they are hearing disproportionately from advantaged constituents. On the contrary, they seem to respond selectively to the affluent. In sum, inequality of political voice is a significant feature of the American political landscape, and it is consequential.

41. James A. Stimson, "The Issues in Representation," in *Who Gets Represented?* ed. Enns and Wlezien, p. 347.

6

The Persistence of
Unequal Voice

If inequality of political voice violates the democratic ideal of equal consideration of the needs and preferences of all citizens, inequality that continues over time would pose an even greater challenge to that democratic ideal.
Persistently loud political voice from some politically significant categories
of citizens coupled with the persistent quiescence of others is a deeper trans-
gression. Policy makers inclined to listen to the messages they receive would
be especially likely to pay attention not simply to the voices they hear but to
the voices they hear now and expect to hear in the future. To the extent that
they are attentive to voters, contributors, or other activists whose assistance
they seek, they would have particular incentives to heed the communications
from those whose support they might solicit in the future.

In this chapter and those that follow, we use several sources of data to
investigate these matters, paying particular attention to the differential voice
of the advantaged and the disadvantaged. We begin by considering whether
the participatory advantage of those who are high in socio-economic status
(SES)—documented by cross-sectional data in Chapter 5—persists over time
and, in particular, whether the widely noted increase in economic inequality
since the late 1970s has been matched by increasing socio-economic stratification of political voice.

Then we use three-wave panel surveys to ask whether ongoing inequalities of political voice reflect not just continuing activity by *the same kinds of
people* but persistent activity by *the same individuals*.[1] We show not only that

1. The literature on the persistence of political engagement has focused more on continuities of partisanship than on continuities in activity. See, for example, M. Kent Jennings and

political voice is characterized on an ongoing basis by bias in the direction of the well educated and affluent but also that, among those who are politically active at any particular time, high-SES political activists are more likely than activists who are lower on the socio-economic ladder to continue to take part politically in the future. In subsequent chapters we extend this analysis of the persistence of political participation by analyzing the processes that lead to continuities of political inequalities across generations and considering the trajectory of political voice over the life cycle.

The Changing Stratification of Participation: What Should We Expect?

What should we expect with respect to whether the social class stratification of political activity has changed over the past several decades? The usual assumption by those who are aware of the kinds of trends discussed in Chapter 3—most important, the attenuation of the labor movement and economic processes such that most of the fruits of economic expansion since 1980 have accrued to a narrow slice of the most affluent—is that the participatory advantage of those at the top in terms of SES would have increased. In light of the well-known role of unions in mobilizing political activity among workers, the attrition in union membership would be expected to contribute to a more pronounced pattern of class stratification in political participation. As we discussed, the decline in union membership has occurred entirely among

Gregory B. Markus, "Partisan Orientations over the Long Haul: Results from the Three-Wave Political Socialization Panel Study," *American Political Science Review* 78 (1984): 1000–1018; Janet M. Box-Steffensmeier, Kathleen Knight, and Lee Sigelman, "The Interplay of Macropartisanship and Macroideology: A Time Series Analysis," *Journal of Politics* 60 (1998): 1031–1049; David O. Sears and Carolyn L. Funk, "Evidence of the Long-Term Persistence of Adults' Political Predispositions," *Journal of Politics* 61 (1999): 1–28.

With respect to political participation rather than political orientations, studies of persistent activity have usually focused on persistent or habitual voters. See Eric Plutzer, "Becoming a Habitual Voter: Inertia, Resources, and Growth in Young Adulthood," *American Political Science Review* 96 (2002): 41–56, and Mark N. Franklin, *Voter Turnout and the Dynamics of Electoral Competition in Established Democracies since 1945* (Cambridge, England: Cambridge University Press, 2004).

In contrast to voting, which can be undertaken only intermittently at designated times, most political activities can be scheduled at the discretion of the activist. Persistent community activists or letter writers can participate whenever, and as often, as they like. For a particularly sensitive analysis of fluctuations in political engagement, see Albert O. Hirschman, *Shifting Involvements: Private Interest and Public Action* (Princeton, NJ: Princeton University Press, 2002).

private-sector workers, a development that has left the unionized workforce not only smaller but also more white collar and better educated. That the union movement has lost factory workers and gained teachers would be expected to reinforce the class-based inequalities in political activity. Furthermore, the spectacular gains in income realized by those in the narrow slice of the most affluent puts them in a position to increase their advantage with respect to the single form of political activity most dependent on financial resources, making donations to political campaigns and causes.

In fact, figuring out how increasing inequality in income should affect participatory inequality in not a simple matter.[2] While many social scientists seem to assume that growing economic inequality would produce increased participatory inequality, several theories with long pedigrees would predict just the opposite. Anthony Downs predicted that, in a democracy where citizens are all enfranchised and have equal votes, the many among the have-nots would gang up on the haves and bring about redistributive policies, a process that would be more likely to occur as the distance between the average and median incomes diverged—as it has in recent decades.[3] In addition, a simplified version of Marxism would suggest that widening gaps in income would generate anger, and even revolt, among those at the bottom of the ladder. Analogously, interest-group pluralists—who inhabited a different part of the political spectrum from Marx—would have predicted that, in reaction to growing income inequality, those being left behind economically would organize themselves into new and numerically powerful interest groups to oppose their increasing relative disadvantage. Of course history provides many fewer examples of such results than have been predicted by the theories. Contrary to the expectation of increasing agitation for redistributive relief, there is even some evidence that increasing economic inequality actually

2. For an extended discussion of this issue, see Henry E. Brady, "An Analytical Perspective on Participatory Inequality and Income Inequality," in *Social Inequality*, ed. Kathryn M. Neckerman (New York: Russell Sage Foundation, 2004), chap. 17. The basic insight is this: In a model of participation we might argue that participation is a positively increasing function of education and income, but this provides no direct insight about how inequality in either one (or in a composite, such as SES) might affect participation. Hence it seems likely both that the amount of inequality must enter as a separate factor that would affect participation and that this amount of inequality is a social fact about the society, not a fact about an individual.

3. See Anthony Downs, *An Economic Theory of Democracy* (New York: Harper and Row, 1957), chap. 10, and Allan H. Meltzer and F. Scott Richard, "A Rational Theory of the Size of Government," *Journal of Political Economy* 89 (1981): 914–927. In Chapter 9 we view Downs's argument in the context of inequalities of political voice.

depresses political discussion and participation instead of increasing them.[4] In sum, we have no clear expectations about the implications of growing economic inequality for participatory inequality in America.

Besides, certain developments would predict an amelioration of the degree of class-based participatory inequality. For one thing, our political parties— which, while never especially powerful in comparison to their counterparts in the democracies of Europe, had entered a period of declining strength beginning in the 1960s—have undergone considerable resurgence in recent years. Although the reinvigoration of the parties is most obvious at the elite level, it has also been associated with efforts to organize on the ground and mobilize the base and with increased ideological coherence and higher levels of partisan voting among citizens.[5] As we shall see in Chapter 15, in recent years the parties have been increasingly likely to get in touch with voters and urge them to go to the polls.

Furthermore, a significant social trend, the aggregate increase in the educational attainment of the American public, would also be expected to weaken the social class structuring of political participation. Of the two components of socio-economic status, education is the real driver when it comes to all forms of political participation except making political contributions, especially large ones. Those who are well educated have multiple characteristics that facilitate political participation now and in the future: they are more likely to hold the kinds of jobs that yield high levels of income and civic skills; to be politically interested, informed, and efficacious; and to be located in the social networks through which requests for political activity are mediated. Those who are lower down on the socio-economic scale are, in absolute terms, better educated than they once were, a trend that might be expected to boost their political activity and, thus, to narrow the participation gap based on class.

The expected increase in aggregate levels of political participation has not materialized, however. Instead, a number of observers have noted a decline in overall rates of political activity—which suggests that *relative* rather than

---

4. Frederick Solt, "Economic Inequality and Democratic Political Engagement," *American Journal of Political Science* 52 (2008): 48–60. There is an extensive literature that analyzes the complex steps between the emergence of a social fact such as income inequality or ethnic group identity and actual political mobilization. Two representative volumes are Sidney Tarrow, *Power in Movement: Social Movements and Contentious Politics*, 2nd ed. (New York: Cambridge University Press, 1998), and Doug McAdam, Sidney Tarrow, and Charles Tilly, *Dynamics of Contention* (New York: Cambridge University Press, 2001).

5. We will take up this theme in Chapter 9.

absolute levels of education are consequential for political participation.[6] Still, because those on the lowest rung of the socio-economic ladder have never been known to be especially politically active, the decrease in political participation cannot derive solely from erosion at the bottom. If so, the decrease in political activity—when combined with the political mobilization of evangelical Protestants, a group that is not especially affluent or well educated—might actually result in some class convergence in participation.

Participatory Inequality over Time

In Chapter 1 we presented illustrative evidence drawn from surveys spanning a half century showing that political participation is not equal with respect to socio-economic status and that this inequality has persisted for a long time. In this section we turn to evidence that extends this tantalizing finding in several directions.[7] We explore whether the ongoing association with SES obtains for separate participatory acts. We inquire whether—in a parallel to what we have already seen for inequality of income—participatory inequality has become more pronounced over time. We also compare political activity with religious attendance to see whether that major involvement in social life is equally stratified by SES and whether that stratification has increased or decreased over time.

For every form of political activity for which we have evidence, we find participatory inequality stretching back across decades. Over time, there have been some ups and downs in participatory inequality that do not seem to track trends in economic inequality or other obvious factors, except per-

---

6. Major works documenting the erosion of turnout and political participation include Ruy A. Teixeira, *The Disappearing American Voter* (Washington, DC: Brookings Institution, 1992); Steven J. Rosenstone and John Mark Hansen, *Mobilization, Participation, and Democracy in America* (New York: MacMillan, 1993); Robert D. Putnam, *Bowling Alone: The Collapse and Revival of American Community* (New York: Simon and Schuster, 2000); Martin P. Wattenberg, *Where Have All the Voters Gone?* (Cambridge, MA: Harvard University Press, 2002); and Stephen Macedo et al., *Democracy at Risk: How Political Choices Undermine Citizen Participation and What We Can Do about It* (Washington, DC: Brookings Institution, 2005). For an argument that it is relative education that matters, see Norman H. Nie, Jane Junn, and Kenneth Stehlik-Barry, *Education and Democratic Citizenship in America* (Chicago: University of Chicago Press, 1996).

7. This section of the chapter updates the analysis in Henry E. Brady, Kay Lehman Schlozman, Sidney Verba, and Laurel Elms, "Who Bowls? The (Un)Changing Stratification of Participation," in *Understanding Public Opinion*, 2nd ed., ed. Barbara Norrander and Clyde Wilcox (Washington DC: CQ Press, 2002), chap. 10.

haps the enhanced political mobilization that accompanies presidential elections. Compared to attendance at religious services, political participation has been, for the past sixty years, much more stratified by social class. Thus, we are struck not so much by any perturbations in the degree of participatory inequality as by the enduring level of that inequality, especially when viewed in the context of the absence of stratification in other forms of social engagement.

To consider these questions, we need data from surveys that ask in the same way over extended periods about political participation and the two components of SES, educational attainment and income. We use two longitudinal data sets that meet these criteria: the American National Election Studies (ANES) cumulative file (1952–2008) and the Roper Social and Political Trends Data (1973–1994) from Roper Starch Worldwide and an updated Roper file (1973–2002).[8]

Inequality in Voting Turnout over Time

We begin with voting. An extensive literature demonstrates substantial socioeconomic bias in voting.[9] Compared to those with lower levels of income, education, and occupational status, those who are better off in terms of income, education, and occupational status are more likely to go to the polls. Using data from the ANES for the fifteen presidential elections between 1952 and 2008 and a measure of socio-economic status based on income and education, Figure 6.1 reproduces this well-known finding.[10] Of all forms of politi-

8. The ANES data begin in 1948, but the participation items beyond voting are available only from 1952 onward.

9. See, for example, Raymond E. Wolfinger and Steven J. Rosentone, *Who Votes?* (New Haven, CT: Yale University Press, 1980); Teixeira, *Disappearing American Voter;* Rosenstone and Hansen, *Mobilization, Participation, and Democracy;* and Arend Lijphart, "Unequal Participation: Democracy's Unresolved Dilemma," *American Political Science Review* 91 (1997): 1–14.

10. Voting turnout in nonpresidential years is inevitably lower than in the highly mobilizing and extremely visible presidential elections. Therefore, although the ANES surveys have been fielded in nearly every midterm election year, we restrict our analysis to the fifteen presidential elections between 1952 and 2008. Besides, ANES did not conduct off–election year studies in 1954 or 2006.

There is a very large literature treating the fact that surveys tend to overestimate turnout. See, for example, Brian D. Silver, Barbara A. Anderson, and Paul R. Abramson, "Who Overreports Voting?" *American Political Science Review* 80 (1986): 613–624; Sidney Verba, Kay Lehman Schlozman, and Henry E. Brady, *Voice and Equality: Civic Voluntarism in American Politics* (Cambridge, MA: Harvard University Press, 1995), pp. 613–619; Henry E. Brady, "Conceptualizing and Measuring Political Participation," in *Measures of Political Attitudes,* ed.

Voting
Percentage

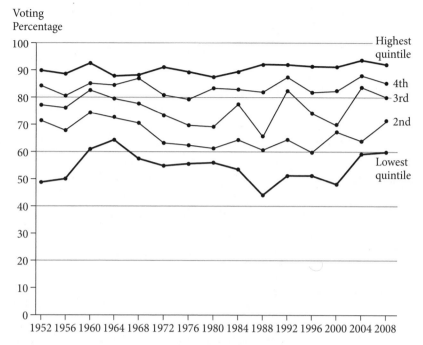

Figure 6.1   Voting over Time for SES Quintiles, 1952–2008

Source: American National Election Studies (1952–2008).

cal participation, voting is the one in which the highest proportion of Americans engage. Because voting turnout is high in comparison to engagement in other participatory acts, voting is—although structured by social class—more egalitarian than other kinds of participation. Still, Figure 6.1 indicates a marked level of inequality. It is striking that the lines tracing voting turnout

John P. Robinson, Philip R. Shaver, and Lawrence S. Wrightsman (San Diego, CA: Academic Press, 1999), vol. 2, chap. 13; Michael P. McDonald, "On the Over-report Bias of the National Election Study Turnout Rate," *Political Analysis* 11 (2003): 180–186. On the problems with survey samples, see, for example, Barry C. Burden, "Voter Turnout and the National Election Studies," *Political Analysis* 8 (2000): 389–398.

An important insight in this literature is the definition of the Voting Eligible Population (VEP) as an alternative to the Voting Age Population (VAP). See Michael P. McDonald and Samuel L. Popkin, "The Myth of the Vanishing Voter," *American Political Science Review* 95 (2001): 963–974. Although the ANES turnout measure that we use is about 16 percentage points higher than the VEP, it is correlated at .878 with the VEP and .747 with the VAP. The ANES turnout measure thus captures the movement in the VEP, but it overestimates the level of turnout. Our analyses are sensitive to this and other problems, but they are inevitably limited by them.

over time for the five SES quintiles array themselves in order from top to bottom and never cross. Turnout in the highest-SES quintile has been rather consistent over the years, hovering around 90 percent. In the middle and the two lower quintiles, there has been considerably more fluctuation; voting in the lowest quintile has varied between 40 percent and just over 60 percent.

Although there is consensus about the socio-economic bias in voter turnout, there is less agreement about how this bias has varied over time. Partly depending upon the time period under consideration, different authors come to different conclusions.[11] In their 1992 paper covering presidential voting between 1964 and 1988, Leighley and Nagler conclude that "with income as a measure of socio-economic class, there has been virtually no increase in class bias between 1964 and 1984 and that 1988 stands out in contrast to that stability."[12] In a 2004 essay, Freeman reanalyzes Leighley and Nagler's data (along with data from some other authors) and concludes that "the evidence supports the proposition that inequality among voters has risen."[13] Finally, in a 2006 paper Leighley and Nagler extend their analysis to 2004 and find, contrary to the conclusion in their earlier paper, that there has been an increase in class bias. However, they argue that it "began only in 1988,"[14] the end point of the data in the earlier paper that had found no growth in income-based inequality in turnout.

To measure representational inequality, we take the ratio of average participation by the top SES quintile to average participation—in this case, voting—by the bottom SES quintile. This ratio can range anywhere from zero to infinity; a ratio of one indicates representational equality between the two quintiles (or any two groups). Ratios greater than one indicate that the top quintile is more active than the bottom quintile. In Figure 6.2 we use this

11. Four articles are especially important: Jan E. Leighley and Jonathan Nagler, "Socio-economic Class Bias in Turnout, 1964–1988—The Voters Remain the Same," *American Political Science Review* 86 (1992): 725–736; Todd G. Shields and Robert K. Goidel, "Participation Rates, Socioeconomic Class Biases, and Congressional Elections: A Crossvalidation," *American Journal of Political Science* 41 (1997): 683–691; Richard B. Freeman, "What, Me Vote?" in *Social Inequality*, ed. Kathryn M. Neckerman (New York: Russell Sage Foundation, 2004), chap. 18; Jan E. Leighley and Jonathan Nagler, "Class Bias in the U.S. Electorate, 1972–2004," paper delivered at the Annual Meeting of the American Political Science Association, Philadelphia, 2006.

12. Leighley and Nagler, "Socio-economic Class Bias in Turnout," 1992, p. 730. Considering congressional turnout until 1994, Shields and Goidel, in "Participation Rates," come to the same conclusion.

13. Freeman, "What, Me Vote?" p. 723.

14. Leighley and Nagler, "Class Bias in the U.S. Electorate, 1972–2004."

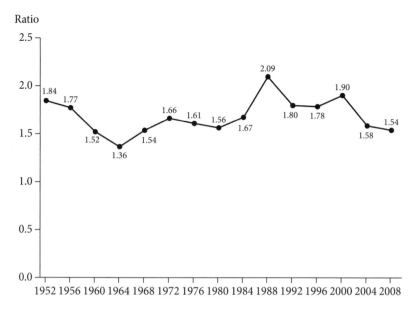

Figure 6.2   Ratio of Percentage Voting, Highest to Lowest SES Quintile over Time, 1952–2008

Source: American National Election Studies (1952–2008).

ratio to show the changes in the degree of inequality in voter turnout between 1952 and 2008.[15]

The pattern in Figure 6.2 is broadly similar to what other authors have found. However, the addition of data from 2004 and 2008 suggests some amendments to their conclusions. We find that, after falling between 1952 and

15. We use a ratio measure of inequality both because we think it best captures what we mean by inequality and because it is adaptable to different kinds of measures of participation—for example, percentages who perform a particular act or indexes of number of acts. Some of the works cited earlier take the difference between the participation levels of the top quintile and the bottom quintile. This measure has the perverse feature that, if on a ten-point scale of participation, the levels of the bottom and top quintiles rise from 1 and 2 respectively to 9 and 10, the difference remains the same, while it seems plain that the second situation is preferable to the first. The ratio measure captures this by decreasing from 2.0 to 1.11. The difference measure fails, but the ratio measure passes, the widely accepted "scale independence" test in which inequality should be construed neither to increase nor to decrease if everyone's activity is doubled. (See Frank A. Cowell and Maria-Pia Victoria-Feser, "Robustness Properties of Inequality Measures," *Econometrica* 64 [1996]: 77–101.) One defect in both the ratio and the difference measures is that errors in the measures for the top and bottom quintiles can lead to severe swings in the resulting measure.

1964, from 1964—and especially from 1968—to 1984, the ratio was fairly stable. Then, in 1988, the ratio spiked upward and remained, through 2000, at a level higher than at any time since 1952. Around 2004 there was a decline in inequality to the level of the 1970s.[16] Across the fifty-six-year period, changes in the level of participatory inequality do not seem to have tracked changes in the level of income inequality with any precision.

When we discussed Figure 6.1, we pointed out that there has been very little variation over time in the turnout of the top quintile, suggesting that changes in the inequality ratio are almost entirely a function of the variation in turnout of the lowest quintile.[17] In fact, the variation in turnout in the bottom quintile is highly positively associated with overall turnout (.786, or 62 percent of the variation), whereas variation in the turnout in the top quintile is only slightly positively associated with overall turnout (.194, or 4 percent of the variation). These results suggest that when overall turnout increases, it increases especially among those in the lowest SES quintile, which has the effect of reducing overall inequality. In other words, at least for voting, fluctuations in the level of activity—which are, in turn, influenced by such political factors as the closeness of an election and the intensity of efforts by parties to mobilize voters—help to explain the degree of participatory inequality.[18]

16. We should recall that our analysis differs from what others have done with respect to data source, the measure of SES, and the measure of inequality. Given such differences, it is noteworthy that there is so much agreement between our results and those in the works cited. Most of the works cited use data from the Current Population Survey (CPS) and not the ANES; while the CPS involves a much larger sample than the ANES, data from the CPS are available only from 1964 onward. In contrast to the other studies, which use income as the measure of SES, we have created a composite SES measure. Finally, most of the other studies use the absolute difference between the turnout of the top and bottom quintiles instead of the ratio of the two. Because the two measures are correlated at .986 and track one another almost perfectly in our data, it turns out that this difference is not very important for voting.

17. The correlation between the inequality ratio and the turnout of the bottom quintile is −.969, whereas the correlation between the inequality ratio and the top quintile is .314, so 94 percent of the variation in the inequality ratio is associated with the turnout of the bottom quintile and only 10 percent with the turnout of the top quintile.

18. The Downsian closeness hypothesis has not fared very well. See John G. Matsusaka and Filip Palda, "The Downsian Voter Meets the Ecological Fallacy," *Public Choice* 77 (1993): 855–878. However, the mobilization hypothesis seems to be on firmer ground. See Donald P. Green and Alan S. Gerber, *Get Out the Vote: How to Increase Voter Turnout*, 2nd ed. (Washington, DC: Brookings Institution, 2008). In fact, mobilization efforts may be a concomitant of closeness. (See Gary W. Cox and Michael C. Munger, "Closeness, Expenditures, and Turnout in the 1982 U.S. House Elections," *American Political Science Review* 83 [1989]: 217–31.) Although mobilization certainly matters and undoubtedly explains some ups and downs

Inequality in Other Electoral Activities over Time

When we move beyond voting to other electoral activities that are more demanding and that, at least in cross-sections, are characterized by a higher degree of stratification by social class, the patterns are somewhat different. Using ANES data for presidential elections over the same period, Figure 6.3 presents for each SES quintile the mean score on a scale of four electoral activities: working in a campaign, giving money to a campaign, going to a campaign meeting or rally, and trying to influence how someone votes.[19] Consistent with what we saw for voting in Figure 6.1, the lines showing mean electoral activity over time for the five SES quintiles array themselves in order from top to bottom and never cross. However, in contrast to what we saw for voting, the data for the five quintiles move more or less in tandem, and the lines are farther apart. Clearly, the past six decades have witnessed substantial and continuing differences among SES quintiles in electoral participation.

How has the class-based inequality in electoral participation varied over time? Figure 6.4 presents, for each presidential election year, the ratio of the average level of electoral participation for the top quintile to the average level for the bottom quintile. The spiked line connects the ratios. One obvious finding from Figure 6.4—which indicates the extent to which electoral activity is structured by social class—is that, in each presidential year, the ratio of the top to the bottom for other electoral activity is higher than the corresponding ratio for voting shown in Figure 6.2.[20] Although the ratios for electoral activity are widely scattered, there is some evidence in Figure 6.4 that inequality has actually decreased over time, especially in the past ten, and perhaps twenty, years.[21] Clearly, when it comes to electoral activity, changes

---

from one election to the next, it may not explain secular trends in turnout. See Kenneth M. Goldstein and Travis N. Ridout, "The Politics of Participation: Mobilization and Turnout over Time," *Political Behavior* 24 (2002): 3–29.

19. A fifth campaign-related item—displaying a candidate button or sign—was added in 1956. However, in order to use the longest possible time series, from 1952 to 2008, we do not use this item in our scale. Including this item has no effect on the results.

20. We replicated this analysis for Republicans and Democrats separately and found no obvious differences between the patterns for the two sets of partisans—except for the fact that Republicans are, on average, consistently higher in SES than Democrats.

21. The difference between the average number of campaign activities for the top quintile and that for the bottom quintile is highly correlated with the ratio measure until 2000, when the two measures start to diverge. A close look at Figure 6.3 shows that in 2004 all quintiles started to participate more in campaign activities, with the greatest increase in the top quintile. However, the bottom quintile increased its activities enough to reduce the ratio between the top

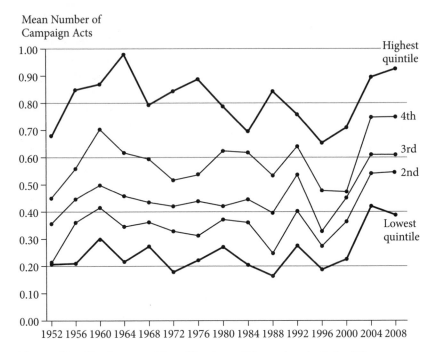

Mean Number of
Campaign Acts

Figure 6.3   Persistence of Stratification of Campaign Activity: Mean
Number of Campaign Acts over Time for SES Quintiles, 1952–2008

Source: American National Election Studies (1952–2008).

Note: Campaign acts: working on a campaign, donating money to a campaign,
going to campaign meetings, or trying to influence someone's vote.

in the degree of participatory inequality have not been hewing closely to
changes in income inequality—either in the overall trajectory over the fifty-
six-year period or in the particulars of the peaks and troughs. A plausible
explanation for the relatively lower levels of participatory inequality beginning in 1992 is the mobilization that occurred during these relatively high-
turnout elections, especially in the high-interest elections of 2004 and 2008.

A Look at Making Campaign Donations

Although voting is relatively egalitarian, giving money is not. In Figure 6.5
we select out from the scale of electoral activity the item about making con-

---

and the bottom quintiles, even though the difference in activity increased. It seems fair to say
that the ratio measure is right in implying that inequality decreased in this instance.

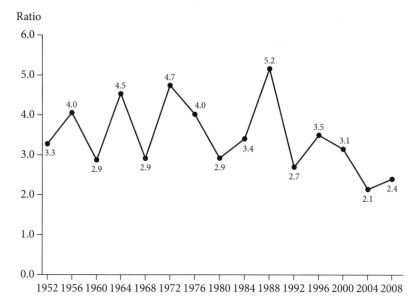

Figure 6.4 Ratio of Number of Campaign Acts over Time for Highest to Lowest SES Quintile, 1952–2008

Source: American National Election Studies (1952–2008).

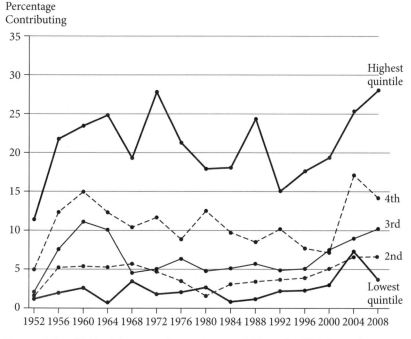

Figure 6.5 Giving Money in Campaigns over Time for SES Quintiles, 1952–2008

Source: American National Election Studies (1952–2008).

tributions to campaigns and show that, while the proportion of donors in the top quintile has varied over time and has sometimes reached nearly 30 percent, less than 5 percent in the lowest quintile typically contribute to political campaigns. The result is an average ratio of the percentage giving in the top quintile to the percentage giving in the bottom quintile of approximately ten to one. Giving campaign money is, quite obviously, highly stratified. What is more, because those in the top SES quintile not only are more likely to donate but are in a position to give much larger amounts when they contribute, were we to weight contributors by the size of their donations, the degree of socio-economic stratification in campaign giving would be much more pronounced.

What Happens at the Very Top?

In view of the income trends over the past three decades, we were interested to learn as much as we could about the political participation of those at the very top of the SES ladder.[22] It is not possible to make extremely fine distinctions with a single survey. As we did in Chapter 5, we combine the respondents from the ANES surveys and array them in terms of very fine SES gradations, percentiles rather than quintiles. In this case, however, to get a rough sense of whether there has been a shift over time in the class stratification of electoral participation, we divide the respondents into two periods, 1952–1980 and 1984–2008.

Figure 6.6 replicates the analysis from Figure 5.2 but presents the results for the two periods separately. Figure 6.6.A shows the data for the period ending in 1980. We see, once again, a sharp uptick in the percentage making donations among those in the highest SES slices. With respect to working in campaigns, the curve also slopes sharply upward for those within, roughly, the top SES quartile.[23] For the twenty-four years since 1984, presented in Figure 6.6.B, the results for making campaign donations show the same striking rise among those in the highest SES percentiles. In fact, were we to superimpose the curves for making campaign donations on each other, the curves for the two periods would be almost indistinguishable. In contrast, the pattern for working in political campaigns is quite different. For the later period, there is no upward trajectory in the highest quartile for working in campaigns. Unlike making campaign donations, working in campaigns became less strati-

22. We are grateful to Andrea Campbell for this suggestion.
23. In order to clarify the patterns, we have omitted the lines for attending campaign meetings. However, the results for attending campaign meetings parallel those for working in campaigns.

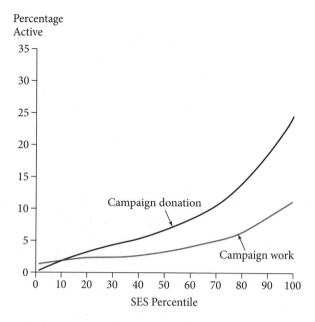

6.6.A   1952–1980

Percentage Active

Campaign donation

Campaign work

SES Percentile

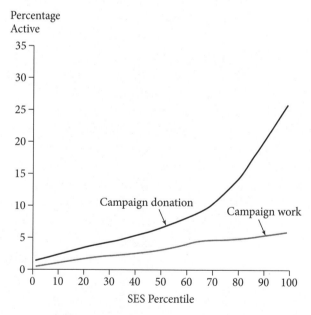

6.6.B   1984–2008

Percentage Active

Campaign donation

Campaign work

SES Percentile

Figure 6.6   Campaign Activity in Two Eras: Percentage Donating or Working by SES Percentile, 1952–2008

Source: American National Election Studies (1952–2008).

Note: Data were smoothed using a LOESS smooth of 40 percent.

fied in the second period, which would explain the finding in Figure 6.4 that the ratio of the highest to the lowest quintiles for electoral participation beyond voting has decreased during the era of increasing economic inequality. Thus the mix of electoral activities for those with very high SES has shifted, and giving money occupies more space in the participatory bundle than does giving time by doing campaign work.

Incorporating Nonelectoral Forms of Participation

Roper data, which contain four items with invariant wording of questions over a three-decade period, allow us to consider forms of participation that go beyond election-related activity.[24] Figure 6.7 presents for each quintile the average on a participation scale that includes two measures relating to elections ("holding or running for a political office" and "working for a political party,") and two measures of nonelectoral participation ("attending a public meeting on town or school affairs," and "signing a petition").[25] Because there have been so many Roper studies, we cannot just connect the dots as we do with the ANES data. We use a LOESS smoothing method to obtain clean and interpretable lines over time.[26] In one respect, the pattern is somewhat different from what we saw for voting and electoral activity. Figure 6.7 shows an uninterrupted downward trend in overall activity. Presumably because the Roper activity scale is weighted in the direction of nonelectoral participation, Figure 6.7 does not show the upward trend in 1992 that we saw for voting and electoral activity. Furthermore, the Roper data extend only through 2002. If there has been a nonelectoral counterpart to the rise in electoral activity that has accompanied the more competitive presidential elections beginning in 2000, we could not use the Roper data to document it. When it comes to the participatory inequality, the pattern looks similar to what we have seen before. Figure 6.7 shows clear and substantial differences in participation by SES quintile; there is a remarkable separation in the lines, which never cross, and even in the location of the individual data points.

Figure 6.8 presents a LOESS fit to the ratios of the top to the bottom quintile for each of the many individual Roper surveys of political participation.

24. Samantha Luks and Laurel Elms are coauthors of this section.

25. The Roper battery contains items about twelve activities, but we use only the four that were explicitly political and were measured in the same way over the entire period.

26. See William S. Cleveland, "Robust Locally Weighted Regression and Smoothing Scatterplots," *Journal of the American Statistical Association* 74 (1979): 829–836, and William S. Cleveland, "LOWESS: A Program for Smoothing Scatterplots by Robust Locally Weighted Regression," *American Statistician* 35 (1981): 54.

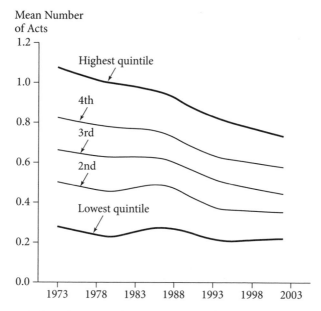

Figure 6.7   Political Activity (Mean Number of Four Political Acts) over Time for SES Quintiles, 1973–2002

Source: Roper Surveys (1973–2002).

Note: Data were smoothed using a LOESS smooth of 40 percent. The figure refers to the mean number of acts on a 4-act scale (holding or running for political office, working for a political party, attending meetings on local issues, or signing a petition).

These activities are highly stratified. The average ratio is very substantial, roughly four to one. Indeed, we should mention that these data underestimate the extent of inequality in political participation because they cover only a small slice of the participatory possibilities. Between 1973 and 1994, Roper collected data about a broader set of twelve political acts. The curve plotting an analogous set of ratios for a twelve-point participation scale over this two-decade period has a shape similar to what we see in Figure 6.8, but all the ratios are higher. For example, the curve in Figure 6.8 peaks in 1980 at just over 4.5. The curve showing the ratios for the more encompassing twelve-point scale also peaks in 1980, but at nearly 7.[27] As we have seen for other ratios over

27. See Figure 10-2 and the accompanying discussion in Brady, Schlozman, Verba, and Elms, "Who Bowls?" pp. 228–230.

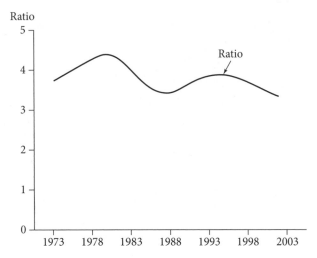

Figure 6.8   Ratio of Political Activity (Mean Number of Four Political Acts) over Time for Highest to Lowest SES Quintile, 1973–2002

Source: Roper Surveys (1973–2002).

Note: Data were smoothed using a LOESS smooth of 40 percent.

time, the curve goes up and down with no obvious longitudinal pattern. The trajectory of participatory inequality has not followed the trend in income inequality, and the expected increase in participatory inequality has not materialized. The curve starts at 4 and ends at approximately 3. In between, it loops up and down, reaching a high point above 4.5 in 1980. Close inspection suggests that there is an overall downward trend in the curve over the time period, amounting to a drop of perhaps .6. In light of the cyclical ups and downs of more than 1.5 units, this diminution in inequality is not especially substantial.[28] Once again, the more important finding is the magnitude of participatory inequality.

A Comparison with Religious Attendance

Is the class-based inequality in political participation simply one manifestation of a larger pattern such that all forms of participation in civil society and politics are highly stratified? One way to gain some perspective on this question is to make a comparison with perhaps the most common form of non-

---

28. A regression fit to the data indicates that there was a drop of –.00226 per study over the course of the 267 studies.

political participation in American society, religious attendance.[29] Religious institutions figure importantly in civil society in America and intersect with politics in many ways. They take stands on public issues. Those who attend religious services are exposed to political cues and to requests for political action. Those who have a deeper involvement in a religious institution—by, for example, taking part in educational, charitable, or social activities—develop civic skills that can be transferred to politics.[30] Religious involvement is also closely related to individual political beliefs and issue positions: most notably, those who attend church regularly are more likely to take conservative positions on social and moral matters.

Figure 6.9 presents data from the ANES that track religious attendance over time.[31] One striking pattern is that religious attendance has dropped over time for all five SES quintiles. What is especially noteworthy in Figure 6.9 is that the lines are so tangled together—especially for the early decades of the period—that it is almost impossible to detect any stratification. Close inspection suggests that, particularly since the mid-1980s, religious participation among those in the top quintile has been generally slightly higher than among those in the bottom quintile, but the differences are quite small.[32] Thus, in contrast to political activity, there seems to be virtually no SES stratification for religious attendance. Figure 6.10, which repeats the curve for the participation ratios for campaign activity from Figure 6.4 and adds a curve showing the ratios for religious attendance, shows the remarkable contrast between the stratification for campaign activity and that for religious attendance. While the ratios for campaign activity range between 2.1 and 5.2, the ratios for religious attendance hover at about 1.1. In sum, participatory stratification is far from preordained or inevitable.

29. In making this comparison, we recognize that these are very different kinds of acts that are measured differently. Religious attendance is measured in terms of how frequently the respondent attends religious services. Political activity is measured by an additive scale consisting of dichotomies measuring whether the respondent has been active at all.

30. On the multiple ways that religious activity fosters political participation, see Verba, Schlozman, and Brady, *Voice and Equality*, pp. 369–390.

31. The question about religious attendance was asked using somewhat different versions over the period. From 1952 through 1968, respondents were asked about the regularity of their attendance at services, and "3" corresponds to "Often." From 1972 through 2008, the options were more specific, and "3" corresponds to "Once or twice a month."

32. We obtain exactly the same result for 1973–2008 when we use data from the General Social Survey. In their massive study of religious behavior in the United States, Putnam and Campbell also note the more recent emergence of an educational gap in religious attendance. See Robert D. Putnam and David E. Campbell, *American Grace: How Religion Divides and Unites Us* (New York: Simon and Schuster, 2010), pp. 252–253.

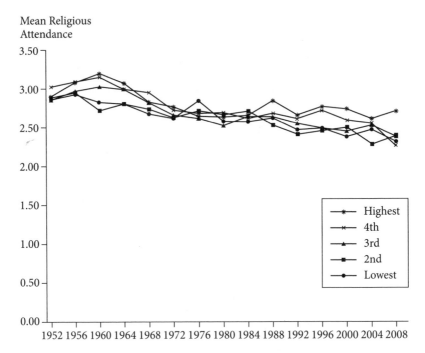

Figure 6.9   Religious Attendance over Time for SES Quintiles, 1952–2008

Source: American National Election Studies (1952–2008).

Note: Religious attendance is a four-point scale: 1 means that one attends "never" or has "no religious preference," 2 "seldom" or "a few times a year," 3 "often" or "once or twice a month," 4 "regularly" or "every week or more."

Political Inequality and the
Persistence of Individual Activity

In light of the extent of participatory inequality that appears in every cross-sectional analysis, we were curious whether the class stratification over time that we have just seen represents a circumstance such that the same kinds of people are politically active over time or one such that the same individuals are active on an ongoing basis. In order to trace the activity of particular individuals over time, we use the three waves of panel data from the 2000–2004 American National Election Study Panel, each of which contains the same battery of questions asking about engagement in nine political acts.[33]

33. The nine acts are voting; talking to others to try to show them why they should vote for or against one of the parties or candidates; giving money to a political party or candidate;

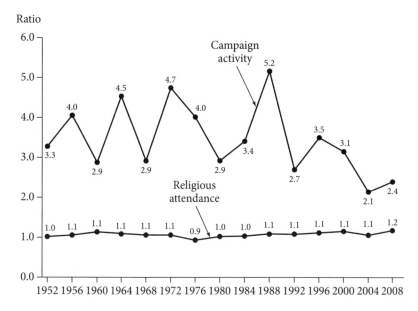

Figure 6.10   Ratio over Time of Highest to Lowest SES Quintile for Campaign Activity and for Religious Attendance, 1952–2008

Source: American National Election Studies (1952–2008).

For each of the three waves, we divided the respondents on the basis of their political activity.[34] The proportions of respondents falling into these categories are quite similar for the three waves. As shown in Table 6.1, using the definitions stated in the table, across the three surveys an average of about 40 percent of the respondents were classified as active and an average of 39 percent of respondents were categorized as inactive.

Table 6.1 presents preliminary data about the persistence of activity by the same individuals across the three waves of the panel. Twenty-two percent of

------

attending political meetings, rallies, speeches, and so on in support of a particular candidate; working for a party or candidate; attending a meeting about an issue facing the community or schools; working with other people to deal with some issue facing the community; contacting a public official; and attending a protest, march, or demonstration on a national or local issue.

34. We categorized the respondents as follows: those who reported having engaged in either no activity at all or one activity, usually voting, were classified as "low" in participation, and those who reported having engaged in three or more of the nine acts were classified as "high" in activity.

Table 6.1   Persistence of Political Activity and Inactivity
across Three Waves of a Panel Study

	Average across 3 Waves (Percent)	Persistence across 3 Waves (Percent)	Expected Persistence across 3 Waves (Percent)	Ratio of Actual to Expected Persistence
Active[a]	40%	22%	6%	3.5
Inactive[b]	39%	18%	6%	3.1

Source: American National Election Studies Panel (2000–2002–2004).

[a] Active in political participation: 3 or more political acts on a 9-act scale.
[b] Inactive in political participation: 0 or 1 political act on a 9-act scale.

the respondents were persistently active, having been categorized as high in activity in each of the waves of the panel, and 18 percent were persistently inactive across all three waves. Political activity entails a good deal of movement in and out; in a subsequent survey, a majority of respondents moved to a participation category different from their initial rating in the first wave of the panel. Nevertheless, these proportions are considerably higher than would be expected if the probability of being active, or inactive, at a subsequent time were independent of the level of activity as measured in the first survey. The right-hand column of Table 6.1 shows the ratio of the actual proportion of respondents who were persistently active, or inactive, to the expected proportion if the level of activity or inactivity were predicted by chance. The data show a good deal more persistence than would be expected if the likelihood of being active given previous activity were random.

Who Is Persistent?

From the perspective of inequality of political voice, the fundamental question is not whether political activity is a persistent commitment for individuals but whether individuals with different characteristics—in particular, different levels of socio-economic status—are differentially likely to be persistently active. To investigate social class differences in the persistence of individual political participation, we combined the top two SES quintiles and the bottom two SES quintiles to divide the sample into three socio-economic

Table 6.2   Average Political Activity and Persistence of Political Activity
by SES across Three Waves of a Panel Study

	Average across 3 Waves		Persistence across 3 Waves	
	Bottom 2 SES Quintiles	Top 2 SES Quintiles	Bottom 2 SES Quintiles	Top 2 SES Quintiles
Active[a]	26%	56%	12%	34%
Inactive[b]	52%	26%	31%	8%

Source: American National Election Studies Panel (2000–2002–2004).

[a] Active in political participation: 3 or more political acts on a 9-act scale.
[b] Inactive in political participation: 0 or 1 political act on a 9-act scale.

levels. The data in Table 6.2 make clear that individuals in the top two quintiles of the socio-economic scale are not only more active at any particular
time but are also more persistently so; conversely, those in the bottom two
quintiles of SES not only are more likely to be inactive but also tend to stay
inactive.

The first and second columns of numbers in Table 6.2 allow us to compare
the top two quintiles in SES to the bottom two quintiles in SES with respect
to the average percentage classified as active or inactive across the three
waves of the study. As expected, compared to those in the lower-SES group,
those in the upper-SES group were, on average, much more likely to be
active—and much less likely to be inactive—in the separate waves of the
panel. The third and fourth columns of numbers show for the two SES groups
the proportions of respondents who were consistently active or inactive
across all three surveys. The difference between the top and bottom SES
groups is especially striking when it comes to persistent activity or persistent
inactivity. Thirty-four percent of those in the upper-SES group, but only 12
percent of those in the lower-SES group, were consistently active. Focusing
on inactivity reverses the findings: 31 percent of those in the lower-SES group,
compared to 8 percent of those in the upper-SES group, were inactive in all
three waves of the panel.

As we did in Chapter 5, we can also define politically relevant groups in
terms of their economic needs. We have argued that those who have deficits
in basic human needs have strong incentives to be politically active. In spite

of those incentives, however, such economically needy individuals are actually less persistent in their activity. For example, among those who reported having experienced difficulties meeting just one basic human need—having been forced to put off medical care because of money problems[35]—16 percent were persistently active and 26 percent were persistently inactive. In contrast, among those who reported no problems meeting such essential needs, 22 percent were persistently active and 16 percent were persistently inactive.

The Persistence of Religious Attendance

Earlier in the chapter we noted the marked contrast between political participation and religious attendance when it comes to the social class structuring of activity over time. Because the socio-economic stratification that characterizes political participation is not an inevitable concomitant of all modes of engagement with civil society, it makes sense to draw out the comparison one step further by investigating the persistence of religious attendance. Each of the three waves of the ANES asked about frequency of religious attendance. Across the three surveys, an average of roughly 26 percent of respondents were active attenders who reported going to religious services every week or more often, and 32 percent were inactive, having reported that they never attend services.

In Table 6.3 we repeat data from Table 6.1 in order to compare political participation with religious attendance in terms of persistence. The differences between religious and political activity with respect to persistence are much smaller than might have been expected: 18 percent of the respondents were persistent religious attenders, and 22 percent were persistent political activists; 20 percent were persistent religious nonattenders, and 18 percent were persistently inactive in politics. It is perhaps surprising that, in spite of the notably deep level of religious commitment in the United States, religious attendance and political participation are so similar in the degree to which individuals are persistently active or inactive.

Table 6.4 brings socio-economic stratification back into consideration, thus rounding out the comparison between political participation and religious attendance when it comes to the persistence of individual activity. As was the case for socio-economic stratification over time, there is a striking

35. Unfortunately, unlike the Citizen Participation Study, the ANES 2000–2004 Panel contained only one item about economic needs (about having "put off medical or dental treatment because you didn't have the money") and none at all on the receipt of government benefits.

Table 6.3 Persistence of Political Participation and Religious Attendance across Three Waves of a Panel Study

	Average across 3 Waves		Persistence across 3 Waves	
	Political Participation	Religious Attendance	Political Participation	Religious Attendance
Active[a]	40%	26%	22%	18%
Inactive[b]	39%	32%	18%	20%

Source: American National Election Studies Panel (2000–2002–2004).

[a] Active in political participation: 3 or more political acts on a 9-act scale; active in church attendance: attend every week or more often.
[b] Inactive in political participation: 0 or 1 political act on a 9-act scale; inactive in church attendance: never attend or attend once or twice a year.

Table 6.4 Persistence of Political Participation and Religious Attendance across Three Waves of a Panel Study by SES

	Percentage Persistent across 3 Waves	
	Political Participation	Religious Attendance
Persistently Active[a]		
Bottom 2 SES Quintiles	12%	18%
Top 2 SES Quintiles	34%	20%
Persistently Inactive[b]		
Bottom 2 SES Quintiles	31%	24%
Top 2 SES Quintiles	8%	17%

Source: American National Election Studies Panel (2000–2002–2004).

[a] Active in political participation: 3 or more political acts on a 9-act scale; active in church attendance: attend every week or more often.
[b] Inactive in political participation: 0 or 1 political act on a 9-act scale; inactive in church attendance: never attend or attend once or twice a year.

contrast between political participation and religious activity. In politics, compared to their counterparts at the bottom of the SES ladder, those in the top two quintiles are much more likely to be persistently active and much less likely to be persistently inactive. With respect to religious attendance, the top and bottom socio-economic groups do not differ substantially in the persistence of either inactivity or, especially, activity.

Is Political Participation Habit-Forming?

Let us take our analysis one step further by inquiring whether political participation is habit-forming. Once having taken part, do individuals become more likely to do so again—by, for example, going to a community meeting, making a campaign donation, or getting in touch with a public official—over and above the personal characteristics that predispose some people to be active in the first place? That is, is political participation itself a factor that predicts higher levels of activity in the future? If political activity is habit-forming, we would expect that the other participatory advantages enjoyed by those of higher socio-economic status would be multiplied by the fact that political participation begets political participation.

To distinguish the participatory impact of habituation requires considerable statistical legerdemain and at least a three-wave panel. We used the four different panels from the ANES and considered three forms of political participation—voting, campaign activity, and nonelectoral activity. In addition, to provide a reality check, we also considered union membership and religious attendance, both of which we expected to show evidence of habituation.[36] Consistent with what we have just seen, voting, campaign activity, and nonelectoral activity, as well as union membership and religious attendance, are all *persistent* activities.[37] That is, someone who voted or who engaged

36. We discuss our technique along with the statistical results in Appendix B. The ANES panels were conducted in the following years: 1956, 1958, and 1960; 1972, 1974, and 1976; 1992, 1994, and 1996; and 2000, 2002, and 2004. Only voting was included in all four panels. Campaign activity (campaign work, campaign contribution, attending campaign meetings, and trying to influence another voter) was not included in 1956, 1958, and 1960; noncampaign activity (contacting political officials, protesting, doing informal community work, and attending a meeting on an issue facing the community) was included only in 2000, 2002, and 2004; union membership was not included in 2000, 2002, and 2004; and religious attendance was not included in 1992, 1994, and 1996.

37. The correlations showing persistence in the four ANES panels are contained in Table B.1 in Appendix B.

in nonelectoral activity at one time was significantly more likely to do so at a future time. However, persistence is not necessarily evidence of *habituation*. The attributes that foster involvement in a particular endeavor at any one time are relatively stable. Therefore, they are likely to be operative the next time an opportunity to take part presents itself, a circumstance that means only that the same factors are acting to enhance participation, but not that there has been habituation.

The evidence for actual habituation—that is, for a process such that the act itself becomes a factor that fosters future engagement—is much less consistent. Not surprisingly, both union membership and church attendance are habitual. Apart from other characteristics that might predispose an individual to be a union member or to attend religious services, being a union member or going to services at one time itself raises the probability of being a union member or going to services when interviewed later. Similarly, like other researchers, we find that voting is habitual.[38] Voting in one election itself enhances the likelihood of going to the polls in subsequent elections. In contrast, although campaign and nonelectoral activity are persistent, they are not habitual. Of the forms of political activity, we find only voting to be addictive. We have seen many ways that people who are high on the SES ladder are able to cumulate their participatory advantages. However, except for voting, political participation does not follow the laws of compound interest.

Conclusion

We began this chapter by posing the question of how social-class structuring of political participation has changed in an era of increasing economic inequality. Although the immediate supposition might be that political voice would have become more unequal along social class lines at the same time

---

38. Using latent growth curve models and a long-term panel covering seventeen years, Eric Plutzer finds evidence for the impact of both life events (such as marriage and church attendance) and habituation on voting turnout. See Eric Plutzer, "Becoming a Habitual Voter: Inertia, Resources, and Growth in Young Adulthood," *American Political Science Review* 96 (2002): 41–56. On the basis of an experimental setup, Alan Gerber, Donald Green, and Ron Shachar provide strong evidence that voting once leads to getting in the habit of voting. See Alan Gerber, Donald Green, and Ron Shachar, "Voting May Be Habit Forming: Evidence from a Randomized Experiment," *American Journal of Political Science* 97 (2003): 540–550. See also Donald Green and Ron Shachar, "Habit Formation and Political Behavior: Evidence of Consuetude in Voter Turnout," *British Journal of Political Science* 30 (2000): 561–573.

that income has become more concentrated at the top, we pointed to other factors, such as the growing strength of the political parties and the increasing levels of educational attainment, that would point in the opposite direction.

The main story in the extensive evidence we have reviewed, however, is less about change than about continuity: political participation in America is highly stratified by social class, and that stratification has been a feature of political activity for as long as we have had surveys to measure it. Participatory inequality is not only pronounced but also enduring, evident in our data as far back as they go, which is the early 1950s. For the political act for which there is the least social class structuring, voting, those in the top quintile are, on average, roughly twice as likely to go to the polls as those in the bottom quintile. When it comes to the political act that is most inegalitarian, making campaign contributions, those in the top quintile are approximately eight times more likely to make a donation to a campaign than those in the bottom quintile.

With respect to the trajectory over time, that SES bias in participation has varied over the years. Additive scales measuring the number of electoral and nonelectoral acts in which an individual has engaged show that, on average, it has not increased, but it has not diminished much either. The ups and downs of participatory inequality do not seem to be related to other obvious factors—in particular, to growing economic inequality. The possible exception is that a competitive presidential election may have a mobilizing impact resulting in some amelioration of participatory inequality with respect to electoral activity. In short, our major conclusion is the substantial and continuing participatory advantage enjoyed by the well-educated and affluent rather than any changes in the level of socio-economic inequality in political activity.

In view of the contradictory expectations we outlined at the beginning of the chapter, the overall stability in participatory inequality is perhaps not a puzzle. In one respect, however, our data point to the possibility of increasingly unequal political voice that is related to increasingly unequal incomes. When we disaggregated the various forms of electoral activity and considered narrower gradations in the SES hierarchy, we noted that the proportion making campaign donations rose rapidly in the highest SES quartile, a regularity that holds for both the period between 1952 and 1980 and the years since 1984. In contrast, with regard to attending campaign meetings and doing campaign work, during the earlier period the increase in participation was not as sharp as for contributing, and during the later period the curves flattened substantially. This configuration explains the apparent decrease in participatory inequality in recent years. For two electoral activities, attending campaign meetings and doing campaign work, involvement is less sharply structured by SES than in the past. This configuration also translates into a circumstance such that making contributions weighs more heavily in the bundle of electoral activities of the very affluent and well educated. The data measure whether individuals made campaign donations, not how much they gave. Because the best predictor of the size of campaign contributions is a respondent's income[39] and because aggregate electoral contributions have soared in recent years, it is reasonable to infer that, when it comes to the most expandable and most unequal form of individual political participation, making campaign contributions, inequality has grown over time in a way that is related to the increase in economic inequality.

Data about religious attendance provide an important point of comparison with political participation. The socio-economic stratification that we find for political participation is not part of an overall pattern of class-based inequality for all forms of civic involvement. On the contrary, over a period of more than half a century, religious attendance has been characterized by only the most minimal class stratification.

When we turned our attention to the question of whether ongoing participatory inequality represents a tendency, on one hand, for certain kinds of people to be politically active or, on the other, for politically active individuals to take part on a continuing basis, we found evidence for both patterns. All those who are politically active at one time—a group that is, of course, shaped by prior socio-economic advantage—are more likely to take part at a subsequent time. However, among activists, upper-SES political participants are more likely than their counterparts lower on the socio-economic ladder to be persistently active. Furthermore, the latter group contains a disproportionate share of consistently inactive citizens. If the occasional activists within the lower-SES quintiles were as likely as those higher on the socio-economic ladder to stick with political participation over the long haul, then the class stratification of political participation would be less pronounced.

We also considered whether individual persistence reflects processes of habituation such that being active itself becomes a factor predicting additional participation in the future—above and beyond the attributes that predispose an individual to take part. We found, as others have, that going to the polls predicts future turnout. However, for other forms of participation we found

---

39. See Verba, Schlozman, and Brady, *Voice and Equality*, pp. 356–361.

no such process of habituation—a rare example where participatory advantage does not cumulate. Thus, except for voting, persistence at the individual level reflects underlying characteristics associated with political activity rather than a self-perpetuating cycle in which participation begets participation.

We have maintained in the past that voting is in many ways sui generis among participatory acts—in its relative frequency, in the particular gratifications it provides, in the factors that explain it.[40] Its very uniqueness is one reason we consider using voting as a surrogate for all forms of political activity to be a mistake. That it seems to be habit-forming renders voting exceptional among political acts in yet another way.

Once again, the comparison with attendance at religious services is instructive. Perhaps surprisingly, there is no substantial difference between religious attendance and political participation with respect to individual-level persistence. That is, those who attend religious services are neither substantially more likely nor substantially less likely than those who undertake political activities to repeat their involvements in the future. Where there is a strong contrast between the two domains of voluntary activity is when it comes to the impact of socio-economic status. The pattern such that upper-SES political activists are also more likely to be persistent political activists does not apply to attendance at religious services. Among those who attend religious services at one time, there is no class structuring with respect to who does so subsequently. Once again, evidence about religious attendance makes clear that SES stratification is not a necessary concomitant to voluntary activity.

In sum, although we have considered the persistence of political participation from a variety of points of view in this chapter, the polar star of this analysis is the power and durability of the class-based stratification of political participation.

40. Verba, Schlozman, and Brady, *Voice and Equality*, pp. 181–182, 358–361.

7

Unequal at the Starting Line: The Intergenerational Persistence of Political Inequality

Our tale so far demonstrates the persistence of political inequality in political voice in many ways. We have seen that a continuing characteristic of political participation is the extent to which it is structured by socio-economic status (SES). In addition, there is persistence at the individual level: those who are active at one point are substantially more likely to be active four years later.

We have also noted that inequalities in the economic domain persist from generation to generation. The promise of the American Dream to the contrary, when it comes to occupational and economic success, we do not start off on an equal footing. We now turn our attention to the analogous intergenerational issue with respect to politics: the transmission of political activity from parent to child.[1]

In Chapter 3 we discussed the fact that, although Americans are quite comfortable with economic inequalities that result from individual differences in

Nancy Burns is coauthor of this chapter.

1. This chapter draws directly from two previously published items: Sidney Verba, Nancy Burns, and Kay Lehman Schlozman, "Unequal at the Starting Line: Creating Participatory Inequalities across Generations and among Groups," *American Sociologist* 34 (2003): 45–69, and Sidney Verba, Kay Lehman Schlozman, and Nancy Burns, "Family Ties," in *The Social Logic of Politics: Personal Networks as Contexts for Political Behavior*, ed. Alan S. Zuckerman (Philadelphia: Temple University Press, 2005). It draws indirectly from Sidney Verba, Kay Lehman Schlozman, and Henry E. Brady, *Voice and Equality: Civic Voluntarism in American Politics* (Cambridge, MA: Harvard University Press, 1995), chap. 15, and Nancy Burns, Kay Lehman Schlozman, and Sidney Verba, *The Private Roots of Public Action: Gender, Inequality and Political Participation* (Cambridge, MA: Harvard University Press, 2001).

talent or effort, they are less accepting of such inequalities if they are passed on across generations from parents to their offspring. Furthermore, Americans are more likely to accept economic than political inequalities; they expect not only that citizens should possess the equal right to be active but also that citizens should express equal political voice on the level playing field of democracy and that public officials should respond equally to all. Thus the transmission of political inequality from one generation to the next would present a double challenge to American ideals, violating both the principle of the equal opportunity to be active politically and the principle of substantive political equality among citizens. Our understanding of equal political voice does not require that all individuals be equally politically active, only that participant publics be representative in their politically relevant characteristics.[2] Still, if the propensity to participate is handed down across generations, the political advantage that accrues at any moment to well-educated and affluent activists will be perpetuated.

Are political inequalities—like economic inequalities—bequeathed from one generation to the next? The persistent class bias in political participation that we demonstrated in Chapter 6 is not necessarily evidence of intergenerational transmission of participatory inequalities. It is possible that ongoing inequalities in political voice represent individual disparities, unrelated to family background, in the desire and capacity to take part. However, it is hard to doubt that family inheritance plays a role in the achievement of elite political status. Political dynasties, on the national, state, and local levels, are numerous and well known. A not insignificant number of members of the U.S. Congress are children of former members,[3] and the 2000 presidential contest pitted the son of a former senator against the son of a former president.

The Legacy of Family for Political Participation

Are the children of politically active parents more likely to take part in politics? If so, how do the families in which they are reared have an impact on

---

2. For discussion of politically relevant categories from the point of view of the representation of political interests, see Verba, Schlozman, and Brady, *Voice and Equality*, chap. 6.

3. In the 111th Congress (2009–2010), thirty-one members of Congress had a parent who had served in the House, the Senate, or both, and eleven of the thirty-one occupied a seat once held by the parent. That Congress also included one married couple, three pairs of siblings, and seven women, most of them widows, whose husbands had served in Congress. See

their political activity as adults? We consider two mechanisms by which the family might operate to influence future political participation. The first emphasizes political learning: in the family, children absorb cues and lessons about politics and the rights and responsibilities of citizens. The second, which has rarely been mentioned by students of political socialization, focuses on the way that the socio-economic status of one's family of origin shapes opportunities for educational attainment, which, in turn, affect the likelihood of acquiring many other attributes that foster political participation.

Although the family does not figure especially importantly in contemporary political science, it once had greater prominence among the concerns of empirical political scientists. During the 1960s and 1970s, students of political socialization considered the family to be one of the institutions that shape the political orientations, attitudes, and behaviors of the young.[4] Among the

---

Chuck McCutcheon and Christina L. Lyons, *CQ Politics in America 2010: The 111th Congress* (Washington, DC: CQ Press, 2009), p. 1147.

4. On political socialization in general—and the role of the family in particular—see, among others, Fred I. Greenstein, *Children and Politics* (New Haven, CT: Yale University Press, 1965); Robert D. Hess and Judith V. Torney, *The Development of Political Attitudes in Children* (Garden City, NY: Doubleday, Anchor Books, 1967), esp. chaps. 5 and 7; Richard E. Dawson and Kenneth Prewitt, *Political Socialization* (Boston: Little, Brown, 1969), esp. chap. 7; David Easton and Jack Dennis, *Children and the Political System: Origins of Political Legitimacy* (New York: McGraw Hill, 1969); James C. Davies, "The Family's Role in Political Socialization," in *Learning about Politics*, ed. Roberta S. Sigel (New York: Random House, 1970), pp. 108–118; Dean Jaros, *Socialization to Politics* (New York: Praeger, 1973), esp. chap. 4; M. Kent Jennings and Richard G. Niemi, *The Political Character of Adolescence: The Influence of Family and Schools* (Princeton, NJ: Princeton University Press, 1974), esp. Parts I, II, and V; M. Kent Jennings and Richard G. Niemi, *Generations and Politics: A Panel Study of Young Americans and Their Parents* (Princeton, NJ: Princeton University Press, 1981); Richard G. Niemi and M. Kent Jennings, "Issues and Inheritance in the Formation of Party Identification," *American Journal of Political Science* 35 (1991): 970–988; Paul Allen Beck and M. Kent Jennings, "Family Traditions, Political Periods, and the Development of Political Orientations," *Journal of Politics*, 53 (1991): 742–763; M. Kent Jennings, Laura Stoker, and Jake Bowers, "Politics across Generations: Family Transmission Reexamined," *Journal of Politics* 71 (2009): 782–799; and Kent Jennings and Laura Stoker, "Generations and Civic Engagement: A Longitudinal Multi-Generation Analysis," paper delivered at the Annual Meeting of the American Political Science Association, San Francisco, September 2001. For reviews of the literature, see Jack Dennis, "Major Problems of Political Socialization Research," *Midwest Journal of Political Science* 12 (1968): 85–114; Paul Allen Beck, "The Role of Agents in Political Socialization," in *Handbook of Political Socialization*, ed. Stanley Allen Renshon (New York: Free Press, 1979), pp. 115–141; and Timothy E. Cook, "The Bear Market in Political Socialization and the Costs of Misunderstood Psychological Theories," *American Political Science Review* 79 (1985): 1079–1093; as well as M. Kent Jennings's thoughtful assessment of the long series of political socialization studies that he and his associates have conducted, "Participation as Seen through the Lens of the Political Socialization Project," paper delivered at the

family characteristics found to be associated with the political development of the young was social class. Children and adolescents who came from higher social class backgrounds or whose parents had high levels of formal education were found to have higher levels of political information and understanding and also to be more politically interested and efficacious, more tolerant, and more politically active.

With respect to the way that family matters—and therefore, the way that the socio-economic status of the family matters—for future political life, the dominant understanding in the socialization literature was a learning model.[5] Children were presumed to look to their parents as role models when it comes to politics; to absorb implicit lessons about authority, autonomy, and decision making from their parents' household management practices and child-rearing styles; and to pick up political orientations and attitudes from the explicit political instruction of their parents.[6] Presumably the connection between parents' social status and their offspring's future political activity would derive from the fact that high-SES parents are more likely to create a politically rich home environment—in which there are frequent political discussions and where politically active parents serve as role models—and children who grow up in such an environment would be distinctive in their political orientations. The lessons that are absorbed in a politically stimulating home would carry on into adulthood, creating citizens who are motivated to take part—who are politically interested, informed, and efficacious. Adults who are psychologically engaged with politics are more likely to take part.

However, being raised by parents who are well educated and affluent is potentially politically enabling in another way, one that is less explicitly political and that is given much less attention in the literature on political socialization.[7] Parents' social class affects the ultimate socio-economic position of

---

Conference on Participation: Building a Research Agenda, Center for the Study of Democratic Politics, Princeton University, Princeton, NJ, October 12–14, 2000.

5. See Hess and Torney, *Development of Political Attitudes*, pp. 110–111.

6. In general, the socialization literature emphasized correspondence between the generations with respect to the content of political attitudes and commitments—in particular, partisanship—rather than the transmission of the orientations and skills that encourage later political activity. In his literature review, "The Role of Agents in Political Socialization," pp. 122–127, Beck concludes that, except in the case of partisan identification, parents' ability to influence the content of their children's political choices is notably weak.

7. Consistent with this perspective, Jennings and Niemi, in *The Political Character of Adolescence*, p. 22, argue that the "social stratification system [that] operates in the nation . . . bequeaths to people of different strata differential access to resources most useful in the

their children—including the education they receive, the jobs they get as adults, and the incomes they earn. Position in the socio-economic hierarchy, in turn, affects the acquisition of such participatory factors as psychological orientations to politics like political interest, knowledge, and efficacy and the civic skills developed in school and in adult institutional settings, as well as the location in networks through which recruitment to political activity takes place. Thus the process of SES transmission implies that the unequal opportunities to stockpile virtually all the factors that facilitate political activity constitute yet another example of the persistence of political inequality rooted in basic social characteristics.

Across the Generations: Some Preliminary Data

Let us begin by considering some preliminary data relevant to these processes.[8] Figure 7.1 presents evidence about parents' education and two characteristics of respondents: the educational level they achieve and the extent of their exposure to politics at home through the political activity of their parents and discussions of politics. Consistent with what we saw in Chapter 3, Figure 7.1.A shows that well-educated parents are able to hand down their educational attainment: the higher the educational attainment of their parents, the more likely are their children to graduate from high school.[9] Ninety-

---

political process." They point out that "the middle class child goes to 'better' schools, interacts with children with greater social competence, has access to more varied learning encounters," and the like. In a similar vein, Stanley Allen Renshon, in "The Role of Personality Development in Political Socialization," in *New Directions in Political Socialization*, ed. David C. Schwartz and Sandra Kenyon Schwartz (New York: Free Press, 1975), p. 48, notes that SES is "a shorthand for a whole range of life and developmental experiences, attitudes, and lifestyles" and that a child who is born into a high-SES family has the advantage of an "expanding choice system."

8. Once again we use data from the 1990 Citizen Participation Study, which turn upside-down the usual problem with socialization studies. Ordinarily, studies present compelling information about youthful experiences that cannot be linked to adult politics. In contrast, we have rich information about the lives, especially the political lives, of our respondents but are forced to rely on weaker retrospective data about their preadult experiences. For wording of all questions and information about the survey; the oversamples of Latinos, African Americans, and those who are active in politics; and the characteristics that allow this study to be treated as a national random sample, see Verba, Schlozman, and Brady, *Voice and Equality*, Appendixes A and B.

9. Parents' education is measured by the average educational attainment of mother and father, converted into five roughly equal quintiles. The measure of exposure to politics at home is an additive scale composed of items that include the respondents' reports about the

7.1.A Percentage of Respondents Graduated from High School by Quintile of Parental Education

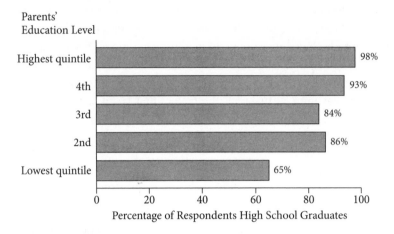

Parents'
Education Level

Highest quintile — 98%
4th — 93%
3rd — 84%
2nd — 86%
Lowest quintile — 65%

Percentage of Respondents High School Graduates

7.1.B Percentage of Respondents Exposed to Politics at Home by Quintile of Parental Education

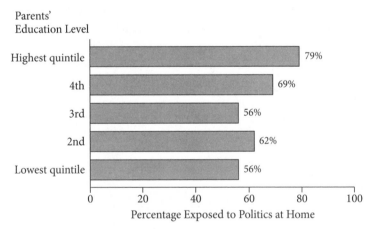

Parents'
Education Level

Highest quintile — 79%
4th — 69%
3rd — 56%
2nd — 62%
Lowest quintile — 56%

Percentage Exposed to Politics at Home

Figure 7.1 The Legacy of Parents' Education

Source: Citizen Participation Study (1990).

Note: Exposure to politics is defined as having at least one parent somewhat or very politically active or reporting sometimes having political discussions at home before respondent's adulthood.

eight percent of children of parents in the top quintile of educational attainment are high school graduates; in contrast, only 65 percent of those in the lowest parental quintile graduated from high school. As shown in Figure 7.1.B, well-educated parents also create homes that are politically stimulating.[10] Those whose parents were highly educated—particularly those whose parents were in the top educational quintile—are substantially more likely to report a home environment that provided exposure to politics: 79 percent of respondents whose parents were in the top educational quintile reported political exposure at home compared with 56 percent of those whose parents come from the bottom educational quintile.

Figure 7.2 connects respondents' youthful experiences to their adult political activity. Figure 7.2.A shows that, as parents' educational level rises, so does the percentage of respondents active in politics—that is, those who take part in two or more acts on an eight-act scale.[11] Similarly, the data in Figure 7.2.B make clear that those who have greater exposure to politics at home are more likely to be politically active.

The Process of Intergenerational Transmission of Political Activity

These simple data show that having well-educated parents is associated with two results known to foster political activity: well-educated parents produce well-educated offspring, and they create politically rich home environments.[12] In previous work we investigated in detail the alternative mechanisms sug-

---

political activity of both parents and about the frequency of political discussion at home—once again, converted into roughly equal quintiles. We would have preferred not to have to rely on respondents' recollections. However, we have reason to believe that these reports are fairly accurate. For a discussion, see Appendix C.

10. Exposure to politics is defined in Figure 7.1.B as reporting political discussion at home and having at least one parent politically active.

11. Activists are defined as those who engage in two or more (usually voting and one other act) of the following eight participatory acts: voting; working in a campaign; contributing to a campaign; contacting a public official; taking part in a protest, march, or demonstration; working with others in the community to solve a local problem; serving on a local community board or regularly attending meetings of such a board; and being affiliated with an organization that takes stands in politics.

12. Presumably the parental legacy operates in other unmeasured ways to affect political participation. For example, all things equal, having parents who were politically and socially well connected or who filled the house with newspapers and periodicals would presumably have consequences for future political activity.

7.2.A Percentage of Respondents Politically Active as Adults by Quintile of Parental Education

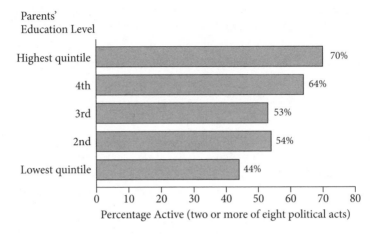

Parents'
Education Level

Highest quintile — 70%
4th — 64%
3rd — 53%
2nd — 54%
Lowest quintile — 44%

Percentage Active (two or more of eight political acts)

7.2.B Percentage of Respondents Politically Active as Adults by Quintile of Political Exposure at Home

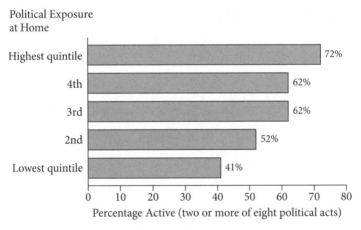

Political Exposure
at Home

Highest quintile — 72%
4th — 62%
3rd — 62%
2nd — 52%
Lowest quintile — 41%

Percentage Active (two or more of eight political acts)

Figure 7.2 The Roots of Adult Political Activity

Source: Citizen Participation Study (1990).

Note: The scale of exposure to politics at home includes the level of political activity of both parents and the amount of political discussion at home before respondent's adulthood.

gested by these associations: the direct political path that leads to political participation from having been nurtured in a politically stimulating home and the indirect path through the educational level of the next generation.[13] We will not replicate the statistical analysis but will instead summarize that discussion and then consider the consequences of the transmission process for our concern with political inequality.

For several reasons, we focus in particular on education as the engine for the socio-economic transmission of political activity from generation to generation, drawing out the consequences of the link between parents' education and the education of their offspring. Education plays a primary role among the factors that foster political activity. In passing on their high levels of educational attainment to their children, educated parents also pass on many other attributes that enhance later political activity. Not only does education have a direct impact on political participation but also level of education affects the acquisition of nearly all the other factors that facilitate participation resources, among them income and civic skills, motivation to use such resources for political purposes, and access to social networks through which requests for political activity are made. In addition, education has advantages in terms of measurement; respondents are probably able to give more accurate estimates of their parents' educational attainment than of their parents' income.[14]

The Impact of Parents' Characteristics

What effect do parental characteristics have on the capacity and propensity of their offspring to take part in politics? In our earlier work we traced out a complex path from early family experiences to adult political activity: from parents' education and the political environment they created at home (the level of parental political activity and the frequency of political discussions at home) to respondent's educational attainment to the participatory factors acquired in adulthood that are fostered by education (civic skills, family income, requests for activity, and psychological orientations to politics such as

13. See Verba, Schlozman, and Burns, "Family Ties," and Verba, Burns, and Schlozman, "Unequal at the Starting Line."

14. As noted earlier, we would have preferred not to have to rely on respondents' reports of their parents' educational attainment and of the political environment at home (their parents' level of political participation and the frequency of political discussions at home). However, as we shall see, we have reason to believe that these reports are fairly accurate.

political interest, knowledge, and efficacy) and finally to political activity.[15] Although the possibility of reciprocal influence with other participatory factors implies that the measures of psychological orientations to politics are uncertainly located in the chain, by and large, the temporal order of these steps that culminate in political activity is fairly clear.

This multistep analysis yields a nuanced understanding of the political path from generation to generation. The data reinforce our contention that the legacy of parental social class operates in at least two ways, one of which is much more explicitly political than the other. Parents' education is associated both with the extent to which the home environment is a politically stimulating one and especially with the educational attainment of their offspring—each of which, in turn, has consequences for adult political activity. The surprise in the analysis is that the learning process emphasized in the literature on political socialization is of secondary importance; that is, growing up in a rich political environment has less powerful consequences for adult political activity than does achieving a high level of education.

In Table 7.1 we summarize the multiple processes through which parental education affects the respondent's political participation by showing the paths by which intergenerational transmission operates.[16] For the sample as a whole, the average number of political acts is 2.11. As shown at the bottom of Table 7.1, about a quarter of the average person's level of activity (0.53 of those 2.11 acts) derives from the various effects of parental education. While the nature of our sample and the uncertainty in the measures of the explanatory and dependent variables imply that we should not overestimate the specificity of that particular number (or any other number in the table), its magnitude is worth noting. While political activity is not fully determined at birth, a significant portion is transmitted from generation to generation. That family background is not the whole story is hardly surprising. Sibling studies have long demonstrated the variation in adult behavior even among those who share genes and environment. Nevertheless, family background exercises an important influence on adult political activity.

Considering these data more closely, we see in the top line of the table that

---

15. This analysis is found in Verba, Schlozman, and Brady, *Voice and Equality*, pp. 416–450.

16. For a full description of our analysis and its results, see the extended description in Verba, Burns, and Schlozman, "Unequal at the Starting Line," esp. Appendix B, pp. 66–69.

Table 7.1   Predicting How Much Participation
Comes from the Effects of Parents' Education

Effects of Parental Education through Political Stimuli	
Politics at Home	0.06 act
Effects of Parental Education through Socio-economic	
Processes	
Respondent's Education	0.20 act ⎤
Family Income	0.06 act ⎟ .34 act
Civic Skills	0.06 act ⎟
Recruitment	0.02 act ⎦
Additional Effects of Parental Education on	
Participatory Acts	<u>0.13 act</u>
Total Effect of Parents' Education	0.53 act

Source: Citizen Participation Study (1990).

one part of the effect of parents' education on activity—a little over one-tenth of the overall impact—is explicitly political. Well-educated parents tend to provide a rich political environment at home, and respondents who have been exposed to politics at home while growing up are more politically active as adults.[17] Even more substantial than the impact of the political environment at home, however, are the effects of socio-economic processes. The single most important of these processes derives from the expected strong relationship between parents' education and that of their offspring and, in turn, the consequence of respondent's education for political participation. In addition, parents' education influences the respondent's political participation through its consequences for subsequent life experiences outside politics: adult family income and civic skills exercised and requests for activity in nonpolitical institutions—on the job, in nonpolitical organizations, and at church. Finally, additional processes that cannot be specified with any preci-

17. Until 1976, the American National Election Studies asked about parents' levels of political interest. We used these data to explore the parental legacy of political involvement, with results consistent with those presented here.

sion account for roughly one quarter of the effect of parental education on political activity.[18] These estimates of parental effects are not insubstantial in light of the number of other variables included in the analysis.[19]

Intergenerational Transmission of Political Activity and Modes of Political Involvement

We can extend our understanding of the difference between the consequences of having well-educated parents and the consequences of coming of age in a politically stimulating home by considering several different modes of adult political involvement that might be influenced by the parental legacy. Tables 7.2 and 7.3 each present the results of regressions predicting two different dependent variables: one of them is a measure of the amount of political activity and the other a measure of psychological engagement with politics. The different aspects of the parental legacy are differentially related to different modes of adult political involvement: having well-educated parents is more closely connected to measures of political activity; growing up in a politically stimulating home is more strongly associated with measures of political concern or engagement.

Let us look more closely at the results. In Table 7.2, the measure of political participation is the same eight-item scale measuring participation that was used in Table 7.1, and the measure of psychological engagement with politics is the strength of party affiliation. For each of these two modes of involvement, in the first column of numbers we show standardized regres-

18. Presumably these additional effects reflect the operation of the unmeasured processes discussed earlier as well as the measurement error in our measures—in particular, the scale measuring home political environment.

19. In data not shown, we took the analysis one step further. For the eight-point scale measuring overall political activity, we substituted two measures of the volume of participation: the amount of time donated to political activity and the amount of money donated to campaigns and other political causes. Our results reinforce the understanding that there are two different mechanisms of intergenerational transmission of political activity. The impact of parents' education that runs through its influence on the political environment at home is manifest for the number of hours given to politics but not for the number of dollars. That is, growing up in a politically stimulating home enhances one's future propensity to give time to politics but has no effect when it comes to giving money. For making political contributions, the single most important factor is family income, for which parents' education has direct consequences—above and beyond its effect on respondents' education. Thus these data strengthen our conclusion that, when it comes to political activity, we are not equal at the starting line. Instead, parents' educational attainment reaches across generations to influence in many ways the political participation of their offspring.

Table 7.2   Predicting Adult Political Activity and Partisan Strength
by Parents' Education and Exposure to Politics at Home: Ordinary
Least Squares (OLS) Regression (Standardized Regression Coefficients)

	Predicting Political Activity[a]		Predicting Partisan Strength[a]	
	Parental Legacy	Adding Adult Characteristics	Parental Legacy	Adding Adult Characteristics
Parents' Education	.22***	.07**	.06	.02
Exposure to Politics at Home	.17***	.13***	.14***	.12***
Respondent's Education		.32***		.06*
Adult Family Income		.15***		.04

Source: Citizen Participation Study (1990).

Note: *Significant at the .05 level; **significant at the .01 level; ***significant at the .001 level.

[a] Gender, race and ethnicity, and age have been included in the equation.

sion coefficients for parents' education and exposure to politics at home derived from an ordinary least squares (OLS) regression that also controls for the respondent's demographic characteristics. The second column presents the coefficients from a regression that adds the respondent's educational attainment and adult family income as intervening factors between the variables measuring youthful home experiences and adult political involvement. Because the latter characteristics clearly come later in time than the first two, we consider them intervening factors in the chain linking youthful experiences to modes of adult political involvement.

The first column of coefficients of Table 7.2 shows that both parental education and exposure to politics at home are significantly associated with adult political activity, but the links to parents' education are more substantial. In the second column, when we take the respondent's SES into account—that is, when we add measures of the respondent's education and adult income to the analysis—the impact of parents' education is reduced substantially, but the effect of political exposure at home remains nearly as strong. Thus both parents' education and the respondent's exposure to politics at home are important for the next generation's political activity, but they operate through

Table 7.3 Predicting the Amount of Political Contributions and the Proportion of All Contributions Given to Politics by Parental Education and Exposure to Politics at Home: OLS Regression (Standardized Regression Coefficients)

| | Amount of Political Contributions[a] | | Proportion of All Contributions Given to Politics[b] | |
	Parental Legacy	Adding Adult Characteristics	Parental Legacy	Adding Adult Characteristics
Parents' Education	.09***	.04	.08***	.01
Exposure to Politics at Home	.06*	−.03	.13***	.12***
Respondent's Education		.04*		.11***
Family Income		.34***		.13***

Source: Citizen Participation Study (1990).

Note: *Significant at the .05 level; **significant at the .01 level; ***significant at the .001 level.

[a] Gender, race and ethnicity, and age have been included in the equation.
[b] Gender, race and ethnicity, and age have been included in the equation. The figures are for those who made a political, religious, or charitable contribution.

different paths. By and large, the consequences of parents' education for adult political activity are indirect, having an impact on adult socio-economic factors that, in turn, have consequences for adult political participation.[20] In contrast, growing up in a politically stimulating home seems to have a direct impact.

We see a different pattern with respect to the strength of partisan commitment, shown in the second pair of columns of Table 7.2. Parental education has neither a direct nor an indirect impact on the strength of party affiliation. Furthermore, such resources as adult income or education are relatively weakly associated with strength of party commitment. Exposure to politics at home, however, has a direct effect that remains strongly significant even after we take into account the possibly intervening factors of adult education and income. Thus, when it comes to partisanship, the intergenerational linkage is much more dependent on exposure to politics at home than on parental edu-

20. A direct effect is one that remains after controlling for all other relevant factors. An indirect effect is one that may exist before controlling for some of these factors.

cation. Although we have stressed the role of SES in relation to political involvement—and have found a strong association between social class and political activity—these data make it clear that SES is not the entire story.

Table 7.3 shows an interesting contrast between two aspects of political contributions: the *amount* of money respondents contribute to political campaigns and causes and the *proportion* of their total voluntary contributions—to charity and religious institutions as well as to politics—that respondents direct to politics. Once again, the first variable is a measure of participation, and the second is a measure of the importance of politics among the respondent's concerns. As a mode of political activity, making political contributions is highly dependent on resources—specifically on income. With respect to the amount of political donations, the data in the first column of coefficients indicate that parental education has a greater impact than does having grown up in a politically stimulating environment. When we introduce the respondent's own education and income into the analysis, shown in the next column, the effect of parents' education—which has worked its influence through the education and income of their offspring—is attenuated. What really matters for the amount of political contributions is the respondent's own income. In contrast, the extent to which voluntary contributions are directed to politics, shown in the two columns at the far right, is more closely connected to exposure to politics at home, a relationship that persists even when education and income as an adult—which are themselves significant—are taken into account.

In sum, our comparison of the intergenerational transmission of the different modes of political involvement underscores the existence of two paths, each of which is significant, from early socialization to politics in adulthood. Both are important for understanding the roots of the intergenerational persistence of participatory inequalities, but the way that the parental legacy operates depends on the particular form of political involvement at stake. Parents who are politically involved transmit their political interest and concern directly to their offspring. In contrast, well-educated parents influence the political activity of their offspring indirectly—and more strongly—by raising children who later turn out to be well educated and affluent.

A Note on the Creation of Group Differences

The intergenerational processes that operate so powerfully to perpetuate class-based inequalities in political voice have complex consequences for disparities in political activity among other politically relevant groups—in particular, political inequality on the basis of gender and race or ethnicity. In Chapter 5 we discussed that men are somewhat more politically active than women and that non-Hispanic whites are more active than African Americans and especially Latinos. In a complex analysis elsewhere, we have explored the roots of those group differences. Here we shall summarize our findings very briefly.[21]

To understand the origins of participatory disparities among groups is a quite different enterprise than to explain individual differences in political activity. To do so requires that we ask questions about both the *level* and the *impact* of the factors, among them parents' education and exposure to politics at home, that foster participation. In terms of level, are there, on average, differences between men and women—or among non-Hispanic whites, African Americans, and Latinos—in the educational attainment of their parents? Are there differences in the extent to which their parents provided a politically rich home environment? If so, such group disparities in the parental legacy would be likely to beget group differences in political activity later on in adulthood.

The data in Figure 7.3 show two different patterns for the parental legacy— one for men and women and another for non-Hispanic whites, blacks, and Latinos. Because boys and girls are born randomly into families, it is hardly surprising that Figure 7.3.A shows no significant difference in the educational attainment of the parents of men and women. In contrast, Anglo white respondents were more likely than African Americans, or especially Latinos, to report that their parents were very well educated.[22] The disparities in relation to exposure to politics at home, shown in Figure 7.3.B, are parallel. There is no appreciable difference in the political richness of the homes in which the women and the men in the sample came of age. When it comes to race or ethnicity, however, the group differences are more pronounced: non-Hispanic

---

21. Once again we invite readers curious about our methods, data, and findings to consult the extended treatment in Verba, Burns, and Schlozman, "Unequal at the Starting Line." See also Sidney Verba, Kay Lehman Schlozman, and Henry E. Brady, "Race, Ethnicity, and Political Participation," in *Classifying by Race*, ed. Paul E. Peterson (Princeton, NJ: Princeton University Press, 1995), chap 15, and Burns, Schlozman, and Verba, *Private Roots of Public Action*.

22. Parents classified as being in the upper educational category in Figure 7.3.A are in the top quintile. Data from the General Social Survey, which include more precise information about the educational attainment of each parent, show that the difference between whites and blacks is a bit under three years of schooling (averaged for both parents) and between Anglo whites and Latinos about five years.

7.3.A Percentage of Respondents Who Reported Having Parents in the Highest Quintile of Education

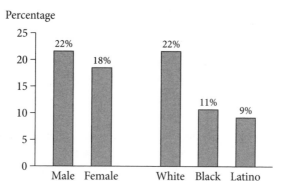

7.3.B Percentage of Respondents Who Reported Some Political Exposure at Parents' Home

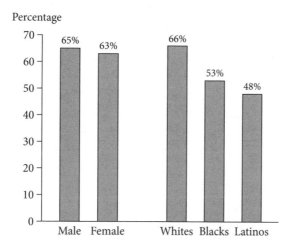

Figure 7.3 Differences in Respondent's Reports of Parents' Education and Political Exposure at Parents' Home by Gender and Race or Ethnicity

Source: Citizen Participation Study (1990).

Note: Political exposure at parents' home is defined as having at least one parent somewhat or very politically active or reporting sometimes having political discussions at home before respondent's adulthood.

whites were more likely than blacks or Latinos to report having had a stimulating political environment at home. The contrast between the two sets of groups is noteworthy. While gender does not seem to confer participatory advantage at birth, there are significant differences in the parental legacy among groups defined by their race or ethnicity.[23]

Still, we should add an important caveat about group differences in an important participatory resource, respondents' educational attainment. On one hand, group differences in parental educational attainment among Anglo whites, African Americans, and Latinos are reproduced across generations and yield corresponding group differences in respondents' educational levels. On the other—reflecting the fact that, until recently, men achieved, on average, higher levels of education than did women—in 1990 there was a gender gap in education among respondents in spite of the similarity between men and women in their parents' educational attainment. Although men's educational advantage has reversed among younger cohorts, the accumulation of several decades during which men's educational attainment surpassed women's implies that the men in the sample were somewhat better educated than the women. This educational disparity was created during men's and women's lifetimes; in contrast, educational differences among groups defined by their race or ethnicity have intergenerational origins.

To understand the role played by intergenerational transmission of political activity in creating group differences in such activity, we need to consider impact as well as level. How are these initial group differences carried over to adult political behavior? A group that begins with an advantage in terms of parents' education might not turn out to be, on average, more politically active in adulthood if there are group differences in the translation of that advantage into political participation. Are there differences among these groups in

---

23. We should note that this similarity between the reports of female and male respondents —in contrast to the different reports across the three groups defined by race or ethnicity— enhances the credibility of the respondents' retrospective reports of the political situation at home while they were growing up. The similarity between males and females lends credence to our claim that these retrospective reports are not unduly contaminated by adult experience. If respondents were projecting backward, we would expect the advantage of male respondents with respect to both educational attainment and political participation to result in recollections of higher levels of educational attainment and political involvement for the parents of male respondents. Instead we find no differences in the reported educational level or political involvement of the parents of male and female respondents, a result consistent with the fact that women and men are born randomly to parents with varying levels of education and political involvement. The same, of course, cannot be said about children of whites, blacks, and Latinos.

the processes by which these factors are converted into political activity? That is, do men and women—or do Anglo whites, African Americans, and Latinos—differ in the extent of the boost given to their political participation by an incremental increase in the level of their parents' educational attainment, exposure to politics at home, or any other participatory factor? To illustrate the importance of the rate of conversion of early experiences into adult participation, consider an extreme example: that of African Americans in the South under segregation. Because blacks were prevented by law, custom, and violence from voting or otherwise taking part in politics, the way that education was translated into political participation in the Jim Crow South must have been very different for blacks and for whites.

To trace the impact of early experiences forward to political activity, we conducted a series of analyses linking parental education to political stimulation at home, to respondents' education, and eventually to political participation—taking into account the intervening effects of other participatory factors.[24] As we did in Table 7.1, we began with parents' education and followed its direct and indirect effects across generations. In order to ascertain whether there are significant group differences in the way that participatory factors are converted into adult political participation, we conducted the analyses separately for men and women and for non-Hispanic whites, African Americans, and Latinos.

The results are clear. In contrast to the racial and ethnic disparities in the levels of participatory factors inherited from parents is the overall similarity across groups in the impact of these and other participatory factors in producing political activity. Each group receives about the same participatory boost from these variables; the conversion rates of the variables differ relatively little from group to group. The correlations between parental education and exposure to politics at home, on the one hand, and respondent activity, on the other, are all positive and not significantly different from each other. When such intervening factors as resources, civic skills, and political recruitment are taken into account, these results are unchanged.

The bottom line is that the intergenerational force of initial parental characteristics is not an important factor when it comes to explaining gender differences in participation. Men and women do not differ in either the kind of families into which they are born or the way that they convert the legacy of

24. Once again, for discussion of our analysis and results, see Verba, Burns, and Schlozman, "Unequal at the Starting Line," Appendix B, pp. 66–69.

their parents' characteristics into political activity. The point is significant. It does not mean that women and men have the same experiences in childhood, adolescence, or adulthood. In fact, the point is often made that siblings may have quite different experiences in the same family, and there is good reason to believe that some of those differences translate into systematic differences between the experiences of sons and daughters. The point is that male–female disparities in participation are created during an individual's life course, not by inheritance from parents' level of education. In contrast, the parental legacy has much more substantial consequences for participatory inequalities among Latinos, African Americans, and non-Hispanic whites. For both blacks and Latinos, group differences in parental education and the political environment at home play an important role in creating a participation gap with non-Hispanic whites.[25]

In short, while processes of intergenerational transmission of political activity operate across the board to create participatory inequalities among individuals and among socio-economic groups, the implications of these processes in creating participatory inequalities for gender differ from those for race or ethnicity. Because boys and girls do not differ systematically in the education of their parents—though they may differ in their experiences as youngsters at home—processes of intergenerational transmission play almost no role in explaining why men are somewhat more politically active than women. In contrast, these processes are crucial in explaining the participatory gap between non-Hispanic whites and Latinos or African Americans.

---

25. To the extent possible, we replicated these analyses using the National Black Election Study and the Latino National Election Study, with results consistent with those presented here. We also replicated the analysis using time-based acts and political contributions as dependent variables. For all five groups, parents' education has an impact on family income, above and beyond its impact on respondent's education, and for all five groups family income is overwhelmingly important in explaining political contributions. Thus we confirm for women and men and for Latinos, African Americans, and Anglo whites the earlier analysis showing multiple streams of influence of parental legacy.

In addition, in order to circumvent the oversimplification of assuming that men and women of the three race and ethnic groups (or that whites, blacks, or Latinos of either sex) are essentially the same, we replicated this analysis for the six groups at the intersection of gender and race or ethnicity: Latinas, Latinos, African American women, African American men, Anglo white women, and Anglo white men. Our results were unchanged. While there are important differences among groups defined by their race or ethnicity in the role played by intergenerational transmission of political activity, there are no important differences in these processes for the men and women within any racial or ethnic group.

Conclusion

The analysis in this chapter demonstrates once more how deeply embedded political inequality is in the social structures of American society and adds another piece to the puzzle of the persistence of unequal political voice. In Chapter 6 we used longitudinal data to show that the bias in political voice has persisted for the past several decades. Not only are the same kinds of people politically active over time but indeed the same individuals tend to take part on a continuing basis. Because the characteristics, orientations, and tastes that foster participation are relatively persistent characteristics of individuals, the same individuals maintain a relatively consistent level of activity over time.

Taking into account information about parents' education and political involvement and about the home political environment adds another dimension to our understanding of the persistence of inequalities of political voice: these processes work across generations. Those who had well-educated parents are, for two reasons, more likely to be politically active as adults. For one thing, they are more likely to have grown up in politically stimulating homes with parents who were politically active and an environment of frequent political discussion. More important but less often noticed, because educational attainment is likely to be handed on across generations, those whose parents were well educated are more likely to become well educated themselves, with consequences for the acquisition of many other factors that encourage political participation.

By demonstrating that the promise of equal opportunity does not hold for political participation, this chapter throws additional light on themes discussed in Chapters 2 and 3. There we discussed the fact that Americans bring contrasting interpretations to economic and political equalities. In the economic domain, as long as we compete on an equal footing, we believe in the promise of equal opportunity and expect that the fleet and the tenacious will fare better. Thus we are willing to accept inequalities of condition in relation to wealth and income. We are more thoroughly egalitarian with respect to the political arena—believing that the promise of democracy requires equal political voice for all. Neither domain, however, is characterized by equality of condition: we are unequal when it comes to both income and political participation. Moreover, we cited evidence showing that differential opportunities for economic success are not independent of initial circumstances and that there is considerable correspondence in the economic outcomes of successive generations. We do not usually ask analogous questions about whether citizens enjoy unequal advantages when it comes to the opportunity to express political voice, but this chapter reports parallel findings for political activity. In neither economy nor politics does equality of opportunity obtain. The transmission of class advantage across generations implies that we are not even equal at the starting line.

8

Political Participation
over the Life Cycle

Elders tut-tutting about the younger generation and its lack of political engagement is an old but recurrent theme:

> The more I am around this generation of college students, the more I am . . . baffled . . . because they are so much less radical and politically engaged than they need to be. . . . America needs a jolt of the idealism, activism and outrage. . . . That's what twentysomethings are for—to light a fire under the country. But they can't e-mail it in.[1]

But then, again, the same was said about Gen X:

> How depressing. A generation ago, young people clamored to reform government and end a war, taking to the streets to fight what they regarded as wrong-headed policies and demanding that the voting age be lowered to 18 so more of them could be enfranchised. Now, many simply tune out politics and tune in TV. . . . That's too bad for democracy.[2]

Indeed, this tune was sung about what ultimately became known as the Greatest Generation:

Jennifer Erkulwater is coauthor of this chapter.

1. Thomas L. Friedman, "Generation Q," *New York Times*, October 10, 2007.
2. "Apathy on the Upswing," *Hartford Courant*, February 3, 1995, p. A14.

The depression generation has scarcely had a chance to be lost. . . . It would be a magnificent thing if many could not only participate, but participate in a real cause rather than in a hollow one.[3]

These periodic lamentations asking, "Why can't they be like we were?"—with or without the follow-up, "perfect in every way"—alert us to another basis for inequality of political voice. Although we have paid attention to group differences in political activity on the basis of race or ethnicity, gender, and especially socio-economic status (SES), we have so far ignored such disparities among age groups, disparities that will become especially important in Chapter 16 when we consider inequalities in Internet-based political participation. The participatory deficit of citizens who have recently entered the electorate raises the same kinds of questions we have been bringing to inequalities of political voice on the basis of socio-economic status: How do we account for disparities in political activity on the basis of age? What are their implications for the representation of the opinions, concerns, and needs of all?

Life-Cycle, Period, and Cohort Effects

Answering these questions poses many methodological challenges. The most familiar is the difficulty of disentangling life-cycle, cohort, and period effects.[4] *Life-cycle effects* refer to the social, psychological, and physical changes that take place as individuals age. In any society, particular experiences tend to correspond to particular stages in the life cycle. For example, in America most people leave school during their late teens or early to midtwenties, and many people in their late forties or early fifties confront an empty nest for the first time. Researchers who study social domains as varied as criminal behavior and market behavior sometimes differentiate among the lasting impact throughout adulthood of what happens in childhood and adolescence; the ongoing changes in income, education, residence, family status, and other events that occur over the life cycle; and the impacts of such experiences as having actually committed a crime, purchased a product, or—more germane to our concerns—participated in politics.[5]

3. "Unfounded Generation," *New Republic*, July 11, 1934, p. 224.
4. The classic exposition of this problem is in Matilda White Riley, "Aging and Cohort Succession: Interpretations and Misinterpretations," *Public Opinion Quarterly* 37 (1973): 35–49.
5. A large literature distinguishes between the impact of "heterogeneity" and that of "state dependence" on behavior. *Heterogeneity* refers to those characteristics that persist over time

We should not exaggerate the extent to which age mates move in lockstep through common experiences. Members of a single cohort do not stay in step as they march, or saunter, toward developmental milestones,[6] and many of the differences within cohorts reflect differences among politically relevant groups rather than the idiosyncrasies of individual choice. For example, among low-skilled black men, high rates of imprisonment mean that incarceration has emerged as a stage in the life cycle, affecting family formation and employment patterns for decades afterward.[7] In addition, the patterns of delayed matriculation in college and the failure to graduate among those who enroll are more typical of men than of women, and especially of those from socio-economically disadvantaged backgrounds.[8] Among women, the tendency to put off childbearing is much more typical of well-educated women than of their less well-educated sisters.[9]

—either those that persist over a lifetime, such as the legacy of childhood (for example, heredity, parents' SES, childhood socialization, experience with student government and other activities during high school, and educational attainment) or those that persist over shorter but still significant periods of time, such as job status, educational attainment, marital status, or residency. *State dependence* focuses on "habituation" that occurs when the performance of a behavior changes the likelihood that a person will perform it again in the future. Those who perform criminal acts, for example, may develop a taste for crime or may learn that they can get away with it. Life-cycle effects may be the result either of relatively short-term changes in a person's characteristics or of habituation. See, for example, James J. Heckman, "Heterogeneity and State Dependence," in *Studies in Labor Markets*, ed. Sherwin Rosen (Chicago: University of Chicago Press, 1981), pp. 91–140; Cheng Hsiao, *Analysis of Panel Data* (Cambridge, England: Cambridge University Press, 1986), chap. 4; Badi H. Baltagi, *Econometric Analysis of Panel Data* (New York: John Wiley and Sons, 1995), chap. 8; and Daniel Nagin and Raymond Paternoster, "Population Heterogeneity and State Dependence: State of the Evidence and Directions for Future Research," *Journal of Quantitative Criminology* 16 (2000): 117–144.

6. See Glen Elder Jr., "Perspectives on the Life Course," in Glen Elder Jr., *Life Course Dynamics: Trajectories and Transitions, 1968–1980* (Ithaca, NY: Cornell University Press, 1985), pp. 31–36, and Ronald R. Rindfuss, C. Gray Swicegood, and Rachel A. Rosenfeld, "Disorder in the Life Course: How Common and Does It Matter?" *American Sociological Review* 52 (1987): 785–801.

7. Becky Pettit and Bruce Western, "Mass Imprisonment and the Life Course: Race and Class Inequality in U.S. Incarceration," *American Sociological Review* 69 (2004): 151–169.

8. See, for example, Robert Bozick and Stefanie DeLuca, "Better Late than Never? Delayed Enrollment in the High School to College Transition," *Social Forces* 84 (2005): 531–554, and John Bound, Michael F. Lovenheim, and Sarah Turner, "Why Have College Completion Rates Declined? An Analysis of Changing Student Preparation and Collegiate Resources," *American Economic Journal: Applied Economics* 2 (2010): 129–157.

9. Ronald R. Rindfuss, S. Philip Morgan, and Kate Offutt, "Education and the Changing Age Pattern of American Fertility: 1963–1989," *Demography* 33 (1996): 277–290.

We must also understand that the participatory consequences of life-cycle events are not necessarily uniform across age mates. For example, the usual assumption is that marriage and family deepen one's commitment to the community and thus enhance political activity. However, among those under age thirty, marriage and children are associated with lower rates of participation, presumably as the result of selection processes such that many who delay these milestones of adulthood have other characteristics, in particular educational attainment, that are germane to participation.[10] Furthermore, marriage and especially having small children at home are associated with greater workforce commitment for men and the opposite for women, with, in turn, implications for the accumulation of such work-based participatory factors as the development of civic skills and exposure to requests for political activity.[11] Thus two of the most significant milestones in emerging adulthood work, on average, in opposite ways for women and men. Such considerations make clear that untangling the relationship between age and political participation is likely to be extremely difficult. Still, the advantage that accrues to the middle aged in terms of their stockpile of participatory factors suggests that they will be more active in politics.

In Chapter 6 we investigated another process that would create disparities among age groups, habituation. There we considered whether engaging in political activity is itself a participatory factor that boosts future political participation—over and above the attributes that predispose some people to take part in the first place. We found that while going to the polls is habit-forming, increasing the probability of turning out in the future, other forms of political activity are not.

Period effects are those occasional shocks that boost or depress political activity more or less across the board. Watergate is sometimes thought to have had a period effect, raising levels of public cynicism among American adults regardless of age. Genuine period effects are probably quite rare. Because they have an impact on everyone—irrespective of age, social class, gender, and so on—at a particular moment, they raise an issue to which we refer fre-

---

10. Raymond Wolfinger and Steven Rosenstone note that turnout is higher among young people who are in college than among cohorts who supposedly take on adult roles by working full time or getting married in *Who Votes?* (New Haven, CT: Yale University Press, 1980), pp. 55–58.

11. See Nancy Burns, Kay Lehman Schlozman, and Sidney Verba, *The Private Roots of Public Action: Gender, Inequality and Political Participation* (Cambridge, MA: Harvard University Press, 2001), chaps. 8 and 12.

quently throughout this inquiry: that changing the level of political activity does not necessarily alter its distribution. Therefore, as important as period effects can be for the political mobilization of citizens, our concern with inequalities of political voice implies that we should put them aside in our discussion.

As students of socialization make clear, we are especially permeable to the effects of early experiences. The kinds of historical events that leave social change in their wake tend to have an especially profound and lasting impact on the young.[12] Thus, *generational* or *cohort effects,* which arise from the shared social and historical experiences of those who were born during the same era, can be understood as a combination of life-cycle effects and period effects.[13] Although we often discuss generational effects in terms of the enduring impact of major historical events—for example, the Depression of the 1930s, World War II, and 9/11—on those who experience them as they come of age, the social forces that create generational effects need not be confined to great historical events. The emergence of Facebook and other social media is a contemporary example of a social development with disproportionate consequences for those who were born in the 1980s and early 1990s.

Some of these generational differences involve differences among cohorts in the timing and sequencing of life-cycle events. Those who came of age during the 1950s were known to marry early and have children, lots of them, at a young age. In contrast, reflecting changing economic constraints, young people today are taking longer than their predecessors to achieve the traditional markers of adulthood: spending more time on their education; delay-

---

12. Period effects can also have a disproportionate effect on groups in society defined by attributes other than their age. For example, the experience of living through the civil rights era of the 1960s might have had a different and more pronounced effect on blacks than on whites. In addition, period effects become generational effects as older people who have been exposed to whatever is producing the period effect die off and are replaced by younger people who have not experienced the source of the period effect.

13. Generational theory was most succinctly put forth in the late 1920s by Karl Mannheim in his essay "The Problem of Generations," in Karl Mannheim, *Essays on the Sociology of Knowledge* (London: Routledge and Kegan Paul, 1952). According to Mannheim, a generational unit is not merely a chronological age unit but a social unit, much like a class. It is formed by an age group, similarly situated in the social and historical processes, whose shared experiences form a common outlook and a sense of solidarity among its members. Mannheim saw the young as particularly impressionable to social, economic, and political change but believed that in order for such change to produce a generational difference, the events must have either a disproportionate impact on the young compared to other segments of the population or must affect the young in ways different from other age groups.

ing marriage, often in favor of cohabitation; and waiting longer before starting a family. They are also more likely to have high levels of debt and to rely on their parents longer for financial support. Compared to earlier cohorts, they are, as we saw in Chapter 3, also seeing their incomes rise less steeply as they age.[14] This generational distinctiveness in what is sometimes called "the changing timetable of adulthood," holds potential long-term consequences for disparities in political participation.

Life-Cycle and Generational Effects: Additional Considerations

As the discussion so far should already have made clear, it is extremely difficult to disentangle life-cycle from generational effects. Using the kind of cross-sectional evidence on which we often rely, it is impossible to do so. The perfect data set for sorting out these matters—a panel, conducted over a long period, that contains a rich array of measures of political participation and the multiple factors that facilitate it—does not exist. Therefore, in this chapter we do the best we can by using several kinds of data: panel data from the American National Election Studies (ANES); the rolling cross-section from the 1952–2008 ANES; cross-sectional data from the U.S. Census; the 1990 Citizen Participation Study; the 2004 Public Agendas and Citizen Engagement Survey (PACES); and the August 2008 election survey of the Pew Internet and American Life Project.

Rendering the task even more complicated for our concern with equality of political voice is that the distinction between life-cycle and cohort effects is germane not only for political activity but also for the factors that foster it and for political preferences and interests. For example, education attainment has both a life-cycle and a generational component. Because many people in their late teens and early twenties are still in school, they are not especially well educated. Although some people do return to school later on, most people today complete their educations by their mid- to late twenties, after which educational attainment is, by and large, stable. The cohort component arises from the extent to which levels of educational attainment have

14. On these themes, see the essays in Richard A. Settersten, Frank F. Furstenberg Jr., and Rubén G. Rumbaut, eds., *On the Frontier of Adulthood: Theory, Research, and Public Policy* (Chicago: University of Chicago Press, 2005), and Sheldon Danziger and Ceclia Elena Rouse, eds., *The Price of Independence: The Economics of Early Adulthood* (New York: Russell Sage, 2007), as well as Frank F. Furstenberg Jr., "On a New Schedule: Transitions to Adulthood and Family Change," *The Future of Children* 20 (2010): 67–87.

risen with successive generations, a pattern that may, for the first time, no longer obtain for the current generation.

Compounding these complexities is the fact that the distinction between life-cycle and cohort effects also pertains to age-group differences in political attitudes, needs, and preferences. In the next section we distinguish differences of opinion among age groups on such matters as, on one hand, funding for education and Social Security, which have roots in the life cycle, and, on the other, sex on television or gay rights, which are characterized by cohort differences.

Do We Really Need to Be Concerned about Age-Group Disparities in Political Voice?

Parents and teachers often reprove younger children, arguing that they need only be patient, and one day the freedoms and privileges exercised by older siblings and schoolmates will be theirs to enjoy. The your-turn-will-come logic underlying this admonition makes clear an important characteristic of disparities in political voice among age groups and suggests that, from the perspective of political voice, perhaps they are not really cause for concern. As the young settle down, finish school, find careers, get married, and acquire children and mortgages, they will pass out of their low-activity phase and catch up to their elders in participation. Thus, for those who live a normal life span, political voice on the basis of age is equalized across the life cycle—in contrast to participatory deficits based on such ordinarily unchanging characteristics as race or ethnicity, gender, and, to a lesser extent, social class. When considered over a lifetime, the participatory playing field of the age-group game appears fair.

But what if age is itself a politically relevant category and there are systematic differences among age groups in their political attitudes and concerns or in their stake in particular public policies? There is evidence for age-related differences that represent a generational phenomenon.[15] Figure 8.1 plots data from the 2004 PACES about whether respondents deem "sex on television" or "being gay" to be problems for society. The data show an age gradient for both, with young people significantly less likely than their elders to consider

15. On the way that "young people have distinct interests," see Peter Levine, *The Future of Democracy: Developing the Next Generation of American Citizens* (Medford, MA: Tufts University Press, 2007), pp. 60–61.

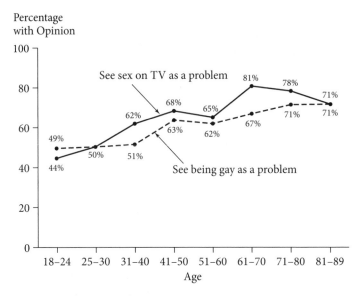

Figure 8.1   Perception of Social Problems by Age: Percentage Who Consider "Sex on Television" or "Being Gay" a Problem for Society

Source: Political Agendas and Citizen Engagement Survey (2004).

either homosexuality or sexual content on television to be a problem. While it is possible that these differences between age groups reflect changes in attitudes over the life cycle, research shows that opinions regarding sexuality change from cohort to cohort over time.[16] Consequently, if younger people are less politically active, political voice will disproportionately reflect the attitudes of older people, creating a "cultural lag" in the political system with

16. On opinion with respect to homosexuality and gay rights, see Jeni Loftus, "America's Liberalization in Attitudes toward Homosexuality, 1973 to 1998," *American Sociological Review* 66 (2001): 762–782; Alison G. Keleher and Eric R. A. N. Smith, "Explaining the Growing Support for Gay and Lesbian Equality since 1990," paper delivered at the Annual Meeting of the American Political Science Association, Boston, August 2008; Robert Andersen and Tina Fetner, "Cohort Differences in Tolerance of Homosexuality: Attitudinal Change in Canada and the United States, 1981–2000," *Public Opinion Quarterly* 72 (2008): 311–330; and Jeffrey R. Lax and Justin H. Phillips, "Gay Rights in the States: Public Opinion and Policy Responsiveness," *American Political Science Review* 103 (2009): 367–386. On attitudes toward sexual issues, see Judith Treas, "How Cohorts, Education, and Ideology Shaped a New Sexual Revolution on American Attitudes toward Nonmarital Sex, 1972–1998," *Sociological Perspectives* 45 (2002): 267–283, and David J. Harding and Christopher Jencks, "Changing Attitudes toward Premarital Sex: Cohort, Period, and Aging Effects," *Public Opinion Quarterly* 67 (2003): 211–226.

respect to views on homosexuality and sexual freedom. Such a cohort effect would lead to a transitory disparity between public attitudes and political voice. Over time, however, public opinion and political voice would come to be in sync.

When coupled with inequalities in political activity, differences of opinion among age groups anchored in life-cycle effects pose a greater challenge to equality of political voice. Many government programs—of which Social Security and public education are obvious examples—target benefits on the basis of age. Figure 8.2 presents PACES data that show age structuring with respect to both opposition to any change in Social Security in the face of President George W. Bush's call for privatization and support for increased funding for K–12 education. Unlike younger people, the elderly—who had lived through the Depression of the 1930s, who would not be able to benefit from decades of appreciation of equity investments for retirement income, and who would be spared the brunt of any long-run insolvency in Social Security—would have reason to support maintaining the defined benefits feature of Social Security.[17] In light of such considerations, it is not surprising that the elderly were most likely to favor retaining a traditional approach to Social Security and younger age groups were more congenial to privatizing Social Security. In contrast, consistent with what we might expect, when it comes to educational funding, support for increases in spending on pre-collegiate education was highest among those who were under age twenty-five and eroded steadily across age groups. Similarly, in Figure 8.3—which repeats the data about support for increases in spending on precollegiate education and adds data about support for aid for students in higher education—the youngest group was the most likely, and the oldest group the least likely, to express support for such aid.

That these age differences in support for education versus Social Security—which make a great deal of prima facie sense—have persisted over time suggests that we are seeing attitudinal differences with life-cycle, rather than generational, roots.[18] The consequence of such continuing age-structured attitudinal differences is that, at least when it comes to political voice through individual activity, such youth-related matters as grants and loans for higher

17. Similarly, an item in the 2008 ANES about allowing people to invest their Social Security payroll taxes in stocks and bonds shows a sharp trajectory of increasing rejection among those over forty.

18. Although there is some disagreement, many studies demonstrate that senior citizens support policies beneficial to their self-interest. See, for example, William Mayer, *The Changing*

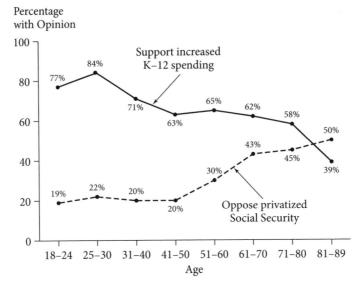

Figure 8.2 Support for Government Spending by Age: Percentage Who Support Increased K–12 Spending or Oppose Social Security Privatization

Source: Political Agendas and Citizen Engagement Survey (2004).

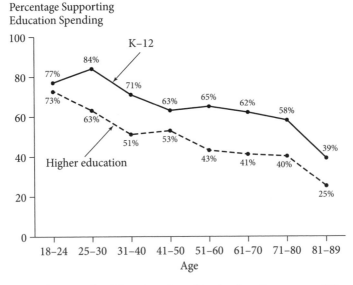

Figure 8.3 Support for Education Spending by Age: Percentage Who Support K–12 and Higher Education Spending

Source: Political Agendas and Citizen Engagement Survey (2004).

education will not achieve their proportionate share of advocacy. In fact, concerns about the continuing failure of the elderly to support education impelled Paul E. Peterson to propose, presumably in jest, that children—who are dependent for political voice and so much else on the kindness of their elders—should be allowed to vote so that they could protect their interests in government programs on their behalf in a manner parallel to the way that seniors have protected Social Security and Medicare.[19] Thus, if political preferences and interests change over the life cycle, enduring participatory differences among age groups would be of concern from the perspective of equality of political voice. Although each cohort would average out any age-related participatory differences over the life cycle, the distinctive concerns and needs of age groups with ongoing deficits in political activity would be underrepresented on a continuing basis—an obvious compromise of equality of political voice.[20]

American Mind: How and Why American Public Opinion Changed between 1960 and 1988 (Ann Arbor: University of Michigan Press, 1992); Susan A. MacManus, *Young versus Old: Generational Combat in the 21st Century* (Boulder, CO: Westview Press, 1996); Andrea Louise Campbell, *How Politics Makes Citizens: Senior Political Activism and the American Welfare State* (Princeton, NJ: Princeton University Press, 2003); and James H. Schulz and Robert H. Binstock, *Aging Nation: The Economics and Politics of Growing Older in America* (Westport, CT: Praeger, 2006).

A great deal of other research suggests that the elderly are less supportive of K–12 education. Cynthia Miller, in "Demographics and Spending for Public Education: A Test of Interest Group Influence," *Economics of Education Review* 15 (1996): 175–185, finds that spending on education increases with the percentage of parents in the state or county. James M. Poterba, in "Demographic Structure and the Political Economy of Public Education," NBER Working Paper W5677, National Bureau of Economic Research, Cambridge, MA, July 1996, and Amy Rehder Harris, William N. Evans, and Robert M. Schwab, in "Education Spending in an Aging America," *Journal of Public Economics* 81 (2001): 449–472, find that it decreases with the fraction of elderly residents in a jurisdiction. For a partly dissenting opinion, see Helen F. Ladd and Sheila E. Murray, "Intergenerational Conflict Reconsidered: County Demographic Structures and the Demand for Public Education," *Economics of Education Review* 20 (2001): 343–357. In "The Guns of Autumn? Age Differences in Support for Income Transfers to the Young and Old," *Public Opinion Quarterly* 52 (1988): 441–466, Michael Ponza, Greg J. Duncan, Mary Corcoran, and Fred Groskind find senior citizens to be less supportive of spending for education and welfare but show complex results for Social Security. Eric Plutzer and Michael Berkman, in "The Graying of America and Support for Funding the Nation's Schools," *Public Opinion Quarterly* 69 (2005): 66–86, agree that surveys have long showed older Americans to be less likely than younger citizens to endorse increased spending on public schools but argue that a cohort effect is in part responsible.

19. Paul E. Peterson, "An Immodest Proposal," *Daedalus* 121 (1992): 151–174.

20. For a philosophical discussion of the issue of how to reconcile the younger self with the older self, see Derek Parfit, *Reasons and Persons* (Oxford, England: Clarendon, 1984).

Why Would Age Groups Differ in Their Participation?

If shared generational experiences result in the widespread mobilization or deactivation of a group of young citizens on a long-term basis, that cohort will be advantaged, or disadvantaged, with respect to political voice in comparison to the generations that precede or succeed it.[21] When the gray of head rue the political apathy of the young, they make an implicit assumption that such generational processes are at work.

Still, there are reasons to expect variations in political participation over the life cycle. It is often argued that the young are less active in politics because they are unsettled and preoccupied with the enterprise of becoming adults. As a study of political participation conducted several decades ago put it: "In the early years one has the problem of 'start-up.' Individuals are still unsettled; they are likely to be residentially and occupationally mobile. They have yet to develop the stake in the politics of a particular locality that comes with extended residence, with home ownership, with children in school, and the like."[22] Some analysts who focus on the participatory consequences of the start-up phase focus on the impact of particular life events—for example, finding a job, getting married, buying a house, and having children. Beyond the ways that such life-cycle milestones function to anchor the unsettled into adulthood, owning a home and having children in school are presumed to give citizens a stake in public outcomes.

Focusing exclusively on life events may distract from the extent to which an array of changes over the life cycle will have repercussions for the accumulation of a variety of factors that foster participation.[23] Table 8.1 shows the differences among age groups with respect to a variety of such factors and gives evidence of both life-cycle and generational phenomena.[24] Because it is so rich in measures of a variety of participatory factors, we use the 1990 Citizen Participation Study. These data, which provide a cross-sectional snapshot, cannot be used to distinguish cohort and life-cycle effects. In fact, the

21. For a discussion of generational and period changes in participation, see Paul Allen Beck and M. Kent Jennings, "Political Periods and Political Participation," *American Political Science Review* 73 (1979): 737–750.

22. Sidney Verba and Norman H. Nie, *Participation in America* (New York: Harper and Row, 1972), p. 139.

23. See Chapter 1 for a discussion of the way that capacity, motivation, and location in social networks operate to foster political participation.

24. Question wording for the items summarized in Table 8.1 can be found in Sidney Verba, Kay Lehman Schlozman, and Henry E. Brady, *Voice and Equality: Civic Voluntarism in American Politics* (Cambridge, MA: Harvard University Press, 1995), Appendix B.

curvilinear patterns in the table could be due to the combined impact of age, period, or cohort effects.[25] Whenever possible, we use the 1952 to 2008 ANES to sort out cohort and life-cycle effects and report these results in footnotes.[26] Although the magnitude of effects may vary over time, we are confident that the pattern shown in Table 8.1 is correct.

Many of these participatory factors show a curvilinear pattern with the young, especially those under twenty-five, and the elderly commanding a much smaller stockpile of participatory factors than those in their forties and fifties. For example, those in their late teens or early twenties are neither especially well educated nor affluent.[27] Many of those who eventually achieve college, and especially post-graduate degrees, have not completed their education at this point. Although increasing numbers of nontraditional students return to college classrooms later on, most people complete their education by their mid-twenties.[28] When it comes to income, the twentysomethings are just beginning to establish their careers and are decades away from their peak earning power.[29] At the other end of the life cycle, the relatively low levels of educational attainment among those who are over age sixty probably represent a generational phenomenon—the fact that, at least until recently, successive cohorts have enjoyed widening educational opportunities—while low levels of family income reflect the life-cycle phenomenon of retirement.[30]

25. See Matilda White Riley, "Aging and Cohort Succession." For several reasons—ranging from necessity to the fact that, in any cross-section, period effects may have consequences for the level of participation without having an impact on its distribution—we neglect period effects in our analysis.

26. We use age and cohort dummy variables in repeated cross-sections to show that there is strong evidence of life-cycle effects even after controlling for cohorts.

27. An age and cohort regression using the ANES data confirms these results and demonstrates that, as discussed earlier, there is both a life-cycle and a cohort effect when it comes to education.

28. Muriel Egerton and Gareth Parry, "Lifelong Debt: Rates of Return to Mature Study," *Higher Education Quarterly* 55 (2001): 4–27; Jerry A. Jacobs and Rosalind Berkowitz King, "Age and College Completion: A Life-History Analysis of Women Aged 15–44," *Sociology of Education* 75 (2002): 211–230.

29. Economists estimate that about 30 percent of income inequality is due to life-cycle effects. See Alan Blinder, *Toward an Economic Theory of Income Distribution* (Cambridge, MA: MIT Press, 1974). Note that the youngest respondents, those under age twenty-five, reported higher family incomes but lower earnings than those in their late twenties. Presumably, a larger share of those in their early twenties are including their parents' incomes in the family incomes they report.

30. Norman H. Nie, Jane Junn, and Kenneth Stehlik-Barry emphasize the importance for political activity of relative rather than absolute levels of education and point out that, as the public has become better educated, levels of political participation have not kept pace. See

Table 8.1 Age and the Factors that Foster Political Activity

	Age Groups						
	18–24	25–30	31–40	41–50	51–60	61–70	71+
Education							
High School Diploma (Percent)	86%	91%	92%	90%	80%	74%	62%
College Graduate (Percent)	9%	29%	29%	30%	26%	18%	18%
Free Time (Mean Number of Hours per Day)	5.8	4.9	4.8	5.4	6.8	10.6	13.1
Income (Thousands of Dollars)							
Mean Family Income	$40.9	$36.4	$41.1	$50.4	$44.4	$33.0	$25.1
Mean Earnings (All Respondents)	$6.6	$17.8	$22.9	$27.2	$23.6	$7.1	$1.1
Mean Earnings (Working Only)	$9.8	$22.7	$27.0	$32.6	$33.1	$26.6	$40.4
Mean Civic Skills[a]							
On the Job	0.85	1.54	1.79	1.98	1.48	0.49	0.04
In a Nonpolitical Organization	0.36	0.50	0.65	0.67	0.68	0.79	0.57
At Church	0.34	0.31	0.48	0.49	0.42	0.52	0.44

Mean Number of Requests for Activity						
On the Job	0.13	0.17	0.23	0.24	0.10	0.04	0.01
In a Nonpolitical Organization	0.06	0.07	0.08	0.08	0.07	0.07	0.07
At Church	0.25	0.26	0.32	0.36	0.27	0.22	0.25
Psychological Engagement with Politics							
Political Interest[b]	3.0	3.5	3.7	4.0	4.0	4.1	3.7
Political Information[c]							
Civic Information (Percent)	56%	57%	60%	61%	54%	56%	48%
Knowledge of Names (Percent)	24%	32%	42%	50%	46%	53%	47%
Political Efficacy[d]	4.7	5.2	5.4	5.6	5.2	5.4	4.6
Strong Partisanship (Percent)	22%	25%	29%	32%	38%	47%	43%

Source: Citizen Participation Study (1990).

[a] Mean on an additive scale including the following: writing a letter, going to a meeting where the respondent took part in making decisions, planning or chairing a meeting, giving a presentation or speech, contacting a government official.
[b] Mean on an additive scale measuring the amount of expressed interest—ranging from "not at all interested" to "very interested"—in national and local politics and affairs.
[c] Percentage correct on each part of a political information scale consisting of five items testing knowledge of government and politics and three asking about the names of public officials
[d] Mean on an additive scale of four items about how much attention a local or national government official would pay if the respondent had a complaint and how much influence the respondent has over local or national government decisions.

Leaving school and getting a full-time job is clearly one of the stepping-stones to adulthood, but it is not so much the fact of having a job as the association between paid work and several of the factors that foster political participation that matters for political participation. Jobs produce income, and those with jobs have opportunities to learn civic skills useful for political activity and become the targets of requests for political involvement. Obviously, such job-related participatory factors are available only to those who are employed, a group that includes relatively few of the elderly. And of course jobs vary not only in the extent to which they provide income, civic skills, and exposure to requests for activity but also in the extent to which opportunities to acquire such participatory factors grow with accumulated workforce experience.

Involvement in nonpolitical organizations and religious institutions functions in a parallel manner to facilitate political participation. Presumably reflecting reduced levels of involvement and leadership in these venues, once again, the young and the elderly are less likely than those in between to gain civic skills or to be asked to take part politically in either of these venues.[31]

When it comes to several measures of psychological engagement with politics—measures not obviously attached to a particular life-cycle event but

---

their *Education and Democratic Citizenship in America* (Chicago: University of Chicago Press, 1996).

31. These deficits in participatory factors among the elderly are consistent with a perspective, called disengagement theory, emphasizing that many of the very elderly have physical infirmities that impair their mobility and thus their ability to be active in civic life. In fact, research has discredited the idea that as people age they disengage from the world in favor of a more nuanced description of withdrawal to activities more appropriate to their age, with potential implications for politics. Norval D. Glenn and Michael Grimes, in "Aging, Voting, and Political Interest," *American Sociological Review* 33 (1968): 563–573, consider but reject disengagement theory, as do M. Kent Jennings and Gregory Markus in "Political Involvement in the Later Years: A Longitudinal Study," *American Journal of Political Science* 32 (1988): 302–316. The latter authors propose (p. 302) "selective withdrawal," in which "participation in the more demanding modes declined following the transition to old age," but point out that these "declines were partly offset by increased involvement of the elderly in age-appropriate activities that can have direct political consequences."

We should also note a measurement issue. In the Citizen Participation Study, the items measuring the exercise of civic skills at work asked those currently in the workforce about such work-based activities as organizing a meeting within the past six months. Respondents who were retired were not asked these questions. Because having exercised civic skills at work might be expected to have a lasting effect into retirement, especially for those with long work histories in highly skilled jobs, the measure of civic skills, on average, underestimates the civic skills of the retired.

very powerful as predictors of political participation—those under age twenty-five show low levels of involvement. The single exception is textbook knowledge of the principles of American government—such matters as whether the Fifth Amendment shields freedom of speech or provides protection from forced confessions or whether the government spends more money on the National Aeronautics and Space Administration or on Social Security. Otherwise, younger respondents show a deficit when it comes to political interest, the knowledge of names of contemporary public officials, political efficacy, and strength of partisanship—all of which are strongly associated with participation in politics.[32]

Free time—that is, time unencumbered by responsibilities to paid work, school, or home and family—is the sole participatory resource for which the youngest, and especially the oldest, age groups are not disadvantaged in comparison to those in between.

Disparities in Participation among Age Groups

Consistent with these considerations and the findings of other researchers, political participation follows a curvilinear pattern across age groups.[33] Let us consider first the disparities among age groups with respect to the political act on which scholarly attention has tended to focus exclusively, electoral turnout. Figure 8.4 presents U.S. Census data from 2008 and shows that voting turnout and voting registration were lowest among the young and increased for each age group before declining somewhat among the elderly.[34]

32. Using the ANES cumulative file to sort out cohort and life-cycle effects for these kinds of factors, we can show that these results are not mostly due to cohort effects. These data show that young people are much less interested than older people and that interest peaks when people are in their fifties or sixties. Similarly, partisan strength is lowest for the youngest age group, and it steadily increases throughout the age groups. The only exception is that data derived from the cumulative ANES about a different measure of political efficacy, this one measuring personal efficacy (that is, how much "say" the respondent has over what the government does), show a completely different pattern, with younger respondents more politically efficacious than their elders.

33. Although this pattern emerges in data from other sources, age-group differences are more pronounced in the Citizen Participation Study. We are not certain whether this difference reflects a generational phenomenon, the particular attention paid to measuring acts of participation in that questionnaire, or something else.

34. Numerous scholarly inquiries have found a genuine life-cycle effect with respect to voting turnout. See Norval D. Glenn and Michael Grimes, "Aging, Voting, and Political Interest," *American Sociological Review* 33 (1968): 563–573; John M. Strate, Charles J. Parrish, Charles D. Elder, and Coit Ford, "Life Span Civic Development and Voting Participation,"

Percentage

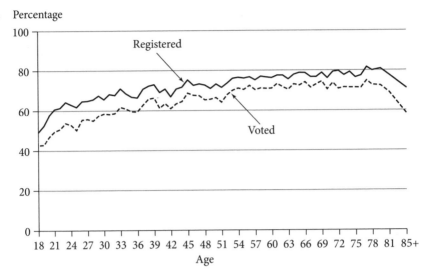

Figure 8.4   Registered and Voting by Age, 2008

Source: U.S. Census Bureau (2008).

This age-related arc for turnout has been observed every election year since survey research on voting began.[35]

Moving beyond the vote to a more expansive understanding of individual political voice, we see a similar trajectory in Figure 8.5, in which we use data from a 2008 survey conducted by the Pew Internet and American Life Project and an additive scale of eight political acts.[36] On average, those in their fifties, who are the most active group, engage in roughly 0.65 more acts than

American Political Science Review 83 (1989): 443–464; Warren E. Miller and J. Merrill Shanks, *The New American Voter* (Cambridge, MA: Harvard University Press, 1996); Richard J. Timpone, "Structure, Behavior, and Voter Turnout in the United States," *American Political Science Review* 92 (1998): 145–158; and Eric Plutzer, "Becoming a Habitual Voter: Inertia, Resources, and Growth in Young Adulthood," *American Political Science Review* 96 (2002): 41–56.

35. In 1948, turnout was 41 percent for those in the youngest group (21–24), rising to 75 percent for those between 45 and 54, then falling back to 59 percent for those between 65 and 74. Similar results hold for each subsequent ANES conducted in a presidential election year.

36. The scale includes the following acts: being registered to vote; working for a political party or candidate; contributing money to a political candidate or party; contacting a government official about an issue; working with fellow citizens to solve a problem in the community; attending a political meeting on local, town or school affairs; attending an organized protest of some kind; and being an active member of a group that tries to influence public policy or government. The point in the life cycle at which participation peaks before declining varies among political acts and across data sets.

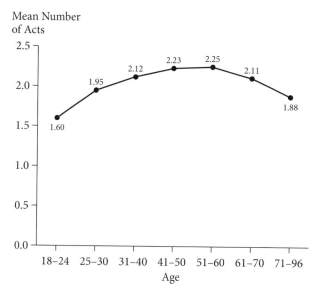

Figure 8.5   Mean Political Acts by Age

Source: Pew Internet and American Life Survey (2008).

Note: The figure indicates the mean number of political acts from an 8-act scale that includes registering to vote; working for a political party or candidate; contributing money to a political candidate or party; contacting a government official about an issue; working with fellow citizens to solve a problem in the community; attending a political meeting on local, town, or school affairs; attending an organized protest of some kind; and being an active member of a group that tries to influence public policy or government.

those under twenty-five and roughly 0.37 more acts than those who are seventy and over. If we separate out the components in the scale measuring overall participation, it becomes clear that individual forms of political activity do not all conform to this pattern. As shown in Table 8.2, the two least common activities—working for a political party or candidate and attending a protest—are the province of the young. Although these two activities are rare in any age group, those in the youngest age group are the most likely to engage in them, and the share declines with age. The participation rates for the remaining six activities all take on a more or less curvilinear shape. There is a particularly steep start-up for younger people when it comes to registering to vote and contacting government officials and a particularly steep "wind-down" for the elderly when it comes to involvement in community affairs.

Table 8.2 Age and Political Participation

	Percentage of Each Age Group Who Engaged in Each Activity							
	18–24	25–30	31–40	41–50	51–60	61–70	71+
Registered to Vote	55%	73%	77%	84%	86%	83%	89%
Worked for a Political Party or Candidate	11%	9%	8%	8%	8%	8%	6%
Made a Political Contribution	7%	13%	18%	20%	23%	22%	21%
Contacted a Government Official	16%	27%	28%	29%	39%	36%	28%
Worked with Others to Solve a Community Problem	25%	30%	30%	33%	27%	27%	21%
Attended a Local Meeting	23%	22%	29%	30%	23%	19%	15%
Attended a Protest	9%	5%	4%	3%	2%	2%	2%
Affiliated with a Group that Takes Stands in Politics	14%	18%	18%	16%	17%	14%	6%

Source: Pew Internet and American Life Project Survey (August 2008).

Accounting for Age Differences in Political Participation

From the perspective of inequalities of political voice, we have observed two critical patterns: there are significant differences in political activity across age groups, and age groups differ in their political attitudes and concerns—in ways that reflect both generation and life cycle. In Chapter 5 we discussed differences in political voice among politically relevant groups—in particular between women and men and among African Americans, non-Hispanic whites, and Latinos. There we made the point that, even if those group disparities could be explained in terms of other factors that are associated with political activity, especially social class, what matters for inequalities of political voice is the fact of the disparities rather than the other attributes that account for them. The same argument can be made here. Still, it seems worth placing participatory differences among age groups in the context of our understanding of the factors that foster political activity.

The differences among age groups with respect to two components of social class, income and education, have obvious consequences for participation. Figure 8.6 shows for SES quintiles the average score on the eight-point scale measuring overall participation for each of seven age groups and confirms an ongoing theme of our inquiry, the strength of the association between social class and participation. The lines for the age groups cluster together and, as expected, for each one, average participation rises sharply with SES.[37]

Considering an Array of Participatory Factors

Our account of participation in politics rests on understanding a variety of attributes in addition to SES that foster political activity. Some of them—for example, exposure to a politically rich home environment, experiences in student government and other organized activities while in high school, and high levels of educational attainment—are more or less fixed in childhood and adolescence and brought into adulthood.[38] Others—for example, income, civic skills, and interest in and knowledge about politics—can vary with adult experiences in such domains as the family, workplace, and church.

---

37. The only obvious exception is the sharp drop in the highest SES quintile for those between eighteen and twenty-four years of age, which is probably sampling error due to the very small sample size of only ten respondents.

38. On the significance for adult political engagement of the nonpolitical voluntary involvement of youth, see Daniel A. McFarland and Reuben J. Thomas, "Bowling Young: How Youth Voluntary Associations Influence Adult Political Participation," *American Sociological Review* 71 (2006): 401–425.

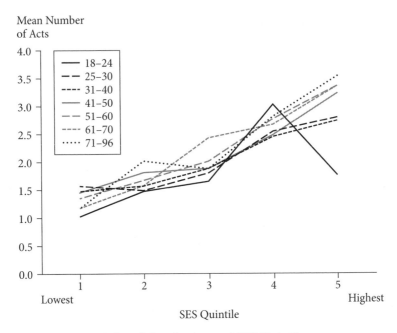

Mean Number
of Acts

Figure 8.6   Mean Political Acts by Age and SES Quintile

Source: Pew Internet and American Life Survey (2008).

Note: For definitions of political acts see note to Figure 8.5.

A number of these variables have a generational as well as a life-cycle component. We have mentioned that, at least until recently, successive generations have become, on average, better and better educated. Furthermore, Robert Putnam has shown substantial generational differences between the long civic generation, born roughly between 1910 and 1940, and Generation X, born between 1964 and 1980, with respect to a variety of attitudinal and behavioral measures of civic commitment and engagement.[39]

To gain a sense of whether differences in these factors explain the participation gaps among age groups, we employ two complementary methods. First we turn to the data from the 1990 Citizen Participation Study. Because these data are cross-sectional, they have serious liabilities for our attempt to

39. Robert D. Putnam, *Bowling Alone: The Collapse and Revival of American Community* (New York: Simon and Schuster, 2000), chap. 14. See also Stephen Bennett, Staci Rhine, and Richard Flickinger, "Young Americans' Attention to Media Accounts of Politics," paper delivered at the Annual Meeting of the Midwest Political Science Association, Chicago, April 2007.

understand the differences among age groups in political activity, in particular, the extent to which such differences reflect generational or life-cycle effects. Still, because they contain such a rich array of relevant measures, they are helpful in illuminating both the relative importance of various factors in explaining political activity and the extent to which age-group differences with respect to these factors explain the disparities in participation. Second we use the ANES cumulative data to separate out life-cycle and cohort effects. Although the ANES lacks many relevant measures, its repeated cross-sections make it possible to control for cohort effects and to identify the remaining effects as due to life-cycle factors.[40]

Table 8.3 presents the results of an ordinary least squares analysis of data from the Citizen Participation Study in which the dependent variable is an eight-point measure of overall political activity. Even with many variables taken into account, several aspects of the legacy of the years before adulthood are significantly associated with political participation: exposure to a politically rich home environment, participation in student government and other activities in high school, and especially educational attainment. In addition, a number of factors related to development during adulthood are associated with political activity: family income, civic skills and requests for activity associated with the workplace, involvement in non-political organizations and religious institutions, and various measures of political engagement—in particular, interest in politics. It is noteworthy that, with these factors controlled, the amount of free time available has absolutely no impact on political participation, a finding that has emerged from these data over and over again.[41]

The evidence for the impact of particular life events is much more mixed. In spite of the frequently heard comment "It wasn't until I had kids in school that I got involved in the issues in this town," we find much more limited confirmation of the hypothesis that lower levels of activity among the young are a function of their not yet having assumed the responsibilities of adulthood—job, marriage, children, and home ownership. On one hand, home ownership and the number of years in the community retain positive effects on activity even with everything else taken into account—suggesting that the stake in the

40. As indicated earlier, we are not treating period effects.

41. Although the amount of available leisure does not predict political participation, among those who take part in politics, spare time does predict how much time is devoted to voluntary political activity. See Verba, Schlozman, and Brady, *Voice and Equality*, pp. 340–341 and 357, and Burns, Schlozman, and Verba, *Private Roots of Public Action*, pp. 256–257.

Table 8.3   Predicting Overall Political Activity:
Ordinary Least Squares Regression

Variable	B	SE B	Beta
Age			
18–24	–.64***	.13	–.12
25–30	–.44***	.10	–.10
31–40	–.02	.08	–.01
41–50	Baseline Group		
51–60	.13	.10	.02
61–70	–.12	.12	–.02
71+	–.32*	.16	–.05
Other Demographic Characteristics			
Female	–.02	.06	–.01
Black	.07	.09	.01
Latino	–.04	.13	–.01
The Legacy of Youth			
Politics at Home	.04*	.02	.04
High School Activity	.10***	.03	.06
Education	.16***	.02	.15
Resources			
Family Income	.04***	.01	.07
Earnings	.01	.01	.02
Free Time	–.01	.01	–.02
Civic Skills	.10***	.02	.14
Nonpolitical Involvements			
Affiliation with an Organization	.02	.06	.00
Church Attendance	–.02	.01	–.03
Requests for Activity	.23***	.03	.13
Political Engagement			
Political Interest	.23***	.02	.22
Political Information	.09***	.02	.10
Political Efficacy	.08***	.01	.11
Partisanship	.08**	.03	.04
Community Roots			
Years in Community	.00*	.00	.05
Own Home	.21***	.06	.06

continued

Table 8.3   Continued

Variable	B	SE B	Beta
Marital Status			
Married	−.09	.09	−.03
Separated or Divorced	−.25*	.10	−.05
Widowed	−.34*	.14	−.06
Single (Never Married)	Baseline Group		
Children			
Preschool Age	−.12	.08	−.03
School Age	−.13	.08	−.03
Employment Status			
Student	−.48*	.20	−.05
Full-Time Work	−.66***	.16	−.20
Part-Time Work	−.57***	.16	−.10
Retired	Baseline Group		
Unemployed or Other	−.59***	.16	−.09
Keeping House	−.37**	.13	−.08
Job Level	−.01	.02	−.01
Constant	−1.08***	.25	

Source: Citizen Participation Study (1990).

Note: The dependent variable is an 8-act measure of political activity that includes the following: voting; working in a campaign; contributing to a campaign; contacting a public official; taking part in a protest, march, or demonstration; working with others in the community to solve a local problem; serving on a local community board or regularly attending meetings of such a board; and being affiliated with an organization that takes stands in politics.
*Significant at the .05 level; **significant at the .01 level; ***significant at the .001 level.

community that accompanies owning a home and long residence does make a difference.

On the other hand, whatever association there is between the role of worker, spouse, or parent and increased participation results either from selection effects such that those who take on adult roles have other characteristics that predispose them to take part or from indirect effects such that these roles lead to greater involvement in civil society or, in particular, increased political engagement. Compared to being retired, being in the workforce, especially full time, which had been presumed to increase an individual's stake in political outcomes and thus to serve as a spur to activity, has a negative impact, as do being a student, being unemployed, or being at home—even with age and leisure time taken into account.[42] However, there is a significant association between political participation and what happens at work in terms of the development of civic skills and exposure to requests for political activity—which are, of course, dependent on having a job.

With respect to marriage and family, although being widowed, divorced, or separated are all negatively associated with political activity compared to being single, marriage and the presence of either preschool or school-aged children at home are not significantly related to political participation. Further analysis shows very modest indirect effects from having children at home, effects that are opposite in direction for men and women.[43] Because, on average, women reduce their workforce commitment when they have children at home, the resultant impact on workplace-based skills and recruitment implies a perceptible but tiny diminution of their political activity. For men, both marriage and children at home enhance their commitment to paid work and their involvement in religious institutions, thus leading indirectly to an increase in political participation that, while still very slight, is more than twice as large as the negative impact of children on women's activity.

Interestingly, accounting for these many factors leaves no statistically significant difference in participation between men and women or among non-Hispanic whites, African Americans, and Latinos. However, it does not go the distance in terms of explaining the participatory gap between the most active age group, those in their forties, and either the young or the elderly:

	Initial Deficit Compared to Those in Their Forties	Deficit Remaining after Accounting for Participatory Factors
Under 25	1.25 acts	0.64 act
25–30	0.88 act	0.44 act
71 and over	0.64 act	0.32 act

42. As indicated in note 31, the Citizen Participation Study did not ask retired respondents about the exercise of civic skills in their previous jobs. We speculate that the positive association between retirement and political activity results from the residual effects of a lifetime of work in terms of civic skills.

43. This analysis is reported in Burns, Schlozman, and Verba, *Private Roots of Public Action*, pp. 316–321.

Once the various participatory factors have been taken into account, the participatory deficits at the near and far ends of the life cycle, while still statistically significant, have been reduced by about half and the familiar curvilinear pattern is harder to discern.

That a variety of participatory factors together account for differences in activity between groups based on gender and on race or ethnicity—but not for disparities in political activity among age groups—is intriguing. One explanation for the participatory gaps that remain is that there are likely to be unmeasured attributes that not only vary systematically with age but have consequences for participation. For example, chronic illness, a variable that was not measured, has been shown to depress participation; we would expect the elderly to be especially likely to face chronic illness. Without appropriate measures, we are able to do nothing more than speculate.[44] Furthermore, there are generational processes at work with differential effects on the various age groups in the 1990 Citizen Participation Study. That is, if, as is often argued, the members of Generation X, who were under thirty at the time of the survey, entered the electorate at particularly low rates of political activity, the participatory factors that account for differences in activity among other groups would be insufficient to account fully for the participatory deficit among the young. We investigate this possibility in the next section.

In Chapter 6 we saw that processes of habituation such that, once having taken part, individuals become more likely to do so again, apart from the other characteristics that predispose them to participate, operate only for voting and not for other participatory acts. Because voting is one of the political acts on the scale and because the young have low rates of turnout, habituation may have a tiny role in explaining the deficit of activity among those under thirty, a role that would be nearly impossible to measure.

How Important Are Life-Cycle Effects for Political Participation?

The other interpretation of the unexplained participatory gaps among age groups is that they represent generational rather than life-cycle phenomena. There is a great deal of evidence that, compared to their predecessors, cohorts that have entered the electorate recently are less likely to vote or to engage in

44. Steven A. Peterson, in "Biosocial Predictors of Older Americans' Political Participation," *Politics and the Life Sciences* 5 (1987): 246–251, finds evidence for a relationship between health status and political orientations and behaviors.

other forms of activity.[45] We are led to ask whether there are any life-cycle effects at all. Unfortunately, the sophisticated econometric methods used in Chapter 6 to seek evidence of processes of habituation have three defects. They require at least three-wave panels in which the same people are interviewed three times in succession. They need very large samples of data to detect effects because they have low statistical power. And, perhaps most important, with measurement periods just four years long, they fall short of the time period required to capture most life-cycle effects. We now turn to a method that, while it has limitations, has the virtue of being simple and straightforward. We use the repeated data cross-sections for all presidential elections from 1952 to 2008 from the ANES to search for life-cycle effects while controlling for cohort effects. To control for cohort effects, we ran regressions that had dummy variables both for age groups and for cohorts.[46]

Figure 8.7 plots for each of five political acts the net life-cycle (or age-group) effects estimated from separate regressions, which include controls for cohort effects, for each act. Because we chose those between forty-one and fifty as the baseline group for the regressions, all the curves for that age group go through zero for ages forty-one to fifty. The values on each curve that can be read off the vertical axis are percentage increases or decreases in the activity from that baseline for each of the other age groups. Because the ANES traditionally focuses on participatory acts related to elections, four of them are electoral. Except for voting, all of them are relatively rare: voting (74 percent); writing a letter to a government official (24 percent); giving money to a candidate or party (10 percent); working for a candidate (4 per-

45. See, for example, William Lyons and Robert Alexander, "A Tale of Two Electorates: Generational Replacement and the Decline of Voting in Presidential Elections," *Journal of Politics* 62 (2000): 1014–1034; Marc Hooghe, "Political Socialization and the Future of Politics," *Acta Politica* 39 (2004): 331–341; Cliff Zukin, Scott Keeter, Molly Andolina, Krista Jenkins, and Michael X. Delli Carpini, *A New Engagement? Political Participation, Civic Life, and the Changing American Citizen* (Oxford, England: Oxford University Press, 2006); Martin P. Wattenberg, *Is Voting for Young People? With a Postscript on Citizen Engagement* (New York: Pearson Longman, 2008); Kaat Smets, "In Need of an Update or Overdue? Re-evaluating the Political Life-Cycle Model," paper delivered at the Annual Meeting of the Midwest Political Science Association, Chicago, April 3–6, 2008; Constance Flanagan and Peter Levine, "Civic Engagement and the Transition to Adulthood," *Future of Children* 20 (2010): 159–179. Various authors point to compensatory factors. Hooghe shows that younger cohorts, although less politically involved, display greater tolerance, and Zukin et al. show that they demonstrate a greater commitment to nonpolitical voluntary activity.

46. See Appendix D for an explication of our methods and their limitations as well as discussion of the reasons that we feel justified in ignoring period effects.

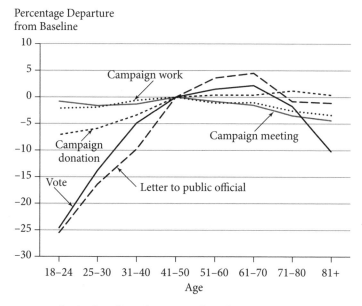

Percentage Departure
from Baseline

Figure 8.7   Life-Cycle Effects for Five Political Acts: Percentage Departure in Activity for Each Act from That of Baseline Age Group (41–50) in Cohort-Corrected Regressions

Source: American National Election Studies (1952–2008).

cent); and attending political meetings, rallies, and the like in support of a candidate (7 percent). For all five of the activities, there are clear processes of start-up for younger people. That is, apart from cohort effects, the youngest citizens are less likely than their middle-aged counterparts to undertake any of the five acts. Not unexpectedly for a set of acts of quite varying frequency, the magnitude of the deficit differs across the acts and is especially pronounced for writing to public officials, voting, and, to a lesser extent, making contributions. On the basis of what we saw earlier in the chapter, had we had access to data about taking part in protests, we would have expected a very different pattern and no shortfall among new voters. We also see processes of wind-down for older people that are particularly marked for the three activities that, under most circumstances, require leaving home to accomplish: voting, working in a campaign, and going to a political meeting. Thus, with the controls for cohort, these data strongly suggest that there are real life-cycle effects at work.

We took this analysis one step further to see if we could explain away life-cycle effects by cohort differences or by changing participatory factors over a lifetime. We constructed a five-act scale of political activity that includes four of the five acts just discussed (all but writing a letter) and that adds another act (talking to people about why they should vote).[47] Using this scale as the dependent variable, we conducted three separate regressions to identify raw life-cycle effects, life-cycle effects adjusted for cohort differences, and life-cycle effects after adjusting for cohort differences and participatory factors.

The solid line in Figure 8.8 shows the highly curvilinear raw life-cycle effects for this five-act scale. Because we are interested only in how the shape of this curve changes as we control for various factors, we set the participation of those in the forty-one to fifty age group at zero even though, in fact, their participation averages 1.4 acts throughout the period. Although those who are a decade older (between fifty-one and sixty years of age) are slightly more active than this baseline group, all other age groups are less active—as much as four-tenths of an act less active for the youngest and oldest age groups, which means that these two groups actually average about one act. The dashed line shows that, once we control for cohort differences, the life-cycle effects for older people are somewhat less pronounced. Adding to the regression participatory factors such as education, income, and various measures of psychological engagement with politics explains even more of the raw life-cycle effects and yields the dotted line at the top of the diagram. Although the arc has about half the depth that we saw for the raw life-cycle curve, the line still retains a curvilinear shape.

Our analyses surely show variation in political activity over the life cycle. Two regressions using somewhat different measures of political participation as dependent variables—one using data from the Citizen Participation Study, which includes an array of participatory factors, and the other adjusting for cohort effects while using the narrower array of participatory factors available in the ANES—conclude that there are life-cycle effects even after controlling for a large number of factors. In addition, the controls in both regressions—such as education, income, partisan strength, and political interest—themselves exhibit life-cycle effects. There can be no question about the reality of true life-cycle differences in political participation.

---

47. We did not use "writing a letter" because it was not asked in all the years. The item asking whether the respondent talked to any people and tried to show them why they should vote was asked throughout the period.

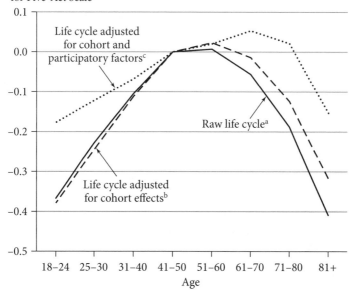

Effect of Life-Cycle
for Five-Act Scale

Figure 8.8   Life-Cycle Effects of Political Activity: Raw Effects, Cohort-Adjusted Effects, and Cohort- and Participatory Factors–Adjusted Effects

Source: American National Election Studies (1952–2008).

Note: The dependent variable is a 5-act scale that includes voting; talking to people about why they should vote; giving money to a candidate or party; working for a candidate; and attending political meetings.

[a] This line indicates how much each age group's average participation on the 5-act scale departs from that of the reference group (41–50).

[b] This line indicates how much each age group's average participation on the 5-act scale departs from that of the reference group (41–50) after a regression adjustment for cohort differences.

[c] This line indicates how much each age group's average participation on the 5-act scale departs from that of the reference group (41–50) after a regression adjustment for participatory factors and cohort differences.

Conclusion

In spite of attention by pundits to the lack of involvement of the younger generation, political scientists have long discerned a curvilinear pattern across the life cycle such that participation is relatively low among those entering the electorate, picks up among those in their thirties, peaks among the middle aged, and tails off among the elderly. We have found that same pattern in several data sets.

From one perspective, the attendant disparities in political voice differ from those rooted in such politically relevant categories as race or gender. To the extent that they are anchored in life-cycle effects, the young need only be patient; with time their levels of political participation will increase in middle age. At the other end of the life cycle, the elderly have had their chance. However, these disparities among age groups in political activity are accompanied by age-related differences in political preferences and concerns. Therefore, even though political voice can be equalized across the life cycle for those who live a normal life span, the age-related gaps in political participation have consequences for inequality of political voice. Furthermore, if there are cohort effects that accompany a particular generation across the life cycle, that group will enjoy a participatory advantage or suffer a participatory disadvantage on a sustained basis. Once again, equality of political voice would be compromised.

Although we do not have a long-term panel containing rich measures of both participatory factors and political acts, which would allow us to solve the puzzles posed by differences among age groups in political activity, we mobilized a number of data sets and some complicated methods in pursuit of that objective. A cross-sectional regression that included a variety of factors known to be associated with participation showed that, with the exception of owning a home and staying put residentially, the milestones of adulthood do not really function as expected in enhancing participation directly. Any discernible participatory consequences of getting a job, getting married, or having children result either from selection effects or from the way that the resulting adult statuses lead to the acquisition of participatory factors in such venues as the workplace or religious institutions and thus indirectly to increased political activity. In fact, the more powerful predictors of political activity among adults are such factors—many of them rooted in social class—as resources, psychological orientations to politics, and location in networks that mediate requests to take part.

That said, these participatory factors were not able to explain fully the disparities among age groups in overall participation. Ordinarily, a model focusing on the role of resources, motivation, and recruitment is able to account for participatory differences among demographic groups. Leaving aside the critical question of why groups distinguished by gender or race differ in class-based participatory factors, we are able to specify what it is about being African American or being female that leads to lower rates of political participation.[48] The disparity in participation between African Americans and Anglo whites disappears when racial differences in education and income are taken into account. The gap in activity between women and men can be fully explained by gender differences in education, income, civic skills, and political engagement. Life-cycle differences seem to persist even after controlling for a large number of factors. In fact, the *unexplained portion* of the disparity between the most and least active age groups is actually twice as large as the initial gap in activity between African Americans and Anglo whites or between women and men—before anything else is taken into account.

Using data from ANES panel studies and from more than a half century of ANES cross-sections, we were able to investigate further the origins of gaps among age groups in participation and found evidence for both cohort and life-cycle effects. Still, as important as it is to distinguish these effects in order to understand the roots of disparities in participation among age groups, from the perspective of equality of political voice, what matters is the fact of those disparities.

48. See, for example, Sidney Verba, Kay Lehman Schlozman, and Henry E. Brady, "Race, Ethnicity, and Political Participation," in *Classifying by Race*, ed. Paul E. Peterson (Princeton, NJ: Princeton University Press, 1995), chap. 15, and Burns, Schlozman, and Verba, *Private Roots of Public Action*, chap. 10.

9

Political Activism and Electoral Democracy: Perspectives on Economic Inequality and Political Polarization

The great instrument of political equality in a democracy is the election. When we think about the operation of elections in America, we focus on the essential equality among voters, each of whom has one vote. We rarely incorporate the fundamental insight of the last several chapters: that year after year, decade after decade, and from one generation to the next, the affluent and well educated have participatory megaphones that amplify their voices in American politics. These class-based participatory inequalities shape what politicians hear about political needs, concerns, and preferences. Not only are those who take part in politics less likely to have unmet needs for health insurance or suitable housing, but they are also less centrist in their political opinions. Placing our understanding of the operation of elections in the context of these obstinate participatory inequalities helps us to rethink political outcomes in America. In this chapter we use survey data to show how the predictions about income distribution and party convergence derived from an influential model of electoral democracy should be reconsidered when viewed in light of the socio-economic characteristics and the distinctive policy preferences of those who become involved politically by voting, working in campaigns, and especially making campaign contributions.

The Downsian Model and the Consequences of Participatory Inequality

We begin with a modified version of one of the most powerful models of American democracy, the model of party competition contained in Anthony

Downs's 1957 volume, *An Economic Theory of Democracy*.[1] The Downsian model rests on the equal weight of voters, who can be arrayed from left to right on a small number of political issues, and on the power of the median or middle position on those issues to dictate what politicians will do, especially in a two-party system. It makes clear that politicians who wish to get elected have an incentive to take voters' issue positions into account. According to Downs, in a two-party, first-past-the-post plurality voting system such as that of the United States, rational, vote-seeking politicians have an incentive to appeal to the median position because that is where elections are decided. Our modification takes into account participatory inequality and its impact on the effective median.[2] We argue that the median voter is not necessarily in the same position as the median campaign volunteer, the median campaign donor, or—because contributors give such different amounts—the person giving the median dollar. We find that American participatory inequalities yield greater pressure for conservative positions on economic policy matters such as income redistribution, somewhat greater pressure for liberal positions on social issues such as abortion and gay rights, and, because Democratic and Republican Party activists of higher socio-economic status (SES) have such different political opinions, increased political polarization.

Downs's model and its implications for politics and policy have engendered a great deal of scholarly attention. They have been the subject of general discussion; they have been elaborated in formal models, and they have been subject to empirical test.[3] But we do not have to come to conclusions

---

1. Anthony Downs, *An Economic Theory of Democracy* (New York: Harper and Row, 1957). See also Duncan Black, *The Theory of Committees and Elections* (Cambridge, England: Cambridge University Press, 1958). A review of the model's contributions is contained in Bernard Grofman, ed., *Information, Participation, and Choice: An Economic Theory of Democracy in Perspective* (Ann Arbor: University of Michigan Press, 1993).

2. The great virtue of the Downsian model is that it combines the informational and incentive aspects of voting into one model that predicts the public policy outcome of political competition. Our modifications of it show how the tilt due to participatory inequality could both convey more upper-class policy positions and provide incentives for politicians to enact policies favoring those positions.

3. A succinct and clear general statement arguing on behalf of the empirical track record of the median vote model can be found in Roger D. Congleton, "The Median Voter Model," in *The Encyclopedia of Public Choice*, vol. 2, ed. Charles K. Rowley and Friedrich Schneider (Boston: Kluwer Academic Publishers, 2004), pp. 382–386. Bernard Grofman, in a review article, "Downs and Two-Party Convergence," *Annual Review of Political Science* 7 (2004): 25–46, argues that, while the "classic comic-book" version of Downs leads to the expectation of party and candidate convergence, a more sophisticated reading of Downs does not. The following are less sanguine about how well the median voter model stands up empirically in

about this vast literature or to adopt all the assumptions, assertions, and predictions that are bundled into what has become known as the "spatial model" of party competition.[4]

Although Downs emphasized politicians' responsiveness to voters, he did not say much about the consequences of other forms of participation, especially those in which activists can multiply the volume of their input. When we incorporate inequalities in political participation beyond voting into our understanding, we not only show how participatory inequality matters but we also shed light on two of Downs's widely discussed predictions about political outcomes in a democracy. First, in order to ensure that they receive the majority of the electorate they need to win, in two-party systems rational, vote-maximizing parties—and, presumably, their candidates—have incentives to converge at the preferences of the median voter.[5] At one level, this insight

---

extended discussions: Morris P. Fiorina, "Whatever Happened to the Median Voter?" paper delivered at the MIT Conference on Parties and Congress, Cambridge, MA, October, 1999, and Ian Shapiro, *The State of Democratic Theory* (Princeton, NJ: Princeton University Press, 2003). These works contain numerous helpful references.

For formal models, see Thomas Romer, "Individual Welfare, Majority Voting, and the Properties of a Linear Income Tax," *Journal of Public Economics* 4 (1975): 163–185, and Allan H. Meltzer and Scott F. Richard, "A Rational Theory of the Size of Government," *Journal of Political Economy* (1981): 914–927. Among the many empirical investigations that examine the size of government and redistribution are William F. Bassett, John P. Burkett, and Louis Putterman, "Income Distribution, Government Transfers, and the Problem of Unequal Influence," *European Journal of Political Economy* 15 (1999): 207–228; Phillip Nelson, "Redistribution and the Income of the Median Voter," *Public Choice* 98 (1999): 187–194; Sultan Ahmed and Kenneth V. Greene, "Is the Median Voter a Clear-Cut Winner? Comparing the Median Voter Theory and Competing Theories in Explaining Local Government Spending," *Public Choice* 105 (2000): 207–230; Branko Milanovic, "The Median-Voter Hypothesis, Income Inequality, and Income Redistribution: An Empirical Test with the Required Data," *European Journal of Political Economy* 16 (2000): 367–410; Tony Addison and Aminur Rahman, "Why Is So Little Spent on Educating the Poor?" Discussion Paper 2001/29, World Institute for Development Economics Research, United Nations University, Helsinki, 2001; and Torben Iversen and David Soskice, "An Asset Theory of Social Policy Preferences," *American Political Science Review* 95 (2001): 875–893. Among those investigating party or candidate convergence at the median voter are Stephen Ansolabehere, James M. Snyder Jr., and Charles Stewart III, "Candidate Positioning in U.S. House Elections," *American Journal of Political Science* 45 (2001): 136–159, and Edward L. Glaeser, Giacomo A. M. Ponzetto, Jesse M. Shapiro, "Strategic Extremism: Why Democrats and Republicans Divide on Religious Values," *Quarterly Journal of Economics* 120 (2005): 1283–1330.

4. For a discussion of the assumptions underlying spatial models and this analysis, see Henry E. Brady, "The Art of Political Science: Spatial Diagrams as Iconic and Revelatory," *Perspectives on Politics* 9 (2011): 311–331.

5. Downs, *Economic Theory of Democracy*, p. 115.

seems obvious. In many democracies, voters cluster at the center of the political spectrum. Hence, it makes sense to appeal to them. However, the Downsian logic goes deeper by arguing that, even if there are not many voters at the center, what matters is the voter who acts as the pivot and provides the party with a majority. That voter is the one at the median on a one-dimensional liberal–conservative issue scale. To win elections, parties on the left and the right will have to move toward the center to appeal to that crucial median voter. Downs's theory is not only intellectually powerful but, because it implies that democracies can solve problems through compromise based on appeals to the median voter, attractive to students of democracy.

Downs's other prediction is that, where the principle of one person, one vote obtains, this convergence to the median is likely to produce redistributive economic policies:

> Government need not regard everyone's money income as given because it has the power to redistribute incomes. In our model, it makes use of this power whenever doing so helps it maximize votes. Clearly, in a society where every citizen has one and only one vote, the best way to gain votes via redistribution is to deprive a few persons of income—thereby incurring their hostility—and make this income available to many persons—thereby gaining their support. Since the pretax distribution of income in almost every society gives large incomes to a few persons and relatively small incomes to many persons, a redistribution tending toward equality accomplishes the very political end government desires. Thus the equality of franchise in a democratic society creates a tendency for government action to equalize incomes by redistributing them from a few wealthy persons to many less wealthy ones.[6]

In a formalization of this insight, Meltzer and Richard proposed that the "left–right" dimension in the Downsian model can be represented by the distribution of incomes with low-income voters on the left and high-income voters on the right.[7] For typically right-skewed income distributions in which the mean income is higher than the median, the median voter can benefit from the setting of a flat-tax rate so as to maximize his or her income from

---

6. Downs, *Economic Theory of Democracy*, p. 198.
7. Meltzer and Richard, "Rational Theory of the Size of Government," pp. 914–927.

tax transfers (mostly obtained from the wealthy) that are then shared equally.[8] Progressive income tax systems can provide even greater benefits to the median voter. The only constraint is ensuring that high tax rates do not discourage too much economic activity. The net effect would be to redistribute income from the rich to the poor.

These models predict that inequality should be greatly ameliorated in American politics through centrist governmental policies.[9] As we saw in Chapter 3, however, political outcomes in America do not follow the Downsian logic. Compared to other countries, America has public policies that are not especially redistributive. In fact, tax policies in the United States have not overcome a trend in recent decades toward increasingly unequal income distribution. In addition, contrary to Downsian logic, American political debate seems highly polarized, with little appeal to the median voter, and the ideological gap separating Republican and Democratic Party elites has been widening rather than narrowing. Increasing political polarization seems to cast further doubt on the classic form of Downs's median voter model.[10] Why, despite growing inequality in incomes, have the lower classes in America not voted more often to "confiscate" the income of the upper classes? Why is American politics now so polarized at both the elite and the mass level instead of converging at the median voter? Why, in short, does the Downsian model seem to fail?

8. "Right-skewed" distributions have long tails on the right, which means, in this case, that there are some very rich people who skew the distribution and its mean to the right.

9. In fact, empirical analyses come to differing conclusions with respect to the question of whether inequality begets redistribution. Contrast the findings in Milanovic, "Median-Voter Hypothesis," pp. 367–410, with those in Addison and Rahman, "Why Is So Little Spent?" or in Jonathan A. Schwabish, Timothy M. Smeeding, and Lars Osberg, "Income Distribution and Social Expenditures: A Cross-National Perspective," Working Paper 350, Luxembourg Income Studies, May 2003.

10. On the increasing polarization of politics in America, see John H. Evans, Bethany Bryson, and Paul DiMaggio, "Opinion Polarization: Important Contributions, Necessary Limitations," *American Journal of Sociology* 106 (2001): 944–959; Stephen Ansolabehere, Jonathan Rodden, and James M. Snyder Jr., "Purple America," *Journal of Economic Perspectives* 20 (2006): 97–118; Nolan M. McCarty, Keith T. Poole, and Howard Rosenthal, *Polarized America: The Dance of Ideology and Unequal Riches* (Cambridge, MA: MIT Press, 2006); Geoffrey C. Layman, Thomas M. Carsey, and Juliana Menasce Horowitz, "Party Polarization in American Politics: Characteristics, Causes, and Consequences," *Annual Review of Political Science* 9 (2006): 83–110; Pietro S. Nivola and David W. Brady, eds., *Red and Blue Nation? Characteristics and Causes of America's Polarized Politics* (Washington, DC: Brookings Institution, 2006), vol. 1; Marc J. Hetherington, "Review Article: Putting Polarization in Perspective," *British Journal of Political Science* 39 (2009): 413–448; and Morris P. Fiorina with Samuel J. Abrams and Jeremy C. Pope, *Culture War? The Myth of Polarized America*, 3rd ed. (Boston: Longman, 2011).

In our view, the Downsian model does not fail, but it does require modification. We need to take account of political activists—who have both high levels of SES and less moderate political opinions—and dimensions beyond economics. Bringing activists, who tend to be well educated and affluent, into the model makes it clear why there is a tilt away from redistributive taxing and spending policies. The median participant, especially the median donor, has a much higher income than the median citizen. Because the income of the median participant is closer to the mean income of the electorate, the median participant has little incentive to engage in income redistribution. Because participants are more extreme in their political opinions than those who are more politically quiescent, considering activists also helps us understand polarization.[11]

We are not the first to observe that disparities in political activity might have implications for inferences that can be drawn from the logic of the median voter. In fact, Downs himself noted that "usually voters with the highest incomes also have the most political power, since in an uncertain world they can use their financial resources to create influence for themselves"—that is, the median participant has a much higher income than the median for all citizens.[12] Others have noted that, because turnout in the United States is hardly universal and because the poor are less likely to go to the polls than those with higher incomes, the median voter would have a higher income than the median citizen.[13] Our contribution is to show systematically the consequences of these observations, not just for voting, but for many forms of activity.

Why No Confiscation in America?

The attempt to understand the failure to redistribute income and the weakness of the welfare state in America is an old and continuing quest. Some of

11. Because participatory inequality has been more or less stable for the last fifty years (see Chapter 6) and polarization has increased only relatively recently, bringing activists into the picture cannot explain the recent increase in polarization.

12. Downs, *Economic Theory of Democracy*, pp. 200–201. See also Shapiro, *State of Democratic Theory*, chap. 5.

13. For an analysis that takes into account differential political activity as a modification of the standard median voter approach in relation to income inequality, see Schwabish, Smeeding, and Osberg, "Income Distribution." See also Iversen and Soskice, "Asset Theory of Social Policy Preferences," p. 878. Others have argued that the tendency for parties and candidates to converge on the median voter would cause those with extreme opinions to abstain. This conjecture receives no empirical support. See Melvin J. Hinich and Peter C. Ordeshook,

the multiple explanations of American exceptionalism focus on characteristics of the citizenry: an American ideology that, as we discussed in Chapter 2, stresses individual opportunity to succeed and is thus tolerant of economic inequality; citizen misunderstanding of economics and who benefits from governmental policies; and conflict and division within a multiethnic and historically racially divided society.[14] Others emphasize institutions: the weakness of labor unions and the absence of a labor or social democratic party, along with the nature of governmental structures and policy processes that inhibit both substantial policy change and coordination among labor, capital, and government.[15]

We add another piece to the puzzle by considering how the prediction about income distribution made by the median voter model changes when we con-

---

"Abstention and Equilibrium in the Electoral Process," *Public Choice* 7 (1969): 81–106, and Fiorina, "Whatever Happened to the Median Voter?" pp. 8–10.

14. The argument here is that few Americans fully understand the nature of tax and transfer policies. They may believe policies will benefit them when in fact they will not. Or they may have eternal hope that, though they are not rich today, they may be in the future—and do not want their new wealth to be confiscated. See Jacob S. Hacker and Paul Pierson, "Abandoning the Middle: The Bush Tax Cuts and the Limits of Democratic Control," *Perspectives on Politics* 3 (March, 2005): 33–53, and Larry M. Bartels, *Unequal Democracy: The Political Economy of the New Gilded Age* (New York and Princeton, NJ: Russell Sage Foundation and Princeton University Press, 2008).

For two reasons, redistributive politics is likely to be inhibited in a multiracial and multiethnic society: first, although united by their poverty, less advantaged citizens may be divided by race or ethnicity and therefore less able to work in concert to influence public policy, and second, better-off citizens may be less willing to support redistributive policies that benefit people who are very different from them in racial and ethnic terms. See, for instance, Martin Gilens, *Why Americans Hate Welfare: Race, Media, and the Politics of Antipoverty Policy* (Chicago: University of Chicago Press, 1999), and Alberto F. Alesina, Edward L. Glaeser, and Bruce Sacerdote, "Why Doesn't the United States Have a European-Style Welfare State?" *Brookings Papers on Economic Activity* (2001): 187–278. Recently the argument has also been applied to differing lifestyles and experiences between affluent and poorer citizens. As income inequality increases and more public services become privatized, there is less comity across social classes that might motivate the more affluent to favor support for the poor. See Schwabish, Smeeding, and Osberg, "Income Distribution and Social Expenditures."

15. On the former point, see, for example, Sidney Verba, Norman H. Nie, and Jae-on Kim, *Participation and Political Equality: A Seven-Nation Comparison* (New York: Cambridge University Press, 1978), and Seymour Martin Lipset and Gary Marks, *It Didn't Happen Here: Why Socialism Failed in the United States* (New York: W. W. Norton, 2000). On the latter, James Madison's solution to the dangers to property of mass political power was to establish governmental institutions that make it easier to block than to make policy change. Recent literature has focused on the packaging of policies in ways that mask the effects on distribution. See, for example, Hacker and Pierson, "Abandoning the Middle," and Suzanne Mettler, *The Submerged State: How Invisible Government Policies Undermine American Democracy* (Chicago: University of Chicago Press, 2011).

sider not just voters but campaign workers and contributors. As does Downs in his discussion of income redistribution, we assume for the moment that arraying voters according to their incomes is politically relevant so that the person with the median income is the median voter.[16] But is the person with the median income pivotal in the electoral process?[17] The electoral process hinges on the person with the median income only if every eligible voter—including the person with the median income—goes to the polls and each voter is endowed with a single vote. Of course, not all eligible citizens vote. Moreover, some members of the electorate enhance their influence on the outcome of the election by virtue of being active in a campaign or making campaign donations. That is, after all, one reason for volunteering in or contributing to campaigns: to have the possibility of controlling more votes than the single one allocated by the democratic process.

The Downsian model depends on an understanding of the strategic calculations made by candidates running for office. Office seekers who wish to maximize votes need support from the activists who work in and fund campaigns. Every hour or dollar contributed to a campaign may help to deliver votes.[18] Thus the rational, vote-maximizing campaigner would have an incentive to take account of the weighted electoral strength of those who are active beyond voting rather than to look to the median person in the population or even to the median voter. The location of the pivotal citizen (the person to whom electoral appeals and policies would be directed) would be determined by the relative positions of those who do nothing but vote (who are weighted as a single unit), campaign workers whose political weight is the sum of the single unit for their own vote plus the number of votes that their work produces, and campaign contributors whose political weight is the single unit for their own vote plus the number of votes their contributions

---

16. Students of American voting behavior typically use a "funnel of causality" metaphor to organize the factors that affect voting. The funnel begins with such sociological attributes as income or demographic characteristics. It then proceeds to psychological states of mind as reflected in individuals' opinions about issues and the candidates and culminates in their vote choices. Even though political issues are among the most proximate causes of vote choices in elections, we start as Downs did, by going back in the funnel of causality and considering income, which allows us to forge a direct link to income distribution. Later in the chapter we move forward to two important issue dimensions, economic policy and social issues.

17. We use income instead of SES because the Downsian model focuses on the role of income as a basic dimension of politics. We obtain very similar results if we use SES.

18. As we discuss in Chapter 10, there is no consensus as to how much influence campaign contributions have on either the electoral outcomes or the behavior of the eventual winner once in office.

deliver. Because they do not contribute to the voting total, those who stay home and do not even vote—who form a sizable share of the American electorate—are weighted as zero. This logic makes clear how far the median voter model, not to mention the weighted participatory median model, is from the median citizen model. Although campaigners cannot know with any precision how many votes are delivered by each hour or each dollar they give to a campaign, rational office seekers know that they cannot ignore the volunteers who donate them.

In light of these considerations, the data in Figure 9.1 help us to think about the position of the pivotal voter in an electoral world in which turnout is not universal and some citizens multiply the weight of their vote by working in or making donations to campaigns. In the figure we use data from the August 2008 survey conducted by the Pew Internet and American Life Project to show, for all respondents, the location of the *median* family income and the *mean* family income. The mean income ($63,000) is more than 40 percent greater than the median ($44,000), indicating that there is clearly room for redistribution from those above the median to those below.[19] Reflecting the widely observed correlation between income and the likelihood of registering and voting, the median registered voter has an income ($48,000) that is greater than that of the median respondent.[20] The median registered

19. Those below the median income, who would be the beneficiaries of the redistribution, have a mean income of $20,500. In contrast, those above the median, whose income would be redistributed, have a mean income of $93,000—suggesting that they are a tempting target indeed.

20. Because the Pew survey was conducted in August before the 2008 election, respondents were asked about registration rather than voting. They were also asked whether they had participated in campaign work or made a donation to a campaign, and, if so, how much they had given. Census data would have more accurate and finely grained information, but the Census does not include the other measures needed for our analysis. Indeed, the Pew study has a critical feature that allows us to undertake this analysis: it contains measures not simply of having made a campaign contribution but of the *amount* of the contribution. The 1990 Citizen Participation Survey, which contained questions about voting as well as registration and a better item about the amount of political contributions, produced results parallel to but even more striking than those presented in Figure 9.1. However, we prefer to show the more recent data.

On the disparity between the mean and the median income of the registered voter, see, among others, Raymond E. Wolfinger and Steven J. Rosenstone, *Who Votes?* (New Haven, CT: Yale University Press, 1980), and Richard B. Freeman, "What, Me Vote?" in *Social Inequality*, ed. Kathryn M. Neckerman (New York: Russell Sage, 2004), chap. 18. Note that it does not matter whether income is a causal factor for voting. Evidence shows that a major reason that the affluent are more likely to vote is their higher education level. What counts here is who votes, not why they do so.

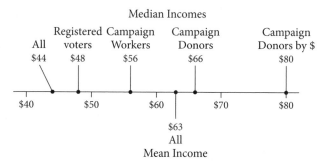

Figure 9.1   Median and Mean Incomes of All Citizens and Median Incomes of Election Activists

Source: Pew Internet and American Life Survey (2008).

voter is still located well below the *mean* income for the sample—suggesting that, in spite of the extent to which income is associated with turnout, voters might still opt to elect policy makers who would redistribute income downward. The situation changes somewhat if we look at the campaign workers, and especially campaign donors, those who are in a position to influence more votes than the single vote allocated to them. The median incomes for these groups of activists are either closer to, or higher than, the population mean of $63,000: at $56,000, the median income for campaign workers is nearer to—and, at $66,000, the median for campaign contributors exceeds— the mean for all respondents. It is worth noting that just over two-thirds of all survey respondents have family incomes below the median for campaign donors.

What is more, as we have noted repeatedly, in contrast to voters who are limited to a single vote, campaign activists can multiply the amount of time or money they give, with implications for the amount of political influence they wield. Because the number of spare dollars that the wealthy can devote to politics is much larger than the number of available hours that the leisured can give, it is possible to multiply the amount of money donated to campaigns to an extent not feasible for the amount of time worked.[21] With this in mind, we show the location of the income of the donor of the median dollar—

21. For an elaboration of this argument and supporting data, see Sidney Verba, Kay Lehman Schlozman, and Henry E. Brady, *Voice and Equality: Civic Voluntarism in American Politics* (Cambridge, MA: Harvard University Press, 1995), chap. 7.

indicated in Figure 9.1 as "Campaign Donors by $." We determine this location in the figure by weighting each campaign donor by the magnitude of his or her contributions.[22] The Pew data show that the median dollar is contributed by someone whose family income is nearly twice the median income for the population, $80,000—not exactly a billionaire but in the top quarter of 2008 family incomes. Thus the pivotal dollar comes from a donor with a family income almost twice the median income of the population. Because the Pew survey did not further specify the size of political contributions over $2,500 or family incomes over $150,000, we cannot discern whether contributions that fall into the highest category were $2,501 or $50,000 and whether family incomes in the highest category are $150,001 or much, much higher. Had we more refined data, we would surely find that the median dollar is contributed by someone with an even higher family income.

Clearly, our data do not tell us about the rate at which campaign dollars are converted into political influence or about the strategic calculations of candidates who need simultaneously to court voters and to satisfy the activists who staff and fund their campaigns. Furthermore, the determinants of policy are very complicated, and vote preferences and issue salience are not dictated by family income. Still, the data in Figure 9.1 cast in a very different light the expectation that the rational, vote-maximizing office seeker will necessarily aim for the median voter or that the process will produce downwardly redistributive economic policies. The data suggest instead that, insofar as political contributions have a significant influence on the distribution of votes, the impulse for redistribution toward the less affluent will be attenuated.

Economic and Social Issues in American Politics

While Figure 9.1 provides powerful evidence that incorporating participatory inequalities into our model helps us to rethink electoral democracy in America, it contains two useful but unrealistic simplifying assumptions: that Americans are arrayed along a single, economic dimension in politics; and that family income is aligned with opinions on economic issues and vote choices. Politics in America is obviously about more than just economic

22. The Pew study did not ask about the number of hours given to politics. In the 1990 Citizen Participation Study, the income of the person contributing the median hour was almost $10,000 higher than the median income of the population. Hence, the median hour is also biased upward.

issues. It engages social and cultural concerns as well. Moreover, family income is associated only imperfectly with economic attitudes and voting preferences. After all, the affluent are not necessarily economic conservatives, and the less economically advantaged are not inevitably economic liberals.

We elaborate by focusing on issue positions, which are notably much closer to vote choices than is family income, and adding a second dimension to capture attitudes on social issues. Figure 9.2 uses data from the 1990 Citizen Participation Study to locate the mean citizen, voter, campaign worker, and campaign contributor—along with the contributor of the mean dollar—in terms of attitudes on economic and social issues.[23] We have constructed two scales: one measuring attitudes on economic issues using three items (two on whether government should guarantee jobs and a decent standard of living and one on taxing and spending), the other measuring attitudes on social issues using items on abortion and prayer in the schools. The closer a group is to the lower left-hand corner of the figure, the more liberal, on average, are its opinions; the further it is to the right on the x-axis, the more conservative it is, on average, with regard to economic issues. The higher on the y-axis, the more conservative it is, on average, in terms of social issues. In spite of the obvious emphasis on the median in the Downsian model, for several reasons having to do with the nature of the scales used to measure attitudes, in this figure—and in subsequent ones that use issue questions or scales—we use the mean rather than the median.[24] When we make the statistically dodgy assumptions needed to calculate the median for data involving issue questions, the overall shape of the results is unchanged.

There are several striking aspects of this diagram. First, the average voter is similar to the average citizen with respect to opinions on social issues but is more conservative than the average citizen on economic issues. Second, opinion on social issues among campaign activists—whether they give time or money—is, on average, more liberal than among voters or all citizens. That is, compared to all citizens and voters, political activists have attitudes that push American politics in a less conservative direction on social issues

23. We use the 1990 Citizen Participation Study because the 2008 Pew study did not include any questions about attitudes on political issues.

24. For family income, we used a ratio scale with many equally spaced categories and a long rightward tail containing the small share at the top who have very high incomes, because the difference between the median and the mean is critical. The scales for issue dimensions are at best interval scales, often with very few categories. The median usually falls within a category. Under those circumstances, to find the median requires interpolation, often within a category containing a large portion of the respondents.

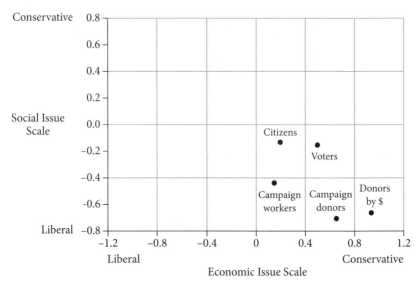

Figure 9.2   Social and Economic Issue Positions of All Citizens and Election Activists, 1990

Source: Citizen Participation Study (1990).

Note: Activity groups are voters, campaign workers, campaign donors, and campaign donors weighted by dollars given.

like abortion. Third, political activists who give money to politics push in a conservative direction on economic policy. In fact, the economic perspective of the person giving the average dollar (the location in Figure 9.2 marked "Donors by $") is far to the right of the average for all citizens and even voters. This result reflects the relatively strong associations among political contributions, income, and economic views: those who make large political contributions are likely to have both high incomes and conservative positions on economic policy.[25] In contrast, those who give time to campaign work are, although more liberal on social issues, close to the average citizen on economic issues.

What is the net result for American politics? The answer depends on the outcome of party competition in two-dimensional issue spaces and on whether activists who give time or money matter more in this competition.

25. These results are confirmed by analyses of data from the American National Election Studies.

Based on the theoretical work on this problem, we assume that the political outcomes in two-dimensional issue spaces are near the average positions.[26] If time and money are equally weighted in politics, political activists, on balance, tilt American politics toward conservative economic policies but towards more liberal policies on social issues such as abortion. If money matters more than time does, the tendency toward conservative economic policies will be even more pronounced.

In Figure 9.3 we update the 1990 results using data from the 2005 Citizenship, Involvement, Democracy (CID) Survey project.[27] Although the study

26. We are aware that classic social choice results show that the power of the median is reduced (or even extinguished) when there are two or more dimensions of contestation. See Gerald Kramer, "On a Class of Equilibrium Conditions for Majority Rule," *Econometrica* 41 (1973): 285–297; Richard D. McKelvey, "Instransitivities in Multidimensional Voting Models and Some Implications for Agenda Control," *Journal of Economic Theory* 12 (1976): 472–82; and Norman Schofield, "Instability of Simple Dynamic Games," *Review of Economic Studies* 45 (1978): 575–594. At the same time, there are two significant bodies of literature that suggest the continued power of the median. One body considers deterministic voting models and shows that equilibriums tend to develop around generalizations of the median (e.g., the "core," the "uncovered set," the "yolk," and other concepts). See Nicholas R. Miller, "A New Solution Set for Tournaments and Majority Voting: Further Graph-Theoretical Approaches to the Theory of Voting," *American Journal of Political Science* 24 (1980): 68–96; J. A. Ferejohn, R. D. McKelvey, and E. W. Packel, "Limiting Distributions for Continuous State Markov Voting Models," *Social Choice and Welfare* 1 (1984): 45–67; Gary W. Cox, "The Uncovered Set and the Core," *American Journal of Political Science* 31 (1987): 408–422; and Scott L. Feld, Bernard Grofman, and Nicholas Miller, "Centripetal Forces in Spatial Voting: On the Size of the Yolk," *Public Choice* 59 (1988): 37–50. Another body of work shows that if voting is probabilistic, multi-dimensional equilibriums are relatively likely, and they typically occur near some central location of the distribution of voters. See Peter J. Coughlin, "Pareto Optimality of Policy Proposals with Probabilistic Voting," *Public Choice* 39 (1982): 427–433; James M. Enelow and Melvin J. Hinich, "A General Probabilistic Spatial Theory of Elections," *Public Choice* 61 (1989): 101–113; and Peter Coughlin, *Probabilistic Voting Theory* (New York: Cambridge University Press, 1992). These results suggest that the median still has power and is worth considering empirically. In addition, John Roemer has proposed a model about how factions within parties might bargain in two-dimensional spaces; see his *Political Competition: Theory and Applications* (Cambridge, MA: Harvard University Press, 2001). This model is applied to trade-offs between economic issues and civil rights issues in John Roemer, Woojin Lee, and Karine van der Straeten, *Racism, Xenophobia and Distribution: Multi-Issue Politics in Advanced Democracies* (Cambridge, MA: Russell Sage Foundation Books and Harvard University Press, 2007). Henry E. Brady and Paul M. Sniderman have argued that the model might be more profitably applied to a two-dimensional space that included social issues; see their "Review of 'Racism, Xenophobia, and Distribution,'" *Perspectives on Politics* 6 (2008): 409–411. These models suggest the power of central locations.

27. See Marc Morje Howard, James L. Gibson, and Dietlind Stolle, "The U.S. Citizenship, Involvement, Democracy Survey," Center for Democracy and Civil Society, Georgetown University, Washington, DC, 2005.

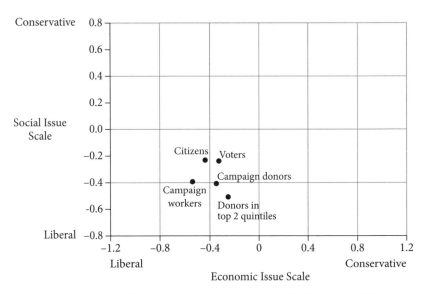

Figure 9.3   Social and Economic Issue Positions of All Citizens and Election Activists, 2005

Source: Citizenship, Involvement, Democracy Survey (2005).

Note: Activity groups are voters, campaign workers, campaign donors, and donors in the top two income quintiles.

lacks at least one important measure of activity, the amount of money given to politics, it contains an ideal question about economic redistribution, which we use to represent the economic dimension. It asks respondents whether the government should take measures to reduce differences in income levels. We use three items, one about abortion and two about gay rights, to form a social issue dimension.[28] The results for 2005 are similar to what we found for 1990. Once again, activists—whether workers or donors—are, on average, considerably more liberal on the social dimension than is the average citizen

28. Questions about abortion and gay rights were equally weighted to form this scale. A question about abortion was scored so that its value varies from minus two to two. (This question asked whether, by law, abortion should never be permitted; abortion should be permitted only for rape / incest / woman's life in danger; abortion should be permitted only after need has been clearly established; or a woman should always able to obtain abortion as a matter of personal choice.) Two questions about gay rights were combined so that they also vary from minus two to two. One was about gay marriage, and the other was about homosexual rights.

or the average voter. Contributors and voters are, on average, less favorably disposed to redistributive economic policies than is the average citizen. One difference between these data and what we saw for 1990 is that those working on campaigns or other forms of political activity are, on average, more liberal on economic redistribution.

Unfortunately, the CID Survey did not ask about the amount contributed to campaigns and other political activities. In order to give some indication of the issue placement of those with the wherewithal to make larger donations, we locate the average position of those contributors in the top two quintiles of the income distribution with the label "Donors in top 2 quintiles." This group, which accounts for more than half the contributors in the study, is both quite liberal on the social dimension and quite conservative on the issue of redistribution.[29]

These diagrams, then, provide an additional way of thinking about the question of why there is no redistribution of income in America. Introducing consideration of participatory inequalities casts doubt on the inevitability of the gravitational pull in the direction of the median voter in a two-party system. Those who do political work or make political contributions are not representative of all citizens, or even of all voters, in their politically relevant characteristics. Not only are they more affluent and well educated but they are also more liberal on social issues. Contributors, especially those who give large amounts, are significantly to the right of citizens on economic matters, including redistribution. Although campaign workers may provide something of a counterweight on the issue of redistribution, the ability of affluent contributors to amplify their voice through large contributions means that the median dollar is contributed by someone with very conservative opinions on economic issues. Of course, we are not claiming that our modification of the Downsian model provides the sole explanation for the absence of redistribution in America, but we think that it adds an important perspective on the matter.

29. In the 2008 Pew study, contributors in the top two income quintiles are responsible for almost three-quarters (72.5 percent) of the total contributions. The top two quintiles of political workers are also somewhat over half the total number of workers, and they are slightly more liberal on the redistribution dimension, at –0.58 versus –0.54, but there is no reason to suppose that they give, on average, many more hours to political activity than do political workers who are lower in the income hierarchy. For discussion of the number of hours given to political activity, see Verba, Schlozman, and Brady, *Voice and Equality*, pp. 190–196.

Why No Convergence in America?
Parties, Activity, and the Pivotal Citizen

The second puzzle that appears in a different light once we introduce inequalities of political voice is the failure of the Downsian model to predict political polarization. If we are to come to grips with the absence of convergence to the median, we must consider political parties. Parties are undoubtedly the most important vehicles for organizing members of the mass public and bringing them into politics, and our treatment of them in this chapter serves as a transition to the next section of the book, in which we consider the other kind of institution that links citizens to policy makers, organized interests. Roughly six of every seven American adults identify with one of the two major parties, and party identifiers—especially those who think of themselves as strong partisans—are more likely to vote for their party's candidates. In turn, the parties compete to gain support from voters and to win elections.

As is widely acknowledged, rank-and-file Republicans and Democrats differ somewhat in their socio-characteristics. We use the standard seven-point party identification question from the 2008 American National Election Study (ANES) and code as partisans both those who indicated an initial preference for one of the parties and the leaners, who said they felt closer to one of the parties.[30] As we have done repeatedly for various forms of political involvement, in Figure 9.4.A we show the percentage of people in each socioeconomic quintile who identify with each party or who are Independents.[31] In these data, about 50 percent of all respondents identified as Democrats and 37 percent as Republicans—with the remaining 12 percent declining to state a preference.[32]

The slopes of the lines make clear that the parties' supporters can be differentiated in terms of social class. The percentage of Democrats in each quintile declines somewhat as SES increases. Democratic identifiers tilt some-

---

30. In the ANES, respondents are asked first: "Generally speaking, do you usually think of yourself as a Democrat, a Republican, an Independent, or what?" Those who indicate a preference for one of the two major parties are asked: "Would you call yourself a STRONG [Democrat or Republican] or a NOT VERY STRONG [Democrat or Republican]?" Those who indicate no preference are asked: "Do you think of yourself as CLOSER to the Republican Party or to the Democratic Party?"

31. Although we have used income up to this point, we use SES ranks here to make this figure comparable to the many similar ones throughout the book. Subsequent notes compare the SES results with those for quintiles of income and education.

32. We place the small proportion of people who favor third parties or who simply have no idea about their party affiliation in the group of Independents.

9.4.A Percentage of Democrats, Independents, and Republicans in Each SES Quintile

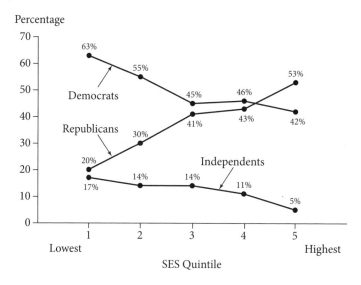

9.4.B Percentage of Democrats, Independents, and Republicans in Each Income Quintile

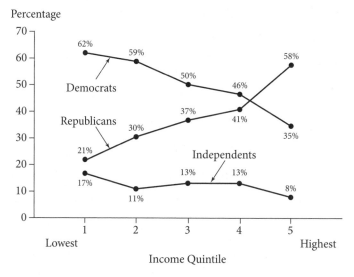

Figure 9.4 Partisan Composition of SES and Income Quintiles

Source: American National Election Study (2008).

what toward lower SES quintiles: slightly under half, 47 percent, come from the bottom two quintiles, and about a third, 35 percent, from the top two quintiles. In contrast, the percentage of Republicans increases with each successive SES quintile, and the upward slope of the line for Republican identifiers is steeper than the downward slope for the Democratic identifiers.[33] A majority of Republican identifiers, 51 percent, come from the top two quintiles, and only about a quarter, 27 percent, come from the bottom two quintiles.[34] It is also worth noting that Independents decline significantly, from 17 per cent in the bottom quintile to 5 percent in the top quintile.[35] Because we have focused on income rather than SES in this chapter, we present parallel data for income in Figure 9.4.B. Although both lines are slightly steeper than in Figure 9.4.A, this figure shows the same pattern for income as for SES.

In short, the major parties are quite different in their composition. Of the two, the Democratic Party would be the obvious vehicle for spearheading the attempts at redistribution that Downs expected. However, because a significant fraction of Democratic identifiers hail from the higher-SES quintiles, we might expect some division over redistribution among Democrats. In contrast, because Republican identifiers are drawn so disproportionately from higher-SES citizens, we might expect them to be more cohesive in opposing attempts to redistribute. The potential ambivalence about redistribution among Democrats and the potential support among Republicans for main-

33. The absolute value of the slope of Republican Party membership (scored as one) regressed on SES ranks scored as one to five is .078, which is 56 percent larger in magnitude than the slope of Democratic Party membership regressed on SES ranks, which is .050. The comparable figures for income are .082 and .067 (22 percent larger), and for education they are .052 and .018 (189 percent larger).

34. In terms of income, 48 percent of Democrats are in the lowest two quintiles and 32 percent in the highest two quintiles, and 28 percent of Republicans are in the lowest two quintiles and 53 percent in the highest two quintiles, so the Republican Party is more stratified by income than the Democratic Party. In terms of education, 42 percent of Democrats are in the lowest two quintiles and 38 percent in the highest two quintiles, and 32 percent of Republicans are in the lowest two quintiles and 49 percent in the highest two quintiles, so the Republican Party is much more stratified by education than the Democratic Party.

Republicans have 2.65 times more people in the top SES quintile than in the bottom; Democrats have 1.48 more people in the bottom SES quintile than in the top. The comparable figures for income are 2.68 for Republicans and 1.80 for Democrats. For education they are 1.91 for Republicans and 1.16 for Democrats.

35. As has been widely noted, the two parties also differ in terms of religious attendance. More than 40 percent of Democrats say they never attend religious services, while only 33 percent of Republicans say this. Thirty-two percent of Republicans, but only 17 percent of Democrats, say they attend church every week or more often.

taining income inequality suggest still another reason why redistribution does not occur in America and why the actual policy median on economic issues is to the right of that of the median citizen.

Still, these regularities do not explain why parties and candidates do not focus on and converge to the same center-right policy with respect to income redistribution. To understand why convergence does not occur, we must return to an observation made earlier to the effect that, if parties are to be effective in the pursuit of electoral victory, they need not only to cater to ordinary voters in the mass public but also to attend to the activists who provide the volunteer labor and dollars that make campaigns possible. Because the chances of losing an election are appreciable, parties and candidates have an incentive to provide ideological and social rewards to volunteers, who tend to be advantaged with respect to SES and to have opinions that are less centrist than those of the median voter. The need to pay attention to high-SES opinionated campaign activists has the potential both to tilt public policy away from the needs of the median voter and to contribute to the polarization that separates Democratic and Republican party elites so dramatically.

What about Political Polarization?

The last decade has witnessed vigorous debate over whether American politics is or is not becoming polarized. The debate involves a number of different issues: Who is becoming more polarized—elites, the mass public, or both? Is polarization occurring with respect to values or to public opinion issues—or both? Should polarization be defined as greater dispersion in people's issue positions or as greater statistical association between their positions and their partisanship?[36]

Observers agree that there is more elite polarization between the political parties in Congress now than there was fifty years ago, even though the current level of polarization may not be higher than the historical norm.[37] The situation for the mass public presents a more complex picture. If we ask

36. Statistical issues are discussed in Paul DiMaggio, John Evans, and Bethany Bryson, "Have Americans' Social Attitudes Become More Polarized?" *American Journal of Sociology* 102 (1996): 690–755; Ted Mouw and Michael E. Sobel, "Culture Wars and Opinion Polarization: The Case of Abortion," *American Journal of Sociology* 106 (2001): 913–943; Dennis J. Downey and Matt L. Huffman, "Attitudinal Polarization and Trimodal Distributions: Measurement Problems and Theoretical Implications," *Social Science Quarterly* 82 (2001): 494–505; and Matthew S. Levendusky, "The Microfoundations of Mass Polarization," *Political Analysis* 17 (2009): 162–176.

37. McCarty, Poole, and Rosenthal, *Polarized America*, and Hetherington, "Putting Polarization in Perspective." On the historical norm, see David W. Brady and Hahrie C. Han,

whether distributions of values or opinions have a greater dispersion—either an increase in their spread (i.e., greater variance) or greater bimodalism (i.e., greater kurtosis)—we do not find much evidence of polarization in the mass public. This conclusion is especially strong if the measure of public opinion is basic values or worldviews, but it also holds for standard public opinion issues. There does not seem to be much evidence that popular opinion is significantly more highly polarized now than in the past.[38]

In contrast to the absence of evidence that the opinions of the mass public have become more extreme is compelling evidence that people have sorted into the political parties so that the two parties are further apart than they used to be. In the not-so-distant past, there were liberal and moderate Republicans like Jacob Javits and Nelson Rockefeller and conservative and moderate Democrats like Strom Thurmond and George Wallace. Neither party contains many such outliers these days. This kind of polarization, which has been called "sorting" by some authors and "consolidation" by others, has occurred at the level of the mass public as well.[39]

Sorting occurs when those with particular politically relevant characteristics —whether income or religious attendance or opinions on taxes, the minimum wage, or school prayer—are increasingly likely to affiliate with one party than the other. Identifying this kind of sorting is simple with the tools that we have been using. It requires only that we compare the median (or mean)

"Polarization Then and Now: A Historical Perspective," in *Red and Blue Nation?* ed. Nivola and Brady, vol. 1, chap. 3.

38. On basic values, see Wayne Baker, *America's Crisis of Values* (Princeton, NJ: Princeton University Press, 2005); Morris P. Fiorina, Samuel J. Abrams, and Jeremy C. Pope, "Polarization in the American Public: Misconceptions and Misreadings," *Journal of Politics* 70 (2008): 568–569; and Hetherington, "Putting Polarization in Perspective," p. 430. On standard public opinion issues, see DiMaggio, Evans, Bryson, "Have Americans' Attitudes Become More Polarized?"; Mouw and Sobel, "Culture Wars and Opinion Polarization"; John H. Evans, "Have Americans' Attitudes Become More Polarized? An Update," *Social Science Quarterly* 84 (2003): 71–90; Ansolabehere, Rodden, and Snyder, "Purple America"; Fiorina, Abrams, and Pope, "Political Polarization in the American Public"; and Fiorina with Abrams and Pope, *Culture War*. For a dissent, see Alan I. Abramowitz and Kyle L. Saunders, "Is Polarization a Myth?" *Journal of Politics* 70 (2008): 542–555. For a rebuttal, see Fiorina, Abrams, and Pope, "Polarization in the American Public," 556–560. Also see Alan Abramowitz, *The Disappearing Center: Engaged Citizens, Polarization, and American Democracy* (New Haven, CT: Yale University Press, 2010).

39. This process is called "sorting" by Fiorina with Abrams and Pope, in *Culture War?*, and Dimaggio, Evans, and Bryson, in "Have Attitudes Become More Polarized?," call it "consolidation." See also Matthew Levendusky, *The Partisan Sort: How Liberals Became Democrats and Conservatives Became Republicans* (Chicago: University of Chicago Press, 2009).

characteristic or opinion of those in the Democratic Party with that of those in the Republican Party. If the means become further apart over time, then there has been sorting.[40] For this type of polarization, there is general agreement that there has been significant sorting over time, which has left the parties more distinctive than they once were in their mass base.[41] Moreover, although the economic fault line that has divided Democrats from Republicans in politics since the New Deal remains the stronger determinant of voting behavior, there is evidence that the most significant recent sorting has occurred on the social dimension.[42]

Centrifugal Tendencies in Electoral Politics

Before proceeding to a consideration of partisan sorting among political activists and its role in political polarization, we should acknowledge that, contrary to the predictions implicit in the Downsian model, parties and candidates have incentives to diverge from the median. Political parties and their candidates are guided by their own policy preferences, the nature of their local constituencies, and the constraints implicit in the need to secure a nomination and to staff and fund a campaign. The result is that they would not inevitably converge at the median voter. Besides, they may not know with

---

40. Another test is whether the correlation between being identified with a particular party and these characteristics or opinions is large or has increased over time. Hence, this kind of polarization is about statistical association.

41. See DiMaggio, Evans, and Bryson, "Have Attitudes Become More Polarized?"; Mark D. Brewer, "The Rise of Partisanship and the Expansion of Partisan Conflict within the American Electorate," *Political Research Quarterly* 58 (2005): 219–229; Alan I. Abramowitz and Kyle L. Saunders, "Why Can't We All Just Get Along? The Reality of a Polarized America," *The Forum* (2005); Ansolabehere, Rodden, and Snyder, "Purple America"; Layman, Carsey, and Horowitz, "Party Polarization"; Morris P. Fiorina and Matthew S. Levendusky, "Disconnected: The Political Class versus the People," in *Red and Blue Nation?* ed. Nivola and Brady, chap. 2; Alan I. Abramowitz and Kyle L. Saunders, "Exploring the Bases of Partisanship in the American Electorate: Social Identity vs. Ideology," *Political Research Quarterly* 59 (2006): 175–187; Fiorina, Abrams, and Pope, "Political Polarization in the American Public"; Hetherington, "Putting Polarization in Perspective"; Alan Abramowitz, *The Disappearing Center;* and Fiorina with Abrams and Pope, *Culture War.*

42. See John P. Hoffman and Alan S. Miller, "Social and Political Attitudes among Religious Groups: Convergence and Divergence over Time," *Journal for the Scientific Study of Religion* 36 (1997): 52–70; Geoffrey Layman and Thomas M. Carsey, "Why Do Party Activists Convert? An Analysis of Individual-Level Change on the Abortion Issue," *Political Research Quarterly* 51 (1998): 723–749; Geoffrey C. Layman, *The Great Divide: Religious and Cultural Conflict in American Party Politics* (New York: Columbia University Press, 2001); Larry M. Bartels, "What's the Matter with What's the Matter with Kansas?" *Quarterly Journal of Political Science* 1 (2006): 201–226; and Bartels, *Unequal Democracy.*

any precision what voters, especially the silent ones, actually want. In short, the assumption of the Downsian model that parties and candidates choose policy positions solely with an eye toward maximizing votes on a national basis and winning two-party elections seems quite unrealistic.[43]

Indeed, the very logic of the median voter model suggests how differences in local constituencies—especially when combined with intraparty candidate selection processes—would lead away from convergence at the national median. With respect to geographic variation, the median voter differs substantially from political jurisdiction to political jurisdiction; that is, the median voter in Wyoming or Houston is very different from the median voter in Maryland or Detroit. By the logic of the median voter model, only a presidential candidate would adopt the position of the national median voter; others would gravitate to the position of the median voter in their constituencies, which might be quite different from the national median. Besides, all candidates have to be nominated as well as elected, and intraparty nomination processes would be likely to produce candidates with less moderate views.[44] In the many constituencies with stable one-party majorities, party nomination is tantamount to election. Therefore, the nominee of the majority party in such a circumstance would be expected to reflect the views of the median voter from the majority party, not the median voter of the constituency as a whole.

Even in competitive districts, election processes contain centrifugal tendencies. The party activists and campaign donors whose support is essential for attaining a party nomination and fielding a campaign tend to have views that are strongly held and that diverge from the political center.[45] Candidates

43. See Kay Lehman Schlozman and Sidney Verba, "Sending Them a Message—Getting a Reply: Presidential Elections and Democratic Accountability," in *Elections in America*, ed. Kay Lehman Schlozman (Winchester, MA: Allen and Unwin, 1987), chap. 1, as well as Grofman, "Downs and Two-Party Convergence."

44. John Aldrich, *Before the Convention: Strategies and Choices in Presidential Nominating Campaigns* (Chicago: University of Chicago Press, 1980); Larry M. Bartels, *Presidential Primaries and the Dynamics of Public Choice* (Princeton, NJ: Princeton University Press, 1988); and Henry E. Brady, "Knowledge, Strategy, and Momentum in Presidential Primaries," *Political Analysis* 5 (1993): 1–38.

45. Herbert McClosky and his coauthors demonstrated that, in the 1950s, Republican Party activists were more conservative than the Republican rank and file, but Democratic Party activists were actually more moderate than the Democratic rank and file. See Herbert McClosky, Paul J. Hoffman, and Rosemary O'Hara, "Issue Conflict and Consensus among American Party Leaders and Followers," *American Political Science Review* 54 (1960): 406–427. According to Norman H. Nie, Sidney Verba, and John Petrocik in *The Changing Ameri-*

would be likely to treat the supporters in their activist base with greater deference than they grant to those who do no more than vote. Besides, turnout in party primaries is notoriously low, and primary voters tend to be more party loyal, and less ideologically moderate, than the electorate as a whole. These factors would be likely to push rational, vote-seeking candidates away from the median.

Additional considerations require that we question the underlying premises of the Downsian model. For example, how voters make up their minds is a much-discussed matter in political science, but the assumption that voters inevitably cast their ballots for the ideologically proximate candidate is far too simple. Instead, a number of factors—ranging from assessments of that candidate's honesty or experience to retrospective evaluations of the performance in office of the incumbent party to voters' standing loyalties to one of the parties—may take precedence.[46] In addition, the assumption that politicians pursue office relentlessly and ignore their own policy views seems unrealistic.[47] Given the uncertainty of ascertaining where the median voter is located,[48] candidates with policy commitments have incentives to edge away from the median voter—thus reducing very slightly the chance of winning but increasing the possibility of being able to implement preferred policies if victorious. In sum, although the median voter—or the median intense participant—holds substantial power, numerous factors work together to push parties, and their candidates, away from the median.

Income and Issue Polarization among Party Activists

Various strands of research about citizens in politics emphasize the important role played by activists—who, for example, tend to be more interested in and knowledgeable about politics and more tolerant of dissenting points of view—in the functioning of American democracy. We find that, because they have, on average, less moderate political views as well as higher incomes than the typical citizen, they also play a role in fostering political polarization.

---

can Voter (Cambridge, MA: Harvard University Press, 1976), pp. 200–209, during the 1960s the pattern reversed for Democrats, and Democratic activists became more liberal than the Democratic rank and file.

46. Melvin J. Hinich and Michael C. Munger, *Ideology and the Theory of Political Choice* (Ann Arbor: University of Michigan Press, 1994).

47. Donald A. Wittman, "Parties as Utility Maximizers," *American Political Science Review* 67 (1973): 490–498.

48. Roemer, *Political Competition*.

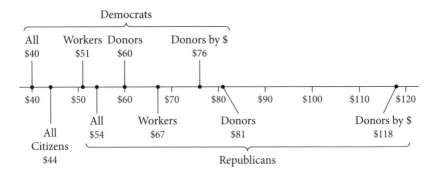

Income in Thousands of Dollars

Figure 9.5   Median Incomes of Democratic and Republican Identifiers and Activists (Thousands of Dollars)

Source: Source: Pew Internet and American Life Survey (2008).

Note: Activity groups are all citizens, registered voters, campaign workers, campaign donors, and campaign donors weighted by dollars given.

In Figure 9.5 we use data from the August 2008 survey conducted by the Pew Internet and American Life Project to replicate for partisans the analysis in Figure 9.1. For Democrats and Republicans separately we show the median incomes of party identifiers, campaign workers, donors, and weighted campaign donors.[49] In addition, we show the position of the median citizen. In each group of partisans, the donor of the median dollar has a higher income than the median for all donors, which is, in turn, higher than the median for campaign workers and rank-and-file partisans. Although the median income for rank-and-file Democrats is lower than the median for all citizens, the medians for all the activist groups, and for Republican partisans, are higher than the median for all citizens. Furthermore, among the various kinds of activists, Republicans have higher median incomes—sometimes much higher —than do their Democratic counterparts. Perhaps most notably, the income of the Republican donor who gives the median dollar is nearly three times that of the median citizen. These placements provide further evidence of how political participation tilts toward those of higher income. Party identifiers and activists from the Democratic and Republican parties are clearly in different locations, and there is even greater polarization—that is, greater income

49. A figure from the 1991 Citizen Participation Study yields a similar picture.

difference—among the various kinds of party activists than among the rank-and-file party identifiers.

Are the party identifiers and activists also polarized with respect to issue positions? Figure 9.6, which shows the results from the 2005 U.S. CID, uses the measures of attitudes on economic redistribution and the scale of social issues from Figure 9.3. Once again, because we are using attitudinal measures, we use means rather than medians. More or less in the middle of the diagram (surrounded by a rectangle) are the citizens, voters, workers, and donors irrespective of party affiliation—including both partisans and those with no ties to either party. In the lower left-hand corner (surrounded by an ellipse)—and thus more liberal than groups of all citizens on both the economic and the social dimensions—are the various Democratic groups. In the upper right-hand corner (surrounded by another ellipse)—and thus more conservative than groups of all citizens on both the economic and the social dimensions—are the various Republican groups.

What is clear in Figure 9.6 is that those who identify as Republicans and Democrats—whether or not they take part in politics—differ substantially in

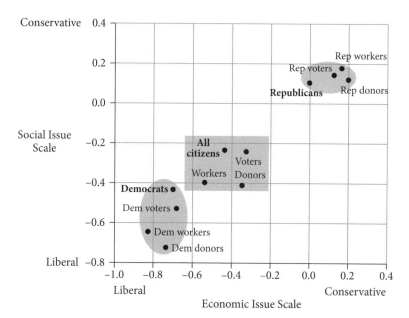

Figure 9.6   Mean Social and Economic Issue Positions of All Citizens and Democratic and Republican Identifiers and Election Activists

Source: Citizenship, Involvement, Democracy Survey (2005).

their views on redistribution and social issues and are far from the mean for all citizens. What is more, the activists of the two parties are even further apart than their respective party identifiers. The details of the patterns differ somewhat between Republicans and Democrats. Although they do not differ appreciably from Republican identifiers on the social dimension, both Republican campaign workers and Republican contributors are more conservative on redistribution. Among Democratic groups, the contributors do not differ appreciably from rank-and-file Democrats on economic redistribution, but both Democratic campaign workers and Democratic contributors are more liberal on social issues. Still, the overall pattern is that party activists pull even further apart parties that are already quite distinctive on both issue dimensions, thus contributing to polarization.

Income, Activity, and Increasing Polarization

While Figure 9.6 shows compelling evidence of partisan polarization, especially among electoral activists, it does not provide evidence for the way that polarization has increased.[50] Figure 9.7 takes us one step further by showing how the identifiers of the two parties grew further apart ideologically between 1973 and 2002 and how income fits into this process.[51] Using Roper data, in Figure 9.7 we present the average score on a scale measuring overall liberalism or conservatism for the lowest and highest income quintiles in the two parties.[52] For the rank and file in both parties, ideological polarization has increased much more substantially among those in the highest income quintile than among those lower down on the income ladder, especially those in the bottom quintile. Republican identifiers at all income levels became more conservative during the last quarter of the twentieth century. However, the ideological swing was most pronounced among those in the highest income group. In these data, the overall ideological shift for Democrats in the

50. Samantha Luks and Laurel Elms are co-authors of this section.

51. In order to simplify a complex presentation, we use an overall measure of liberalism or conservatism. This scale ranges from very liberal (scored as minus two) to very conservative (scored as plus two), with simply liberal, no preference, or conservative in between. By this measure, 21 percent of the Roper respondents are liberals and 44 percent conservatives. The same pattern emerges when we use ANES data to separate the economic and social dimensions.

52. The data were "smoothed" by combining all respondents for five-year periods (1973–1977, 1978–1982, and so on to 1998–2002). Each period had between 61,000 and 100,000 observations. The values on the ideology index for the other quintiles generally array themselves between the highest and lowest quintiles in the expected fashion.

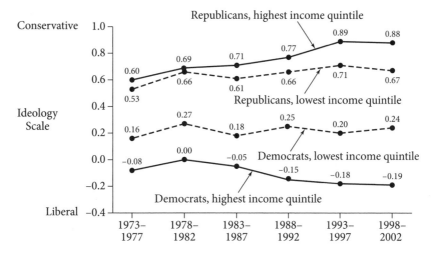

Figure 9.7 Ideology over Time for Partisans in Highest and Lowest Income Quintiles: Mean Score on Conservative–Liberal Scale, 1973–2002

Source: Roper Surveys (1973–2002).

direction of liberalism is seen to have been less sharp than the corresponding conservative shift for the Republicans. However, it is notable that the ideological shift among Democrats derives from the increasing liberalism of the most affluent Democrats, especially those in the highest income quintile.

Figure 9.8 presents the results of a parallel analysis—using the same Roper data, the same measure of overall liberalism or conservatism, and an eight-point scale measuring political activity—stratifying by activity rather than by income.[53] We divide the rank and file for each party into groups on the basis of the number of participatory acts in which they engaged: the least active undertook none of the eight acts; the most active undertook at least five.[54] The pattern for activity is very similar to that for income. The most active in both parties have moved apart more sharply than their more politically

53. The eight participation items on the additive scale are sufficiently similar over time so that we feel comfortable comparing them over the period. Fifty-seven percent of the Roper respondents did none of these things, 33 percent did one or two, 7 percent did three or four, and 2 percent did five or more.

54. To simplify the presentation, we present results only for the most and least active groups. If we add two more groups, those who performed one or two acts and those who took part in three or four, their ideological scores are between those of the least and most active in just the way we would expect.

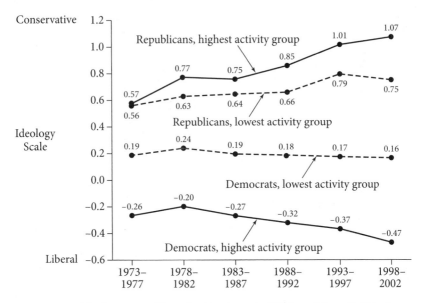

Figure 9.8 Ideology over Time for Partisans in High and Low Political Activity Groups, 1973–2002

Source: Roper Surveys (1973–2002).

Note: The low activity groups engaged in zero of eight acts and the high activity groups engaged in five or more. The eight acts are running for office, engaging in political party work, signing a petition, going to a public meeting, giving a speech, writing an article, being on an organizational committee, and being an organizational officer.

quiescent fellow partisans. As in the case of income, although the drift toward conservatism is particularly noteworthy among the most active Republicans, even the least active Republicans have moved to the right. For Democrats, the movement in a liberal direction is less striking than the corresponding conservative movement among Republicans but is even more concentrated among the most active Democratic identifiers. If we were to superimpose Figure 9.8 on Figure 9.7, we would see, in addition, that the polarization between the activists from the two parties has been even more pronounced than the polarization between their upper-income adherents.

As interesting as these details might be, we should emphasize the bigger picture: in both parties, the relative affluence and the distinctive preferences of activists have driven the increasing polarization of the parties at the level of the mass public, with the result that not only are Republicans and Democrats further apart than in the past but the activists in each party have grown away from their less active identifiers.

Conclusion

In this chapter we have used evidence about political activity to shed light on two puzzles: In a two-party system with equal voting, why, contrary to the logic of the median voter model, does the majority who have incomes at the lower end of the economic ladder not use their voting power to foster public policies that redistribute wealth from those above the median? And why do the two parties and their candidates not converge at the preferences of the median voter but instead offer genuine policy alternatives? We have shown that voters are not equal in their voting strength. Instead, those who work in or donate to campaigns—whose economic position, economic needs, and policy preferences do not reflect those of the median voter—are in a position both to have additional influence on the outcome of an election and to send direct messages to candidates about their preferences. Vote-seeking candidates, therefore, do not converge at the median voter. Instead, the requirements of running and funding a campaign force parties and candidates to be responsive to political activists—whose circumstances and perspectives have been communicated to them.

Within the electorate as a whole, as well as within each of the major parties, the median voter, campaign worker, and campaign contributor are more affluent than and less inclined to support income redistribution than is the median citizen. What is more, the donor of the median dollar is even further, often much further, from the median citizen. These findings about the greater affluence and economic conservatism of political participants provide an important perspective on why, the Downsian model to the contrary, there is no income confiscation in America. Political aspirants seeking the political support needed to be nominated by their parties and to run an effective campaign will be drawn away from the median voter, with clear consequences for policy outcomes.

Moreover, parties and candidates do not converge either at the position of the median voter or at some weighted average that accounts for differences in activity and political voice. Instead—reflecting the constraints imposed by a variety of factors including differences among geographical constituencies, processes of candidate selection, the need to appeal to party activists, and the fact that office seekers do not inevitably place their desire to maximize votes before their ideological commitments—the parties differ. When we considered the data for Democrats and Republicans separately, we saw that, at each level of political activity, the partisans differ from those who are less active in their income and their views on economic and social issues. Furthermore, the activists in each party are more affluent and less centrist in their views than the rank and file, and they have become even more so in recent decades, thus contributing both to the increased polarization of the parties and to a circumstance such that the gaps in income and ideology between the median party identifier and the median party activist have grown.

However influential the Downsian model and however compelling its logic, its predictions miss important aspects of current political realities. When we modify the model by introducing an understanding of the stratification of political participation, we not only improve its capacity to account for contemporary political outcomes but also clarify the significance of unequal voice in political life. Without a consideration of unequal voice, Downs's model is misleading; without an analysis of the electoral process that begins with Downs, the implications of unequal voice are not as clear.

PART III

Inequality of Political Voice and Organized Interest Activity

10

Political Voice through Organized Interests: Introductory Matters

Since long before Tocqueville famously noted the American propensity to form associations in pursuit of joint ends, political and otherwise, organizational activity has served as an important channel for the expression of political voice. The political messages conveyed through the medium of individual citizen participation are paralleled by a flood of messages emanating from organized interests. We construe citizen voice and organized interest voice not as separate topics but as closely related modes of communicating the preferences and interests of the public to public officials. In part, these two channels for the expression of political voice are linked by the fact that many individual participatory acts—for example, making a contribution to an electoral campaign through a political action committee or writing a letter to a government official at the behest of a union or professional association of which one is a member—are undertaken in the context of organizations. As we shall emphasize throughout, however, because a majority of organizations active in political life have no members in the usual sense of the word, individual political activity within membership associations does not constitute the sum total of organized interest involvement in politics.

This chapter introduces a section in which we inquire into the kinds of interests that are represented by organizations in national politics, the extent to which that configuration approximates equality of political voice, the way that it has changed over the past generation, and the various activities undertaken by organizations in politics.[1] In the chapters that follow we shall use

1. The chapters in this section draw from the intellectual framework contained in Kay L. Schlozman and John T. Tierney, *Organized Interests and American Democracy* (New York:

systematic evidence about the organizations that become involved in Washington pressure politics to describe the dazzling array of organized interests and measure the weight of their activity in lobbying, making donations to political action committees (PACs), testifying at congressional hearings, and filing amicus briefs before the Supreme Court.

We would be naïve to expect organized interest politics to show patterns of inequality of political voice any less pronounced than what we have been describing for individuals. In fact, although it is difficult to imagine how this proposition could be tested empirically, it is probably fair to say that, of the various forms of collective political voice—through political parties, social movements, or organizations—expressions of preference through organized interest activity are least likely to represent all citizens equally and that the economically advantaged speak especially loudly and clearly in organized interest politics.

Collective political efforts raise the same kinds of questions about inequalities of political voice that we have been considering with respect to individual activity. When political organizations assume a major share of the burden of articulating citizen needs and preferences, questions about representation assume particular relevance and take on additional complexities. We want to know what kinds of organizations are involved, for whom they speak, and how much they say.

Before proceeding to the data in subsequent chapters, we pause in this chapter to consider several matters that complicate the understanding of inequalities of political voice through organized interests. First, we differentiate between, on the one hand, the view of organized interest influence that emerges from the periodic scandals involving the use of illicit cash and favors to buy policy benefits from public officials and, on the other, what we would consider the ordinary, and completely legal, inequalities intrinsic to organized interest politics. The newsworthy incidents that, understandably, engage the attention of the media contrast with our subject: the ongoing activity, the

---

Harper and Row, 1986), chap. 4. Further discussion and additional bibliography are contained in William C. Mitchell and Michael C. Munger, "Economic Models of Interest Groups: An Introductory Survey," *American Journal of Political Science* 35 (1991): 512–546; Andrew McFarland, "Interest Groups and the Policymaking Process: Sources of Countervailing Power in America," in *The Politics of Interests*, ed. Mark P. Petracca (Boulder, CO: Westview Press, 1992), chap. 3; Frank R. Baumgartner and Beth L. Leech, *Basic Interests: The Importance of Groups in Politics and in Political Science* (Princeton, NJ: Princeton University Press, 1998), chaps. 5 and 6; and David Lowery and Virginia Gray, "A Neopluralist Perspective on Research on Organized Interests," *Political Research Quarterly* 57 (2004): 163–175.

overwhelming share of it legal, of thousands of organizations that seek policy influence in Washington politics.

We also discuss the multiple factors—not least of which is the fact that *less than one-eighth of the organizations active in national politics are membership associations of individuals*—that make it even more difficult than it is for individual input to identify in practice when a circumstance of equal political voice has been achieved for organized interest input.

As difficult as it is to measure departures from equal voice for organized interest activity, what we eventually find clearly does not even approximate equal voice. As background for our empirical inquiry, in this chapter we review briefly the political science theories about the processes that impose barriers to the organization of like-minded publics and their participation in politics and the implications of those processes for the shape of organized interest input into politics.

Finally, a large section of this chapter is devoted to discussing a question parallel to one we posed about individual participation: Does organized interest activity make a difference for political outcomes? As in the case of individual participation, inequalities of political voice become consequential when linked to policy influence. It seems obvious that there must be some impact from the efforts of the thousands of persons spending millions of hours and billions of dollars on attempts to influence Washington policy. Nevertheless, measuring organized interest influence turns out to be a more complicated task than is sometimes assumed.

Bribery and the Politics of Extraordinary Inequalities

Cigar in hand, he gazes out from the cover of the August 4, 1888, *Harper's Weekly* with icy self-satisfaction. His elbow rests on a table containing a dish of cigarettes, various snifters and flasks, and an array of glasses—some drained, some half filled—the right size and shape for libations from whiskey to champagne. The caption announces his occupation: "The Lobbyist." Organized interests and their representatives enjoy low esteem with the American public, and in the popular imagery, organized interest activity is firmly linked to corruption of the political process. Of the many flavors of American political scandal—sometimes involving electoral chicanery, sometimes the abuse of office, and, of course, sometimes sex—one recurrent form of political corruption involves bribery of public officials. When it is uncovered, bribery inevitably elicits explosions of appropriate public indignation.

The Teapot Dome scandal, which emerged during the administration of Warren Harding and contributed to its low repute among historians, is in many ways typical of the bribery scandals that have emerged with regularity in Washington politics.[2] A scandal of Byzantine complexity that requires a scorecard to follow, Teapot Dome involved the decision taken in 1922—one that dismayed conservationists—by Secretary of the Interior Albert Fall, to lease drilling rights to private oil companies in the naval petroleum reserves at Elk Hills in California and Teapot Dome in Wyoming. After investigations by Congress and the press, it emerged that Fall had received a loan of $100,000—a figure worth considerably more than $1 million in current dollars—from Edward Doheny of the Pan-American Petroleum and Transport Company, whose son had delivered the money "in cash, 'in a little black bag.'"[3] Further revelations demonstrated that Fall had also received even more substantial sums from Harry Sinclair of Mammoth Oil. Eventually, the leases were ruled illegal by the courts, and Fall, who had refused to testify during the Senate hearings on the grounds of self-incrimination, was convicted of accepting bribes. Penniless, broken, and unrepentant, he served nine and a half months of his one-year prison sentence, most of it in the prison hospital, and never paid his $100,000 fine. Fall's conviction for bribery to the contrary, both Doheny and Sinclair were acquitted and walked out of court as free men.[4]

In one respect, Teapot Dome is distinctive as a national bribery scandal. More commonly, it is members of Congress rather than the executive branch who are accused of taking bribes. In other respects, Teapot Dome was more typical. As always when political corruption is exposed, members of the press and the public were infuriated by the scandal. One concern that inevitably emerges when an influence-peddling scandal makes news is the impact on the public confidence in government. Teapot Dome was no exception. Thoughtful observers worried that the scandal might undermine the people's trust in their leaders. Wrote Albert J. Beveridge, former Republican senator, from his retirement in Indiana: "I am gravely concerned about the state of

2. This account is drawn from Burl Noggle, *Teapot Dome: Oil and Politics in the 1920s* (Baton Rouge: Louisiana State University Press, 1962).

3. The current value of the loan was calculated from the Bureau of Labor Statistics Web site, http://www.bls.gov/data/inflation_calculator.html (accessed March 31, 2010). Details on the transaction come from Noggle, *Teapot Dome*, p. 75. For a detailed chronology, see chap. 5.

4. Noggle, *Teapot Dome*, pp. 201, 210–213. Because he refused to testify in the Senate hearings, Sinclair was jailed briefly for contempt of the Senate and criminal contempt of court (pp. 145, 185–186).

the public mind. Out in this neck of the woods, ordinary citizens are [concluding] that nobody is straight about anything."[5]

As is well known, Americans have a limited attention span, and public outrage does not last forever; at some point, as other issues dominate the headlines, public concern moves elsewhere. The response to a second series of the Teapot Dome hearings, focusing on new and even more problematic revelations, typified this pattern.[6] Although the sums involved were even more substantial than before, this round of Teapot Dome never gained public traction—perhaps because the financial machinations were even more complicated, perhaps because the public suffered from scandal fatigue.

Although political scandals involving money always generate at least temporary public opprobrium, we rarely inquire why this form of corruption offends so deeply. As James C. Scott explicates succinctly, in a modern democratic polity, corruption "seems especially damaging since it undermines both the egalitarian assumptions of majority rule and the principles of even distribution of civil and social rights of which we normally approve. Under liberal democratic regimes, corruption represents an additional and *illegal* advantage of wealthy interests over and above the *legal* advantages they normally enjoy by virtue of large campaign contributions, muscle in the courts, and so forth."[7]

In essence, a concern with bribery partakes of the same set of concerns that underlie the democratic principle of one person, one vote. Of the resources for political persuasion and influence—skills, time, and money— money is not only the most unevenly distributed but also the one whose distribution hews most closely to fault lines of political conflict. Given how unequal our bank accounts are, to allow cash gifts or preferments to public officials from the stakeholders in a policy controversy is to place citizens on a

5. Noggle, *Teapot Dome*, p. 122.

6. Noggle, *Teapot Dome*, chap. 9.

7. James C. Scott, "Handling Historical Comparisons Cross-Nationally," in *Political Corruption: Concepts and Contexts*, 3rd ed., ed. Arnold J. Heidenheimer and Michael Johnston (New Brunswick, NJ: Transaction, 2002), p. 135, emphasis in the original. In a similar vein, Mark E. Warren asserts that "corruption of democracy is a violation of the norm of equal inclusion of all affected by a collectivity" in "What Does Corruption Mean in a Democracy?" *American Journal of Political Science* 48 (2004): 334. See also Michael Johnston, *Syndromes of Corruption: Wealth, Power, and Democracy* (Cambridge, England: Cambridge University Press, 2005), chaps. 1–2, esp. pp. 8–9. Susan Rose-Ackerman, in "When Is Corruption Harmful?" in *Political Corruption*, ed. Heidenheimer and Johnston, pp. 353–371, considers the economic as opposed to the political consequences of corruption.

very unequal footing when it comes to potential political influence. The principles that govern markets are not always applicable to democracy. We expect that, in a capitalist economy, rare gems and real estate will be sold to the highest bidder but rightly outlaw that principle when it comes to the making of public policy in a democracy. Of course, in a functioning democracy principles other than majority rule often obtain when decisions are made. Constitutional principles are not subject to simple majority rule. Moreover, public officials may depart from the principle of majority rule by deferring to the preferences of an intense minority, to their own judgment of the long-term good of all, or to the dictates of neutral criteria of competence or expertise. Still, if there is any distinction between politics and markets in a democracy, winners should not be determined by the number of dollars they bring to the table.

Organized Interests and Ordinary Inequalities

As a scandal, Teapot Dome was in most ways typical; as an example of organized interests in politics, it was anything but business as usual. Of course, we cannot know how common the shenanigans characteristic of the periodic lobbying scandal are in American politics. Presumably, cover-ups are sometimes successful, and thus such behavior occurs more frequently than we know. Nevertheless, we believe that illegal influence peddling is not the norm—an assessment that is substantiated by the fact that the United States consistently ranks quite well as rated by the Transparency International Corruption Perceptions Index.[8]

Furthermore, we depart from popular stereotypes of pressure politics by recognizing that organized interest representation is essential both for democratic governance and for the formation and legitimation of sound public policy. Almost by definition, any polity that aspires to be considered a democracy must permit citizens to organize in order to communicate their prefer-

8. According to the Web site of Transparency International, http://www.transparency.org/policy_research/surveys_indices/cpi/2008 (accessed July 17, 2008), scores are constructed on the basis of ratings in surveys of businesspeople and country analysts. The United States is fairly consistently at the bottom of the top decile (behind most of the countries of Northern Europe as well as Canada, New Zealand, Australia, and Singapore) and ranked eighteenth out of 180 countries in 2008. For a discussion of the difficulties in measuring corruption and the criticisms of the Transparency International scale, see Eric M. Uslaner, *Corruption, Inequality, and the Rule of Law* (Cambridge, England: Cambridge University Press, 2008), pp. 11–17.

ences to office holders, to have an impact on the peaceful and lawful selection of public officials, and to influence policy outcomes. But organized interests are not merely to be tolerated in a democracy; they also have a central part to play in its functioning. Representatives of organized interests perform a crucial role in providing information in the policy-making process: they call attention to issues, furnish evidence about how problems are being experienced on the ground, and provide expertise about the anticipated consequences—both substantive and political—of proposed solutions. Furthermore, by making possible a two-way process of communication, organized interests facilitate the acceptance and legitimation of policies by interested stakeholders.

While we cannot know how often the unsavory practices exposed during lobbying scandals occur in American politics, we can know more about inequalities of political voice characteristic of the day-to-day, completely legal, functioning of organized interest politics. If we look systematically—and we don't often—we can understand more about the ordinary inequalities of pressure politics.

The Puzzle of Political Equality
when Representation Is by Organizations

We discussed in the introduction how difficult it would be to specify what political equality among individuals would look like. However, when political advocacy is by organizations rather than by individuals, a number of additional complicating factors are introduced, making it even more difficult to know when a condition of political equality has been achieved. Still, it is possible to identify when we have substantial departures from political equality and to make comparative assessments of relative inequality. Moreover, the domain of organized interest representation is fundamentally so far from a circumstance approximating equality of political voice that the appropriate intellectual task is not to specify what an ideal model of equal political voice would look like but to explore systematically the boundaries of a very unequal system.

Any attempt to consider matters of equality of political voice must immediately raise several caveats. We mentioned in the introduction that equal political voice does not require universal activity, only representative activity. We also pointed out several problems that make it difficult to know how to assess degrees of inequality of political voice: different participatory acts involve different, and not easily compared, metrics of input—for example, hours versus dollars, a big check versus a small one, or a well-reasoned letter versus a cursory one; even the same act can vary in both volume and effectiveness. In addition, we referred to the dilemma of how to treat the problem of intensity—that is, how to weigh the opinions of those who care deeply relative to the views of the less strongly committed.

The question of what political equality would look like if representation were collective is even more complicated. When we considered the inequalities of political voice through individual activity, we began with the adult population of the United States—which can be enumerated, perhaps imperfectly, by the Census—and assessed the extent to which individual political participation is representative of that population. When it comes to organizations, there is no such natural population to serve as a baseline. In fact, as we shall see later in the chapter, both the free rider problem and the resource problem function as barriers to the natural emergence of organizations among those who have common interests and concerns. Thus, if it were possible to enumerate all existing organizations, that census would yield a set of organizations that is already stratified by several criteria. The set of politically active organizations drawn from the already partial group of all organizations is further skewed. Thus the two-stage process by which organizations may or may not come into being and then may or may not get involved in politics makes it very difficult to assess the representativeness of political voice through organizational activity.

Besides, moving from consideration of individuals to consideration of groups that are arrayed along a variety of dimensions of political cleavage and that have radically different numbers of members—and sometimes no members at all in the ordinary sense—introduces additional complexities. With respect to norms of political equality, how do we compare the relative political weight of the AARP (formerly the American Association of Retired Persons), which has more than thirty million members, and the American Beekeeping Federation, which has twelve hundred?[9] Of course, in a circumstance parallel to what we have already seen for individuals, organizations differ in their resources, especially money. Such disparities in resources are not necessarily proportional to the number of their members, the number of politically relevant issues with which they are concerned, or the intensity of

9. These figures were taken from the online version of *Encyclopedia of Associations*, http://galenet.gale.com.proxy.bc.edu/a/acp/db/grr/extendedorg.html (accessed November 27, 2006).

their political concerns. Budgetary resources are especially important because they can be converted into a wide variety of inputs into the policy-making process: among them, such traditional lobbying activities as undertaking policy-related research, seeking to inform and persuade policy makers, drafting bills, testifying at hearings, issuing policy statements and reports, and the like; making campaign contributions; grassroots lobbying; and influencing public opinion through issue advertising, funding friendly authors and think tanks, and placing news and opinion pieces in the mass media. Moreover, organizations with deep pockets can spend more generously in hiring the talent to undertake these activities.

A further dilemma in seeking to understand the implications of collective representation for political equality is that even groups of people who have important attributes in common are rarely uniform in their interests, needs, and preferences. Those who focus on what is sometimes called "intersectionality" point out the tendency to overlook such differences within groups. We would expect, for example, veterans who served during the Korean War to have different health care needs from those who served in Iraq, Hispanics to be divided along lines of national origin, and elderly people with pensions to have different concerns than those who rely solely on Social Security.[10]

That the preferences and concerns of the members of an association are unlikely to coincide on all relevant issues implies that there may be ambiguity in knowing for whom the organization is speaking. For one thing, as Robert Michels famously pointed out a century ago, the leaders of a membership group develop their own interests, which may conflict with those of the rank and file.[11] Besides, among the rank and file, it is easy to imagine circumstances in which, say, younger workers and retirees in the Service Employees International Union or chemists in industry and chemists at universities in the American Chemical Society might part company with one another. Such divisions of opinion and interest are even more common when a voluntary

10. While the concept is relevant to all groups regardless of circumstance of advantage, the term *intersectionality* is typically used to refer to internal divisions within groups of the disadvantaged. There is now a large literature on intersectionality. For brief discussions and bibliographical references, see Nancy Burns, Kay Lehman Schlozman, and Sidney Verba, *The Private Roots of Public Action: Gender, Equality and Political Participation* (Cambridge, MA: Harvard University Press, 2001), pp. 274–276, and Dara Z. Strolovitch, *Affirmative Advocacy: Race, Class, and Gender in Interest Group Politics* (Chicago: University of Chicago Press, 2007), pp. 24–28.

11. Robert Michels, *Political Parties: A Sociological Study of the Oligarchical Tendencies of Modern Democracy*, trans. Eden and Cedar Paul (New York: Dover, 1959).

association implicitly seeks to represent a constituency beyond its dues-paying members. The activists who join and run membership associations often have opinions that are, if not different in direction, more intensely held and more extreme than do others within the larger constituency. For example, while there is a substantial range of opinion on Middle Eastern policy among Jewish Americans, the most prominent and vocal organizations of American Jews tend to be supportive of hard-line Israeli foreign policy. In each of these cases, when an organization takes a stand in politics, there are ambiguities as to whose voice is being heard.

Such ambiguities are multiplied when we move beyond associations of individuals. In fact, the majority of organizations in the pressure system are not associations of individuals.[12] They may be institutions like corporations or museums, which have no members at all, or associations of institutions like the Snack Food Association, which has firms as members, or the National Association of Children's Hospitals.[13] That the preponderance of organizations in the pressure system have no members in the ordinary sense raises knotty questions for equality of political voice. When representation is by institutions like corporations or universities, whose concerns and preferences are being represented? As Justice John Paul Stevens put it in his dissent in the campaign finance case *Citizens United* v. *FEC* (2010):

> It is an interesting question "who" is even speaking when a business corporation places an advertisement that endorses or attacks a particular candidate. Presumably it is not the customers or employees, who typically have no say in such matters. It cannot realistically be said to be the shareholders, who tend to be far removed from the day-to-day decisions of the firm and whose political preferences may be opaque to management. Perhaps the officers or directors of the corporation have

12. On this point, which is often overlooked in discussions of organized interest politics, see David Lowery, Virginia Gray, Jennifer Anderson, and Adam J. Newmark, "Collective Action and the Mobilization of Institutions," *Journal of Politics* 66 (2004): 684–705.

13. Following Robert H. Salisbury, who in "Interest Representation: The Dominance of Institutions," *American Political Science Review* 78 (1984): 64–76, first pointed to the significance of institutions in interest representation, we use the term *institution* in a specialized way to refer to any of a large category of for-profit and not-for-profit economic entities—many of which become involved in the Washington pressure community. Even though it is perfectly reasonable to refer to Congress or the Department of Agriculture as political institutions, when we refer to institutions in this context we mean such entities as corporations, universities, hospitals, and museums.

the best claim to be the ones speaking, except their fiduciary duties generally prohibit them from using corporate funds for personal ends.

Similar questions can be raised about a university: whose interests are being represented—those of the administration, professors, staff, graduates, or students? Surely, there are many occasions when the interests of these various stakeholders coincide. Still, evidence that ranges from the number of labor–management disputes before the National Labor Relations Board to student protests over tuition hikes suggests that what is good for one part of an institutional constituency is not necessarily good for all.[14]

An additional complexity is that the set of organizations that take stands in politics is structured around multiple axes of cleavage. It is complicated enough to characterize political equality considering only the dimension around which the largest portion of organized interest representation takes place, economic interests associated with making a living. It becomes even more so when the framework includes the many other dimensions around which interests are organized. In achieving equality of political voice, how much of the total organizational space should be allocated to organizations based on race? Sexual orientation? Attitudes toward capital punishment or the rights of homeowners? Hobbies?

Still, as difficult as it might be to specify the requirements for equality of political voice when interest representation is by organizations, it is unambiguous that our systematic data analysis in the next few chapters will show a configuration of organized interests and distributions of organized interest activity that depart substantially from a circumstance of equal political voice.

The Emergence of Groups: Theoretical Approaches

Although America is often characterized as being "a nation of joiners," in recent decades scholars have paid a great deal of attention to the *barriers* to the emergence of interest groups. This literature sometimes assumes that it is obvious why a student of democracy should pay attention to the difficulty of getting a nascent interest group off the ground or to the conditions under which the effort is likely to be successful. Given our concern with political

14. See Robert M. Skinner, *More than Money: Interest Group Action in Congressional Elections* (Lanham, MD: Rowman and Littlefield, 2007), for examples of the internal complexities of active interest organizations and the impact of internal characteristics on the functioning of such groups.

voice, we should make explicit why we care about the circumstances under which interest groups emerge: because organized interests are such an essential part of the process by which policy makers in a democracy learn about the preferences and needs of citizens, barriers to entry into the political fray have potential consequences for the representation—and, in particular, for the equal representation—of citizen interests. Thus we need to pay attention not only to explaining where groups come from but also to understanding the kinds of interests and concerns that have vigorous representation—and those that do not.[15] It is not simply the size but the shape of the organized interest system that counts.

As a prelude to our empirical investigation of changes in the size and shape of the organized interest system, let us consider briefly the various theoretical approaches to the explanation of how organizations emerge and become politically active. While the central focus in these accounts is on where interest groups come from and the factors that encourage or inhibit their emergence, the several intertwined strands of explanation of their origins are germane to our concern with inequalities of political voice.[16]

The once-dominant analysis of American politics, interest group pluralism —an approach associated with Arthur Bentley and David Truman—placed interest groups at the center of policy making and emphasized the low barriers to entry to the organized interest system and its fluid nature.[17] Thus

15. Further discussion of these issues and additional bibliography are contained in McFarland, "Interest Groups and the Policymaking Process," and Baumgartner and Leech, *Basic Interests*, chaps. 5 and 6.

16. Helpful discussions of the various explanations for the emergence of interest groups can be found in Anthony J. Nownes, "The Population Ecology of Interest Group Formation: Mobilizing for Gay and Lesbian Rights in the United States, 1950–1998," *British Journal of Political Science* 34 (2004): 49–58, and Andrew S. McFarland, "Neopluralism," *Annual Review of Political Science* 10 (2007): 53–57.

17. Among the most significant works from an interest group pluralist point of view are Arthur F. Bentley, *The Process of Government* (Chicago: University of Chicago Press, 1908); David B. Truman, *The Governmental Process: Political Interests and Public Opinion*, 2nd ed. (New York: Knopf, 1951); Earl Latham, *The Group Basis of Politics* (Ithaca, NY: Cornell University Press, 1952); and Robert A. Dahl, *A Preface to Democratic Theory* (New Haven, CT: Yale University Press, 1956). The authors of these works differ from one another in important respects, and no single work serves as the definitive text for interest group pluralism. Thus the brief rendition of the interest group pluralist perspective in this paragraph is a caricature that, while frequently set up as a straw man by detractors, was never espoused by interest group pluralists. In particular, Robert A. Dahl, in *Who Governs?* (New Haven: Yale University Press, 1961), gave a less central place to interest groups in his understanding of political contestation and never subscribed to the belief that the competing pressures comprise the

organized interests supposedly emerge more or less automatically in response to disturbances in the political environment and regularly enter and leave the pressure system as dictated by their concerns about the particular issues at stake in politics at any given time. Because of the ease of entry and exit from pressure politics, the absence of advocacy for a particular point of view in a political controversy was interpreted as an indication of a corresponding absence of political concern on the part of those who might be expected to, but do not, articulate a collective opinion on a policy matter.

The interest group pluralist argument about the absence of barriers to the emergence of political groups was challenged by two influential though quite different analyses, one by E. E. Schattschneider and the other by Mancur Olson. As we note in our epigraphs, Schattschneider famously observed— and we echo in our title—that "the flaw in the [organized interest] heaven is that the heavenly chorus sings with a strong upper-class accent."[18] In an analysis that speaks directly to our concern with equality of political voice, he argued that what he called the "pressure system" is biased in favor of groups representing the well off, especially business, and against groups representing two other kinds of interests.

According to Schattschneider, broad public interests or public goods constitute the first kind of interest that is unlikely to achieve organized representation. These are objectives like safer streets or safer consumer products, cleaner water or cleaner government, enhanced domestic security or reduced domestic violence that are broadly beneficial to all in society. Schattschneider argued that, while everyone has a stake in such broad public interests, relatively few people care intensely about them or give them the highest political priority.

In an influential formal analysis, Mancur Olson reached through logical deduction the same conclusion about advocacy on behalf of public interests that Schattschneider had reached by empirical observation. Olson pointed out that large, diffuse groups lacking the capacity to coerce cooperation or to provide selective benefits often face severe collective action problems that prevent them from organizing on behalf of their joint political concerns.[19]

---

sum total of political forces in making policy. For a discussion of the many uses of the term *pluralism*, see McFarland, "Neopluralism."

18. E. E. Schattschneider, *Semi-Sovereign People* (New York: Holt, Rinehart and Winston, 1960) p. 35.

19. See Mancur Olson Jr., *The Logic of Collective Action: Public Goods and the Theory of Groups* (Cambridge, MA: Harvard University Press, 1965).

According to Olson, the rational individual has an incentive not to spend scarce resources of money and time in support of favored causes but rather to free ride on the efforts of others. Only when an organization has the capacity to force a potential free rider to support group efforts or when it supplies benefits available only to those who assist in the collective effort will an organization emerge and prosper.[20] Moreover, contrary to the understanding common in democratic theory that the larger the jointly interested constituency, the more likely it is to be represented by an organization, the free rider problem is exacerbated when the potential group is large.[21] Thus Olson's logic gives a formal foundation to Schattschneider's observation that the proportion of people who take part in an organization seeking public goods is far smaller than the proportion that would benefit from those conditions.

In an observation that has generated less discussion by social scientists, Schattschneider pointed to a second kind of interest that would be less well represented in politics, one that links directly to our findings with respect to inequalities of political voice among individuals, that of the disadvantaged. While Olson's argument rests on the notion that there are costs to starting an organization or keeping one going, he neglected the disparities among groups in the capacity to assume those costs. In contrast, Schattschneider understood that not all potential constituencies are in a position to bear the costs of political organization and advocacy.

20. Olson construed the problem of interest group formation as a form of "Prisoner's Dilemma." More recently, in works that are not especially well known in political science, others have argued that this construction is too limited. Reconceptualizing the problem in terms of multiple production functions, they discuss how different kinds of production functions are related to different kinds of games: in particular, how accelerating production functions are related to assurance games (sometimes referred to as coordination games). See Russell Hardin, "Collective Action as an Agreeable n-Prisoners' Dilemma," *Behavioral Science* 16 (1971): 472–81; Pamela Oliver, Gerald Marwell, and Ruy Teixeira, "A Theory of the Critical Mass, I: Interdependence, Group Heterogeneity, and the Production of Collective Action," *American Journal of Sociology* 91 (1985): 522–556; Michael Taylor, *The Possibility of Cooperation* (New York: Cambridge University Press, 1987); Douglas D. Heckathorn, "The Dynamics and Dilemmas of Collective Action," *American Sociological Review* 61 (1996): 250–277; Peter Kollock, "Social Dilemmas: The Anatomy of Cooperation," *Annual Review of Sociology* 24 (1998): 183–214; Pamela E. Oliver and Gerald Marwell, "Whatever Happened to Critical Mass Theory? A Restrospective and Assessment," *Sociological Theory* 19 (2001): 292–311; and Russell Hardin, "Normative Methodology," in *Oxford Handbook of Political Methodology*, ed. Janet M. Box-Steffensmeier, Henry E. Brady, and David Collier (New York: Oxford University Press, 2008), chap. 2.

21. This point is made by Matthew Grossmann, who points out that "democratic theory generally suggests that large groups should be represented more extensively than small groups." See his *The Not-So-Special Interests: Interest Groups, Public Representation, and American Governance* (Stanford, CA: Stanford University Press, forthcoming), p. 66.

Olson's collective action model has elicited many efforts that meet it on its own terms and seek to square its compelling logic with empirical reality. Clearly, the political arena contains many large organizations that are not in a position to force members to join and that do not provide selective benefits of significant economic value. Moreover, ongoing groups that do offer selective benefits to induce membership had to overcome the free rider problem at the outset in order to get off the ground. In a penetrating discussion of the problem of organizational maintenance and the difficulties confronting someone who wishes to found a membership group or keep one going, James Q. Wilson points to a broader array of selective benefits that organizations can provide in place of material ones—in particular, the solidary benefits that derive from working with others and enjoying their fellowship and esteem and the purposive benefits that arise from the satisfaction associated with supporting a cherished cause.[22] Another perspective emphasizes the role of entrepreneurs—the costs they bear, the rewards they reap, and the constraints they face—in founding and nurturing new organizations.[23] Jack L. Walker Jr. focuses on the significance of patrons—for example, foundations or even governments—that encourage and subsidize the founding of new organizations, especially organizations that seek public goods.[24] Anthony J. Nownes argues that even more important than external patrons are large donors among members.[25] Because large donors are more likely to value the fellowship and recognition that accompany organizational involvement and leadership, they are more likely than outside patrons to stick around for the long run.

An approach from a quite different tradition points to the roots of many political organizations in social movements. A distinctive aspect of politics in America is that citizens' movements seeking to supplement mass action with more readily sustained forms of participation ordinarily form organizations and move into pressure politics. The pressure community in Washington politics contains hundreds of such "social movement organizations"—the

---

22. James Q. Wilson, *Political Organizations* (New York: Basic Books, 1973), esp. chaps. 2–3.

23. See, for example, Robert H. Salisbury, "An Exchange Theory of Interest Groups," *Midwest Journal of Political Science* 13 (1969): 1–32, and Norman Frolich, Joe A. Oppenheimer, and Oran R. Young, *Political Leadership and Collective Goods* (Princeton, NJ: Princeton University Press, 1971).

24. Jack L. Walker, *Interest Groups in America: Patrons, Professions, and Social Movements* (Ann Arbor: University of Michigan Press, 1991), esp. chap. 5.

25. Anthony J. Nownes, "Patronage and Citizen Groups: A Reevaluation," *Political Behavior* 17 (1995): 203–221.

National Organization for Women, the Human Rights Campaign, the National Council of La Raza, and the Friends of the Earth, to name a few—that grew out of protest movements.[26] Social movements do not necessarily leave conventional political organizations in their wake, but the literature on movements provides clues as to the circumstances under which such organizations are likely to emerge. In particular, resource mobilization theorists draw attention to the requirement for certain basic resources—among them leadership capacity and access to some financial backing.[27] Although the resource mobilization perspective focuses more explicitly on the role of resource availability in the success of social movements, the lesson is directly applicable to the domain of political organizations and has relevance for our concern with the representation of the disadvantaged by organized interests.

Still another perspective, that of population ecology theory, draws from insights in the biological sciences and shifts the focus from the micro-level processes that lead to the formation of individual organizations to a macro-level consideration of organized interest communities.[28] Focusing on "density" and "diversity," David Lowery and Virginia Gray use state-level data on the organizations active in state politics and emphasize that changes in the

26. Students of social movements usually differentiate social movement organizations (SMOs) from other organizations that take part in pressure politics. However, they do not make clear in what ways, if any, such organizations are distinctive other than their origins in social movements. Analysts of social movements disagree as to whether moving from protest to organization, on one hand, represents a form of cooptation and decreases a movement's effectiveness by taking the pressure off—a position associated, in particular, with Frances Fox Piven and Richard A. Cloward in *Poor People's Movements: Why They Succeed, How They Fail* (New York: Vintage Books, 1977)—or, on the other, permits issue activists to achieve sustained vigilance, follow-through, and a place at the table. For a brief review of the controversy and bibliographical references, see David Meyer, *The Politics of Protest: Social Movements in America* (Oxford, England: Oxford University Press 2007), pp. 36–37.

27. See, in particular, John D. McCarthy and Mayer N. Zald, "Resource Mobilization and Social Movements: A Partial Theory," *American Journal of Sociology* 82 (1977): 1212–1241, and Mayer N. Zald and John D. McCarthy, *Social Movements in an Organizational Society* (New Brunswick, NJ: Transaction, 1987).

28. Although sociologists have used population ecology theory to study various kinds of organizations, Virginia Gray and David Lowery, in *The Population Ecology of Interest Representation* (Ann Arbor: University of Michigan Press, 1996), have pioneered its application to political organizations. Since the publication of their book-length treatment, they have elaborated their model in many ways. For a brief presentation and references to their many journal articles, see Lowery and Gray, "Interest Organization Communities: Their Assembly and Consequences," in *Interest Groups Politics*, 7th ed., ed. Allan J. Cigler and Burdett A. Loomis (Washington, DC: CQ Press, 2007). While their work is more theory driven and less descriptive than ours and they have different intellectual concerns, to the extent that our analyses intersect, our findings are similar.

size and shape of the organized interest community depend on a variety of contextual influences, including the size and shape of the existing organized interest community. Thus organized interest "populations are more than an accumulation of mobilization events."[29] The number of organizations responds, in particular, to the number of potential constituents in a particular interest domain and to the availability of resources for organizations. With respect to diversity, both the extent to which the organizations within a particular community are diverse and the specific mix of kinds of organizations within that diversity respond to many influences. Presumably a single set of variables is not sufficient to account for each of the many kinds of organizations that comprise a diverse organized interest community.

As shown by this brief summary, those who discuss the problem of the formation of organizations sometimes elide the issue of why students of politics should care about the issue. To state what is obvious: because organizations perform a crucial function in representing citizen concerns before public officials, it matters for equal protection of interests if there are barriers to organizational formation.

Do Organized Interests Influence Public Policy?

Toward the end of *The Once and Future King,* T. H. White's rendering of the legend of King Arthur, the just order that has been created in Camelot is falling apart. Mordred, King Arthur's illegitimate son, whose actions are the source of the discord, proposes that, instead of resorting to combat to ascertain the truth of the allegations about an adulterous affair between the knight Lancelot and Queen Guenever, the matter be put to a jury. The dispirited King replies:

> You are still very young, Mordred. You have yet to learn that nearly all the ways of giving justice are unfair. If you can suggest another way of settling moot points, except by personal combat, I will be glad to try it. . . .
>
> You see, moot points have to be settled somehow, once they get thrust upon us. If an assertion cannot be proved, then it must be settled some other way, and nearly all these ways are unfair to somebody. It is not as if you would have to fight the Queen's champion in your own

---

29. Lowery and Gray, "Interest Organization Communities," p. 137.

person, Mordred. You could plead infirmity and hire the strongest man you knew to fight for you, and the Queen would, of course, get the strongest man she knew to fight for her. It would be much the same thing if you each hired the best arguer you knew, to argue about it. In the last resort it is usually the richest person who wins, whether he hires the most expensive arguer or the most expensive fighter, so it is no good pretending that this is simply a matter of brute force.[30]

In political controversies that involve organized interests, do those who are in a position to hire the most expensive arguers—and many of the arguers are, indeed, very expensive—inevitably prevail?

When we discussed inequalities of political voice among individuals in Chapter 5, we made the point that such inequalities would be of little consequence for democratic equality if the silent were no different from activists with respect to politically relevant preferences and concerns or if the messages conveyed through the medium of political voice had no impact on public policy.[31] These same considerations pertain to inequalities of political voice through organizations. We examine the first of these conditions—the representativeness of political expressions through the medium of organized interest activity—at length in the next four chapters. Before embarking on that extensive investigation, we consider the second question about the requisites for interest group impact: Are policy makers responsive to the voice of the organized interests? If, for whatever reason, organized interests have no influence on policy, no matter how unrepresentative their political voice, it would make no difference for democratic equality.

From one perspective, we might be led to expect limited consequences from organized interest efforts to influence policy. The widely recognized gravitational pull of the policy status quo would have the effect of restricting the impact not only of organized interests but also of many other political forces seeking policy change. A recurring theme in the analysis of American

---

30. T. H. White, *The Once and Future King* (New York: Berkley Books, 1939), p. 557.

31. When we posed this matter in Chapter 5, we posited a third circumstance that would imply that inequalities of political voice do not result in unequal treatment. If policy makers were sensitive to the silences—that is, if they sought to identify the kinds of individuals from whom they were not hearing—and sought to engage in compensatory responsiveness, inequalities of political voice would not lead to inequalities of political responsiveness. However, as we saw, the opposite obtains. Policy makers are more responsive to the opinions of the advantaged than to those of the disadvantaged. Thus, rather than compensating for the weaker voice of the disadvantaged, they amplify the voice of the better off.

politics is that a variety of factors, starting with a set of constitutional arrangements designed to circumvent majority tyranny, establish multiple veto points at which interested parties—whether public officials or representatives of opposing organized interests—can throw up roadblocks to policy innovation. Even if the organized interests seeking policy change are more numerous and active and deploy more resources than their opponents, the status quo usually prevails, with the result that organized interest activity does not always produce the desired outcome.[32] However, to assume that this circumstance indicates the impotence of organized interests ignores the extent to which the status quo that exerts so much power reflects, among many other forces, past organized interest activity. Organized interests have previously had a voice in the construction of the policy status quo.[33] Besides, this circumstance means that organized interests seeking to preserve the policy status quo may be scoring unnoticed victories in blocking unwelcome policy changes.

Organized interests do not behave as if their efforts come to naught. The inertial force of the policy status quo to the contrary, there is plenty of evidence of extensive activity by organized interests both in Washington and in the state capitals. According to the records of the Senate Office of Public Records, in 2009, 13,746 individuals registered as lobbyists and $3.49 billion was spent on lobbying activity.[34] As Beth Leech puts it in an overview of the impact of lobbies: "Nearly $3 billion is spent each year on lobbying and political action committee (PAC) campaign contributions in apparent attempts to influence public policy. Hundreds of thousands of people mobilize for hundreds of different causes—demonstrating, writing letters, and making phone calls to officials. If all of these efforts are so lacking in influence, why does anyone bother?"[35]

32. Frank R. Baumgartner, Jeffrey M. Berry, Marie Hojnacki, David C. Kimball, and Beth L. Leech, *Lobbying and Policy Change: Who Wins, Who Loses, and Why* (Chicago: University of Chicago Press, 2009), Tables 11.6 and 11.7. In their study of ninety-eight policy controversies, the authors find (p. 241–243) that that the usual outcome is no change at all.

33. Baumgartner et al., *Lobbying and Policy Change*, p. 240. The literature on path dependency is also relevant. A policy decision at one point of time is affected by what came before and will affect what comes next. See Paul Pierson, "Path Dependence, Increasing Returns, and the Study of Politics," *American Political Science Review* 94 (2000): 251–267.

34. Figures are taken from the Web site of the Center for Responsive Politics, www .opensecrets.org/lobby (accessed June 23, 2010).

35. Beth Leech, "Lobbying and Influence," in *The Oxford Handbook of American Political Parties and Interest Groups*, ed. L. Sandy Maisel and Jeffrey M. Berry (Oxford, England: Oxford University Press, 2010), p. 535.

Why do they bother? According to most observers—from political reporters and commentators to political officials to lobbyists themselves to the public at large—organized interests are powerful. Thus they bother because they make a difference when it comes to political outcomes. They may not always be victorious, and their impact may be marginal rather than complete. And they are hardly the only factor that matters in determining policy outcomes. Still, that organized interests have an effect on policy is axiomatic in many quarters.

In contrast, political scientists do not always find evidence for organized interest influence. We examined two kinds of studies by political scientists, in-depth case studies of particular issue areas or particular lobbying organizations and multivariate studies of the efforts of organized interests to influence policy. We expected that the case studies would have found that organized interest activity has consequences for policy and that the statistical studies would be quite mixed. While it is difficult to make an overall assessment across many studies that differ from one another in important ways, we were surprised to find that the two kinds of studies differ less notably than we might have predicted. On balance, the same précis applies to both case studies and statistical studies. Sometimes the evidence shows an impact, and sometimes it does not. And even when there is clear evidence of the policy influence of organized interest activity, the connection of organized group activity to policy outcomes is weaker than the researchers had expected at the outset. As Leech puts it, "The search for a definitive statement about the power of lobbyists has become the Holy Grail of interest group studies. All seek it, but are being forever led astray."[36]

In the remainder of this chapter we consider the matter of the influence of organized interests on policy outcomes. We do not present any new data on the policy impact of organized interests. Instead we draw on the existing literature, including several general overviews, to summarize the present state of knowledge on the effectiveness of organized interests in national politics.[37] We shall not shy from pointing to the uncertainties and contradictory evidence.

36. Leech, "Lobbying and Influence," p. 534.
37. One of the best recent overviews is in Leech, "Lobbying and Influence." See also Frank R. Baumgartner, "Interest Groups and Agendas," in *The Oxford Handbook*, ed. Maisel and Berry, chap. 27. Other works offering summaries of the literature include Richard Smith, "Interest Group Influence in the U.S. Congress," *Legislative Studies Quarterly* 20 (1995): 89–139; John R. Wright, *Interest Groups and Congress: Lobbying, Contributions, and Influence*

Do Organized Interests Influence Policy?
The View from the Media

Anyone who opens a daily newspaper or watches the news will see references to organized interests of all sorts at the center of the policy-making process, along with detailed descriptions of their activities. Lobbyists for business interests routinely justify their high salaries on the basis of their ability to produce a return on investment from political action that dwarfs any reasonable expectation of payoff from even the most successful economic venture.[38] To a regular reader of national newspapers, that organized interest activity has an impact on policy outcomes seems obvious. Some snippets from the press culled from a manila folder into which newspaper articles about organized interests had been tossed in a somewhat haphazard manner will illustrate the range of examples that exist. These examples are but a tip of the iceberg.[39]

- The commercial education industry, which includes such for-profit institutions as the University of Phoenix, used well-placed lobbyists and strategically placed campaign contributions to win over key members of Congress, and a provision ending the 50 percent rule, a 1992 requirement that colleges could deliver no more than half their courses online rather than on campus, was inserted into a budget bill.[40]

- Companies and lobbyists representing a diverse array of interests including airlines, Wall Street firms, and local rural electric

(Boston: Allyn and Bacon, 1996), chap. 1; Thomas Stratmann, "Some Talk: Money in Politics; A (Partial) Review of the Literature," *Public Choice* 124 (2005): 135–156; and Paul Burstein and C. Elizabeth Hirsh, "Interest Organizations, Information, and Policy Innovation in the U.S. Congress," *Sociological Forum* 22 (2007): 174–199.

38. These are more likely to be claims made to their clients or employers than more generally. Their public face is often more modest; they claim that they inform decision makers but do not influence them.

39. It is hard to ignore the amount of coverage of lobbying activity in the press. A search of Lexis-Nexis for articles mentioning lobbies or organized interests during the year when we were finishing this book found a stunning 1,269 articles in the *New York Times* (an average of three and a half per day) and 1,049 in the *Washington Post*. And if one moves away from New York and Washington, one finds numerous such references: *Denver Post*, 260; *San Francisco Chronicle*, 267; and *Atlanta Journal-Constitution*, 257. These articles are on a range of major, and sometimes minor, issues.

40. Sam Dillon, "Online Colleges Receive a Boost from Congress," *New York Times*, March 1, 2006.

cooperatives persuaded legislators to weaken substantially a bill originally designed to shore up the nation's private pension system by ensuring that companies set aside sufficient money to fund their promised pensions.[41]

- Residents of Treasure Island, Florida (population 7,514), avoided higher bridge tolls and a tax increase when a lobbying firm they hired on retainer succeeded in persuading the chair of the House Appropriations Committee to place into an omnibus bill an earmark for a $50 million new toll-free bridge.[42]

- After intense lobbying by the trucking industry, the Federal Motor Carrier Safety Administration—headed by a former top official of the American Trucking Associations—loosened the rules governing the number of hours truckers can be on the road.[43]

- In what was described as "a David-and-Goliath struggle," a comprehensive immigration reform bill collapsed after Numbers USA, an anti-immigration grassroots citizen group, generated a million faxes to the Senate.[44]

- With the help of legislators representing districts far from sugar-growing areas—all of whom had benefited from political contributions from PACs representing sugar growers and refiners—a House farm bill retained a generous subsidy for sugar growers and other provisions protecting them from Mexican competition.[45]

- The Air Transport Association beat back a proposed $5 airline departure fee.[46]

- Justifying a contract for a highway monitoring system that had been awarded without competitive bidding on extremely favorable

41. Mary Williams Walsh, "Major Changes Raise Concerns on Pension Bill," *New York Times*, March 19, 2006.

42. Jodi Rudoren and Aron Pilhofer, "Hiring Lobbyists for Federal Aid, Towns Learn That Money Talks," *New York Times*, July 2, 2006.

43. Stephen Labaton, "As Trucking Rules Are Eased, a Debate on Safety Intensifies," *New York Times*, December 3, 2006.

44. Robert Pear, "A Million Faxes Later, a Little-Known Group Claims a Victory on Immigration," *New York Times*, July 15, 2007.

45. Dan Morgan, "Sugar Industry Expands Influence," *Washington Post*, November 3, 2007.

46. Jeffrey H. Birnbaum, "Mickey Goes to Washington," *Washington Post*, February 17, 2008.

terms to Traffic.com, the Transportation Department "cited nine letters from members of Congress—many of whom had received frequent campaign contributions from executives at Traffic.com."[47]

- Forty-two House members inserted into the *Congressional Record* statements supporting a provision in the 2010 health care bill regarding the manufacture of biologic drugs that had been drafted, at least in part, by lobbyists for Genentech, a major producer of such drugs.[48]

The issues addressed in these examples are diverse, but—with the exception of immigration, pension reform, and health care—relatively narrow and low profile. The organizations involved include a citizen group and a small municipality along with a large number of mainstream economic organizations—corporations, trade associations, and farm groups. The number of examples is small, and a different selection would produce a different array of outcomes. But each of these examples shows an unambiguous policy payoff from political action, supporting the view that lobbying is a potent force.

Even so, the narratives of these policy controversies contain mixed evidence on the success of lobbying. The ranks of active organizations include losers as well as winners. Consumer groups and candy manufacturers opposed the sugar subsidy. A diverse coalition of organizations including the United States Chamber of Commerce, the Roman Catholic Church, and representatives of the hotel, restaurant, construction, and high-tech industries had put lobbying muscle behind the unsuccessful immigration reform. The travel industry had proposed the airline departure fee to help finance a program of federal government support for increased foreign tourism, a program that has not gotten off the ground.

While a number of organizations—including powerful ones that are used to getting their way in national politics—were not successful in realizing their policy goals, their political efforts did not backfire. They were not worse off for having entered the political fray. Besides, even some of the losers ended up better off for having become involved politically. For example, representatives of such "specialty crops" as fruits, vegetables, and nuts were dis-

47. Eric Lipton, "U.S. System for Tracking Traffic Flow Is Faulted," *New York Times*, December 14, 2009.

48. Bennett Roth, "Arguing for Teva's Brand: Critics Say Pharmaceutical Firm Lobbies Both Sides," *Roll Call*, November 18, 2009.

appointed by their treatment in the farm bill that protected not only sugar subsidies but other commodity crops including cotton, corn, and wheat. However, while organized advocates for specialty crops did not achieve what they had hoped, they fared better in the 2007 farm bill than they ever had in the past.[49] Thus a consistent reader of the national press would gain the impression that, while politically active organized interests do not always get everything they ask for, political action usually produces positive policy results.

Do Organized Interests Influence Policy?
Empirical Inquiries

Moving from journalism to academic inquiry, we find a large literature on organized interest activity. The literature is of two types. On the one hand, there are numerous case studies by scholars—mostly political scientists but also historians and other social analysts—that focus intensely on a single political organization or issue. On the other is a set of multicase systematic statistical studies of some aspect of interest group activity. Each approach has strengths and liabilities. Case studies provide in-depth analyses that can encompass many aspects of the role of interest organizations in the making of public policy, but such studies face the twin problems of generalizability and potential selection bias. In contrast, studies involving multivariate analysis have weaknesses when it comes to the measurement of critical variables. Each of these complementary approaches has something to contribute to our understanding of organized interests in politics. We begin with the case study literature and then turn to the more systematic literature to see what the two modes of analysis tell us and why they sometimes differ.[50]

What the Case Studies Say

To provide an overview of what such cases can tell us about the impact of organized interests on public policy, we selected a set of such studies—some

---

49. Andrew Martin, "Lean Crop of Dollars," *New York Times*, October 4, 2007.

50. On the value of case studies and their relation to causal quantitative analysis, see Gary King, Robert O. Keohane, and Sidney Verba, *Designing Social Inquiry: Scientific Inference in Qualitative Research* (Princeton, NJ: Princeton University Press, 1994), and Thomas J. McKeown, "Case Studies and the Limits of the Quantitative World View," in *Rethinking Social Inquiry: Diverse Tools, Shared Standards*, ed. David Collier and Henry E. Brady (Lanham, MD: Rowman and Littlefield, 2004), chap. 6. See also Harry Eckstein, "Case Study and Theory in Political Science," in *Handbook of Political Science*, ed. Fred Greenstein and Nelson Polsby

on a particular issue area, some on a particular organization, and some on both.[51] These cases are a heterogeneous bunch and encompass issues that range from agricultural policy to trucking regulation, from campaign finance to the environment, from smoking to gun control. The organizations involved range from the American Trucking Association to the Catholic Church to Common Cause.

The clear advantage of a close case analysis of a domain of organized interest activity is that it makes it possible to present in all its complexity the process by which organized interests engage with other actors in the making of public policy. Case studies usually incorporate thorough consideration of the relevant backstory of the organization or issue; pertinent aspects of the political context, such as the existence of a hostile administration in office; the varied stakeholders, including, for example, policy makers in various branches of government, the media, other organized interests—sometimes in alliance, often

---

(Reading, MA.: Addison-Wesley, 1965), vol. 7, chap. 5; and John Gerring, "What Is a Case Study and What Is It Good For?" *American Political Science Review* 98 (2004): 341–354. Case studies may also include systematic data within the framework of their analysis, thereby blurring the distinction between the case study and more systematic studies.

51. The examples cover a wide range: David Vogel, *Lobbying the Corporation: Citizen Challenges to Business Authority* (New York: Basic Books, 1978); Sar A. Levitan and Martha R. Cooper, *Business Lobbies: The Public Good and the Bottom Line* (Baltimore, MD: Johns Hopkins University Press, 1984); Dorothy L. Robyn, *Braking the Special Interests: Trucking Deregulation and the Politics of Policy Reform* (Chicago: University of Chicago Press, 1987); William Paul Browne, *Private Interests, Public Policy, and American Agriculture* (Lawrence: University Press of Kansas, 1988); Timothy A. Byrnes, *Catholic Bishops in American Politics* (Princeton, NJ: Princeton University Press, 1991); Josh Sugarman, *National Rifle Association: Money, Firepower, and Fear* (Washington, DC: National Press Books, 1992); Lawrence S. Rothenberg, *Linking Citizens to Government: Interest Group Politics at Common Cause* (Cambridge, England: Cambridge University Press, 1992); Douglas R. Imig, *Poverty and Power: The Political Representation of Poor Americans* (Lincoln: University of Nebraska Press, 1996); David Vogel, *Kindred Strangers: The Uneasy Relationship between Politics and Business in America* (Princeton, NJ: Princeton University Press, 1996); Darrell M. West and Burdett A. Loomis, *The Sound of Money: How Political Interests Get What They Want* (New York: W. W. Norton, 1998); Kelly D. Patterson and Matthew M. Singer, "The National Rifle Association in the Face of the Clinton Challenge," in *Interest Group Politics*, 6th ed., ed. Allan J. Cigler and Burdett A. Loomis (Washington, DC: CQ Press, 2002), 55–78; Sheldon Kamieniecki, *Corporate America and Environmental Policy: How Often Does Business Get Its Way?* (Stanford, CA: Stanford University Press, 2006); Allan M. Brandt, *Cigarette Century: The Rise, Fall, and Deadly Persistence of the Product that Defined America* (New York: Basic Books, 2007); Peggy Lopipero, Dorie E. Apollonio, and Lisa A. Bero, "Interest Groups, Lobbying, and Deception: The Tobacco Industry and Airline Smoking," *Political Science Quarterly* 122 (2007–2008): 635–656; and Robert J. Spitzer, *The Politics of Gun Control*, 4th ed. (Washington, DC: CQ Press, 2008).

in opposition—or the public and the relative resources at their command; the complete process of policy formation, including the critical agenda-setting phase; and possible causal links between the actions of organized interests and policy outcomes. Because the focus of each study is on a single case, the emphasis is not on all factors that might matter but rather on those that actually do matter. The result is that each of these thorough accounts covers many relevant aspects of the case in question, but the various cases do not all cover the same aspects.

While case studies of organized interests in action may provide fuller accounts of the links between attempts at influence and policy outcomes, they also have well-known liabilities. One is generalizability: the difficulty of specifying the larger class of instances to which a single case can be generalized. Another is related to selection effects: the distinct possibility that researchers will not bother with cases in which organized interests are unsuccessful or, indeed, with small and narrow issues in which few actors are involved and the stakes—though high for the particular participants—do not have a large public impact or arouse much public concern.[52] Similarly, researchers may forgo cases in which presumed stakeholders do not take part. In light of the potential for positivity bias in the set of policy controversies that become the objects of detailed case studies, it would be risky to aggregate across many, many case studies and assume that it is then possible to generalize about the extent of the influence of organized interest.

Our choice of cases was in no way systematic. In particular, we did not seek cases with any bias in the direction of finding organized interest impact. Indeed, in several cases the interest organization at the center was not as successful as it would have wished or as the researcher had originally anticipated. As Sheldon Kamieniecki writes in the preface to his book on business and environmental policy:

> When I first began working on this book . . . I anticipated finding that American corporations are regularly involved in environmental agenda building and policymaking and that they exert a great deal of influence over government decision making. Like many, I accepted the conventional wisdom that business frequently opposes proposals that will improve environmental quality in order to protect its profits. . . . Of course, good social scientists are supposed to remain objective. . . .

52. See Leech, "Lobbying and Influence," pp. 540–541.

As the data show, business interests do not participate in environmental policy debates at a high rate and, when they do, they have mixed success in influencing policy outcomes.[53]

Critics of this literature sometimes argue that authors of case studies systematically select cases showing organized interest influence. Our survey suggests that, while such authors may gravitate to subjects that are substantively interesting, they are not necessarily choosing cases that demonstrate the power of organized interests.

Who Wins? Who Loses?

What did we learn from the case studies about the impact of organized interest activity? Taken together, they most certainly do not demonstrate that policy is determined by contending organized interests to the exclusion of such obviously significant political factors as the political climate of the times, public opinion, the preferences of relevant public officials, positions taken by the parties, or the institutional maintenance needs of governmental institutions. The cases make clear that policy making and the role of organizational advocates in the process warrant the complexity of a case study.

Political influence involves cause and effect.[54] In none of these cases is there a clear-cut dyadic relationship between an interest organization and a policy maker with a simple "accept or reject" policy outcome to what the lobby proposed.[55] For a variety of reasons, even under the magnifying glass

53. Kamieniecki, *Corporate America and Environmental Policy*, pp. ix–x. This formulation does not mean that the business was not involved or, when involved, had no influence. When the issue was important, business was active and often held sway. See p. 257.

Our group of mostly book-length case studies does not include examples—if, indeed there are any—of an important domain of lobbying in which an interest organization, operating more or less beneath the radar of other policy makers and the public, seeks a narrow public policy benefit. Later in the chapter, in the section on earmarks and regulatory changes, we shall discuss such policies.

54. Robert A. Dahl, in *Modern Political Analysis*, 4th ed. (Englewood Cliffs, NJ: Prentice-Hall, 1984), p. 23, makes clear the causal link by positing that "A influences B to the extent that he or she changes B's actions or predispositions in some way." There is some controversy over the use of the terms "power" and "influence" in Dahl's work—with "power" referring to intended effects sought by the power wielder and "influence" referring to any causal relationship of A's behavior on B. Because the word *influence* is used often in discussions of the role of organized interests, we use *influence* to refer to intended causality. On the terminology of causality, power, and influence, see McFarland, "Neopluralism," pp. 46–47.

55. As we show later in the chapter when we discuss studies of earmarks and regulatory changes, there are instances that approximate the more straightforward dyadic lobby and

of the case study, that kind of causality may be difficult to prove. Given the complexity of the policy-making process, it may not be possible to establish definitively that the outcome was the result of the actions of a particular corporation or professional association seeking to shape policy by inserting a clause in pending legislation or passing a favorable amendment. Was the clause inserted or did the amendment pass as the result of organized interest actions? As the result of the intervention of a powerful subcommittee chair with strong personal convictions or a particular constituency need? As the result of a threatened presidential veto? Or as the result of all of these working together?

One barrier to demonstrating such cause and effect is that, to understand whether an organized interest gets what it wants, we need to understand its goals, which are often ambiguous. For example, there may be several objectives in play at the same time. The leaders and staff of an organization may be pursuing one policy aim while holding another back or may be pursuing both at once. In addition, political organizations have institutional maintenance goals. Moreover, as we discussed earlier in the chapter, many organized interests are not internally homogeneous. For example, Catholic bishops share a profession, a religion, and a commitment to its principles, but they differ internally in terms of the priority they give to those principles.[56] Pursuing a number of liberal domestic and international public interest goals can lead to internal divisions among members of Common Cause, divisions they do not always understand.[57] Such internal discord can affect an organization's political effectiveness and make it difficult to know precisely whether it has been successful in achieving its goals.

In the context of a case study, it is also possible to provide evidence about the many techniques, some of which would be difficult to measure systematically, that organized interests use to influence what happens during many stages of policy making in many institutional venues.[58] Some of the activities

---

policy-maker situation. These are more likely to be found in relation to narrow issues of importance to a particular interest group. Authors of book-length case studies are less likely to be attracted to cases of this sort.

56. Byrnes, *Catholic Bishops*, pp. 6–8.

57. Rothenberg, *Linking Citizens to Government*, p. 261 et passim.

58. For a discussion of the several stages of the policy-making process and examples of the way in which different results will be found depending on the stage studied, see Erik K. Godwin, R. Kenneth Godwin, and Scott Ainsworth, "Is Corporate Lobbying Rational or Just a Waste of Money?" in *Interest Group Politics*, 7th ed., ed. Cigler and Loomis, p. 266.

in which organized interests engage—for example, testifying at congressional hearings or filing amicus briefs—are officially documented and therefore measurable. But much of what organized interests do—not only the informal networking and socializing but also such vital activities as grassroots lobbying, conducting research, and providing information to policy makers—is not formally recorded and is therefore extremely difficult to measure across issues and organizations. That the relevant actors sometimes prefer their activities to be unobserved renders measurement even more problematic. In the introduction to a selection in one of their edited volumes, Allan J. Cigler and Burdett A. Loomis observe:

> Political scientists have regularly struggled to assess the importance of lobbying; many analyses have been simplistic, even useless. Much of the difficulty comes from a lack of understanding of what lobbyists actually do. How do you quantify "schmoozing" or assess the implicit bargains that transpire between lobbyists and legislators over an obscure bit of tax law? Moreover, neither legislators nor lobbyists want to fully acknowledge their reliance on each other, even when such reliance is central to decision making in a complex democratic society.[59]

Just as the objectives and advocacy methods are complex and varied, so are the outcomes. Whether an organization has prevailed may not always be clear. A desired provision may be buried as a detail in an amendment. The objective might have been to block action, in which case success may not be obvious without close scrutiny of the process. Advocates often settle for half loaves. Suppose a new tax passes in spite of vigorous opposition by a reputedly powerful organization. However, in response to the lobbying, the rate is half what was originally proposed. Is that a victory or a loss?

Case studies are able to provide much fuller information about such potentially ambiguous outcomes than are more systematic statistical studies using a large sample of cases. The kind of up-close and in-detail observation about who did what when and where that is possible in a case study gives us a chance to connect the dots and therefore to make inferences about the extent to which the policy result was shaped by the actions of an organized interest. Although they differ in many ways, the cases before us do allow us to draw some significant conclusions about the impact of lobbying.

59. Allan J. Cigler and Burdett A. Loomis, in *Interest Group Politics*, 6th ed., ed. Cigler and Loomis, p. 225.

Case Studies: The Bottom Line

What is the bottom line? Our reading of cases supports several conclusions. First, *organized interests do not always win.* None of the case studies presents a picture of a lobby dominating an issue area without opposition, a finding that holds regardless of whether we are considering poverty groups, which are notoriously weak; the National Rifle Association (NRA), an organization with a reputation as a powerhouse; or the various business organizations concerned about agricultural policy or trucking, tobacco, or environmental regulation.

That said, *organized interests very often get their way.* The organizations in the cases were successful a good deal of the time. In short, neither polarized position about the influence of lobbies is correct. This mixed conclusion— which is consistent with the heterogeneity and complexity of the case studies —is perhaps unsatisfying. However, there is a third finding that seems compatible with what the cases show. In all cases involving legislative or regulatory politics—win, lose, or a bit of each—*organizations are never worse off, and are usually better off, for having gotten involved than they would have been if they had not been at the table.* Had they ceded the process to the other actors, they would either have gained less or lost more.[60]

Two cases, both involving losses by powerful political organizations, illustrate this proposition: the passage of a bill banning semiautomatic firearms over the opposition of the NRA and the passage of regulations requiring health warnings on cigarette packs, a regulation strongly opposed by the once-powerful trade association the Tobacco Institute. In each case, the involvement of the "defeated" lobbies modified the result. In the gun control case, the NRA delayed the decision and managed to narrow the gun control section of the bill in question.[61] In the cigarette case, the label to appear on each pack was "watered down to read 'Caution: Cigarette Smoking May Be Hazardous to Your Health.' Indeed, such ambiguity—'may be'—made it a warning in name only, all but officially retracting the findings of the surgeon general's committee."[62]

60. This generalization does not necessarily hold for the judicial branch. The nature of judicial decisions is such that organizations that go to court—usually because they have been sued but even because they have initiated legal action—can end up worse off than they were to start.

61. Patterson and Singer, "The National Rifle Association in the Face of the Clinton Challenge," pp. 60–61.

62. Brandt, *Cigarette Century*, p. 256. According to Robyn, in *Braking the Special Interests*, p. 233, even the serious defeat dealt to the American Trucking Association (ATA) in trucking

A final principle illustrated by the case studies is that, *even when it is over, it is not over.* Policy matters are rarely settled once and for all, and the issues that were the occasions for apparent victories or defeats may reappear with different results. Although the NRA may have lost in its 1994 confrontation with the administration of Bill Clinton over semi-automatic weapons, the assault weapons ban lapsed in 2004, and as of this writing, the NRA has been successful in defeating numerous efforts to restore it.[63] With regard to the tobacco case, the Public Health Cigarette Smoking Act of 1969 substituted a less ambiguous cigarette package label with wording closer to that originally proposed in 1964: "Warning: The Surgeon General Has Determined That Cigarette Smoking Is Dangerous to Your Health."[64] Still, the cigarette lobby was largely able to contain its policy losses for decades until the settlement in 1997 of the suit brought on behalf of several states by a group of attorneys general. In an unusual development, the Tobacco Institute was dissolved as part of the settlement.[65] Even though the settlement constituted a policy defeat for the tobacco industry, according to one account, "the industry emerged . . . decidedly intact ready to do business profitably at home and abroad."[66] In light of the ever-unfinished nature of policy disputes, the organized interest that stays ready for action on the ground is in a better position to recoup a loss in the next round.

Do Organized Interests Influence Policy?
What the Statistical Studies Say

Statistical studies in political science are perhaps even more mixed in their conclusions about the impact of organized interest activity on policy. Case

---

deregulation—the result of faulty tactics and bad timing by the ATA—was tempered by the avoidance of even harsher outcomes.

63. Michael Isikoff, "A Ban Gets Shot Down," *Newsweek*, April 6, 2009, p. 6.

64. A. Lee Fritschler and Catherine E. Rudder, *Smoking and Politics: Bureaucracy Centered Policymaking*, 6th ed. (Upper Saddle River, NJ: Pearson Education, 2007), pp. 67 and 83.

65. See Martha A. Derthick, *Up in Smoke: From Legislation to Litigation in Tobacco Politics*, 2nd ed. (Washington, DC: CQ Press, 2005), p. 86.

66. Brandt, *Cigarette Century*, p. 445. In more recent times, the cigarette manufacturers have been challenged by victims of smoking-related illnesses or by their relatives, who want damages. But the industry has gathered support from state governments in limiting damages from such claims. Cigarette manufacturers have done so by supplying revenue to states through support of state taxes on cigarettes, the support of which loses them less in sales than would losses to successful suits with punitive damages.

studies find evidence for significant lobbying impact by taking into account many aspects of a single case and emphasizing the ones that are significant. Statistical studies use systematic data about a narrower set of characteristics of organized interest activity across many cases.

That statistical studies do not always show policy consequences for organized interest involvement has occasionally led political scientists to adopt a flippant counterorthodoxy, to the effect that there is no evidence for organized interest influence on policy. Such a conclusion is a caricature of the mixed results of the multivariate studies. Some of them find significant influence; others show no significant influence. However, there are none that demonstrate a significant negative impact of organized interest activity on policy. Thus a superficial summary of these studies, taken together, would reach a conclusion not very different from what we gleaned from the case studies. It is inaccurate to conclude that policy influence is inevitable; it is also inaccurate to conclude that statistical studies show no evidence of policy influence from the political activity of organized interests.

The Problem of Selection

While they have obvious virtues, multivariate analyses do not necessarily escape all the problems that bedevil case studies. For example, when it comes to the matter of generalizability, quantitative studies of organized interests in action often focus on a single policy area or agency and adduce systematic data about the activities of many organizations or the comportment of all members of the House and Senate. It is widely recognized that organized interest politics do not fall into a single pattern.[67] Because we would expect, for example, different politics depending on whether what is at stake is government procurement or financial regulation, policy-specific statistical studies would not necessarily yield the same results about the nature and extent of organized interest influence. A recent study by Frank Baumgartner, Jeffrey Berry, Marie Hojnacki, David C. Kimball, and Beth Leech comes as close as possible to solving the problem of specifying a random set of policy contro-

---

67. Two important statements about patterns of conflict and cooperation in organized interest politics are found in Theodore J. Lowi, "American Business, Public Policy, Case Studies, and Political Theory," *World Politics* 16 (1964): 677–715, and Wilson, *Political Organizations*, chap. 15. For discussion, see Schlozman and Tierney, *Organized Interests*, pp. 82–85 and 279–283. Anthony J. Nownes, in *Total Lobbying: What Lobbyists Want (and How They Try to Get It)* (Cambridge, England: Cambridge University Press, 2006), builds into his study of lobbying an understanding of the concept that different policy domains are characterized by different patterns of organized interest activity and conflict.

versies to examine by assembling a weighted random sample of organizations that lobby in Washington and then asking a government relations liaison in each organization to name the issue on which he or she had been working most recently, thus generating a random selection of issues of concern to lobbyists in national politics.[68]

These authors' substantive findings about organized interest influence are complex, defying simple assumptions about the relationship between the efforts of political organizations and policy payoff. Similarly, a somewhat earlier major study of organized interest influence in four policy domains of national politics notes that "private interests confront pervasive uncertainty in national policy-making systems. . . . Despite historically unparalleled levels of investment in attempts to shape national policy, the return on that investment is highly uncertain and often intangible."[69]

The Problem of the Political Agenda

Still, Baumgartner and colleagues note that, by selecting issues on which Washington representatives are actually working, they fail to consider policy matters that do not make it into the policy-making process: "'What wasn't there?' The research design allowed us to capture a range of issues lobbyists were trying to convince Congress or an agency to pay attention to, but what of problems that weren't even on the periphery of the agenda?"[70] The result is that their analysis cannot take into account an important form of organized interest influence—having an impact on the composition of the political agenda as opposed to determining the outcome once controversies become objects of political contention. In fact, an earlier study by one of the authors, Jeffrey Berry, demonstrates the impact on the political agenda of the rise of liberal public interest groups.[71]

The political agenda is not simply a reflection of the issues that engage the attention of policy makers or the American public. Instead the construction of the political agenda is a political process in which organized interests take

68. Baumgartner et al., *Lobbying and Policy Change*.

69. John P. Heinz, Edward O. Laumann, Robert L. Nelson, and Robert H. Salisbury, *The Hollow Core: Private Interests in National Policymaking* (Cambridge, MA: Harvard University Press, 1993), pp. 4–5. The authors generated data by interviewing samples of Washington representatives, public officials, and clients who hire Washington representatives in four policy domains: agriculture, energy, health, and labor.

70. Baumgartner et al., *Lobbying and Policy Change*, p. 254.

71. Jeffrey Berry, *The New Liberalism: The Rising Power of Citizen Groups* (Washington, DC: Brookings Institution, 1999), chap. 4.

part. In his research on agenda setting in American policy making, John Kingdon finds "many examples of items on the government agenda because of interest group activity" but notes that "a substantial portion of the interest group effort is devoted to negative, blocking activities," pre-emptive action designed to keep unwanted issues off the policy agenda.[72] In a similar vein, writing about "agenda denial," Roger W. Cobb and Marc Howard Ross present strong evidence that established organized interests seek to keep

> new issues off the formal or public agenda. The first observation about the opponents [of new entrants into the policy process] is that they were powerful actors, especially the economic pressure groups interested in maintaining the status quo. In all cases but two [of a wide range of issues studied] powerful economic forces were arrayed against the challengers; in the regulatory cases, the accounting and securities industries, the pharmaceutical and medical industries, and the Catholic Church; in the public health cases, the insurance and medical industries and local developers. These groups are not accustomed to losing political battles without a fight.[73]

Using the term "agenda bias," Baumgartner et al. point out the extent to which the set of policy issues under consideration reflects the realities of political power. When they compare the list of policy matters in their sample with the issues that concern the public as revealed in public opinion surveys, they note the "relative paucity of issues relating to the poor and to the economic security of working-class Americans. . . . Although some marginalized constituencies—ethnic and racial minorities, gays, women—have organized with beneficial results, the same cannot be said of those who are simply poor. . . . There could be no more vivid evidence of the relationship between class and voice than the nature of the issues in our sample."[74] This observation about the difference between the policy agenda and the issue concerns of the public foreshadows the findings in subsequent chapters of this book about the skew in political voice as expressed through organized interests. At

---

72. John W. Kingdon, *Agendas, Alternatives, and Public Policy* (Boston: Little Brown, 1984), p. 52.

73. Roger W. Cobb and Marc Howard Ross, *Cultural Strategies of Agenda Denial: Avoidance, Attack, and Redefinition* (Lawrence: University of Kansas Press, 1997), p. 208. See also Kamieniecki, *Corporate America and Environmental Policy.*

74. Baumgartner et al., *Lobbying and Policy Change*, p. 255.

this point, it is essential to note that systematic studies of organized interest influence take the policy agenda as a given and do not account for the issues that never reach the agenda because they have been kept off by powerful political forces or because those concerned about them lack political voice.

The Problem of Measurement

Our discussion of the case studies pointed to another difficulty, the variations in the information available for systematic comparison about the many aspects of organized interest activity and the many forms that policy takes. The intellectual project in statistical studies of organized interest influence on policy—to establish causal links between inputs in the form of organized interest activity and policy outputs, demonstrating that the policy outcome would not have occurred had the organized interest activity not taken place—turns out to be, for some of the reasons we have already considered for the case studies, a very complicated business. We have already discussed the complexities in specifying an organization's policy objectives, in measuring certain kinds of advocacy efforts, and in assessing whether a policy setback is necessarily evidence of an absence of policy influence.

When it comes to the policy outputs for which links to organized interest activity are sought, because they are readily observable, votes on the floor of the House or Senate are often used as the indicator of organized interest influence. However, as we shall discuss later in the chapter, it is often argued that organized interest influence is more likely to be manifest long before legislation reaches the stage of roll-call voting—in decisions by favorably disposed legislators to expend time and political capital on an issue, in the alteration of details when a bill is marked up, and so on.[75] Furthermore, the major policy action may be undertaken in other venues—for example, when regulations for meat inspections are written at the Department of Agriculture or procurement decisions for a weapons guidance system are made at the Department of Defense. In short, like organized interest inputs, policy outputs are complex and difficult to measure.

Lobbying as Service Provision: Measurement Issues

Analysts of lobbying often focus on services of various kinds as a form of assistance that organized interests have to offer to policy makers. The following description of a lobbyist active on a medical privacy bill makes clear the

---

75. See Leech, "Lobbying and Influence," pp. 541–544.

multiple ways that Washington representatives can help policy makers, especially those in Congress:

> The corporate lobbyist, though not a witness, had been instrumental at every other step: she was heavily involved in drafting the bill, helping sign up congressional cosponsors, organizing the hearing and strategizing with staff about its timing and composition (she identified several witnesses and wrote testimony for two of them), and meeting with staffers during the hearing to clarify points and scribble questions for legislators to ask witnesses: all this even though the medical privacy issue was only a distant concern to the corporation she represents.[76]

In providing such services, which are very difficult to document and measure, lobbyists seek simultaneously to enhance access, to frame policy positions in ways that are congenial, and to leave grateful policy makers in their wake.[77]

Among the most important of these services is the provision of information.[78] Professional lobbyists often have access to substantive expertise and

76. Rogan Kersh, "Corporate Lobbyists as Political Actors," in *Interest Group Politics*, 6th ed., ed. Cigler and Loomis, p. 227.

77. On the significance of service provision in the lobbying process and the importance of the information function of lobbying, see, for example, Lester W. Milbrath, *The Washington Lobbyists* (Chicago: Rand McNally, 1963), chap. 15; Raymond A. Bauer, Ithiel de Sola Pool, and Lewis Anthony Dexter, *American Business and Public Policy* (Chicago: Aldine, 1963), chap. 24; Schlozman and Tierney, *Organized Interests*, pp. 297–301; Keith Krehbiel, *Information and Legislative Organization* (Ann Arbor: University of Michigan Press, 1991); David Whiteman, *Communication in Congress: Members, Staff, and the Search for Information* (Lawrence: University of Kansas Press, 1995); Richard L. Hall and Alan V. Deardorff, "Lobbying as Legislative Subsidy," *American Political Science Review* 100 (2006): 69–84; and Godwin, Godwin, and Ainsworth, "Is Corporate Lobbying Rational?"

78. In light of the amount of information about policy matters that arises from organized interests, the question is often raised about whether such information is accurate. It is possible to cite instances of outright obfuscation. The denial by the tobacco lobby of the health effects of passive smoking reported by Lopipero, Apollonio, and Bero in "Interest Groups, Lobbying, and Deception" constitutes a notorious example. On one hand, there is general agreement that a reputation for credibility is essential for effective lobbying and that knowing prevarication is rare. On the other hand, there is a long continuum separating blatant dishonesty from dispassionate analysis. Wittingly or unwittingly, representatives frame policy arguments in ways that support congenial results by presenting information that is at once accurate and selective. See, for example, Smith, "Interest Group Influence"; Rogan Kersh, "Corporate Lobbyists"; Nownes, *Total Lobbying*, pp. 26–28; and Burstein and Hirsh, "Interest Organizations, Information, and Policy Innovation," pp. 174–178.

political information that would be very costly for government officials and their staffs to generate on their own. Policy-relevant substantive information helps policy makers to understand whether proposed policy changes are technically feasible and whether they are likely to work out as expected. Political information may give policy makers a better understanding of the progress of policy proposals in the political process; the views and actions of other stakeholders, including public officials, other organized interests, constituents, and the public; the electoral and political consequences of supporting or opposing the policy at stake; and the electoral and political fallout should it be enacted.[79]

The case studies we reviewed contain many examples in which information provided by organized interests had an impact on either the overall shape or the details of policy. However, in contrast to such measurable forms of organized interest activity as dollars contributed to campaigns by PACs or amicus briefs filed with the Supreme Court, there is no obvious procedure for quantifying inputs of information and connecting them to policy outcomes, and research measuring the policy impact of information is relatively sparse.[80]

79. In emphasizing the way that Washington representatives provide information to policy makers, we should not overlook the ways that the transmission of information is a two-way process. In "The Paradox of Interest Groups in Washington—More Groups, Less Clout," in *The New American Political System,* 2nd ed., ed. Anthony King (Washington, DC: AEI Press, 1997), chap. 7, Robert Salisbury reminds us that lobbyists also rely on information that they receive from officials. Furthermore, the information path also runs from lobbyists to their clients and constituents: Washington representatives seek to explain and interpret government policy and to moderate their expectations as to what is politically realistic and substantively feasible. On this theme, see Lewis Anthony Dexter, *How Organizations Are Represented in Washington* (Indianapolis, IN: Bobbs-Merrill, 1969), chap. 6.

80. Burstein and Hirsh, "Interest Organizations, Information, and Policy Innovation," pp. 176–177. There are few studies that, with mixed results, focus on testimony at congressional hearings as the vehicle for the provision of information. Burstein and Hirsh, in "Interest Organizations, Information, and Policy Innovation," p. 192, find that testimony in support of a measure on the basis of arguments for its effectiveness is related to a clear increase in the likelihood of the enactment of the proposal. In contrast, Nina Therese Kasniunas, in "Impact of Interest Group Testimony on Lawmaking in Congress," Ph.D. dissertation, Loyola University, Chicago, 2009, reports more ambiguous results. As we shall see in Chapter 14, the process by which organized interests come to testify at congressional hearings is quite different from the process by which they come to lobby. Therefore, the patterns that obtain for congressional testimony are unlikely to obtain for other forms of information provision. Note, by the way, that the corporate lobbyist cited in the earlier example as having been so active with respect to a congressional hearing on medical privacy did not herself testify at the hearing.

The Problem of Establishing Influence

A further difficulty is determining whether the input and output are causally related and establishing the direction of causality between lobbying activity and policy outputs. The usual assumption is that what organizations do affects policy, but it is well known that "policy makes politics." That is, policy also affects organized interests: organizations may be formed or, if in existence, become politically active in response to government policy initiatives.[81] Furthermore, as we mentioned when we discussed the case studies, policy influence is not the same as policy victory. The interactive nature of the policy-making process implies that an organization's goals may change along the way; an organization may give up some things to gain others. Even the loser in a policy controversy may be better off, or less badly off, for having been on the scene than it would have been had it not been involved at all.

The result is a large number of well-executed studies that, taken together, have heterogeneous findings that are not altogether different from those contained in the case studies. The varied conclusions derive not so much from flawed research as from the fact that the studies focus on different aspects of a complex phenomenon. In her review of the unresolved debate in the literature on the effects of interest groups, Beth Leech finds striking continuity in the disagreements in current research, noting: "Modern-day quantitative studies of the influence of lobbying and PACs are as contradictory as the classic cases were."[82] She elaborates, noting:

> There are almost as many ideas about why studies of interest group influence disagree as there are studies that disagree. . . . [There are] a series of methodological problems, including a tendency to study one or a handful of issues, failure to include relevant variables, modeling influence as dichotomous, as well as a lack of attention to the political

---

81. See Beth L. Leech, Timothy LaPira, and Nicholas A. Semanko, "Drawing Lobbyists to Washington: Government Activity and Interest-Group Mobilization," *Political Research Quarterly* 58 (2005): 19–30; Virginia Gray, Matthew Fellowes, and Jennifer Anderson, "Understanding the Demand Side of Lobbying," *American Politics Research* 33 (2005): 404–434; and the essays in *Remaking America: Democracy and Public Policy in an Age of Inequality*, ed. Joe Soss, Jacob S. Hacker, and Suzanne Mettler (New York: Russell Sage Foundation, 2007); and Frank R. Baumgartner, Virginia Gray, and David Lowery, "Federal Policy Activity and the Mobilization of State Lobbying Organizations," *Political Research Quarterly* 62 (2009): 552–567.

82. Leech, "Lobbying and Influence," p. 537.

context of the issues in question . . . [and, in addition,] a tendency to select on the dependent variable, a tendency to focus on the end stage of the policy process, misconceptions about what it is that interest groups actually do, and misconceptions about how the policy process actually works.[83]

Policy Influence on Low-Profile Issues

On balance, the evidence seems to be stronger for lobbying influence when it comes to relatively narrow issues that do not receive a great deal of attention from the media. Two examples of such below-the-radar matters that have significant consequences for particular stakeholders are targeted allocations by the government to specific projects in specific districts, commonly referred to as "earmarks,"[84] and executive branch regulations.

Earmarks, district-specific projects sponsored by individual members of Congress, have traditionally elicited concern and activity by political organizations and provided legislators with opportunities to shore up local electoral support.[85] Each of the individual, targeted items was likely to involve a relatively small allocation compared to big-ticket budget items like defense or Social Security. Still, when aggregated, they added up: Congress inserted 12,881 earmarks worth $18.3 billion into 2007 spending bills, $14.8 billion of which were disclosed by lawmakers.[86] A large-scale statistical study underscores the influence of organized interests in generating earmarks. Data about federal earmark spending and organized interest activity in seven issue areas

83. Leech, "Lobbying and Influence," p. 540.

84. Such discretionary funds are defined on the Web site of the Office of Management and Budget, http://earmarks.omb.gov/earmarks-public (accessed September 28, 2010) as "programs, or grants where the purported congressional direction (whether in statutory text, report language, or other communication) circumvents otherwise applicable merit-based or competitive allocation processes, or specifies the location or recipient, or otherwise curtails the ability of the executive branch to manage its statutory and constitutional responsibilities pertaining to the funds allocation process."

85. For a general overview of earmarks and their origins, see Robert M. Stein and Kenneth N. Bickers, *Perpetuating the Pork Barrel: Policy Subsystems and American Democracy* (New York: Cambridge University Press, 1995); and Kenneth N. Bickers and Robert M. Stein, "The Electoral Dynamics of the Federal Pork Barrel," *American Journal of Political Science* 40 (1996): 1300–1346.

86. Figures compiled by Taxpayers for Common Sense, February 14, 2008, reported on http://www.taxpayer.net/search_by_category.php?action'view&proj_id'996&category'Earmarks&type'Project (accessed September 28, 2010). See also Paul Kane, "Candidates' Earmarks Worth Millions," *Washington Post*, February 14, 2008.

over an eight-year period show clearly that "the allocation of federal discretionary grants depends on the demands expressed by organized interests, and not just the self-serving manipulations of well-placed political actors."[87] After recent attention by politicians and the media to the general issue of earmarks, Congress abandoned earmarks early in 2011. However, early soundings suggest that the substantive impact of this procedural change has been limited.[88]

Like earmarks, rules promulgated by government agencies often combine low public salience with narrow but important effects on particular interests. Under federal "notice and comment" procedures, proposed rule changes must be publicly announced and comments invited. Research on regulations is significant for its focus on the narrow "everyday business" of regulation. While previous studies had found little evidence of greater business effect on regulations compared with other sources of comment, a recent study—with a larger sample, a focus on smaller-scale regulations, and a better measure of policy outcomes—found a significantly greater business impact. Businesses, which submitted the majority of the comments, received a positive response 90 percent of the time, a much higher level of positive response than for comments from other sources.[89] These results, which would hardly be surprising to journalistic or public observers of politics, confirm the impact of organized interests in two low-visibility but significant arenas of federal policy making.

87. Robert C. Lowry and Matthew Potoski, "Organized Interests and the Politics of Federal Discretionary Grants," *Journal of Politics* 66 (2004): 530.

88. See, for example, Ron Nixon, "Cost-Cutters, Except When the Spending Is Back Home," *New York Times*, July 21, 2011.

89. Jason Webb Yackee and Susan Webb Yackee, in "A Bias Towards Business? Assessing Interest Group Influence on the U.S. Bureaucracy," *Journal of Politics* 68 (2006): 128–139, collected 1,693 comments about forty rules promulgated by seven agencies over a four-year period. In contrast to comments from other sources, comments from business have a statistically significant effect. The success of business intervention does not appear to be related to its capacity to supply expert information and advice. For the earlier sources on rule making, see Wesley Magat, Alan Krupnick, and Winston Harrington, *Rules in the Making: A Statistical Analysis of Regulatory Agency Behavior* (Washington, DC: Resources for the Future, 1986); Maureen L. Cropper, William N. Evans, Stephen J. Berardi, Maria M. Ducla-Soares, and Paul R. Portney, "The Determinates of Pesticide Regulation: A Statistical Analysis of EPA Decision Making," *Journal of Political Economy* 100 (1992): 175–197; Marissa Martino Golden, "Interest Groups in the Rule-Making Process: Who Participates? Whose Voices Get Heard?" *Journal of Public Administration Research and Theory* 8 (1998): 245–270; and David C. Nixon, Robert M. Howard, and Jeff R. De Witt, "With Friends Like These: Rule-Making Comment Submissions to the Securities and Exchange Commission," *Journal of Public Administration Research and Theory* 12 (2002): 59–76.

Dollars and Policy Influence

As we indicated earlier in the chapter, money plays an especially significant and complicated role in any consideration of equality of political voice.[90] Observers in the public and the media pay attention to the use of money in politics and often seem to assume that we live in a "pay-to-play" environment in which political spending has a direct and significant impact on policy. Concern about the possibility of an explicit or implicit quid pro quo has led to regulations of the use of money to influence electoral and policy outcomes that have no equivalent for the full mobilization of resources like time or skills to achieve favorable outcomes. The special status of money as a political resource has led political scientists to use sophisticated statistical approaches in order to investigate its political impact—with results that are rarely straightforward and sometimes surprising. The large multi-issue study of lobbying by Baumgartner and colleagues presents compelling evidence that there is a very weak relationship between a variety of measures of resources devoted to lobbying on a particular issue and policy success.[91] Still, in an explanation of "why resources matter but appear not to," the authors discuss the many factors that also need to be considered in addition to resources and remark that their "findings do not suggest that it is better in politics to be poor than rich."[92]

In particular, contributions to electoral campaigns by PACs, which function as the political giving arm of many organized interests, raise concerns about contributions that arrive with a clear return address and the possibility of an implicit policy agenda. While data about expenditures on lobbying—which, in fact, involve much greater sums than PAC giving does—date back only to the late 1990s and lobbying reports do not specify who was lobbied, we have a time series for several decades that documents the size of PAC contributions and, equally important, connects donors to recipients. These data

90. For a wide-ranging narrative account of the persistent role of business in shaping policy on the economy for thirty years beginning in the 1970s—that is, through periods of Democratic and Republican control in Washington—see Jacob S. Hacker and Paul Pierson, *Winner-Take-All Politics: How Washington Made the Rich Richer—And Turned Its Back on the Middle Class* (New York: Simon and Schuster, 2010). The authors discuss, for example, the success of business lobbyists in defeating a Carter administration proposal to create an Office of Consumer Representation, a proposal with strong majority support in both Congress and the public (pp. 126–127) and the role of the National Federation of Independent Business in undercutting the Clinton health plan (pp. 205–207).

91. Baumgartner et al., *Lobbying and Policy Change*, chap. 10.

92. Baumgartner et al., *Lobbying and Policy Change*, p. 212.

make possible quantitative studies that seek to link PAC contributions to the political actions of legislators. When it comes to the consequences of PAC donations for floor votes in Congress, statistical studies show either no effect at all or, at most, small and inconsistent effects for PAC contributions and point to the expected trio of factors—ideology, party, and constituency—as the important influences on roll-call voting.[93] Making a summary assessment, Stephen Ansolabehere, John de Figueiredo, and James Snyder remark: "The evidence that campaign contributions lead to a substantial influence on votes is rather thin."[94]

In rejoinder, Michael Malbin argues that "the last place we should expect to find a change in a Member's behavior would be on a public roll-call vote."[95] Often the act of making a political donation represents only one part of an overall lobbying strategy.[96] The impact would be manifest in less visible ways—

93. See, for example, Jonathan I. Silberman and Garey C. Durden, "Determining Legislative Preferences on the Minimum Wage: An Economic Approach," *Journal of Political Economy* 84 (1976): 317–329; Henry W. Chappell, "Campaign Contributions and Voting on the Cargo Preference Bill: A Comparison of Simultaneous Models," *Public Choice* 36 (1981): 301–312; Henry W. Chappell, "Campaign Contributions and Congressional Voting: A Simultaneous Probit-Tobit Model," *Review of Economics and Statistics* 62 (1982): 77–83; W. P. Welch, "Campaign Contributions and Legislative Voting: Milk Money and Dairy Price Supports," *Western Political Quarterly* 35 (1982): 478–495; James B. Kau and Paul H. Rubin, *Congressmen, Constituents, and Contributors* (Boston: Martinus Nijhoff, 1982); John R. Wright, "PACs, Contributions, and Roll Calls: An Organizational Perspective" *American Political Science Review* 79 (1985): 400–414; Woodrow Jones and K. Robert Keiser, "Issue Visibility and the Effects of PAC Money," *Social Science Quarterly* 68 (1987): 170–176; Jean Reith Schroedel, "Campaign Contributions and Legislative Outcomes," *Western Political Quarterly* 40 (1987): 371–389; Gerald Keim and Asghar Zardkoohi, "Looking for Leverage in PAC Markets: Corporate and Labor Contributions Considered," *Public Choice* 58 (1988): 21–34; Janet Grenzke, "Shopping in the Congressional Supermarket: The Currency Is Complex," *American Journal of Political Science* 33 (1989): 1–24; Frank J. Sorauf, *Inside Campaign Finance: Myths and Realities* (New Haven, CT: Yale University Press, 1992); Heinz et al., *The Hollow Core*, chap. 11; Gregory Wawro, "A Panel Probit Analysis of Campaign Contributions and Roll-Call Votes," *American Journal of Political Science* 45 (2001): 563–579; Stephen Ansolabehere, John M. de Figueiredo, and James M. Snyder, Jr., "Why Is There So Little Money in U.S. Politics?" *Journal of Economic Perspectives* 17 (2003): 105–130; and John Samples, *The Fallacy of Campaign Finance Reform* (Chicago: University of Chicago Press, 2006). For a helpful review essay, see Richard A. Smith, "Interest Group Influence in the U. S. Congress," *Legislative Studies Quarterly* 20 (1995): 89–139.

94. Ansolabehere, de Figueiredo, and Snyder, "Why So Little Money?" p. 116. However, there are systematic empirical analyses that find positive results for the effects of contributions. See Stratmann, "Some Talk: Money in Politics."

95. Michael Malbin, "Rethinking the Campaign Finance Agenda," *The Forum* 6, no. 1 (2008): 2, http://www.bepress.com/forum/vol6/iss1/art3 (accessed June 23, 2010).

96. See, for example, John R. Wright, "Lobbying and Committee Voting in the U.S. House of Representatives," *American Political Science Review* 84 (1990): 417–438, and Wendy L.

for example, in the particular issues to which legislators devote time and attention, in the lobbyists to whom legislators and their staff grant face time, or in such low-key actions as planning legislative strategy or specifying details. In particular, contributions are considered to enhance access.[97] According to Richard Smith, the "purpose of campaign contributions is to buy access rather than votes."[98] Thus, even if PAC contributions do not change the way legislators vote, donations may influence whom legislators talk to, the amount of energy they devote to particular issues, and what they do in informal settings, committee hearings, and markup sessions. As John Wright puts it, "Representatives may 'hear you better,' for example, when a contribution precedes lobbying."[99]

Testimony from lobbyists and corporate leaders in the court case testing the Bipartisan Campaign Reform Act gives anecdotal, if not systematic, sup-

Hansen and Neil J. Mitchell, "Disaggregating and Explaining Corporate Political Activity: Domestic and Foreign Corporations in National Politics," *American Political Science Review* 94 (2000): 891–903.

97. Among the works demonstrating this point are James F. Herndon, "Access, Record, and Competition as Influences on Interest Group Contributions to Congressional Campaigns," *Journal of Politics* 44 (1982): 996–1019; Laura Langbein, "Money and Access: Some Empirical Evidence," *Journal of Politics* 48 (1986): 1052–1062; Janet Grenzke, "Shopping in the Congressional Supermarket: The Currency Is Complex," *American Journal of Political Science* 33 (1989): 1–24; Richard L. Hall and Frank W. Wayman, "Buying Time: Moneyed Interests and the Mobilization of Bias in Congressional Committees," *American Political Science Review* 84 (1990): 797–820; M. Margaret Conway, "PACs in the Political Process," in *Interest Group Politics*, 3rd ed., ed. Allan J. Cigler and Burdett A. Loomis (Washington, DC: Congressional Quarterly, 1991), p. 211; Sorauf, *Inside Campaign Finance*, p. 168; James M. Snyder Jr., "Long-Term Investing in Politicians; or, Give Early, Give Often," *Journal of Law and Economics* 35 (1992): 15–43; Janet M. Box-Steffensmeier and J. Tobin Grant, "All in a Day's Work: The Financial Rewards of Legislative Effectiveness," *Legislative Studies Quarterly* 24 (1999): 511–524; Wawro, "Campaign Contributions and Roll-Call Votes"; and Richard L. Hall and Alan V. Deardorff, "Lobbying as Legislative Subsidy," *American Political Science Review* 100 (2006): 69–84. For an extended discussion with numerous citations, see John R. Wright, *Interest Groups and Congress: Lobbying, Contributions and Influence* (Boston: Allyn and Bacon, 1996), chap. 5. In contrast, Michelle L. Chin, Jon R. Bond, and Nehemia Geva, in "A Foot in the Door: An Experimental Study of PAC and Constituency Effects on Access," *Journal of Politics* 62 (2000): 534–549, find that scheduling requests are equally likely to be successful when they come from a group associated with a PAC as when they come from a group unassociated with a PAC.

98. Smith, "Interest Group Influence," p. 93. On the difficulty of distinguishing access from influence, especially when access is unequal, see Schlozman and Tierney, *Organized Interests*, pp. 164–165, and Frank J. Sorauf, "Political Action Committees," in *Campaign Finance Reform: A Sourcebook*, ed. Anthony Corrado, Thomas E. Mann, Daniel R. Ortiz, Trevor Potter, and Frank J. Sorauf (Washington, DC: Brookings Institution, 1997), pp. 121 and 127.

99. Wright, "Lobbying and Committee Voting," p. 418.

port to the notion that contributions are viewed as a means of having an impact on public policy and makes clear that "buying access" is a first step to gaining influence, especially if unequal access means that only one side of a story is told.[100] According to Robert Rozen, a lobbyist for corporations, individuals, and trade associations: "The large contributions enable donors to establish relationships, which increases the chances they will be successful with their public policy agendas. Compared to the amounts that companies spend as a whole, large political contributions are worthwhile because of the potential benefit to the companies' bottom line."[101] The testimonies also make clear that donors often feel pressured by office holders to make contributions, a perspective that changes the understanding of the origins of the implicit bargain between funders and elected officials but not the implications for equality of political voice.

The pattern of which particular legislators receive donations from which PACs also suggests that the goal is not necessarily to influence the direction of legislators' floor votes. Many PAC donations are directed at incumbents who are not in immediate electoral danger and are already favorably inclined to the interest in question.[102] Although the evidence that PACs target legislators on relevant committees is somewhat mixed, when politicians' committee assignments change, so does the composition of the PAC donations they receive.[103]

100. See the testimonies of Robert Rozen, Gerald Greenwald, Robert W. Hickmott, Wade Randlett, Peter L. Buttenweiser, and Steven L. Kirsch in *Inside the Campaign Finance Battle: Court Testimony on the New Reforms*, ed. Anthony Corrado, Thomas E. Mann, and Trevor Potter (Washington, DC: Brookings Institution, 1997), pp. 297–316.

101. Robert Rozen, "Large Contributions Provide Unequal Access," in *Inside the Campaign Finance Battle*, ed. Corrado, Mann, and Potter, p. 297.

102. Herndon, "Access, Record, and Competition"; Hall and Wayman, "Buying Time"; Kevin Grier, Michael Munger, and Brian Roberts, "The Industrial Organization of Corporate Political Participation," *Southern Economic Journal* 57 (1991): 727–738; Kevin Grier and Michael Munger, "Corporate, Labor, and Trade Association Contributions to the U.S. House and Senate, 1978–1986," *Journal of Politics* 55 (1993): 614–643; Kevin Grier, Michael Munger, and Brian Roberts, "The Determinants of Industry Political Activity, 1978–1986," *American Political Science Review* 88 (1994): 911–926.

103. On the evidence that PACs target legislators, see J. David Gopoian, "What Makes PACs Tick? An Analysis of the Allocation Patterns of Economic Interest Groups," *American Journal of Political Science* 28 (1984): 259–281; Janet Grenzke, "Shopping in the Congressional Supermarket: The Currency Is Complex," *American Journal of Political Science* 33 (1989): 1–24; Grier, Munger, and Roberts, "Industrial Organization of Corporate Political Participation." On the change in composition of the PAC donations, see Thomas Romer and James M. Snyder Jr., "An Empirical Investigation of the Dynamics of PAC Contributions," *American Journal of Political Science* 38 (1994): 745–769.

If You're Not at the Table, You're on the Menu: Does Not Taking Part in the Process Have Consequences?

A final difficulty further complicating any attempt to assess definitively the extent to which organized interests have policy influence is that models do not encompass organizations that are not at the table. Investigations of the impact of individual political participation on policy use public opinion surveys to capture the preferences and interests of both political activists and inactive citizens who express no political voice. Systematic studies of the policy impact of organized interests attempt, insofar as possible, to measure the inputs of organized interest activity and to relate them to policy outputs. However, such measurements are difficult in the organized interest domain because there is no universe of potential interests from which to sample. Thus the silent voices cannot be taken into account, and the consequences of not taking part remain outside the purview of the inquiry. As Heinz, Laumann, Nelson, and Salisbury put it in their study of the role of organized interests in policy making: "We have no way to catalogue the segments of society that lack a voice in discussions of policies affecting them or who are unable even to initiate discussion of their concerns. Thus, despite the great range and diversity in the political orientations of the interest groups [we have studied] . . . we cannot conclude that national policy systems have overcome the problems of exclusiveness and limited participation noted by so many scholars."[104]

It is often said in Washington, "If you're not at the table, you're on the menu." It is undoubtedly too extreme to claim that interests not represented in the policy-making process will be roasted, sauced, and consumed. Nevertheless, close scrutiny of actual policy controversies demonstrates that, even if the organized interests that take part do not always win, they are better off for having gotten involved. By being in the process, they are in a position to achieve partial gains and to avoid the even larger losses that might have ensued had they not been on the scene. The interests that never get to the table are not in a position to engage in such defensive maneuvering or to realize even such limited objectives.

A Bottom Line on Organized Interest Influence?

As we embark on an extended inquiry into the expression of political voice through organized interests, we raise questions that parallel those discussed

104. Heinz et al., *The Hollow Core*, p. 409.

with regard to the political voice of individuals. Less than full mobilization of organized interests jeopardizes equality of political voice if either of two conditions is met. One is that the set of active organizations is not representative, a condition that is difficult to specify in the abstract and that we shall investigate with detailed empirical evidence in the next four chapters. The other is that organized interest activity has consequences for policy outcomes, a proposition that we were able to examine in this chapter by considering the extensive political science literature on the subject.

What we have learned confirms neither the view, widely disseminated in the media and the public, that investments in political action by organized interests inevitably pay off nor the counterorthodoxy, sometimes espoused by political scientists, that systematic assessments show organized interests to be paper tigers whose activity consists of a lot of motion to impress clients and constituents without having an effect on policy. Our reading of the literature suggests that neither stereotype captures what is a complex reality.

Of the various kinds of scholarly inquiries that seek to establish the extent to which organized interest activity has policy influence, case studies permit the examination of multiple factors up close and in detail and make it possible to draw inferences about whether there really are causal links between the actions of organized interests and eventual policy change. However, case studies have the well-known liability that it is difficult to specify the class of political controversies to which they can be generalized. Furthermore, the possibility that a selection effect such that researchers would systematically avoid choosing cases in which nothing happens implies that, taken together, case studies may overestimate the extent to which organized interests affect policy.

In contrast, quantitative studies—which adduce systematic data across cases—have other liabilities. For one thing, it is difficult to measure such critical inputs as energy devoted to mobilizing the grassroots or behind-the-scenes efforts to inform and persuade policy makers. Similarly, when it comes to policy outputs, while roll-call votes are readily quantified, such less visible outputs as decisions to devote time and attention to an issue or to alter details of policy in a markup session are more difficult to measure. In addition, without digging deeply, it may be difficult to establish the causal links between inputs and outputs that demonstrate actual influence. Moreover, the models in systematic studies begin with issues that have made their way onto the political agenda and include only organizations that are actively involved. Thus they do not account for the political process by which the agenda is constructed, a process in which organized interests are often engaged. Furthermore, they cannot assess the consequences of absence for interests, not represented at the table, that are affected by a particular policy outcome.

Perhaps unexpectedly, these contrasting kinds of inquiries converge on conclusions that are similar. Clearly, lobbyists do not always get what they want. However, the literature does substantiate Anthony J. Nownes's maxim that "lobbyists sometimes get what they want."[105] In fact, lobbyists often get at least some of what they want and more than they would have gotten had they not entered the fray. Therefore, it makes sense to inquire about the shape of political voice through organized interests, a question that we shall investigate in detail in the next several chapters. As we do so, our inquiry will be guided by the theoretical expectations contained in the literature discussed earlier in the chapter about the barriers to the emergence of organizations among jointly interested people, especially if they are resource deprived or if they are concerned about a public good. These expectations suggest that the biases in political voice expressed through organizational advocacy will reinforce those we found for individual activity.

105. Nownes, *Total Lobbying*, p. 32.

11

Who Sings in the Heavenly Chorus?
The Shape of the Organized Interest System

Fittingly, in the nation whose birth cry opposed taxation without representation, citizens in American democracy seek political voice not only individually but jointly. Having outlined in the preceding chapter some of the complexities that make the measurement of inequalities of voice especially difficult when representation is collective, in this chapter we use systematic data that we collected for the Washington Representatives Study to inquire into the kinds of interests that are represented by organizations in national politics and the extent to which that configuration approximates equality of political voice.

Is Organized Interest Representation Universal?

"One answer to the question, 'Who is in government relations?' might be 'Almost everybody.'"[1] This assessment, which was originally made in the 1960s, would seem to be supported by the array of organized interests referenced in *The National Journal* during one three-month period. Of the dozens and dozens of organizations mentioned, Table 11.1 presents examples of some of the common kinds—along with the issues on which they were working during the period from early May to late July, 2006—and makes clear the broad range of organizations and policy concerns. The policy issues embrace both domestic and foreign policy concerns. For each of the issues, there is at least

Traci Burch and Philip Edward Jones are coauthors of this chapter.

1. Lewis Anthony Dexter, *How Institutions Are Represented in Washington* (Indianapolis: Bobbs-Merrill, 1969), p. 17.

Table 11.1   Examples of Organized Interests and Their Policy Concerns

Organization	Policy Issue
ExxonMobil	Gas prices
Tuna Foundation	Mercury levels in canned tuna
National Federation of Independent Businesses	Estate tax
American Immigration Lawyers Association	Immigration reform
Air Line Pilots Association	Request by Virgin Atlantic to start a new airline
State of Alaska	Drilling in the Arctic National Wildlife Refuge
Taipei Economic and Cultural Representatives Office	U.S.–Taiwan free trade agreement
Natural Resources Defense Council	Oil company profits
Christian Coalition	Internet gambling

Sources: The organizations listed were all mentioned in articles in *National Journal* 38, nos. 18–29, during a three-month period. The articles include: Bara Vaida, "The Death Tax Won't Die," May 6, 2006; Randy Barrett and Bara Vaida, "Petro PR," May 6, 2006; Lisa Caruso, "High Stakes on Web Gambling," May 13, 2006; Bara Vaida, "Alaska's Pumping ANWR," May 13, 2006; Bara Vaida, "Domestic Virgin," June 10, 2006; Bara Vaida, "Getting Her Sea Legs," June 17, 2006; Bara Vaida, "Taiwan's Last Move," July 22, 2006; and Neil Munro, "The Immigration Bar," July 22, 2006.

one organization that is animated by an economic concern; for several, at least one organization is motivated by a non-economic objective.

The last policy matter listed in Table 11.1, a proposed bill outlawing most forms of online gambling and prohibiting financial institutions from processing illegal bets placed on the Internet, involved an especially large number of organizations in an especially complex configuration.[2] Not surprisingly,

2. Lisa Caruso, "High Stakes on Web Gambling," *National Journal* 38, no. 19, May 13, 2006. Although it involves a public issue but not government action and therefore may be less germane to this discussion, a particularly interesting combination of organizations emerged from an article about the reactions to the decision of the International Astronomical Union to demote Pluto from "planet" to "dwarf planet" status. Not surprisingly, a spokesman for the U.S. Space and Rocket Center in Huntsville, Alabama, was quoted to the effect that "Pluto wants a recount." But so were representatives of Pluto's, a salad and sandwich

the Poker Players Alliance, a grassroots organization initiated by a group of poker champions, was opposed—as were various parts of the Internet gambling industry, technology firms like Gtech and eLottery, and trade groups like the Interactive Alliance and the Interactive Gaming Council. On the other side, the proposed bill was supported by the National Collegiate Athletic Association and the major sports leagues, which welcomed protection from any involvement with gambling, as well as representatives of financial institutions, the American Bankers Association, MasterCard, Visa, PayPal, and Citigroup. As would be expected, social conservatives like the Family Research Council, Focus on the Family, the Christian Coalition, the Eagle Forum, Concerned Women of America, and the Ethics and Religious Liberty Commission of the Southern Baptist Convention also lined up in support.

After that, the alignments became more complicated. Unlike most conservative groups, the Traditional Values Coalition opposed the bill as containing too many loopholes. Presumably because they face competition from online betting, representatives of other parts of the gambling industry—for example, the National Thoroughbred Racing Association, the American Greyhound Track Operators Association, and the National Association of Convenience Stores—were supportive. In contrast, the trade association of the commercial casino industry, the American Gaming Association, stayed neutral. The National Indian Gaming Association focused on the wording of narrow provisions that would exempt bets placed on tribal lands where gambling is allowed. And, while forty-nine of the fifty state attorneys general were on board, the North American Association of State and Provincial Lotteries, which maintains that regulation of all forms of gambling is within the purview of the states, took no position.

Although these examples might suggest that representation in Washington is universal, periodically our attention is called to a notable political silence. According to an analysis by Gretchen Morgenson, in the aftermath of the 2008 banking crisis, the Federal Reserve maintained a policy of low interest rates in order to "shore up troubled banks' financial standing," a policy disadvantageous to savers, investors, and those on fixed incomes. Why weren't

---

shop in San Francisco ("Pluto gets no respect, man"), Walt Disney Parks and Resorts ("We're certainly not changing Pluto's name"), and the American Federation of Astrologers ("As far as I'm concerned, Pluto is still an effective energy source that's [sic] influence is felt on this earth.") Jesse McKinley, "Ex-Planet's Fans Voice Dismay and Sorrow," *New York Times*, August 25, 2006.

such policy consequences being brought to the attention of public officials? According to Morgenson, "One reason it's not a priority is that savers and people living on fixed incomes have no voice in Washington. The banks, meanwhile, waltz around Washington with megaphones."[3]

This example recalls our discussion in Chapter 10 of the theories of the origins of groups, which brings into question the notion that everybody is represented by organized interests in Washington. What we might call "the free rider problem" and "the resource problem" suggest that organized interest representation will be anything but universal. As discussed, E. E. Schattschneider and Mancur Olson use quite different intellectual approaches—the former acute empirical observation, the latter formal analysis—to converge in finding that political organizations are likely to underrepresent broad public interests that are widely beneficial to all in society.[4] According to economists, the defining characteristic of a public good—endangered species preservation, protection from terrorism, or a reduction in the sales tax—is that if it is available to some member of a society, it cannot be withheld from everyone else. In many controversies, a broad public interest is opposed by a well-organized private interest with a substantial stake in the outcome: for example, organizations representing steel manufacturers and electric utilities are more likely to be active in opposition to air quality regulations than are environmentalists to be active in support—even though everyone shares an interest in breathing clean air and public opinion data consistently demonstrate widespread popular support for environmental preservation.

Although we commonly refer to such public goods as public interests, we should make clear that those who advocate on behalf of public interests have no monopoly on virtue. Just like supporters of policies that benefit particular constituencies—whether the deductibility of business lunches or agricultural crop supports or Medicare—advocates of broad public interests can be sanctimonious and, even, not fully forthcoming. Furthermore, there is no such thing as a single public interest. In any controversy involving a public interest on one side, there is usually a competing public interest on the other.[5] Those

---

3. Gretchen Morgenson, "Debt's Deadly Grip," *New York Times—Sunday Business*, August 22, 2010.

4. E. E. Schattschneider, *The Semi-Sovereign People* (New York: Holt, Rinehart, and Winston, 1960), and Mancur Olson Jr., *The Logic of Collective Action: Public Goods and the Theory of Groups* (Cambridge, MA: Harvard University Press, 1965).

5. This point is made by Andrew S. McFarland in *Public Interest Lobbies: Decision Making on Energy* (Washington, DC: American Enterprise Institute, 1976), chap. 2.

who adduce publicly interested foreign policy or environmental concerns to promote an energy tax may be opposed by equally publicly interested supporters of low energy costs. Similarly, the environmentalists who argue for wilderness and wildlife preservation may be opposed by other public interest advocates who champion the freedom for snowmobilers to enjoy the national parks in winter. Moreover, many political conflicts find supporters of public and private goods on the same side. In the snowmobiling example, manufacturers of cross-country skis might find themselves allied with the environmentalists against snowmobile dealers. When a controversy brings together advocates for both public and private interests, the latter often attempt to cloak their policy positions in the mantle of the public good. However, even though all of them may be sincere in their support for the public good in question, it is possible to distinguish analytically between the cross-country ski manufacturer and the environmentalist when it comes to wilderness preservation or between the defense contractor and the advocate for national security when it comes to military preparedness. In each case the former stands to benefit selectively from the policy in question in a way that the latter does not.

As we noted in Chapter 10, Schattschneider took his discussion of organized interest representation one step further. In an observation that is especially germane to our concern with equality of political voice, he also noted the "strong upper-class accent" of the "heavenly chorus" of organized political interests.[6] That is, Schattschneider pointed to the political underrepresentation of the disadvantaged. In contrast to Olson, whose discussion of the costs of organization did not differentiate among politically concerned individuals with respect to their ability to bear those costs, Schattschneider understood the way that resource differences shape the capacity to assume the costs of political organization and advocacy. Although money is surely a necessity, these costs are not simply financial. Not only are the affluent and well educated able to afford the financial costs of organizational support but they are also in a better position to command the skills, acquire the information, cultivate the media, and use the connections that are helpful in getting an organization off the ground or keeping it going. In short, a group of jointly interested citizens that is reasonably well endowed with a variety of kinds of resources—for example, veterans—is more likely to overcome the hurdle posed by the logic of collective action than is a group of similar size and simi-

---

6. Schattschneider, *Semi-Sovereign People*, p. 35.

lar intensity of concern that is resource poor, say public housing tenants or nursing home residents.

Schattschneider's observations help us to interpret notable political silences. It is sometimes argued that the absence of organized representation for what would seem to be a politically relevant interest is prima facie evidence for an absence of political concern on the part of those who might be presumed to have joint political interests. However, if baggage handlers, convenience store clerks, office receptionists, and gas station attendants do not have organized representation, it does not necessarily mean that they are satisfied with current public policies or that they would rather spend their time and energy going fishing, attending the opera, or putting in more hours on the job. The barriers to group mobilization, especially when the group in question is relatively large and not well endowed with political resources, imply that it is erroneous to assume that the amount of organization activity is a surrogate for the intensity of group political preferences or that the paucity of organized political groups that represent the resource disadvantaged indicates indifference to political outcomes.

The Washington Representatives Study

Since Schattschneider and Olson wrote, much has changed in Washington politics, and many of the changes have potential implications for organized interest politics. Thus the time seems ripe to take a systematic look at the contours of political input through collective representation. To do so we have built an extensive data archive containing information about the characteristics, organizational histories, and political activity of organizations involved in national politics. This new database covers the thousands of organizations listed in the 1981, 1991, 2001, or 2006 *Washington Representatives* directory as having a presence in national politics—either by maintaining an office in the capital or by hiring Washington-based consultants or counsel to manage their government relations activities.[7] Although the *Washington Representatives* directory contains extensive listings, it includes neither organizations that drop in on Washington politics occasionally but do not maintain an ongoing presence nor organizations whose participation is confined to writing checks

7. The directory *Washington Representatives* (Washington, DC: Columbia Books), is published annually. For more information about the directory and the database we constructed from it, see Appendix E. We are grateful to Valerie Sheridan, the editor of the *Washington Representatives* directory, for her assistance and for her forthcoming answers to our questions.

to campaigns or filing amicus briefs. Such politically active organizations are also included in the database. In addition, the directory does not list organizations active only in state or local politics, an omission with possible consequences for our concern with the socio-economic inequalities of political voice. It is possible that the disadvantaged achieve greater voice—for example, through neighborhood groups—in local politics than in national politics.

Given our concern with political voice, a crucial part of this data collection was to place each organization into one or more of 96 organizational categories. These categories were designed to capture the nature of the interest being represented—business, an occupation, a foreign government, a group of universities, a religious or ethnic group, a conservative think tank, and so on—as well as something about its organizational structure. In contrast to most studies of organized interests that rely on highly aggregated categories, we deliberately proliferated the number of categories in order to capture fine distinctions.

The significance of the large number of categories is worth underlining. Observers of American politics have emphasized the emergence of large numbers of citizen groups over the last generation. However, this aggregate category obscures important distinctions with theoretical importance for the understanding of American politics: for example, between organizations that seek public goods and organizations that seek benefits for more limited constituencies; between organizations that seek liberal and conservative public interests; or between organizations that advocate on behalf of the disadvantaged on the basis of economic need as opposed to some noneconomic identity such as race, religion, or gender, which may, in fact, be associated with economic need.

The Contours of Organized Interest Representation

The organizations in our database make clear that the range of organizations active in Washington is nothing short of astonishing. It includes individual institutions such as United Airlines, Villanova University, and Children's Hospital of Boston;[8] the governments of places as diverse and far-flung as

---

8. Throughout this chapter and the ones that follow, we use the names of real organizations. However, the names listed in the 2001 *Washington Representatives* directory may have changed since then. In addition, as we shall see in the next chapter, organizations do sometimes go out of business. Some of the organizations chosen for illustrative purposes may no longer be in existence.

Abilene, Texas, the state of Montana, and Tonga; organizations of pineapple growers, magazine photographers, hang gliders, home health agencies, bicycle manufacturers, urban transit authorities, exporters of Austrian hard cheeses (as well as exporters of Austrian soft cheeses), Pakistani-American businessmen, advocates for causes that range from the protection of ducks to the rights of smokers, and crusaders seeking to expose the governmental conspiracy to suppress scientific information about the reality of UFOs; organizations based on how people earn a living, how they spend their leisure, and how they define themselves in religious or ethnic terms; organizations, especially corporations, that have billions in assets and others that live from hand to mouth; organizations with liberal views; and organizations with conservative views.

Taken together, this diverse group of organizations demonstrates the inappropriateness of using *interest groups* or *pressure groups* as umbrella terms to denote the organizations that seek to influence political outcomes. Such organizations do include membership groups with many members and groups with few members; however, they also include institutions—most notably corporations, but also universities, hospitals, think tanks, and the like—that have no members in the ordinary sense. We mentioned in Chapter 10 that most of the organizations in the pressure system are not membership associations of individuals. In fact, as shown in Table 11.2, in 2001 only a small fraction, about 12 percent, of the organizations listed in the *Washington Representatives* directory were associations of individuals; about 17 percent were associations of institutions such as trade and other business associations; and fully 65 percent were governments (12 percent) or institutions such as corporations, hospitals, or universities (53 percent).[9] To repeat, less than a third of the organizations listed were membership associations of any kind, and about one in eight was a classic voluntary association composed of individual members.

For all the number and diversity of organizations, it turns out that both the free rider problem and the resource constraint problem have profound

9. The procedures we used to ascertain the membership status of organizations are described in Appendix E. There we also explain that a final cleaning of the data eliminated duplications, with the result that the total numbers of organizations in Table 11.3 and elsewhere are slightly different from the figures contained in preliminary publications based on the Washington Representatives Study. Throughout this chapter we present data from 2001, which is the baseline year of the Washington Representatives Study. In the next chapter we consider the changing distribution of organizations in Washington pressure politics over the generation from 1981 to 2006.

Table 11.2   Membership Status of Washington Organizations[a]

Organizational Membership Status	Distribution of Organizations
Associations of Individuals	11.9%
Institutions[b]	52.7
Associations of Institutions	17.0
Governments[c]	12.4
Mixed	2.7
Other or Unknown	3.2
Total	99.9%
N	11,651

Source: Washington Representatives Study (2001).

[a] The table includes all organizations listed in the 2001 *Washington Representatives* directory.
[b] For example, corporations, universities, or hospitals.
[c] Includes foreign as well as domestic governments and associations of governments.

effects on whose voices are heard through the medium of collective representation. The data in Table 11.3, which summarizes—in all its multidimensional complexity—the distribution of the organizations listed in the *Washington Representatives* directory in 2001, make it clear that the essential outlines of Schattschneider's analysis of the pressure system still pertain today and that the set of organized political interests continues to be organized principally around economic matters. In this domain—which includes large numbers of membership associations, for example, unions and professional associations, that join people on the basis of their shared occupations—the representation of business is dominant.[10]

10. For a cogent critique of the possibility of drawing inferences from counts of organizations and extensive bibliographical citations, see David Lowery and Virginia Gray, "Bias in the Heavenly Chorus: Interests in Society and before Government," *Journal of Theoretical Politics* 16 (2004): 5–29. For all their criticisms, many of which had been noted in earlier works—including Kay Lehman Schlozman and John T. Tierney, *Organized Interests and American Democracy* (New York: Harper and Row, 1986), chap. 4—it is interesting to note the following in their conclusion (p. 23): "First, we are certainly not suggesting that counts of interest organizations and their behaviors are uninteresting data, useless for understanding the nature of interest representation. . . . Second, and most emphatically, we are not arguing that business interests are under-represented within interest communities or that their predominance in numbers has declined over time."

Table 11.3   Interests Represented by Organizations in Washington Politics[a]

Categories of Organized Interests	Distribution of Organizations
Corporations[b]	34.9%
Trade and Other Business Associations	13.2
Occupational Associations	6.8
Unions	1.0
Education	4.2
Health	3.5
Social Welfare or Poor	0.8
Public Interest	4.6
Identity Groups[c]	3.8
State and Local Governments	10.4
Foreign	7.8
Other	7.7
Unknown	1.4
Total	100.1%
N	11,651

Source: Washington Representatives Study (2001).

[a] Distribution of organizations listed in the 2001 *Washington Representatives* directory.
[b] Includes U.S. corporations, U.S. subsidiaries of foreign corporations, and for-profit firms of professionals such as law and consulting firms.
[c] Includes organizations representing racial, ethnic, or religious groups; the elderly; women; or lesbian, gay, bisexual, or transgender (LGBT) sexual orientation.

Consistent with Schattschneider's analysis, just as in individual political participation, the economically disadvantaged are underrepresented in pressure politics. Even those with ordinary jobs and middle-class incomes are vastly underrepresented. Organizations of the poor themselves are extremely rare, if not nonexistent, and organizations that advocate on behalf of the poor are relatively scarce.[11] In addition, the number of public interest groups is relatively small, accounting for less than 5 percent of the organizations active in

11. See Douglas R. Imig, *Poverty and Power: The Political Representation of Poor Americans* (Lincoln: University of Nebraska Press, 1996), and R. Allen Hays, *Who Speaks for the Poor?* (New York: Routledge, 2001).

Washington. In contrast, Table 11.3 makes it clear that a number of other kinds of organizations that are less often featured in discussions of Washington pressure politics—in particular, state and local governments in the United States and a variety of kinds of foreign interests—also have a substantial organizational presence.

Although this brief synopsis is a helpful summary of the ongoing inequalities in political voice, the highly aggregated nature of the categories in Table 11.3 obscures a great deal. Therefore, it seems useful to take a closer look at some of the more important categories of interest organizations.

Economic Organizations in Washington Politics: A Closer Look

More than two-thirds of the organized interests in Washington are institutions or membership associations directly related to the joint political concerns that arise from economic roles and interests.[12] Among the thousands of organizations in this remarkably diverse sector, those representing business—domestic and foreign corporations, the multiple kinds of business associations, occupational associations of business executives, and business-oriented think tanks and research organizations—constitute the overwhelming share, more than three quarters. Put another way, of all the organizations active in Washington, more than half, 53 percent, represent business in one way or another.[13] And of these business groups, corporations are by far the most numerous. In fact, American corporations accounted for nearly two-thirds of business organizations and more than a third of all the organizations with Washington representation in 2001.[14] Although they are, by a factor of more

12. This figure includes corporations (both domestic and foreign), trade and other business associations (again, both domestic and foreign), farm organizations, occupational associations, labor unions, and institutions and organizations in the health and educational sectors. (Foreign corporations and foreign trade and other business organizations are contained within the category of foreign organizations. Farm organizations are contained within the category of other organizations.)

13. Using data coded from approximately 19,000 1996 lobbying reports, Frank R. Baumgartner and Beth L. Leech, in "Interest Niches and Policy Bandwagons: Patterns of Interest Group Involvement in National Politics," *Journal of Politics* 63 (2001): 1191–1213, find (as shown in Tables 1–2) a distribution of lobbying organizations not very different from that described here. Echoing our findings, they conclude (p. 1207): "Unions, non-profits, and citizen groups will sometimes make their voices heard, but will often be absent. Rarely do these groups lobby alone. That may be the clearest statement of the privileged place of business."

14. The umbrella category "corporations" includes partnerships and sole proprietorships as well as corporations.

than three, the most numerous of the organizations active in Washington, it is interesting to note that only a small proportion of American corporations are represented.[15]

Trade and other business associations, which have for-profit American corporations as members, make up most of the remainder of business organizations and constitute 13 percent of all organizations in the Washington pressure system. Trade associations include well-known heavyweights like the American Bankers Association and PhRMA (the Pharmaceutical Research and Manufacturers of America) along with such smaller fry as the Athletic Footwear Association, the Door and Hardware Institute, the American Fishing Tackle Manufacturers, and the National Frozen Pizza Institute. They bring together companies in a single industry, companies that are ordinarily marketplace competitors, to work together on common problems. Part of their mission is nonpolitical: trade associations often provide technical services on such nonpolitical matters as accounting practices or employee benefits. However, their shared concerns usually also include political matters, in particular the kinds of regulatory issues on which government action affects an entire industry. As we shall see in Chapter 12, trade associations, of which more than a thousand are active in Washington politics, at one time provided a greater share of representation for the corporate sector.

In addition to trade associations, there is a smaller but more diverse group of associations that also bring together American firms. Some of these are peak associations like the U.S. Chamber of Commerce; the National Federation of Independent Businesses, made up of many small businesses—especially in services, retail, or construction—a majority of which have fewer than six employees; or the Business Roundtable, a group of fewer than two hundred very large publicly traded corporations, represented by their CEOs. In contrast to the peak associations is a somewhat eclectic group of business associations like the Calorie Control Council, which sponsors studies of and encourages "the approval of additional safe low-caloric sweeteners, fat substi-

15. This point is made by a number of analysts of the role of business in organized interest activity. Even Fortune 500 firms are not necessarily represented in Washington politics by lobbyists or political action committees. See, for example, John L. Boies, "Money, Business, and the State: Material Interests, Fortune 500 Corporations, and the Size of Political Action Committees," *American Sociological Review* 54 (1989): 821; David Lowery, Virginia Gray, Jennifer Anderson, and Adam J. Newmark, "Collective Action and the Mobilization of Institutions," *Journal of Politics* 66 (2004): 684–705; Holly Brasher and David Lowery, "The Corporate Context of Lobbying Activity," *Business and Politics* 8, no. 1 (2006): 3; Jeffrey M. Drope and Wendy L. Hansen, "Does Firm Size Matter? Analyzing Business Lobbying in the United States," *Business and Politics* 8, no. 2 (2006): 7.

tutes, and other dietary ingredients," and the Coalition for Vehicle Choice—with members drawn from, among others, the automotive, construction, and insurance industries; farm groups; and the law enforcement community —"working to preserve Americans' access to safe and affordable cars and light trucks to meet diverse personal and professional transportation needs."[16] These sometimes ephemeral, often issue-specific, business groups bring together companies across industries to work together on particular issues—ranging from intellectual property rights to postage rates to environmental regulation to health care costs—of joint concern.

We should make clear that our emphasis on the sheer number of organizations that represent business interests in national politics should not be interpreted as implying that business speaks with one voice.[17] Some analysts view the absence of business unity as evidence of business weakness.[18] However, it is important to recognize that the many issues on which business interests are active involve varying patterns of organized interest interaction, not a single structure of power. Very few issues involve the mobilization of the entire business community. While there are issues—for example, competition among military suppliers for a defense contract—that involve conflict among business interests, much more common are issues on which a portion of the business community is opposed by interests drawn from outside business or by no organized interests at all.[19]

Other Economic Sectors

The educational and health sectors contribute a much smaller but still notable set of organizations. In both cases, roughly two-thirds of the organiza-

16. Information and quotations taken from the following Web sites (accessed September 26, 2006): http://www.healthfinder.gov/orgs/HR1137.htm and http://www.wildwilderness.org/docs/climad.htm.

17. There is widespread agreement on this point, even among scholars who disagree in their assessment of the aggregate weight of business interests in politics. A helpful review article is David M. Hart, "'Business' Is Not an Interest Group: On the Study of Companies in American National Politics," *Annual Review of Political Science* 7 (2004): 47–69.

18. See, for example, Mark A. Smith, *American Business and Political Power: Public Opinion Elections and Democracy* (Chicago: University of Chicago Press, 2000). For a contrary account of the activity and success of business in influencing policy, see Jacob S. Hacker and Paul Pierson, *Winner-Take-All Politics: How Washington Made the Rich Richer—and Turned Its Back on the Middle Class* (New York: Simon and Schuster, 2009).

19. Baumgartner and Leech, in "Interest Niches and Policy Bandwagons," p. 1204, find that on many issues only one or two interests are involved and that "business advantage, while great overall, is even more striking in the cases where the fewest interest groups are active."

tions are individual institutions. In the education sector, these are overwhelmingly universities—with public and nonprofit private universities more or less equally represented, along with a handful of for-profits. All three of our employers—Boston College, Harvard University, and the University of California—are listed, the latter two with their own offices in Washington. Health institutions include hospitals, clinics, nursing homes, and other institutions that care for the infirm or disabled. The health sector has a much more substantial, and often difficult-to-discern, component of for-profit institutions. In both the education and the health fields there are a variety of associations, the functional equivalent of trade and other business associations, that bring together institutions with joint concerns—for example, the Council of Graduate Schools, the National Association of Independent Schools, the Federation of American Hospitals, and the Eye Bank Association of America—along with various other relevant organizations.

A much smaller yet nonetheless highly important set of organizations represents the agricultural sector. Farm organizations constitute little more than 1 percent of all organizations in the Washington pressure system.[20] Most of these are crop-specific organizations like the American Peanut Council, the American Soybean Association, and the United Egg Producers. Such organizations often include processors and equipment manufacturers along with individual farmers and corporate agricultural producers. There is also a small number of peak agricultural associations like the American Farm Bureau Federation and the National Farmers Union, as well as their state affiliates.

Labor Unions and Other Occupational Associations

The organizations in the economic sector are overwhelmingly either for-profit or nonprofit institutions or associations of such institutions. Still, individuals gain significant representation through their memberships in various kinds of occupational associations. Because occupational hierarchies are so deeply rooted in disparities in education and income, the many membership associations that organize people on the basis of what they do for a living are clearly central to our concern with the relationship of socio-economic status to inequalities of political voice. Those who do work that requires high levels of education—and, to a lesser extent, confers high levels of income—are very likely to be represented by an organization in Washington. In contrast, with

---

20. Following the categorization used by the Census, we include fishing and forestry along with farming.

the exception of unions, those who do unskilled work have no occupationally based membership groups at all to represent them.[21]

Labor unions are one category of occupational association that traditionally receives attention in discussions of Washington representation. We use a single criterion to distinguish labor unions from the many other membership associations that bring together people who share a common occupation: if an organization bargains collectively on behalf of its members, we consider it to be a union. The members might be professionals as defined by the Census; many white-collar unions—for example, unions of teachers or nurses—are made up of professionals, especially professionals employed in the public sector. Beyond this single defining characteristic, unions can be differentiated from other occupational associations in that, on average, they have larger memberships and enroll members from a broader array of occupations. That said, as shown in Table 11.4, unions are not especially numerous. Unions comprise only 12 percent of the occupational membership associations, or 1 percent of all organizations, in the Washington pressure community. Because there are so few of them, and because there are so few other organizations that represent the economic interests of nonprofessional and nonmanagerial employees, their political efforts are spread thinly across a wide range of issues.[22]

We mentioned in Chapter 3 that, considering individuals rather than organizations, rates of union membership are much higher for workers in the public sector than in the private sector. Rates of unionization also vary quite substantially across occupations and industries. Interestingly, because public-sector professional workers like teachers are relatively likely to be unionized, professionals have, overall, higher rates of union membership than do service, sales, or production workers. Within the private sector, workers in construction, transportation, and telecommunications have much higher rates of membership than those in agriculture or financial services.[23]

Most of the membership associations that represent individuals on the basis of their occupations do not bargain collectively. By far the most

21. On the role of unions as "vigorous champion on pocketbook issues" for middle- and working-class Americans, see Hacker and Pierson, *Winner-Take-All Politics*, p. 143.

22. Frank R. Baumgartner, Jeffrey M. Berry, Marie Hojnacki, David C. Kimball, and Beth L. Leech, *Lobbying and Policy Change: Who Wins, Who Loses, and Why* (Chicago: University of Chicago Press, 2009), pp. 10–11.

23. Figures are taken from the Web site of the Bureau of Labor Statistics, www.bls.gov/news.release/union2.t03.htm (accessed September 27, 2006).

Table 11.4   Occupational Membership Associations[a]

	Distribution of Organizations
Union	
White-Collar Unions	3.0%
Blue-Collar Unions	5.3
Mixed and Other Unions	4.0
Nonunion	
Professional Associations	48.7
Associations of Managers and Professionals in Business	9.4
Associations of Administrators of Nonprofits	3.7
Associations of Public Employees[b]	16.4
Other Occupational Associations	9.5
Total	100.0%
N	908

Source: Washington Representatives Study (2001).

[a] Distribution of occupational organizations listed in the 2001 *Washington Representatives* directory that have individuals as members.
[b] Includes associations of military employees.

numerous such organizations—accounting for nearly half—are professional associations. These organizations unite people—for example, criminal defense lawyers, plant physiologists, landscape architects, historians, audiologists, transportation engineers, and thoracic surgeons—on the basis of a shared occupation that requires a prescribed course of educational training and at least a college degree.[24] Alone among the categories of occupational associations, professional associations include large numbers of organizations uniting members who share not only their profession but some other characteristic as well. There are, for example, associations of Hispanic journalists, black psychologists, women highway safety engineers, Jewish lawyers and judges, and gay and lesbian physicians. We shall look more closely at such organizations later in the chapter.

24. In categorizing occupational associations as professional associations, we followed the Census definition of professional occupations, which includes certain occupations—for example, professional athlete—that do not fully conform to this criterion.

Similar to professional associations, though much smaller in number, are the occupational associations that represent executives, managers, and professionals working in the for-profit sector. There are organizations representing bank directors, lobbyists, investment managers, funeral directors, real estate executives, and home economists working in business. In addition, there are analogous organizations of managers and administrators in nonprofit settings: health care administrators, academic deans, research administrators, art museum directors, and the like. Such nonunion government employees as court reporters, planners, crime lab directors, circuit court judges, police officers, and postal supervisors are also organized.

Of particular relevance to our concern with the relationship between disadvantage and political voice is the 10 percent of occupational associations, or less than 1 percent of all organizations in the Washington pressure community, that bring together those in nonprofessional and nonmanagerial occupations. Examples of such groups include associations of realtors, master printers, meeting planners, travel agents, medical sonographers, and pilots.

When we compare the list of these organizations with the Census list of all occupations, what is immediately evident is the extent to which even the associations that enroll nonprofessional and nonmanagerial workers tend to represent those in occupations that demand relatively high levels of skill, pay, and status.[25] Unless they are unionized, there are no associations representing many occupations: bellhops, telemarketers, hotel desk clerks, laundry workers, bus drivers, bartenders, custodians, bank tellers, or tool and die makers. A conservative estimate is that for only one-eighth of the more than 90 million American workers in nonprofessional and nonmanagerial occupations is there an occupational association, other than a union, that brings together people in their occupation. Indeed, other than unions, there are *no occupational associations at all* to organize those who labor at low-skill jobs.

Figure 11.1, which allows us to acquire some understanding of the degree of political inequality in collective representation with respect to economic roles, reinforces the message that economic organizations in Washington politics overrepresent the interests of the affluent, well educated, and highly skilled. The left-hand column shows the distribution of adults in the baseline year, 2001: 64 percent were in the labor force in various kinds of jobs; 3 per-

---

25. The remainder of the paragraph is based on a comparison of the data about other occupational associations in our database with U.S. Census data found at www.census.gov/compendia/statab/labor_force_employment_earnings/ (accessed September 26, 2006).

Percentage

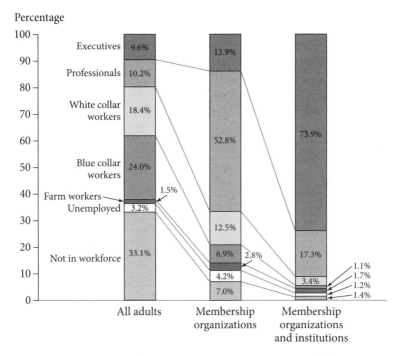

Figure 11.1   Distribution of Adult Workforce Statuses, Parallel Membership
Organizations, and All Economic Organizations

Source: Statistical Abstract (2002), pp. 381–383, as reported on the Web site of the
U.S. Census, http://www.census.gov/prod/2003pubs/02statab/labor.pdf, and Washington Representatives Study (2001).

cent were out of work; and 33 percent were out of the workforce by virtue of
being in school, at home, disabled, or retired.[26]

The middle column shows the distribution for the subset of organizations
in the 2001 *Washington Representatives* directory organized around economic
roles that are membership organizations. It is essential to recognize that the
correspondence between the people in the column on the left and the organizations is at best approximate. It is extremely difficult to match all the relevant organizations in the middle column to the economic roles in the left-hand

26. These data, which are for the civilian workforce and the noninstitutionalized adult
population, are taken from the 2002 Statistical Abstract, pp. 381–383, as reported on the Web
site of the U.S. Census, http://www.census.gov/prod/2003pubs/02statab/labor.pdf (accessed
September 28, 2006).

column. For example, we have already seen that white-collar unions may organize professionals like teachers, nurses, and social workers rather than lower-level white-collar workers. Moreover, we have mentioned that, compared to the various occupational associations that organize professionals or business executives, unions—though few in number—have much larger memberships. Wherever possible we made assumptions that would have the effect of coding against the expected patterns in the data.[27]

Whatever the imperfections in the data, the overall pattern is clear. When it comes to the number of organizations representing adults in various economic roles, professionals are very substantially overrepresented and managers are somewhat overrepresented. In contrast, blue-collar and service workers, along with those out of the workforce, are very substantially underrepresented.

When we add data about institutions in the right-hand column, the pattern shifts somewhat and becomes more pronounced. We have noted the puzzle of inferring representation when an organization is an institution that has no individual members. In the right-hand column we make the perhaps unwarranted assumptions that corporations and trade associations represent the interests of managers and executives only and that all the organizations in the educational and health sectors represent the interests of the professionals that staff such institutions only. In addition, we include any organization that might possibly represent the interests of those outside the workforce. For example, not one of the organizations that represent women in Washington politics focuses exclusively on the preferences and needs of women at home. However, in the right-hand column we include as representing women at home all organizations of women listed in the directory—even though many of them bring together women in a particular occupation.

Comparing the distribution in the right-hand column with the distribution of economic roles of adults produces striking results. The 10 percent of adults who work in an executive, managerial, or administrative capacity are represented by 74 percent of the economic associations and institutions. Professionals constitute 10 percent of adults and are represented by 17 percent of

27. For example, although there are no organizations in the Washington pressure system that explicitly represent the concerns and needs of the unemployed, we considered all social welfare organizations and those concerned with the poor to represent the unemployed. One difficulty was fitting occupational associations of administrators of nonprofits into this scheme. Because these organizations—which, if included, would constitute a very small proportion of the economic organizations—seem to represent the interests of neither business nor professionals, they have been omitted.

economic organizations. The remaining 80 percent of adults—a group that includes lower-level white-collar, blue-collar, and service workers as well as those who are unemployed, in school, at home, disabled, or retired—are represented by a mere 9 percent of the economic organizations. In short, however the data are arranged or rearranged, the conclusion is inescapable: when it comes to economic organizations, those representing business are vastly disproportionate in their numbers, and the vast majority of adults who work in service, blue-collar, or lower-level white-collar jobs or who are out of the workforce entirely have a very small share of organized representation.

Organizations that Represent the Less Privileged

We must entertain the possibility that, by focusing on how adults are represented in terms of their occupations or workforce status, we may have overlooked other forms of representation of the economic needs of those who are on the middle and lower rungs of the economic ladder, many of whom have experienced heightened economic insecurity over the past few decades. As we saw in Chapter 3, we live in an era in which workers, even highly skilled ones, are squeezed by many trends designed to cut labor costs.[28] These range from the export of jobs overseas to the outsourcing of service functions to the increased use of part-timers and independent contractors. Such developments create potential economic constituencies—for example, workers whose company pensions are in jeopardy or workers whose jobs provide neither health care benefits nor protection from disability or job loss. However, those who share these statuses have no Washington representation by groups organized around such joint nonoccupationally defined economic interests.

Furthermore, like those who work in jobs requiring little in the way of skills and commanding little in the way of pay, those at the bottom of the economic ladder are also underrepresented in pressure politics. We saw in Table 11.3 that less than 1 percent of the organizations active in Washington in 2001 fell into the category we label as "social welfare or poor." We divided organizations that represent the poor into three types. Nearly two-thirds are providers of direct services like the Food Bank of Virginia Peninsula, Goodwill Industries, the Indianapolis Neighborhood Housing Partnership, Meals on Wheels, or the American Red Cross. Many of these agencies—for example,

---

28. See, for example, Michael B. Katz, *The Price of Citizenship: Redefining the American Welfare State* (New York: Henry Holt, 2001), chaps. 7–8, and Jacob S. Hacker, *The Great Risk Shift* (New York: Oxford University Press, 2006).

the Haitian Refugee Center, Gospel Rescue Ministries of Washington, or the Jewish Family Service Association of Cleveland—have a religious or ethnic tie. The remainder are organizations that advocate on behalf of the poor in the United States or in favor of more comprehensive guarantees with respect to basic human needs. Such organizations, which may or may not also attempt to organize the poor, include the Coalition on Human Needs, the Food Research and Action Center, and the Center on Budget and Policy Priorities.[29]

Finally we looked for organizations of recipients of social welfare or tax benefits—for example, jobless workers, public housing tenants, or those who benefit from the Earned Income Tax Credit—advocating on their own behalf. These are needy constituencies with an obvious stake in policy outcomes. A very few such organizations—for example, the Full Employment Action Council and the Section 8 Housing Group—had appeared in earlier directories. However, of the more than 11,000 organizations enumerated in the 2001 directory, *not one* was an association of beneficiaries of means-tested government benefits representing themselves.[30] Furthermore, as Jeffrey Berry points out, the health and human service nonprofits that have as clients "constituencies that are too poor, unskilled, ignorant, incapacitated, or overwhelmed with their problems to organize on their own" are constrained by the 501(c)3 provisions in the tax code from undertaking significant lobbying.[31]

Another aspect of organizational underrepresentation of resource-poor constituencies is made clear by an analogy with the elderly. The wag who once observed, "You are only old once" made a powerful observation about the possibilities for organized advocacy. There are a number of explanations for the potent organization of the elderly and their ability to protect government benefits that assist them economically: benefits for the elderly are not

29. Many such organizations not only engage in advocacy but also provide direct services. Coders were instructed to consider the overall balance in organizational activities in placing an organization into one of the two categories.

30. Beginning in 1967, an organization composed of current and former recipients of public assistance, the National Welfare Rights Organization, advocated on behalf of the poor. Its Washington office closed in 1974. A successor organization, the National Welfare Rights Union, was founded in 1987. However, the National Welfare Rights Union concentrates on protest activity and does not maintain a presence in Washington. On the National Welfare Rights Organization, see Lawrence Neil Bailis, *Bread or Justice: Grassroots Organizing in the Welfare Rights Movement* (Lexington, MA: Lexington Books, 1974).

31. Jeffrey M. Berry with David Arons, *A Voice for Nonprofits* (Washington, DC: Brookings Institution, 2003), p. 65. In his analysis of the impact of the tax code on lobbying by nonprofits, Berry points out that a little-known tax provision of which nonprofits are not aware, the possibility of H election, gives them autonomy in undertaking political action.

means-tested, and therefore many of the beneficiaries are not poor; the elderly have high rates of electoral turnout; AARP (formerly the American Association of Retired Persons) has found a formula for generating a large membership based on the provision of selective benefits. Still another is that —in contrast to the other age-related statuses through which we pass—we do not graduate from being elderly. There is a lesson in this analogy for the organized representation of resource-deprived constituencies. Organized advocacy by the economically disadvantaged acting on their own is especially unlikely when economic need results from conditions that are unforeseen or expected to be temporary—for example, unemployment, mortgage foreclosure, or medical emergency not covered by insurance. The elderly know that they will always be dependent on Medicare and Social Security and act accordingly in politics.

Organizations that Represent Identity Groups

The evidence about the representation of economic interests in pressure politics is compelling: the overwhelming share of organizations represent the well-off. We should, however, note an important qualification to this pattern. When it comes to the sets of groups constellated around noneconomic axes of cleavage—for example, race, ethnicity, nationality, religion, age, sexual orientation, or gender—it is not the dominant groups in society that receive the lion's share of explicit organizational representation. In contrast to the circumstance that obtains for economic need, it is the less advantaged among the identity groups that have whatever organizational representation there is.[32] Numerous groups represent the interests of, for example, women, the elderly, Muslims, Asian Americans, or African Americans, and few, if any, are explicitly organized around the interests of men, the middle aged, or WASPs. Nevertheless, the interests of middle-aged white men are surely well represented in the mainstream economic organizations that form the bulk of the organized interest community.

These organizations are remarkable for their diversity. While most of them are membership associations of individuals, some, especially in the religious domain, are not: examples include the United Church of Christ, the United

---

32. We are aware that the term *identity groups* is a contested one and use it to denote institutions and associations in which the organizing principle is some noneconomic demographic characteristic.

States Conference of Catholic Bishops, and the National Association of Evangelicals. Identity organizations rest on a continuum in terms of the extent to which politics is central to the organizational mission. A few such organizations that are listed in the directory—for example, the Sons of Italy and the Lithuanian American Council—are essentially fraternal associations. More common are organizations, like the National Alliance of Senior Citizens and the American-Arab Anti-Defamation Committee, that give greater focus to politics as a means of promoting group interests. While most of these political groups have broad political agendas, some—for example, the Jewish Peace Lobby or Women for Tax Reform—focus on a single issue. There are also organizations at the intersection of more than one identity: the Older Women's League and the Brethren/Mennonite Council for Lesbian, Gay, Bisexual and Transgender Interests are examples. We have already mentioned a common kind of identity group—of which the Nisei Farmers League, the American Association of Blacks in Energy, and the National Association of Minority Contractors are examples—that weds an occupational status to a racial, ethnic, religious, or gender affiliation.

To what extent can identity groups—whether on the basis of race, ethnicity or nationality, religion, gender, age, or sexual orientation—substitute for class-based groups in advocating for economically needy members of constituencies defined by other affinities? As shown in Table 11.5.A, for all their diversity, organizations representing racial, ethnic, or nationality groups; religious groups; women; the elderly; and gays and lesbians comprise only a tiny proportion of the organizations in the pressure system. They constitute 2.3 percent, 0.8 percent, 0.4 percent, 0.2 percent, and less than 0.1 percent, respectively, of the organizations listed in 2001. Table 11.5.B gives more detail about the distribution of racial, ethnic, and religious groups.

Interestingly, nearly half of the organizations in this category are organizations representing Native Americans. By a factor of six, organizations representing Native Americans outnumber those representing African Americans, a group traditionally viewed as the vanguard with respect to minority politics, with, according to the 2010 Census, nearly fourteen times the Native American population. We probed this striking result further and discovered that 74 percent of these organizations are federally recognized tribes, which makes them in some ways more analogous to the state and local governments in the intergovernmental lobby than to the kinds of civil rights organizations that traditionally represent racial and ethnic groups. The number of Native American tribes that have Washington representation reflects not

Table 11.5 Representation of Identity Groups
among Organized Interests, 2001

11.5.A   Organizations Representing Identity Groups as a Proportion of All
Organizations Listed

	Proportion of All Organizations
Racial, Ethnic, or Nationality	2.3%
Religious	0.8
Women	0.4
Elderly	0.2
LGBT	0.1
Total	3.8%

11.5.B   Distribution of Racial, Ethnic, Nationality, and Religious Groups

	Distribution of Racial, Ethnic, and Religious Groups
"Minorities"	2.6%
African Americans	7.7
Latinos	5.9
Asians	3.2
Native Americans	48.2
European Ethnic Groups	4.5
Arab or Islamic Nationality Groups	1.6
Jewish	5.7
Islamic Religious Groups	0.5
"Christian"	3.3
Mainline Protestant	4.3
Evangelical Protestant	2.3
Catholic	5.2
Interfaith	1.4
Other Nationality or Religious Groups	3.6
Total	100.0%
N	366

Source: Washington Representatives Study (2001).

only the legacy of historical engagement with the federal government but also more proximate events. The 1988 Indian Gaming Regulatory Act (IGRA) stimulated the political involvement of Indian nations both because it enhanced their stake in public policy and because the resources that accrued to them through gaming have given them the wherewithal to undertake political action. In fact, 83 percent of the federally recognized tribes with Washington representation are involved with casino gambling.[33]

Public Interest Groups

We have discussed the fact that the free rider problem implies that public goods will receive less vigorous organized advocacy and noted that the number of public interest groups is relatively small, accounting for less than 5 percent of the organizations active in Washington. Although they are not especially numerous, the causes they advocate are remarkably diverse. Table 11.6.A gives examples of various kinds of public interest groups. Table 11.6.B shows the distribution of such organizations and makes it clear that these broad public interests are not inevitably liberal.

As we have mentioned, discussions of public interests often overlook how often, in any real political controversy, there is competition between opposing conceptions of the public interest: for example, wilderness preservation versus economic growth, consumer product safety versus low prices, and national security versus low taxes. It is extremely difficult to make a simple characterization of the overall ideological position of the diverse organizations that seek to represent the public interest. The set of organizations representing public goods probably leans somewhat to the left. Still, Table 11.6 makes clear that there is also considerable representation of conservative public goods. In fact, explicitly ideological public interest groups—for example, anti- or pro-gun control groups on the domestic front or pro–national security or pro-peace groups in the international domain—are balanced between conservative and liberal organizations. Moreover, many of the pub-

---

33. See Richard Witmer and Frederick J. Boehmke, "American Indian Incorporation in the Post–Indian Gaming Regulatory Act Era," *Social Science Journal* 44 (2007): 127–145. Especially as interpreted by the Supreme Court, the IGRA has increased the political involvement of tribal governments with state governments. See the essays in *The New Politics of Indian Gaming*, ed. Kenneth N. Hansen and Tracy A. Skopek (Reno: University of Nevada Press, 2011), in particular Tracy A. Skopek and Kenneth N. Hansen, "Afterword: The Death of Indian Gaming and Tribal Sovereignty," pp. 209–216.

lic interest groups in various presumptively liberal categories are, in fact, either ideologically neutral or conservative. Examples include consumer groups like the American Automobile Association and the American Motorcyclist Association, wildlife organizations like Pheasants Forever, and government reform organizations like the Citizens against Government Waste. Furthermore, compared to advocates of liberal public interests, conservative

Table 11.6　Public Interest Groups in Washington Politics

11.6.A　Examples of Public Interest Groups

Environmental and Wildlife	Environmental Working Group
	Greenpeace, U.S.A.
	Izaak Walton League
Consumer	Center for Auto Safety
	Consumer Federation of America
	National Association of Investors Corporation
Government Reform	Campaign Reform Project
	Citizens against Government Waste
	Project on Government Oversight
Civil Liberties	American Civil Liberties Union
	Council on Religious Freedom
	Electronic Privacy Information Center
Citizen Empowerment	Center for Voting and Democracy
	Close Up Foundation
	Speak Out! USA
Other Liberal Groups	Amnesty International
	Death with Dignity National Center
	Religious Coalition for Reproductive Choice
Other Conservative Groups	American Security Council
	Americans for Tax Reform
	Citizens for Law and Order
Other	Americans for Divorce Reform
	Federation for American Immigration Reform
	National Safety Council

continued

Table 11.6   Continued

11.6.B   Distribution of Public Interest Groups

	Distribution of Public Interest Groups
Environmental and Wildlife	23.8%
Consumer	6.0
Government Reform	5.1
Civil Liberties	2.2
Citizen Empowerment	3.5
Other Liberal Groups	15.7
Other Conservative Groups	16.0
Other	27.7
Total	100.0%
N	531

Source: Washington Representatives Study (2001).

public interest organizations are more likely to find themselves on the same side of a policy controversy as an intense private interest—for example, a corporation or trade association representing real estate developers or the manufacturers of infant car seats.

State and Local Governments

Discussions of the pressure system do not usually focus on governments as advocates in federal politics. However, other than business interests, representatives of state and local governments are the most common organized interests. State and local governments often carry out federal policy—sometimes with funding and always with strings attached. Given the extent to which the national government is a source of both financial largesse and regulatory headaches, subnational governments have incentives to establish a presence in Washington. Three-fifths of the organizations in what is sometimes called the "intergovernmental lobby" are local and county governments and their affiliated departments and authorities: Lake County, Illinois; the city of Huntsville, Alabama; the Eugene, Oregon, Water and Electric Authority; and so on. All but one of the nation's twenty most populous cities, and all but seven of the fifty most populous, either have an office in Washington or hire outside counsel to represent their interests. Similarly, every state but Kansas, New Hampshire, Rhode Island, Tennessee, and Vermont is represented in some way. For two-thirds, the state itself has an office or hires outside counsel or consultants; for the remainder, it is units of state government—the department of transportation, the turnpike commission, the department of environmental quality, and so on—that are represented.

Because activity in Washington by subnational governments is a form of enhanced citizen representation, it is appropriate to consider who enjoys this form of added political weight.[34] With 233 governmental entities having representation in Washington, California dwarfs every other state. The second-largest delegation in the intergovernmental lobby is Florida's, with 6 percent (55 entities) of the total. New York and Texas, with 5 percent (43 entities) each, also weigh heavily. That these states have a large number of representatives in the Washington pressure system is not surprising. After all, they are the four most populous states.

Adjusting for population size allows us to capture the extent to which the inhabitants of the states are over- or underrepresented in the Washington pressure system. The number of subnational units in the Washington pressure system is far from proportional to their states' populations. Alaska is the heavy hitter. The 25 governmental entities representing Alaska constitute a share of organizations that is 12.7 times Alaska's share of the population. Nevada (3.1 times), Oregon (2.4 times), California (2.2 times), and Louisiana and North Dakota (2.1 times each) are also overrepresented. On balance, western states tend to be overrepresented in terms of their delegations of state and local units in federal politics. Although New York and Texas have a relatively large number of governmental entities in Washington, their delegations to the intergovernmental lobby are actually smaller than would have been expected on the basis of population.

It is tempting to adduce post hoc explanations for these patterns. The overrepresentation of western states seems sensible. After all, a perennial source of political tension in the West is the fact that the federal government is a large landowner there. Still, one might expect that states like Michigan, Ohio, and Pennsylvania, which have aging economic infrastructures and aging populations, or Georgia and South Carolina, which have substantial military installations, would also be well represented. Clearly, there are elements of serendipity in the extent to which the people in a particular location

---

34. Appendix F contains the data on which this paragraph and the next one are based.

have a geographically based voice in federal politics. It clearly helps to be in the right place.

Other Organizations

Our review of the kinds of organizations that are represented in Washington politics has omitted a few categories that deserve mention. Given the global era in which we live and the impact of what happens in the United States on other nations and their citizens, it is not unexpected that nearly 8 percent of the organizations listed in the 2001 *Washington Representatives* directory are foreign. Of these, 24 percent represent foreign governments from Albania to Zimbabwe and their ministries. The majority, 74 percent, represent foreign corporations and foreign business associations. Like their American counterparts, these include familiar names like Alitalia and Honda, along with smaller firms and the trade and other business associations that represent them. The remaining foreign organizations include a small number of international organizations like the Organization of American States and the European Space Agency and a variety of other foreign organizations ranging from Hebrew University of Jerusalem to the Liberal Party of Japan to Interns for Peace International.

Table 11.3 lists 7.7 percent of the organizations in the 2001 directory as "Other." In fact, most of the organizations obscured under this rubric fall into small but significant categories. For example, a variety of kinds of organizations that are concerned with children and young people—ranging from the Boy Scouts to the Child Nutrition Forum to the National Center for Missing and Exploited Children—comprise less than 1 percent of all the organizations. Although their political clout is well known, veterans' organizations such as the American Legion and the Retired Officers Association constitute an even smaller share, a mere 0.3 percent of the 2001 organizations. A residual group of 0.3 percent of the 2001 organizations—of which the Coin Coalition, a heterogeneous coalition that embraces advocates for the blind as well as vending machine manufacturers in support of the minting of a dollar coin, is an example—could be identified but not placed in one of the other categories.

Mixed-Category Organizations

Our coding rules permitted us to place an organization into as many as three categories. Our purpose in so doing was not to allow us to hedge our bets in the many cases in which we were uncertain where to place an organization. Rather we recognized a need to accommodate organizations that, in the nature of their organizational mission, membership, or structure, really do belong in more than one category. We were curious as to the impact of these "mixed-category organizations" on the distribution of political organizations within aggregate categories.

A mixed-category organization is one that has been coded into at least two of the 96 categories. Organizations like the Veterans Education Project (other education + veterans' association), the Visually Impaired Piano Tuners (other occupational association + particular illness or disability), or the National Coalition for Minority Business (other business + "minorities") do not really straddle categories; they join them.[35] We consider an organization to be mixed-category even if the categories into which it is classified fall within a single aggregated category. Therefore, an intersectional organization like the National Council of Negro Women is a mixed-category organization even though both parts of the mixture are identities.

Although mixed-category organizations occur relatively infrequently and amount to only 4.8 percent of all organizations, there are 555 such organizations in the 2001 directory. Of the thousands of possible combinations, hundreds are actually represented. As shown in Table 11.7, they are dispersed, though far from evenly, across the various kinds of organizations. Perhaps unexpectedly, mixed-category organizations constitute a larger share within several aggregate categories that figure importantly in our discussion because of their relative underrepresentation in the pressure system: public interest groups, social welfare organizations and organizations of the poor, and identity-based organizations.[36] Nearly half of the organizations that are categorized, at least in part, as social welfare organizations and more than half the organizations categorized, at least in part, as identity-based organizations are mixed-category organizations.

To a small extent, the set of organizations in Washington would be even more skewed away from such interests if there were only single-category orga-

35. The organizations used as examples in this section of the chapter were chosen because their names indicate the nature of the organization without additional explanation. Although all are organizations contained in our data base, they are not necessarily all listed in the 2001 directory.

36. There is also a disproportionate number of mixed-category organizations among health organizations, but they are mostly of two readily definable types: for-profit medical care systems (corporation + health institution) and medical schools (educational institution + health institution).

Table 11.7   Mixed-Category Organizations

	Percentage of All in Category[a]	N[b]
Corporations[c]	1.4	56
Trade and Other Business Associations	3.1	49
Occupational Associations	9.3	78
Unions	11.8	14
Education	17.5	93
Health	23.0	107
Social Welfare or Poor	45.9	56
Public Interest	19.9	118
Identity Groups[d]	52.6	312
State and Local Governments	1.4	17
Foreign	1.6	15
Other	17.1	165

Source: Washington Representatives Study (2001).

[a] Percentage of all organizations within a particular aggregated category (for example, identity groups) that have been coded into more than one of the 96 organizational categories, even if the categories in the mix are within that same aggregate category (for example, a group representing elderly women); includes all organizations listed in the 2001 *Washington Representatives Directory.*
[b] Number of organizations within a particular aggregated category that have been coded into more than one of the 96 organizational categories.
[c] Includes U.S. corporations, U.S. subsidiaries of foreign corporations, and for-profit firms of professionals, such as law and consulting firms.
[d] Includes organizations representing racial, ethnic, or religious groups; the elderly; women; or LGBT sexual orientation.

nizations and no mixed-category organizations.[37] The set of single-category organizations leans slightly more in the direction of the corporations, trade and other business associations, and state and local governments that weigh so heavily in the set of all organizations that are active in Washington politics.

Identity groups play a special role among mixed-category organizations. Earlier we noted that, in contrast to the circumstance for economic groups, identity groups do not represent dominant social groups. Taking all mixed-

37. The data on which this paragraph is based are contained in Table F.2 of Appendix F.

category organizations together, more than half have an identity group as one part of the mixture. In contrast to what is the case for public interest and social welfare organizations, there is a much more substantial presence of identity groups in the mixed-category organizations in the aggregated categories that have traditionally figured so importantly in pressure politics: corporations, trade and other business associations, and occupational associations. There are, for example, companies like the American Indian National Bank or Hispanic Broadcasting Inc. and trade associations like the Association of Hispanic Advertising Agencies that have an identity group as part of the mix.

Especially noteworthy are what we call "occupational caucuses" that bring together an occupational association or union with an identity-based organization. Examples of occupational caucuses include the National Asian Pacific American Bar Association, the National Hispanic Medical Association, the Association of American Foreign Service Women, and the National Association of Black Accountants, along with union consortia such as the Coalition of Black Trade Unionists and the Coalition of Labor Union Women.[38] Although such organizations span a variety of kinds of occupations, occupational caucuses are especially likely to represent those in occupations that require high levels of education or confer high levels of income. That is, compared to the set of all unions and occupational associations, organizations representing private-sector managers and professionals constitute an even larger share of the occupational caucuses—and the other occupational organizations that represent workers further down the occupational ladder constitute an even smaller share. Not one of the occupational caucuses is an identity-based organization of workers in a lower-white-collar or a blue-collar occupation.

Thus the mixed-category organizations that, in their organizational membership or mission, amalgamate two or three of the 96 organizational categories do have a small impact on the overall distribution of organizations that take part in Washington politics. Because such organizations are relatively likely to have a public interest, social welfare, or identity group as part of the mix, the distribution of single-category organizations is even more skewed in the direction of the corporations, trade and other business associations, and

---

38. The mixed-category organizations that join a union and an identity-based organization are not operating unions. Rather they are special coalitions or caucuses associated with a particular identity group and with the union movement in general.

occupational associations that have traditionally dominated the ranks of organized interests. Still, the extent to which they ameliorate the strong bias in the pressure system is quite marginal, and, with the exception of the occupational caucuses, the organizational couplings rarely involve the linking of a public interest, social welfare, or identity group, on the one hand, with a corporation, trade or other business association, or occupational association on the other.

Conclusion

Consistent with our ongoing concern with political voice, we began our consideration of political representation through organizations with a quotation asserting that "almost everybody" is in government relations, a circumstance that—if true—would surely contrast with our results about citizen voice expressed through individual activity. Our exploration of the contours of the organized interests in Washington politics has unearthed an astonishing number of organizations representing an astonishing number of interests. In the course of our discussion of the organizations in pressure politics, we have cited dozens of actual organizations. Of the organizations in the pressure system, some are well known, others obscure. Some command large staffs and budgets, others very limited resources. But all have a stake in the outcome of some policy controversy and a legitimate story to tell to the public officials whose decisions affect their lives and livelihoods. To an extent not always acknowledged, very few of these organizations that are sometimes gathered under the rubric of "interest groups" are membership groups, and only a tiny minority, about one in eight, are associations composed of individual members.

Nevertheless, our survey has made clear that, for all the variety in the interests represented by organizations in Washington, the pressure system is far from universal. Many constituencies with a seeming interest in federal policies—parents of children in Head Start programs, women at home, office receptionists, Wal-Mart associates, criminal defendants awaiting trial, recipients of Temporary Assistance for Needy Families benefits or food stamps, parking lot attendants—have no organization of their own.

What is more, both the free rider problem and the resource constraint problem imply that organized interest representation in Washington is riddled with everyday inequalities. It is true that the political voices of underrepresented groups would register even more softly were it not for the presence of mixed-category organizations, which are disproportionately likely to be found among public interest groups, social welfare organizations and organizations of the poor, and identity-based organizations. Still, these mixed-category organizations have only a marginal impact on the distribution of organizations.

The free rider problem implies that public goods like automobile safety, crime reduction, an end to capital punishment, or lower taxes are less likely to receive organizational support unless the organizational advocates are very small or have the capacity to coerce support or to dispense selective benefits. When we considered the set of organizations that act on behalf of such public goods, we saw, on the one hand, that a wide variety of such causes receive organized advocacy. On the other hand, public goods–seeking organizations are less common than might be expected on the basis of the number of people who would potentially benefit from the conditions being sought.

In other respects, the public interest groups active in Washington defy some popular conceptions. The visibility of certain public interest groups—for example, environmental groups—leads to the conclusion that the public interest sector is uniformly liberal. In fact, in most controversies involving a public good, there is an alternative public good at stake, usually on the opposite side of the ideological spectrum: for example, consumer product safety is balanced by low consumer prices. Taken together, the public interest groups in the pressure system lean in a much less decisively liberal direction than is sometimes imagined.

This observation leads to a second point, one that fits with the themes that emerged in our consideration of inequalities of political voice among individuals. While they take seriously the costs of founding and maintaining an organization, formal presentations of the free rider problem often miss the differences among constituencies in their ability to bear those costs. The size of a potential constituency is not the only factor that influences whether it achieves organizational representation. Instead, resource constraints have a powerful impact on which voices are heard through the medium of collective advocacy.

Compared to those well endowed with resources, especially business interests, economically disadvantaged constituencies—including economically disadvantaged groups defined by another characteristic, such as race or gender—have limited representation in pressure politics if they are represented at all.[39] Two especially notable findings in this regard bear repeating: first, unless they are members of a union, those whose work is unskilled have no occupational associations at all to represent their interests in Washington, and, second, although there are a small number of organizations that advocate for the poor, there is not a single organization that brings together recipients of means-tested government benefits such as Medicaid acting on their own behalf. Such gaps in organized interest representation imply that the voices in the heavenly chorus continue to sing with an upper-class accent.

39. In his study of the relationship between the characteristics of individual members of social groups and the number of political organizations that represent those groups, Matthew Grossmann, in "One Person, One Lobbyist? American Public Constituencies and Organized Representation," paper delivered at the Annual Meeting of the Midwest Political Science Association, Chicago, April 2006, p. 19, finds that "the mean socio-economic status of a constituency . . . is significantly correlated with the number of organizations and staff representing it."

12

The Changing Pressure Community

Our snapshot view of the composition of the pressure system as of 2001 obscures its essential fluidity. The next step is to do for political organizations what we did for individuals in Chapter 6: extend our analysis over time to consider the evolution of the Washington pressure community, assessing changes in the number and distribution of active organizations over a twenty-five-year span. Of special concern is whether the patterns we have described—in particular, the strong representation of business interests in contrast to the economic interests of less economically advantaged—are unique to 2001 or are a persistent aspect of organized interest representation in Washington.

In an era in which the costs of transportation and communications have fallen in relative terms and electronic technologies make it easier to stay in touch with both those at an organization's headquarters and the folks at the grassroots, organizations can move in and out of politics relatively easily. However, there have been more entries than exits over the twenty-five-year period for which we have data, with the result that there has been substantial growth in the number of organizations that take part in Washington politics, a development that has been noted by political observers. The increase in the number and influence of citizen groups—a broad category that includes a variety of kinds of membership associations such as identity groups and public interest groups—has been well documented.[1] What has garnered less attention is the explosive growth in the number of state and local govern-

1. See, in particular, Jeffrey M. Berry, *The New Liberalism* (Washington, DC: Brookings Institution, 1999).

ments as well as established but previously apolitical institutions—for example, hospitals and museums—that are active in Washington.

In delineating the changes in the number and distribution of organized interests, we delve into the processes of organizational birth and death, political mobilization and deactivation, behind these population changes. What we find is a vast expansion in the number of organizations and a great deal of continuity in the kinds of interests they represent.

In previous chapters we reviewed a number of theories explaining where interest groups come from and the factors that encourage or inhibit their emergence and noted that various strands of explanation of the origins of interest groups are germane to our concern with inequalities of political voice.[2] These various theoretical perspectives lead to some expectations as to the shape of the organized interest system. Mancur Olson's analysis and the literature it has spawned make clear the severe collective action problems that prevent large, diffuse groups from organizing on behalf of their joint political concerns. In spite of the undoubted significance of Olson's analysis, for several reasons the "free rider problem" is not the whole story. For one thing, the resource mobilization perspective reminds us of the variations among potential constituencies in the capacity to bear the costs of political organization and advocacy. It is not simply that some potential constituencies have patrons who are willing to shoulder a disproportionate share of the costs. Even when there is no such patron on the scene, some sets of collectively concerned citizens are much better positioned to command the resources needed to get an organization off the ground or keep it going. In addition, any perspective that focuses exclusively on group formation as the key to the shape of the pressure system misses the fact that, as was made clear in the preceding chapter, only a small fraction of the organizations in pressure politics are associations of individuals.

Organizational formation is only the first step. Organizations must then become involved in politics. That is, the composition of the pressure community is affected not only by organizational births and deaths but also by decisions of previously apolitical organizations to enter the political fray and of politically active organizations to exit politics and revert to apolitical status.

---

2. For discussion of the theories of organizational formation, see Anthony J. Nownes, "The Population Ecology of Interest Group Formation: Mobilizing for Gay and Lesbian Rights in the United States, 1950–1998," *British Journal of Political Science* 34 (2004): 49–58; and Andrew S. McFarland, "Neopluralism," *Annual Review of Political Science* 10 (2007): 53–57.

Olson's analysis provides no explanation for why an organization that is in a position to provide collective goods or coerce membership would take the step of devoting resources to political action. In fact, the logic of collective action obtains for decisions made by organizations—institutions as well as membership groups—at this stage as well.[3] As we shall see, most of the organizations new to the pressure community are not organizations that never existed before; rather, they are organizations that have been outside of politics and, for reasons that are less well studied, are activated into politics. Thus the shape of the pressure community is influenced by a number of factors—of which an important one, but far from the only one, is the set of processes by which new political organizations come into being.

The Ever-Expanding Pressure System

In spite of the barriers to organization, perhaps the most inescapable change in the pressure system between 1981 and 2006 is the expansion in the number of active organizations. Compared to the 1981 *Washington Representatives* directory, the 2006 directory lists more than twice the number of organizations. From one perspective, we would expect the number of listings to have grown. The population of the United States has grown, and with more people we would expect more policy concerns and claims on the government. Moreover, as indexed by federal expenditures, governmental activity has also increased—although, in a noteworthy development to the contrary, the number of civilian federal employees, including the number of employees in the legislative branch, actually fell over the quarter century covered. Yet the rate of increase in the number of organizations listed far outpaced the rate of increase in population, which grew by less than one-third over the period. It also beat the increase in federal expenditures, which nearly doubled. The only benchmark with which it did not quite keep up is the increase in real gross domestic product.[4] Across the quarter century, the rate of increase in the number of organizations was somewhat uneven. The number of entries increased by 19 percent from 1981 to 1991, by 47 percent from 1991 to 2001, and by 19 percent in the five-year period from 2001 to 2006.

3. Focusing on the motivations and actions of organization entrepreneurs, Robert H. Salisbury, in "An Exchange Theory of Interest Groups," *Midwest Journal of Political Science* 13 (1969): 1–32, and James Q. Wilson, in *Political Organizations* (New York: Basic Books, 1973), pp. 195–198, propose answers to this puzzle.

4. These inferences are based on the data on the Web site of *Statistical Abstract of the United States*, http://www.census.gov/compendia/statab/ (accessed October 6, 2010).

There are two discontinuities in the data: one has the effect of deflating the total number of organizations in the enumeration, the other the effect of inflating the total. The first of them occurred in the late 1980s, with consequences for the 1991 census of organizations. At the time that the 1981 directory was assembled, its editor gathered information from the dockets of such regulatory agencies as the Federal Trade Commission, the Nuclear Regulatory Commission, and the Federal Maritime Commission about organizations that used outside attorneys to represent their interests before the agency. Later on, this practice was discontinued because the reward in terms of additional organizations listed was deemed too costly to justify the effort involved.[5] This change of procedure would have had the effect of systematically overlooking organizations that hired outside counsel to deal with executive branch agencies but not with Congress. We have good reason to suspect that such organizations are not distributed evenly across organizational categories and that, in particular, the number of corporations is diminished by this modification.

The second discontinuity in the data derives from the impact of the 1995 Lobbying Disclosure Act (LDA). The LDA closed loopholes in the 1946 Federal Regulation of Lobbying Act and extended coverage in a variety of ways.[6] Not unexpectedly, the result was to increase the number of registered lobbyists. From 1995 to 1996, the number of entries increased 12 percent. Obviously, some of this increase reflects the jump in the number of registrations. Still, the number of entries increased by 19 percent between 2001 and 2006, a period in which no external factor would have affected the enumeration of organizations.

From one perspective, the growth in the number of organizations active in Washington is not surprising. The process by which increasing numbers of organizations have come to be involved in Washington politics has a self-reinforcing quality. One small category of organization that has grown steadily over the twenty-five-year period is firms of professionals—especially law firms. A not insubstantial portion of these firms of professionals specialize in

5. Valerie Sheridan, editor of the *Washington Representatives* (Washington, DC: Columbia Books) directory, explained this change of procedure in response to our query about the decrease in the absolute number of corporations from the 1981 to the 1991 directory.

6. On the provisions of the LDA, see Jonathan D. Salant, "Highlights of Lobby Bill," *Congressional Quarterly Weekly Report*, December 2, 1995, p. 3632. For further discussion of the LDA, see Chapter 14. Valerie Sheridan, editor of the *Washington Representatives* directory, indicated that the act had a substantial impact on her operation. She describes having more or less started over from scratch in putting together the 1996 directory.

government relations. These government relations specialists have an interest in generating new clients and thus in demonstrating to organizations without Washington-based representation the benefits such representation can confer. Similarly, an important function of the in-house government relations professionals in organizations with offices in Washington is to provide intelligence to their employers about the relevance of unfolding political developments. In the process, they are likely to find reasons that the organization needs to continue to have a presence in Washington—which has the effect of simultaneously justifying their existence and protecting the organizations that employ them.

From another point of view, however, the steady increase in the number of organizations active in Washington is unexpected because it seems to contradict a widely documented trend in American society, the decline in affiliations with membership associations. Although they make somewhat different arguments and use somewhat different kinds of evidence, both Robert Putnam and Theda Skocpol demonstrate an erosion in participation in voluntary associations and articulate serious concerns about the consequences of that erosion for democracy in America.[7] Putnam uses a variety of measures—ranging from the decrease in membership in organizations like PTAs to the dwindling of attendance at club meetings—to document a decrease in associational involvement. He considers the trend in organizational activity to be a crucial component of the deterioration of social capital, a wider phenomenon entailing a diminution of many kinds of formal and informal social connectedness as well as an erosion of social trust. Skocpol focuses on the increasing significance of staff-led checkbook organizations at the expense of what she calls cross-class membership associations and discusses the consequences of these developments for the experience of democratic governance and cultivation of democratic habits. Although Skocpol and Putnam differ in the nature of their language and their data, they converge in their concern about the implications of their findings for the democratic capacities of citizens.

While Putnam and Skocpol point to an important trend, we see no contradiction between diminishing organizational involvement at the individual level and an ever-increasing number of organizations active in pressure poli-

---

7. See Robert D. Putnam, *Bowling Alone: The Collapse and Revival of American Community* (New York: Simon and Schuster, 2000), esp. chap. 3, and Theda Skocpol, *Diminished Democracy: From Membership to Management in Civic Life* (Norman: University of Oklahoma Press, 2003), esp. chaps. 3–6.

tics. There is overlap, but not congruence, between the political organizations with which we are concerned and the membership groups on which Putnam and Skocpol focus. These sets of organizations differ in two important ways: the nature of their memberships and their involvement in politics. First, Putnam and Skocpol are discussing developments with respect to *voluntary associations of individuals*, and, as we saw in the preceding chapter, only a small minority of organizations that are active in Washington pressure politics are associations with individuals as members. Second, while the majority of membership associations are not active in politics on any level, especially nationally, the organizations that we have been discussing are defined by their involvement in Washington politics.

The Growth of the Pressure System

The figures in Table 12.1 contain two messages. First, over the two and half decades under consideration, the number of organizations active in politics increased substantially. Second, the expansion of the pressure system was quite uneven across various categories of organizations. Not unexpectedly, the data in the left hand column of numbers show above-average growth rates among the several kinds of citizen organizations: identity groups, public interest groups, and organizations that provide social welfare services or that advocate on behalf of the poor. However, other striking changes seem to have gone unnoticed by Washington watchers. One is the extraordinary growth both of organizations in the health and educational sectors and of state and local governments. Another is the failure of the kinds of organizations that have traditionally dominated in pressure politics—business organizations and occupational associations—to keep pace with the overall rate of increase in the number of organizations in Washington politics. Especially striking is the fact that the number of labor unions is unchanged. Indeed, unions are the *only one* of the aggregated categories in Table 12.1 not to register an increase over the quarter-century period. In addition, the increase in the number of trade and other business associations and the number of occupational associations did not keep up with the overall rate of growth of the Washington pressure community.

We were puzzled to note that the absolute number of corporations listed actually *fell* by one-eighth from 1981 to 1991 before rebounding substantially from 1991 to 2006. This pattern does not extend to the 500 large corporations included in the Standard and Poor's (S&P) Index, whose growth rate in the

Table 12.1   Growth in the Pressure System, 1981–2006

Categories of Organizations	Relative Increase (Percent)	Absolute Increase (Number)
Corporations[a]	62%	1,898
Trade and Other Business Associations	41%	429
Occupational Associations	32%	172
Unions	0%	0
Education	612%	643
Health	883%	547
Public Interest	123%	313
Identity Groups[b]	192%	347
Social Welfare or Poor	291%	95
State and Local Governments	382%	1,292
Foreign	54%	315
Other	312%	896
Don't Know	186%	149
Total	106%	7,096

Source: Washington Representatives Study (1981–2006).

[a] Includes U.S. corporations, U.S. subsidiaries of foreign corporations, and for-profit firms of professionals, such as law and consulting firms.
[b] Includes organizations representing racial, ethnic, or religious groups; the elderly; women; or the lesbian, gay, bisexual, or transgender (LGBT) sexual orientation.

directory listings was essentially flat between 1981 and 1991 and varied in a very narrow range over the entire period: 67.6 percent of the S&P 500 were listed in 1981, 67.2 percent in 1991, 71.4 percent in 2001, and 68.3 percent in 2006. Moreover, from 1991 to 2001 and from 2001 to 2006, the increase in the number of corporations outpaced the increase in the overall number of organizations. We entertained several hypotheses to explain why the number of corporations listed dropped off during the 1980s. Although the 1980s were known as an era of a great deal of merger and acquisition activity, the diminution in the number of corporations in the pressure system does not seem to reflect a smaller number of corporations. One possibility is that, after the well-documented march to Washington by business in the 1970s, the more politically friendly Washington environment provided by the Reagan administration made it less necessary for corporations to be on the scene.[8] Our suspicion is that the decline reflects the fact that the *Washington Representatives* directory included the dockets of the regulatory agencies as a source of information in its 1981 enumeration but not in its 1991 enumeration.[9]

The right-hand column of Table 12.1, which shows the changes in the absolute number of organizations listed, tells a somewhat different story. A high rate of increase may not imply many new organizations, and vice versa. For example, a fairly high rate of increase for organizations that provide social services and advocacy for the economically needy masks a quite small absolute increase. In contrast, for subnational governments and organizations in the health and education sectors, high rates of increase produced large absolute numbers of newly active organizations. In a different pattern, although the relative rate of increase for organizations representing business lagged, their absolute increase was the most substantial. Even considering the fact that the procedural change that excluded clients appearing before regulatory agencies after the 1981 directory may have artificially depressed the number of corporations, there were 1,898 more corporations and 429 more trade and other business associations in the 2006 directory than in 1981. Taken together, these changes mean that, in absolute terms, the increases in the kinds of organizations traditionally well represented in pressure politics—corporations, trade and other business associations, occupational associations of professionals and managers, and the like—dwarf the increases in the kinds of organizations that we have seen to be less well represented, public interest groups and organizations representing the less advantaged.

---

8. David Vogel, in *Fluctuating Fortunes: The Political Power of Business in America* (New York: Basic Books, 1989), chap. 8, documents the massive increase in the government relations capacity of business and the resultant policy victories by business interests during the late 1970s. He also discusses (chap. 9) that, after the honeymoon during the first two years of the Reagan administration, the business community was not as unified and therefore was not as successful in realizing its objectives later in the decade. However, he does not mention a diminishing business *presence* during that period.

9. In the search for an explanation of the decline in the absolute number of corporations between 1981 and 1991, Lee Drutman noticed a precipitous decline in the number of radio and television stations listed in the two directories. By rough count, there were more than 800 stations in the 1981 directory—all of which were listed as hiring outside counsel rather than as having their own offices in the capital—and fewer than 150 in the 1991 directory. This gap alone more than accounts for the drop-off of just over 400 corporations from 1981 to 1991. It was the curious evaporation of the radio and television stations that led us to follow up with Ms. Sheridan, the editor of the directories. We extend our appreciation to Lee for being so observant.

The Changing Distribution of Organizations

Table 12.2, which presents data about the distribution of organizations in the pressure system for each of the years in our study, summarizes the effects of these processes. On balance, the overall pattern shows a great deal of continuity. Organizations representing broad publics and the disadvantaged continue to constitute only a small share of organized interest representation in Washington. The economic organizations that have traditionally dominated in the pressure system—corporations, trade and other business associations, occupational associations, and labor unions—continue to represent a majority of organizations active in national politics. Nevertheless, these traditionally dominant sectors command a smaller share of the pressure system than they did in 1981. As we discussed in the previous chapter, several categories of organizations represent the interests of the for-profit sector: corporations, both domestic and foreign; trade and other business associations, again both domestic and foreign, which have corporations as members; occupational associations of business executives and professionals; and business-related think tanks and research organizations. These various kinds of organizations representing business constituted 69.2 percent of all organizations listed in 1981 but only 51.5 percent in 2006—a substantial drop. Part of this decline presumably reflects the procedural change by the editor of the *Washington Representatives* directory.[10] Even if we ignore the impact on the data of the change in procedure, however, there were 2,540 more business-related organizations active in Washington politics in 2006 than in 1981—a substantial increase. In fact, combining all the unions, public interest groups, identity groups, and organizations representing the economically needy listed in 2006 yields a total that is just over half the number of *additional* organizations representing the private sector.

The diminution of the share of the pressure system occupied by traditional business and occupational organizations has not been accompanied by

10. In fact, the share of business organizations dropped much less substantially between 1991 and 2006. While the number of corporations listed declined between 1981 and 1991, in no other category was there a decrease over this period in the absolute number of organizations. Across all categories other than corporations, the number of organizations increased by 56 percent from 1981 to 1991. Had the number of corporations kept pace with this rate of growth—a not unreasonable assumption given that the growth in the number of corporations surpassed the rate for the pressure community as a whole from 1991 to 2001 and from 2001 to 2006—the share of organizations representing business in 2006 would actually have increased very slightly from 1981.

Table 12.2 Organized Interests in Washington Politics, 1981–2006

Categories of Organizations	Share of Washington Organizations (Percent)				Change in Share (Percent)
	1981	1991	2001	2006	
Corporations[a]	45.9%	33.8%	34.9%	36.1%	-9.8%
Trade and Other Business Associations	15.5	14.8	13.2	10.7	-4.8%
Occupational Associations	8.1	8.6	6.8	5.2	-2.9%
Unions	1.6	1.5	1.0	0.8	-0.8%
Education	1.6	3.0	4.2	5.4	+3.8%
Health	.9	2.4	3.5	4.4	+3.5%
Social Welfare or Poor	0.5	0.7	0.8	0.9	+0.4%
Public Interest	3.8	4.8	4.6	4.1	+0.3%
Identity Groups[b]	2.7	3.5	3.8	3.8	+1.1%
State and Local Governments	5.1	7.0	10.4	11.8	+6.7%
Foreign	8.7	10.2	7.8	6.5	-2.2%
Other	4.3	7.0	7.7	8.6	+4.3%
Don't Know	1.2	2.7	1.4	1.7	+0.5%
Total	99.9%	100.0%	100.1%	100.0%	
N	6,681	7,925	11,651	13,777	

Source: Washington Representatives Study (1981–2006).

[a] Includes U.S. corporations, U.S. subsidiaries of foreign corporations, and for-profit firms of professionals, such as law and consulting firms.

[b] Includes organizations representing racial, ethnic, or religious groups; the elderly; women; or LGBT sexual orientation.

a corresponding enlargement in the share of the kinds of organizations that are traditionally underrepresented in pressure politics: organizations representing broad publics and the disadvantaged. Instead there has been explosive growth of subnational governments, especially local governments, and institutions, especially in the health and education sectors. Taken together, the share of organizations in the pressure system accounted for by subnational governments and the health and educational sectors rose nearly three times over the twenty-five-year period. With respect to the kinds of organizations that are traditionally underrepresented in national pressure politics, the share of organizations representing public interests increased very slightly, from 3.8 to 4.1 percent. The small share of organized interests that represent people in terms of their shared identities—racial, religious, ethnic, age, gender, and sexual orientation—was also slightly higher in 2006 than it had been in 1981.

Several kinds of organizations represent the economic interests of the less affluent: social welfare and poor people's organizations, occupational associations of nonprofessionals, and labor unions. Throughout the quarter-century period under discussion, this group of organizations accounted for only a tiny fraction of the pressure system. However, between 1981 and 2006 that share decreased from 2.9 percent to 2.2 percent. Decomposing that figure into its constituents, the minute share of organizations representing the poor and social welfare increased slightly. In contrast, the share of organizations representing the occupational interests of the vast majority of American workers diminished. Moreover, as we saw earlier in Chapter 3, when it comes to union strength, what is even more important than the number of unions is the decline in the number of members and the share of the workforce unions enroll.

The Changing Pressure System: A Closer Look

When we put these data under a microscope and peer inside the subcategories that make up some of these aggregates, we find that an increase in the numbers of organizations in an aggregate category can be driven by especially strong growth in a particular subcategory. Consider, for example, the data in Table 12.3, which divides the public interest category into its constituent parts. The rate of increase was particularly sharp for "other public interest groups"—both domestic ones like the Air Bag and Seat Belt Safety Campaign, Security on Campus, and the Coalition for the Prevention of Alcohol

Table 12.3   Growth in Numbers of Public Interest Groups, 1981–2006

Categories of Public Interest Groups	Relative Increase (Percent)	Absolute Increase (Number)
Environmental and Wildlife	116%	67
Consumer	12%	4
Government Reform	179%	17
Civil Liberties	–8%	–1
Citizen Empowerment	486%	17
Other Liberal Groups	160%	67
Other Conservative Groups	84%	41
Other Public Interest Groups	200%	112

Source: Washington Representatives Study (1981–2006).

Problems and, especially, nonideological organizations focused on problems abroad. In contrast, growth in the numbers of consumer and civil liberties organizations, traditionally important components of the public interest community, has been very limited. Table 12.3 also indicates that the increase in other liberal public interest groups has outpaced somewhat the growth in other conservative public interest groups. Even more finely grained analysis demonstrates that the divergence occurred during the five years at the end of the period—between 2001 and 2006, a time when the Republicans controlled both the presidency and Congress and liberals were feeling besieged.

The aggregate category of identity groups also illustrates the extent to which subcategories may have differing patterns of growth. Among identity groups, organizations representing people who are lesbian, gay, bisexual, or transgender (LGBT) registered the strongest growth rate in percentage terms, representing a jump from 1 organization to 10! In spite of the impressive growth rate for LGBT organizations, much of the growth in identity groups from 1981 to 2006 can be attributed to the additional 168 organizations, mostly federally recognized tribes, representing Native Americans. That the increase in the number of organizations representing Native Americans was especially sharp between 1991 and 2001 suggests the impact of the 1988 Indian Gaming Regulatory Act and the significance of issues surrounding casino gambling in the political activation of Native Americans. For the other subcategories of identity groups—organizations of women, the elderly, various racial and ethnic groups, and diverse religious denominations—the numbers of additional organizations are very small. When the aggregate category of identity groups is considered apart from Native American organizations, the growth rate just tracks the overall twenty-five-year growth rate for the pressure system.[11]

The only aggregate category not to register an increase in absolute terms over the quarter-century period is organized labor. In fact, over the two and a half decades the number of public-sector unions (both white- and blue-collar), white-collar unions (both public- and private-sector), and mixed unions all increased, albeit at very modest rates. These increases were offset by a decline in the number of blue-collar, private-sector unions from 58 to 40.

The robust growth in the number of subnational governments active in Washington politics similarly reflects the change in a single subcategory, local governments. In this case, the various subcategories each registered increases.[12] However, nearly three-quarters of the net gain results from the additional local governments listed in the 2006 *Washington Representatives* directory.

One other pattern emerges from scrutiny of the subcategories out of which the aggregate categories are built: in spite of the fact that the rate of growth for corporations lagged behind that for the pressure system as a whole, other organizational subcategories composed principally of institutions registered impressive gains. The growth in the numbers of institutions in the educational and health sectors is especially notable. From 1981 to 2006, the number of public educational institutions, mostly universities, listed in the directory skyrocketed 2,355 percent—from 11 to 270; the number of private educational institutions, again mostly universities, listed in the directory rose 1,353 percent—from 19 to 276; and the number of health institutions grew 2,713 percent—from 15 to 422. Arts and cultural organizations, a diverse category that encompasses a number of museums and other arts and cultural institutions, shows a similar though less dramatic increase, rising from 27 to 188 for an increase of 596 percent.

11. Excluding organizations representing Native Americans, identity groups constituted 2.1 percent of all organizations listed in 1981 and 2.3 percent of organizations listed in 2006.

12. The components of this aggregate category include state governments (and agencies of state governments), county and local governments (and their agencies), consortia of governments of various kinds, government corporations and various kinds of public–private partnerships, airports, and miscellaneous other governmental entities, including governments of U.S. territories. See Appendix E for descriptions of the 96 categories into which organizations were sorted.

The tendency for subcategories dominated by institutions to be characterized by relative growth extends, perhaps surprisingly, even to the organizations that represent the poor in national politics. This aggregate category
includes three kinds of organizations: organizations of recipients of means-
tested social welfare or tax benefits advocating on their own behalf, organizations that advocate on behalf of the economically needy, and providers of
direct services to economically needy publics, most of which are nonprofit
institutions and many of which are government contractors. Considering the
first of these, organizations *of* the poor, the directories listed only one of these
in 1981, three in 1991, and not a single one in either 2001 or 2006. In contrast,
although not very numerous, the latter two kinds of organizations that represent the poor in politics registered gains over the twenty-five-year period.
However, while they were less numerous than advocates for the poor in 1981,
the rate of increase of social service providers was considerably higher, with
the result that in 2001 and 2006 social service providers outnumbered organizations advocating on behalf of the economically disadvantaged.[13]

A Note on the Decline of Labor Unions

When viewed in the context of other developments, the trends we have outlined have implications for the social class accent of the heavenly chorus. We
mentioned that, alone among all the aggregate categories of organized interests, labor unions did not register an absolute increase in the number of organizations, an outcome that results from the absolute decrease in the number
of unions that organize blue-collar workers in the private sector. These findings dovetail with the findings in Chapter 3 about the steady decline in the
proportion of private-sector employees who are unionized and the increasing share of union members with college degrees, especially among women.
The result, as Theda Skocpol demonstrates, is a growing gap between the
proportion of college-educated Americans who are members of a professional society and the proportion of non-college-educated Americans who
are union members.[14]

The erosion of union membership within the working class also has consequences for the changing accent of political voice through individual-level

13. The number of social service providers rose 438 percent—from 13 to 70. The number
of organizations advocating on behalf of the poor grew more modestly, 200 percent, from 17
to 51.

14. See Skocpol, *Diminished Democracy*, pp. 212–219.

political participation. Surveys conducted over a three-decade period allow us to track the proportion of all political activity undertaken by individuals that arises from union members. Because the surveys include somewhat different measures and somewhat different political acts, we should not reify any particular number.[15] However, the pattern of steady decrease is unmistakable. In 1967, 25 percent of all political acts were performed by union members. By 1990, this figure had decreased to 18 percent. It had fallen to 13 percent in 2000 and then to 11 percent in 2006. This decline is especially noteworthy in light of the gains over the period in the share of the unionized workforce that is college educated. What is also striking is the erosion in the share of political activity that arises from union members lower down on the ladder of socio-economic status (SES). In 1967, 4.6 percent of all political acts originated with union members in one of the two lower SES quintiles. In 2006, the corresponding figure was 2.5 percent. In short, what we observe for individual activity accords with our findings about the pressure system.

In and Out: Turnover in the Pressure System

In one respect, our data lend some confirmation to the pluralist orthodoxy. The set of organizations in the Washington pressure system is extremely fluid, with a great deal of turnover from year to year. The net increase in organizations active in Washington politics obscures complex processes by which individual organizations enter and leave the pressure system. Even when there is no change in the number of organizations from one year to the next, there is a great deal of churning of the particular organizations that are active.

Discussions of political organizations in politics have often focused solely on the initial step in what is, at least in the abstract, a two-step process involving organizational formation and then entry into politics—a step sometimes overlooked by the formal theorists who emphasize the barriers to the formation of organizations. Analogously, the biological metaphors that are some-

---

15. The data are drawn from the following studies: 1967, "Participation in America Survey"; 1990, "Citizen Participation Study"; 2000, "Social Capital Community Benchmark Survey," Saguaro Seminar, Kennedy School of Government, Harvard University; and 2006, "Social Capital Community Survey," Saguaro Seminar, Kennedy School of Government, Harvard University. These surveys are available at the major political science data repositories, including the Interuniversity Consortium for Political and Social Research. While the specific acts differ somewhat from survey to survey, each of these surveys contains a set of questions about such political acts such as voting, contacting officials, or taking part in campaigns.

times used to describe the population of politically active organized interests emphasize organizational births and deaths. However, in contrast to populations of plants and animals, the set of organizations that constitute the pressure system at any given moment results from processes of organizational politicization as well as of organizational births and deaths. That is, new entrants into pressure politics can be either entirely new organizations or, more likely, existing organizations that have been outside politics. Similarly, organizations that exit from pressure politics may continue as organizations outside politics, or they may go out of business altogether.[16]

In order to probe these processes, we traced the previous histories of the individual organizations listed in the 2006 *Washington Representatives* directory. Unfortunately, for several reasons we could not reconstruct back to 1981 the histories of the corporations listed in 2006 and are forced to omit them from this discussion.[17] However, we did locate information about the political whereabouts in 1981 of 87 percent of organizations, other than corporations, listed in 2006: 17 percent of them were, in fact, listed in the 1981 directory; 30 percent were not yet alive; and a majority, 53 percent, existed as organizations but were not listed in the directory. Of the organizations that were listed in 2006 but not in 1981, fully 64 percent were alive in 1981—just not in politics. Only 36 percent of the organizations listed in 2006, but not in 1981, are new organizations that did not exist in 1981. When we disaggregate these figures, we find considerable variation across particular categories of organizations. Of the organizations new to the 2006 list, those for which political objectives weigh especially heavily in the organizational mission—in particular, public interest groups and organizations for the economically disadvantaged—are more likely to be newly hatched rather than existing but newly mobilized.[18] These figures suggest not only that it is easier to move an

16. For a sophisticated analysis making extensive use of the biological model that recognizes that understanding the population of active organized interests requires tracing processes of organizational entries and exits as well as organizational births and deaths, see Virginia Gray and David Lowery, *Population Ecology of Interest Representation* (Ann Arbor: University of Michigan Press, 1996), esp. chap. 6.

17. There are several reasons that we are forced to omit corporations, both domestic and foreign, from this discussion. The period covered by our study witnessed huge changes in corporate identities—mergers, acquisitions, spin-offs, and changes in names. While such organizational transformations are described for associations at their Web sites and in such sources as Associations Unlimited, this information is harder to locate for corporations. For the large number of listed corporations that are privately owned and not publicly traded, this information is even more difficult to find.

18. Full data on which this discussion is based can be found in Appendix F.

existing organization into politics than it is to start a political organization from scratch but also that, at any time, the political mobilization of existing organizations is only partial. Whether they sit out politics because they have no politically relevant concerns or because they are daunted by the resource requirements, many existing organizations are not part of the political fray.

We can gain additional perspective on the processes by which organizations go in and out of politics by starting at the other end, with the organizations listed in the 1981 directory. Once again, we were unable to trace the subsequent histories of the corporations listed in the 1981 directory. However, we were able to figure out what happened to 83 percent of the other organizations listed in 1981. Contrary to the received wisdom that "once in politics, always in politics," only a bare majority of these organizations, 51 percent, were listed in the 2006 directory, and only 37 percent were in all four directories.[19] When organizations exit the pressure system, they leave politics, but, consistent with organization theories that stress the resilience of organizations, they are very unlikely to go out of business entirely. Of the no-longer-listed organizations about which we could find information, fully 86 percent were still alive, though not in politics; only 14 percent had gone out of business entirely. Of course, the 17 percent of the 1981 listings for which we were unable to trace subsequent history probably include a disproportionate share that were no longer alive. Still, it is striking what a relatively high proportion of the 1981 organizations had exited the pressure system without going out of business. Moreover, in contrast to what we might expect on the basis of pluralist theory, the fluid pressure system is characterized by relatively low levels of *reentry*. That is, of the organizations that were listed in 1981 that we know were still in existence as of 2006, only 9 percent were absent from a subsequent directory and then listed again thereafter.

When we looked more closely at the political activation and deactivation of the organizations that were listed in the 1981 *Washington Representatives* directory, we found that the categories we have been examining were not especially helpful in discerning patterns. Instead, as shown in Table 12.4, two other variables seem to have implications for the movement of an organization in and out of Washington politics: first, whether it has Washington representatives on its in-house staff or relies exclusively on outside public relations, consulting, or law firms to handle its government affairs business,

---

19. These figures, which are for all organizations listed in 1981 for which we have information about their 2006 status, once again omit domestic and foreign corporations.

Table 12.4 Movement In and Out of the Washington Pressure System[a]

	Years Organizations Were Listed in the *Washington Representatives* Directory (1981, 1991, 2001, 2006)					
	Listed in 1981 Only (Percent)	Listed in 2 or 3 Directories, Then Out for Good (Percent)	Listed in 1981, Then Out, Then Back In (Percent)	Listed in All 4 Directories (Percent)		
Kind of Washington Representation						
In-House Washington Representatives	17%	25	4	53	= 99%	(1,446)
No In-House Washington Representatives	41%	22	15	22	= 100%	(1,103)
Membership Status						
Voluntary Association of Individuals	29%	26	6	39	= 100%	(732)
Voluntary Association of Institutions	27%	28	8	36	= 99%	(857)
Institution	42%	24	16	17	= 99%	(127)
Government or Association of Governments	38%	16	19	28	= 99%	(355)

Source: Washington Representatives Study (1981–2006).

[a] The table includes organizations listed in the 1981 *Washington Representatives* directory and known to be alive as organizations in 2006; it does not include either domestic or foreign corporations.

and second, its membership status. For each of the organizations listed in 1981 that we knew to be alive twenty-five years later, we coded whether it was listed in the 1981 directory only; listed in the 1981 directory and at least one subsequent directory before disappearing permanently; listed in the 1981 directory, absent from at least one directory, and then listed again in at least one subsequent directory; or listed in all four directories.[20]

Not unexpectedly, the top portion of Table 12.4 shows that organizations listed in 1981 as having made the political investment of establishing an office in Washington and hiring an in-house Washington representative were much more likely to be listed in all four directories and much less likely to have been listed only in the first directory than were organizations that relied exclusively on outside counsel or lobbyists. Making such a commitment requires substantial resources that would not be justified in the absence of a level of sustained political concern and ongoing issues with the federal government. Furthermore, having government relations professionals in Washington would predispose an organization to continued political activity—whether because having eyes and ears on the scene enhances an organization's capacity to anticipate issues that might be germane to its interests or because canny in-house staff are alert to opportunities to demonstrate the importance of what they do.

The bottom portion of Table 12.4 makes clear the relationship between an organization's path in and out of politics and its membership status, that is, whether it is a voluntary association of individuals, a voluntary association of institutions, an institution, or a government or consortium of governments. The voluntary associations, whether composed of individuals or institutions, show a similar trajectory. If in politics at all, they tend to be somewhat more likely to be in for the long haul. Once they disappear from the directories, they rarely show up again. In contrast, institutions like universities, hospitals, and think tanks are less likely to get into politics for the duration and more likely to move in and out of politics—and even to move in, out, and back in again strategically. The data for governments and consortia of governments, whether domestic or foreign, show a similar, if less pronounced, pattern. These tendencies are not surprising. Institutions and governments are ongoing enterprises with infrastructure and public relations staff that can easily be redirected toward government affairs in Washington and, usually, the bud-

---

20. The data in Table 12.4 once again include all organizations listed in 1981 for which we have information about their 2006 status except for domestic and foreign corporations.

getary wherewithal to hire outside lobbyists on a temporary basis. While they resemble voluntary associations in having a basic need to stay solvent, they are not subject to the free rider problem in the same way. This configuration of circumstances makes it easier for institutions and governments to move nimbly into, and out of, Washington politics.

With respect to the membership status of organizations, the most substantial change over the quarter-century period studied was the increase in the share of state and local governments, from 5.8 percent of all organizations listed in 1981 to 13.1 percent in 2006. The growth in the share of state and local governments came at the expense of organizations of institutions, which fell from 18.8 percent to 14.5 percent. The proportions of institutions, just over half, and membership associations of individuals, about an eighth, were virtually unchanged.

Conclusion

This chapter has considered in detail the changing pressure community over the past quarter century. The essential message in this welter of detail is that the march to Washington by organized interests entails expansion but not metamorphosis. The overall distribution of kinds of organizations listed in the *Washington Representatives* directory shows a great deal of continuity. Throughout the period, the representation of business was robust, and the kinds of organizations that Schattschneider observed as less well represented—public interest groups and organizations representing the less advantaged—were only a very small share of the organizations active in Washington politics.

If overall continuity in the distribution of organizations is the main story, several kinds of change are relevant to our basic themes. For one thing, continuity in the kinds of organizations that are active obscures the amount of churning among individual organizations. Organizations—especially those that do not establish an office in Washington but instead rely exclusively on outside counsel or consultants—enter and leave the pressure community quite readily. Organizations listed in the directory in a single year are not necessarily committed for the long run, and less than a third of the organizations listed in 1981 appeared in all four directories. Such fluidity can be construed as evidence for the pluralist contention that American politics has few barriers to entry by a group of jointly interested citizens, and therefore that the absence of organized representation is prima facie evidence of absence of collective concern. However, the evidence shows that the organizations that were not listed in 1981 but had entered politics by 2006 were much more likely to be previously existing but politically inactive organizations that were mobilized into politics than to be newly formed organizations, and more likely to be institutions or governments than to be membership associations. Thus the processes we describe call into question the pluralist claim that membership associations will be formed almost automatically when individuals have a common political interest.

That it is much harder to get a new organization off the ground than to take an ongoing organization into politics is evidence that Mancur Olson was on to something when he discussed how the free rider problem inhibits organizational formation. However, to the student of politics rather than of organizational behavior, an exclusive focus on organizational formation neglects important parts of the story of political voice through organized political representation in which voluntary associations made up of individuals and institutions are less numerous than institutions and governments, in which the political activation of existing organizations figures more importantly than the founding of new ones, and in which the processes by which organizations enter into politics are themselves a puzzle requiring explanation. Moreover, the continuing dearth of organizations representing the disadvantaged suggests that the free rider problem is not the only hurdle on the path to entry into organized interest politics; the resource deficit problem also operates to raise barriers to organized political activity. Potential stakeholders are not equally likely to be mobilized into pressure politics.

In spite of the barriers to the formation of new membership groups and taking them into politics, the pressure community has expanded substantially. An important theme of this analysis is the striking increase in the number of organizations active in Washington politics: more than twice as many organizations were listed in the *Washington Representatives* directory in 2006 as in 1981. Although we have stressed the extent to which this expansion has been accompanied by stability in the kinds of organizations that are involved in politics, we should make it clear that more of the same is not necessarily the same.

Interestingly, in relative terms the rate of increase in some of the kinds of organizations that have traditionally formed the backbone of pressure politics—trade and other business associations, occupational associations, and unions—has not kept pace with the rate of increase in other kinds of organizations. However, the growth rates for the kinds of organizations that have traditionally been less well represented—public interest groups and organizations representing the less advantaged—have not been especially noteworthy. Instead, the marked expansion in the number of politically active organizations derives disproportionately from the education and health fields, categories dominated by institutions rather than voluntary associations, and from state, and especially local, governments.

Focusing exclusively on relative rates of increase obscures the implications of changes in the absolute numbers of organizations. In one important way, the impact of increased numbers of organizations is contrary to the overall bias of the pressure system. In his study of the policy impact of increasing numbers of citizen groups, Jeffrey Berry makes clear that larger numbers of citizen groups acting as advocates for postmaterialist concerns—in particular, environmental groups—have had an appreciable influence on policy.[21]

In other ways, the proliferation of organizational advocates reinforces the tendencies we have been emphasizing. While the growth rates for the various kinds of organizations representing business were not remarkable, the absolute changes were substantial.

During this period the number of unions did not grow, a function of a decline in the number of blue-collar, private-sector unions. In the context of the declining proportion of the private-sector workforce enrolled in unions and the relative increase in the educational attainment of union members, these developments suggest a weakened political voice on behalf of the economic interests of those lower down on the economic ladder. At the same time, in absolute terms, the increases in organizations representing business dwarf the increases in organizations advocating on behalf of either public goods or the disadvantaged. Indeed, nearly twice as many organizations representing the private sector were added over the period as there were unions, public interest groups, identity groups, and organizations representing the economically needy listed in 2006.

From a different perspective, the expansion of the organized interest community has consequences for political voice. As we shall see in Chapter 14, because pressure politics relies so heavily on the services of paid professionals, it is a domain that facilitates the conversion of market resources into political advocacy. Our findings in Chapter 6 confirm those of other political scientists who have shown that, in the aggregate, political participation by

21. Berry, *New Liberalism.*

individuals has diminished in recent decades.[22] The simultaneous growth in activity in pressure politics thus shifts the relative weight of individual and organized input into politics and implies that the section of the heavenly chorus with an especially pronounced upper-class accent is singing relatively more loudly. Thus, even though the distribution of organizations has not changed appreciably, the alteration in the balance of individual and organizational voices may have the effect of exacerbating inequalities of political voice.[23]

What is the bottom line? A reader of the manuscript for this volume asked whether we were describing "a new and disturbing trend or an old and disturbing process."[24] Our detailed consideration of the complicated and sometimes contradictory trends over the past quarter century makes it clear that we are dealing with an expanded version of an old and disturbing process. Throughout the period we have considered, pressure politics has been a domain hospitable to the representation of the interests of the advantaged, especially business. Any amelioration or exacerbation of its upper-class accent is secondary to the fact that the chorus has unambiguously become larger.

22. See, in particular, Steven J. Rosenstone and John Mark Hansen, *Mobilization, Participation, and Democracy in America* (New York: MacMillan, 1993), and Putnam, *Bowling Alone*.

23. We thank Archon Fung for making this point.

24. We thank Frank Baumgartner for posing this question.

13

Beyond Organizational Categories

Evidence about the organizations active in Washington makes a compelling case for the way that both the free rider problem and the resource problem operate to shape collective representation. Still, we wondered whether, in relying on organizational categories—even categories that are very refined—we might be overlooking additional factors implying that the distribution of organizational types exaggerates or underestimates the paucity of organized representation for the resource deprived. In this chapter we consider several kinds of data that might show evidence of reinforcing or ameliorating tendencies. We investigate whether, within any category, the organizations that have Washington representation are stratified by organizational size or budget. We use survey data about individual members of voluntary associations to query whether those who are active or are mobilized to political action in organizations and those who consider that the organization represents them are representative of all organization members. Finally, we scrutinize evidence gathered from organizations' Web sites to inquire whether the resource disadvantaged are gaining representation from other, perhaps more privileged, organizations in the pressure system. Taken together, these disparate sources of information suggest that, if anything, data about the distribution of organizational categories understate the upper-class accent of the organizational chorus.

Big Organizations–Little Organizations: Looking Inside Categories

One possibility is that the politically active organizations in a particular category are in some way atypical of all organizations in that category. It is not clear how to establish, across the many categories of organizations in the pressure system, the universe of organizations from which organizations active in politics are drawn. However, for several important categories of organizations we have been able to assemble data demonstrating that processes of organizational selection into politics reinforce the bias in favor of the resource advantaged.

The data presented in Table 13.1 indicate unambiguously that, within any category, larger organizations are more likely than smaller ones to be listed in the *Washington Representatives* directory. Sections A–C of Table 13.1 present information about the organizations contained in a sample of the more than 7,300 trade associations, occupational associations, and labor unions listed in the 2001 edition of a directory that essays to list all such organizations—irrespective of their involvement in Washington politics.[1] When the organizations in one of these categories—whether trade and other business associations, occupational associations, or labor unions—are stratified by budget size, it becomes clear that organizations with large budgets are much more likely to be listed in the 2001 *Washington Representatives* directory as having a presence in politics: at least three-quarters of the affluent organizations with budgets over $25 million, but no more than 6 percent of the organizations with budgets under $100,000, were listed.[2] Section D of Table 13.1 shows an analogous pattern for a sample of institutions of higher education as categorized by the Carnegie Foundation for the Advancement of Teaching. Half of the research universities that produce large numbers of doctoral degrees have Washington representation compared to only 2 percent of the two-year colleges that award associate's degrees. Smaller research universities and master's and baccalaureate institutions are in between. Of course the large universities that have medical schools and extensive scientific facilities receive substantial federal funding and are subject to federal regulation and thus intersect with federal policy more extensively than do smaller institutions. Nevertheless, the community colleges that comprise the large share of associate's colleges enroll a disproportionate share of economi-

---

1. Buck Downs, ed., *National Trade and Professional Associations of the United States* (Washington, DC: Columbia Books, 2001).

2. Although Jeffrey M. Drope and Wendy L. Hansen, in "New Evidence for the Theory of Groups: Trade Association Lobbying in Washington, D.C.," *Political Research Quarterly* 62 (2009): 303–316, are principally concerned to test Olson's logic with respect to whether the market structure of an industry affects trade association political activity, consistent with Table 13.1, their data show that an even more powerful explanatory variable is industry size.

Table 13.1 Organization Size and Washington Representation: Percentage of All Organizations in Each Category that Are Listed in the 2001 *Washington Representatives* Directory

A. Trade and Other Business Associations
Ranked by Budget[a]

$25 Million or More	77%	(47)
$5–25 Million	69%	(93)
$1–5 Million	50%	(139)
$100,000–1 Million	30%	(112)
Less than $100,000	5%	(58)

B. Occupational Associations Ranked by Budget[a]

$25 Million or More	75%	(41)
$5–25 Million	63%	(109)
$1–5 Million	51%	(129)
$100,000–1 Million	23%	(165)
Less than $100,000	6%	(169)

C. Unions Ranked by Budget[b]

$25 Million or More	94%	(16)
$5–25 Million	88%	(24)
$1–5 million	59%	(32)
$100,000–1 Million	0%	(6)
Less than $100,000	0%	(4)

D. Colleges and Universities[c]

Large Doctoral/Research Universities	50%	(50)
Smaller Doctoral/Research Universities	44%	(50)
Master's Colleges and Universities	12%	(100)
Baccalaureate Colleges	15%	(100)
Associate's Colleges	2%	(100)

E. Standard and Poor's 500 Corporations
Ranked by Number of Employees[d]

Top 50	86%
51–100	82%
101–200	82%
201–300	72%
301–400	64%
401+	49%

continued

Table 13.1   Continued

F. Cities Ranked by Population[e]

Top 50	82%
51–100	52%
101–150	46%
151–200	18%

Source: Washington Representatives Study (2001). See also the sources in the notes.

[a] Organizations were listed in groupings by size of budget in Buck Downs, ed., *National Trade and Professional Associations of the United States* (Washington, DC: Columbia Books, 2001), pp. 769–795. Organizations were sampled randomly at ratios ranging from 1:1 for the most affluent organizations listed to 1:7 for the least affluent organizations listed. Numbers in parentheses represent the actual number of organizations in a particular category that were checked.

[b] Unions were listed in groupings by size of budget in Buck Downs, ed., *National Trade and Professional Associations of the United States* (Washington, DC: Columbia Books, 2001), pp. 769–795. All unions were checked.

[c] Colleges and universities were sampled randomly at ratios ranging from 1:2 for the smaller research universities to 1:12 for associate's colleges for the institutions of higher education listed in *The Carnegie Classification of Institutions of Higher Education* (Menlo Park, CA: Carnegie Foundation for the Advancement of Teaching, 2001). Definitions of the categories of institutions can be found on p. 1. The two kinds of doctoral/research universities are differentiated by the number of doctoral degrees awarded annually in a minimum number of fields, not by the size of the student body, faculty, budget, or endowment.

[d] Data about number of employees, taken from the Compustat database, are missing for 22 of the corporations listed by Standard and Poor's in 2001.

[e] Cities were ranked by 2000 population as recorded by the U.S. Census, www.census .gov/population/cen2000/phc-t5/tab02.pdf (accessed July 25, 2007).

cally needy students who would qualify for Pell Grants. Therefore, the dearth of political representation of associate's colleges cannot simply be attributed to an absence of a stake in federal politics.

Sections E and F of the table present data about the likelihood that corporations included in the 2001 Standard and Poor's (S&P) 500 and the nation's 200 largest cities would be listed as having representation in Washington politics. In contrast to the data about trade associations, occupational associations, unions, and institutions of higher education in the upper part of the table, which are drawn from what are purported to be comprehensive listings, these data are derived from listings that have already been screened for size—corporations that are publicly traded and are large and important enough to be included in a major stock index and big cities. Even within these censored samples, however, size is associated with Washington representation. The corporations with the most employees and the cities with the most people were very likely, and corporations with fewer employees and cities with fewer people were much less likely, to be listed in the directory as having a presence in pressure politics.

The association between size and having a presence in Washington politics has consequences for equality of representation. On one hand, it might seem natural for the probability of being in politics to grow with size. After all, if New York City, the nation's most populous city, is not active in Washington politics, the results have a potential impact on many more people than if Beaumont, Texas, listed as the two hundredth largest city, takes a pass on federal politics. On the other hand, these are all large entities. All of the cities in the top two hundred had populations above 100,000. In 2001 only five companies in the S&P 500 had fewer than 1,000 employees, and all of them surely have both the wherewithal to field Washington representation and sufficient interaction with the federal government to justify it. Besides, there are the thousands of firms that do not make it into the S&P 500 and thousands of cities and towns with fewer residents than Beaumont. Leaving aside the knotty issue of who is represented when a corporation is politically active, it is worth noting that in 2001, 53.2 percent of nongovernment workers worked for employers having fewer than 100 employees and only 13.7 worked for employers having 1,000 or more employees.[3] Similarly, in 2000, 56.9 percent

3. Calculated from U.S. Census data found at http://www.census.gov/compendia/statab/business_enterprise/establishments_employees_payroll/, table 738 (accessed August 25, 2007).

of those residing in incorporated places lived in cities and towns with fewer than 100,000 people, and nearly six million students attended two-year colleges.[4]

We should make clear that membership associations often function as very effective advocates for smaller units that do not have their own Washington representation. Such associations—of which the National League of Cities or the National Federation of Independent Business are prime examples—act as eyes and ears for the unrepresented, undertaking grassroots campaigns and lobbying when the occasion demands and scoring impressive policy victories. Still, it is striking that almost all of the individual companies in the Alliance of Automobile Manufacturers have their own Washington representation, usually in the form of an office in the capital. When Ford and General Motors vie for a government contract to purchase trucks, a trade association is not the right vehicle to make the case. Similarly, a municipality may be seeking a disaggregated benefit—for example, the earmark for a $50 million new toll-free bridge secured by Treasure Island, Florida, to which we referred in Chapter 10—for which no consortium of towns would be useful as an advocate. As impressive as the track record of the associations that represent small entities might be, it is difficult to argue that organizations are better off when they rely solely on the activity of an effective association and do not field representation on their own behalf. Thus the underrepresentation of small entities introduces a further bias into organized interest politics beyond that manifest in data about categories of organizations.

Inside Organizations: Who Is Active? Who Gets Mobilized? Who Feels Represented?

While a great deal about the kinds of interests that are represented within organized interest politics can be inferred from the distribution of organizations, we have made clear how difficult it is to know who is represented by an organization. While the matter of organizational representation is especially

4. Calculated from U.S. Census data found at http://www.census.gov/prod/2002pubs/01statab/pop.pdf (accessed August 25, 2007). This figure omits those living in unincorporated places. Although they might be represented in Washington politics by their counties or states, those who reside in unincorporated places are very unlikely to be represented by a municipality. The number of students in two-year colleges was taken from U.S. Census data found at http://www.census.gov/prod/2004pubs/03statab/educ.pdf (accessed November 20, 2007).

puzzling for political organizations that do not have individuals as members, it is germane even for that minority of politically active organizations that are membership associations of individuals. Analysts of organizational life at least since Robert Michels called attention to the Iron Law of Oligarchy have been aware that internal processes within organizations imply that members of organizations are not uniform in their opinions and interests and that they differ in their activity and influence over organizational matters.[5] In this section we link our concern with the political voice of individuals to our analysis of political organizations. In order to assess whether what goes on inside organizations replicates or alters the representation of members' preferences and interests, we use information about individuals—both their activities and experiences of being mobilized within political organizations and their perceptions of the extent to which they feel represented by those organizations.

Survey data about organizational affiliations and activities of individuals, which are based on a random sample of the public, differ in an important way from the data we analyze about the organizations that are active in Washington.[6] In contrast to the information gleaned from the population of thousands of political organizations, survey data allow us to establish a baseline for the citizenry as a whole and thus to understand the extent to which political voice through the medium of organizational activity is representative.

Everything that we have seen so far both about the extent to which individual political participation is associated with income and education and about the dearth of political organizations representing the disadvantaged would lead us to expect social class stratification in organizational membership and activity. Furthermore, a number of observers—in particular, Theda Skocpol—have commented on the extent to which increasing numbers of membership organizations are professionally managed national organizations requiring little of their members other than financial support and drawing their members very disproportionately from among the well educated.[7] Such "checkbook organizations" clearly broaden the set of interests repre-

5. See Robert Michels, *Political Parties: A Sociological Study of the Oligarchical Tendencies of Modern Democracy*, trans. Eden and Cedar Paul (New York: Dover, 1959), and Grant McConnell, *Private Power and American Democracy* (New York: Knopf, 1966), chap. 5.

6. The survey data used in this chapter are taken from the 1990 Citizen Participation Study, which we use because it contains an unusually extensive battery of questions about organizational membership and activity.

7. See Theda Skocpol, "Voice and Inequality: The Transformation of American Civic Democracy," *Perspectives on Politics* 2 (2004): 3–20, fig. 3.

sented in a pressure system dominated by economic organizations, most of them representing the interests of economic haves, and bring into the political conversation perspectives that might otherwise go unvoiced—for example, those of advocates on behalf of public goods of both the left and the right or on behalf of groups organized around a shared identity. Still, more often than not, such citizen groups reinforce the class bias in organized political voice.[8]

Figure 13.1 presents, for five groups classified by socio-economic status (SES), information about affiliation with and activity in organizations that take stands in politics.[9] Whatever the measure, there is a strong relationship to socio-economic status: those at the top of the SES ladder are much more likely than those lower down to be affiliated with a political organization and to indicate that they have attended a meeting, that they have been active (that is, that they have served on a committee, given time to special projects, or helped organize meetings), or that they have served as a board member or officer of an organization that takes stands in politics.

That attendance at meetings, organizational activity, and service on the board of a political organization rise with socio-economic status follows naturally from the way that affiliation with political organizations is structured by SES. What is equally striking is the way that the internal processes within these organizations give further advantage to those with higher levels of education and income. Figure 13.2 repeats the data in Figure 13.1 just for those who are affiliated with a political organization. The association between socio-economic status and activity in organizations that take stands in politics is not driven solely by the relationship between SES and affiliation with

8. A similar point is made by Jeffrey M. Berry in *The New Liberalism: The Rising Power of Citizen Groups* (Washington, DC: Brookings Institution, 1999), pp. 57 and 169.

9. For each of twenty categories of organizations, respondents were asked whether they are members of or make contributions to an organization of that type. (If respondents indicated affiliation with more than one organization in a particular category, they were asked the follow-up questions about the single organization in that category with which they were most involved.) Then they were asked about attending meetings, being active, and having served on the board or as an officer of that organization. They were also asked whether that organization ever takes stands in politics. It should be noted that the designation of an organization as political does not depend on the substantive category into which it fell. This strategy has the advantage that politically active organizations in seemingly nonpolitical categories—for example, the local gun club that lobbies on the state level for the relaxation of gun laws, discussed by a respondent under the rubric of "hobby clubs"—are appropriately construed as political. It has the disadvantage that respondents did sometimes make mistakes.

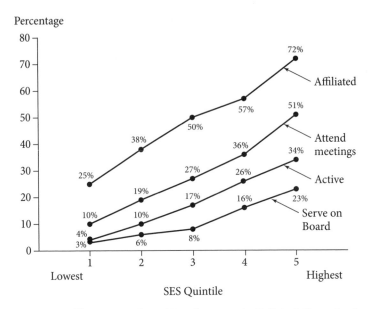

Figure 13.1   Affiliations with and Involvement in Political Organizations by SES Quintile

Source: Citizen Participation Study (1990).

Note: Affiliated: either was a member of or contributed money to an organization that takes stands in politics; Meetings: attended a meeting of an organization; Active: served on a committee, gave time to special projects, or helped organize meetings; Board: served as a member of the board or an officer of an organization.

such organizations. When we restrict our purview to members of political organizations, we find that, compared to those in the lowest SES quintile, those in the highest quintile are nearly twice as likely to have attended a meeting, nearly three times as likely to have been active, and more than three times as likely to have served on the board or as an officer.

Who Feels Represented by Political Organizations?

We can gain additional perspective on the thorny issue of who is represented by the membership organizations that take part in politics by considering the extent to which the perception of being represented by those organizations hews to lines of socio-economic status. After respondents had been asked about all the organizations with which they were affiliated, they were asked to

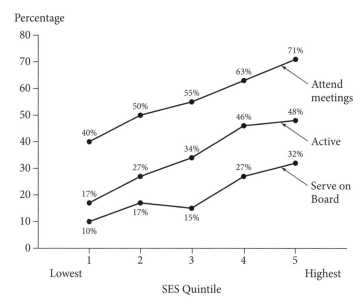

Figure 13.2   Involvement in Political Organizations among Members by SES Quintile

Source: Citizen Participation Study (1990).

choose one organization as the most important to them.[10] A series of follow-up questions were asked, including four about how well they feel that this organization represents them: whether the organization has asked the respondent's opinions on issues; whether the respondent agrees strongly with the organization's policies; whether the respondent feels at least some control over the organization; and whether the respondent has volunteered an opinion about an issue confronting the organization at a meeting.[11] As measured

10. The "most important" or "main" organization was selected as follows: respondents who reported affiliation with only one organization were asked the follow-up battery about that organization; respondents affiliated with more than one organization were asked to choose the one in which they are most active and the one to which they give the most money; if the two organizations were different, they were asked which organization is most important to them. For a full explanation of the selection of the most important organization, see Sidney Verba, Kay Lehman Schlozman, and Henry Brady, *Voice and Equality* (Cambridge, MA: Harvard University Press, 1995), pp. 542–549.

11. In constructing the organizational representation scale, one point was given for each positive answer. Respondents who received three or four points were considered to perceive themselves as well represented by their most important organization.

by an additive scale based on these four items—which measures what members perceived and not necessarily what organizations actually did—just over a third, 35 percent, of those whose most important organization takes stands in politics feel that they are represented by the organization.

Figure 13.3 presents striking data about the probability that organization members feel well represented—within the subset of respondents who chose a political organization as the one most important to them, a group that is already highly skewed in the direction of the affluent and well educated. The bottom line, which shows the percentage who feel well represented among all who chose an organization that takes political stands as their most important, rises sharply with socio-economic status.[12] Thus compounding the impact of selection processes such that upper-SES individuals are substantially more likely to be affiliated with political organizations in the first place are processes within these organizations that leave their upper-SES members substantially more likely to feel well represented. The upper line in Figure 13.3 shows the percentage who feel well represented for the smaller group of those who are organizational activists. Even within this group of organizational activists—which, as we saw in Figures 13.1 and 13.2, overrepresents upper-SES individuals even more substantially—those in the lowest SES quintile are the least likely to feel well represented.

In short, these data show the interaction between individual and organizational data and demonstrate how internal processes within political organizations operate cumulatively to reinforce the upper-class accent of the heavenly chorus. Not only are the well educated and affluent more likely to be affiliated with political organizations but, even among members, they are also more likely to be active in those organizations and to serve on the board or as officers. Consequently, they are more likely to feel that these organizations speak for them.[13]

---

12. The following data show the proportion of all respondents (including those who had no organizational affiliations at all) in each SES quintile who chose an organization that takes stands in politics as their most important organization:

Lowest SES	1	2	3	4	5	Highest SES
	16%	24%	28%	40%	40%	

13. Melissa K. Miller demonstrates the joint effect of stratification in citizen choices to join and become active in organizations coupled with the actions of organizational leaders in privileging their stratified members in "Membership Has Its Privileges: How Voluntary Groups Exacerbate the Participatory Bias," *Political Research Quarterly* 63 (2010): 356–372.

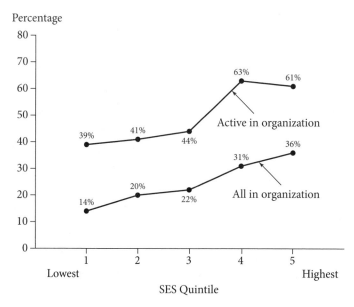

Figure 13.3   Feeling Represented by a Political Organization by SES Quintile

Source: Citizen Participation Study (1990).

Note: The table reflects the percentage who reported feeling represented among only those respondents who chose as their most important organization one that takes stands in politics.

Representing the Disadvantaged: What Organizations Actually Do

These data about individuals within political organizations dovetail with our findings about how small a share of the pressure system is occupied by organizations representing those who are disadvantaged on the basis of shared identity—for example, race or ethnicity, gender, or sexual orientation —or economic circumstances. Dara Strolovitch's research on the organizations that advocate on behalf of these disadvantaged groups adds another piece to the puzzle by making clear that such organizations are more vigorous in their efforts to represent the interests of the more advantaged subgroups, as opposed to the less advantaged subgroups, within their differentiated constituencies.[14] Thus in another way the distribution of organizations in Wash-

14. See Dara Z. Strolovitch, *Affirmative Advocacy: Race, Class, and Gender in Interest Group Politics* (Chicago: University of Chicago Press, 2007), esp. chap. 3.

ington politics understates the extent of bias within the system, and internal processes within political organizations have a multiplier effect in amplifying the voice of the relatively advantaged over the less advantaged.

Strolovitch uses the results of a survey of 286 economic and social justice organizations as well as face-to-face, open-ended interviews with staff and board members at such organizations to examine how such organizations represent the more and less advantaged parts of their constituencies. She shows that leaders of these organizations take seriously their responsibility to represent the many subgroups within their constituencies—even, sometimes, to represent disadvantaged groups that go beyond the organization's defined constituency. For example, she quotes a policy specialist at a labor organization about the commitment of his organization to "the advancement of working people. Not only our members, but generally."[15] Such professions of support seem sincere, not mere lip service.

Still, Strolovitch shows that, when it comes to actual organizational priorities, measures that would benefit the even more disadvantaged subgroups within an already disadvantaged constituency take a back seat. For example, after the chair of the board of a civil rights organization had discussed his organization's vigorous policy advocacy to combat racial profiling and to support affirmative action in higher education, Strolovitch asked him about welfare reform. He replied somewhat ruefully that his organization had not been particularly active in 1996 when welfare reform was being proposed and did not plan to get deeply involved when it was up for renewal.[16] She multiplies such examples of organizations neglecting issues with an impact on a large number of particularly disadvantaged people within their constituencies: for instance, the failure of an organization advocating for the lesbian, gay, bisexual, and transgender population that had been active with respect to HIV/AIDS to get involved in the efforts to make sure that low-income people who are HIV positive have access to AIDS medications on a reduced-cost basis and the avoidance by an Asian–Pacific–American organization of the issue of violence against women.

Systematic analysis of the data from Strolovitch's survey backs up these anecdotes: these social and economic justice organizations are significantly more active on issues that would affect the relatively advantaged parts of their

15. Strolovitch, *Affirmative Advocacy*, p. 67.
16. The examples in this paragraph are taken from Strolovitch, *Affirmative Advocacy*, pp. 76–78, 108, and 99.

constituencies than on issues that would affect the relatively disadvantaged parts—even when the number of people affected by the latter is demonstrably greater.[17] In her discussion Strolovitch is sensitive both to the organizational maintenance needs and to the external political constraints that work to produce this outcome. Yet she shows that organizations do not always eschew controversy, particularly when an issue resonates with advantaged subgroups. Furthermore, she demonstrates the ways that such issues may be framed as being germane to the entire group rather than simply to a more advantaged subgroup. Such framing is less likely to be invoked for issues relevant to disadvantaged subgroups.

We have often referred to the difficulty of knowing who is represented by organizations that do not have individuals as members—institutions like corporations and hospitals or associations that enlist such institutions as members. These considerations remind us that even voluntary associations made up of individuals raise issues of whose interests are being represented. In any membership association, there are likely to be divisions of interest and preference. Strolovitch's work on economic and social justice organizations suggests that the advocacy of the relatively small number of organizations that do the most to diversify the perspectives brought into pressure politics not only ameliorates bias but simultaneously exacerbates it.

Surrogate Advocacy: A Look at Organizations' Web Sites

One way that the relatively small number of organizations representing disadvantaged groups could enhance their clout is if other better-endowed organizations act as their surrogates. Even if the disadvantaged speak only in a whisper in the cacophony of voices represented through individual participation and organizational activity, might not other organizations speak on their behalf? That is, might mainstream organizations with other concerns and other constituencies also speak for those who are less likely to speak for themselves?

In his analysis of the politics of social welfare policy between 1970 and 1997, R. Allen Hays demonstrates that a number of kinds of organizations were active in support of the poor and that the configuration varied depending on the particular policy—housing, food, or welfare.[18] On the basis of a

17. Strolovitch, *Affirmative Advocacy*, pp. 83–93.
18. R. Allen Hays, *Who Speaks for the Poor?* (New York: Routledge, 2001), chaps. 3–4. The listing of groups perceived as most influential is contained in table 4-11, p. 146.

1998 survey of organizations active in testifying on these issues in Congress, Hays listed the ten groups rated as being the most influential in each of the three policy areas. The groups perceived as influential included only three organizations—for example, the Food Research and Action Center—dedicated to advocacy for the poor. Other advocates deemed influential included several consortia of state and local governments such as the National League of Cities and the National Council of State Housing Authorities (both listed as influential in housing policy), organizations like the U.S. Catholic Conference (influential in food policy and welfare policy) that were active on behalf of the poor as a matter of social justice, organizations like the Children's Defense Fund and the National Association for the Advancement of Colored People (both influential in welfare policy) that represent constituents with a disproportionate number of poor people, and organizations like the National Association of Home Builders and the Mortgage Bankers Association (both influential in housing policy) that were motivated to support the poor out of self-interest.

A large number of organizations testified in opposition to federal social policy. Although testimony in opposition to federal social policy was far less common than testimony in support, the organizations in opposition are, like those who acted as surrogate advocates for the poor, a diverse set. The most frequent testifier was the Heritage Foundation, followed, in order, by the U.S. Chamber of Commerce, the American Enterprise Institute, the National Association of Manufacturers, and the Southern Baptist Convention.[19]

In order to gain additional perspective on whether, out of self-interest or altruistic concern, organizations that represent particular constituencies also speak for other constituencies that are less noisy in organized interest politics, in 2006 we scrutinized the Web sites of organizations that are active in Washington politics for evidence of such surrogate advocacy. We noted references both to particular groups of people who are not especially well represented in politics—for example, children, women, or the poor—and to policies that have an impact on those groups, of which Head Start, mandated coverage of childbirth leave, and adjustments in eligibility for the Earned Income Tax Credit are examples.

Clearly, coding whether an organization's Web site mentions concerns or issues relevant to people who are not its core constituency is a weak and imperfect measure of actual political voice. It is easy to imagine both kinds of errors of interpretation. It is possible that, fearing pushback from members,

19. Hays, *Who Speaks for the Poor?* p. 138.

organizations do not necessarily want to advertise when they become involved politically on behalf of disadvantaged, and potentially unpopular, groups. In such cases, the silence on the Web site would lead us to infer, incorrectly, a lack of support and action. The opposite scenario strikes us as being even more likely. Because it is cheap and easy to put a nod in the direction of a needy constituency on a Web site, even a sincere statement of support may not be followed up with action. Indeed, Strolovitch's findings about the failure of organizations of the disadvantaged to act on behalf of their even more disadvantaged constituents gives us reason not to give too much credence to the significance of such surrogate Web site support.[20]

In our coding we focused on a strategically selected subset of the various kinds of organizations and, because of the problems in knowing whom they represent, excluded altogether such institutions as corporations, universities, hospitals, and museums.[21] We also noted whether any such mentions are displayed in a relatively prominent location—on the organization's home page, in its mission statement, or on the "About Us" tab—or are buried more deeply in the Web site. Furthermore, we recorded whether references to a needy constituency encompass all members of that group or refer just to the members of the needy constituency who share the characteristic that is core to the mission of the organization. For example, if the Web site of a union mentions issues of race, is the reference to racial minorities generally or just to racial minorities among members of the union? Analogously, if the Web site of a professional association mentions women, is the reference to women generally or just to women members of the profession?

20. For a contrary view asserting the significance of other advocates' substituting for organizations of the poor acting on their own behalf, see Jack Walker Jr., *Mobilizing Interest Groups in America* (Ann Arbor: University of Michigan Press, 1991), pp. 30, 40, and 154.

21. We considered Web sites from the following categories of organizations:

	N
Economic Organizations	
Trade associations	424
Professional associations	227
Unions	119
Other Potential Surrogates	
Religious organizations	155
Liberal public interest	58
Conservative public interest	90
Organizations of the Disadvantaged	
Organizations of racial and ethnic minorities	119
Women's organizations	78
Social welfare organizations and the poor	38

In our discussion we focus on what the Web sites tell us about surrogate advocacy on behalf of three particular groups whom we consider disadvantaged: the poor or economically needy; racial and ethnic minorities, under which rubric we include references to African Americans, Latinos, and Asian Americans along with references to "minorities" or "persons of color"; and women. We begin by showing in Table 13.2 the extent to which the Web sites of organizations in perhaps the three most important kinds of membership associations in Washington politics—trade associations, professional associations, and labor unions—provide surrogate advocacy. Reading across the rows of Table 13.2 shows the percentage of organizations of a particular type that expressed some support for each of the three disadvantaged groups. Reading down a column shows for each of the three kinds of economic organizations the percentage that expressed some support for a particular kind of disadvantaged group.

The central message of Table 13.2 is that there is very little surrogate advocacy for the economically needy, minorities, or women from the economic

Table 13.2   Percentage of Economic Organizations Mentioning the Disadvantaged on Their Web Sites

| | Percentage of Organizations Mentioning Each Type of Disadvantaged | | |
	The Poor	Minorities	Women
All Mentions on Web Sites of			
Trade Associations	4%	5%	2%
Professional Associations	16%	19%	17%
Unions	13%	20%	18%
Prominent Mentions[a] on Web Sites of			
Trade Associations	1%	3%	1%
Professional Associations	1%	4%	2%
Unions	4%	4%	4%

Source: Washington Representatives Study (2001).

[a] A prominent mention is one on the organization's home page, in its mission statement, or on the "About Us" tab.

organizations that form the backbone of the membership associations in the pressure system—and almost none at all from trade associations. What is more, as shown in the lower portion of the table, very few of the mentions of these disadvantaged groups appear prominently on the Web sites—that is, on the home page, in the mission statement, or on the "About Us" tab—of these economic membership organizations. It is interesting to note that unions, which historically position themselves as advocates for the economic interests of little guys, very rarely mention the economically needy on their Web sites.

Table 13.3 elaborates these data further, showing whether these references are inclusive—that is, whether the references to members of a disadvantaged constituency are confined to "just us," those who are members of the organization, or whether they encompass "everybody," all members of the needy constituency irrespective of their relationship to the organization that is doing the mentioning. The pattern is similar for professional associations

Table 13.3   Inclusivity of Mentions of the Disadvantaged
on the Web Sites of Economic Organizations

	Percentage of Organizations Mentioning Each Type of Disadvantaged		
	The Poor	Minorities	Women
Professional Associations			
Just Us[a]	2%	11%	8%
Everybody[b]	14%	8%	9%
Unions			
Just Us[a]	1%	10%	12%
Everybody[b]	13%	7%	7%

Source: Washington Representatives Study (2001).

[a] Entries in the cells are the percentage of mentions that refer just to the members of the needy constituency who share the characteristic that is core to the mission of the organization, that is, just those in the disadvantaged group who are members of the organization or the occupations it represents.

[b] Entries in the cells are the percentage of mentions that refer to all members of the disadvantaged group regardless of whether they are members of the organization or the occupations it represents.

and unions.[22] On one hand, when a union or professional association mentions the poor on its Web site, the reference is likely to be to "everybody" and is not confined to poor union or professional association members—who are, in any case, very unlikely to be poor—or to those in the occupations it represents. On the other, when the Web site of a professional association or especially a union mentions minorities or women, the reference is quite likely to be confined to "just us"—that is, to women or persons of color who are members of the organization or the occupation it represents.

In light of the fact that mentions of the disadvantaged are relatively infrequent, the fact that they are often buried in less prominent Web site locations, and the fact that they sometimes refer to "just us," surrogate advocacy by mainstream economic organizations does not seem to be adding substantially to the voice of the disadvantaged in politics. This conclusion is reinforced by the data in Table 13.4, which shows the same measures for the relatively small number of religious organizations in politics. Religious organizations are more likely to mention needy groups, especially the poor, on their Web sites. Furthermore, those mentions are more likely to be in prominent locations on the Web site and are more likely to encompass "everybody" rather than just members of the denomination that the organization represents. Even so, the fact that religious organizations are so few in number, coupled with the fact that only a small fraction of religious organizations mention disadvantaged groups, implies that the gain in volume of political voice for the needy arising from religious organizations is quite limited.

The same conclusion obtains when we consider surrogate advocacy by public interest organizations and organizations of the needy. Table 13.5 presents data for public interest organizations.[23] Recognizing the differences in the policy agendas of what we have called "other liberal" and "other conservative" public interest organizations, we separate them in the analysis. Given that public interest groups advocate on behalf of public goods—which are available to all in society, irrespective of their circumstance of social, political, or economic advantage or disadvantage—it is notable that other liberal public interest organizations are more likely than any kind of organization reviewed so far to mention the poor, minorities, or women on their Web

22. Because of the ambiguity of who is represented in politics by a corporation, we omit trade associations, which have corporations as members, from Table 13.3.

23. We include only public interest organizations with concerns about domestic issues and omit those that focus on international issues.

Table 13.4   Percentage of Religious Organizations
Mentioning the Disadvantaged on Their Web Sites

	Percentage of Organizations Mentioning Each Type of Disadvantaged		
	The Poor	Minorities	Women
All Mentions on Web Sites	24%	16%	20%
Just Us[a]	1%	1%	3%
Everybody[b]	23%	15%	17%
Prominent Mentions[c] on Web Sites	8%	5%	6%

Source: Washington Representatives Study (2001).

[a] Entries in the cells are the percentage of mentions that refer just to the members of the needy constituency who share the characteristic that is core to the mission of the organization, that is, just those in the disadvantaged group who are members of the organization or the denomination it represents.
[b] Entries in the cells are the percentage of mentions that refer to all members of the disadvantaged group regardless of whether they are members of the organization or the denomination it represents.
[c] A prominent mention is one on the home page, in the mission statement, or on the "About Us" tab.

sites. Not unexpectedly, references to these groups, particularly the poor and minorities, are much less frequent on the Web sites of other conservative public interest organizations. Still, it is worth noting that other conservative public interest organizations are only slightly less likely than other liberal ones to mention children on their Web sites: 34 percent of the other liberal public interest organizations and 28 percent of the other conservative ones mention children. In addition, other conservative public interest organizations are slightly more likely to mention the elderly on their Web sites: 12 percent of the other conservative public interest organizations and 9 percent of the other liberal ones do so.

Finally we inquired whether the small number of organizations advocating on behalf of disadvantaged groups use their Web sites to support one another. Table 13.6 shows the share of organizations advocating on behalf of a particular disadvantaged group that mention a different disadvantaged

Table 13.5 Percentage of Other Liberal and Other Conservative Public Interest Organizations Mentioning the Disadvantaged on Their Web Sites

	Percentage of Organizations Mentioning Each Type of Disadvantaged		
	The Poor	Minorities	Women
Other Liberal Public Interest Groups	28%	29%	31%
Other Conservative Public Interest Groups	2%	2%	7%

Source: Washington Representatives Study (2001).

Table 13.6 Percentage of Organizations of the Disadvantaged Mentioning Other Disadvantaged Groups on Their Web Sites

	Percentage of Organizations Mentioning Each Type of Disadvantaged		
	The Poor	Minorities	Women
All mentions on Web sites of			
Organizations for Economically Needy	—	16%	5%
Minority Organizations[a]	25%	—	14%
Women's Organizations	24%	20%	—
Prominent Mentions[b] on Web Sites of			
Organizations for Economically Needy	—	8%	0%
Minority Organizations[a]	9%	—	6%
Women's Organizations	5%	5%	—

Source: Washington Representatives Study (2001).

[a] Minority organizations include organizations for African Americans, Latinos, and Asian Americans as well as organizations for "minorities" in general
[b] A prominent mention is one on the home page, in the mission statement, or on the "About Us" tab.

group.[24] The data show levels of support comparable to what we found for religious groups but slightly lower than what we found for liberal public interest groups. As we have seen with respect to the Web sites of trade associations, professional associations, unions, and religious organizations, when organizations of the disadvantaged mention other disadvantaged groups, such references are relatively unlikely to be placed prominently on the Web site. The data about overall mentions in the top part of Table 13.6 are interesting in another way as well. Women's organizations are frequently berated for focusing exclusively on the issues germane to white, middle-class women. However, at least in terms of total mentions, women's organizations are no less likely to mention the economically needy and minorities than either organizations for the poor or minority organizations are to mention women.

In summary, earlier in the chapter we made the point that the distribution of organizational categories tends to underestimate the bias in pressure politics in two ways: first, selection processes operate in such a way that large and affluent organizations in any category are overrepresented, and, second, processes internal to organizations operate in such a way that, among those affiliated with membership associations, higher-SES members are more likely to be active and to feel represented. That organizations, even mainstream economic organizations like trade associations, professional associations, and unions, sometimes mention such disadvantaged groups as the poor, racial and ethnic minorities, or women is perhaps compensatory. Nevertheless, the compensatory impact is likely to be extremely limited. For one thing, mentioning a disadvantaged group on a Web site is a very weak measure of actual support. We have no guarantee of what kind of action, if any at all, resulted from the verbal support. For another, the proportion of organizations that mentioned disadvantaged groups is relatively low. In some categories— including liberal public interest groups, religious organizations, and organizations of other disadvantaged groups—mentions were somewhat more frequent, but these are categories containing very few organizations. Besides, many of the references were buried in obscure locations on the Web sites, and a substantial share—especially those that mentioned women or minorities—

24. In Chapter 11 we discussed mixed-category organizations, of which the National Council of Negro Women, an organization of African American women, is an example. This organization would have been categorized as both an African American organization and a women's organization. As such it would not have been categorized as providing *surrogate* advocacy for either of these groups. However, if the Web site had mentioned Latinas or poor women, that reference would have been coded.

applied to "just us," that is, to disadvantaged members of the organization rather than to all members of the disadvantaged group. In brief, what we learned from reading Web sites suggests that disadvantaged constituencies should not count on organizations representing other groups or interests to advocate on their behalf.

Conclusion

This chapter has addressed from several perspectives the question of whether there are, obscured beneath the distribution of aggregate organizational categories, other factors influencing the accent of the heavenly chorus. The weight of the evidence reviewed suggests that, if anything, the distribution of organizational categories underestimates the extent to which groups with limited resource capacity are represented in organized interest politics.

Possibly indicating greater representation of the disadvantaged is evidence gleaned from Web sites about the extent to which other organizations act as surrogates for the disadvantaged. However, the organizations most likely to mention disadvantaged groups are drawn from categories with small numbers of organizations and constituencies with limited resources, which suggests that the compensatory effect is very limited. Mainstream economic associations, especially trade associations, are very unlikely to mention disadvantaged groups on their Web sites.

Much more compelling is the evidence in the other direction, indicating the extent to which tendencies that further exaggerate the imbalances in organized interest representation are buried within the distribution of organization categories. Data about organizations demonstrate that, within any particular category of organizations, large and well-heeled organizations are much more likely to be represented in Washington politics. In addition, survey data show that beyond the unmistakable socio-economic stratification in affiliation with organizations that take stands in politics are processes within organizations that operate in such a way that the probability that an organization member will be an organizational activist, will be asked to get involved in politics outside the organization, or will feel represented by the organization rises steeply with SES. In short, rather than overestimating the extent of bias in the pressure system, the distribution of organizations into categories seems to make the opposite error.

14

Political Voice through Organized Interest Activity

The pitch and amplitude of political voice depend not only on the number of organizations of any particular type but also on what and how much they do. In this chapter we use extensive systematic empirical data to map the terrain of political activity by organizations and thus to understand something about the political voice emerging from organized involvement in various domains of national politics. For various domains of organizational activity, we characterize categories of organizations with respect to the likelihood that organizations are active and, if active, how much they do. In the process we clarify the strategic considerations and resource constraints that shape the involvement of different kinds of organizations in different arenas. When we aggregate activity and show the distribution of activity in any arena across various kinds of organizations, it will become apparent that the policy makers in different institutional settings hear quite different mixes of messages. Although we present many unexpected findings, the overall message reinforces our understanding of the upper-class accent of the heavenly chorus.

Organizational Voice in Various Political Arenas

The governing structure in Washington was deliberately designed by the Founders to establish multiple, often overlapping, institutions and therefore multiple points of access for those who seek a hearing by policy makers. Organizations seeking to influence policy may have no option but to lobby

Philip Edward Jones and Traci Burch are coauthors of this chapter.

the senators on the subcommittee currently holding hearings, to file a report with the executive agency that regulates the industry, or to respond in the appropriate court if sued.

Still, there are usually choices. The first question is whether, and if so how intensely, to become involved—an assessment requiring a variety of strategic and tactical considerations including the availability of appropriate resources and skills, the importance of an issue to the organization or its members, the likelihood of support or opposition from other organizations, and the probability of achieving the desired policy objectives. When the necessary resources are lacking, the possibilities for policy influence are remote, the political configuration is unfavorable, or the issue does not justify the cost, the decision may be to do nothing—a decision that may send signals to the organization's members, if any; to other organized interests; and to policy makers.[1]

Organizational leaders need to make choices not only about whether to act but also about the location of their political actions. These decisions reflect many further considerations—among them, the mission of the governmental arena in question, its rules for handling political matters, its receptivity to particular points of view, and the resource requirements for an organized interest that seeks to be active. Organizations frequently engage in forum shopping, seeking to locate a controversy in the institutional setting that, by dint of institutional mission or the particular incumbents in place, promises the greatest likelihood of a favorable outcome.

The choice of venue has consequences for the tactics used. As we shall see, many of the tactics that are appropriate when lobbying Congress—for example, meeting personally with those responsible for making policy or doing favors for them—are proscribed when dealing with the federal judiciary.[2] Furthermore, within any venue there may be choices about which particular policy makers to target. No single strategy obtains for all organizations, for all issues, or for approaches to all policy makers.[3] Although it seems logical to

1. Thomas Holyoke, in "Choosing Battlegrounds: Interest Group Lobbying across Multiple Venues," *Political Research Quarterly* 56 (2003): 325–336, considers the multiple factors that shape decisions by organized interests about whether and where to be politically active and differentiates between an organization's decision about whether to get involved and its decision about how intensely to get involved.

2. For a concise summary of the various tactics of influence at the disposal of organized interest representatives and the policy venues in which they can be marshaled, see Anthony J. Nownes, *Total Lobbying* (Cambridge, England: Cambridge University Press, 2006), pp. 16–26.

3. On the alternative mechanisms for influence that justify engaging in lobbying of one form or another, see the arguments made and the literature cited in, for example, Beth L.

focus on persuading a legislator who is on the fence, it may be worth attempting to persuade a legislator who seems to be opposed, especially if a link to affected interests in the district can be demonstrated. It may be productive to work with allies, for example, urging them to give higher priority to the matter at stake or helping them to shape legislative strategy. Just to make matters more complicated, none of these are mutually exclusive options. Organizations may create synergies by combining tactics, for example, grassroots lobbying or spending by political action committees (PACs) with direct attempts at influence.[4] Or they may play simultaneously in more than one institutional arena: for example, corporations use political expenditures aimed at Congress to signal to a bureaucratic agency that overly rigorous regulatory treatment will result in an appeal for relief from Congress.[5]

Using 2001 as the base year, we recorded data from the 2001 *Washington Representatives* directory, organizations' Web sites, congressional sources, the Federal Election Commission (FEC), Supreme Court records, opensecrets.org, and politicalmoneyline.com about the resources and political activities of organizations active in national politics. These data permit us to measure whether organizations became involved in a particular way—and, if so, how much they did—with respect to the following: using their Web sites to inform potential supporters about policy issues and urge them to take political action, spending on lobbying, testifying at congressional hearings, filing amicus briefs with the Supreme Court; and making PAC donations.[6]

Leech and Frank R. Baumgartner, "Lobbying Friends and Foes in Washington," in *Interest Group Politics*, 5th ed., ed. Allan J. Cigler and Burdett A. Loomis (Washington, DC: CQ Press, 1998), chap 10; Marie Hojnacki and David C. Kimball, "The Who and How of Organizations' Lobbying Strategies in Committee," *Journal of Politics* 61 (1999): 999–1024; and Richard L. Hall and Alan V. Deardorff, "Lobbying as Legislative Subsidy," *American Political Science Review* 100 (2006): 69–84.

4. See, for example, Hojnacki and Kimball, "Organizations' Lobbying Strategies," and Stephen Ansolabehere, James M. Snyder Jr., and Micky Tripathi, "Are PAC Contributions and Lobbying Linked? New Evidence from the 1995 Lobby Disclosure Act," *Business and Politics* 4 (2002): 131–155. For an alternative perspective, see Nolan McCarty and Lawrence S. Rothenberg, "Commitment and the Campaign Contribution Contract," *American Journal of Political Science* 40 (1996): 872–904.

5. See Sanford C. Gordon and Catherine Hafer, "Flexing Muscle: Corporate Political Expenditures as Signals to the Bureaucracy," *American Political Science Review* 99 (2005): 245–261.

6. We were thus able to generate data about attempts to influence through the electoral process as well as through the direct expression of preferences. Unfortunately, we were unable to find an analogous source that would allow us to aggregate data about organizational activity in the executive branch.

Organizational Resources for Political Action

Students of organized interests point to a large number of resources that are relevant for political advocacy—ranging from having an appealing message to having skilled personnel on staff. These resources vary in the extent to which they can be substituted for one another in the policy fray, but it is usually assumed that, of all politically relevant resources, money is the most fungible. A large budget can be used to purchase talented personnel. Although there are limits on the extent to which a sow's ear can be transformed into a silk purse, a carefully crafted campaign can even be used to shape political debate and thus to reduce the liability imposed by a political message that lacks natural appeal. Organizations vary substantially in the size and composition of the arsenal of resources they bring to the political fray. Some organizations have large staffs and deep pockets, and others are much leaner operations. Besides, some organizations have millions of members, others have thousands, and the majority have none at all. Fortunately, the *Washington Representatives* directories contain a valuable surrogate measure of an organization's political capacity, the number of in-house lobbyists it has on staff and the number of outside law, public relations, or consulting firms it hires.[7]

Washington lobbyists are often characterized as fat cats with bottomless war chests to fund their political operations. Indeed, many organizations have substantial operations to look after their political business. In the 2001 directory, Verizon listed 28 in-house employees and 28 outside firms; Lockheed listed 27 and 34; Edison Electric, the trade association for shareholder-owned electric utility companies, listed 31 and 29; the U.S. Chamber of Commerce listed 39 and 4; and Boeing listed 34 and 28, respectively. Nevertheless, most organizations fielded much smaller staffs. In fact, nearly three-fourths, 74 percent, of the organizations in the directory were what could be characterized as low capacity, either hiring only a single outside firm or having only one or two people on staff in Washington and hiring no outside firms. In fact, with the exception of unions, a majority of the organizations in

---

7. For descriptions of these differing kinds of paid political advocates, see Clive S. Thomas, "Lobbyists: Definitions, Types and Varying Designations," in *Research Guide to U.S. and International Interest Groups*, ed. Clive S. Thomas (Westport, CT: Praeger, 2004), pp. 151–153, and Ronald G. Shaiko, "Making the Connection: Organized Interests, Political Representation, and the Changing Rules of the Game in Washington Politics," in *The Interest Group Connection: Electioneering, Lobbying, and Policymaking in Washington*, 2nd ed., ed. Paul S. Herrnson, Ronald G. Shaiko, and Clyde Wilcox (Washington, DC: CQ Press, 2005), pp. 12–16.

every category could be considered low in capacity, and 48 percent of the unions fell into the low-capacity category.[8]

With respect to the number of in-house lobbyists or the number of outside firms retained, there is substantial variation across individual organizations and aggregate categories. The number of inside lobbyists and outside firms hired also varies with whether an organization has members. Institutions such as hospitals, museums, or corporations rely in large part on outside firms. A majority of membership associations have in-house lobbyists. Membership associations with institutions as members—in particular, trade associations—are especially likely to use both. Overall, only 30 percent of the organizations listed in the directory have offices in Washington with in-house lobbyists. Most organizations, 70 percent, do not have offices in Washington and rely on outside firms for their Washington representation. Just over one in eight, or 13 percent of all organizations, have both in-house and outside lobbyists.

A number of factors might predispose an individual organization to choose in-house or outside representation: the limitations it faces in locating its headquarters, the extent to which political representation is central or peripheral to its mission, and the volume of its business with the federal government.[9] Organizations differ in the extent to which they have choices when it comes to the location of their headquarters. Neither New York University nor the Metropolitan Museum of Art can feasibly relocate to the Washington area, but the headquarters of Association of American Universities and the American Association of Museums are there. Analogously, while it would be impractical for a company like Freeman United Coal Mining to uproot to Washington, the United Mine Workers and the National Mining Association have headquarters in the capital.

A corollary is that organizations for which Washington politics are a central focus are much more likely to maintain an office or locate their headquarters in the capital than are organizations for which involvement in federal politics is secondary to the main organizational purpose—whether manufacturing tires, educating aspiring scientists and engineers, caring for cancer

---

8. Using the individual lobbyist as the unit of analysis puts these data in a somewhat different light. Nearly a third of the in-house lobbyists are in Washington offices with ten or more in-house lobbyists.

9. On the decision whether to open an office in Washington or to hire outside counsel or consultants, see Lee Drutman, "The Business of America Is Lobbying," Ph.D. dissertation, University of California, Berkeley, 2010, chap. 3.

patients, or governing the people of Cleveland. Furthermore, when the political task of an organization is substantial—for example, because the organization is in an industry that is heavily regulated or dependent on government contracts or because the organization's constituents rely in some way on federal largesse—it inevitably opens an office, though not necessarily a headquarters, in the Washington area. Many organizations with only sporadic need for political representation in Washington or relatively limited political concerns hire an outside firm or two to conduct their political business in the capital and work with their hired guns from home. However, organizations with offices in Washington often hire outside lobbying professionals who command specialized expertise or useful contacts. Moreover, very few organizations that hire three or more outside firms to assist in political representation fail to have an office of their own to coordinate and supplement these political efforts by outsiders.

The figures in Table 14.1, which shows the political capacity of organized interests measured in terms of the average number of in-house lobbyists on the staff of an organization's Washington office and the average number of outside law, public relations, or consulting firms retained as listed in the directory for 2001, reflect these considerations. Because the tables in this chapter contain a lot of numbers, in this table and the ones that follow we focus on a truncated set of organizational categories: economically based organizations including corporations, trade and other business organizations, occupational associations, unions, and organizations that provide services or advocacy for the economically disadvantaged; identity groups; public interest organizations; and state and local governments. When we consider the distribution of organized interest activity in different domains, we bring back the full set of organizational categories. Furthermore, in our discussion we refer to other kinds of organizations on an eclectic basis where relevant.

What is striking in Table 14.1 is not so much the differences among categories of organizations in the average number of in-house employees or outside firms they hire as the fact that different kinds of organizations tend to emphasize one or the other kind of Washington representation. For corporations, as well as organizations in the education and health fields— mainly universities and hospitals or clinics—and state and local governments, the balance tilts in the direction of hiring outside firms.[10] Membership associations—trade

10. The figure for in-house lobbyists hired by corporations is increased by our having included firms of professionals such as lawyers or architects. Included in this group are the

Table 14.1 Political Capacity of Organized Interests: Average Number of In-house Lobbyists and Outside Firms Hired[a]

Categories of Organized Interests	In-House Lobbyists	Outside Firms
Corporations[b]	0.7	1.4
Trade and Other Business Associations	1.6	1.3
Occupational Associations	1.6	0.7
Unions	3.1	0.8
Social Welfare or Poor	1.5	0.6
Identity Groups[c]	1.1	0.8
Public Interest	1.9	0.5
State and Local Governments	0.3	1.1
All[d]	0.9	1.2

Source: Washington Representatives Study.

[a] The figures are the averages for all the organizations in each category that were listed in the 2001 *Washington Representatives* directory, of the number of in-house lobbyists and outside firms hired.
[b] Includes U.S. corporations, U.S. subsidiaries of foreign corporations, and for-profit firms of professionals such as law and consulting firms.
[c] Includes organizations representing racial, ethnic, or religious groups; the elderly; women; or lesbian, gay, bisexual, and transgender (LGBT) sexual orientation.
[d] Includes all organizations in the 2001 *Washington Representatives* directory, including organizations in categories not shown in the table.

groups, occupational associations, and labor unions—as well as public interest groups and organizations representing racial, ethnic, or religious groups, the elderly, women, the lesbian, gay, bisexual, or transgender (LGBT) population, or the economically needy are more likely to have their own offices in Washington and to rely on in-house lobbyists.

Washington-based law and consulting firms that are hired by others to represent their interests in politics. For many of these firms, the directory lists a large number of in-house lobbyists, with the megafirm of Patton, Boggs, and Blow topping the charts with 132 in-house lobbyists. We included in the analysis the 68 firms of professionals with one or more in-house lobbyists on staff (all but 14 of which were listed in the 2001 directory as being firms that represent clients in politics). When these firms are removed from the tally, the average for corporations is decreased to 0.5 in-house lobbyists.

Informing and Activating Potential Supporters

One time-honored tactic of organizational political influence is grassroots lobbying: communicating with the public or with organization members and supporters in order to highlight issues, to shape opinions, or to generate communications to public officials in support of favored political positions.[11] In contrast to direct lobbying efforts, which usually involve paid professional advocates and specialized or technical information, grassroots lobbying can be used to call attention to policy matters deemed important to a political organization and to provide legislators with a sense of public, or especially constituency, opinion. When there are powerful antagonists in government or other organizations, such tactics can function to expand the scope of the conflict by bringing in special publics, or the public at large, as allies.[12] Organized interests often use such outsider strategies in tandem with traditional insider tactics.[13] The kinds of arguments made by organized interests when they lobby become more compelling in the context of evidence of constituent opinion and concern about an issue.

Given the natural predilection of elected officials, especially legislators, to feel a need to listen and respond to constituents, grassroots lobbying is an obvious tactic for associations that have individuals as members. However, because messages delivered by individuals whose lives are affected by government action are so much more effective, institutions like corporations, universities, or museums and associations of such institutions use the technique effectively as well, mobilizing employees who want to protect their jobs, customers who seek to protect a valued product—for example, vitamin supplements—that is threatened with federal regulation or taxation, or stockholders or executives who wish to protect a company's profits.[14] Corporations

---

11. On grassroots lobbying, see Thomas L. Gais and Jack L. Walker Jr., "Pathways to Influence in American Politics," in Jack L. Walker Jr., *Mobilizing Interest Groups in America* (Ann Arbor: University of Michigan Press, 1991), chap. 6; Diana M. Evans, "Lobbying the Committee: Interest Groups and the House Public Works and Transportation Committee," in *Interest Group Politics,* 3rd ed., ed. Allan J. Cigler and Burdett A. Loomis (Washington, DC: CQ Press, 1991), pp. 257–276; and Ken Kollman, *Outside Lobbying* (Princeton, NJ: Princeton University Press, 1998).

12. Evans, "Lobbying the Committee," p. 258. On the way that expanding the scope of political conflict can alter political outcomes, see E. E. Schattschneider, *The Semisovereign People* (New York: Holt, Rinehart, and Winston, 1960), chap. 1.

13. Hojnacki and Kimball, "Organizations' Lobbying Strategies," p. 1000.

14. On the increase in grassroots lobbying by business, see Drutman, "The Business of America Is Lobbying."

and other resource-endowed organizations perceive constituent lobbying as so effective that they sometimes weigh in on public debates surreptitiously by undertaking "astroturf lobbying"—hiring public relations firms to manufacture artificial grassroots campaigns.[15] These grassroots mobilization strategies not only facilitate the pursuit of policy objectives but also serve organizational maintenance functions. Grassroots tactics can be used to raise the visibility of an organization and to attract new members or supporters.[16] Furthermore, they can be used to reassure existing members or supporters—demonstrating that the organization's leadership and staff are busy fighting the good fight on behalf of shared goals.[17]

In spite of the obvious political benefits of grassroots lobbying, there are, as always, trade-offs. Grassroots efforts can be costly in terms of time and resources.[18] Besides, going public entails the risk of activating opponents as well as supporters.[19] Furthermore, once a grassroots campaign has been initiated, it may be difficult to control, and the organization may lose control of both the membership and the message.[20] In fact, if the policy views of an organization's members and staff conflict, mobilizing the membership to lobby can be downright counterproductive.[21]

Because there is no obvious source of systematic information across organizations and issues about grassroots lobbying efforts, we were unable to assemble data about grassroots lobbying analogous to the data we present about other forms of organized interest activity and are forced to rely on a surrogate measure. One of the many ways that the Internet has expanded the possibilities for individual political involvement is that organizations use the capacity of the Internet to communicate with interested individuals—informing them of pending political issues and encouraging them to take

15. Sharon Beder, "Public Relations' Role in Manufacturing Artificial Grass Roots Coalitions," *Public Relations Quarterly* 13 (1998): 20–23, and Thomas P. Lyon and John W. Maxwell, "Astroturf: Interest Group Lobbying and Corporate Strategy," *Journal of Economics and Management Strategy* 13 (2004): 561–597.

16. Linda L. Fowler and Ronald G. Shaiko, "The Grass Roots Connection: Environmental Activists and Senate Roll Calls," *American Journal of Political Science* 31 (1987): 485.

17. Hojnacki and Kimball, "Organizations' Lobbying Strategies," p. 1004.

18. Gais and Walker, "Pathways to Influence," p. 258.

19. Evans "Lobbying the Committee," p. 259.

20. R. Kenneth Godwin, *One Billion Dollars of Influence: The Direct Marketing of Politics* (Chatham, NJ: Chatham House, 1988).

21. William P. Browne, "Organized Interests, Grassroots Confidants, and Congress," in *Interest Group Politics*, 4th ed., ed. Allan J. Cigler and Burdett A. Loomis (Washington, DC: CQ Press, 1995), pp. 284–285.

action when appropriate. An August 2008 survey conducted by the Pew Internet and American Life Project found that 56 percent of Americans who are members of a civic or political group use electronic means—for example, e-mail or the group's Web site—to communicate with other group members. In 2008 we investigated whether the organizations in the 2001 *Washington Representatives* directory use their Web sites in any of several ways to inform and activate potential political supporters.[22] Among the organizations for which we could find a Web site, 37 percent use the site to discuss current political issues. Twenty-two percent facilitate activity in one or more ways: 17 percent encourage those who visit the Web site to take a specific political action, such as getting in touch with their legislators in Congress; 14 percent offer visitors the option of uploading an e-mail address so that they can receive e-mail updates about issues of concern to the organization or about its political activities; and 4 percent include information—for example, an interactive map—to help visitors to register or vote. In addition, 8 percent include a password-protected link leading to political information available only to those who are members or who register to gain access.

While only a minority of the organizations for which we found Web sites use them as a conduit for political information and activation, there are wide disparities among organizations. For one thing, an organization's status as an association of individuals, an institution, or an association of institutions, once again has considerable explanatory power. Only a small minority of institutions, 17 percent, discuss political issues on their Web sites, and an even smaller minority, 9 percent, use their Web sites to mobilize visitors to get involved politically by urging them to take political action, encouraging them to sign up for e-mail updates, or helping them to register or vote. In contrast, whether they have individuals or institutions as members, more than two-thirds of the membership associations include discussions of political issues on their Web sites. Half the membership associations of individuals and a third of the membership associations with institutions as members use their Web sites for political activation. These figures suggest that an organization's members are one of its most important resources in politics—often

22. Unfortunately, the idea for this data collection did not come to us until the spring of 2008. Even so, we were able to find Web sites for 78 percent of the organizations listed in the 2001 directory—ranging from 69 percent of the foreign organizations to 95 percent of the educational organizations listed in 2001—or 83 percent of the 2001 organizations not known to be out of existence. Because their Web sites are used to inform the public about the issues currently under consideration, we did not include state and local governments in this analysis.

compensating for deficits when it comes to financial resources—and underline the theme that it is very difficult to define an institution's constituents and to know for whom it speaks when it is active in politics.

Considering the particular categories of organizations in Table 14.2, we see that corporations are very unlikely to use their Web sites for political information and activation. In contrast, labor unions, public interest organizations, occupational associations, trade and other business associations, and social welfare organizations and organizations on behalf of the poor are quite likely to do so. Some of these are organizations that have messages that can

Table 14.2   Organized Interests Using a Web Site
for Political Information and Activation[a]

Categories of Organized Interests	Web Site Discusses Public Policy Issues (Percent)	Web Site Facilitates Political Action[b] (Percent)
Corporations[c]	8%	3%
Trade and Other Business Associations	68%	33%
Occupational Associations	73%	47%
Unions	87%	72%
Social Welfare or Poor	64%	48%
Identity Groups[d]	58%	37%
Public Interest	84%	66%
All[e]	37%	22%

Source: Washington Representatives Study.

[a] The figures are for all organizations in the 2001 *Washington Representatives* directory for which Web sites could be found in spring 2008; state and local governments have been omitted.
[b] Web site encourages individuals to take specific political action, invites submission of an e-mail address in order to receive a newsletter or periodic updates about policy matters, or includes links to facilitate voter registration.
[c] Includes U.S. corporations, U.S. subsidiaries of foreign corporations, and for-profit firms of professionals such as law and consulting firms.
[d] Includes organizations representing racial, ethnic, or religious groups; the elderly; women; or LGBT sexual orientation.
[e] Includes all organizations in the 2001 *Washington Representatives* directory, including organizations in categories not shown in the table.

be framed in appealing ways or more extensive resources when it comes to members than when it comes to dollars.

The figures for identity groups that organize people on the basis of race, ethnicity, or nationality, religion, gender, age, or sexual orientation are affected by the fact that organizations, mostly tribes, representing Native Americans—which form such a large proportion of these groups—are quite unlikely to use their Web sites in these ways. When organizations representing Native Americans are excluded, 69 percent of the identity groups discuss political issues on their Web sites and 52 percent use their Web sites to facilitate political activity.

The differences among categories of occupational associations are interesting from the perspective of our concern with political voice. Associations of private-sector executives and professionals are quite likely to use their Web sites in these ways: 71 percent of the Web sites of associations of business professionals discuss political issues, and 39 percent seek to activate individuals politically. The analogous figures for professional associations that bring together physicians, professors, engineers, and so on are 74 percent and 46 percent. In contrast, the other occupational associations that bring together workers who are not professionals, managers, or administrators are much less likely to use their Web sites for political information or activation: only 39 percent discuss policy issues, and 19 percent facilitate political involvement by urging them to take political action, offering the option of e-mail updates about public affairs, or helping them to register or vote. Thus, once again, if they are not union members, those who work in nonmanagerial or nonprofessional positions are less likely to achieve political voice.

Organizational Activity in Washington

For each organization in the 2001 directory we used archival sources to code information about the extent of their involvement in four forms of Washington political activity. Not unexpectedly, organizations vary in the number of activities in which they engage. Although there are differences with respect to organizational membership status, they are less pronounced than what we saw for use of the Web site for political information and activation: institutions like corporations or hospitals engage in fewer activities than do membership associations of institutions or especially membership associations of individuals. Seventeen percent of the institutions did at least two of the following: spent at least $10,000 on lobbying in 2000 and 2001; testified before a congressional committee or subcommittee in 2001 or 2002; filed an amicus brief during the 2000–2001 or 2001–2002 Supreme Court terms; or made a PAC donation in a federal election between 1999 and 2002.[23] The analogous figures for membership associations of institutions and membership associations of individuals are 27 percent and 34 percent, respectively.

Greater than the differences among organizations distinguished by their membership status is the disparity between organizations that have Washington offices and those that hire outsiders only; 39 percent of the former—in contrast to 14 percent of the latter—engaged in two or more of the four activities. Presumably, these disparities reflect a variety of causal linkages. Organizations with significant ongoing business to transact with government would be more likely to set up an office in Washington. Once there they would become enmeshed in the networks through which coalitions are formed and requests for testimony, amicus briefs, and PAC donations are mediated and thus would be recruited to political action. Furthermore, the in-house lobbyists who staff such a Washington office would have incentives to be active in order to justify their salaries to the membership or the bosses at the organization's headquarters.

With respect to particular organizational categories, Table 14.3 shows considerable disparities. Public interest organizations—which, if they are organized as nonprofits under tax law, are limited with respect to lobbying—and corporations engage in relatively few of the four activities in the table. At the other extreme are unions—in particular, public-sector unions of white-collar workers—which, on average, undertake the greatest number of the four activities. Otherwise, the categories of organizations vary in a relatively narrow range with respect to the number of activities they undertake.

---

23. The sources used to compile these data are as follows: lobbying expenses for 2000 and 2001 of all organizations listed in the 2001 *Washington Representatives* directory as presented on the publicly accessible Web site of the Center for Responsive Politics, opensecrets.org; all congressional hearings from the 107th Congress (2001–2002) as listed in *Congressional Information Services Abstracts;* all cases with amicus activity in which petitions of certiorari were submitted to the Supreme Court between October 1, 2000, and September 30, 2002 (the 2000–2001 and 2001–2002 terms) as recorded in the *U.S. Supreme Court Records and Briefs* microfiche collection; PAC contributions as contained in the Itemized Committee Contributions Files of the FEC for the 1999–2000 and 2001–2002 electoral cycles. For testifying at congressional hearings, signing amicus briefs, and making PAC contributions, we are able to enumerate the activity of all organizations that took part, regardless of whether they were listed in the directory. For lobbying expenses, we were able to compile information only for those organizations listed in the directory. Where appropriate, we add further information about the sources used.

Table 14.3   Number of Political Activities by Organized Interests[a]

Categories of Organized Interests	Percentage Engaging in Various Numbers of Activities				Total Percentage
	0	1	2	3–4	
Corporations[b]	29%	53	13	5	= 100%
Trade and Other Business Associations	31%	41	17	11	= 100%
Occupational Associations	42%	28	20	11	= 101%
Unions	15%	29	24	32	= 100%
Social Welfare or Poor	31%	39	24	6	= 100%
Identity Groups[c]	30%	38	24	8	= 100%
Public Interest	41%	34	15	9	= 99%
State and Local Governments	25%	54	18	4	= 101%
All[d]	33%	46	15	6	= 100%

Source: Washington Representatives Study.

[a] Number of the following four activities in which organizations engaged: spent $10,000 or more on lobbying in 2000 or 2001 (or both), testified before a congressional committee in 2001 or 2002 (or both), filed an amicus brief in the 2000–2001 or 2001–2002 term (or both), made political action committee (PAC) donations in the 2000 or 2002 electoral cycle (or both).

[b] Includes U.S. corporations, U.S. subsidiaries of foreign corporations, and for-profit firms of professionals such as law and consulting firms.

[c] Includes organizations representing racial, ethnic, or religious groups; the elderly; women; or LGBT sexual orientation.

[d] Includes all organizations in the 2001 *Washington Representatives* directory, including organizations in categories not shown in the table.

Spending on Lobbying

The political voice of organized interests is shaped not only by how many activities they undertake but also by how much they do when they become involved. Starting with spending on lobbying, let us examine the four activities for which we have information about the organizations in the 2001 *Washington Representatives* directory.

For all organizations in the 2001 directory we recorded the amount spent on lobbying in 2000 and 2001 as reported in the lobbying registrations filed under the Lobbying Disclosure Act (LDA) of 1995.[24] Of the four activities we consider, spending on lobbying is the one that permits an organization to use its financial resources on its own initiative—constrained only by the registration requirements under the LDA and the restrictions on lobbying by non-profits.[25]

The LDA superseded the relatively toothless 1946 Federal Regulation of Lobbying Act, which covered only lobbyists who devoted a majority of their time to lobbying activities and only those who lobbied members of Congress, exempting representatives of American subsidiaries of foreign-owned companies and lawyer lobbyists for foreign entities. The LDA, which covers communications, both oral and written, about legislative or administrative issues, extended coverage to foreign agents and expanded the list of targets to encompass not just members of Congress but also their staff members as well as high-level policy makers in the White House and executive branch agencies.[26] As passed in 1995, the LDA required those who spend more than 20 percent of their time in a six-month period on lobbying and who receive more than $5,000 and organizations that spend more than $20,000 in a six-month period to register—sums that are adjusted periodically to account for inflation. Under the LDA, lobbyists must list the congressional chamber or executive agency lobbied and the issues involved but do not have to name the specific government officials who were contacted. Organizations are expected to divulge only their expenditures on legislative and executive lobbying and not the amounts spent on such political activities as monitoring political developments, grassroots lobbying, conducting and publicizing research, holding fundraisers, or filing amicus briefs—activities that can absorb substantial amounts of organizational resources, time, and skills. Therefore, the reports cover only part, and often a very small part, of the funds spent by an organization in pursuit of political influence. Furthermore, these exemptions imply that the number of registered lobbyists is only a fraction of the number

24. The Center for Responsive Politics discusses its sources and coding methods at http:// www.opensecrets.org/lobbyists/methodology.asp. If opensecrets.org did not have any information about the lobbying spending of an organization, we also consulted the data contained at politicalmoneyline.org (now CQMoneyLine).

25. On the LDA of 1995, see Shaiko, "Making the Connection," pp. 17–19, and Jonathan D. Salant, "Highlights of the Lobby Bill," *CQ Weekly Online*, December 2, 1995, p. 3632. For additional details, including definitions and specific provisions, see "Provisions: Bill Targets Lobbying Law Loopholes," *CQ Weekly Online*, November 11, 1995, pp. 3477–3478. The Lobbying Disclosure Technical Amendments Act of 1998 clarified certain aspects of the LDA and closed certain loopholes.

26. "Lobbying—Lobbyists on a Leash," *National Journal*, February 3, 1996.

of individuals who are associated with the business of influencing policy outcomes but whose activities—for example, conducting research—do not fall under the definition of lobbying in the LDA.[27]

For several reasons, we were able to find information about lobbying expenditures for less than two-thirds of the 2001 organizations. First, compliance with the 1995 LDA is voluntary, and therefore those who are potentially covered make different judgment calls about the need to register.[28] Because organizations that spend less than the specified amounts are not required to file reports, lobbying expense data omit the expenditures not only of relatively inactive organizations but also of small and impecunious ones. Finally, unless they establish a parallel, non-tax-deductible 501(c)4 arm, organizations that fall into the 501(c)3 designation under the tax code—that is, nonprofits for which contributions are tax deductible—are legally enjoined from undertaking significant lobbying, though not from engaging in many other kinds of political activity.[29] In terms of our categories, 501(c)3 organizations are concentrated among educational, health, social service, and arts or cultural institutions; public interest groups; identity groups; and groups advocating for the poor. In some of these categories, there is also likely to be a disproportionate share of organizations that are small and resource deprived. Thus the fact that, in certain categories, a relatively low proportion of organizations report lobbying expenses is neither a matter of missing data nor an indicator of organizational failure to comply but is substantively important for our understanding of the sources of political voice through lobbying.

Data from lobbying registrations show that, even when we omit organizations that registered no lobbying expenses, the vast bulk of spending on lob-

27. In 2006, political scientist James Thurber estimated that about one hundred thousand people were involved in government influence, a figure roughly three times the number of registered lobbyists at the time. Quoted in Lisa Caruso, "What's in a Number?" *National Journal*, March 26, 2006.

28. This inconsistency, along with the fact that they found errors in some reports, led Gordon and Hafer, in "Flexing Muscle," pp. 251–252, to use PAC expenditures as their measure of political effort. That measure, however, is quite limited as a measure of total effort to influence federal policy. Besides, Frank R. Baumgartner and Beth L. Leech, in "Interest Niches and Policy Bandwagons: Patterns of Interest Group Involvement in National Politics," *Journal of Politics* 63 (2001): 1194, argue that compliance with the LDA is likely for several reasons: organizations are reluctant to give their political opponents an opportunity to exploit any failure to register; in addition, hired lobbyists in law, public relations, and consulting firms have an incentive to advertise that they do a lot of business.

29. See Jeffrey M. Berry with David F. Arons, *A Voice for Nonprofits* (Washington, DC: Brookings Institution, 2003). The authors demonstrate (pp. 54–65) that an arcane tax provision, "H election," can permit nonprofits to ignore lobbying limits.

bying is concentrated among a very small share of political organizations. Of the nearly $3 billion spent on lobbying during 2000 and 2001 by the registered organizations listed in the 2001 *Washington Representatives* directory, nearly a third, 33 percent, was spent by the top 1 percent of lobbying spenders. Fully 75 percent was spent by the top 10 percent of lobbying spenders and a mere 3 percent by the bottom 50 percent of lobbying spenders. Had we been able to include in the denominator the organizations that did not register because their lobbying expenses fell below the threshold in the LDA, these figures would have shown even greater concentration of lobbying spending.

Table 14.4 shows the proportion of organizations in the 2001 directory that spent at least $10,000 on lobbying over the two-year period and, for

Table 14.4   Lobbying Expenses of Organized Interests[a]

Categories of Organized Interests	Percentage Spending at Least $10,000 on Lobbying	Average Spent by Organizations Spending at Least $10,000
Corporations[b]	68%	$468,000
Trade and Other Business Associations	64%	$625,000
Occupational Associations	49%	$563,000
Unions	59%	$555,000
Social Welfare or Poor	51%	$116,000
Identity Groups[c]	53%	$287,000
Public Interest	39%	$334,000
State and Local Governments	69%	$154,000
All[d]	61%	$394,000

Source: Washington Representatives Study.

[a] The figures in the first column of numbers are for all the organizations in each category that were listed in the 2001 *Washington Representatives* directory; the figures in the second column of numbers are for organizations with at least $10,000 in reported lobbying expenses in 2000 or 2001 (or both).

[b] Includes U.S. corporations, U.S. subsidiaries of foreign corporations, and for-profit firms of professionals such as law and consulting firms.

[c] Includes organizations representing racial, ethnic, or religious groups; the elderly; women; or LGBT sexual orientation.

[d] Includes all organizations, including organizations in categories not shown in the table.

those that spent more than $10,000, the average amount spent. The data make clear both the striking differences among kinds of organizations with respect to their spending on lobbying and the high levels of spending among those organizations traditionally known to be heavy hitters. Public interest organizations—along with foreign organizations, which also face legal constraints on lobbying—are the least likely to spend at least $10,000 on lobbying. With respect to the average amounts spent by organizations that spent at least $10,000, trade and other business associations reported spending, on average, $625,000, more than five times more than the organizations that provide services and political representation to the economically needy—which spent, on average, $116,000. Organizations representing economic interests associated with making a living, occupational associations and unions, and corporations are also, on average, big lobbying spenders. In contrast, the spending reported by state and local governments was much more modest.

Buried within these aggregate categories are additional disparities in average lobbying expenditures. Among occupational associations, while associations of managers and professionals in business spent, on average, $814,000, professional associations spent $649,000, and other occupational associations spent $673,000, associations of military employees spent, on average, only $71,000 on lobbying. The differences among organizational subcategories are particularly interesting for organizations that represent identity groups or that seek public goods. As we see in Table 14.5, among the former, organizations representing Native Americans are by far the most likely to spend at least $10,000 on lobbying. However, they are not, on average, big spenders. Organizations representing the elderly, led by AARP, and the handful of LGBT organizations have far higher average spending. At the other end of the spectrum, it is notable that organizations representing African Americans and women—two groups strongly associated with the rights revolution of the 1960s and 1970s—are relatively unlikely to spend $10,000 on lobbying. Among the organizations that do, the average amounts spent are notably low.

Among organizations seeking public goods, civil liberties groups spend, on average, ten times as much as the citizen empowerment groups that encourage citizens to become involved in politics.[30] The imbalance in spending on lobbying between liberal and conservative organizations is noteworthy: the "other liberal groups" spend, on average, $159,000—about one-sixth of the average spent by the "other conservative groups," $904,000.

---

30. Note that this statement is based on a very small number of cases.

Table 14.5   Lobbying Expenditures of Identity and Public Interest Groups[a]

	Percentage Spending at Least $10,000 on Lobbying	Average Spent by Organizations Spending at Least $10,000	Total Number[b]
A. Identity Groups			
Native Americans	78%	$169,000	(176)
Other Racial, Ethnic, or Nationality	35%	$209,000	(97)
Religious	38%	$268,000	(90)
Women	33%	$133,000	(45)
Elderly	41%	$2,004,000	(29)
LGBT	25%	$1,691,000	(8)
B. Public Interest Groups			
Consumer	52%	$168,000	(33)
Environmental and Wildlife	55%	$211,000	(126)
Civil Liberties	25%	$903,000	(12)
Government Reform	22%	$645,000	(27)
Citizen Empowerment	26%	$90,000	(19)
Other Liberal Groups	36%	$159,000	(84)
Other Conservative Groups	31%	$904,000	(85)
Other	36%	$316,000	(147)

Source: Washington Representatives Study.

[a] The figures in the first column of numbers are for all the organizations in each category that were listed in the 2001 *Washington Representatives* directory; the figures in the second column of numbers are for organizations with at least $10,000 in reported lobbying expenses in 2000 or 2001 (or both).
[b] Number of organizations in the 2001 *Washington Representatives* directory.

Testifying before Congress

At the discretion of their chairs, congressional committees and subcommittees hold hearings that give organized interests an opportunity to state a public case either by sending written comments or by testifying in person.[31] While

31. On testifying as a form of advocacy by organized interests, see Kevin M. Leyden, "Interest Group Resources and Testimony at Congressional Hearings," *Legislative Studies*

organizations retain control over whether and how much they lobby, when it comes to congressional testimony the initiative rests with legislators and their staffs. Depending on the underlying purposes of the hearing—whether, for example, to explore policy alternatives and their consequences or to create a public record in favor of one approach—the list of witnesses may be balanced among various perspectives or stacked in one direction. Although the financial resources involved cannot be multiplied in the way that spending on lobbying can reach stratospheric heights, testifying does entail costs. An obvious direct cost is travel. Perhaps even more important are resources devoted to monitoring policy developments and to cultivating committee staffers to persuade them that the information commanded by an organization or its distinctive perspective deserve to be aired during a hearing.[32]

When it comes to testifying before congressional committees and subcommittees, patterns of organized interest activity are quite different from what we saw for spending on lobbying.[33] Of the organizations listed in the 2001 *Washington Representatives* directory, there is a sharp disparity between

---

Quarterly 20 (1995): 431–439, and John R. Wright, *Interest Groups and Congress* (Boston: Allyn and Bacon, 1996), pp. 40–43. We were disappointed not to be able to locate an analogous measure—for example, a measure of comments submitted during the notice and comment period—of participation by organized interests in the executive branch. While it is possible to construct such a measure for a particular agency, a limited number of issues, or certain kinds of organizations, we were unable to do so across the gamut of government agencies, issues, and organizational types. A useful summary containing helpful bibliographical suggestions can be found in Suzanne J. Piotrowski and David H. Rosenbloom, "The Legal-Institutional Framework for Interest Group Participation in Federal Administrative Policymaking," in *The Interest Group Connection*, ed. Herrnson, Shaiko, and Wilcox, chap. 14.

32. See Leyden, "Interest Group Resources and Testimony," p. 433. With respect to executive branch lobbying, Scott R. Furlong, in "Exploring Interest Group Participation in Executive Policymaking," in *The Interest Group Connection*, ed. Herrnson, Shaiko, and Wilcox, p. 284, makes the point that, even with the *Federal Register* now available online, keeping tabs on executive branch activity is likely to be time consuming and expensive.

33. We mentioned earlier that for three forms of activity we were able to locate and code the activity of all organizations that took part—including organizations not listed in the 2001 *Washington Representatives* directory, which lists only 32.2 percent of the organizations that testified in Congress, 29.5 percent of those that filed an amicus brief, and 47.7 percent of those that made a PAC donation during the specified periods. There are reasons other than error that the directory is not a complete listing for these forms of activity. According to Valerie Sheridan of Columbia Books, organizations move in and out of Washington politics, and the directory for any year is a snapshot as of a particular date. Therefore, because our measures for testifying, filing briefs, or making PAC donations each cover at least two years, it is likely that some of the active organizations were listed on the Web site of the directory or in a directory for another year but not in the 2001 directory. Besides, the directory does not list

those that have in-house lobbyists on staff in their Washington offices and those that hire outside lobbyists only: 35 percent of the former, as opposed to 11 percent of the latter, testified over the two-year period. Moreover, among organizations in the directory that testified, those with in-house lobbyists testified an average of 4.2 times—in contrast to 1.9 times for organizations that hired outside firms only. There are also differences among organizations distinguished on the basis of their membership type. Presumably reflecting congressional need to be responsive to the public, associations of individuals are nearly three times more likely than institutions to testify: 34 percent of the associations of individuals—compared to 12 percent of the institutions and 23 percent of the associations of institutions—testified at least once during the two-year period.

Table 14.6 shows the data for different categories of organizations.[34] In contrast to what we observed for spending on lobbying, the traditional heavy hitters are not necessarily the most likely to testify or, among those who do, the most frequent testifiers. While labor unions are the most likely to testify and, among organizations that testify, score the highest average number of testimonies, corporations are relatively unlikely to testify; corporations that do testify do not, on average, testify very often. Three sets of organizations that have engaged our ongoing attention—organizations representing broad public interests, identity groups, and social service providers and advocates for the poor—are relatively likely to testify, although, among testifiers, the frequency of their testimonies is not remarkable.

Looking within these aggregate categories, among organizations representing people on the basis of identity, Native American organizations are both numerous and frequent testifiers. When they are omitted from the analysis,

---

organizations that testify but do not have a Washington presence or PACs that are not run out of an office in Washington.

It is important to recognize that, as indicated in the notes to Tables 14.6–14.10, the columns refer to different sets of organizations: the left-hand column of numbers shows the proportion of organizations listed in the directory that were active; the right-hand column shows the average activity for all active organizations, whether or not they were listed in the directory.

34. We should note that a witness—for example, a professor whose research is relevant to the policy under consideration—might be testifying as an expert rather than as an organizational representative. When it was not obvious in what capacity an individual was testifying, we read the text of the hearing to ascertain whether the witness was testifying on behalf of the organization and coded only organizational representatives, not experts. Obviously those testifying as experts often have strong points of view and are not necessarily "impartial."

Table 14.6   Organized Interests Testifying before Congress

Categories of Organized Interests	Percentage Testifying[a]	Average Number of Testimonies (among Testifiers)[b]
Corporations[c]	10%	1.4
Trade and Other Business Associations	23%	2.6
Occupational Associations	30%	2.5
Unions	52%	3.9
Social Welfare or Poor	40%	1.6
Identity Groups[d]	33%	1.8
Public Interest	32%	2.1
State and Local Governments	20%	1.9
All[e]	18%	1.9

Source: Washington Representatives Study.

[a] The percentage of all the organizations listed in the 2001 *Washington Representatives* directory that testified before Congress in 2001 or 2002 (or both).

[b] Average number of testimonies by organizations that testified, including those not listed in the 2001 *Washington Representatives* directory.

[c] Includes U.S. corporations, U.S. subsidiaries of foreign corporations, and for-profit firms of professionals such as law and consulting firms

[d] Includes organizations representing racial, ethnic, or religious groups; the elderly; women; or LGBT sexual orientation.

[e] Includes all organizations that testified, including organizations in categories not shown in the table.

the likelihood that an identity organization testified drops to 28 percent. The figures in Table 14.7 show that, with the exception of citizen empowerment organizations that seek to teach adults about politics or to give children and adults hands-on training for political involvement, all the subcategories of public interest organizations were relatively heavy testifiers. It is interesting to observe that, although Congress was organized by the Republicans during the period covered, there was a rough balance between other liberal and other conservative public interest organizations. In fact, among testifiers, those from what we call other liberal public interest organizations testified a little more frequently than those from other conservative ones. Other kinds of organizations that are likely to testify include obvious stakeholders in gov-

Table 14.7   Public Interest Organizations Testifying before Congress

	Percentage Testifying[a]	Average Number of Testimonies (among Testifiers)[b]	Total Number[c]
Consumer	34%	2.8	(32)
Environmental and Wildlife	47%	2.0	(126)
Civil Liberties	33%	4.0	(12)
Government Reform	41%	2.8	(27)
Citizen Empowerment	16%	2.1	(19)
Other Liberal Groups	29%	2.2	(83)
Other Conservative Groups	31%	1.8	(85)
Other	23%	1.7	(147)

Source: Washington Representatives Study.

[a] Percentage of all the organizations listed in the 2001 *Washington Representatives* directory that testified before Congress in 2001 or 2002 (or both).
[b] Average number of testimonies by organizations that testified, including those not listed in the 2001 *Washington Representatives* directory.
[c] Number of organizations in the 2001 *Washington Representatives* directory.

ernment policy and organizations whose representatives would probably elicit sympathy: among them, associations of government employees including military employees (40 percent); organizations representing veterans and members of the military reserves (49 percent); organizations advocating on behalf of particular diseases or medical conditions or on behalf of the disabled more generally (40 percent).

To summarize, the balance of congressional testimony by organizations seems not only to favor those on the scene with Washington offices but also to tilt less obviously in the direction of the kinds of organizations that are especially numerous in Washington politics. In particular, because congressional testimonies are a form of voice for which the initiative rests with the people's elected representatives, congressional committees seem to be more receptive to statements from organizations representing public goods; from organizations representing individuals, including individuals who are not especially privileged and who have a clear stake in public outcomes; and from those who would be deemed "deserving."

Filing Amicus Briefs

As is well known, the courts have special characteristics as a forum for organized interest activity. In contrast to the legislatures, which function so importantly as arenas for organized interest efforts to influence policy, courts cannot initiate political action. Litigants do. Going to court requires a real dispute, not a hypothetical concern, in which the contending parties have a stake. The adversarial nature of the judicial process implies that the sides are sharply defined in a way that they are not always in legislative matters, and the outcomes are more likely to be zero sum.

Although they cannot engage in conventional lobbying of judges and their clerks, organized interests that seek to influence federal judicial outcomes have several options. They can focus on nominees to the bench and attempt to have an impact on Senate confirmation processes. They can file suit. Or they can file an amicus curiae brief.[35] The filing of amicus briefs has a long legal history, dating back to the Middle Ages in England and at least to 1823 in the United States.[36] Although any party wishing to file an amicus brief must secure the permission of the Court, scholars agree that the Supreme Court is unlikely to deny permission and that amicus briefs are becoming more and more common, especially at the merits stage of Supreme Court cases.[37]

As a form of organized interest advocacy, filing amicus briefs is quite explicitly about the expression of political voice. In that sense, it can be thought of as the judicial counterpart of legislative lobbying.[38] However, in contrast to legislative lobbyists, who can increase their leverage by linking a forceful presentation to inducements—including campaign donations and other favors—those filing amicus briefs can deliver nothing more than a compelling argument.

Under ordinary circumstances, the objective in filing an amicus brief is to influence the outcome of the decision—whether a decision to grant certiorari

35. An especially clear account of organized interest activity in the courts can be found in Lee Epstein, "Courts and Interest Groups," in *The American Courts: A Critical Assessment*, ed. John B. Gates and Charles A. Johnson (Washington, DC: CQ Press, 1992), chap. 13.

36. On the history of the use of amicus curiae briefs, see Frank M. Covey Jr., "Amicus Curiae: Friend of the Court," *DePaul Law Review* 9 (1959): 30–37, and Karen O'Connor and Lee Epstein, "Court Rules and Workload: A Case Study of Rules Governing Amicus Curiae Participation," *Justice System Journal* 8 (1983): 35–45.

37. See, for example, Epstein, "Courts and Interest Groups," and Joseph D. Kearney and Thomas W. Merrill, "The Influence of Amicus Curiae Briefs on the Supreme Court," *University of Pennsylvania Law Review* 148 (2000): 751–754.

38. On this point, see Lucius J. Barker, "Third Parties in Litigation: A Systemic View of the Judicial Function," *Journal of Politics* 29 (1967): 53 ff.

or a decision on the merits. However, even when organized interests have no expectation of changing which side prevails in the present case, they may seek to have an impact on how the argument in the decision is framed, to influence details of the decision if not its overall direction, to shape the direction of dissenting opinions, or to alter the terms of future debate not only in judicial proceedings but in the media or in other political arenas. While amicus briefs often repeat and reinforce the arguments made by one of the parties to the case, they ordinarily provide additional information to justices who are aware that the decision in the case in question will have implications beyond its impact on the immediate litigants. An amicus brief can make arguments that litigants cannot make, inform the court of the broader implications of the case, provide additional background information, indicate the lineup of political and social forces concerned about the case, and clarify who besides the immediate litigants might be affected by the outcome.[39] Any party who wishes to serve as an amicus must file a "statement of interest," which brings the alignment of concerned forces into especially sharp focus.[40]

Because filing an amicus brief is expensive, organizations often make strategic calculations.[41] Beyond seeking to influence what cases the Supreme

---

39. See Bruce J. Ennis, "Effective Amicus Briefs," *Catholic University Law Review* 33 (1984): 606; Gregory A. Caldeira and John R. Wright, "Organized Interests and Agenda Setting in the U.S. Supreme Court," *American Political Science Review* 82 (1988): 1111; Donald Songer and Reginald S. Sheehan, "Interest Group Success in the Courts: Amicus Participation in the Supreme Court," *Political Research Quarterly* 46 (1993): 351–352; Kevin T. McGuire and Barbara Palmer, "Issue Fluidity on the Supreme Court," *American Political Science Review* 89 (1995): 696; James F. Spriggs II and Paul J. Wahlbeck, "Amicus Curiae and the Role of Information at the Supreme Court," *Political Research Quarterly* 50 (1997): 371–373; Luther T. Mumford, "When Does the Curiae Need an Amicus?" *Journal of Appellate Practice and Process* 1 (1999): 281–282; and Paul M. Collins, "Friends of the Court: Examining the Influence of Amicus Curiae Participation in U.S. Supreme Court Litigation," *Law and Society Review* 28 (2004): 813.

40. Gregory A. Caldeira and John R. Wright, "Amici Curiae before the Supreme Court: Who Participates, When, and How Much?" *Journal of Politics* 52 (1990): 786.

41. Caldeira and Wright give two different estimates of the cost of drafting an amicus curiae brief: $15,000–20,000 ("Organized Interests and Agenda Setting in the U.S. Supreme Court," p. 1112) and $10,000–15,000 ("Amici Curiae before the Supreme Court," p. 800). It may be that the higher set of figures refers to estimates "from the general counsels of several large organizations with headquarters in Washington, DC . . . for a single brief prepared by a reputable law firm." According to the Web site of the American Institute for Economic Research (http://www.aier.org/research/col.php, accessed October 6, 2010), to express these figures in 2010 dollars, they should be multiplied by roughly 1.7. On the strategic calculations made by those who file amicus briefs, see Lisa A Solowiej and Paul M. Collins Jr., "Counteractive Lobbying in the U.S. Supreme Court," *American Politics Research* 37 (2009): 670–699.

Court hears and how they are decided, organized interests may be animated by additional concerns. Analyses that seek to account for why organizations might undertake this costly activity often emphasize the organizational maintenance needs of membership associations. Filing briefs is a way of reassuring members or donors of the association's vigorous efforts in promoting its objectives.[42] In addition, it is well known that a substantial share of individual political participation originates in a request for activity.[43] There is evidence that litigants often encourage the filing of amicus briefs and that those who plan to file amicus briefs often encourage others to sign along with them—as a way of forging alliances with organizations having similar political predispositions, demonstrating wider support before the Court, and sharing the costs.[44] Regardless of the organizational maintenance pressures that might impel organized interests to file amicus briefs, however, amici do not seem to select cases that are sure winners in which to participate.[45]

In spite of the multiple differences between the Supreme Court and Congress as institutions, there are perhaps unexpected similarities between the tendencies for different kinds of organizations to file amicus briefs in Supreme Court cases and what we saw in Tables 14.6 and 14.7 about testifying before congressional committees. The data in Table 14.8 make clear both that only a small share of organizations listed in the 2001 *Washington Representatives* directory filed an amicus brief in a case in which a petition of certiorari was filed during either the 2000–2001 or the 2001–2002 term and that the share

42. On this point, see Lee Epstein and C. K. Rowland, "Debunking the Myth of Interest Group Invincibility in the Courts," *American Political Science Review* 85 (1991): 206, and Thomas G. Hansford, "Information Provision, Organizational Constraints, and the Decision to Submit an Amicus Curiae Brief in a U.S. Supreme Court Case," *Political Research Quarterly* 57 (2004): 219–230.

43. See Steven J. Rosenstone and John Mark Hansen, *Mobilization, Participation, and Democracy in America* (New York: Macmillan, 1993), esp. chaps. 2, 4, 6, and 7; Kay Lehman Schlozman, Sidney Verba, and Henry E. Brady, "Civic Participation and the Equality Problem," in *Civic Engagement in American Democracy*, ed. Theda Skocpol and Morris Fiorina (Washington, DC: Brookings Institution, 1999), pp. 444–456; and Henry E. Brady, Kay Lehman Schlozman, and Sidney Verba, "Prospecting for Participants: Rational Expectations and the Recruitment of Political Activists," *American Political Science Review* 93 (1999): 153–168.

44. In a mail survey of lawyers who represented petitioners before the Supreme Court at the agenda stage, Kevin T. McGuire, as recounted in "Amicus Curiae and Strategies for Gaining Access to the Supreme Court," *Political Research Quarterly* 47 (1994): 825, found that 23 percent of them solicited amicus briefs on their clients' behalf.

45. See Kevin T. McGuire and Gregory A. Caldeira, "Lawyers, Organized Interests, and the Law of Obscenity: Agenda Setting in the Supreme Court," *American Political Science Review* 87 (1993): 723–724, and Collins, "Friends of the Court."

Table 14.8   Organized Interests Filing Amicus Briefs

Categories of Organized Interests	Percentage Filing Briefs[a]	Average Number of Briefs Filed (among Filers)[b]
Corporations[c]	3%	1.2
Trade and Other Business Associations	8%	2.1
Occupational Associations	12%	2.0
Unions	17%	1.7
Social Welfare or Poor	14%	1.5
Identity Groups[d]	22%	2.0
Public Interest	15%	2.3
State and Local Governments	11%	5.8
All[e]	8%	2.3

Source: Washington Representatives Study.

[a] Percentage of all the organizations listed in the 2001 *Washington Representatives* directory that filed an amicus brief with the Supreme Court in the 2000–2001 or 2001–2002 terms (or both).
[b] Average number of briefs filed by organizations that filed briefs, including those not listed in the 2001 *Washington Representatives* directory.
[c] Includes U.S. corporations, U.S. subsidiaries of foreign corporations, and for-profit firms of professionals such as law and consulting firms.
[d] Includes organizations representing racial, ethnic, or religious groups; the elderly; women; or LGBT sexual orientation.
[e] Includes all organizations that filed briefs, including organizations in categories not shown in the table.

varies substantially across various kinds of organizations. Unions were relatively likely to file amicus briefs. In contrast, business organizations—in particular, corporations—were not especially likely to have done so, a pattern that might have changed since the period covered by our data. There is evidence that, since then, business organizations, especially the U.S. Chamber of Commerce, have discovered the utility of filing briefs before the business-friendly Roberts Court.[46]

46. See Adam Liptak, "Justices Offer Receptive Ear to Business Interests," *New York Times*, December 19, 2010.

With respect to the average number of briefs filed, it is state and local governments that are the outliers. Because Supreme Court decisions so often involve issues of federalism or consequences for the states, it is not surprising that this result turns out to be driven by the state governments: 23 percent of the state governmental units that are listed in the 2001 directory filed a brief; of those that filed, including state government units not listed in the directory, the average is a whopping 15.6 briefs. In a parallel to testifying before Congress, organizations that are not known to be powerhouses in the organized interest domain—organizations representing diffuse public interests, identity groups, and social service providers and advocates for the poor—are relatively likely to file briefs with the Supreme Court. Their average numbers of briefs, however, are not notably high, especially for organizations representing service providers and the poor.

Table 14.9 allows us to peer inside these aggregate categories and shows the extent to which the propensity to file amicus briefs is shaped by the substance of the issues that are the subjects of Supreme Court decisions. Given the significance of the courts in matters surrounding civil rights and nondiscrimination, it is not surprising that organizations based on identity are likely to file amicus briefs and, if they file, to do so relatively frequently. When it comes to filing amicus briefs, the organizations of Native Americans, mostly tribes, which are by far the most numerous of the identity organizations, are not especially active—in contrast to what we have seen for other kinds of organizational involvement in Washington politics. If organizations of Native Americans are omitted from the analysis, the proportion of identity organizations that filed briefs rises further, to 26 percent.

In a result that is hardly unexpected, among organizations representing public interests, the handful of civil liberties organizations are, by a substantial margin, the most likely to file amicus briefs; among filers, they file, on average, a relatively high number of briefs. The data in Table 14.9 show the same relative balance between other liberal and other conservative public interest organizations in the likelihood of filing that we saw for testifying in Congress. However, when it comes to the average number of briefs filed, the other conservative public interest organizations outpace the other liberal public interest organizations by a significant margin.

Making PAC Donations

Organizations often supplement their attempts to influence policy through direct communications to public officials with actions targeted at elections.

Table 14.9 Identity and Public Interest Organizations Filing Amicus Briefs

	Percentage Filing Briefs[a]	Average Number of Briefs Filed (among Filers)[b]	Total Number[c]
A. Identity Groups			
Native Americans	15%	1.2	(177)
Other Racial, Ethnic, or Nationality	24%	2.0	(98)
Religious	26%	1.8	(90)
Women	33%	2.9	(45)
Elderly	17%	3.6	(29)
LGBT	57%	1.5	(7)
B. Public Interest Groups			
Consumer	22%	2.1	(32)
Environmental and Wildlife	13%	1.3	(127)
Civil Liberties	42%	3.2	(12)
Government Reform	11%	1.3	(27)
Citizen Empowerment	5%	1.5	(19)
Other Liberal Groups	24%	2.0	(84)
Other Conservative Groups	25%	3.2	(85)
Other	7%	1.4	(148)

Source: Washington Representatives Study.

[a] Percentage of all the organizations listed in the 2001 *Washington Representatives* directory that filed an amicus brief with the Supreme Court in the 2000–2001 and 2001–2002 terms.
[b] Average number of briefs filed by organizations that filed briefs, including those not listed in the 2001 *Washington Representatives* directory.
[c] Number of organizations in the 2001 *Washington Representatives* directory.

Organizations become involved in elections in a variety of ways—by, for example, recruiting and assisting candidates; communicating with and mobilizing their own members; and especially if, like labor unions, they have large memberships, providing campaign volunteers to work on behalf of favored candidates.[47] The most common organizational strategy for electoral action, however, is making contributions to candidates and parties.

47. On the multiple ways that organizations get involved in campaigns, see Paul S. Herrnson, "Interest Groups and Campaigns: The Electoral Connection," in *The Interest Group Connection*, ed. Herrnson, Shaiko, and Wilcox, chap. 2.

The vehicle used to collect campaign contributions from individuals and stamp them with the organization's imprimatur is the political action committee or PAC. By conventional standards, many political practices used at the end of the nineteenth century—including more or less free-for-all campaign giving—would now be considered ethically questionable. Part of the Progressive-era reaction to these practices was the 1907 Tillman Act, which outlawed direct campaign contributions in federal elections by corporations. In 1943, unions were proscribed from making direct contributions by the Smith-Connolly Act or the War Labor Disputes Act, a ban that was made permanent in 1947 by the Taft-Hartley Act. At the urging of labor unions that wanted to ensure that the political action committees that serve as their campaign finance arms would not be put out of business, the 1974 amendments to the Federal Election Campaign Act gave legal sanction to the creation of political action committees. In the aftermath, corporations sought clarification as to whether they also had the right to establish political action committees. In its 1975 *Sun Oil* decision, the FEC gave corporations a green light to use resources from the corporate treasury to establish and administer political action committees and solicit managers and shareholders to make contributions.

After the *Sun Oil* decision, PAC giving—by corporations and a variety of other kinds of institutions and associations—took off quickly. In 1977 there were 1,360 PACs, of which 550 were associated with corporations and 234 with labor unions. By 2009 the total number of PACs had risen to 4,611. For corporations and labor unions the 2009 totals were 1,598 and 272, respectively. PAC spending increased even more rapidly over the period. In constant dollars, total PAC expenditures shot up from $77.4 million to $1.18 billion. Corporate PAC expenditures multiplied more than fourteen-fold, from $15.2 million to $298.6 million, and labor PAC expenditures grew from $18.6 million to $265.0 million.[48] Not only are the dollar amounts considerable but they are also concentrated. The figures are strikingly similar to what we saw for spending on lobbying. During the 1999–2000 and 2001–2002 electoral cycles, the top 1 percent of PACs accounted for nearly a third, 32 percent, of PAC contributions and the top 10 percent accounted for fully 70 percent. The bottom half of PAC contributors were responsible for only 4 percent of the total contributions.[49]

48. FEC data taken from Harold W. Stanley and Richard G. Niemi, *Vital Statistics on American Politics 2009–2010* (Washington, DC: CQ Press, 2010), pp. 91 and 93.

49. Unless otherwise noted, figures cited are based on FEC data for the 1999–2000 and 2001–2002 electoral cycles. Our concern with organizational voice in politics leads us to use

In spite of the substantial sums involved, PAC contributions are not the most significant, much less the sole, source of money for campaigns. Contributions from individuals weigh much more heavily in candidates' war chests. In the 2000–2006 election cycles, PAC donations accounted for 36 percent of all contributions to candidates for the U.S. House and 14 percent of contributions to Senate candidates.[50] Moreover, the aggregate sums for PAC giving are dwarfed by the amounts spent on lobbying.

While PAC giving is far from the most important source of campaign funds in terms of aggregate dollar amounts, it generates concern about the possibility of undue influence on electoral results or policy outcomes by interests with deep pockets and identifiable policy agendas. As we have argued, forms of political expression that rely fundamentally on inputs of money rather than on such resources as time or skill raise particular concerns. Citizens are much more unequal with respect to the size of their bank accounts than with respect to the amount of their leisure or the acuity of their skills. What is more, differences in income are more likely to hew to the fault lines of contentious political issues than are differences in other kinds of political resources. Besides, with respect to individual forms of political participation, while a series of factors such as educational attainment or political interest and efficacy predict political acts based on inputs of time, a single factor, family income, predicts making political contributions. The public shares such concerns about PACs. Public opinion surveys have repeatedly found that Americans are both distrustful of PACs and concerned that PAC contributions to federal candidates lead to "a great deal of influence" in Congress, especially by corporate and labor interests, and that they favor limits on the amounts that candidates may accept from PACs in any election.[51]

Discussions of PAC spending usually delineate two possible strategic objectives in making contributions. An organization may seek to influence the

---

the same 96 categories that we apply to political organizations for PACs and omit certain categories of PACs from the data we present: candidate PACs, party PACs, and leadership PACs, which are PACs sponsored by politicians that funnel money to other candidates for office. For this reason, the figures in our tables do not map onto the figures published by the FEC.

50. FEC figures cited in Gary C. Jacobson, *The Politics of Congressional Elections*, 7th ed. (New York: Longman, 2009), p. 67.

51. David B. Magleby and Kelly D. Patterson, "The Polls—Poll Trends: Congressional Reform," *Public Opinion Quarterly* 58 (1994): 419–427; Harris Interactive, "PAC Money, Big Companies, News Media, Political Lobbyists All Seen by Large Majorities as Having Too Much Power and Influence in Washington," press release, February 24, 1999, http://www .harrisinteractive.com/harris_poll/index.asp?PID=37, accessed March 2, 2010.

outcome of an election and thus to retain an office holder who is congenial to its policy goals or to replace one who is hostile. An organization that seeks to affect who holds office—for example, a labor union PAC or a PAC seeking a public good like environmental preservation or gun rights—will focus its donations on competitive elections in which additional resources might have the potential to make a difference in who wins. PAC contributions may also have a second objective: to influence what the eventual winner will do once in office. In order to gain a hearing for a political story that they inevitably believe to be persuasive and fair, organizations may seek to make sure that they will have access to elected officials who will be dealing with policy matters with consequences for the organization and its stakeholders.

While, as we saw in Chapter 10, some political scientists are skeptical that PAC contributions can be seen as facilitating access, there is no doubt that many PACs, especially big ones, target their giving in patterns that are inconsistent with the goal of influencing election outcomes. They often make contributions to sure winners—even to candidates who have no opposition at all. Organizations, especially ones that lobby extensively, frequently donate to incumbents holding positions of power, including committee chairs and party leaders. They are also more likely to give to candidates from both parties, sometimes in the same race, and to candidates of all ideologies.[52] The behavior of corporate PACs during the mid-1990s exemplifies such a pragmatic contribution strategy. Although we would expect corporations to be more favorable to the market-oriented Republicans, in the 1994 election cycle corporate PACs directed 57 percent of their contributions to Democrats, then in control of Congress. After the 1994 election produced a Republican majority in both the House and the Senate, corporate PACs made 70 percent of their contributions to Republicans in the next election cycle.[53]

Those who doubt whether there is a link between PAC contributions and lobbying access point out, correctly, that most organizations that lobby do not have an affiliated PAC.[54] Others, however, make clear that political heavy-

52. In "Are PAC Contributions and Lobbying Linked?" Ansolabehere, Snyder, and Tripathi find that groups that spend relatively little on lobbying tend to contribute to candidates on the basis of electoral circumstances and ideological persuasion, in contrast with the "big hitters" who account for the bulk of organized interests' lobbying expenditures.

53. Herrnson, "Interest Groups and Campaigns," pp. 38–39.

54. See, for example, Thomas Gais, *Improper Influence: Campaign Finance Law, Political Interest Groups, and the Problem of Equality* (Ann Arbor: University of Michigan Press, 1996), chap. 4.

weights tend both to make PAC contributions and to spend on lobbying. As shown in Figure 14.1, the probability that an organization that lobbies will have an associated PAC is quite low for most organizations that lobby but rises quickly among those that spend the most on lobbying. If we array all the organizations in the 2001 *Washington Representatives* directory that reported lobbying spending in 2000 or 2001 by their total spending on lobbying over the two-year period, just 7 percent of the organizations in the lower four quintiles of lobbying spenders had an affiliated PAC that made contributions in the 2000 or 2002 electoral cycle. In contrast, more than three-quarters, 78 percent, of the top 1 percent of lobbying spenders had an affiliated PAC that made contributions. In fact, organizations listed in the 2001 directory that registered both PAC contributions and lobbying spending accounted

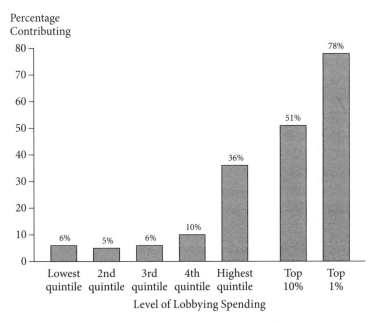

Figure 14.1   Is Making PAC Contributions Associated with Spending on Lobbying?

Source: Washington Representatives Study.

Note: For organizations that reported spending on lobbying in 2000 or 2001, the bars show, for each level of total lobbying spending in 2000 and 2001, the percentage of organizations with an affiliated PAC that made contributions in the 2000 or 2002 election cycle.

for 74 percent of the PAC contributions—and 53 percent of the lobbying expenditures—made by the organizations in the directory.

In light of our concern with equal representation through political voice, it is noteworthy that the list of the PACs that spent the most in the two-decade period from 1989 to 2009, which appears below, encompasses a wide range of interests and seems to give greater weight to organizations that represent ordinary people than do most lists of Washington big leaguers. It includes large corporations as well as associations representing smaller local businesses like beer distributors and auto dealers, highly paid professionals like doctors and trial lawyers, public employees, skilled blue-collar workers, and even low-wage service employees. The ranking of these PACs and the dollar amounts they spent are as follows:[55]

1	AT&T Inc.	$43,225,567
2	American Federation of State, County, and Municipal Employees	$40,965,173
3	National Association of Realtors	$35,059,763
4	Goldman Sachs	$31,111,912
5	American Association for Justice	$30,733,929
6	International Brotherhood of Electrical Workers	$30,733,491
7	National Education Association	$29,908,375
8	Laborers Union	$28,201,600
9	Service Employees International Union	$27,510,607
10	Carpenters and Joiners Union	$27,368,258
11	Teamsters Union	$27,151,254
12	Communications Workers of America	$26,633,246
13	Citigroup Inc.	$26,545,405
14	American Medical Association	$26,188,799
15	American Federation of Teachers	$25,994,021
16	United Auto Workers	$25,403,502
17	Machinists and Aerospace Workers Union	$24,793,477
18	National Auto Dealers Association	$23,987,908
19	Altria Group	$23,849,491
20	United Food and Commercial Workers Union	$23,742,074

55. These figures, based on FEC data released on May 12, 2009, aggregated by money spent by the PACs themselves, their affiliates, and their subsidiaries, were taken from the Web site of the Center for Responsive Politics, http://www.opensecrets.org/orgs/list.php?order=A, accessed August 11, 2009.

21	United Parcel Service	$23,517,045
22	American Bankers Association	$21,734,466
23	National Association of Home Builders	$21,401,355
24	EMILY's List	$20,911,560
25	National Beer Wholesalers Association	$20,301,345

Table 14.10 considers not the biggest givers among PACs but instead the universe of PAC giving for a more limited period—the 1999–2000 and 2001–2002 electoral cycles.[56] Of the organizations listed in the 2001 *Washington Representatives* directory, the kinds of organizations that traditionally form the backbone of organized involvement in Washington politics—corporations, trade and other business associations, occupational associations, and labor unions—are especially likely to have an affiliated PAC that made a contribution during the four-year period. However, in a pattern we have not observed for any other form of organizational political activity, labor unions outpace all other kinds of organizations by a wide margin in terms of both the likelihood of having an affiliated PAC that made contributions and the average size of the total donations made: 57 percent of the unions—compared to 14 percent of the corporations and 15 percent of the trade and other business associations—had an affiliated PAC that made donations; the average for union PACs was $1,385,000, in contrast to $160,000 for corporations and $228,000 for trade associations. Furthermore, considering the subcategories of unions underlines the extent to which PAC giving is not simply the province of the well heeled: 85 percent of the private-sector, blue-collar unions had an affiliated PAC that made donations, with an average total of $1,110,000.

Still, it is essential to recognize that each labor union represents a very large number of members. To give some examples of large, though not necessarily the largest, unions, figures from the Department of Labor show that in 2008 the Service Employees International Union had 4.7 million members; the American Federation of State, County, and Municipal Workers had 2.8 million; and the Laborers International Union had 1.3 million.[57] The large

56. The data in Table 14.10 include PACs that are associated with organizations such as Google Inc. NetPAC or VenturePAC, the PAC of the National Venture Capital Association, as well as a limited number of stand-alone PACs that make clear that they are funding candidates with particular characteristics or points of view. Examples of the latter include the League of Conservation Voters and the anti-Castro U.S.–Cuba Democracy PAC.

57. Data from the Office of Labor–Management Standards, http://kcerds.dol-esa.gov/query/getOrgQry.do, accessed March 3, 2010.

Table 14.10   PAC Donations by Organized Interests

Categories of Organized Interests	Percentage Donating[a]	Average PAC Donations among PAC Donors[b]
Corporations[c]	14%	$160,000
Trade and Other Business Associations	15%	$228,000
Occupational Associations	11%	$464,000
Unions	57%	$1,385,000
Social Welfare or Poor	1%	$185,000
Identity Groups[d]	4%	$159,000
Public Interest	7%	$341,000
State and Local Governments	0%	$166,000
All[e]	10%	$258,000

Source: Washington Representatives Study.

[a] Percentage of all the organizations listed in the 2001 *Washington Representatives* directory that made PAC donations in the 2000 or 2002 election cycle (or both); candidate- and party-based PACS are excluded.
[b] Average PAC donations by organizations that made PAC donations, including those not listed in the 2001 *Washington Representatives* directory; candidate- and party-based PACS are excluded.
[c] Includes U.S. corporations, U.S. subsidiaries of foreign corporations, and for-profit firms of professionals such as law and consulting firms.
[d] Includes organizations representing racial, ethnic, or religious groups; the elderly; women; or LGBT sexual orientation.
[e] Includes all organizations, including organizations in categories not shown in the table.

sums in the coffers of union PACs represent the aggregation of a large number of small individual donations. In contrast to union PACS, which represent a lot of people, each of whom contributes a little, some PACs function by collecting donations from far fewer people, each of whom gives a lot more. Besides, recalling that contributions from individuals figure much more importantly in campaign finance than do contributions from PACs, we glean a different impression of the kinds of organizations that are represented in campaign contributions by focusing on the organizations with which generous campaign donors are affiliated, usually as employees. The following is a list of organizations for which at least one affiliated individual made donations totaling $50,000 or more to federal candidates or parties during at least one electoral cycle.[58] The number in parentheses indicates the number of individuals who donated at least $50,000.

Altria Group

American Financial Group (2)

American International Group (3)

Amway/Alticor Inc. (3)

Archer Daniels Midland

Bank of America (2)

BellSouth Corp.

Boeing Co.

Bristol-Myers Squibb (2)

Citigroup Inc. (5)

Credit Suisse Group (7)

Deloitte Touche Tohmatsu

Eli Lilly and Co. (3)

EMILY's List (2)

Enron Corp. (3)

Freddie Mac (2)

General Electric

Goldman Sachs (17)

MBNA Corp. (2)

MCI Inc.

Merrill Lynch

MetLife Inc. (2)

Microsoft Corp. (9)

National Rifle Association

Time Warner (17)

Union Pacific Corp.

Vivendi (4)

Walt Disney Co. (3)

We must make clear that the big givers do not necessarily make their contributions with the intention of promoting the interests of the organizations with which they are connected. Still, the list of organizations for which affiliated individuals made contributions of at least $50,000 stands in striking contrast to the list of the PACs that have given the most. With the exception of the National Rife Association and EMILY's List, every single organization is either a corporation or a for-profit partnership.

The Distribution of Organizational Activity

We have reviewed a great deal of data about how different kinds of organizations become involved in different arenas of Washington politics. Now we wish to put these data together to characterize the accent of the heavenly

58. This list includes any organization for which an affiliated individual contributed at least $50,000 to federal candidates and parties during one or more election cycles while affiliated with the organization. The list is based on FEC data released on May 12, 2009, and were taken from the Web site of the Center for Responsive Politics, http://www.opensecrets.org/orgs/indivs.php, accessed August 11, 2009.

chorus in various domains of national politics. That is, we seek to investigate how different forms of organizational activity give different weight to different kinds of voices—a function of the number of organizations in a particular category, the likelihood that they are involved in that arena, and the average amount of activity of organizations that are involved. As we proceed, we shall make comparisons among kinds of organizational involvement with respect to the distribution of organized interest activity and their permeability to the kinds of organizations that are expected to be underrepresented in Washington—in particular, organizations advocating on behalf of diffuse public interests, the economically deprived, and identity groups.

Table 14.11 presents the distribution of organized interest activity for each of the kinds of activity we have discussed. One striking aspect of the data in Table 14.11 is the sheer volume of activity. The figures at the bottom of the table show that organizational political action is a massive enterprise involving nearly 12,000 listed organizations, nearly 11,000 in-house lobbyists and more than 13,000 contracts with outside firms, nearly $3 billion in spending on lobbying, more than 12,000 congressional testimonies, nearly 7,000 signings of amicus briefs, and more than $550 million in PAC donations.[59]

In interpreting the figures in Table 14.11, it is important to keep in mind that, only in the left-hand column of numbers, which shows the now familiar distribution of organizations in the 2001 *Washington Representatives* directory, is the organization the unit of analysis. Other columns show the distribution of the number of in-house lobbyists on staff in organizations' Washington offices, outside lobbying firms hired, dollars spent on lobbying, testimonies before congressional committees and subcommittees, signings of amicus briefs filed before the Supreme Court, and dollars of PAC spending. Although it will be useful to compare the share of activity in any realm for a particular category of organization with its share for all organizations, it is critical not to reify the distribution of organizations in the second column of numbers. Although a census of organizations, it cannot be considered any kind of natural population. We discussed in Chapter 10 the multiple reasons why it is

---

59. The data for political organizations, in-house lobbyists, and outside firms hired are derived from the 2001 *Washington Representatives* directory and thus represent the situation as of spring 2001. The figures for lobbying spending, testimonies, and amicus briefs represent two-year periods. The figures for PAC spending represent two two-year electoral cycles. Because the base year was 2001, the figures would presumably be considerably higher if collected today. After all, as we saw in Chapter 12, the number of organizations listed in the directory increased by 19 percent between 2001 and 2006.

Table 14.11 Distribution of Political Activity by Organized Interests[a]

	All Organizations	In-House Lobbyists	Outside Firms	Lobbying Expenditures	Congressional Testimony[b]	Amicus Briefs[b]	PAC Donations[b]
Corporations	35%	20%	44%	46%	16%	6%	34%
Trade and Business	13	25	15	22	13	8	14
Occupational	7	13	4	8	9	11	11
Unions	1	4	1	1	3	1	26
Education	4	2	4	3	3	4	<1
Health	4	2	3	4	3	1	1
Social Welfare	1	1	<1	<1	2	2	<1
Identity Groups	4	5	3	3	6	10	2
Public Interest	5	10	2	3	11	13	9
State and Local Governments	10	3	10	5	18	36	<1
Foreign	8	2	8	3	2	1	1
Other	8	12	5	3	15	8	4
Don't Know	1	<1	1	<1	1	<1	1
	101%	99%	100%	101%	102%	101%	103%
N	11,651	9,996	13,246	$2,844,784,000	12,619	6,894	$558,361,000

Source: Washington Representatives Study.

[a] Distributions for all organizations listed in the 2001 *Washington Representatives* directory.

[b] Includes all organizations that undertook this activity whether or not they are listed in the 2001 *Washington Representatives* directory; figure for PAC donations does not include candidate or party PACs.

impossible to specify what a representative distribution of organizations would look like. Nevertheless, we concluded that the existing distribution is anything but representative. Most obviously, it underrepresents the economic interests of all but the most affluent Americans—not just needy ones like recipients of means-tested government benefits but nonunionized workers in nonprofessional, nonmanagerial occupations. In addition, the interests of a variety of noneconomic groups—ranging from students to women at home to non–English speakers to supporters of various public goods—receive scant representation through organizations.

The next two columns bring together information about the distribution of organizations into categories with information about these measures of political capacity. The bottom line is that the share of political capacity—whether in-house lobbyists or outside firms—of any particular category of organization reflects, first and foremost, the number of such organizations and thus their weight in the overall distribution of organizations.[60] That is, categories with many organizations have a substantial share of political capacity; categories with few organizations have limited political capacity. Compared to their share of all organizations, corporations and state and local governments—which have good reasons for being located in places other than Washington and for which dealings with the federal government can facilitate, but do not define, their overall mission—field a smaller share of in-house lobbyists and hire a larger share of outside firms. For occupational associations, labor unions, organizations representing public interests, and groups based on identity, the opposite is true. It is striking that trade and other business associations claim a larger portion—and the organizations that assist and represent the poor a smaller one—of both in-house lobbyists and outside firms than of organizations.

The next two columns—which show the distributions for the two congressionally based activities, spending on lobbying and testimonies—stand in striking contrast with one another. When it comes to the distribution of money spent on lobbying, spending by corporations and trade or other business associations is substantially higher than the already notable share of organizations and dwarfs the share of spending by any other kind of organi-

---

60. The figure for the share of in-house lobbyists for corporations does not include those who work for Washington law, public relations, and consulting firms that represent clients before the government. If they are included, the corporate share rises to 27 percent and the shares for other kinds of organizations are reduced proportionally.

zation.[61] Of the $2.84 billion spent on lobbying by the organizations listed in the 2001 *Washington Representatives* directory, 46 percent was spent by corporations and 22 percent by trade and other business associations. In contrast, reflecting their more limited resources and, in some cases, restraints on lobbying by tax-exempt organizations, organizations advocating on behalf of public goods spent $70.0 million, those advocating on behalf of African Americans and Latinos $4.9 million, and those advocating on behalf of social welfare benefits or the poor $1.7 million—of which not a single penny came from a group of recipients of means-tested benefits acting on their own behalf.

When it comes to testifying in Congress, a form of activity for which financial resources are less central and for which the balance of the initiative rests more with policy makers in Congress than with the organizations, the distribution manifests the representation of a broader set of interests and a quite different skew. The modal testifier represents a subnational government or consortium of governments. Corporations and trade and other business associations, which together accounted for more than two-thirds of the dollars expended on lobbying, account for a much smaller share of the testimonies: 16 and 13 percent, respectively. At 11 percent of the testimonies, advocates of broad public interests constitute a much larger share of the testimonies than of the lobbying dollars. A similar point can be made about organizations representing identity groups, 6 percent of the testimonies, and organizations representing social service providers and the economically needy, 2 percent of the testimonies. Indeed, for the first time we see a trace of activity by an organization of means-tested public benefits recipients: 8 of the nearly 13,000, or 0.06 percent, of the testifiers represented such an organization.

These same tendencies are even more pronounced when it comes to the distribution for the signings of amicus briefs.[62] State and local governments, which account for more than a third of the signings, are by far the biggest hitters. At 6 and 8 percent respectively, corporations and trade and other business associations account for a much smaller share of the signings than for any other form of political activity in the table. Reflecting the kinds of issues that are brought to the Supreme Court, organizations representing public goods, 13 percent of the signings, and identity groups, 10 percent of the sign-

61. This finding is similar to that contained in Baumgartner and Leech, "Interest Niches and Policy Bandwagons," Table 3.

62. Because many briefs were signed by more than one organization, we refer to signings as the unit of analysis rather than to signers or to briefs.

ings, figure even more importantly in signing briefs than in testifying in Congress. Organizations that provide services to or advocacy on behalf of the economically needy constitute, as they did for testimonies, 2 percent of the signings. Still, there is a trace of activity attributable to organizations of recipients of means-tested benefits: 29 of the 6,922 signings, or 0.4 percent, came from such groups, usually representing public housing tenants.

In certain respects, the distribution for PAC spending hews to the pattern that we have seen for other domains that are dependent on financial resources. The organizations that are known as providing the backbone for Washington-based organizational activity—in particular, corporations and trade and other business associations but also the various kinds of occupational associations—form a substantial part of the distribution. Organizations representing identity groups and the economically needy barely register.

However, in one respect the distribution of PAC giving departs strikingly from the other distributions in Table 14.11: union PACs account for fully 26 percent of PAC giving by organizations. As we have proceeded through our discussion of organizational involvement in various domains of Washington politics, we have often noted that unions are very active. Labor unions were least likely to be categorized as low capacity—that is, to hire only one outside firm or to have only one or two in-house lobbyists on staff. With respect to the number of activities, unions outpaced all other kinds of organizations. Still, unions are such a small part of the pressure system, constituting 1 percent of all organizations active in Washington in 2001, that even though active, they barely register in the distributions for other measures. Even when they figured most importantly, they accounted for only 4 percent of the in-house lobbyists and 3 percent of the testimonies. Thus it is quite notable that they account for a quarter of the PAC giving, a relative weight that is, by far, the most substantial on behalf of the economic interests of ordinary workers seen anywhere in the table.

Another noteworthy aspect of the distribution is that advocates of broad public interests constitute 9 percent of PAC donations, a figure that is triple their share of lobbying spending. The list of electorally oriented advocates for public goods includes an array of organizations supporting causes as diverse—and sometimes conflicting—as environmental preservation, abortion (both sides), gun control (again, both sides), foreign policy concerns in locales ranging from Cuba to the Middle East, marijuana legalization, and the consumer rights of snowmobilers to buzz through national parks and motorcyclists to ride without helmets.

Organizations Representing Identity
Groups and Public Goods

Because so many kinds of identity and public interest groups are buried within these two aggregate categories, it might be useful to understand the distribution of their activity in the various arenas of organizational involvement. Table 14.12 shows the relative shares of various kinds of organizations in each of the kinds of organizational activity. For organizations representing identity groups, the distribution of groups, shown in the far left-hand column of figures, is an imperfect predictor of the distribution for any particular arena. The departures from proportionality are noteworthy. The Native American organizations that are so numerically dominant in this category and weigh heavily when it comes to spending on lobbying and congressional testimonies contribute only a small share of the amicus brief signings and a minuscule share of the small number of PAC dollars that come from organizations representing identity groups. Groups representing the elderly are responsible for a large share, 42 percent, of the lobbying spending. In contrast, other racial, ethnic, and nationality groups as well as religious and women's organizations figure more importantly when it comes to amicus brief signings. Once again, PAC donations show a distinctive pattern. Of the small pool of PAC dollars deriving from identity group organizations, more than half came from PACs representing women (30 percent) and LGBT groups (22 percent) taken together.

For organizations representing broad public interests, there is, overall, a clear relationship between the distributions for the separate activities and the distribution of all public interest organizations, shown in the far left-hand column of numbers. There are, however, a few departures that merit mention. Presumably reflecting the relative significance of Congress and the courts in environmental policy making, environmental organizations—which are quite numerous among advocates of diffuse public interests—figure much more importantly in congressional testimonies than in amicus brief signings. Not unexpectedly, civil liberties advocates weigh more heavily in amicus signings than in any other activity. In addition, it is not surprising that supporters of government reform, whose good government instincts include skepticism about the use of money in elections, barely register in PAC giving.

Also noteworthy is the relative balance between what we have been calling the "other liberal" and "other conservative" public interest organizations—categories that include single-issue domestic and foreign policy advocates as well as conservative and liberal multiple-issue groups. In our initial discus-

Table 14.12 Distribution of Political Activity by Organizations Representing Identity Groups and Public Interests[a]

	All Organizations	In-House Lobbyists	Outside Firms	Lobbying Expenditures	Congressional Testimony[b]	Amicus Briefs[b]	PAC Donations[b]
A. Identity Groups							
Native Americans	43%	3%	65%	32%	44%	7%	1%
Other Racial, Ethnic, or Nationality	17	24	14	8	18	28	11
Religious	23	36	11	10	16	28	19
Women	10	18	5	2	10	21	30
Elderly	7	14	5	42	10	7	17
LGBT	1	6	<1	5	<1	8	22
	101%	101%	100%	99%	98%	99%	100%
N	396	477	338	$88,223,000	748	691	$10,014,000

B. Public Interest Organizations

Consumer	6%	6%	5%	4%	7%	3%	<1
Environmental	24	23	29	21	45	6	21
Civil Liberties	2	3	2	4	5	13	<1
Government Reform	5	5	4	6	4	2	<1
Citizen Empowerment	4	3	3	1	1	1	<1
Other Liberal	16	20	10	7	13	17	36
Other Conservative	16	20	10	34	8	33	39
Other	28	21	36	24	18	25	4
	101%	101%	99%	101%	101%	100%	100%
N	531	1,017	271	$69,975,000	1,332	925	$48,121,000

Source: Washington Representatives Study.

[a] The table reflects the distributions for all organizations listed in the 2001 *Washington Representatives* directory.

[b] Includes all organizations that undertook this activity whether or not they are listed in the 2001 *Washington Representatives* directory.

sion of advocacy on behalf of public goods in Chapter 11, we noted that when a diffuse public interest is at stake in a political controversy, there is usually a competing one on the other side: for example, consumer product safety versus low consumer prices or energy independence versus available supplies of fossil fuels. Furthermore, while public interest organizations in the aggregate lean in a liberal direction, there is substantial representation of conservative public interests. With respect to several measures—in-house lobbyists, outside firms, and PAC donations—the share represented by other liberal and other conservative public interest organizations is in rough balance. With respect to congressional testimonies, an area of activity in which such organizations do not weigh particularly heavily, other liberal public interest organizations, with 13 percent of the testimonies, have an edge over other conservative ones, with 8 percent of the testimonies. However, when it comes to lobbying expenditures and amicus brief signings, arenas in which such organizations figure more importantly, other conservative public interest organizations dominate their liberal counterparts: the competing public interest organizations account for, respectively, 34 percent and 7 percent of the lobbying expenditures and 33 percent and 17 percent of the amicus brief signings.

Distribution of Organized Interest Activity: Summing Up

A series of pie charts in Figure 14.2 summarizes the many numbers in Table 14.11 with special emphasis on the categories of organizations to which we have paid special attention: organizations representing business, the economically less privileged, identity groups, and broad public interests.[63] For the latter two categories we use the definition that we have used throughout. Business organizations include U.S. and foreign corporations, U.S. subsidiaries of foreign corporations, for-profit firms of professionals such as law and consulting firms, U.S. and foreign trade and other business associations, and business-affiliated research organizations. We define organizations repre-

---

63. The figure includes all organizations listed in the 2001 *Washington Representatives* directory. Business organizations include U.S. and foreign corporations, U.S. subsidiaries of foreign corporations, for-profit firms of professionals such as law and consulting firms, U.S. and foreign trade and other business associations, and business-affiliated research organizations; less privileged groups include blue-collar and white-collar unions, social service providers, organizations advocating on behalf of the poor, and other occupational associations; identity groups include organizations representing racial, ethnic, or religious groups; the elderly; women; or persons who are lesbian, gay, bisexual, or transgender.

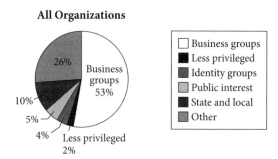

All Organizations

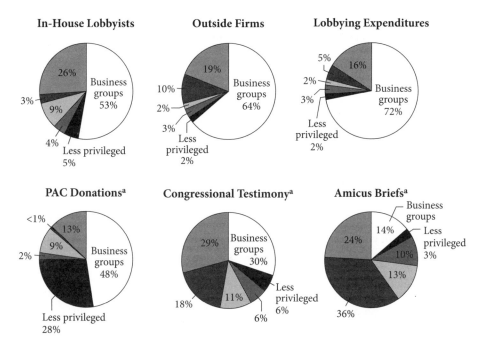

In-House Lobbyists

Outside Firms

Lobbying Expenditures

PAC Donations[a]

Congressional Testimony[a]

Amicus Briefs[a]

Figure 14.2   Distribution of Various Political Activities for Types of Organized Interests

Source: Washington Representatives Study.

[a] Includes all organizations that undertook this activity whether or not they are listed in the 2001 *Washington Representatives* directory; the figure for PAC donations does not include candidate, party, or leadership PACs.

senting the economic interests of the less privileged very broadly and include blue-collar and white-collar unions, social service providers, organizations advocating on behalf of the poor, and other occupational associations. Because they figure so importantly in certain kinds of activity—in particular, signing amicus briefs—we also include state and local governments.

Figure 14.2 makes clear that different sections of the heavenly chorus sing with somewhat different accents but that, in the aggregate, business interests are very well represented—and the interests of broad publics and the less privileged, whether defined in terms of economic well-being or identity, are much less well represented—in organized interest politics. This formulation is particularly apt for spending on lobbying, a domain in which economic resources are paramount. Nearly three-quarters of the dollars spent on lobbying in the two-year period originated with business. In contrast, business interests weigh much less heavily in the total when it comes to congressional testimonies and signings of amicus briefs. In fact, the latter is the only domain of organized interest involvement in which the combined share of organizations representing the less economically privileged, identity groups, and public goods is larger than that representing business.

With respect to PAC spending, we see a complicated relationship to equality of political voice. Campaign giving is the realm of participation in which financial inequalities among individuals matter most. Besides, PAC spending is a form of campaign finance in which the political priorities of donors are most explicit. However, PAC spending is the only realm in which the activity of the economically less privileged registers at all significantly: 28 percent of PAC donations represent unions; occupational associations of those in non-managerial, nonprofessional jobs; or the economically needy. If we eliminate white-collar unions and other occupational associations from our expansive definition of economic have-nots, we reduce the share of in-house lobbyists, outside firms hired, lobbying expenditures, congressional testimonies, and amicus brief signings attributable to the less economically privileged by a percentage point or two. Even with this more restricted definition, however, the less economically privileged account for 15 percent of PAC spending, a far higher share than in any other domain. For no other form of political activity does a list of the most active organizations encompass such a wide range of kinds of citizens and such a sizable share from the less affluent. Still, as would be expected in an arena that depends on the deployment of financial resources, business is well represented when it comes to campaign contributions from PACs.

Political Voice through Organized
Interest Activity: The Bottom Line

In this chapter we have translated what we have learned about the kinds of organizations that are active in Washington politics into multiple measures of political voice. Before we attempt to summarize the dizzying number of microfindings that have emerged from detailed descriptions involving 96 categories of organizations and a half-dozen measures of organizational capacity and political involvement, let us recall a few of the findings from earlier chapters that help us to understand the contours of political voice through organized interest advocacy.

The appellation *interest groups* and the scholarly attention to the puzzle of how voluntary associations get off the ground have left the misimpression that the primary units of the pressure system are membership associations. Instead, the modal organization active in pressure politics is an institution like a corporation, hospital, university, or think tank. Less than a third of the organizational advocates are membership associations of any kind, and only about an eighth are membership associations of individuals.

With respect to the interests represented, the representation of politically relevant interests is anything but inevitable. The shape of the pressure system reflects both the free rider problem and the resource constraint problem, with the result that broad public interests—whether liberal or conservative or neither—and the economically disadvantaged have limited organizational representation. These patterns are long-standing ones. The most important change in the pressure system is the expansion in the number of active organizations rather than a change in the distribution of those organizations. This increase in the number of organized interests has coincided with erosion in individual activity, thus altering the balance between the two forms of political voice.

Because we were concerned that our categories, even though detailed, might be obscuring compensatory tendencies, we looked more closely. In fact, we found considerable evidence pushing in the opposite direction. To the extent that there are appropriate data available, we found that within any particular category of organizations, organizations that are large and affluent are much more likely to be represented in Washington politics. In addition, survey data show, not surprisingly, that members and supporters of organizations that take stands in politics are stratified by social class. Furthermore, even among those affiliated with such organizations, those who are affluent and well educated are more likely to be activists and to feel represented by the organization. Thus the distribution of organizations into categories does not so much overestimate the extent of bias in the pressure system as, perhaps, understate it.

Against this background, let us summarize briefly the principal findings that shed light on political voice through the medium of organized interest activity:

- Most of the interest organizations in Washington politics do not conform to a stereotype of the well-heeled operation with resources to burn. On the contrary, a majority involve one or two in-house lobbyists or the services of a single outside firm.

- Whether they have individuals or institutions as members, membership organizations are much more likely than institutions to use an organizational Web site to discuss political issues or to seek to generate political involvement. The contrasts between membership and nonmembership organizations underline that an organization's members are one of its most important resources in politics—often compensating for deficits when it comes to financial resources.

- Although the weight of advocacy by organizations representing business interests varies across domains of organized interest activity, in no case is it outweighed by the activity of either organizations representing the less privileged or public interest groups. The weight of business advocacy is particularly notable when it comes to forms of input in which the metric is dollars. It is striking that 72 percent of expenditures on lobbying originate with organizations representing business.

- In no domain of organized interest activity does activity by organizations that provide services to or political representation of the poor register more than a trace. Activity on their own behalf by recipients of means-tested benefits barely exists at all. Unless nonprofessional, nonmanagerial workers are union members, their economic interests of receive very little representation in any arena of organized interest activity. The interests of unskilled workers receive none at all.

- As individual organizations, unions are very politically active. However, because there are so few of them, they register as a significant share of organized interest activity only when it comes to PAC giving.

- Identity groups are, across the board, also a very small share of organized interest activity.

- In the multidimensional issue space of American politics, it is impossible to specify what share of activity should represent public goods. However, in no domain does activity by public interest organizations outweigh activity by organizations representing business, and activity by conservative public interest organizations is a more substantial share of activity on behalf of public interests than is generally acknowledged.

In short, our extensive review of organized interest activity in Washington leads to the conclusion that the heavenly chorus does sing with an upper-class accent and that the voices of advocates of broad publics and the less privileged are much more muted. As a medium for the expression of political voice, pressure politics contrasts with political participation by individuals in the extent to which financial resources can be used to purchase professional advocacy in order not only to enlarge the number of voices but also to substitute skilled professionals for citizen amateurs.

PART IV

Can We Change the Accent of the Unheavenly Chorus?

15

Breaking the Pattern
through Political Recruitment

Our narrative has had a consistent theme. Whether we have looked across generations or through the life cycle, at individuals or organizations, we have found that political voice in America is biased in the direction of those who are already socially and economically advantaged. We were concerned to investigate whether there were ways to break a cycle deeply embedded in ongoing social and political processes. One possibility is that the processes by which people are recruited to political activity might act as the circuit breaker.[1] That is, to what extent can political recruitment bring in a more representative set of activists and thus moderate the accent of the political chorus?

Social scientists have long paid attention to the way that social movements —whether composed of assembly line workers, civil rights activists, environmentalists, advocates of school prayer, or opponents of higher taxes—can function as vehicles for the political activation of those who would otherwise be quiescent. Our concern is somewhat different: to understand the effect on the shape of political voice of the ordinary processes by which friends, neighbors, coworkers, and strangers who call during dinner recruit others to become

---

1. This chapter is based on an earlier article: Henry E. Brady, Kay Lehman Schlozman, and Sidney Verba, "Prospecting for Participants," *American Political Science Review* 93 (1999): 153–168.

Political scientists ordinarily use the term *recruitment* to signify the process by which citizens are selected for inclusion among political elites. We use it, in much the same sense, in relation to citizen activity. Other terms, in particular *mobilization*, have multiple meanings and therefore might lead to misunderstanding as to the process we are discussing.

politically active. To anticipate our story, we find that there is a process that we call rational prospecting in which those who wish to get others involved in politics follow a strategy of seeking out those prospects who are likely to assent to a request for political activity and to participate effectively when they do, with the result that ordinary processes of recruitment are actually amplifying the class bias in political voice rather than reducing it.

Social Movements and Recruitment to Politics

Although social movements take on many forms in the amorphous space between categories of people with common characteristics, beliefs, or needs and structured organizations with membership rules, official leadership, and administrative apparatus, scholars of social movements agree that, by speaking for and mobilizing outsiders, social movements serve to bring both new issues and new publics into politics.[2] Social movements unite people who challenge the workings of the political, economic, or social system. As one analysis puts it: "No social movement or social movement organization is part of an established order that governs, maintains, or changes social, political, religious, or economic norms and values. . . . Social movements exist and operate primarily from *outside* established institutions."[3]

The outsider status of social movements is directly related to another aspect of these movements, their contentiousness: "The irreducible act that lies at the base of all social movements, protests, and revolutions is *conten-*

---

2. The vast literature on the nature and explanation of social movements is in many ways as contentious as the movements being studied. For representative examples of the various views, see, among others, Hadley Cantril, *The Psychology of Social Movements* (Huntington, NY: R. E. Krieger, 1941); Anthony Oberschall, *Social Conflict and Social Movements* (Englewood Cliffs, NJ: Prentice-Hall, 1973); Aldon Morris and Carol McClurg Mueller, eds., *Frontiers of Social Movement Theory* (New Haven, CT: Yale University Press, 1992); Anthony Oberschall, *Social Movements: Ideologies, Interests, and Identities* (New Brunswick, NJ: Transaction, 1993); Sidney G. Tarrow, *Power in Movement: Social Movements and Contentious Politics* (New York: Cambridge University Press, 1998); Doug McAdam, Sidney Tarrow, and Charles Tilly, *Dynamics of Contention* (New York: Cambridge University Press, 2001); Jeff Goodwin and James M. Jasper, eds., *Rethinking Social Movements: Structure, Meaning, and Emotion* (Lanham, MD: Rowman and Littlefield, 2004); Gerald Davis, Doug McAdam, Mayer N. Zald, and W. Richard Scott, eds., *Social Movements and Organization Theory* (New York: Cambridge University Press, 2005); Charles Tilly and Sidney Tarrow, *Contentious Politics* (Boulder, CO: Paradigm, 2007); David S. Meyer, *The Politics of Protest: Social Movements in America* (New York: Oxford University Press, 2007).

3. Charles J. Stewart, Craig Allen Smith, and Robert E. Denton Jr., *Persuasion and Social Movements*, 4th ed. (Prospect Heights, IL: Waveland, 2001), pp. 5–6, emphasis in the original.

tious collective action . . . because it is the main and often the only recourse that ordinary people possess against better-equipped opponents or powerful states."[4] In an influential work, Frances Fox Piven and Richard A. Cloward argue that those outside of ordinary channels of activity have no choice but to engage in disruption.[5] They argue that "poor people could achieve little through the routines of electoral or interest group politics. What remained as their main resource was . . . disruption, the breakdowns that resulted when people defied the rules and institutional routines that ordinarily governed life."[6] Thus movements can bring into politics people who would not otherwise be active and therefore can act as a counterforce to the ordinary processes of social and economic life that foster political inequality.[7]

American history has been punctuated by social movements—of which agrarian radicalism, the labor movement, and the civil rights movement are notable examples—that have organized outsider constituencies to effect social change.[8] Although there is a long-standing tradition in the United States and elsewhere of social movement activism on the left, the causes on behalf of which social movements advocate span the ideological spectrum. In fact, a number of important recent social movements—including the pro-life move-

4. Sidney Tarrow, *Power in Movement*, p. 2, emphasis in the original.

5. Frances Fox Piven and Richard A. Cloward, *Poor People's Movements: Why They Succeed, How They Fail* (New York: Pantheon, 1977).

6. Frances Fox Piven, "Retrospective Comments," in "Symposium: Poor People's Movements," *Perspectives on Politics* 1 (2003): 707.

7. Recent work on movements has taken a different approach, focusing less on the mobilization of individuals to action than on collective action events. This work departs somewhat from the emphasis on individual activity in much of the social capital tradition and from the emphasis on disruptive events in much of the social movement tradition. With respect to the role of collective action in relation to poor and disadvantaged people, the results are remarkably similar to our conclusions about the voice of the less advantaged. According to Robert J. Sampson, Doug McAdam, Heather MacIndoe, and Simón Weffer-Elizondo, in "Civil Society Reconsidered: The Durable Nature and Community Structure of Collective Civic Action," *American Journal of Sociology* 111 (2005): 708: "Although the [social movement] literature tends to equate movement activity with disruptive protest in the context of loosely coordinated national movements waged by disadvantaged minorities, our study fails to confirm this stylized picture. Protest and collective civic engagement events tend to be overwhelmingly mundane, local, initiated by relatively advantaged segments of society, and devoid of major conflict. Conditioned to view movements as highly contentious and disruptive national struggles on behalf of the disadvantaged, it appears movement analysts have largely missed this . . . far more moderate form of social action."

8. The remainder of this section of the chapter draws from Kay Lehman Schlozman, Benjamin I. Page, Sidney Verba, and Morris P. Fiorina, "Inequalities of Political Voice," in *Inequality and American Democracy*, ed. Lawrence R. Jacobs and Theda Skocpol (New York: Russell Sage Foundation, 2005), pp. 66–67.

ment, the Christian right, the militia movement, and, most recently, the Tea Party movement—are on the right, not the left. Like many of their progressive counterparts, they mobilize alienated nonelites to activity in contentious politics and confront entrenched adversaries.

While they face well-organized and resource-endowed opponents both inside and outside the government, the challenging groups that coalesce around social movements are not necessarily socially and economically disadvantaged. There is in the United States a long tradition of middle-class protest movements. The nineteenth-century abolition and temperance movements, the peace movement of the 1960s, and the contemporary environmental and animal rights movements are examples of movements that have involved oppositional activism on behalf of initially overlooked or unpopular ideas by foot soldiers drawn from the middle class. While their causes rendered them political outsiders, the individual supporters of each of these movements were not socially or economically disadvantaged.

Furthermore, in a parallel to what we saw in Chapter 13 for political organizations, even when a movement appeals to a disadvantaged group, it rarely mobilizes those who are worst off in absolute terms.[9] Resource mobilization theorists have argued convincingly that certain basic resources—for example, organizational networks, leadership capacity, and access to some financial backing—are required in order to launch and sustain a movement.[10] Lacking a stake in the system, a sense that they can make a difference, and the skills and resources that facilitate political participation, the worst off in disadvantaged groups usually do not join social movements. Thus even though social movements serve as vehicles for those who lack conventional political resources, they may be characterized to some degree by the same kind of participatory stratification that we have seen in other forms of political activity.

Similar patterns may obtain for the internal dynamics of social movements. For example, in the student movements of the left during the 1960s, women resented the dominance of men, who occupied the leadership positions. Within the civil rights movement, black members of the Student Nonviolent Coordinating Committee chafed under the leadership of white counterparts while black women fought against sexual stereotyping from

9. As we noted there, Dara Z. Strolovich, in *Affirmative Advocacy: Race, Class and Gender in Interest Group Politics* (Chicago: University of Chicago Press, 2007), makes this point about political organizations that represent disadvantaged groups.

10. See John D. McCarthy and Mayer N. Zald, "Resource Mobilization and Social Movements: A Partial Theory," *American Journal of Sociology* 82 (1977): 1212–1241.

both black and white men. During the 1960s and 1970s, Filipino Americans complained that the Asian American movement was being run by the numerically dominant Chinese and Japanese Americans, who presumed, inappropriately, to speak for all Asian Americans. Although social movements often challenge the status quo from the vantage point of disadvantaged groups, they inevitably favor some voices in these groups over others.[11]

It is widely accepted that social movements have difficulty maintaining a high level of fervor over the long run. Occasionally they fade away without having much impact. More commonly, they are absorbed into a political party or—especially in the United States, where the pressure system is quite permeable—they leave political organizations in their wake. Social scientists tend to disagree about whether the natural evolution of social movements into more sustainable forms undermines their capacity to activate and represent the disadvantaged. On one hand is the view that, because the ardor inevitably cools, some kind of ongoing organizational presence is the only alternative to oblivion. On the other is the perspective that the certain concomitant of organization is compromise of movement purpose.[12]

Ordinary Recruitment

Social movements fascinate precisely because they involve new issues and new publics and thus are not simply political business as usual. Studies of social movements, whether they concentrate on a single movement or encompass a range of movements, typically focus on a movement itself and its mobilization activities. By investigating who is recruited by a movement and whether movement activists are experienced participants or new to citizen activity, this strategy provides a rich understanding of one kind of mobilization.

However, our objective is somewhat different: to understand the less colorful—and less often studied—ordinary processes by which friends, friends of friends, and even strangers mobilize others to become active politically. These ordinary processes might entail a request to attend a meeting to sup-

11. See, for example, Jo Freeman, *The Politics of Women's Liberation* (New York: David McKay, 1975); Yen Le Espiritu, *Asian American Panethnicity: Bridging Institutions and Identities* (Philadelphia: Temple University Press, 1992); and Belinda Robnett, *How Long? How Long? African-American Women in the Struggle for Civil Rights* (New York: Oxford University Press, 1997).

12. The view that organization destroys the spirit and purpose of movements is associated, in particular, with Piven and Cloward, *Poor People's Movements*. For alternative perspectives, see the essays in "Symposium: Poor People's Movements."

port a local school bond referendum or to oppose a zoning change that will bring more commercial development to the neighborhood; a request to give a campaign donation to a business associate who is running for state treasurer; a request to volunteer in the campaign of his opponent; a request to write a legislator about the impact of cuts in National Science Foundation funding on research in the social sciences; or a request to attend a pro-life demonstration. These solicitations may be associated with a social movement, but ordinarily they are not.

To attain this broader view of the solicitation of citizen activity, we start with the population, not with the successfully mobilized. That is, in order to look closely at everyday recruitment, we begin not with a particular movement but with a random sample of the public.[13] We are able to establish patterns of recruitment across the entire citizenry and thus not only to understand the workings of the recruitment process more generally but also to gain some perspective on the consequences of that process for inequalities in participation.[14]

We find that, when taken as a whole, the process by which citizens are asked by others to take part politically does not, by and large, mobilize excluded constituencies to politics. Rather, the overall thrust is to reinforce the tendencies of a participatory process anchored in long-term, ongoing participatory factors. Those who are, by dint of their motivation, capacity, and social location, more likely to be politically active are also more likely to be the targets of appeals for activity. In short, when viewed in its entirety, the process of citizen recruitment brings into politics activists who closely resem-

13. As we have at various points in this volume, in this chapter we use data from the Citizen Participation Study of 1990. As usual, we do so because it is the only survey that includes the array of variables needed for our analysis. Furthermore, it was conducted as a three-wave panel study. In this chapter we use the first two waves to assess the impact of participation in the past on political activity at a later time.

14. It may be useful to differentiate our use of surveys based on random population samples from the experimental strategy used by Alan S. Gerber and Donald P. Green to study voter mobilization. In an innovative field experiment, they considered the differential effect of three modes of mobilization: face to face, mail, and telephone. As they point out, randomly applying these different experimental treatments eliminates the bias that may exist in the selection process by which potential voters are chosen for contact. In contrast, because we are interested in precisely the processes they appropriately sought to control, we use a random sample to determine whether some kinds of people are more likely to be asked than others. Our interests converge with those of Gerber and Green when we ask, at the next stage of our analysis, who says yes in response to requests. See Alan S. Gerber and Donald P. Green, "The Effects of Canvassing, Telephone Calls, and Direct Mail on Voter Turnout: A Field Experiment," *American Political Science Review* 94 (2000): 653–663.

ble those who would have taken part spontaneously and does not mobilize the marginal and dispossessed.

How Much Recruitment?

Respondents in the Citizen Participation Study were asked whether, over the past twelve months, they had received any requests to take part in a campaign (to work in the campaign, to contribute money, or both); to contact a government official; to take part in a protest, march, or demonstration; or to take some active role in a public or political issue at the local level. If so, they were asked whether they said yes to the request—or to the most recent request if they had received more than one.[15] In addition, follow-up questions probed the characteristics of people making requests and the nature of their connections to respondents. We should make clear that the resulting data provide information about recruitment attempts and that what we know about the characteristics of recruiters is derived from reports of targets. Thus, to the extent that we are making inferences about the intentions of recruiters, we are doing so—in the best tradition of economists—on the basis of revealed preferences.

Appeals for political participation figure importantly across a variety of activities. As shown in Table 15.1, which presents a brief summary of these data, just over half of the respondents in our survey, 52 percent, reported having received a request over the past year to take part in at least one of the five kinds of activity about which we asked; of those asked, 53 percent said yes to at least one request. There is substantial variation across acts in terms of both the proportion asked to take part and the proportions who acceded to requests. Requests to contact public officials are both the most frequent and the most likely to be met with assent. In contrast, requests to protest are relatively infrequent and are much less likely to elicit cooperation.

Table 15.2 gives, for each form of participation, figures for the proportion of activists who acted spontaneously (that is, who either received no requests

15. The Citizen Participation Survey also posed questions about recruitment in particular venues: in a religious institution, in a voluntary association, or on the job. Because they yield much more detail about the range of requests for activity, throughout most of the rest of the chapter, we have used the responses to the recruitment questions about particular acts rather than those to the questions about particular recruitment venues. To check our results, we replicated the analysis using data about institution-based requests. The two approaches produce parallel results.

Table 15.1   Recruitment to Politics[a]

Type of Activity	Percentage Asked to Take Part	Percentage Who Said Yes (among Those Asked)
Campaign Work	12%	48%
Campaign Contribution	29%	32%
Contact	29%	57%
Protest	11%	28%
Community Activity	19%	50%
Any of These Five Activities	52%	53%

Source: Citizen Participation Study (1990).

[a] N = 2,517.

Table 15.2   Recruited and Spontaneous Political Activity[a]

	Percentage Active Spontaneously[b]	Percentage Active in Response to a Request[c]
Campaign Workers	63%	29%
Campaign Contributors	42%	31%
Contactors	51%	38%
Protesters	49%	43%
Community Activists	60%	30%
Those Participating in Any Activity	70%	42%

Source: Citizen Participation Study (1990).

[a] N = 2,517.
[b] Respondent either received no requests for activity or received one request and denied it.
[c] Respondent received at least one request to which he or she assented. Rows do not add up to 100 percent because cases in which the respondent received more than one request for a particular activity and declined the most recent one have been omitted.

to become active in that particular way or were asked once and did not say yes) and the proportion who acted in response to a recruitment attempt (that is, who assented to the most recent solicitation).[16] Once again, there was variation across acts, with campaign work and community involvement most likely—and making campaign contributions least likely—to be unambiguously spontaneous. In addition, 70 percent of those who engaged in any of the five listed activities undertook at least one spontaneously; 42 percent of those who engaged in any of the activities undertook at least one in response to a request. The data make clear that recruitment is an important factor in generating political activity—and therefore in influencing the accent of political voice—in the United States.

Recruitment and Equality: Who Is Recruited?

Our concern, however, is not with the question of how much recruitment there is but with the matter of who is targeted—not, that is, with the level but with the distribution of recruitment. Figure 15.1 sheds light on the issue of the impact of political recruitment on participatory stratification. For respondents in each of five groups defined by socio-economic status (SES)—that is, their education and income—Figure 15.1.A shows the percentage who were asked to take part in any of the five acts listed in Tables 15.1 and 15.2 and the percentage who undertook at least one of these five acts. As expected, the share who reported activity rises steeply across SES groups—as does the share who reported receiving at least one request for activity, which tracks actual activity quite closely. The data in Figure 15.1.B, which show the proportion in each socio-economic quintile that engaged in at least one such act as the result of a request and the proportion who engaged in at least one spontaneously, are more striking and perhaps more surprising. Predictably, those at the low end of the SES scale are least likely to be active, whether as the result of having been asked or on their own. What is noteworthy is that, across the SES quintiles, the variation in the likelihood of activity from a request is much greater than the variation in the likelihood of spontaneous action. Compared to those in the bottom SES quintile, those in the top SES quintile are six times as likely to have been active in response to a request and

---

16. We omit from the table those ambiguous cases in which the respondent reported more than one request for a particular kind of activity but said no to the most recent one. In these cases we cannot ascertain whether there had been assent to a previous request—even though the most recent one was turned down.

15.1.A Percentage Asked to be Active and Percentage Active

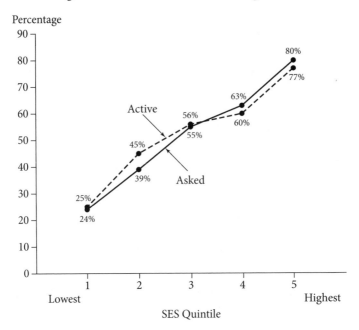

15.1.B Percentage Who Engaged in Recruited and Spontaneous Acts by SES Quintile

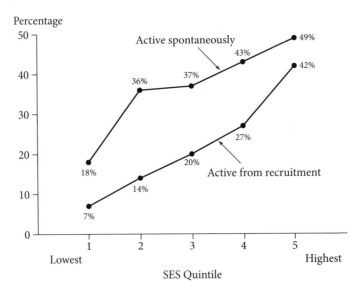

Figure 15.1 Political Recruitment and Political Activity by SES Quintile

Source: Citizen Participation Study (1990).

Note: The figure reflects the percentage asked to engage in at least 1 of 5 acts—working on a campaign, making a campaign contribution, contacting an official, protesting, taking part in community activity—and the percentage who engaged in at least one of the acts.

less than three times as likely to report having been active spontaneously. Thus, contrary to what might have been expected, processes of ordinary recruitment do not merely replicate the stratification of political participation but actually exaggerate it.

What about the recruitment of political contributions? We have made the point that, while a variety of factors predict most forms of political activity, a quite different configuration of variables predicts making financial contributions.[17] Not unexpectedly, compared to activities that depend more heavily on time rather than money, family income plays a much more important role with respect to making political contributions. Not only is family income a powerful variable in predicting who makes a contribution, but it is the overwhelming variable when it comes to predicting the *size* of the contribution. Because political recruiters so often seek cash, we wanted to assess the extent to which rational prospecting for contributions exacerbates participatory stratification. Those who make political contributions are, on average, more affluent than those who do not. Because those who ask others for political contributions target potential givers with large bank accounts, those who gave in response to a request are especially well heeled—with average family incomes of $56,400, compared with $48,000 for those who contributed spontaneously and $35,300 for those who did not contribute at all.[18]

Considering the size of the donation rather than the size of the pocketbook of the donor demonstrates especially clearly that recruiters look where the money is and find it. Contributions given spontaneously average $119—only a fraction of those given in response to a request, which average $350.[19] The three pie charts in Figure 15.2 make clear that the process by which contributors are recruited reinforces the participatory overrepresentation of the well heeled. Figure 15.2.A shows the share of campaign donors coming from each of the five SES quintiles. Figures 15.2.B and C shift the unit of analysis from individuals to dollars and present data on the proportion of campaign money that is contributed either spontaneously or in response to a request by each of these income groups. As expected, those with the highest socio-

17. Sidney Verba, Kay Lehman Schlozman, and Henry E. Brady, *Voice and Equality: Civic Voluntarism and American Politics* (Cambridge, MA: Harvard University Press, 1995), chap. 12. Voting also differs somewhat from other political acts with respect to the model that predicts activity. However, we do not have data on requests to go to the polls and thus cannot test whether the model that predicts voting turnout also predicts being asked to vote.

18. Note that these family incomes reflect the fact that the Citizen Participation Study was conducted in 1990.

19. Income predicts who is asked to donate, not who will say yes. Hence the pattern in these data reflects processes of selection by recruiters, not decisions to say yes by their targets.

15.2.A Distribution of Contributors by SES Quintiles

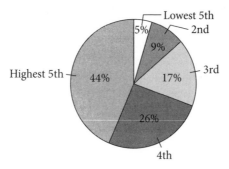

15.2.B Distribution of Political Dollars Given Spontaneously from SES Quintiles

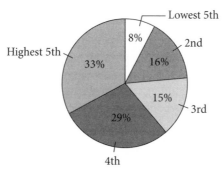

15.2.C Distribution of Political Dollars Given as a Result of Recruitment from SES Quintiles

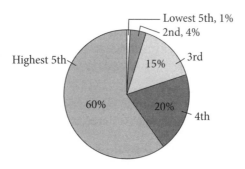

Figure 15.2 Where Do the Political Dollars Come From?

Source: Citizen Participation Study (1990).

economic status are more likely to make campaign contributions: 44 percent of the contributors come from the highest SES quintile and 5 percent from the lowest SES quintile. Of course, not only are those in the highest quintile more likely to give but they also write bigger checks when they contribute.

What is especially striking is the distinction between the dollars that are donated spontaneously and the dollars contributed in response to requests. The highest SES donors are responsible for 33 percent of all campaign money given spontaneously, while the lowest are responsible for only 8 percent. However, of the funds contributed in response to requests, three-fifths derive from the highest SES quintile and only 1 percent from the lowest SES quintile. Thus political contributions made spontaneously, while drawn disproportionately from the affluent, are, in fact, less sharply stratified by socioeconomic status than are those made as the result of assenting to a request.

Rational Prospecting:
The Everyday Process of Recruiting Participants

In an oft-quoted—and probably apocryphal—remark, Willy Sutton is said to have replied when asked why he robbed banks, "Because that's where the money is." The straightforward data presented in Figures 15.1 and 15.2 have made clear that, unlike processes of social movement mobilization, the ordinary processes through which people are asked to take part do not help to overcome the class bias in individual political voice. They do not even involve scattershot practices in which targets are selected at random, thus reproducing the socio-economic structuring of participation. It seems that those who wish to recruit others to politics—from professional fund-raisers in search of large campaign contributions to community residents concerned about the local crime rate—are heeding Sutton's advice. They act as "rational prospectors," seeking to expend their time and effort as efficiently as possible. The implicit strategy of the rational prospector would be to maximize the probability that the people they ask to get involved are the kinds of people who would be likely to say yes and, upon assenting, to participate effectively—by, for example, making a large rather than a small contribution or writing a compelling letter rather than an incoherent one.

Thus we conceive of the process of recruitment as having two stages: finding likely prospects to ask and then getting them to say yes in reply. In the first stage, the rational prospector uses information to assess whether potential targets are likely to have the capacity and inclination to be active. In the second stage, the rational prospector seeks to get these recruits to say yes by apprising them of participatory opportunities and of the gratifications attendant to activity.

We examine both parts of the process, delineating the characteristics of individuals that make them attractive prospects and then the characteristics that make them likely to say yes. In so doing, we are able to assess the impact of the recruitment process on the kinds of people who participate and thus on the kinds of people from whom the government hears. The process appears to reinforce rather than to diminish the participatory inequalities we have seen so consistently throughout our inquiry.

Stage 1: Using Information to Find Prospects

How does a rational prospector decide whether a particular prospect is likely to become active in response to a request to participate and, beyond that, whether the person has the capacity and motivation to participate in an effective manner? First, and most obviously, because previous activity is such a good indicator of the likelihood of future activity, a recruiter would want to know whether an individual has been active in the past. Beyond that, however, a canny recruiter would want to know whether prospects have other characteristics that might predispose them to take part in politics: the resources of time, money, or skills needed to take effective political action, as well as psychological engagement with politics—that is, political interest, knowledge, and efficacy. (We would, of course, like to believe that recruiters read the literature in political science but surmise that they use past experience rather than academic research to guide their quest.)

These characteristics—past activity, resources, and psychological engagement with politics—are, however, not equally apparent to the naked eye of the political recruiter. For example, because occupation and lifestyle are relatively observable, it would probably be easier to make a reasonably accurate guess about someone's income than about, say, his or her politically relevant civic skills or interest in politics. The amount of information a recruiter has about a prospect will depend on the prior relationship of the recruiter to the prospect. Information about the participation potential of targets of recruitment is enhanced by being socially close to the targets.

Stage 2: Getting to Yes

Having chosen a target, a recruiter needs to obtain acquiescence. Of course, selecting promising prospects maximizes the probability of assent. But, having made the selection, the rational recruiter can use two further tactics to obtain a positive response. First, the recruiter can apprise the prospect of participatory opportunities: a town meeting the prospect might want to attend, a phone bank that needs volunteers, or a campaign that could use some financial support. The recruiter may be providing new information or simply jogging the prospect's memory—as in the common "Just a reminder that the election is tomorrow."

Second—and perhaps more important—the recruiter can use various inducements to get the prospect to say yes. These can be of many sorts, including selective material benefits as well as such social rewards as meeting new friends or working with people one enjoys or the purposive gratifications attendant to fulfilling a civic obligation or furthering a worthwhile policy goal. Of special interest to us are inducements that involve some form of *leverage:* instances in which the relationship to a particular recruiter gives the prospect a special incentive to say yes. Relationships that entail the possibility of leverage might be of several kinds. Most obviously, when the person making the request has control over rewards or punishments, the appeal is more likely to be successful. An employer or supervisor is an example of someone commanding this kind of leverage. (It is for this reason that federal campaign finance regulations include many provisions concerning the circumstances under which employees can be solicited for donations to political action committees.)

We also need to consider an additional aspect of the relationship of the recruiter to the prospect. The likelihood of having good information and wielding some kind of leverage would seem to vary with the *closeness* of the recruiter to the prospect. In contrast to the recruiter who approaches a stranger, or even a friend of a friend, the recruiter who is personally acquainted with the prospect is certainly more likely to know about characteristics of the prospect that are relevant to participation—not just relatively visible ones like income but less apparent ones like political interest or concern about policy issues. In addition, close relationships enhance leverage. We tend to trust and to want to please those we know best. Devoting attention to targets to whom they are close has another virtue as well to rational prospectors, efficiency. Not only does closeness imply the likelihood of greater information and an enhanced ability to elicit affirmative responses, but rational prospectors will presumably find it easier to locate, connect with, and get the message across to those with whom they have close relationships. Connection through networks thus plays a role in finding prospects and getting them to say yes.[20]

---

20. There are numerous studies of processes of political activation through networks. On the effects of close interpersonal networks on participation, see David Knoke, "Networks of

To summarize the two-stage process, the rational prospector uses whatever information is available about activity in the past, participatory resources, and engagement with politics in order to locate likely prospects. Having located a prospect, the recruiter provides information about participatory opportunities and gratifications to get the prospect to say yes. The target of the request is more likely to acquiesce when there is leverage, perhaps in the form of a relationship—which may be of several kinds—that gives the recruit a special reason to say yes to this particular recruiter. The recruiter who is close to the target is more likely both to have information about the prospect's participatory potential and to be able to elicit assent.

Our analysis of the process by which political recruiters select their quarry sheds light on two underlying issues. The first is the one we have emphasized throughout: the consequences of that process for inequalities of citizen activity. The second is the rationality of political action. Political scientists have reached no consensus regarding whether citizens make rational cost–benefit analyses in choosing whether to take part politically.[21] Whether or not they engage in a rational process of balancing costs and benefits, it is clear that there is an array of possible rewards from political participation. These benefits can range from gaining a selective material benefit such as a job or government contract to feeling the satisfaction that comes from doing one's part to enjoying camaraderie with other activists. Like political activists, those who act as political recruiters may be pursuing a variety of benefits. Some become recruiters because they are paid to do so, others because they believe in a policy or cause or candidate, others because they have themselves been asked by a friend whom they do not want to offend. Regardless of whether the decision to become a recruiter involves a rational calculus, it seems fairly

Political Action: Toward Theory Construction," *Social Forces* 68 (1990): 1041–1063. Among the few studies of networks and electoral mobilization is Robert Huckfeldt and John Sprague, "Political Parties and Electoral Motivation: Political Structure, Social Structure, and the Party Canvass," *American Political Science Review* 80 (1992): 70–86. The important role of mobilization in explaining activity is stressed by Steven J. Rosenstone and John Mark Hansen in *Mobilization, Participation and Democracy in America* (New York: Macmillan, 1993). In contrast to our emphasis, they focus not on the more proximate interpersonal networks within which citizens live but on the role of strategic elites in mobilizing citizens. For a review of contextual studies, see Robert Huckfeldt and John Sprague, "Citizens, Contexts, and Politics," in *Political Science: The State of the Discipline,* 2nd ed., ed. Ada W. Finifter (Washington, DC: American Political Science Association, 1993), pp. 281–303.

21. On this ongoing debate and references to the literature, see Kay Lehman Schlozman, Sidney Verba, and Henry E. Brady, "Participation's Not a Paradox: The View from American Activists," *British Journal of Political Science* 25 (1995): 1–36.

clear that, once they have made that decision, recruiters behave rationally in locating targets. They seek out prospects who are likely to acquiesce to a request and who will be effective as political participants when they are active.

Finding Likely Activists

Even if rational recruiters do not rush to the library to consult the scholarly literature on the subject, the factors on which they base their predictions as to who would be an attractive target should match fairly closely the factors that actually predict participation. Thus, in choosing potential recruits who can and will participate effectively, they would look for targets who are psychologically engaged with politics—who are politically interested, informed, and efficacious. In addition, they would seek those who command politically relevant resources, in particular education, money, and civic skills—the organizational and communication skills that are acquired in school and, during adulthood, on the job, in church, and in nonpolitical organizations.

Table 15.3 presents the results of three analyses, all of which include a scale measuring psychological engagement with politics and such political resources as education, income, and civic skills, along with controls for standard demographic characteristics (gender, race or ethnicity, and age). The models in sections A and B of Table 15.3 allow us to compare the role of these participatory factors in predicting, first, political participation and, then, recruitment to political activity. In section A, the dependent variable is a scale of the number of political acts in which the individual engaged over the past twelve months; in section B, the dependent variable is a scale of the number of requests for political activity that a respondent received in the same time period.[22] If our argument is correct, these factors should perform similarly in explaining both actual political activity and requests for activity.

The analyses make clear that, in selecting individuals to contact, recruiters use criteria quite similar to the factors that predict participation. They target those who are psychologically engaged with politics—interested, informed, and efficacious—and those who have the critical political resources of education, money, and skills. That the same factors that propel political activity also affect being asked to take part in politics is consistent with the notions of

---

22. The dependent variable in Table 15.3.A includes the five political acts for which we asked the questions about recruitment (voting, doing campaign work, making campaign contributions, contacting an official, and taking part in a protest). The dependent variable in Table 15.3.B is the number of requests for these five activities.

Table 15.3 Predicting Activity and Recruitment:
Ordinary Least Squares (OLS) Regressions

	B	SE B	Beta
A. Predicting Activity[a]			
Education	.09***	.02	.13
Family Income	.03***	.01	.10
Political Engagement	.08***	.01	.32
Political Skills	.08***	.01	.17
(Constant)	−1.30***	.13	
B. Predicting Recruitment[b]			
Education	.16***	.02	.20
Family Income	.04***	.01	.10
Political Engagement	.07***	.01	.26
Political Skills	.07***	.01	.14
(Constant)	−1.28***	.14	
C. Predicting Activity from Recruitment[a]			
Previous Activity	.40***	.02	.39
Education	.02	.01	.03
Family Income	.00	.01	.01
Political Engagement	.03***	.00	.14
Political Skills	.03***	.01	.07
Recruited	.26***	.02	.29
(Constant)	−.49***	.10	

Source: Citizen Participation Study (1990).

Note: *Significant at the .05 level; **significant at the .01 level; ***significant at the .001 level.

[a] Dependent variable: five-act additive scale of political participation (the acts were voting, doing campaign work, making campaign contributions, contacting an official, and taking part in a protest). Gender, race, ethnicity, and age were included in the equation but not reported.
[b] Dependent variable: five-act additive scale of requests for political participation. Gender, race, ethnicity, and age were included in the equation but not reported.

rational expectations.[23] In addition, the fact that the criteria recruiters use to select potential participants are similar to the characteristics that would ordinarily lead people to participate strongly suggests that whatever biases are built into the processes of becoming active will be mirrored—indeed perhaps magnified—in the mobilized population.

Section C of Table 15.3 uses many of the same variables to ask a different question, one that underlies this whole enterprise: Does recruitment lead to participation? If requests for participation do not generate activity, we do not need to worry about their consequences for political equality. Section C adds two additional factors to the model predicting political participation, a measure of past political activity, which imposes a tough test, and the number of participatory acts (of the five in the dependent variable) for which the respondent received a request. Section C shows that, even after we account for a respondent's activity in the past, being asked to take part is closely related to activity.[24]

Closeness and Recruitment

We have suggested that recruiters who have close relationships to those they approach have two advantages: they are more likely to have information about the activity potential of the targets and more likely to have the leverage that makes acquiescence to a request probable. Thus a close relationship between prospector and quarry has implications for both steps of the two-stage process

23. We should note that rational expectations models usually require something much stronger: expectations must not only be formed using all available information but they must also use this information in an efficient and unbiased way. See Steve Sheffrin, *Rational Expectations* (New York: Cambridge University Press, 1983), and Clifford L. F. Attfield, David Demery, and Nigel W. Duck, *Rational Expectations in Macroeconomics: An Introduction to Theory and Evidence* (Oxford, England: Blackwell, 1991). If all prospectors had the same information about prospects—a very strong and unlikely assumption—this conception of rational expectations requires not only that expectations be based on the same factors that appear in the predictive equation for activity but that the factors be combined in the same proportions for the two equations, because this provides the most efficient and unbiased estimate of who might participate. For a test for this proportionality, see Brady, Schlozman, and Verba, "Prospecting for Participants," Appendix D.

24. The dependent variable, political activity, is measured in our second-wave survey, as are the recruitment measure political engagement, civic skills, and the other demographic controls. By using an activity measure from our first wave as a control in this regression we increase the likelihood that the positive relationship between recruitment and activity that we find in our second-wave survey reflects the effect of recruitment on activity rather than an effect of contemporaneous activity on recruitment.

of recruitment—facilitating the location of attractive prospects and enhancing the likelihood that they will say yes. In this section, where we focus on explaining who is asked to take part, we consider whether a close relationship seems to increase information; in the next section, where we turn to the issue of eliciting a positive reply, we consider whether it seems to increase leverage.

Included in the battery of items about attempts at political recruitment were questions about whether the person making the request for activity was someone known personally, someone in a secondary network (that is, a friend of a friend or someone whose name was recognized), or a complete stranger. Thus we can look separately at the factors that predict recruitment by a stranger and the factors that predict recruitment by someone whom the recruiter knows. This should provide a powerful test of our model of the way in which recruiters use available information to seek out potential activists. While strangers would have to rely for their cues on more visible characteristics, recruiters who have close relationships with those they approach would probably be in a better position to assess less readily apparent characteristics related to participation.

To explore what information a rational recruiter might use to predict participation, and thus to choose people to contact, we use the set of variables in Table 15.3, including the measure of the prospect's past political activity. We distinguish these variables in terms of the likelihood that they would be visible to a stranger or only to someone who is known personally:

- *More visible characteristics:* Among the characteristics that are sufficiently visible that even a stranger might have information about them are the recruit's educational level and family income. Prospects' past political activity is probably more visible than is their political interest or efficacy or their willingness to cooperate. Even strangers, especially those with ties to political parties or organizations, might have information about previous activity from, for example, lists of contributors or volunteers.

- *Less visible characteristics:* Among the characteristics less likely to be known by strangers than by persons who are close to the potential recruit—or by an interviewer who has spent a couple of hours in face-to-face discussion with a respondent—are the potential recruit's civic skills and psychological engagement with politics (as measured by a scale that includes political interest, information, and efficacy).

Table 15.4   Predicting Recruitment by Someone Known
or by a Stranger: OLS Regressions

	B	SE B	Beta
A. Predicting Recruitment by a Stranger[a]			
Previous Activity	.02*	.01	.05
Education	.07***	.01	.20
Family Income	.01*	.00	.05
Political Engagement	.01	.00	.04
Political Skills	.00	.01	.01
(Constant)	−.21	.07	
B. Recruitment by Someone Known[a]			
Previous Activity	.24***	.01	.35
Education	.02*	.01	.05
Family Income	.00	.00	.00
Political Engagement	.02***	.00	.11
Political Skills	.03***	.01	.09
(Constant)	−.40***	.09	

Source: Citizen Participation Study (1990).

Note: *Significant at the .05 level; **significant at the .01 level; ***significant at the .001 level.

[a] Dependent variable: The five-act additive scale of requests for political participation (the acts were voting, working in a campaign, making campaign contributions, contacting an official, and taking part in a protest). Gender, race, ethnicity, and age are included in the equation but not reported.

Table 15.4 reports the results of regression analyses using these factors to predict receiving requests for activity from strangers (A) and from people known to the respondent (B).[25] The differences between the factors that predict being asked by someone known personally and by a stranger are quite striking and consistent with our expectations. Strangers seem to rely on visible aspects of social status—in particular, education—but do not appear to use information about less visible characteristics such as the target's civic

25. The dependent variables are the number of times (out of five possible) a respondent was asked to be active either by a stranger or by someone known personally.

skills or degree of psychological engagement with politics.[26] In contrast, recruiters who have personal relationships with their targets make less use of visible characteristics. Unlike strangers, friends and acquaintances rely heavily on less visible characteristics such as the recruit's civic skills and psychological engagement with politics. Note, finally, that past activity predicts requests from both strangers and, especially, friends.

The overall pattern of these data offers strong support for the role we ascribe to information in our rational prospecting model. Close relationships appear to improve information, information that is useful in making decisions about whom to approach with requests for activity.

Closing the Deal

Along with salesmen and fund-raisers, those who seek to recruit others to political activity must, as we have said, go through a two-stage process: they must locate the prospect; then they must close the deal. We have considered the first stage, in which rational prospectors select whom to approach. Now we turn to the issue of whether, and under what conditions, requests for activity are successful.

We might expect that what leads prospects to assent to requests would be similar to whatever led to their being asked. After all, rational recruiters select prospects they deem most promising. Nevertheless, the fact that this is a two-stage process suggests that we should be sensitive to differences between the stages. Indeed, if recruiters have done their work well in stage one, the characteristics that led them to choose whom to ask should be relatively useless in predicting acquiescence. If recruiters have perfect—or at least very good—information about the likelihood of acquiescence, then there would be no systematic variables predicting acquiescence among those contacted because these factors would have been taken into account in the process of deciding whom to ask. That is, knowing the key variables that predispose someone to be active and selecting targets on the basis of these variables means that the initial selection criteria should be of little use in predicting who will assent once asked. Whether the recruitment attempt is successful in eliciting a yes will depend on random factors or unmeasured variables not built into the selection process.

---

26. This is not to say that anonymous recruiters necessarily know the level of education or occupational status of all of those they contact. Rather, such impersonal recruiters may use surrogate measures—for example, zip code—to make reasonable inferences.

We can clarify this logic by drawing an analogy to the selection process in college admissions. If SAT scores and high school grades are good predictors of the ability to do well in college and they become the selection criteria for admissions, they are no longer potent predictors of who, among the admitted class, will do well in college.[27] In short, the better the selection process, the less well the variables used in that process will do in predicting the next stage— whether the outcome in that stage is academic success in college or agreement to become politically active.

Of course, predictive models are never perfect. There are always variables that cannot be measured well and that may, therefore, have an effect on stage two. Information on SATs or high school grades is easily available, but information on the potential for adjustment to college or perseverance may be harder to acquire. These less visible factors may then play a greater role in determining how well someone does in college. Similarly, when it comes to requests for activity, the rational prospector has better information on some characteristics than on others. Presumably it is easier to ascertain—or estimate—the demographic characteristics of potential activists than to know what they think. We may know that someone lives in a large house in a neighborhood where most people have gone to college, traits obviously associated with high levels of political participation. It is more difficult to know about someone's interest in politics or sense of political efficacy. Thus, if recruiters are doing their jobs well, they will make good use of measurable information in selecting prospects, which, in turn, will make those characteristics less useful for predicting the second stage, saying yes. However, the characteristics that are less well measured by the recruiter should still have predictive power.

In addition, we have argued that rational prospectors should select people over whom they have some leverage or with whom they have some kind of relationship that would enhance the likelihood that the prospects would say yes *to them*. As mentioned, several kinds of relationships suggest themselves as having the potential for giving a targeted recruit added incentive to comply with a request. Anyone who controls important rewards or punishments—a boss is an obvious example—would seem to be in a privileged position when making requests.[28] Similarly, because we ordinarily seek not to offend those to whom we are close, when there is a close relationship between recruiter

27. See Christopher Achen, *The Statistical Analysis of Quasi-Experiments* (Berkeley: University of California Press, 1986).

28. In fact, supervisors at work have the highest success rate: fully 70 percent of those asked by a supervisor acceded to the request.

and prospect, the probability that the request will be met with assent should increase. In addition, the potential bonds of identification created by congruence of race or gender should also raise the likelihood of a positive response to a request.[29]

To test these expectations, we turn our attention to predicting successful recruitment, not just recruitment. In order to see how various characteristics affect obtaining a positive answer—especially when those characteristics involve some relationship of the recruiter to the recruit—we must connect the characteristics of prospectors and targets. We asked about the relationship of the recruiter to the recruit separately for each request received by the respondent. Because, for example, the request to contact an official came from a neighbor while the one to contribute to a campaign came from a stranger who phoned, we must make that linkage separately for each request. Thus in Table 15.5 we change the unit of analysis from the individual respondent to a particular request and the dependent variable from the number of requests received by an individual to saying yes to that particular request.[30] The explanatory variables are the set of factors we have used to explain requests for participation plus additional variables capturing the relationship of the recruiter to the recruit.[31]

Consider first the variables that we have used thus far to explain the receipt of a request: the visible and less visible characteristics of the recruit. Earlier we saw that such overt characteristics as income and education play a significant role in predicting who will be asked to become active in politics. However, the data in Table 15.5 make clear that, when it comes to predicting who will say yes once asked, these factors recede in significance and

29. The addition of leverage to our analysis illustrates another way in which our approach involves assumptions other than those in standard rational expectations work. Standard uses of that approach do not assume any market power on the part of the individual. An individual may forecast the inflation rate but is not expected to be able, as an individual, to influence that rate. In the political recruitment case, the recruiter is in a position to influence the outcome.

30. The dependent variable is, in fact, a trichotomy: saying no, saying yes in part, and saying yes.

31. To perform this regression, we first identified all those cases in which an individual was asked to perform an activity. If a respondent was not asked to perform any activity, the respondent does not appear in the regression. If the respondent was asked to perform one or more activity, he or she appears in the analysis once for each act for which there was a request. We then stacked the requests for each activity into one regression equation to constrain the independent variables to have the same impact across all of the activities. To allow for different baseline rates of saying yes, we included separate intercepts for all but one of the activities. For additional technical information, see Brady, Schlozman and Verba, "Prospecting for Participants," p. 160, n. 19.

Table 15.5 Getting to "Yes"—Predicting a Positive Response
to a Request to Become Involved Politically: OLS Regression

	B	SE B	Beta
Visible Characteristics			
Education	−.01	.01	−.02
Family Income	.00	.00	.04
Job Level	.00	.01	.02
Organized Affiliations	−.02	.02	−.02
Less Visible Characteristics			
Civic Skills	.01	.00	.04
Engagement	.02***	.00	.12
Cooperativeness	.04*	.02	.04
Personal Leverage of Recruiter			
Personal Friend or Relative	.28***	.03	.28
Secondary Connection	.08**	.03	.08
Job Supervisor	.16**	.05	.06
Demographic Similarity or Difference			
Black Asked Black	.12*	.06	.04
Black Asked White	.09	.07	.03
White Asked Black	.04	.07	.01
Woman Asked Woman	.11***	.03	.09
Woman Asked Man	.09*	.04	.05
Man Asked Woman	.05	.03	.04
(Constant)	−.46***	.14	

Source: Citizen Participation Study (1990).

Note: Weighted sample size: 2,210. *Significant at the .05 level; **significant at the
.01 level; ***significant at the .001 level. Citizenship status, whether English was
spoken at home, working or retired status, Catholic religious preference and
religious attendance, and age dummies as well controls for the particular act for
which the request was made were also included but not reported.

the less conspicuous factor of the recruit's psychological engagement in politics comes to the fore.[32]

With respect to the relationship of the recruiter to the recruit, we add two dummy variables measuring personal closeness. The first is positive if the

---

32. We have not included past activity among the characteristics that might predict a person's saying yes to a request. We used it in the analysis that predicted being asked to be active

recruit reported having been solicited by someone who was known personally. The second is positive if the recruit reported having been solicited by
someone with a secondary connection, that is, someone who knows someone whom the recruit knows. Recruiters who are not personally acquainted
with their targets can often establish a connection by mentioning someone
known in common.[33] We also include a dummy variable that is positive if the
recruiter is the prospect's supervisor at work. Finally, we include several variables measuring correspondence between recruiter and recruit in terms of
gender and race.[34]

The results presented in Table 15.5 indicate that recruiters will make significant improvements in the probability of a positive response if they target
people with whom they have close relationships. Compared to those who
make requests of strangers, recruiters who know their targets personally are
substantially more likely to elicit a positive reply. Recruiters who have a secondary connection also do better than strangers, although, as we would expect,
not as much better as those who ask someone they know. Targeting someone
over whom one exercises supervisory authority at work also increases the
likelihood of a yes. In addition, compared to a white person asking a white
person, recruitment across race lines—a black person asking a white person
or vice versa—does not affect the likelihood of acceptance. However, recruitment between African Americans tends to be more successful. Finally, when
women ask one another, they are somewhat more likely to get a positive
answer than when men make requests of each other.[35] In short, a rational

under the assumption that this was information for a recruiter to use in deciding whom to
ask. In this instance, it seemed to us to represent a redundancy, because the impact of previous activity had been felt at the first stage. We did analyze the data in Table 15.5 with the measure of previous activity in the analysis, and the general contours of the results are similar.
Including that measure does not change our overall story.

33. The omitted category in relation to these two dummy variables is requests from
strangers.

34. One set of dummy variables measures various combinations with respect to gender (a
woman asking a woman, a woman asking a man, a man asking a woman), with a man asking
a man as the omitted category. Another measures various combinations of racial similarity (a
black being asked by a black, a black being asked by a white, and a white being asked by a
black). The omitted category, which includes people of other races as well as cases in which
the race of the recruiter is unknown, overwhelmingly consists of cases in which both the
recruiter and the target were white.

35. Further analysis demonstrates that requests for activity disproportionately bring together recruiters and targets who share gender or race or ethnicity. When the gender or race
or ethnicity of the recruiter does not match that of the target, there is an additional pattern:

prospector will benefit from having a personal connection, from being boss, and, to some extent, from certain kinds of demographic congruence.

Because those who ask others to become active politically seek individuals with characteristics—among them, high levels of income and education—that would predispose them to participate in politics, we now can understand the fallacy of our original conjecture that processes of recruitment might operate to overcome the ordinary biases in political participation in favor of the advantaged. If the same factors are associated with both being asked to be politically active and actually being politically active, those who take part as the result of requests would not differ from those who act on their own. That many participatory acts result from requests by people who know their targets personally reinforces these processes. If they use any information they have based on personal connections to find recruits and their personal ties to induce potential recruits to say yes, those who focus their recruitment efforts on those to whom they are close are especially likely to generate political activity from the ranks of the SES-advantaged group. Thus, in contrast to social movements, which sometimes activate less advantaged groups into politics, ordinary processes of recruitment seem to exaggerate the patterns already evident in political participation.

Political Parties and the Recruitment of Activity

Political parties function as an important engine of political recruitment. In a democracy, an important function of political parties, especially parties of the left, is the mobilization of ordinary citizens—in particular, those who might not otherwise be active. During the nineteenth century, strong political parties played a critical role in organizing and mobilizing voters in America—or at least the white males among them—regardless of class or immigrant status. Recent scholarship about the role of American parties in mobilizing publics for political action has focused, in particular, on immigrants. There is recognition that the incorporation of the foreign born into politics depends on a variety of factors, including their nation of origin, the length of their stay in the United States, their command of English, and many aspects of the communities in which they settle.[36] Nonetheless, no one argues that contem-

---

men are more likely to ask women than vice versa and Anglo whites are more likely to ask African Americans or Latinos than vice versa.

36. See the analyses and references in, among others, Janelle Wong, *Democracy's Promise: Immigrants and American Civic Institutions* (Ann Arbor: University of Michigan Press, 2006),

porary American political parties mobilize lower-SES or immigrant voters as effectively as they once did. Besides, they are well known for being weak and fragmented, and there are no working-class or peasant parties.

In order to assess the parties' efforts to mobilize voters, we use an item in the American National Election Studies (ANES) asking respondents whether anyone from the political parties had gotten in touch with them about the campaign.[37] In Figure 15.3 we combine the respondents from the ANES from 1956 to 2008 and array them in terms of SES percentiles. The data make clear that a majority of respondents never hear from someone connected with either of the parties but that the probability that a voter has been contacted rises sharply with socio-economic status. Both parties are more likely to attempt to mobilize upper-SES voters than those in the middle or, especially, in the lowest SES ranks. The curve is, not surprisingly, especially steep for the Republican Party. Still, it is striking that the Democrats are also acting as rational prospectors—targeting those higher on the SES ladder.[38]

Although the combined ANES data allow us to understand the pattern of party mobilization over very fine gradations of SES, these data conflate party efforts over more than a half century. By disaggregating these data, we can investigate the trajectory over time. The failure of modern parties to get voters to the polls has been linked to the low levels of voter turnout in the last decades of the twentieth century. Relying on the same ANES question, Rosenstone and Hansen noted in a 1993 book that this kind of party-based voter recruitment began to decline dramatically for both parties starting in

---

esp. chaps. 3 and 9; S. Karthick Ramakrishnan and Irene Bloemraad, "Introduction: Civic and Political Inequalities," in *Civic Hopes and Political Realities*, ed. S. Karthick Ramakrishnan and Irene Bloemraad (New York: Russell Sage Foundation, 2008), chap. 1; and Kristi Andersen, *New Immigrant Communities: Finding a Place in Local Politics* (Boulder, CO: Lynne Rienner, 2010), esp. chaps. 1, 2, and 5.

The received wisdom of the effectiveness of the historical urban party machines in bringing immigrants into politics has come in for some revision. See, for example, Steven Erie, *Rainbow's End: Irish Americans and the Dilemmas of Urban Machine Politics, 1840–1985* (Berkeley: University of California Press, 1988), and Gerald Gamm, *The Making of New Deal Democrats* (Chicago: University of Chicago Press, 1989).

37. The ANES item is worded as follows: "As you know, the political parties try to talk to as many people as they can to get them to vote for their candidate. Did anyone from one of the political parties call you up or come around and talk to you about the campaign this year?"

38. The parties act as rational prospectors in another way. Data not shown indicate, not surprisingly, that these processes of strategic recruitment are likely to occur within parties. The Republican Party is more likely to get in touch with Republicans in the electorate and the Democratic Party to get in touch with Democrats.

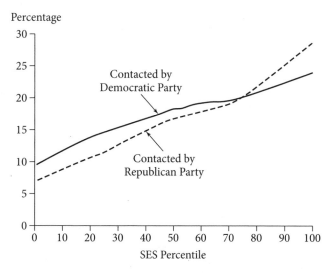

Percentage

Figure 15.3 To Whom Do the Parties Talk during a Campaign? Percentage of Respondents Contacted by Democratic Party or Republican Party by SES Percentiles

Source: American National Election Studies (1956–2008).

Note: Data smoothed using a LOESS smooth of 40 percent.

the 1970s and argued that a major cause of turnout decline was the decrease in mobilization by the political parties.[39]

Figure 15.4.A shows for Republicans, and Figure 15.4.B for Democrats, the rates of contacting over a half century for three groups of voters—the top, middle, and lowest SES quintiles—bringing the data up to 2008. It turns out that Rosenstone and Hansen's book was published just when party recruitment efforts were at their low point. In fact, the contacting of voters rebounded dramatically in both parties in the 1990s. Moreover, Figure 15.4 makes clear that the pattern we observed in Figure 15.3 obtains across the entire period:

39. Rosenstone and Hansen, *Mobilization, Participation and Democracy in America.* Rosenstone and Hansen's claim is disputed by Kenneth M. Goldstein and Travis N. Ridout, who in "The Politics of Participation: Mobilization and Turnout over Time," *Political Behavior* 24 (2002): 3–29, argue that the rate of contacting had not declined significantly as of 1996 even though turnout had declined. Their article suggests that the story of turnout decline may be more complicated than simply the decline in party efforts to get out the vote, but they do not really dispute the notion that party efforts to contact people can get them to turn out to vote. Their study does not include more recent data presented here.

15.4.A Contacting by Republican Party

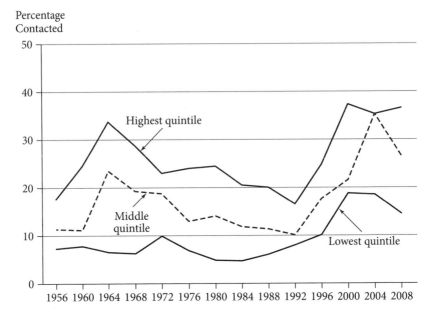

15.4.B Contacting by Democratic Party

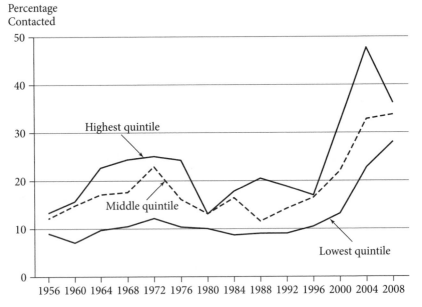

Figure 15.4 Contacting over Time by Republican Party and Democratic Party for SES Quintiles, 1956–2008

Source: American National Election Studies (1956–2008).

the parties are considerably more likely to target upper-SES voters. Because upper-SES voters are disproportionately likely to vote Republican, it is not unexpected that, as shown Figure 15.4.A, Republican Party efforts to contact voters show a class gap throughout the period. It is noteworthy that the class stratification of Republican Party efforts to mobilize voters seems to have diminished somewhat in recent years. Strikingly, the strategy of targeting upper-SES voters obtains for the Democratic Party as well. Consistent with Figure 15.3, the pattern shown in Figure 15.4.B is less pronounced than for the Republican Party; however, Democrats are very unlikely to seek to mobilize the lower-SES voters, whose enhanced turnout would, presumably, be electorally helpful to them.[40]

Figure 15.5, which shows the ratio of the top quintile to the bottom quintile separately for recruitment by the Republican Party and the Democratic Party, uses LOESS smoothing and clarifies the patterns. As we have seen, while the socio-economic stratification in voter contacts is more pronounced, though diminishing, for the Republican than for the Democratic Party, both parties engage in class-based rational prospecting.

Data from the 1990 Citizen Participation Study about requests from fellow partisans for more demanding forms of electoral involvement reinforce our conclusions about the implications for political voice of recruitment through partisan networks. Table 15.6 shows, not surprisingly, that Republican identifiers had incomes that were, on average, higher—and Democratic identifiers had incomes that were, on average, lower—than the average for the population. It also shows, again not surprisingly, that those who were recruited to work in campaigns—and especially those who were recruited to contribute to campaigns—had higher-than-average incomes, higher even than the average for Republican identifiers.

Focusing more narrowly on requests by fellow partisans, the intraparty nexus involves recruitment of targets who were, on average, higher in income than the average for their respective parties.[41] While the partisan difference is

---

40. We would have liked to repeat this analysis separating native born from foreign born. Unfortunately, however, the ANES has not asked about immigrant status consistently over time.

41. In contrast to the items from the ANES, the questions about requests for political activity from the 1990 Citizen Participation Study asked about the party leanings (if known) of the person making the request. Thus a request from a fellow partisan might have been made on behalf of the party, or it might have come from a neighbor or coworker who happened to share party loyalties.

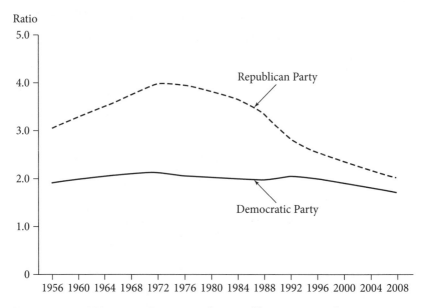

Figure 15.5   SES Bias in Contacting by Republican Party and Democratic Party: Ratio of Contacting over Time for Highest to Lowest SES Quintile, 1956–2008

Source: American National Election Studies (1956–2008).

Note: Data smoothed using a LOESS smooth of 70%.

also present in this instance—with Republican activists more affluent than Democratic ones—it is clear that rational prospecting within the parties does not broaden the spectrum of political activists. For contributions, the pattern is especially noteworthy. Those asked by a fellow partisan had, on average, incomes that were quite high. When Democrats solicited Democrats—and especially when Republicans solicited Republicans—the targets of the requests had family incomes that were not only higher than the average incomes for their fellow partisans but also higher than the average for all who were asked to contribute.

In short, while parties have unambiguously played an important historical role in mobilizing voters who might otherwise not go to the polls and in representing the concerns of broad groups whose views might otherwise not be voiced, in terms of who they bring in as activists, the result is more mixed. Especially when seeking contributions, the parties hunt where the ducks are and target the affluent among their supporters.

Table 15.6 Family Income and Recruitment to Campaign Activity—
The Partisan Connection

	Average Family Income
All Respondents	$40,400
All Republican Identifiers	$46,500
All Democratic Identifiers	$36,300
All Who Were Asked to Work in a Campaign	$50,000
Republican Asked by a Republican	$55,700
Democrat Asked by a Democrat	$52,800
All Who Were Asked to Contribute to a Campaign	$52,700
Republican Asked by a Republican	$59,300
Democrat Asked by a Democrat	$56,400

Source: Citizen Participation Study (1990).

A Note on Recruitment within
Religious Institutions

In Chapter 6 we noted a contrast between religious and political life: the former is much less likely to be structured by socio-economic status than is the latter. In view of the extent to which participation in religious institutions is equal across the SES hierarchy, we were curious to know how processes of recruitment to politics operate within religious institutions. Figure 15.6 shows that, while attendance at religious services does not vary with socio-economic status, the absence of SES structuring does not extend to the recruitment of political participation.[42] The solid line shows that there is essentially no variation across SES quintiles in the proportion of respondents who reported attending religious services at least once a week. In contrast, the dashed line shows a fairly sharp increase across SES quintiles in the proportion of frequent church attenders who indicated having been asked by someone in their church, synagogue, or other religious institution—a member of the clergy or someone in an official position—to take some political action on a

42. In Chapter 6 we noted that the past decade has witnessed the emergence of a slight positive relationship between education and religious attendance that does not show up in these 1990 data. See also Robert D. Putnam and David E. Campbell, *American Grace: How Religion Divides and Unites Us* (New York: Simon and Schuster, 2010), pp. 252–253.

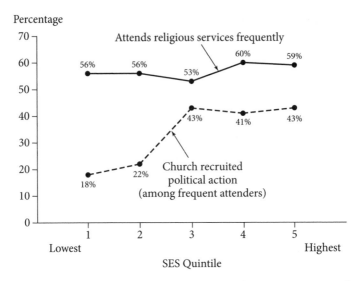

Figure 15.6   Attendance at Religious Services and Recruitment to Politics within a Religious Institution by SES Quintile

Source: Citizen Participation Study (1990).

Note: Recruiting refers to being asked by someone in one's church, synagogue, or other religious institution—by a member of the clergy or someone in an official position—to take some political action on a local or national political issue, such as signing a petition, writing a letter, going to a meeting, attending a protest or march, or getting in touch with a public official.

local or national political issue such as signing a petition, writing a letter, going to a meeting, attending a protest or march, or getting in touch with a public official.

Because religious institutions have so often provided the infrastructure for political and social protest, especially for African Americans, we were curious to know whether the pattern of church-based strategic targeting obtained within racial and ethnic groups. As shown in Figure 15.7, which once again presents data about those who attend services at least once a week, non-Hispanic whites and Latinos show a similar upward trajectory across SES quintiles. The data about blacks are particularly striking—showing both a high level and a remarkably class-structured pattern of church-based political recruitment. Clearly there is rational prospecting within religious institutions as well as outside them.

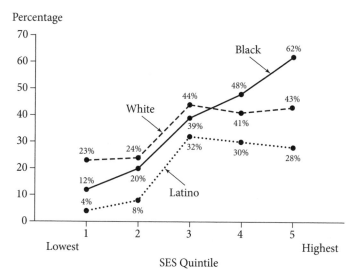

Figure 15.7   Political Action Suggested within a Religious Institution by Race or Ethnicity and SES Quintile: Percentage Asked to Take Political Action (Frequent Religious Service Attendees Only)

Source: Citizen Participation Study (1990).

Note: Recruiting refers to being asked by someone in one's church, synagogue, or other religious institution—by a member of the clergy or someone in an official position—to take some political action on a local or national political issue such as signing a petition, writing a letter, going to a meeting, attending a protest or march, or getting in touch with a public official.

Recruitment and the Bias in Citizen Participation

Social scientists are often interested in social movements and processes of political mobilization because they bring into politics new and unrepresented publics. We have undertaken a novel approach to the political mobilization and recruitment of citizens. Rather than looking at particular social movements, we started with a random sample of the population to see how the recruitment process, seen comprehensively, brings citizens to politics. Our results illustrate, once again, that methods count: conclusions based on systematic sampling modify those based on case studies. It is not that studies of social movements are inaccurate; they just give a partial picture.

We have presented the contours of a structured process by which rational prospectors seek targets with the characteristics that would predispose them to agree to a request for activity and to take part effectively when they do. The implicit model is one that mirrors the process by which citizens self-select into politics spontaneously. Whether they use as cues the socio-economic characteristics associated with participation in politics—or use what is perhaps the best indicator of future potential to participate, previous activity in politics—recruiters target citizens who are politically engaged and who have the resources to be active. In addition to selecting people who might participate on their own, they seek prospects over whom they have some leverage—some connection that would make the targets feel a special constraint to say yes. Critical to the process is information. The more recruiters know, the more likely they are to select promising targets. Because close relationships increase information and leverage, rational recruiters look close to home—contacting people they know. When they do so, they are more likely to locate targets with the relevant characteristics, to elicit a positive reply, and to produce effective participation.

Taken in its totality, the process by which individuals are asked by others to become active politically appears to parallel the process by which individuals come to participate on their own. However, because rational prospectors target recruits who possess attributes that are associated with participation, those brought into politics by recruiters actually exaggerate the traits characteristic of activists. Although this pattern holds for all forms of participation, it pertains especially to campaign contributions. Money is the most unequally distributed of inputs into American politics, and political recruiters exacerbate participatory inequalities by locating an affluent group of potential donors who proceed to give especially generously. The result is that policy makers in America hear even more disproportionately from those who command the resources that make participation possible. In the aggregate, processes of recruitment whereby citizens are asked by others to become involved are less likely to transform than to replicate the representational outcomes of a participatory system in which the privileged speak more loudly than the disadvantaged.

16

Weapon of the Strong?
Participatory Inequality and the Internet

The Internet has changed the way we shop, play games, make airline reservations, and keep up with friends. Among the still unfolding consequences of the Internet are the possibilities it opens up for disseminating messages to large numbers of like-minded people and coordinating them for joint action.[1] An early and still amusing example of the Internet's capacities for viral communication is contained in Jonah Peretti's account of his attempt to take advantage of Nike's 2000 offer to order customized shoes over the Internet. As a way of making a statement about Nike's labor practices, he sought to have his shoes customized with the word *sweatshop*. What ensued was a series of e-mails in which Peretti politely challenged each of Nike's successive excuses for refusing to fill his order. After it became clear that Nike would not honor an order for "sweatshop" shoes, Peretti fired off a final request—to which, not surprisingly, he received no reply—asking, "Could you please send me a snapshot of the ten-year-old Vietnamese girl who makes my shoes?" Then he forwarded the exchange to a few friends for their entertainment. They, in turn, passed it on until eventually an estimated 11.4 million people received the e-mails.[2]

---

1. This chapter draws directly from two previously published articles: Kay Lehman Schlozman, Sidney Verba, and Henry E. Brady, "Weapon of the Strong? Participatory Inequality and the Internet," *Perspectives on Politics* 8 (2010): 487–510, and Kay Lehman Schlozman, Sidney Verba, and Henry E. Brady, "Who Speaks: Citizen Political Voice on the Internet Commons," *Daedalus* 140 (2011): 121–139.

2. Jonah Peretti (with Michele Micheletti), "The Nike Sweatshop E-mail: Political Consumerism, Internet, and Culture Jamming," in *Politics, Products, and Markets*, ed. Michele

Since then, it has become clear how the capacities of the Internet can be mobilized in the name of organizing political action. The results have been especially dramatic in authoritarian systems in which oppositional parties and organizations are banned and the media are controlled by the regime in power. The Internet and its children—among them Facebook and Twitter—have brought down regimes by making it possible to communicate incendiary messages to large numbers of citizens who lack the usual institutional infrastructure for democratic political mobilization.[3]

Closer to home, the possibilities for using the Internet to bring about more conventional political actions were discovered considerably earlier. The Help America Vote Act, passed in response to the irregularities associated with the 2000 election, resulted in the replacement of old-fashioned punch card and lever voting systems with optical scan and direct record electronic systems (DREs). Then, beginning in 2003, an Internet-based movement among computer scientists led to questions about the security of electronic voting systems and the potential for electronic corruption of DREs. Skeptics established Web sites such as http://verifiedvoter.org and then moved into more traditional forms of advocacy in opposition to paperless electronic systems. By 2007, twenty-seven states had adopted provisions mandating a paper trail.[4]

This story—a textbook example of a jointly concerned group of citizens working together to have an impact on government—has been used as evidence of the positive consequences of the Internet for democracy. The claim is made that "the Internet changes everything," functioning as "the great equalizer," even "the people's lobby" and "our last, best chance to rekindle the great American dream."[5] Among its predicted salutary effects on democratic

---

Micheletti, Andreas Follesdal, and Dietlind Stolle (New Brunswick, NJ: Transaction, 2004), p. 128. The entire humorous exchange can be found at http://www.shey.net/niked.html (accessed December 17, 2011).

3. Among the many examples, see Jennifer Preston, "Movement Began with Outrage and a Facebook Page That Gave It an Outlet," *New York Times*, February, 5, 2011. Of course it must be recognized that not all such Internet-based protests have been successful—sometimes because the regimes in power are able to use the same capacities of the Internet to identify protesters and then arrest them.

4. For a brief version of this story, see Paul Herrnson, Richard G. Niemi, Michael J. Hanmer, Benjamin B. Bederson, Frederick C. Conrad, and Michael W. Traugott, *Voting Technology* (Washington, DC: Brookings Institution, 2008), pp. 11–12.

5. The quotes are from the title of an article by Stephen M. Johnson, "The Internet Changes Everything: Revolutionizing Public Participation and Access to Government Information through the Internet," *Administrative Law Review* 50 (1998): 277–337; Howard Rheingold, "The Great Equalizer," *Whole Earth Review* (Summer 1991): 6, quoted in Bruce Bimber,

governance is the capacity of the Internet to permit ordinary citizens to short-circuit political elites and deal directly with one another and public officials, a process known, awkwardly, as "disintermediation"; to foster deliberation, enhance trust, and create community;[6] and—of special concern to us —to facilitate political participation.

In this chapter we consider the potentially democratizing impact of the Internet on political participation, asking about both individuals and organizations the same kinds of questions we posed when we considered whether processes of political recruitment alter familiar participatory patterns: if the Internet is bringing new people and new organizations into politics, is it bringing *new kinds of people* and *new kinds of interests* into political activity? Even if the Internet is effective in generating additional political activity, is the new activity simply replicating the same participatory inequalities that have emerged over and over in this volume?

We, too, were hopeful that, as access to the Internet is disseminated more and more widely, the Internet might act as the trip wire interrupting the patterns of participatory inequality we have documented so consistently. Still, our optimism was tempered by our recognition that, compared to other Internet experts, political scientists who have been studying the impact of the Internet on politics tend, on the whole, to be more cautious in their assessments. According to one such perspective, "Far from revolutionizing the conduct of politics and civic affairs in the real world . . . the Internet tends to reflect and reinforce the patterns of behavior of that world" and constitutes "politics as usual conducted mostly by familiar parties, candidates, interest groups, and news media."[7]

Besides, everything we have seen so far about political activity renders the political success of what began as an Internet-based movement among com-

---

"The Internet and Political Transformation: Populism, Community, and Accelerated Pluralism," *Polity* 31 (1998): 138; William Wresch, *Disconnected: Haves and Have-Nots in the Information Age* (New Brunswick, NJ: Rutgers University Press, 1996), p. 237; and Daniel Burstein and David Kline, *Road Warriors: Dreams and Nightmares along the Information Highway* (New York: Dutton, 1995), p. 360, quoted in Richard Davis, *Politics Online: Blogs, Chatrooms, and Discussion Groups in American Democracy* (New York: Routledge Taylor and Francis Group, 2005), p. x.

6. A strong statement of this theme is contained in Steve Davis, Larry Elin, and Grant Reeher, *Click on Democracy: The Internet's Power to Change Political Apathy into Civic Action* (Boulder, CO: Westview, 2002).

7. Michael Margolis and David Resnick, *Politics as Usual: The Cyberspace "Revolution"* (Thousand Oaks, CA: Sage, 2000), p. vii.

puter professionals as not fully unexpected. While computer nerds are hardly the most visible group in American politics, they have characteristics—in particular, high levels of education—that predispose them to take part in politics should the occasion arise. Although the young are clearly much more willing and able to use electronic technologies than their elders, the association between social class and participation is powerful and durable. Internet access is far from universal among American adults, a phenomenon widely known as the "digital divide," and the contours of the digital divide reflect in certain ways the shape of participatory input. Moreover, access to the Internet does not necessarily mean use of the Internet and, even more important, use of the Internet for political activity.

While researchers have investigated the impact of the Internet on levels of political activity, the extent to which the biases in online political activity ameliorate or merely reflect, or even exaggerate, the familiar biases in offline political activity has been a distinctly secondary concern. In order to investigate this matter, during the summer of 2008 we collaborated with Lee Rainie and Scott Keeter of the Pew Internet and American Life Project to design a survey to collect information about Internet use and about political activity both off and on the Internet.[8] The survey, which was conducted in August 2008, provides an opportunity to consider whether online political activity—including newer forms of online activity on blogs and social networking sites—has the possibility of remedying the inequalities of political voice so characteristic of traditional offline participation.

All studies of the impact of the Internet on some aspect of democratic politics are hampered by the fact that they report on a phenomenon that is very much a moving target—a technology that is, according to Matthew Hindman, "in its adolescence."[9] Not only does the set of people with Internet access continue to expand, a development with potential consequences for participatory stratification, but there has also been a rapid increase in the amount of political material from a variety of sources. Moreover, technology has continued to develop. Improvements in Web browsers make it much easier to find information and to locate Web sites. The impact of innovations like social

8. We are very grateful to Lee Rainie and Scott Keeter for having responded to our suggestion about the importance of collecting systematic national data comparing online and offline participation, for allowing us to be partners in the design of the questionnaire, and for making those data available to us.

9. Matthew Hindman, *The Myth of Digital Democracy* (Princeton, NJ: Princeton University Press, 2009), p. 129.

networking and Twitter, which have powerful capacities to link like-minded people, and YouTube, which facilitates the instantaneous dissemination of audio and visual material, continues to unfold. In 1998 Bruce Bimber observed cautiously that it would be some time before the full political impact of the Internet would becomes apparent.[10] That modest assessment continues to be appropriate.

With respect to our focus on inequalities in political participation, another consideration—that the survey on which we rely was conducted at a particular point, in August 2008, after the parties had selected their presidential candidates but before the candidates had been officially nominated and before the campaign was in its final autumn sprint—is, in fact, probably less cause for concern. Surely the 2008 presidential campaign had some unusual characteristics, including significant activity by younger adults and a candidate who made self-conscious efforts to incorporate the Internet into his campaign. Still, it is plausible to argue that President Obama's experience as a community organizer and his obvious appeal to the young and to persons of color imply that this single survey would be *more likely to understate than to overstate* the extent of class- and age-based participatory inequalities.

Does the Internet Increase Citizen Participation?

Because the Internet lowers barriers to citizen political activity, observers have been optimistic that the Internet would raise political participation.[11] Certain forms of political participation—in particular, making campaign donations and contacting public officials—are simply easier on the Internet.[12] The networking capacities of the Internet are also suited to facilitate the process of forming political groups, recruiting adherents and sympathizers, and mobilizing them to take political action—either on- or offline.[13] Moreover, the

10. Bimber, "The Internet and Political Transformation," 159. On this theme, see also Michael Xenos and Patricia Moy, "Direct and Differential Effects of the Internet on Political and Civic Engagement," *Journal of Communications* 57 (2007): 705–706.

11. A succinct and sober estimate of the participation-enhancing capacities of the Internet is contained in Richard Davis, *The Web of Politics* (New York: Oxford University Press, 1999), pp. 20–27.

12. On campaign fundraising on the Internet, see Davis, Elin, and Reeher, *Click on Democracy*, pp. 55–65, and Bruce Bimber and Richard Davis, *Campaigning Online* (New York: Oxford University Press, 2003), pp. 38–39 and 60–62.

13. These points are made by a number of authors, among them Bimber, "The Internet and Political Transformation," p. 156; Arthur Lupia and Gisela Sin, "Which Public Goods Are

Internet provides a wealth of political information and opportunities for political interaction, discussion, and position taking.[14] Just about every offline source of political information—whether sponsored by governments, candidates, or the media—is now on the Web, usually without charge, available to be consulted, downloaded, and saved at the user's convenience.

However, the effect of the Internet may be not to increase political activity but instead to repackage it.[15] That is, instead of citizens undertaking political action that they ordinarily would not, people who would have participated anyway might simply be taking their activity online. For example, between early 1996 and late 2007, the proportion of Americans who reported that the Internet was one of their two most important sources of campaign news rose from 2 to 26 percent; at the same time, the proportion who made the equivalent assessment of newspapers as a source of campaign news declined from 49 to 30 percent.[16] In fact, investigations of whether Internet use enhances political activity show mixed results.[17]

Endangered: How Evolving Communication Technologies Affect 'The Logic of Collective Action,'" *Public Choice* 117 (2003): 319–321; and Andrew Chadwick, *Internet Politics: States, Citizens and New Communications Technologies* (New York: Oxford University Press, 2006), pp. 139–142. For examples, see Davis, Elin, and Reeher, *Click on Democracy*, chaps. 6–9.

14. On the information made available online, see, among others, Pippa Norris, *Digital Divide: Civic Engagement, Information Poverty, and the Internet Worldwide* (Cambridge, England: Cambridge University Press, 2001), chap. 6; Michael Margolis and David Resnick, *Politics as Usual: The Cyberspace 'Revolution'* (Thousand Oaks, CA: Sage Publications, 2000), chap. 3; Bimber and Davis, *Campaigning Online*, chap. 3; and the essays in Andrew Paul Williams and John Tedesco, eds., *The Internet Election: Perspectives on the Web in Campaign 2004* (Lanham, MD: Rowman and Littlefield, 2006). On online discussions, see Davis, *Politics Online*.

15. For alternative ways of thinking about the impact of the Internet on political activity, see Norris, *Digital Divide*, pp. 229–231.

16. Figures taken from Pew Research Center for the People and the Press, "Internet's Broader Role in Campaign 2008," January 11, 2008, http://www.pewinternet.org/Reports/2008/The-Internet-Gains-in-Politics.aspx?r=1 (accessed June 16, 2010).

17. On one hand are studies that show no increase in political participation as the result of exposure to the Internet. See, for example, Bruce Bimber, "Information and Political Engagement in America: The Search for Effects of Information Technology at the Individual Level," *Political Research Quarterly* 54 (2001): 53–67; Bruce Bimber, *Information and American Democracy* (Cambridge, England: Cambridge University Press, 2003), p. 5; M. Kent Jennings and Vicki Zeitner, "Internet Use and Civic Engagement," *Public Opinion Quarterly* 67 (2003): 311–334; Cary Coglianese, "Citizen Participation in Rulemaking: Past, Present, and Future," *Duke Law Journal* 55 (2006): 943–966; and Stuart Minor Benjamin, "Evaluating E-Rulemaking: Public Participation and Political Institutions." *Duke Law Journal* 75 (2006): 934–935.

Internet Political Activity and Participatory Inequality

Even if it were unambiguous that Internet use increases political participation, a higher level of political participation does not necessarily imply a less unequal distribution of political activity.[18] While we often associate the use of the Internet as a tool of citizen activation with emergent groups and underdog candidates needing to operate on a shoestring, use of the Internet is now nearly universal among established as well as emergent interests. As Pippa

---

On the other hand are studies that find a positive association between Internet use and measures of civic engagement. See, for example, Dhavan Shah, Nojin Kwak, and R. Lance Holbert, "'Connecting' and 'Disconnecting' with Civic Life: Patterns of Internet Use and the Production of Social Capital," *Political Communication* 18 (2001): 141–162; Caroline Tolbert and Ramona S. McNeal, "Unraveling the Effects of the Internet on Political Participation?" *Political Research Quarterly* 56 (2003): 175–185; Xenos and Moy, "Direct and Differential Effects of the Internet"; and Karen Mossberger, Caroline Tolbert, and Ramona McNeal, *Digital Citizenship: The Internet, Society, and Participation* (Cambridge, MA: MIT Press, 2008), chap. 4. For brief reviews of this literature, see Mossberger, Tolbert, and McNeal, *Digital Citizenship*, pp. 77–78, and Hindman, *Myth of Digital Democracy*, p. 9.

18. While our concern is to assess the extent to which Internet-based political activity ameliorates or replicates offline participatory inequalities, researchers have considered the consequences of the Internet for inequalities of other kinds. Two significant books consider implications of the Internet for inequalities in domains quite different from the one considered here. In a wide-ranging inquiry, Yochai Benkler, in *The Wealth of Networks: How Social Production Transforms Markets and Freedom* (New Haven, CT: Yale University Press, 2006), esp. chap. 9, considers, among other issues, how the "networked information environment" might improve the health and well-being of those who are not well off. For example, he discusses (pp. 320–323) the potential ramifications of free software for those in developing countries. Matthew Hindman, in *Myth of Digital Democracy*, treats several issues more directly related to politics, including (chap. 6) that, although the barriers to entry of establishing a political blog are low, only a small number of blogs attract many readers, and widely read bloggers "are quite unrepresentative of the broader electorate" (p. 103).

Among the inquiries that touch on the issue raised here are those of Markus Prior, who in *Post-Broadcast Democracy* (Cambridge, England: Cambridge University Press, 2007) argues that the impact of the Internet is to exacerbate inequalities in political interest and knowledge and therefore in turnout, and Mossberger, Tolbert, and McNeal, who in *Digital Citizenship* focus in particular on inequalities in "digital citizenship," defined as daily Internet use, and conclude that "the patterns of inequality in society are clearly being replicated online" (p. 146). Xenos and Moy, in "Direct and Differential Effects of the Internet," find that the association between use of the Internet for political information and offline political participation is stronger among the politically interested. Although they do not discuss the meaning of this result for participatory inequalities, the inference can be drawn that the information-rich online environment is not reducing inequalities in political activity. Thus, while the data have never before been available to permit comparison between online and offline political participation with respect to political inequalities, previous research contains few indications that the Internet is an equalizing force.

Norris notes, if the increase in political participation derives from the same people, or the same kinds of people, who are already active, a possible consequence of the process is the replication, or even the exacerbation, of existing political inequalities.[19]

The Digital Divide

For more than a decade, social observers have been concerned that the digital divide is leaving behind a substantial portion of the public—with implications for equal opportunity in economic life and equal voice in political life. Concern about unequal access to the Internet led to a mandate in the Telecommunications Act of 1996 specifying that "elementary and secondary schools and classrooms, health care providers, and libraries should have access to advanced telecommunication services"[20] and created a program of federal grants under the E-Rate program. According to a September 2000 report by the Department of Education, fully 75 percent of all public schools and districts and 50 percent of libraries had applied for funds under the E-Rate program.[21] By the turn of the twenty-first century, 95 percent of public libraries offered Internet access to patrons.[22]

Although the metaphor of the digital divide originally referred to lack of hardware access and suggests a chasm separating cyber haves from the cyber have-nots, it is more appropriate to think of a continuum ranging from, at one end, those who have no Internet access or experience to, at the other, those who have broadband access at home, use the Internet frequently, and are comfortable with a variety of online techniques.[23] Use of the Internet to

19. Norris, *Digital Divide*, pp. 230–231.

20. Quoted in Bruce Bimber, *Information and American Democracy* (Cambridge, England: Cambridge University Press, 2003), p. 151. On the history and remarkable politics of E-Rate, see Bimber, *Information and American Democracy*, pp. 150–161. See also Jeffrey Benner, "Bush Plan 'Digital Distortion,'" *Wired*, 2002, http://www.wired.com/politics/law/news/2002/02/50279 (accessed February 16, 2008).

21. Figure cited in Bimber, *Information and American Democracy*, p. 159.

22. Figure cited in Karen Mossberger, Caroline J. Tolbert, and Mary Stansbury, *Virtual Inequality: Beyond the Digital Divide* (Washington, DC: Georgetown University Press, 2003), p. 129. Such progress led some observers to argue that the digital divide has become a nonissue. See Benjamin M. Compaine, "Declare the War Won," in *The Digital Divide: Facing a Crisis or Creating a Myth*, ed. Benjamin M. Compaine (Cambridge, MA: MIT Press, 2001), pp. 315–335.

23. Anthony G. Wilhelm, *Democracy in the Digital Age* (New York: Routledge Taylor Francis, 2000), pp. 67 ff. See also Anthony G. Wilhelm, "Civic Participation and Technological Inequality: The 'Killer Application' Is Education," in *The Civic Web*, ed. David M. Anderson and Michael Cornfield (Lanham, MD: Rowman and Littlefield, 2002).

learn about politics and to be politically active requires not simply access to hardware but an array of skills: the capacity both to operate a computer and to seek and understand political information on the Web.[24] But what is critical for our concern with participatory inequalities is not simply that some Americans have been left out of the technological advances of recent decades but that the contours of the digital divide hew so closely to the socioeconomic stratification that has been widely observed as characteristic of political activity in the United States.[25]

Data from the 2008 Pew Internet and American Life survey that provide the basis for our analysis confirm the unevenness in access to the Internet. Reflecting patterns that have emerged from earlier studies, these data show that the attributes associated with access to hardware are in many ways familiar ones that, in important respects, track the individual characteristics that predict political participation—in particular, the class stratification that has such powerful implications for political participation.[26] As of 2008, roughly half of those in the lowest income category—who had family incomes below $20,000 in 2007—were online; that is, they either used the Internet or sent or received e-mail, at least occasionally. In contrast, at least occasional Internet or e-mail use was nearly universal among those in the highest income cate-

24. Mossberger, Tolbert, and Stansbury, in *Virtual Inequality*, pp. 40–50, call these capacities, respectively, "technical skills" and "information literacy." In an interesting study that parallels what we find here, Samuel Best and Brian Krueger, in "Analyzing the Representativeness of Internet Political Participation," *Political Behavior* 27 (2005): 183–216, demonstrate that online skills (measured as the sum of whether the respondent has designed a Web page, sent an attachment via e-mail, posted a file to the Internet, or downloaded a program from the Internet) function in predicting Internet-based political activity in just the same way that organizational and communications civic skills (using the measure in Sidney Verba, Kay Lehman Schlozman, and Henry E. Brady, *Voice and Equality* [Cambridge, MA: Harvard University Press, 1995]) do in predicting offline activity.

25. For discussion of inequalities in access to and use of the Internet and citations to the literature, see Paul DiMaggio, Eszter Hargittai, Coral Celeste, and Steven Shafer, "Digital Inequality: From Unequal Access to Differentiated Use," in *Social Inequality*, ed. Kathryn M. Neckerman (New York: Russell Sage Foundation, 2004), and Mossberger, Tolbert, and McNeal, *Digital Citizenship*, chap. 1.

26. For a general discussion, see Michael Alvarez and Thad E. Hall, *Point, Click, and Vote* (Washington, DC: Brookings, 2004), pp. 44–53. Other data sets show similar patterns to those presented here. See the October 2003 Current Population Survey contained in U.S. Department of Commerce, Economics and Statistics Administration, National Telecommunications and Information Administration, *A Nation Online: Entering the Broadband Age*, September 2004 (Table A-1), and John B. Horrigan and Aaron Smith, "Home Broadband Adoption 2007," Pew Internet and Public Life Project, http://www.pewinternet.org/Reports/2007/Home-Broadband-Adoption-2007.aspx?r=1 (accessed May 18, 2010).

gory, who had family incomes of $150,000 or more in 2007. Similarly, only 38 percent of those who did not graduate from high school, compared to 95 percent of those with at least some graduate education, were online in 2008.

In terms of the Internet's political capacities for providing opportunities for participation, access to information, and requests for activity, there is a difference between having Internet access at home and elsewhere—say, at work or the local library. In addition, even for those with Internet access at home, there is a difference between dial-up and broadband access. The Pew data indicate that three-quarters of those who were online in 2008—or 56.5 percent of all respondents—had high-speed Internet at home. Once again, there is a sharp socio-economic gradient: 30 percent of those in households with annual incomes below $20,000, compared to 88 percent in households with annual incomes above $150,000, reported having high-speed Internet access at home; the analogous figures in terms of education are 22 percent for respondents who did not finish high school as opposed to 81 percent for those with education beyond college.[27] Figure 16.1.A summarizes the data for the five quintiles of socio-economic status (SES) and makes clear that Internet use and access increase steadily with SES.[28]

27. Every other survey of Internet access and use shows that non-Hispanic whites have higher levels of computer use and access than do African Americans or Latinos. For reasons we cannot explain, the 2008 Pew data differ in showing high levels of access for Latinos, finding the following for non-Hispanic whites, African Americans, and Latinos, respectively: 75 percent, 70 percent, and 78 percent for using the Internet or e-mail at least occasionally and 57 percent, 46 percent, and 55 percent for having high-speed Internet at home.

Previous studies have differed in terms of whether the Internet deficits of blacks and Latinos can be explained completely as a function of group differences in education and income. In view of the changing nature and rapid diffusion of relevant technologies, it is difficult to make comparisons between surveys conducted at different times and using different measures of Internet access or use. See, for example, Mossberger, Tolbert, and Stansbury, *Virtual Inequality*, p. 33. On the basis of their 2001 survey, they find that, even with a variety of other characteristics taken into account, blacks and Latinos are less likely to have home access to the Internet than are whites or Asian Americans. In contrast, using data from the 2000 American National Election Study, Bimber, in *Information and American Democracy*, p. 218, finds that, once education has been taken into account, race has no effect on whether a respondent saw campaign information on the Internet.

A multivariate analysis shows that, even with a variety of characteristics including education, family income, and age taken into account, African Americans are significantly less likely to have access to broadband at home. Still, we must emphasize that, if the concern is equality of political voice, what really matters is whether a group suffers a continuing digital deficit rather than whether racial disparities result from socio-economic differences.

28. As usual, we use a scale based on education and family income and divide respondents into rough quintiles. Although the data about educational attainment are nearly com-

16.1.A   By SES Quintile

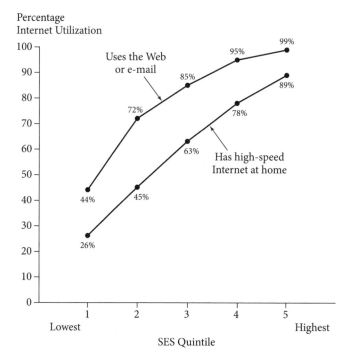

16.1.B   By Age Group

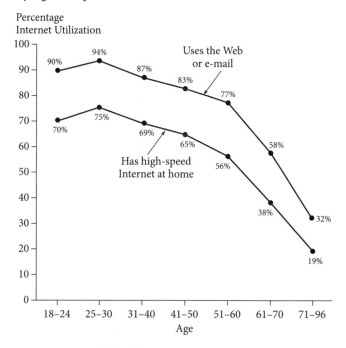

Figure 16.1   Internet Use by SES Quintile and Age

Source: Pew Internet and American Life Survey (2008).

There is, however, an important exception to the pattern, such that Internet use and broadband access are associated with characteristics that predict political participation. We saw in Chapter 8 that the young are relatively inactive politically. They are, however, more likely than their elders to use the Internet. Every study of Internet access and use, no matter what the measure, shows a steady, sharp decline with age. Figure 16.1.B shows that 90 percent of those between eighteen and twenty-four years of age, compared with only 32 percent of those seventy-one and over, use the Internet or e-mail at least occasionally. The corresponding figures are 70 percent and 19 percent for having broadband at home.[29] In light of the wide and unexplained disparities in participation between the young and their elders, this constitutes a potentially significant counterstratificational effect of the Internet. Moreover, as members of the younger generation come of age and replace their tech-phobic elders, the extent to which there is an age-related digital divide may be ameliorated.[30]

Using the Internet versus Using the Internet for Politics

Beyond access to and skillful use of the Internet is the inclination to use it for political purposes. The overwhelming share of Internet use is for nonpolitical activities that range from finding directions to viewing pornography to keeping up with friends on a social networking site. Studies of political participa-

---

plete, we do not have information about family income for 19 percent of respondents. While the respondents for whom family income is missing are distributed fairly evenly along the educational hierarchy, they are somewhat less active politically—especially with respect to online political activity—than are those who reported a family income.

29. It is interesting to note that, when it comes to broadband access, young adults (those eighteen to twenty-four) are divided on the basis of whether they are in school. Census data from 2003 showed that, in this age group, those in school were nearly twice as likely as their out-of-school peers to have broadband at home. National Telecommunications and Information Administration, *A Nation Online*, 2004, Table A-1.

30. An aspect of uneven Internet access and use that has received somewhat less attention —the disparity between suburban and urban dwellers, on the one hand, and rural residents, on the other—maps less well onto participatory inequalities. See Horrigan and Smith, "Home Broadband Adoption," pp. 4–8. In the 2008 Pew data, 40 percent of rural dwellers, compared to 57 percent of urban dwellers and 62 percent of suburbanites, reported having high-speed Internet at home.

Previous studies indicate that the rural deficit reflects a lack of availability of broadband connections rather than an absence of interest or a concern with costs. In fact, Wilhelm, in *Democracy in the Digital Age*, p. 106, describes a pattern of "digital redlining" by the telecommunications industry because fiber optic networks were initially bypassing both rural areas and inner-city neighborhoods with large minority populations.

tion make clear that the predisposition to devote leisure time—that is, time not spoken for by obligations at home, school, or work—to political activity is structured by both age and socio-economic status. We were suspicious that, beyond the demographic biases in access to hardware, online political participation might function less to redefine the kinds of people who are active politically than to replicate the widely acknowledged stratification in offline participation.[31]

The Representativeness of Online and Offline Political Participation

The results of the 2008 Pew survey make it possible to investigate whether political participation on the Internet overcomes the representational biases that have long been observed to characterize offline political activity. The survey asked about a series of political activities, five of which can be performed either online or offline: contacting a national, state, or local government official; signing a petition; sending a "letter to the editor"; communicating with fellow members of a political or community group; and making a political contribution. Using these items, we constructed three activity scales: the first two contain five items each and measure either online activity or offline activity in the acts with online counterparts; the third contains eleven items and measures overall activity.[32] Sixty-three percent of respondents took part

31. There are so many different paths by which the Internet might influence political activity that we have no reason to expect that studies focusing on different participatory acts or on Internet mobilization as opposed to online participation would find identical results. Nevertheless, all studies of particular political acts have found that online participants are not representative of the public as a whole. See, for example, Bruce Bimber, "The Internet and Citizen Communication with Government: Does the Medium Matter?" *Political Communication* 16 (1999): 409–428; Michael Alvarez and Jonathan Nagler, "The Likely Consequences of Internet Voting for Political Representation," *Loyola of Los Angeles Law Review* 34 (2001): 1115–1154; John Clayton Thomas and Gregory Streib, "The New Face of Government: Citizen-Initiated Contacts in the Era of E-Government," *Journal of Public Administration Research and Theory* 13 (2003): 83–102; and Davis Schlosberg, Stephen Zavestoski, and Stuart W. Schulman, "Democracy and E-Rulemaking: Web-Based Technologies, Participation, and the Potential for Deliberation," *Journal of Information Technology and Politics* 4 (2007): 37–55.

32. The three scales include items asking respondents whether they did the following: *Offline activity*—contacted a national, state, or local government official in person, by phone, or by letter about an issue that is important to you; signed a paper petition; sent a "letter to the editor" through the U.S. Postal Service to a newspaper or magazine; communicated with others [in the political or community group in which you are MOST involved] by having a face-to-face meeting, by print letter or newsletter, or by phone; contributed money to a polit-

in at least one of the eleven acts on the overall measure of political participation, and the average is 1.87 acts. With respect to the five political activities for which there are online and offline counterparts, respondents average 0.64 on the scale of five online acts, and about a third, 34 percent, engage in at least one of them. For offline political acts, the analogous figures are somewhat higher: the average is 0.97, and just over half of respondents, 52 percent, engage in at least one of the five offline acts. Online and offline activity are associated with one another.[33]

Figure 16.2 presents data for five groups based on socio-economic status and makes obvious that, no matter how political participation is measured, political activity rises sharply with socio-economic status. Figure 16.2 shows the percentage who engage in at least one participatory act as measured by these three scales: the top line shows the proportion who engage in at least one of the eleven activities on the scale of overall participation; the next line shows the proportion who undertake offline at least one of the five activities with online and offline versions; the bottom line shows the proportion who take part in at least one of the online counterparts of these five activities.

The additional line in Figure 16.2, which is between the second line and the bottom line, shows the proportion who engage in at least one of the five Internet-based political activities *among Web users*—that is, among those who use the Internet or e-mail at least occasionally.[34] On one hand, because

---

ical candidate or party or any other organization or cause in person, by phone, or through the mail. *Online activity*—sent an e-mail to a national, state, of local government official; signed a petition online; e-mailed a "letter to the editor" or your comments to a newspaper or magazine; communicated with others [in the political or community group in which you are MOST involved] by e-mail, using the group's Web site, instant messaging, using a social networking site; contributed money to a political candidate or party or any other organization or cause on the Internet. *Overall activity*: attended a political rally or speech; attended an organized protest of any kind; attended a political meeting on local, town, or school affairs; worked or volunteered for a political party or candidate; made a speech about a community or political issue; was an active member of any group that tries to influence public policy or government, not including a political party; worked with fellow citizens to solve a problem in your community; contacted a national, state, or local government official (either on- or offline); signed a petition (either on- or offline); sent a "letter to the editor" or your comments to a newspaper or magazine (either on- or offline); contributed money to a political candidate or party or any other organization or cause (either on- or offline).

33. The Pearson correlation for the pair of five-item scales is .586.

34. Mossberger, Tolbert, and McNeal, in *Digital Citizenship*, p. 1, define "digital citizens" as those who use the Internet on a daily basis and demonstrate the impact on various outcomes, including political participation, of digital citizenship. We choose a much lower threshold because we are interested in filtering out those who, through lack of access, interest, or capacity, do not use the Internet at all.

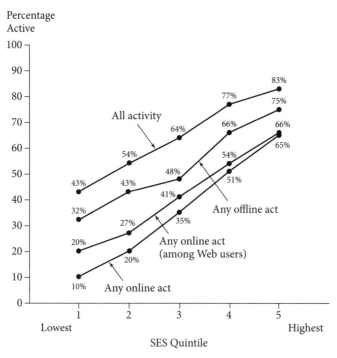

Percentage
Active

Figure 16.2   Online and Offline Political Activity by SES Quintile

Source: Pew Internet and American Life Survey (2008).

access to and use of the Internet have a social class component, when we consider the online political activity of Internet users only, the SES gradient is less sharp than when we consider all respondents. On the other, Figure 16.2 makes clear that lack of access is only part of the story of the class structuring of online political activity. Even when we omit those who are not online and consider only those who use the Internet or e-mail, we see a strong association between political participation and socio-economic status. Among those who use the Internet or e-mail, the percentage who undertake at least one online political act is substantially lower at the bottom of the SES hierarchy than at the top. Because fewer than half of those at the lower end of the SES rankings use the Internet or e-mail, their levels of Internet-based political activity show the potential effects of lack of Web access. While lack of access to the Internet obviously makes online political activity impossible, we suspect that those who lack Internet access would not necessarily use it for political activity if they were to get connected. Still, the digital divide presumably depresses levels of online political activity further down the SES ladder. In contrast, at the upper end, where Internet use was nearly universal, the level of online activity was not affected by lack of access to hardware. Thus it seems that, far from acting as a great equalizer, the possibility of political activity on the Internet replicates familiar patterns of socio-economic stratification not only because the digital divide has a social class component but because the SES disadvantaged among those online are not using the Internet for political participation.[35]

In Figure 16.3 we show parallel data for a single political act, getting in touch with a public official. The top portion presents data for SES quintiles about contacts with public officials by e-mail and contacts by phone or in person. The bottom portion repeats the data about e-mail contacts for all respondents and adds information about e-mail contacts for those who are Internet or e-mail users. Once again, we see a strong association with socio-economic status—even when we consider electronic communications among those who used the Internet or e-mail, at least occasionally. Very few people who are low in SES contact public officials, a pattern that is partially, but only partially, explained by the fact that they are less likely to be online.[36]

The patterns for age groups, shown in Figure 16.4, are quite different. The top line shows, for overall political participation, the same roughly curvilinear pattern over the life cycle that we saw in Chapter 8. Age, however, is much less powerful in structuring political activity than is socio-economic status: the distance between the most active of the seven age groups and the least active age group is much smaller than the distance between the lowest and highest of the SES quintiles.

35. Lu Wei and Douglas Blanks Hindman present data from the 2008–2009 American National Election Study on the use of the Internet to obtain political and social information. As we do, they find that, while access to the Internet is stratified by socio-economic status, there is greater stratification by socio-economic status of the use of the Internet for gathering political and social information. Furthermore, the information gap across SES levels is greater for information from the Internet than for information from newspapers and television. SES stratification does not equalize across social class; just the opposite. See Lu Wei and Douglas Blanks Hindman, "Does the Digital Divide Matter More? Comparing the Effects of New Media and Old Media Use on the Education-Based Knowledge Gap," *Mass Communication and Society* 14 (2011): 216–235.

36. It is interesting to note that there is virtually no difference between online and offline contacts with respect to either the probability of receiving a response or the probability of being satisfied with the reply. Among the 21 percent of respondents who contacted a public official by e-mail, 66 percent indicated having received a response; of the e-mail contactors who received a reply, 66 percent were satisfied. For the 29 percent of respondents who contacted a public official in person, by mail, or by phone, the analogous figures are 69 percent and 69 percent.

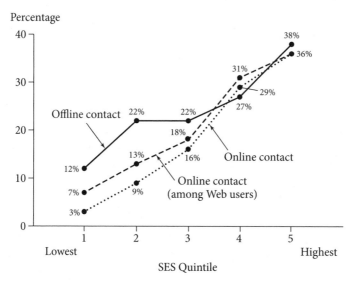

Figure 16.3 Contacting Officials Online and Offline by SES Quintile

Source: Pew Internet and American Life Survey (2008).

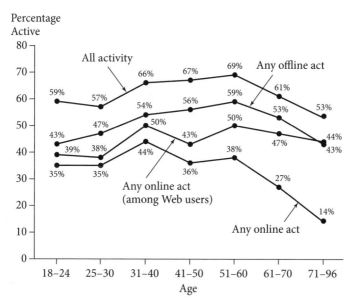

Figure 16.4 Online and Offline Political Activity by Age Group

Source: Pew Internet and American Life Survey (2008).

The curvilinear pattern is replicated for the scale of five offline acts for which there are online counterparts, shown in the second line. However, when it comes to online activity, shown in the bottom line, we see a contrasting pattern that includes an unusual element of counterstratification. For online political activity, the participatory gap between the youngest group and their elders up to age sixty is relatively small with little relationship between age and online political activity. The likelihood of undertaking online political activity, however, is lower among the elderly, especially among those over seventy. In contrast to what we observed for offline political activity, the absence of online activity among the elderly represents, we assume, not a fall-off from previous Internet-based participation but instead a never-was. This suspicion gains credence when we consider the online activity of those who use the Internet or e-mail at least occasionally, shown in the third line from the top. Among those who use the Internet and e-mail, the young are actually the least likely to be politically active online. Thus the digital divide has its greatest impact among older respondents. The small number of Web users among older respondents—a group that surely is not a random selection —are actually quite politically active on the Internet.

These findings are underscored by the data in Figure 16.5, which replicates for Internet-based activity the analysis shown earlier in Figure 8.6. Each line represents the average online political participation for the SES quintiles of a single age group for respondents who use the Internet or e-mail at least occasionally.[37] The overall pattern shows the impact of socio-economic status and the irrelevance of age. Even after we have accounted for lack of Internet access and use, the five lines are bunched quite closely and rise in tandem with social class. For all the age groups there is the expected association between socio-economic status and political activity, but within any SES quintile there is much less variation among age groups and little consistent pattern as to which age group is the most active.

These straightforward figures speak to our concern that the impact on inequalities of participatory voice depends on whether political activity takes place on the Internet or off. The data suggest that offline and online participant publics are not appreciably different with respect to SES but that, in contrast, the age profile of political participation on the Web differs from the age profile of offline activity. To nail down these findings, we sought statistical

---

37. In order to facilitate the graphic presentation, we have reduced the number of age groups from seven to five.

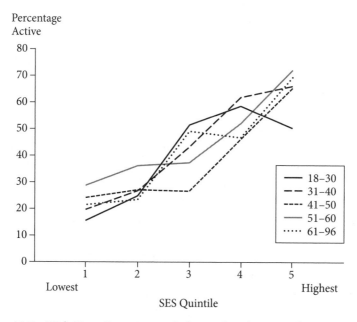

Figure 16.5   Web Users Engaging in Online Political Activity by SES Quintile for Age Groups

Source: Pew Internet and American Life Survey (2008).

confirmation.[38] Our techniques permit us to differentiate between two processes: the impact of the factors related to Web access and the impact of the factors related to political participation.

The analysis demonstrates that income and education appear to have the same stratificational impact for online acts as for offline acts: there is no evidence that the relationship between Web-based participation, on the one hand, and education or income, on the other, is different from the relationship between offline political participation and these SES factors. In contrast, age affects access to the Internet (and thus political participation based on the Internet), but once someone has access to the Internet, there is no difference in how age affects offline versus online political activity. Thus the extent to which the young are less underrepresented with respect to political participation via the Internet is related to their greater likelihood to be Web users

---

38. Discussion of these statistical tests and accompanying data can be found in Appendix H.

rather than to any enhanced propensity to use the Internet politically once on the Web.

We should add one caveat. This survey was conducted during a particular campaign—a campaign notable both for its special attempts to use electronic technologies to mobilize young activists and for its historic outcome. If the overall shape of participatory input was somehow unusual during the 2008 campaign, we might speculate that it would have been less stratified with respect both to age and to socio-economic status. We find it difficult, however, to speculate how any amelioration of class and age bias in political activity would have been expressed in the *relative weight of offline and online participation*. When it comes to SES, lack of access to and use of the Internet reinforces for online political activity the well-known SES stratification of conventional offline participation. In contrast, when it comes to age, the group that is typically underrepresented in political activity, young adults, is more likely to use the Internet. Teasing out this logic requires complex models and longitudinal data about online and offline political activity that have not at this point ever been collected. In the meantime, we would not expect conclusions drawn from survey conducted in 2008 to exaggerate the extent of either age or social class bias in political participation.

Political Contributions On- and Offline

Because making political contributions is the form of political activity most obviously dependent on access to financial resources and because a great deal of attention has been paid to the success of some candidates in raising large numbers of small donations over the Web, we were particularly interested to look more carefully at political giving. The Pew data—which, we should recall, were collected in August of 2008, before Obama's Web-based September fundraising blitz—contain helpful items about political giving that allow us to ascertain not only whether but also how much respondents gave in political contributions, both offline and on the Web.[39] These 2008 data show that Internet contributions were less common than offline donations: 6 per-

---

39. The Pew survey is the first large-scale survey to collect data about the *size* of political contributions since the 1990 Citizen Participation Study. However, the two-stage design of the Citizen Participation Study permitted the oversampling of those who made large contributions, thus facilitating the analysis of political activity in which the input is money rather than time. Because there are very few large donors in the Pew survey, we do not feel comfortable in drawing conclusions about those who make very large contributions.

cent of respondents made an online—and 15 percent an offline—contribution. The data also suggest that behind the widely discussed success of Internet-based fundraising in collecting political money in smaller amounts is a more complex pattern. On one hand, the average total offline contribution was larger than the average total online contribution, and 74 percent of the political dollars donated offline—in contrast to 49 percent of the political dollars contributed on the Internet—were given in amounts over $250. On the other hand, the percentage of contributions that were $50 or less—38 percent made online and 39 percent made offline—was virtually identical, as was the proportion of contributions that were between $51 and $100—28 percent made online and 29 percent made offline.

What is clear is that the very large donations that figure so importantly in campaign war chests are much less likely to come over the Web: less than 1 percent of the online contributions—as opposed to nearly 5 percent of the offline contributions—were for amounts over $1,000. We are not certain why big givers are less likely to use the Internet. One speculation is that, out of security concerns, they are reluctant to put a credit card number attached to a large donation on the Web. Others are that big donors like to be invited to events where they can rub elbows with politicos and celebrities or that they like to contribute in such a way as to allow a friend or political ally to get credit for the donation.[40]

Figure 16.6 allows us to probe the differences between those who make donations over the Internet and the larger group of traditional donors who write checks. Figure 16.6.A presents data about the proportion of respondents in various family income groups who made political contributions and shows a familiar pattern.[41] Regardless of whether we are considering offline or online political donations, the share of respondents who contribute rises sharply with family income and is more than five times greater in the highest family income group than in the lowest. When it comes to age, Figure 16.6.B shows that the proportion making donations offline starts at a low level among the young—with only 4 percent of those under twenty-five making offline contributions—and rises fairly steadily across the age groups, remaining high among those over seventy, a group that is otherwise not especially politically

40. We thank Michael Malbin for the first suggestion and Daniel Schlozman for the second.

41. Because the size of political contributions has been shown to be a function of family income rather than education, we substitute categories based on family income for SES quintiles.

16.6.A Contributing by Family Income

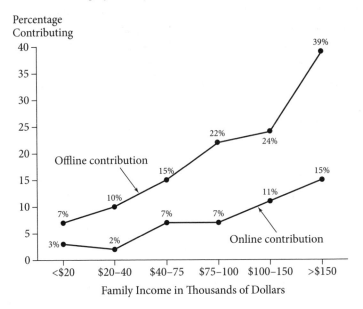

16.6.B Contributing by Age Group

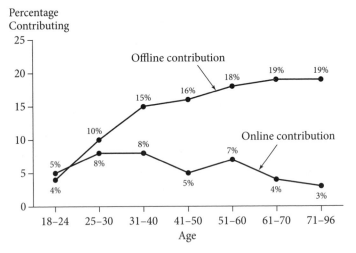

Figure 16.6 Online and Offline Campaign Donations by Family Income and by Age

Source: Pew Internet and American Life Survey (2008).

active. In contrast, when it comes to making contributions online, there is no particular pattern among younger and middle-aged groups. However, the proportion of respondents who use the Internet to make political donations is much lower among the oldest respondents, those over seventy.[42]

Many analysts of campaign finance emphasize expanding the ranks of small donors as the solution to the conundrum of money in democratic politics. Because small donations are unlikely to arrive with a set of policy instructions attached and can exercise limited leverage even when they do, small donations seem to ameliorate the possibilities for compromise of political equality in a campaign finance system that relies so heavily on contributions from individuals. Hence, we were concerned to learn whether small donors—especially those who contribute over the Web—are distinctive in their characteristics. The bar graphs in Figure 16.7 present distributions by family income and age for three groups: all respondents, those who made donations of $50 or less offline, and those who made donations of $50 or less over the Internet. Two patterns emerge from the data about income. First, as shown in Figure 16.7.A, higher income groups are overrepresented among those who make campaign donations, even what would seem to be very small ones.[43] While they are less exclusively affluent than big donors, those who make small donations are relatively unlikely to be drawn from the lower rungs of the income ladder. Second, and more germane to our immediate concerns, online contributors who donate small amounts are not markedly less affluent than their offline counterparts. If anything, they are actually somewhat better off financially. Thus it seems that the Internet may be bringing in *more* small donors, but it is not bringing in a *less affluent* set of small donors.

With respect to age, Figure 16.7.B indicates that the youngest respondents, those between eighteen and twenty-four, are underrepresented among those making political contributions of $50 or less. However, while they are nearly invisible among offline small donors, the extent of their underrepresentation is much less substantial when it comes to online contributions. While the next age group, those between twenty-five and thirty, is also underrepresented

---

42. For those who use the Internet or e-mail at least occasionally, there is no consistent relationship between age and the proportion making online political contributions. In fact, among those online, those under age twenty-five are least likely to use the Web to donate.

43. Although the Pew data contain very few cases of those who make very large campaign contributions, and we are therefore reluctant to draw any conclusions, the fact that the Pew respondents who indicated having made campaign contributions of more than $2,500 are drawn almost uniformly from the highest income category is consistent with earlier studies.

16.7.A   Distribution of All Respondents and of Online and Offline Donors of $50 or Less by Family Income Groups

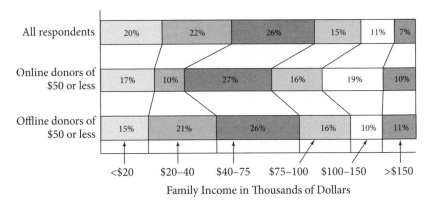

16.7.B   Distribution of All Respondents and of Online and Offline Donors of $50 or Less by Age Groups

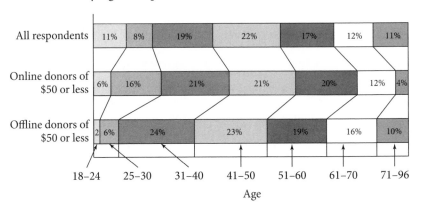

Figure 16.7   Who Makes Small Donations Online and Offline?

Source: Pew Internet and American Life Survey (2008).

among those who make small contributions offline, these late twentysome-things are actually overrepresented among those who make small donations on the Web. Thus it seems that, although making campaign contributions, even small ones, is not an activity of the young, the possibility of making those donations online renders small donors a somewhat more representative group with respect to age.

Alternative Paths to Participation via the Internet

Earlier we mentioned that the Internet has potential for indirect influence on political participation—either online or offline—in other ways: by acting as a venue for political conversation, by providing easy access to political information, and by facilitating recruitment to political activity.[44] However, we have also made clear that to raise the level of political participation is not necessarily to ameliorate inequalities in political participation.

As we discussed in Chapter 5, engaging in political discussions has a complex relationship to political participation. For one thing, it occupies a space at the penumbra of political activity: though not aimed at direct or indirect influence on public authorities, talking about politics is still more active than such psychological orientations as being politically interested or efficacious. For another, its causal relationship to political activity is presumably reciprocal: while discussions about politics stimulate political activity, experiences of actually taking part in politics also generate political talk.

The Pew survey asked respondents how often they discuss politics and public affairs on the Internet (by e-mail or instant message, on a social networking site, or in an online chat) as well as offline (in person, by phone, or by letter). Replicating our analysis for political discussion yields results parallel to what we have seen for political participation. People are much more likely to engage in political discussions offline than on the Internet. In addition, echoing what we saw in Chapter 5, the propensity to engage in political discussion, whether online or offline, is positively associated with socioeconomic status. As with more active forms of political participation, some of the social class gradient with respect to online political conversations results from the association between Internet use and socio-economic status. However, even among Internet users, those at the top of the SES ladder are roughly twice as likely as those at the bottom to engage in Web-based political discussion. There is no such clear pattern when it comes to the relationship of age to talking about politics. With respect to offline political discussion, other than that those under twenty-five are the least likely to engage in political discussions, there is no other discernible pattern. Political discussions online, which are markedly less frequent than political conversations in person or on the phone, diminish sharply with age—a pattern that is not repeated among Internet users.

44. For an explanation of why we are not dealing with use of the Internet to find political information, see Schlozman, Verba, and Brady, "Weapon of the Strong?"

When it comes to political mobilization, various digital media, ranging from e-mail to social networking to Twitter, make it nearly costless to multiply the number of specially crafted messages to selected publics and thus to facilitate the recruitment of political activists. In fact, the level of Internet-based political recruitment has already expanded to the point that it approaches that for offline recruitment. Furthermore, as we demonstrated in Chapter 15, those who seek to get others involved in politics engage in rational prospecting, with the result that their requests for political participation are structured by the same variables, including socio-economic status, that predict offline political participation.

When we consider requests for political activity that come by phone or by e-mail in Figure 16.8, what we find echoes the findings about rational prospecting in Chapter 15 and parallels what we have seen so far with respect to the SES and age stratification of political participation. In Figure 16.8.A, the probability that a respondent reported a request for political activity by phone at least once a month rises steadily with socio-economic status. The curve for monthly e-mail requests to take part politically is, in fact, much steeper, suggesting that the digital revolution has not democratized processes of political recruitment.

Once again, we see evidence that the Internet may have a counterstratificational impact when it comes to age. As shown in Figure 16.8.B, while those under twenty-five are somewhat less likely than their elders to receive a phone call at least once a month asking them to take political action, they are considerably more likely to have received monthly e-mail requests to take part politically. In short, what we have seen about the capacities of the Internet to stimulate political participation by providing a forum for political discussion or by serving as a medium through which requests for political activity are transmitted reinforces what we saw earlier with respect to online political activity. On one hand, we find no evidence that politics on the Web is ameliorating the class-based inequalities in political participation that have so long characterized American politics. On the other, the generational digital divide may have the consequence of reducing the participatory under-representation of the young.

Citizen Politics on the Changing Web

The activities we have just considered are political acts that existed before the advent of the Internet—which, of course, is what allows us to compare them

16.8.A Percentage Receiving Requests for Political Activity by SES Quintile

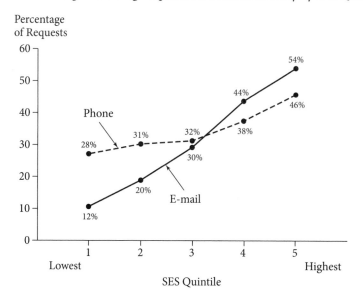

16.8.B Percentage Receiving Requests for Political Activity by Age Group

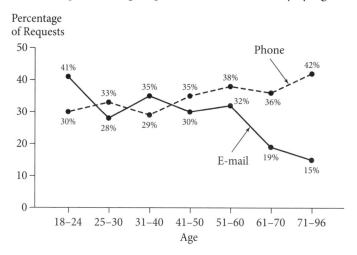

Figure 16.8 Requests for Political Activity by Phone or E-mail

Source: Pew Internet and American Life Survey (2008).

Note: Phone: received a phone call requesting involvement in a political activity; e-mail: received an e-mail requesting involvement in a political activity.

in their off- and online manifestations. There are, of course, modes of Internet-based engagement that have no direct offline counterpart, including posting comments on blogs—whether one's own or someone else's—and using social networking sites like Facebook or LinkedIn.

Most people who write in blogs or, especially, join social networking sites do so for reasons having nothing to do with politics. Figure 16.9 gives information about the proportion of respondents in each of the age groups who reported blogging or using social networking sites—*whether or not for politics*. Figure 16.9 makes clear that the young are much more likely to exploit these relatively recent and rapidly developing Internet capabilities. Especially striking are the data for social networking, which show that, in 2008, the overwhelming majority of respondents under age twenty-five were social networkers, a proportion that has undoubtedly grown since the survey was conducted.

These forms of Internet engagement can also be used for political purposes. Of the two, blogging seems to require skills analogous to those needed for offline position taking. Writing one's own blog has affinities to being an

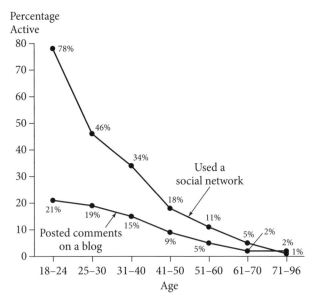

Figure 16.9   Using a Social Network or Posting Comments on a Blog by Age Group

Source: Pew Internet and American Life Survey (2008).

op-ed columnist—though with lower barriers to entry.[45] Posting comments on someone else's blog is akin to writing a letter to the editor—though with guaranteed publication and minimal requirements for civility of tone, coherence of argument, or the niceties of grammar and spelling.

While blogging originated around the turn of the twenty-first century and came into its own during the 2004 election, social networking is a more recent and rapidly evolving phenomenon. At this point, the possibilities for political engagement through social network sites such as Facebook do not simply reproduce participation as we have always known it but instead reflect some of the distinctive civic tastes of post-Boomer cohorts: their preference for participatory forms that are anchored in nonhierarchical and informal networks and that eschew such traditional political intermediaries as campaigns, parties, and interest groups.[46]

Age, Social Class, and New Modes of Web Activity

The Pew study asked explicitly about political forms of engagement on blogs and social networks: that is, both about writing about a political or social issue on a blog, either in one's own blog or, more frequently, on someone else's, and about doing any of the following on a social networking site— looking for campaign or candidate information, starting or joining a political group or group supporting a cause, signing up as a "friend" of a candidate, or posting political news for friends or others to read.

It is not surprising that, as Figure 16.10 makes clear, blogging about political and social issues and political social networking are closely connected to age. The lower two lines—which show the percentage in various age groups reporting that, in the past year, they had posted comments about a political or social issue on a Web site or on a blog and the percentage reporting that they had undertaken at least one of the four political activities on a social

45. Matthew Hindman, in *Myth of Digital Democracy*, chap. 6, demonstrates that, in spite of the low barriers to entry, the work of few bloggers is actually read. Readership of blogs is even more concentrated than readership of op-ed writers, and bloggers with large readerships share the elite educations and other characteristics of well-known op-ed writers. Richard Davis, in *Typing Politics: The Role of Blogs in American Politics* (New York: Oxford University Press, 2009), pp. 4–7, points out that, while the number of blogs has proliferated rapidly in the past decade, more than 70 percent of blogs are personal journals and, according to one survey, only 11 percent of bloggers reported that politics or public affairs were the main subject of their blogs.

46. See, for example, Cliff Zukin, Scott Keeter, Molly Andolina, Krista Jenkins, and Michael X. Delli Carpini, *A New Engagement? Political Participation, Civic Life, and the Changing American Citizen* (Oxford, England: Oxford University Press, 2006), chap. 4.

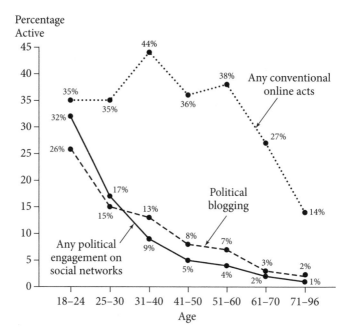

Figure 16.10   Forms of Political Engagement Online by Age Group

Source: Pew Internet and American Life Survey (2008).

Note: Political use of a social networking site includes looking for campaign or candidate information, starting or joining a political group supporting a cause, signing up as a "friend" of a candidate, or posting political news for friends or others to read.

networking site—fall sharply from the levels for those under twenty-five. Figure 16.10 also repeats the data from Figure 16.4 about the proportion of respondents who engaged in the online version of one of the "conventional" political activities such as making a political contribution or getting in touch with a public official. As before, the pattern is quite different. Although there is a steep drop-off among those over age sixty, the youngest groups are not especially politically active online.

Although these possibilities for political engagement through social network sites do not simply reproduce participation as we have always known it, they may lead to forms of online and offline political participation as conventionally understood. Besides, in the period since the Pew survey was conducted, these modes of involvement have become less exclusively the province of the young and have continued to evolve. There is a well-known pattern such that new technologies initially look a lot like the older technologies they eventually replace before their unique capacities are developed. For example, before the power of visual images was refined, early campaign ads on television used talking heads with wordy messages suitable for radio. In certain ways, as increasing numbers of politicians move from maintaining Web sites to establishing a presence on Facebook, what is happening is almost the opposite. More conventional forms of political discourse and advocacy have also established a beachhead in this brave new world.

Do these Web 2.0 phenomena have the potential to overcome the structuring of political participation by social class? Figure 16.11 shows data, analogous to those in Figure 16.10, about the association between socio-economic status and writing about political and social issues on a blog, engaging in political social networking, and engaging in the online versions of traditional political acts. As we saw in Figure 16.2, the relationship of more traditional political activity carried out on the Internet slopes sharply upward

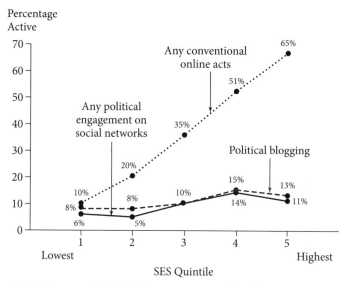

Figure 16.11   Forms of Political Engagement Online by SES Quintile

Source: Pew Internet and American Life Survey (2008).

Note: Political use of a social networking site includes looking for campaign or candidate information, starting or joining a political group supporting a cause, signing up as a "friend" of a candidate, or posting political news for friends or others to read.

with socio-economic status. The lines for political social networking and blogging about political and social issues also rise with SES, but the increase is much less pronounced.

Before we conclude prematurely that new forms of political engagement on the Web will break the long-standing association between social class and political participation, let us go one step further. Most of the political bloggers and political social networkers are twentysomethings. Measuring SES among younger respondents is tricky, especially if they are still in school. In answering questions about income, they may consider their family income to be that derived from their own earnings or, especially if they are still living at home, that of their birth family. Particularly among those who have not finished their educations, their own current incomes may not be especially predictive of their future earning power. Their socio-economic status is under construction: if they graduate, the educational component of their eventual SES will, by definition, rise; their measured incomes are artificially depressed by their student status but their incomes will, in the future, be likely to rise more sharply than those of members of their cohort who leave school earlier. Forty-two percent of the respondents under thirty in the Pew survey reported still being in school either full or part time. Thus we consider it premature to conclude, as others have suggested, that interactive forms of online political participation hold the key to unlocking the association between political participation and socio-economic status.

Table 16.1 allows us to look more closely at how these respondents under thirty use the Internet. In addition to asking about their use of social networks to engage in political activities, the 2008 Pew study queried respondents about their use of the Internet for personal purposes—using the Internet to learn more about people they knew or might meet or using online dating sites. Instead of focusing on socio-economic status, we compare groups based on educational attainment: those who were still full-time students and, among those no longer in school, high school graduates, those with some college, and college graduates. It is noteworthy that, even in an election year that witnessed an upsurge of activity by younger citizens, under-thirties were considerably more likely to use the Internet for personal objectives—to find information about people or to find dates—rather than to use social networks for political purposes. In addition, when it comes to personal use of the Internet, there is no association with current student status or, for non-students, with educational attainment. The pattern for use of social networking sites for political purposes is quite different. Those who

Table 16.1   Personal and Political Use of the Internet
(among Web Users under Age 30)

Educational Status	Percentage Making Personal Use of the Internet[a]	Percentage Making Political Use of a Social Network[b]	N
Currently a Student	54%	43%	94
Highest Grade Achieved			
High School or Less	60%	18%	129
Some College	58%	25%	62
College Graduate	62%	36%	49

Source: Pew Internet and American Life Project (2008).

[a] Personal use of the Internet: use the Internet to learn more about people they knew or might meet or use online dating sites.
[b] Political use of a social networking site: seek political information on a social network site, join a political group, sign on as a "friend" of a candidate, or post political messages.

were still students were the most active, and, among nonstudents, the higher the educational attainment, the more likely someone was to have taken political actions on the Internet. This finding is especially germane to our concern with class-based inequalities of political voice and suggests that even these new forms of Internet-based political involvement may not act as the circuit breaker interrupting the long-standing connection between SES and citizen political activity.

Politicians and Social Media

We are reluctant to draw firm conclusions from the August 2008 Pew data about the extent to which such Web 2.0 phenomena as blogging and social networking have the potential to overcome the structuring of political participation by age and SES. With astonishing rapidity, new possibilities for communication and the dissemination of information are being created. The opportunities for digital political engagement continue to proliferate both in ways that mimic older forms of political participation and in ways that were not imagined even a few years ago, when the Pew survey was conducted. Just as we were putting the finishing touches on this manuscript, President Obama, whose 2008 presidential campaign had been marked by pioneering use of digital technologies, held a first-ever Twitter town hall in which he spent more than an hour responding live from the East Room to questions that had been submitted via Twitter. White House Communications Director Dan Pfeiffer commented, "If you're going to communicate with the broad public, it is no longer sufficient to simply do it through traditional mainstream media."[47]

Major political figures now all have Facebook pages as well as Web sites. In June 2011 we visited the Facebook pages of twenty national politicians. Given that Facebook is fundamentally about self-presentation, it is remarkable how widely these politicians' Facebook pages ranged in almost every respect. Much of the variation had little to do with such traditional political fault lines as partisanship or ideology and much more to do with differences in the balance between the personal and various versions of the political. At that time nearly twenty-two million people "liked" President Barack Obama and fewer than two thousand liked former Vice President Dick Cheney (whose Facebook page was very spare and may have been under construction). House Speaker John Boehner (R-OH) and former Democratic Vice President Al Gore included very little information about their personal likes and dislikes. In contrast, Republican presidential aspirant Mitt Romney listed a dozen books that ranged from *Huckleberry Finn* to *The World Is Flat* to *The Purpose Driven Life;* President Obama revealed his broad taste in music, including John Coltrane, Bob Dylan, and J. S. Bach; Senate Minority Leader Harry Reid (D-NV) liked the Grateful Dead and Joan Baez; and Senator John Kerry (D-MA) listed *Animal House* as one of his favorite movies. The material they post varies substantially not only in the frequency with which it is updated but also in its emphasis on the substance of policy, partisan promotion, campaigning, or daily comings and goings. Some political figures post photos—which vary widely in their content and their relative emphasis on the personal or the political.[48] Some link to the politicians' Web sites or to other political material.

The comments posted in response to postings vary in length, wit, quality of spelling and grammar, and the extent to which they engage political issues.

47. Quoted in Michael D. Shear, "Live from the White House, a Twitter Town Hall," *New York Times*, July 7, 2011.
48. Two of us who live in the same congressional district appreciated that, uniquely among the Facebook pages we consulted, our representative in the House listed his employer as "the people of the 4th District of Massachusetts."

Informal perusal suggests that the more a politician's postings focus on the substance of policy and the fewer people who like the politician on Facebook, the higher the proportion of comments that engage policy matters rather than involve personal cheerleading or vilification. Still, even the comments that deal with policy issues rarely rise to the level of what a citizen would put in a letter or e-mail about the same subject.

Postscript: A Preliminary Look at the Digital Organization

When we began this project, neither Facebook nor Twitter existed.[49] As we concluded, we recognized that not only are politicians, even politicians who came of age in the era of radio, learning to take advantage of the communications capacities of rapidly changing social media but political organizations are confronting the prospects offered by—and the potential threats posed by—social media. Although scholars have begun to investigate politicians' use of social media, we know of no inquiries that focus on whether and how the thousands of organizations that seek influence in Washington are engaging with these potentially transformative technologies. Throughout our inquiry we have seen consistently that overrepresentation of the advantaged in individual participation is paralleled by an even more pronounced overrepresentation of the advantaged in organized interest activity. In order to enrich our understanding of the consequences of changing digital technologies for inequalities of political voice, we decided to add data about organizations to our extensive existing database. Thus we are able to consider in a preliminary way for organizations the same questions about the accent of the heavenly chorus that we have just posed about individuals.

In Chapter 14 we saw that some organized interests use their Web sites as a tool for political communication and activation. Regardless of whether they are composed of individuals or institutions, more than two-thirds of the membership associations include discussions of political issues on their Web sites. Half the membership associations of individuals and a third of the membership associations having institutions as members use their Web sites to urge political action. Labor unions and public interest groups are particularly likely to include explicitly political material on their Web sites. In contrast, because they have good reason to appear nonpartisan, institutions like universities and

---

49. Daniel Nadler and Sounman Hong are coauthors of this section.

corporations are unlikely to use their Web sites either to discuss political issues or to suggest that visitors to their Web sites take some political action.

To investigate the ways organizations are using social media, we returned in the summer of 2011 to the set of organizations listed in the 2001 *Washington Representatives* directory, whose political activity is reported in Chapter 14. Because we were not in a position to code all the more than 11,000 organizations in the directory, we focused on categories of organizations that are dominated by membership associations and that had been found to use their Web sites to present political content: trade and other business associations, professional associations, other occupational associations (which have as members people who are in nonprofessional and nonmanagerial occupations and who are not unionized), labor unions, social welfare organizations and organizations advocating on behalf of the poor, identity groups, and public interest groups.[50] In order make the task more manageable, we sampled 100 of the professional associations; 100 of the racial, ethnic, and nationality groups (including Native American groups); and 500 of the trade and other business associations. We assembled information on social media use for more than 1,700 organizations. Although the data we assembled in the summer of 2011 are far more extensive than any we know about, we should make clear that we consider this to be a preliminary report on a constantly evolving domain.

We were concerned that, over the course of a decade, many organizations would have gone out of business as the result of the natural processes of the organizational life cycle. These concerns were reinforced by predictions made by some observers of social media that the possibilities for lateral communications among like-minded people obviate the need for formal organizations. We need not have worried. Predictions of the imminent demise of formal organizations turn out to be premature: the survival rate for organizations in the decade since they were listed in the 2001 directory is remarkable.[51] With one perhaps ironic exception—"only" 78 percent of the organizations of the elderly listed in 2001 were alive in 2011—in every category, more than 80 percent of the organizations listed in 2001 could be located ten years later. Professional associations had an especially notable rate of survival: 97 percent.

50. For descriptions of these categories, see Chapter 11. There we noted that, although the members of "other occupational associations" work in nonprofessional, nonmanagerial occupations, they tend to be very skilled.

51. We consider an organization to have survived even if it has changed its name or merged with another organization.

Organized Interests and Digital Technologies

Table 16.2, which presents data about the extent to which organizations have adopted digital technologies, shows notably high levels of use. Not surprisingly, the overwhelming share of organizations active in politics in 2001 and still active as organizations in 2011 were found to have Web sites. In a pattern that obtains not only for all the categories of organizations in Table 16.2 but also for such detailed subcategories as women's organizations or consumer groups, organized interests are less likely to have Facebook pages than Web sites and still less likely to have Twitter accounts than either Facebook pages or Web sites.[52] In Chapter 14 we saw that trade and business associations are, in general, very politically active—having, for example, the highest average lobbying spending among the categories of organizations listed in the table. We also saw that, if they have a Web site, they are relatively likely to use it to discuss policy issues. Thus it is interesting that trade and other business associations are laggards when it comes to embracing these media—the least likely to have a Web site or, especially, a Facebook page or a Twitter account.

When we pry open these aggregated categories, we find some marked differences among the more detailed categories that comprise them. In particular, there are disparities among the various kinds of identity groups in their use of these technologies, especially Twitter. The digital champions are the handful of lesbian, gay, bisexual, and transgender (LGBT) groups, each of which has a Web site, a Facebook page, and a Twitter account. In contrast, only 37 percent of the organizations representing the elderly and only 13 percent of the organizations, most of which are tribes, representing Native Americans have Twitter accounts. Unlike the identity groups, the various kinds of public interest groups—which are, collectively, quite active in the use of these technologies—show much less variation. A majority of all the organizations in each of the subcategories of public interest groups have a Web site, a Facebook page, and a Twitter account. Also notable is the fact that 78 percent of the small number of organizations that advocate on behalf of the poor use Twitter.

Organizations on Facebook

Politically active membership associations are increasingly likely to establish a presence on Facebook. The Facebook pages created by organizations—and,

---

52. Of the more than 1,700 organizations, only 11 have either a Facebook page or a Twitter account but no Web site. Thirty-two are on Twitter but not Facebook.

Table 16.2   Organized Interests Using Digital Technologies, 2011[a]

Categories of Organized Interests	Percentage of Organized Interests Using Each Technology		
	Web Site	Facebook	Twitter
Trade and Other Business Associations	85%	47%	31%
Professional Associations	97%	66%	59%
Other Occupational Associations	94%	62%	50%
Unions	91%	64%	55%
Social Welfare or Poor	97%	77%	65%
Identity Groups[b]	95%	66%	38%
Public Interest	95%	73%	64%

Source: Washington Representatives Study (2001).

[a] The table shows, for organizations listed in the 2001 *Washington Representatives* directory that were still operative as organizations in June or July 2011, the percentage that had a Web site, a Facebook account, or a Twitter account; smaller random samples were searched for trade and other business associations (500 organizations), professional associations (100 organizations), and identity groups representing racial, ethnic, and nationality groups (100 organizations); for all other categories, all organizations were searched.

[b] Includes organizations representing racial, ethnic, or religious groups; the elderly; women; or lesbian, gay, bisexual, or transgender (LGBT) sexual orientation.

for that matter, politicians—differ in an important respect from those set up by individuals. While individuals ordinarily make at least some of the information on their Facebook pages available only to their Facebook "friends," the information on organizations' Facebook pages is usually open to all and can be accessed using Google.

Like their Web sites, organizations' Facebook pages are quite varied along a number of dimensions, including the extent of their political content. Although the information on an organization's Facebook page is usually more limited than on its Web site and often replicates it, Facebook offers intriguing possibilities for conveying information and generating support among potential organizational supporters.

Just as they can with politicians, individuals who are on Facebook can register their approval of an organization by "liking" what they see on its Facebook page. This support becomes part of individuals' Facebook profiles, information that, in turn, becomes available to all their Facebook "friends," who average 130 in number.[53] When Facebook users click through their Facebook friends' "likes," they become aware of an organization's existence and, if they delve further, its message. This process uses the power of social networks to provide not only access to information but implicit endorsement. Just as requests for political activity from friends and acquaintances are more likely to produce results than requests from strangers, presumably a recommendation by someone who is known personally carries greater weight in validating an organization's message and significance. Thus, while the content of an organization's Facebook postings is not necessarily "political" in the old-fashioned sense, Facebook provides an infrastructure that can immediately be converted into a mechanism for disseminating political information and requests for political action.

In addition, Facebook has interactive capacities. An organization's Facebook "wall" affords opportunities for supporters to comment on the material posted by the organization. Similar to the comments that are posted to politicians' Facebook walls, the comments tend to be relatively brief and not unduly concerned with the niceties of grammar, spelling, or sometimes civility. Although some might function as brief letters to the editor, in general the emphasis is on the personal and expressive.

Table 16.3 presents data about the number of supporters of the Facebook pages of various kinds of membership associations. The left-hand column of numbers, which shows the proportion of each kind of organization with a Facebook account, repeats information from Table 16.2. The next column shows the average number of Facebook supporters for the organizations in each category *among the organizations with Facebook accounts.* The next column shows the total number of Facebook "likes" for the organizations in that category, a figure that reflects the average number of supporters for those organizations and the number of such organizations. Because Facebook users are not limited in the number of organizations to which they can give a thumbs-up, the unit of analysis is the "like," and the totals in this column do not represent unique individuals. Still, they indicate the phenomenal reach of Facebook, and thus its potential as a tool for organizations that are politically active.

53. Figure given on http://www.facebook.com/press/info.php?statistics (accessed August 26, 2011).

Table 16.3 Organized Interests on Facebook and Their Supporters, 2011

Categories of Organized Interests	On Facebook[a]	Average Number of Supporters[b]	Total Number of Supporters[c]	N[d]
Trade and Other Business Associations	47%	74,220	43,913,065	1,301
Professional Associations	66%	2,447	731,161	431
Other Occupational Associations	62%	3,407	151,615	74
Unions	64%	4,111	263,249	99
Social Welfare or Poor	77%	7,474	456,100	78
Identity Groups[e]	66%	7,647	2,429,605	398
Public Interest	73%	30,006	9,212,170	432

Source: Washington Representatives Study (2001).

[a] Among organizations listed in the 2001 *Washington Representatives* directory that were still operative as organizations in June or July 2011, the percentage that had a Facebook account; smaller random samples were searched for trade and other business associations (500 organizations), professional associations (100 organizations), and identity groups representing racial, ethnic, and nationality groups (100 organizations); for all other categories, all organizations were searched.

[b] The average number of people who said that they liked the Facebook pages of the organizations in a particular category—among the organizations that have Facebook pages (i.e., the average excludes organizations without Facebook pages).

[c] The total number of people who said that they liked the Facebook pages of the organizations in a particular category.

[d] The number of organizations listed in the 2001 *Washington Representatives* directory that were still operative as organizations in June or July 2011, weighted to account for organizations that were in more than one category (see Chapter 11); for categories of organizations for which a random sample of organizations was searched—trade and other business associations, professional associations, and identity groups representing racial, ethnic, and nationality groups—the number of living organizations was inferred from the results for the sample.

[e] Includes organizations representing racial, ethnic, or religious groups; the elderly; women; or LGBT sexual orientation.

The surprise in Table 16.3 is that, although trade and other business associations are relatively unlikely to have Facebook accounts, they have, by far, the greatest Facebook support—a function of the fact that there are so many of them and that they have, on average, so many supporters. Also notable is the limited Facebook reach of unions. Throughout our investigation we have seen that unions tend to have very high levels of political activity but that the total volume of union action is bounded by the fact that there are so few of them in comparison to other kinds of organizations, especially corporations. Even though their membership rosters have diminished substantially since peaking in the 1950s, one resource that unions bring to the political fray is their large numbers of members. Compared to other kinds of membership associations that organize people on the basis of their shared occupations, unions have, on average, much larger memberships, whom they have always sought to mobilize to take part in politics. Indeed we saw earlier (Table 14.2) that, among organizations with Web sites, unions were the most likely to use their Web sites both to discuss political issues and to facilitate political activity by, for example, encouraging individuals to take specific political action, inviting submission of an e-mail address in order to receive a newsletter or periodic updates about policy matters, or including links to facilitate voter registration. Thus the unions' limited Facebook penetration is striking.

We should acknowledge that the remarkable Facebook reach of trade and other business associations reflects the presence of the National Basketball Association (with roughly 10 million supporters) and the National Football League (with nearly 4 million)—as part of the sample of five hundred such organizations we examined. If we make the quick and overly compensatory fix of omitting these two organizations from the tally of total Facebook supporters, we reduce the number of Facebook supporters very substantially, to just under 1.6 million.[54] Even so, trade and other business associations are left with more Facebook supporters than unions.

Once again, looking within these aggregated categories is revealing and shows disparities among different kinds of organizations in their emphasis on Facebook—and among their different constituencies in their propensity to use Facebook—as an interactive medium. Although organizations representing Native Americans are the most numerous of the identity groups and

54. The mathematically minded reader who is attempting to reconcile these numbers with those in the table is reminded that the numbers in Table 16.3 have been weighted to adjust for the sampling ratio.

an organization representing the elderly, AARP, is by far the largest membership association, neither category registers very substantially in terms of Facebook support. Native American organizations generate only 3 percent, and organizations representing the elderly only 2 percent, of Facebook support for identity groups. In contrast, although LGBT organizations are a tiny category, containing very few organizations, all of them are on Facebook, and together they account for nearly half of the Facebook supporters of identity groups. This outcome reflects the roughly 900,000 Facebook supporters of the Human Rights Campaign, the LGBT organization that represents more than a third of the Facebook support for identity groups.

While the various kinds of public interest groups are all quite likely to have a Facebook presence, environmental and wildlife groups account for nearly half, 48 percent, of the Facebook supporters for public interest groups. It is worth noting that, although other liberal public interest groups are somewhat more likely to be on Facebook than are other conservative public interest groups, the Facebook pages of the latter attract, on average, more than twice as many likes, with the result that the volume of Facebook support for other conservative public interest groups is nearly twice that for other liberal public interest groups.

Organizations representing social service providers and the poor are among the most likely to have Facebook accounts, but there are very few of them, and their total Facebook support is about half that of the LGBT Facebook powerhouse, the Human Rights Campaign. Besides, Facebook support for these organizations is driven by a single organization, the American Red Cross. Its Facebook supporters represent about three-quarters of the Facebook supporters of these organizations. Even within a category that barely registers in aggregate measures of the volume of political activity by organizations, advocates for the poor constitute only 11 percent of the Facebook supporters of organizations representing social service providers and the poor.

In thinking about organizations on Facebook, it is important to reiterate that the Facebook pages of organizations that are very politically active contain much material that is only marginally political. In addition, aggregate results in these data about political organizations' Facebook use and support show the dominance of particular organizations with large numbers of supporters. Still, these data contain striking findings. On the one hand, Facebook provides opportunities to reach groups that are not well represented in organized interest politics. The kinds of citizen groups that have made their presence felt recently in American politics—identity groups and especially public interest groups—are effective in using Facebook to link to supporters.

On the other hand, our findings reinforce the overall conclusions about the contours of political representation through membership organizations. Organizations representing business have a substantial presence that overshadows the representation of the economic interests of the poor and the bulk of the workforce, which is in nonprofessional, nonadministrative occupations.[55]

Organizations on Twitter

Earlier in the chapter we cited the example of how the account of Jonah Peretti's attempt to order customized Nike shoes—emblazoned with the word *sweatshop*—quickly reached millions of people though e-mail. Twitter amplifies substantially the possibilities for real-time dissemination of messages. A Twitter account allows an organization to broadcast short messages—no more than 140 characters—to all its "followers," thus lowering to nearly zero the transaction costs of disseminating content simultaneously and instantaneously to a large number of followers. In turn, messages on Twitter can be rebroadcast by recipients to the followers of their own accounts, thus creating the potential for a massive amplification of a message or a piece of content across an interconnected population. Ordinarily, individuals and organizations with Twitter accounts are simultaneously both followed and followers; that is, not only do they have followers who trail them but Twitter users are followers themselves, following others on Twitter.[56] To followers, messages will appear in a "stream" of messages that aggregates in real time all the messages of all the accounts they are following. Like Facebook, Twitter makes it possible to discover information indirectly by browsing the content of accounts being followed. However, it is even easier on Twitter than on Facebook to stay up to date with the content and messages of friends, celebrities, politicians—and politically active organizations.

How Do They Tweet? We were also not surprised that organizations' Facebook pages bear some relation to their Web sites or that those Facebook pages vary in the extent to which they contain political content. We had fewer

---

55. This pattern is consistent with Jeffrey Berry's analysis of the way that the ascendancy of liberal citizen groups has not included advocacy on behalf of liberal economic issues. See Jeffrey M. Berry, *The New Liberalism: The Rising Power of Citizen Groups* (Washington, DC: Brookings Institution, 1999), pp. 55–57.

56. We collected data for two measures of network influence: amplification, which is a measure of the extent to which others act on someone's tweets, and "Klout Score." The Klout Score is the online influence of an organization as determined by Klout, which makes a calculation on the basis of a secret proprietary formula. Because we could not verify what was being measured, we decided not to present these data. For information about amplification and Klout scores, see http://klout.com/corp/kscore (accessed September 4, 2011).

expectations when it comes to Twitter. In order to gain some perspective on the different ways that political organizations use Twitter to present themselves and their political commitments, generate support, mobilize action, and interact with potential supporters, we surveyed the Twitter accounts of forty membership organizations—all of them known as heavyweight political actors—drawn from the range of organizational types we have been discussing. To some extent, all these organizations use their social media accounts to convey information about the organization and its mission and to provide daily or weekly updates on its activities, including campaigns and fundraising events, as well as to mobilize followers to take action—ranging from the call by the NAACP urging backers to show up at a rally to the request from the National Association of Realtors to attend a regularly scheduled membership meeting.

As expected, however, we discovered a substantial degree of variation in the mix of objectives that organizations pursue using Twitter and in the tone, politicization, and partisanship of their tweets. Even highly politically active organizations use their messages to promote members' interests in nonpolitical ways. For example, the American Federation of Teachers posted a reminder to "Check to see when your local @Staples is having its Teacher Appreciation," and the American Bar Association, which tends to be nonpartisan and reticent in its social media use, keeps members up to date regarding organization activity and reports on litigation statistics across the United States. Still, we were struck by the extent to which these organizations use Twitter to take political positions and urge political action. AARP, for example, uses its Twitter account both to organize congressional lobbying ("Tell Congress: Cut wasteful spending & close tax loopholes, not SS & Medicare benefits *aarp.us/rhdz0Y*") and to broadcast concrete policy suggestions ("8 cuts the Congress deficit committee might make to #Medicare and #Medicaid *http://aarp.us/pvnWME*"). Perhaps ironically, the American Automobile Association used its Twitter account to inform its membership about text messaging laws on the road ("34 states + D.C. currently ban text messaging for all drivers. Do you know the laws in your state? *http://ow.ly/5UljR* #dwd").

Many organizations take a more strident tone. The National Rifle Association does post helpful information like the following: "Texas Deer Hunting Leases, Deer Hunting Tips *bit.ly/pDP6vu* #spo #texas." However, it also broadcasts a steady stream of highly politicized messages, such as "Obama Administration Resorts to Mob Tactics to push gun control agenda." Similarly, the

American Civil Liberties Union often sends out impassioned and even vitriolic messages: "Cheney has no regrets, even tho [*sic*] the policies he wants his legacy to rest upon have been recognized as illegal http://bit.ly/pLlWvF." Even the Business Roundtable—a peak business association composed of CEOs of leading U.S. companies, not otherwise known for a pugnacious political style—builds an argument across its various broadcasts, some of which are highly politicized and partisan.

We also investigated the extent to which these organizations use their accounts to engage in dialogue with other users in the Twittersphere. While we found considerable willingness among these organizations to rebroadcast the messages that we sent when those messages were supportive of their priorities, we found little disposition to use the public forum of Twitter to engage in direct "conversations" with us.

Who Tweets? Table 16.4 presents data about the Twitter followings of various categories of membership associations. The left-hand column of numbers repeats data from Table 16.2 about the proportion of organizations in each category that have Twitter accounts. The next column shows for each category the average number of tweets per week *among organizations that post on Twitter*. Overall, organizations that post on Twitter do so quite often, usually every day. Across these categories, the average frequency of Twitter feeds, which is not strongly associated with the probability that an organization in that category has a Twitter account, varies somewhat. Among organizations that tweet, public interest groups and trade and other business associations post on Twitter roughly twice as often as professional associations or the other occupational associations (which have as members nonunion workers in nonprofessional and nonmanagerial occupations). The next column shows, again for organizations that post on Twitter, the average number of followers. In all categories except one, the average number of Twitter followers is lower, sometimes markedly, than the average number of Facebook supporters. What is especially noteworthy, however, is the variation among kinds of organizations, which is substantial.

The next column shows the total Twitter volume for the various categories of organizations. Twitter volume is measured by the total number of tweets delivered per week by the organizations in a particular category—which reflects the number of tweets per week, the number of followers, and the number of organizations in that category. Although the particulars differ, the overall shape of the relationships tracks what we saw for Facebook. Although trade and other business associations are less likely than other kinds

Table 16.4 Organized Interests on Twitter and Their Followers, 2011

Categories of Organized Interests	On Twitter[a]	Average Tweets per Week[b]	Average Number of Followers[c]	Total Weekly Tweet Hits[d]	N[e]
Trade and Other Business Associations	31%	11	36,468	1,605,485,558	1,301
Professional Associations	59%	6	1,659	4,217,164	431
Other Occupational Associations	50%	6	1,441	640,569	74
Unions	55%	8	1,704	1,230,056	99
Social Welfare or Poor	65%	9	10,736	4,503,937	78
Identity Groups[f]	38%	8	1,380	11,107,701	398
Public Interest	64%	12	6,326	66,536,063	432

Source: Washington Representatives Study (2011).

[a] Among organizations listed in the 2001 *Washington Representatives* directory that were still operative as organizations in June or July 2011, the percentage that had a Twitter account in June or July 2011; smaller random samples were searched for trade and other business associations (500 organizations), professional associations (100 organizations), and identity groups representing racial, ethnic, and nationality groups (100 organizations); for all other categories, all organizations were searched.

[b] The average number of tweets sent per week—among the organizations that send tweets (i.e., the average excludes organizations that do not tweet).

[c] The average number of followers of the organizations in a particular category—among the organizations that send tweets (i.e., the average excludes organizations that do not tweet).

[d] The total number of Twitter connections made per week by the organizations in a particular category (i.e., the sum for each category of the number of tweets per week times the number of followers times the number of organizations in the category).

[e] The number of organizations listed in the 2001 *Washington Representatives* directory that were still operative as organizations in June or July 2011, weighted to account for organizations that were in more than one category (see Chapter 11); for categories of organizations for which a random sample of organizations was searched—trade and other business associations, professional associations, and identity groups representing racial, ethnic, and nationality groups—the number of living organizations was inferred from the results for the sample.

[f] Includes organizations representing racial, ethnic, or religious groups; the elderly; women; or LGBT sexual orientation.

of membership organizations to use Twitter, they are much more numerous than other kinds of organizations, tweet relatively frequently, and have, on average, extremely large numbers of followers. Once again, the staggering number of Twitter connections reflects the high number of Twitter followers for the National Basketball Association (NBA) and the National Football League (NFL). Still, as with Facebook, unions have not been successful in exploiting the possibilities of social media. Even if we omit the NBA and the NFL from the calculation, an action we consider overly conservative, the total volume of Twitter feeds for trade and other business associations—while reduced substantially—is still more than twice the total for organizations advocating on behalf of the poor, unions, and other occupational associations taken together.

The patterns for the different kinds of organizations within these categories are also similar to what we saw for Facebook support. Once again, the very small number of LGBT organizations—which represent 37 percent of the weekly Twitter connections for identity groups—generate substantial volume within that category. With 18 percent of the total volume for identity groups, organizations representing the elderly carry more weight with respect to Twitter than with respect to Facebook. Organizations representing Native Americans, the most numerous among identity groups, account for less than 1 percent of the total weekly Twitter connections made by identity groups.

Regarding public interest groups, with 65 percent of the weekly Twitter connections in that category, environmental and wildlife organizations are even more dominant than on Facebook. There is an interesting reversal from what we saw for Facebook support when it comes to the relative balance between what we call "other liberal" and "other conservative" public interest groups. Although the latter are slightly more likely to post on Twitter, the former have many more followers. When all the factors have been taken into account, other liberal public interest groups have a volume of weekly Twitter connections that is 4.6 times that of their conservative counterparts.[57]

57. It is interesting to note that Republican senators and members of the House seem to be more likely than their Democratic counterparts to use Twitter to communicate with constituents. See Matthew Eric Glassman, Jacob R. Straus, and Colleen J. Shogan, "Social Networking and Constituent Communication: Member Use of Twitter during a Two-Week Period in the 111th Congress," Congressional Research Service, February 3, 2010, at http://www.fas.org/sgp/crs/misc/R41066.pdf CRS Report.R40823 (accessed September 4, 2011), and Colleen J. Shogan, "Blackberries, Twitter Messages, and YouTube: Technology and the Future of Communicating with Congress," *PS: Political Science and Politics* 43 (2010): 231–233.

With respect to social welfare providers and organizations representing the poor, the roughly half a million Twitter followers of the American Red Cross account for a substantial share of the weekly Twitter connections for organizations in this category. Still, organizations of and on behalf of the poor account for a greater share, 20 percent, of the volume of weekly Twitter connections than of total Facebook support in this category.

In short, although the details vary, the overall shape of Twitter connections by membership associations that get involved in politics conforms to patterns that obtain not only for Facebook support but also for political activity more generally: organizations representing business are well represented, and among citizen groups, public interest and identity groups figure more importantly than such advocates for the economic interests of nonelites as labor unions, other occupational associations, and social service providers and advocates for the poor.

Conclusion

Technological innovations seem always to combine transformation with continuity and to have uneven consequences across various domains of human endeavor. In the brief span of their history, the implications of rapidly evolving digital technologies have already been felt in venues as disparate as the streets of Cairo and the divorce courts of the United States. They are also having an impact on the practice of American democracy.

If we began this chapter modestly hopeful that the political possibilities of the Internet might disrupt long-standing patterns of participatory inequality in American politics, what we have found has, by and large, showed those expectations to be unfounded. Whether we considered participatory acts—including the making of political contributions—that can be undertaken online, political discussions on the Internet, or political recruitment by e-mail, we have found little evidence that, for individuals, the association between social class and political activity is any different when politics is on the Internet. Not only does the digital divide mean that those who are lower on the socio-economic ladder are less likely to use the Internet or e-mail at least occasionally or to have broadband access at home, but among Internet users, there is a strong positive relationship between SES and—with the possible exception of political social networking—every measure of Internet-based political engagement we reviewed.

In contrast, the Internet seems to have the potential to ameliorate the well-known participatory deficit of those individuals who have just joined the electorate. When it comes to online politics—whether political activity, political discussion, or requests for political action on the Internet—younger respondents are less underrepresented than they are offline. In fact, they are more likely than their elders to receive requests for political activity by e-mail, and they dominate on blogs and in politically relevant uses of social networking. However, we should note that these counterstratificational tendencies are anchored in the digital divide. As is well known, young adults are much more likely than their elders to be comfortable with electronic technologies and to use the Internet. Their advantage is less obvious when those who do not use the Internet are eliminated from the analysis. In fact, the relatively few elderly Web users are particularly likely to exploit the political capacities of the Internet. Moreover, within generational groups, we found sharp socioeconomic stratification in online activity.

These findings about individuals should be placed in the context of an understanding that the survey on which they are based was conducted during a historic presidential campaign. With respect to the particularities of the 2008 campaign, we might expect the campaign to have had a special appeal both to younger citizens and to those who are lower down on the SES ladder, thus ameliorating both forms of stratification ordinarily associated with political activity. Yet, when it comes to online activity, the consequences are more complicated, for younger citizens are advantaged—and those in lower SES groups disadvantaged—by the digital divide.

We extended our exploration of the implications of social media for inequalities of political voice with systematic data about membership associations. Our inquiry, though preliminary, suggests that, contrary to predictions that their ability to facilitate lateral communications among members will make political organizations obsolete, social media are unlikely to put politically engaged organizations out of business. Social scientists have long known that organizations tend to be resilient. Besides, it would be difficult for ordinary individuals acting on their own to engage in many of the activities undertaken, usually by professionals, by organized interests in politics—among them, providing expert policy information, filing amicus briefs, and testifying at committee or agency hearings. Even when individuals take part politically—by, for example, funding candidates or contacting public officials—their actions may be coordinated by organizations. That said, social media may influence the relationship between organizational leaders and rank and file and may lead to greater emphasis on forms of political engagement that are more personal and more expressive than are characteristic of traditional participatory acts.

With respect to inequalities of political voice, in their broad outlines, data about the Facebook support and Twitter followings of membership associations listed in the 2001 *Washington Representatives* directory and still active as organizations in 2011 hew closely to the findings in the first part of this chapter about individual political participation on the Internet and in Chapter 14 about the distribution of organized interest activities. Just as individual political participation on the Internet ameliorates the age structuring of individual activity but replicates the socio-economic stratification, the possibilities for membership associations on Facebook and Twitter permit new voices—for example, those of LGBT groups or environmental organizations—to be heard. However, they leave untouched a circumstance in which the perspectives of business receive much fuller representation than the concerns and needs of the poor and those who work in nonprofessional, nonmanagerial occupations.

We should repeat that our findings might soon be considered obsolete. The political capacities of the Internet and other digital media continue to develop with astonishing rapidity. In particular, we do not yet know the full implications for political involvement—and for the inequalities of political activity—of social media. After all, even though neither Facebook nor Twitter existed when we began this study, a recent opinion piece about Facebook in the *New York Times* announced ironically, "It's Over."[58]

Part of the question is the meaning of new technologies for the way that citizens experience politics. For example, politicians' diverse Facebook pages —which blur the lines between the personal and the political and between politics and entertainment—suggest that it is not clear whether social media will redefine the meaning of political engagement. Many forms of political engagement in these venues do not fall squarely under the rubric of a definition of political participation as "activity that has the intent or effect of influencing government action—either directly by affecting the making or implementation of public policy or indirectly by influencing the selection of people who make those policies."[59] Will a social networking site like Facebook facilitate the dissemination of political information and encourage modes of online and offline political participation, as conventionally understood? Or will these rapidly changing forms of digital interaction dilute the meaning of politically engaged citizenship? Although "liking" a candidate is

58. Curtis Sittenfeld, "I'm on Facebook. It's Over." *New York Times*, September 4, 2011.
59. Verba, Schlozman, and Brady, *Voice and Equality*, p. 38.

not the same as taking part in a campaign, will it become the first step in that direction? Can the political groups formed on a social networking site become the basis for sustained political action as well as an infrastructure for mobilization?

As for the issue of how the possibilities provided by social media for political discussion and mobilization affect the mix of voices in the heavenly chorus, at present, political engagement on blogs and social networking sites clearly overcomes the historical underrepresentation of younger citizens with respect to political activity. As older cohorts quickly register on social networking sites, there is no guarantee that the young will continue to dominate these venues to the extent they do today. In the two years after the Pew survey used in this chapter was conducted, the number of people using social networking sites doubled and the proportion of social networkers over age thirty-five rose from roughly a third to more than half.[60] Besides, we cannot know whether the current techno-savvy generation will be trumped by their successors, who are now in elementary school. Thus, in part the consequences of the Internet for inequalities of political voice depend on what happens with the aging of the current cohort of younger adults.

When it comes to the impact of these changing technologies on the socioeconomic stratification of participation, we are similarly uncertain. We consider it premature to conclude, as others have suggested, that interactive forms of online political participation hold the key to unlocking the association between political participation and socio-economic status. The links between social class and political participation have proved to be powerful and enduring. We are not ready to wager that the Internet will sunder them. The data reviewed in this chapter suggest that, whether composed of individuals or organized interests, whether singing on or off the Internet, the heavenly chorus sings with an accent that seems to persist.

60. See Keith N. Hampton, Lauren Sessions Goulet, Lee Rainie, and Kristen Purcell, "Social Networking Sites and Our Lives," Pew Research Center's Internet and American Life Project, June 16, 2011, http://pewinternet.org/Reports/2011/Technology-and-social-networks .aspx (accessed July 17, 2011).

17

What, if Anything, Is to Be Done?

A book like this one that diagnoses a problem in democratic governance usually concludes with a chapter that looks forward by making suggestions for procedural change. Consistent with our habit of sticking closely to the data, when we have considered such issues in the past we have never availed ourselves of the opportunity to propose reforms that might ameliorate the circumstances that we have gone to such lengths to analyze. In a break from our prior reticence, in this chapter we consider some of the political, educational, and social changes that might overcome partially the inequalities of political voice that previous chapters have documented in such detail.

Our more reform-minded readers will probably not find our exploration to be fully satisfactory. In the space of a single chapter, we cannot give thorough consideration to the various procedural changes—many of which, like campaign finance reform and voter registration, have been the subjects of multiple volumes and extensive scholarly writing—that might address political inequalities among citizens. Rather than propose a laundry list of reforms, we hope to provide some analytical hooks to facilitate systematic thinking about the various strategies that might reduce inequalities of political voice. Moreover, as signaled by the title of the chapter, we have not abandoned entirely our previous prudence. As we proceed, we shall emphasize repeatedly why political change is so difficult to realize and why it is so often a disappointment when it is achieved. Hence this chapter makes no pretense of being the final word on what is to be done.

Shauna Shames is coauthor of this chapter.

We should make clear that our purview in this chapter is not the entire landscape of political reform. There are many proposed changes to American political procedure—for example, term limits for members of Congress, a defined period of campaigning for federal elections, or a greater role for elected officials at party conventions—that might or might not be desirable but that are not germane to our central concern. In fact, we are not even concerned with the full range of reforms that might bear on citizen political participation. The agenda of procedural reforms contains items, of which voting by mail is an example, that seem to have the effect of *raising the level of activity* without *decreasing inequalities of political voice.*[1] In fact, because most people are not especially active in politics, and thus the channels that transmit messages from citizens to public officials run at far below full capacity, it is possible simultaneously to increase both the amount of activity and the extent to which it is unrepresentative.

Our focus is on changes that would have the result of making the participatory input from individuals and organizations more representative of the American public in terms of a variety of politically relevant attributes—not only such demographic characteristics as social class, race, gender, or age but also preferences and needs for government policy. As we have maintained throughout, our concern with equality of political voice does not prescribe any particular inflection point along the continuum of elite autonomy or populist control in policy making, only that the expressions of political voice —through which citizens inform public officials about their circumstances and opinions and persuade them to listen—represent all equally.

The Uphill Road to Reform

As political scientists, we have reason to be leery of wholehearted endorsement of political reform. Not only are there multiple barriers to effecting political change but political history is littered with examples of procedural reforms that did not deliver on their initial promise. As we discussed in Chapter 10, one of the axioms of political analysis is the strong gravitational pull exerted by the political status quo in America. As every textbook points out, our political system was constructed from the outset to diminish the possibilities for hasty change. The checks and balances intrinsic to separation

1. See Adam J. Berinsky, Nancy Burns, and Michael W. Traugott, "Who Votes by Mail? A Dynamic Model of the Individual-Level Consequences of Voting-by-Mail Systems," *Public Opinion Quarterly* 65 (2001): 178–197.

of powers and federalism have been reinforced by institutional mechanisms that disperse power—for example, the committee system in Congress and a traditionally weak bureaucracy—with the result that inaction is more likely than policy innovation. Not only do institutional arrangements present an impediment to policy change but it is also the case that "policy makes politics." That is, existing policies usually create stakeholders with an interest in maintaining those policies. Their support for existing policies is an additional factor militating against policy change.

Moreover, federalism implies that many of the political arrangements with implications for inequalities of political voice—ranging from the laws mandating the disenfranchisement of felons to the regulation of corporate giving in state elections—are governed by state, not national, law. Some states have a track record of innovation when it comes to political arrangements. State-level experiments can yield important evidence to guide procedural reform on a more widespread basis regarding such matters as ballot access and campaign finance. However, the very unevenness that is the essence of federal arrangements implies that sometimes these procedural arrangements—for example, poll taxes in the South or restrictive local regulations governing protests—act as barriers to equal voice instead of facilitating it.

Bringing about changes on a national basis involves changing up to fifty sets of laws—and perhaps myriad local ones—which is much more challenging than altering a single federal statute. One way to overcome the impact of federalism and bring about change on a national basis is by constitutional amendment. Historically, the cause of greater equality of political voice has been furthered by constitutional amendments enfranchising former slaves in 1870 and women in 1920, outlawing the poll tax in 1964, and enfranchising young adults in 1971. However, the number of failed constitutional amendments—including, most recently, the attempt to establish equality under the law irrespective of gender through the Equal Rights Amendment—demonstrates how high a hurdle is imposed by the requirement for congressional supermajorities and passage in three-fourths of the states.

An additional barrier to certain kinds of political changes is the nature of the American political tradition. Distrust of government and a liberal celebration of the individual apart from inherited statuses mean that certain political arrangements that are common across democracies to overcome political inequalities—for instance, registration of voters by the government or reservation of seats in the legislature for underrepresented groups such as women —would be less likely in the American context.

Anatole France wrote famously: "The law, in its majestic equality, forbids the rich as well as the poor to sleep under bridges, to beg in the streets, and to steal bread." Still another political obstacle to procedural reform is contained in the observation that, even when fairly applied, the rules of politics are rarely neutral in their political effects, and thus a quarrel about the rules of American politics often masks a dispute over substance. Most observers of American democracy do care deeply about the frequently conflicting values at stake in disputes about procedure. Nevertheless, there is often a remarkable coincidence between political self-interest and the competing democratic norms to which contestants appeal in debates about political arrangements. For example, laws aimed at combating vote fraud that require voters to present a photo ID at the polls are thought by many to pose a more substantial deterrent to turnout by voters of limited education or English language skills. Under the circumstances, it is hardly surprising that Democrats are less likely than Republicans to consider vote fraud to be a serious problem and less enthusiastic about voter ID laws as a possible remedy. Of the 2,018 legislators across nine states that considered voter ID bills between 2005 and 2007, 95.3 percent of the Republicans and 2.2 percent of the Democrats voted in favor.[2]

Political Reform: Results or Consequences?

When it comes to political reform, it is a truism that "you want results and you get consequences." For a variety of reasons, political innovations frequently do not work out as expected. As commonly noted about public policies, and many other matters, "The devil is in the details." Assessments of the consequences of procedural reforms often contain the caveat that they have their intended impact "if correctly designed," thus attesting to the central role played by details of program design in determining their effectiveness. It is often possible to find loopholes that can be exploited to subvert the best intentions for political change—a circumstance that seems to be the rule, not the exception, when it comes to campaign finance law. For example, the impact of limitations on the sums that individuals can donate to campaigns is weakened when smaller checks are "bundled" together.[3]

2. Figure cited in Chandler Davidson, "The Historical Context of Voter Photo-ID Laws," *PS: Political Science and Politics* 42 (2009): 94.
3. Fred Wertheimer and Susan Weiss Manes, "Campaign Finance Reform: A Key to Restoring the Health of Our Democracy," *Columbia Law Review* 94 (1994). Wertheimer and

Furthermore, it is one thing to legislate and another to implement. In many cases, the implementation of political reforms has been spotty. For example, on the principle that low-income and disabled voters would be less likely to have cars or driver's licenses, the 1993 National Voter Registration Act (NVRA) contained provisions directing states to provide for voter registration not only at motor vehicle bureaus but also at public assistance agencies. According to a report issued by Project Vote and Dēmos, nongovernmental organizations concerned with voter participation, compliance with the mandate for voter registration at public assistance agencies declined precipitously in the decade after the NVRA was passed and first implemented. Comparing two presidential election cycles (1995–1996 and 2003–2004) shows a decrease of 60 percent in the number of registrations at public assistance agencies over the eight-year period.[4]

In addition, procedural changes often bequeath unintended consequences. For example, in seeking to establish the direct party primary early in the twentieth century, Robert La Follette reasoned that, if parties were no longer controlled by bosses driven by desire for patronage, they would be more likely to be united behind policy programs. However, if anything, the introduction of direct primaries left the parties less disciplined and cohesive. Similarly, in seeking to make the Democratic presidential nominating process less removed from the rank and file, the McGovern-Fraser Commission (1969–1972) did not intend to spur the widespread introduction of state presidential primaries. Nonetheless, that was surely one consequence of its guidelines.[5]

Manes note (pp. 1140–1141) that, although checks within a "bundle" originate from many sources, the "bundler"—that is, the person, group, or corporation gathering the checks together and delivering them to a candidate or campaign—gets the credit.

4. Douglas R. Hess and Scott Novakowski, *Unequal Access: Neglecting the National Voter Registration Act*, February 2008, http://www.demos.org/pubs/UnequalAccessReport-web.pdf (accessed August 8, 2008), p. 5. The report (p. 6) takes care to consider and discredit explanations other than uneven implementation for the decline in the number of registrations at public assistance agencies. For example, it might be thought that by reducing the number of recipients of public assistance, welfare reform would have obviated the need for voter registration in public assistance offices. However, although the number of recipients of Temporary Assistance for Needy Families funds did decrease over the period, the number of food stamp recipients increased substantially.

5. Austin Ranney, *Curing the Mischiefs of Faction: Party Reform in America* (Berkeley: University of California Press, 1975), pp. 205–206. Ranney, who served as a member of the McGovern-Fraser Commission, gives a number of examples of party reforms that have led to unexpected consequences. On the proliferation of primaries, see also Nelson W. Polsby, *Consequences of Party Reform* (Oxford, England: Oxford University Press, 1983), pp. 56–59.

Still another example of a government initiative that worked out in unanticipated ways—one that touches our concerns very directly—was the controversial mandate for "maximum feasible participation" of the poor in the community action programs of the federal poverty program of the 1960s. According to one analysis of this casually legislated attempt to address "political poverty"—that is, the political powerlessness and quiescence of the poor—the pushback against community participation by urban blacks came from a somewhat surprising source. It came "not from businessmen antagonistic to changes in class relationships nor from white groups resisting racial equality" but instead from "Democratic politicians who had often relied on black electoral support and encouraged specific black advances within their cities" and who resisted threats to established patterns of authority and to their own political power.[6]

Not only do reforms sometimes produce unexpected results but a procedural reform in the name of one democratic value may, in fact, jeopardize others. For instance, opponents of same-day voter registration, a procedural reform that increases turnout, argue that it increases vote fraud. Surely the integrity of the electoral process, which requires restricting access to the ballot to eligible voters, is also an important democratic principle. As we shall see, among the most notable examples of the way that political reforms may involve trade-offs among cherished democratic values is campaign finance regulation.

Our discussion so far leads us to be circumspect about the possibilities for reducing political inequalities through procedural reform both because there are political barriers to the realization of such reforms and because they so often go awry if adopted. There is a final reason that we are dubious about what can be achieved by procedural reform. Our analysis of the roots of political inequalities makes clear how deeply embedded they are in social, educational, and economic inequalities. If this volume has any theme, it is the power and durability of the impact of stratification by socio-economic status (SES) on individual and collective political participation. Addressing

---

6. J. David Greenstone and Paul E. Peterson, *Race and Authority in Urban Politics: Community Participation and the War on Poverty* (New York: Russell Sage Foundation, 1973), p. 13. This government effort to increase participation by the disadvantaged elicited widely differing assessments. For contrasting views, see Daniel P. Moynihan, *Maximum Feasible Misunderstanding: Community Action in the War on Poverty* (New York: Free Press / Macmillan, 1969), and Milton Kotler, "Discussions," in *A Decade of Federal Antipoverty Programs: Achievements, Failures, and Lessons*, ed. Robert H. Haveman (New York: Academic Press, 1977), pp. 281–283.

such inequalities of income and education is not a matter of mere institutional tinkering but would constitute a political and social revolution requiring a level of patience and a commitment of resources that have not been characteristic of American policy and that would seem out of step with the current political climate. It is difficult to overestimate what would be required to cut through the web of interconnected political, social, economic, and educational circumstances that reinforce inequality in contemporary America. Not only would the radically egalitarian policies designed to level the SES playing field be politically unlikely but it is doubtful that they could be fine-tuned in such a way as to bring about the desired outcomes without other disastrous consequences.

Strategies for Ameliorating Inequalities of Political Voice

Thus chastened, we shall spend the remainder of the chapter discussing a series of changes that might have the effect of reducing inequalities of political voice. Once again, our survey of reforms is not intended to be a comprehensive treatment of possible democratic reforms. It is not even a survey of possible reforms that have some bearing on political voice. Instead we focus much more narrowly on those that, if implemented, have a chance of reducing inequalities of political voice. The qualifiers *if implemented* and *chance* reflect our understanding of the barriers to enacting and implementing reforms and the frequent surprises in how they actually work out.

Table 17.1 presents a series of six strategies for reducing inequalities in political voice and, for each, gives examples of the kinds of political arrangements or public policies that are in place in the United States and in some other developed democracy. Those strategies are as follows:

- Ensuring votes of equal weight
- Mandating a participatory ceiling
- Establishing a participatory floor
- Lowering barriers to activity
- Recruiting activity
- Developing civic capacity

We developed these rubrics as a tool in organizing a complex discussion of the multiple policies that contain the possibility of ameliorating inequalities

Table 17.1 Strategies for Reducing Inequalities of Political Voice in the United States and Other Developed Democracies

	Strategy	
	United States	Other Developed Democracies
Ensuring Votes of Equal Weight	One person, one vote	Proportional representation electoral systems
Mandating a Participatory Ceiling	Limits on lobbying Limits on campaign contributions	Full public financing of elections
Establishing a Participatory Floor	Intervenor funding	Compulsory voting
Lowering Barriers to Activity	Voter registration at public assistance agencies	Election day a national holiday
Recruiting Activity	Get-out-the-vote drives	Strong labor unions
Developing Civic Capacity	Civic education	Educational and social services Redistributive economic policies

of political voice, but we do not wish to reify these categories. It would be easy to slice and dice the relevant proposals in other ways. There are surely alternatives with respect to the rubrics under which relevant policies could be grouped.

Ensuring Votes of Equal Weight

An obvious source of political inequality is any set of electoral arrangements in which votes do not count equally. Until a series of Supreme Court decisions in the 1960s declared the practice an unconstitutional violation of the Equal Protection Clause of the Fourteenth Amendment, legislative districts often differed substantially in population, with the result that those living in districts with fewer people, usually rural districts, enjoyed greater representation.[7] The effect of these Court decisions was to end such mathematical malapportionment for state and local legislatures, and eventually for the U.S. House.

However, the U.S. Senate remains as a clear example of unequal representation of individual citizens, with, at this writing, the most populous state, California, having the same number of senators—and more than seventy times the number of inhabitants—as the least populous, Wyoming. At times in the past, the equal representation of states in the Senate has had the political effect of protecting particular minority interests, such as the interests of slaveholders. At present, altering the composition of the U.S. Senate—which, because Article V of the U.S. Constitution requires that "no State, without its Consent, shall be deprived of its equal Suffrage in the Senate"—is extremely politically remote.[8]

Support for altering the other visible manifestation of unequal votes, the Electoral College, arises from time to time—usually in response to an election in which the peculiar operation of the Electoral College threatens to produce deadlock or to elect as president a candidate who did not win a plurality of the popular vote rather than in response to an abstract concern about the way that popular votes may weigh unequally.[9]

7. On these decisions and their consequences, see Stephen Ansolabehere and James M. Snyder, Jr., *The End of Inequality: One Person, One Vote and the Transformation of American Politics* (New York: W. W. Norton, 2008).

8. See Robert A. Dahl, *How Democratic Is the American Constitution?* (New Haven, CT: Yale University Press, 2002), pp. 13–18 and 144–148.

9. At this time, the supporters of National Popular Vote are seeking a reform that would circumvent the possibility that workings of the Electoral College will deny the presidency to the national plurality winner. According to its Web site, "Under the National Popular Vote

In discussions of the Electoral College, voters in three different sets of states are deemed to be advantaged by the way that the Electoral College works in presidential elections:

- Small states, because the apportionment of electoral votes as the total of a state's delegation to the U.S. House and Senate implies that each electoral vote represents fewer popular votes

- Large states, because the unit rule in the casting of electoral votes to the plurality winner in the state makes winning a large state much more valuable in the Electoral College tally

- Competitive states, because candidates do not pay much attention to states that they know they will definitely lose—or win[10]

In addition, the common wisdom has traditionally been that the biases in the operation of the Electoral College accrue to the advantage of urban interests, especially blacks.[11] However, there is reason to question this conclusion. The states in which African Americans are an especially large share of the voter-eligible population tend to be in the South and to be medium sized. They do not fall into any of the categories—the small, the large, or the competitive—said to be privileged in presidential elections. Thus, contrary to the received opinion, African Americans do not seem to be placed at a political advantage by the Electoral College.

It can be argued that the most substantial affront to votes of equal weight is the system of single-member legislative districts with winner-take-all elec-

---

bill, all of the state's electoral votes would be awarded to the presidential candidate who receives the most popular votes in all 50 states and the District of Columbia. The bill would take effect only when enacted, in identical form, by states possessing a majority of the electoral votes—that is, enough electoral votes to elect a President (270 of 538)." See http://www .nationalpopularvote.com/pages/explanation.ph (accessed March 23, 2010).

10. On the biases in the way the Electoral College operates, see Lawrence D. Longley and Neal R. Peirce, *The Electoral College Primer 2000* (New Haven, CT: Yale University Press, 1999), chap. 5, and Robert L. Lineberry, Darren Davis, Robert Erikson, Richard Herrera, and Priscilla Southwell, "The Electoral College and Social Cleavages: Ethnicity, Class, and Geography," in *Choosing a President: The Electoral College and Beyond*, ed. Paul D. Schumaker and Burdett A. Loomis (New York: Chatham House, 2002), chap. 11.

11. For an example of the common wisdom, see Nelson W. Polsby and Aaron Wildavsky with David A. Hopkins, *Presidential Elections*, 12th ed. (Lanham, MD: Rowman and Littlefield, 2008), p. 243. The argument made in this paragraph is less obviously applicable to Latinos, who are concentrated in such large states as California, Florida, and Texas and in certain swing states like New Mexico.

tions. Under these arrangements, which have long been critiqued by reform-minded scholars, politicians, and activists, the votes of those who cast ballots for any candidate other than the one gaining a plurality of the vote have essentially no weight at all. In contrast, in systems using proportional representation, parties attracting votes beyond a specified threshold, even if not a plurality, gain legislative representation, and therefore voters supporting minority viewpoints are not shut out. According to Robert Dahl, "Because the governing coalitions [in proportional systems] will generally include representatives from minority parties, governing majorities are likely to be more inclusive than in a majoritarian system. Thus, a proportional system comes closer than a majoritarian system to providing equal representation—an equal say—for all."[12] That said, the political obstacles to bringing about a change in the procedures for presidential elections are, to say the least, formidable.

Mandating a Participatory Ceiling

Much more common than inequalities of political voice deriving from electoral arrangements in which votes count unequally are those that derive from inequalities in the resources of skills, time, and money that make it possible for individuals and organizations to be politically active and from differences in the desire to use those resources in the pursuit of political objectives. With the exception of voting—for which the principle of one person, one vote mandates equality of political input among individual participants—all forms of political activity can be multiplied to the limits of a participant's capacity and inclination to take part. Thus one way to limit inequalities of

---

12. Dahl, *How Democratic Is the American Constitution?* p. 101. A similar sentiment is expressed by Arend Lijphart in "Reforming the House: Three Moderately Radical Proposals," *PS: Political Science and Politics* 31 (1998): 10: "That PR provides more accurate representation than majoritarian election methods is not controversial." See also G. Bingham Powell Jr., *Elections as Instruments of Democracy: Majoritarian and Proportional Visions* (New Haven, CT: Yale University Press, 2000), chap. 10. Powell shows that, on average, the policies in proportional systems come closer to the policy positions of the median citizen than those in majoritarian systems. For the impact of PR on increasing equality for women and minorities, see Joseph F. Zimmerman, "Underrepresentation of Women and Minorities in Elective Office in the United States," in *Electoral Systems in Comparative Perspective: Their Impact on Women and Minorities,* ed. Wilma Rule and Joseph F. Zimmerman (Westport, CT: Greenwood Press, 1994), pp. 101–114; Ian McAllister and Donley T. Studlar, "Electoral Systems and Women's Representation: A Long-Term Perspective," *Representation* 39 (2002): 3–14; and Pippa Norris, "The Impact of Electoral Reform on Women's Representation," *Acta Politica* (Special Issue) 41 (2006): 197–213.

political voice is to place constraints on the use of resources in participation or the amount of activity in which an individual or organization is permitted to engage.

By way of explanation, consider Kurt Vonnegut's short story "Harrison Bergeron."[13] Lest anyone take advantage of special gifts in Vonnegut's dystopia, the Handicapper General imposes equality of capacities by reducing all to the least common denominator: an intelligent man has a small radio in his ear that emits frequent noises so as to prevent him from thinking too hard; a particularly graceful ballerina is forced to wear weights on her arms; a beautiful one wears a mask that is unsightly. There is no precedent in American politics for the Handicapper General's strategy of leveling downward. Except under unusual circumstances that will be discussed, individuals are free to spend as much time as they like on participatory acts intended to influence politics: while others pass their leisure time shooting hoops or attending the ballet, activists can spend their spare time working for a candidate for office, composing letters to public officials, or serving on the local zoning board. The most important boundaries are those imposed by the limits on participants' time, attention, and commitment. In general, when it comes to reducing inequalities by imposing a participatory ceiling, it has been much more common to regulate forms of activity that depend on money than those that depend on time or especially skills.

From the perspective of inequalities of political voice, the unfettered use of money as a medium of participatory input poses special problems.[14] When a Monet is sold at Sotheby's, we expect the highest bidder to prevail. Why do we impose a different standard when it comes to political transactions? As we mentioned when we considered the organizations that are active in Washington politics, we do not ordinarily bother to ask why bribery is offensive in a democratic political system except to say, somewhat tautologically, that we are concerned about "corruption" or "the integrity of the political process." Presumably, the reason that bribery is an affront to democracy has something to do with the fact that, when political preferments and policy outcomes are apportioned in response to bribes, an important principle of democratic equality is violated: political decisions are no longer made in response to the

13. Kurt Vonnegut Jr., "Harrison Bergeron," in *Welcome to the Monkey House* (New York: Dell, 1970), pp. 7–13.

14. On the contrast between time and money as resources for politics, see Sidney Verba, Kay Lehman Schlozman, and Henry E. Brady, *Voice and Equality: Civic Voluntarism in American Politics* (Cambridge, MA: Harvard University Press, 1995), pp. 289–295.

will of the majority or as the result of deliberation on the merits but on the basis of who has the capacity to pay, and therefore democracy is no longer a level playing field on which citizens are equal.

Under certain circumstances, the use of money to achieve political goals is completely proscribed. For example, it is unlawful to bribe a voter. Similarly, everywhere in the United States it is illegal to pay a public official to take some desired action—a set of provisions that are generally, though hardly universally, honored. In the same spirit, there are complicated laws and regulations governing the nature and value of gifts, services, and entertainment that public officials can accept from constituents and representatives of organized interests. U.S. House rules prevent representatives from accepting any present valued above $50, any gifts that are cumulatively valued above $100 from a single source in a calendar year, or any gifts from registered lobbyists.[15] Analogous rules vary depending on the political jurisdiction and the branch of government in question. A former Maryland state legislator reported that in his state, under rules enforced by the Maryland Ethics Commission, he was not allowed to accept a cup of coffee from a lobbyist.[16]

Campaign Finance

Both more controversial and more highly technical than the laws that make it illegal to bribe a public official are the many restrictions that seek to equalize political voice by placing limits on campaign contributions.[17] Campaign finance regulations take many forms. Some of them—for example, overall caps

15. U.S. House of Representatives, "The House Gift Rule," U.S. House of Representatives Committee on Standards of Official Conduct, 2010, http://ethics.house.gov/Subjects/Topics.aspx?Section=24 (accessed January, 6, 2011).

16. John Hurson, quoted in David D. Kirkpatrick, "States Take Lead on Ethics Rules for Lawmakers," *New York Times*, January 1, 2007, p. A-1. Even within the boundaries of strict adherence to such regulations, lobbyists are in a position to do valuable favors for legislators— for example, by holding fund-raisers or otherwise assisting with raising campaign funds or by donating money in support of a party convention.

17. The literature on campaign finance reform and its effects is quite substantial. Extensive references to recent literature can be found in the bibliography to Malbin, ed., *The Election after Reform: Money, Politics, and the Bipartisan Campaign Reform Act* (Lanham, MD: Rowman and Littlefield), pp. 271–281, and in the references to the articles in "The Forum: Has the U.S. Campaign Finance System Collapsed?" Berkeley Electronic Press 6, no. 1 (2008), http://www.bepress.com/forum/vol6/iss1 (accessed November 28, 2010). A helpful review of the literature on the effects of campaign finance regulation in the states is Nolan L. Reichl, "What We Know and What We Don't: A Review of the Literature Empirically Analyzing the Effects of State Campaign Finance Reform Laws," Senior Thesis, Stanford Law School, Stanford, CA, 2006.

on what a campaign can spend—are not really germane to our concern with equal political voice among citizens. However, several forms of campaign finance regulation bear directly on the matter of diminishing inequalities of political voice. Among them are restrictions on campaign giving from certain sources such as labor unions, corporations, and government; restrictions on the size of contributions from individuals and political action committees; and schemes for the public funding of elections. In addition to federal laws regulating campaign finance are diverse regulations on the state and local levels. Forty-five states impose some type of campaign contribution limits, and twenty-three have some sort of public funding of electoral campaigns or political parties.[18] Furthermore, a number of large cities provide either full or partial public funding for citywide elections.[19] Viewed cross-nationally, the American system of campaign finance is unique among developed democracies in the extent to which it relies on contributions from individuals and organized interests.[20] Every other democracy of the Organisation for Economic Co-operation and Development (OECD) uses some form of public funding to conduct its elections.[21]

18. On contribution limits, see National Conference of State Legislators, "Contribution Limits," 2010, http://www.ncsl.org/Portals/1/documents/legismgt/limits_candidates.pdf (accessed November 28, 2010). On public funding for campaigns or parties, see Jessica Levinson, "State Public Charts," Center for Governmental Studies, Los Angeles, CA, 2009, http://cgs.org/images/publications/cgs_state_pfc_050409.pdf (accessed November 28, 2010). See also Steven Levin, "Keeping It Clean: Public Financing in American Elections," Los Angeles, CA: Center for Governmental Studies, 2006, http://cgs.org/images/publications/Keeping_It_Clean.pdf (accessed November 28, 2010). For more information, see the series of public election financing and other reports from the Center for Governmental Studies, http://www.cgs.org/.

19. Levin, "Keeping it Clean," and Jessica Levinson, "Local Public Financing Charts," Center for Governmental Studies, Los Angeles, CA, 2009). These cities include, among others, Albuquerque, Austin, Chapel Hill, Long Beach, New York, Los Angeles, Oakland (CA), Portland (OR), Sacramento, San Francisco, and Tucson.

20. For an overview of the literature on comparative political finance, see Susan E. Scarrow, "Political Finance in Comparative Perspective," *Annual Review of Political Science* 10 (2007): 193–210. Scarrow points out that most of the literature is not genuinely comparative but consists instead of single-country studies. There are several edited volumes containing chapters on party and campaign finance arrangements in various countries, among them Arthur B. Gunlicks, ed., *Campaign and Party Finance in North America and Western Europe* (Boulder, CO: Westview Press, 1993); Herbert E. Alexander and Rei Shiratori, eds., *Comparative Political Finance among the Democracies* (Boulder, CO: Westview Press, 1994); and Robert Williams, ed., *Party Finance and Political Corruption* (New York: St. Martin's Press, 2000).

21. With the exceptions of Chile and New Zealand, which use indirect public funding through free media access, every other OECD country uses direct public funding given to the parties. Chile also has another form of indirect public funding of parties; it grants parties

Fundamental to the controversy over campaign finance regulation is the extent to which campaign finance arrangements entail complex trade-offs among democratic values. As students of democracy, we ask a great deal of elections: among other things, to be free of corruption, to be competitive, to involve a large share of the eligible voters, to increase the voters' faith in the political process, and to allow maximum opportunities for individuals to express—and to persuade others to heed—their views. Depending on whether what is at stake is a cap on individual contributions or public funding and depending on just how the regulations are specified, procedural arrangements that might ameliorate inequalities of political voice have possible consequences for a number of these desirable qualities for elections. In particular, political scientists have examined, with mixed results, the implications of various forms of campaign finance regulation for the competitiveness of elections.[22]

No fancy statistical studies are needed to ascertain that ceilings on contributions have the effect of preventing those who are so inclined from devot-

---

a special tax status. The United States stands out among OECD nations in that it provides for no direct or indirect public funding of parties. See the Political Finance Database of the International Institute for Democracy and Electoral Assistance, http://idea.int/parties/finance/db/index.cfm, or download the 2003 handbook at http://idea.int/publications/funding_parties/upload/full.pdf (accessed November 28, 2010).

22. In "What We Know and What We Don't," Nolan L. Reichl reviews a number of studies of the consequences for the competitiveness of elections of regulations at the state level. See also Donald A. Gross, Robert K. Goidel, and Todd G. Shields, "State Campaign Finance Regulations and Electoral Competition," *American Politics Research* 30 (2002): 143–165, and Donald A. Gross and Robert K. Goidel, *The States of Campaign Finance Reform* (Columbus, OH: Ohio State University Press, 2003).

On the implications of public funding, see also Kenneth R. Mayer and John M. Wood, "The Impact of Public Financing on Electoral Competitiveness: Evidence from Wisconsin, 1964–1990," *Legislative Studies Quarterly* 20 (1995): 69–88; Patrick D. Donnay and Graham P. Ramsden, "Public Financing of Legislative Elections: Lessons from Minnesota," *Legislative Studies Quarterly* 20 (1995): 351–364; and Patrick Basham and Martin Zelder, "Does Cleanliness Lead to Competitiveness? The Failure of Maine's Experiment with Taxpayer Financing of Campaigns," Policy Analysis 456, Cato Institute, Washington, DC, October 16, 2002.

Researchers disagree about the consequences of contribution limits. See Robert E. Hogan, "The Costs of Representation in State Legislatures: Explaining Variations in Campaign Spending," *Social Science Quarterly* 81 (2000): 941–956; Thad Kousser and Ray LaRaja, "The Effect of Campaign Finance Laws on Electoral Competition: Evidence from the States," Policy Analysis 426, Cato Institute, Washington, DC, 2002; Kedron Bardwell, "Campaign Finance Laws and the Competition for Spending in Gubernatorial Elections," *Social Science Quarterly* 84 (2003): 811–825; Thomas Stratmann and Francisco J. Aparicio-Castillo, "Competition Policy for Elections: Do Campaign Contribution Limits Matter?" Social Science Research Network, 2001, http://papers.ssrn.com/sol3/papers.cfm?abstract_id=274470 (accessed August 22, 2007); and Keith E. Hamm and Robert E. Hogan, "Campaign Finance Laws and Candidacy Decisions in State Legislative Elections," *Political Research Quarterly* 61 (2008): 458–467.

ing whatever resources they have to campaign donations. Such restrictions are unambiguously a constriction of individual liberty and are therefore to be taken seriously by anyone concerned about democracy. Whether such constraints constitute an infringement of free speech, however, is a more complicated—and more highly contested—matter. The Supreme Court first declared spending money to be a form of speech in *Buckley* v. *Valeo* (1976). Reviewing the 1974 amendments to the Federal Election Campaign Act, the Court stated in the majority opinion:

> A restriction on the amount of money a person or group can spend on political communication during a campaign necessarily reduces the quantity of expression by restricting the number of issues discussed, the depth of their exploration, and the size of the audience reached. This is because virtually every means of communicating ideas in today's mass society requires the expenditure of money. The distribution of the humblest handbill or leaflet entails printing, paper, and circulation costs. Speeches and rallies generally necessitate hiring a hall and publicizing the event. The electorate's increasing dependence on television, radio, and other mass media for news and information has made these expensive modes of communication indispensable instruments of effective political speech.[23]

Within the principle that spending money is a form of constitutionally protected expression, the Court ruled that it would not permit certain kinds of restrictions—most importantly, on independent spending that is not coordinated with a candidate—but allowed many others. For three decades the Court hewed to this course, emphasizing the relevance of the First Amendment to campaign finance laws while permitting various forms of regulation. In *McConnell* v. *FEC* (2003), a divided court upheld most of the provisions of the Bipartisan Campaign Reform Act (BCRA).

With the personnel changes that brought Justices John Roberts and Samuel Alito to the bench, the Supreme Court has tacked in a more antiregulatory direction since then.[24] In a series of five decisions, the Court struck down several campaign finance laws: strict state and local limits on

---

23. *Buckley* v. *Valeo* (1976), p. 9. On the *Buckley* decision, see Frank J. Sorauf, *Money in American Elections* (Glenview, IL: Scott Foresman, 1988), pp. 235–246.

24. On recent campaign finance decisions by the Supreme Court, see Richard Briffault, "Decline and Fall? The Roberts Court and the Challenges to Campaign Finance Law," *The Forum* 6, no. 1, Article 4, 2008, Berkeley Electronic Press, http://www.bepress.com/forum/

contributions in Vermont (*Randall* v. *Sorrell* [2006]); restrictions, sustained a few years earlier in *McConnell*, on the use of corporate and union funds to pay for electioneering communications (*FEC* v. *Wisconsin Right to Life, Inc.* [2007]); BCRA's "Millionaire's Amendment" that lifted limits on what could be contributed to a House or Senate candidate whose self-funded opponent had spent personal funds over a specified amount (*Davis* v. *FEC* [2008]); and Arizona's provision, passed by ballot initiative, for escalating matching funds to candidates who accept public financing (*Arizona Free Enterprise Club* v. *Bennett* [2011]).[25] In contrast to other recently disallowed provisions, the Millionaire's Amendment and the Arizona's Citizens Clean Election Act did not restrict political expenditures; in fact, it facilitated them.

The most significant and controversial decision was handed down in early 2010, when the Court struck down limits on corporate independent expenditures on political campaigns in its decision in *Citizens United* v. *FEC*.[26] The case concerned a documentary produced in 2008 by a nonprofit corporation, Citizens United, and the television advertisements for this documentary, both of which were highly critical of then–presidential candidate Hillary Clinton. The FEC argued that such negative advertising was an unlawful independent expenditure under BCRA. Reversing a lower court's decision, the Supreme Court held that the BCRA provisions limiting corporate independent expenditures constituted an "outright ban on speech" and had a "substantial, nationwide chilling effect" on free speech.[27] In a reference that made unusually clear the value trade-offs inherent in campaign finance regulation and their consequences for equal political voice, Justice Roberts cited "*Buckley*'s explicit repudiation of any government interest in 'equalizing the relative ability of individuals and groups to influence the outcome of elections.'"[28] In his

---

vol6/iss1/art4 (accessed January 13, 2011), and Adam Liptak, "Justices Reject Another Campaign Finance Law," *New York Times*, June 28, 2011.

25. The issues at stake in *Davis* are discussed in Briffault, "Decline and Fall?" pp. 8–9, which was written before the Court had ruled. The decision is discussed in Matthew Mosk and Robert Barnes, "High Court Deals Blow to Campaign Finance Law: 'Millionaire's Amendment' Is Ruled Unconstitutional," *Washington Post*, June 27, 2008, p. A 4.

26. Liptak, "Justices Reject Another," shows that five justices (Roberts, Alito, Kennedy, Scalia, and Thomas) voted together in all five decisions and were joined only once, by Breyer in *Randall*.

27. *Citizens United* v. *Federal Election Commission* (2010), U.S. Sup. Ct. 08-205, opinion of the Court, written by Justice Kennedy.

28. Concurring opinion (p. 8), written by Justice Roberts. Justice Kennedy included a similar comment (p. 34) in his majority opinion. For contrasting views on the consequences of

State of the Union address not long afterward, President Obama drew attention to the potential impact of the decision on political equality: "I don't think American elections should be bankrolled by America's most powerful interests, or worse, by foreign entities. They should be decided by the American people."[29]

Undergirding the *Citizens United* decision is the legal status of corporations as persons. Since the late nineteenth century the Court has extended rights to corporations as persons under the Fourteenth Amendment—among them First Amendment rights.[30] As we saw in Chapter 14, corporations are active in lobbying government, and neither their right to do so nor their right to deduct the expenses associated with lobbying has been contested by political reformers. *Citizens United* recognized and enhanced the free speech rights of corporations. Corporate personhood to the contrary, the rights and responsibilities of corporations are not coterminous with those of individual citizens. Corporations pay taxes, but they do not sit on juries. They can be sued but do not carry guns. In fact, to spoof the notion that corporations are entitled to the same political rights as human persons, those involved with Murray Hill Inc., a small public relations firm in the Maryland suburbs of Washington, decided that the company should run for Congress. "'Until now, corporate interests had to rely on campaign contributions and influence-peddling to achieve their goals in Washington,' the candidate, who was unavailable for an interview, said in a statement. 'But thanks to an enlightened Supreme Court, now we can eliminate the middle-man and run for office ourselves.'"[31]

There is a nascent movement among those concerned about corporate political power to strip corporations of their status as persons. While the move-

---

Citizens United for equality, see Samuel Issacharoff, "On Political Corruption," and Mark Alexander, "*Citizens United* and Equality Forgotten," in *Money, Politics, and the Constitution: Beyond Citizens United*, ed. Monica Youn (New York: Century Foundation Press, 2011), chaps. 8 and 10.

29. "Remarks by the President in State of the Union Address," January 27, 2010, http://www.whitehouse.gov/the-press-office/remarks-president-state-union-address (accessed March 11, 2010).

30. The original case, *Santa Clara County* v. *Southern Pacific Railroad* (1886), involved taxation of railroads. Although the railroad raised the issue of whether corporations were considered "persons" under the Fourteenth Amendment, the Court did not rule on this matter in its decision. However, language asserting the personhood of corporations was included in a preface to the decision.

31. John Wagner, "Campaign Stunt Launches a Corporate 'Candidate' for Congress," *Washington Post*, March 13, 2010.

ment uses populist, anti-corporate rhetoric, it is less clear exactly how the rights of corporations to engage in political advocacy would change if they were no longer construed as persons and how much effect those changes would have on inequality of political voice.[32]

The nature and extent of the consequences of the *Citizens United* decision depend upon what the courts do to interpret and apply the decision with respect, for example, to state and local laws, what Congress does to introduce statutory and constitutional changes to blunt the effects of the decision, and what organized interests do to take advantage of their new electoral rights. At this point, it seems that the campaign finance environment after *Citizens United*—and the subsequent appellate court decision in *SpeechNow.org* v. *FEC* (2010)—is changing dramatically in ways that, if anything, render the playing field even less level. Although spending traditionally drops in off-year elections, independent spending in 2010 reached unprecedented levels. As we finish this work, media attention is focusing on the avalanche of money pouring into the 2012 Republican primaries and on the preferred vehicle for independent spending, the Super PAC, which permits unlimited donations, often difficult to trace, by individuals, corporations, and unions.[33]

Restrictions on Voting

When political participation requires time or skills rather than money, individuals and organizations are generally free to be as active as they like—

32. On the legal consequences of corporate personhood, see Daniel J. H. Greenwood, "Essential Speech: Why Corporate Speech Is Not Free," *Iowa Law Review* 83 (1997–1998): 995–1070; Thomas W. Joo, "The Modern Corporation and Campaign Finance: Incorporating Corporate Governance Analysis into First Amendment Jurisprudence," *Washington University Law Quarterly* 79 (2001): 1–88; Thom Hartmann, *Unequal Protection: The Rise of Corporate Dominance and the Theft of Human Rights* (Rodale, NY: St. Martin's Press, 2002); Kellye Y. Testy, "Capitalism and Freedom: For Whom? Feminist Legal Theory and Progressive Corporate Law," *Law and Contemporary Problems* 67 (2004): 87–108; Adam Winkler, "Corporate Law or the Law of Business? Stakeholders and Corporate Governance at the End of History," *Law and Contemporary Problems* 67 (2004): 109–133; Kenneth Lipartito and David B. Sicilia, eds., *Constructing Corporate America: History, Politics, Culture* (New York: Oxford University Press, 2004); and Arun A. Iyer, "The Missing Dynamic: Corporations, Individuals and Contracts," *Journal of Business Ethics* 67 (2006): 393–406. A helpful summary of the relevant issues and links to other materials can be found at http://www.pbs.org/now/politics/corprights .html (accessed March 10, 2010).

33. See Adam Liptak, "Courts Take On Campaign Finance Decision," *New York Times,* March 26, 2010; Eduardo Porter, "How the Big Money Finds a Way In," *New York Times,* September 18, 2011; Nicholas Confessore and Michael Luo, "Campaign Finance Reports Show 'Super PAC' Donors," *New York Times,* January 31, 2012; and Nicholas Confessore and Michael Luo, "Secrecy Shrouds 'Super PAC' Funds in Latest Filings," *New York Times,* February 1, 2012.

constrained not by policy but only by the limits on their talents and their leisure time. Thus politically committed activists can write as many letters to public officials, attend as many rallies, or labor as hard as a member of the school board as they like. However, even forms of political activity that do not rely on money are sometimes restricted. Limitations on such activity do not always have the intent or the effect of ameliorating inequalities of political voice. On the contrary, depending on the circumstances, ceilings may actually exacerbate such inequalities.

The vote is the single form of political participation for which there is an upper bound on the amount of activity in which any individual may engage, and one person, one vote is one of the most important democratic principles in the name of equal political voice. There is another form of limitation on the vote, however—the disenfranchisement of citizens in particular categories. Historically, citizens have been barred from voting on the basis of, most notably, property, race, and sex. Conventional history points to the onward, if protracted, process of incorporating disenfranchised groups into the electorate: Jacksonian-era reforms removed property qualifications; the Fifteenth and Nineteenth Amendments eliminated race- and sex-based qualifications, respectively; and various measures during the 1960s outlawed poll taxes, literacy tests, and other discriminatory policies and practices. However, as Alexander Keyssar makes clear, the process of incorporating a greater share of adult citizens into the electorate has entailed periodic retreats as well as advances and efforts to place barriers to access to the polls on the basis of class.[34] The post–World War II era has witnessed the establishment of a nearly universal right to vote for adult citizens.

Nevertheless, access to the franchise is still limited for those who appear to lack either the instrumental or the moral competence to make decisions relevant to participation: children, some of the mentally incapable, and felons.[35] With the enfranchisement of eighteen-year-olds by the Twenty-sixth Amendment in 1971, age restrictions on the vote are no longer controversial. In contrast, state laws disenfranchising felons are the subject of contention. With the exception of Maine and Vermont, all states have some provision for

---

34. Alexander Keyssar, *The Right to Vote: The Contested History of Democracy in the United States* (New York: Basic Books, 2000).

35. On votes for those with developmental disabilities and serious mental health problems, see Erica Goode, "Gentle Drive to Make Voters of Those With Mental Illness," *New York Times*, October 13, 1999, pp. A1ff, and Jeremy Peters, "Who Is Fit to Vote? A Vote Will Decide," *New York Times*, October 14, 2007, sec. 14 NJ, p. 2.

the disenfranchisement of felons, and fourteen states deny access to the ballot to some or all ex-felons who have completed their sentences and no longer have contact with the criminal justice system.[36] States with high proportions of African Americans are especially likely to have stringent laws, and there is good reason to believe that racial considerations played a significant role in their enactment. With felon disenfranchisement laws that are far more punitive than in other developed democracies and incarceration rates that are six to ten times higher, the United States is unique—both in barring large numbers of nonincarcerated felons from the polls and in the share of the electorate that is affected. At the time of the 2004 election, more than five million people, or more than 2 percent of the voting-age population, were denied access to the polls. Although there is no consensus as to whether the disenfranchisement of felons has an impact on actual electoral outcomes, there is agreement that the burden of such laws falls disproportionately on young males—in particular, young African American males—and represents a serious compromise of equality of political voice.[37]

Limiting Contacts with Policy Makers

The First Amendment to the contrary, another form of political activity, communicating with public officials, is, under certain circumstances, subject to regulation. The policy-making process is said to be enhanced by the free exchange of views between such public officials and those who know about and are affected by government policies, and concerned individuals and organizational representatives are free to approach legislators, elected executives, and their political staff to discuss policy matters. However, different values are invoked for the judicial branch. When it comes to judges, impartiality and fairness take precedence. Thus, in contrast to the possibility of informal contacts with a senator, governor, or mayor when policies are under consideration, informal communications are proscribed when cases are pending before a judge. Individuals or representatives of politically concerned organizations do not take the initiative to get in touch with a judge;

---

36. Material in this paragraph is taken from Jeff Manza and Christopher Uggen, *Locked Out: Felon Disenfranchisement and American Democracy* (New York: Oxford University Press, 2006).

37. On the issue of whether felon disenfranchisement laws actually alter election outcomes, compare Manza and Uggen, *Locked Out*, chap. 8, and Traci Burch, "Punishment and Participation: How Criminal Convictions Threaten American Democracy," PhD Dissertation, Harvard University, Cambridge, MA, 2007.

instead the exchange of views takes place in the ritualized and rule-bound setting of a hearing. Although the relative skills of the parties—or their relative abilities to pay for skilled counsel—may provide an advantage to one side or the other, the structured setting and the requirements for due process put the parties on a more nearly equal footing.[38]

The expectations that judges act impartially and the substantial efforts they make to shun even the appearance of conflict of interest seem to be at odds with the fact that, in many states, candidates for elected judicial office are permitted to accept campaign contributions from lawyers and litigants who might appear before them. In thirty-nine states, some if not all judges are elected in what can be expensive campaigns, and elected judges do not necessarily recuse themselves in cases involving campaign contributors. Judges for the state's highest court are elected in twenty-one states, and in eight of those states the elections are partisan.[39] In a 2009 decision, a divided Supreme Court ruled five to four that an elected West Virginia judge should have disqualified himself in a case in which the defendant had spent $3 million on television advertisements urging the electoral defeat of the judge's opponent.[40] It is noteworthy that the First Amendment arguments offered by those opposed to the Court's decision in this case have not been invoked as a justification for permitting litigants and their attorneys to engage in informal contacts with judges when cases are pending.

A different kind of limitation has a clearer impact in terms of political voice when it comes to advocates of broad public interests. There are restrictions on the amount of lobbying that so-called 501(c)3s—such nonprofits as

---

38. With respect to these matters, federal executive agencies—which have quasi-legislative functions when they make rules and quasi-judicial functions when they decide cases—occupy a space between these poles. Administrative law judges, who preside over hearings that dispense with cases, are subject to rules parallel to those that govern the behavior of judges. However, with respect to administrative rule making, there is no simple analogy to Congress or the White House. In contrast to the practices that obtain for Congress, greater transparency is expected in the executive branch and agencies, which are required to keep records of contacts with stakeholders. Once again, alternative democratic values are invoked without discussion of their appropriateness for different institutional settings or the trade-offs involved. On ex parte rules, which govern contacts with executive branch agencies, see Richard J. Pierce Jr., Sidney A. Shapiro, and Paul Verkuil, *Administrative Law and Process*, 4th ed. (New York: Foundation Press, 2004), chap. 9.

39. Robert Barnes, "Politics Enters the Courtroom," *Washington Post Weekly Edition*, November 5–11, 2007, p. 16.

40. On the decision in *Caperton v. A. T. Massey Coal Company*, see Adam Liptak, "Judges Tell Judges Not to Rule in Major Backers," *New York Times*, June 8, 2009.

museums, universities, clinics, and social service agencies, contributions to which are tax deductible under section 501(c)3 of the federal tax code—are permitted to undertake.[41] In fact, these regulations do not erect a wall between nonprofit executives and government officials, especially those in the executive branch. Instead there is a complex and contradictory dance in which those in nonprofits cultivate relationships with policy makers but feel constrained from using the full arsenal of tactics of advocacy that other organizations mobilize—lest their tax status be jeopardized. This chilling effect potentially exacerbates inequalities of political voice among organizations representing different kinds of interests.

The rhetoric surrounding restrictions on lobbying by 501(c)3s and the limitations on campaign contributions illustrates the truism that behind every procedural disagreement in American politics lurks a dispute over substance. Although they have been joined by such First Amendment hawks as the American Civil Liberties Union, it is conservatives who have been most concerned about the implications of campaign finance regulations for freedom of expression. However, periodic conservative efforts to use the prohibition on lobbying by nonprofits as a mechanism to "defund the left" and thus weaken a set of liberal institutions have not engaged a parallel deference to the First Amendment.[42] Reciprocally, liberals demonstrate the same inconsistency in the opposite direction, exhibiting less concern with free speech when it comes to campaign finance than with respect to the restrictions on lobbying by nonprofits. Of course the 501(c)3s that are constrained from lobbying by the tax code are unlikely to be uniform in their political perspectives. Still, it is liberals rather than conservatives who have suggested loosening the rules.

Regulating Protests

The restrictions on the First Amendment "right of the people peaceably to assemble" take a different form. There is no ceiling on the number of protests or marches that an individual may attend. However, public authorities sometimes prevent such activities from taking place—if, for example, they threaten

41. The argument in this paragraph is taken from Jeffrey M. Berry with David F. Arons, *A Voice for Nonprofits* (Washington, DC: Brookings Institution, 2003). Berry probes the relationship between nonprofits and government and the impact of 501(c)3 tax status. He also discusses (pp. 54–65) the way that an obscure tax provision, H election, permits greater freedom in approaching public officials.

42. On the effort to "defund the left," see Berry, *A Voice for Nonprofits*, pp. 81–85.

to become disorderly. The rules governing public protests and rallies vary from city to city and are often contested. In one locale a permit may be required for a protest of 250 people, in another for a protest of 300. In New York City, for example, public protests are generally allowed without permits as long as the protest does not block streets, sidewalks, or building entrances and does not use amplified sound.[43]

There is, however, an irony to this form of ceiling on activity. Unlike caps on campaign contributions, raising barriers to protests has the potential to exacerbate inequalities of political voice. Although the United States has a tradition of middle-class protest movements, as we saw in Chapter 5, the SES bias characteristic of all kinds of political participation does not obtain for taking part in protests and demonstrations. Protest is traditionally viewed as the weapon of the weak, and protest activities sometimes bring new and challenging ideas into politics. Moreover, if local policies are complex, legalistic, or not widely known or if they are zealously or selectively enforced, groups with limited skills and resources are especially likely to be affected.

Establishing a Participatory Floor

The opposite strategy for reducing inequalities of political voice is to give a boost to the silent by placing a floor under the activity of those who participate least. Such participatory floors are quite unusual, but not unknown, in American political arrangements. One policy that can be construed as creating such a floor emerged from the 1963 Supreme Court decision in *Gideon* v. *Wainwright* establishing the right of an indigent defendant in a felony trial to be represented by counsel, a decision that can be thought of as creating a floor that equalizes voice in a setting in which matters involving individual offenders are resolved.

A short-lived and less well-known example in a domain in which policy is made, intervenor funding, derives from the world of administrative agencies. Under these arrangements, which were in place in a number of agencies from the mid-1970s, citizen groups that did not command the resources or the expertise needed to participate in protracted and complex rule-making hearings were subsidized to take part. In the process, perspectives that might

---

43. New York Civil Liberties Union (NYCLU), "Know Your Rights: Demonstrating in New York City," NYCLU pamphlet, 2009, http://www.nyclu.org/files/publications/nyclu_pub_demonstrating_in_nyc.pdf (accessed January 17, 2011).

otherwise not have come to the attention to public officials were given voice.[44] Although most of the intervenor funding programs were killed early in the Reagan administration, some government agencies—for example, the Environmental Protection Agency (EPA)—continue to solicit public participation in the making of policy.[45]

Another proposal that would have the effect of placing a floor under political participation is for a publicly funded campaign voucher program that would issue to every citizen a voucher for a set amount—proposals range from $10 to $100—that could be assigned to any (registered) political party, other campaign funding organization, or candidate.[46] Citizens would be per-

---

44. On intervenor funding, see Joan B. Aron, "Citizen Participation at Government Expense," *Public Administration Review* 39 (1979): 477–485; Jeffrey Berry, "Citizen Groups and Alternative Approaches to Regulatory Reform," *Review of Policy Research* 1 (1982): 505; Barry B. Boyer, "Funding Public Participation in Agency Proceedings: The Federal Trade Commission Experience," *Georgetown Law Journal* 70 (1981–1982): 51–172; William T. Gormley Jr., "Regulatory Issue Networks in a Federal System," *Polity* 18 (1986): 595–620; and Kay L. Schlozman and John T. Tierney, *Organized Interests and American Democracy* (New York: Harper and Row, 1986), pp. 351–353; William T. Gormley Jr., *Taming the Bureaucracy: Muscles, Prayers, and Other Strategies* (Princeton, NJ: Princeton University Press, 1989), pp. 77–81; and Richard A. Harris and Sidney M. Milkis, *The Politics of Regulatory Change*, 2nd ed. (New York and Oxford: Oxford University Press, 1996), pp. 173–180.

Australia and Canada have had intervenor funding programs. See, for example, Michael I. Jeffrey, "Intervenor Funding as the Key to Effective Citizen Participation in Environmental Decision-Making: Putting the People Back into the Picture," *Arizona Journal of International and Comparative Law* 19 (2002): 643–677; and Michael I. Jeffrey, "Environmental Governance: A Comparative Analysis of Public Participation and Access to Justice," *Journal of South Pacific Law* 9 (2005), available at http://www.paclii.org/journals/fJSPL/vol09no2/2 .shtml (accessed July 29, 2009).

45. As of 2003, the EPA mandated "public involvement" in decision making, and certain EPA regulations dictated more specific public participation requirements. See EPA, "Public Involvement Policy," available at the EPA Web site at http://www.epa.gov/publicinvolvement/ pdf/policy2003.pdf (accessed November 29, 2010).

46. Various versions of the voucher plan have been proposed. See, for example, David W. Adamany and George E. Agree, *Political Money: A Strategy for Campaign Financing in America* (Baltimore, MD: Johns Hopkins University Press, 1975); Bruce Ackerman, "Crediting the Voters: A New Beginning for Campaign Finance," *American Prospect* 13, March 21, 1993, 71–90; Edward B. Foley, "Equal-Dollars-per-Voter: A Constitutional Principle of Campaign Finance," *Columbia Law Review* 94 (1994): 1204–1257; Richard Hasen, "Clipping Coupons for Democracy: An Egalitarian/Public Choice Defense of Campaign Finance Vouchers," *California Law Review* 84 (1996): 1–59; and Bruce Ackerman and Ian Ayres, *Voting with Dollars: A New Paradigm for Campaign Finance* (New Haven, CT: Yale University Press, 2002). A related suggestion involves small-donor matching funds, which would have the effect of diluting large contributions in state elections. See Michael J. Malbin, Peter W. Brusoe, and Brendan Glavin, "Public Financing of Elections after *Citizens United* and *Arizona Free Republic*," Campaign Finance Institute, Washington, DC, 2011.

mitted to divide the total and assign varying amounts to different groups or candidates. Earlier proposals varied in terms of whether candidates would be permitted to accept private money in addition or would be limited to voucher receipts, an alternative that, most likely, would not now pass constitutional muster with the Supreme Court.[47] Proposals for campaign vouchers have not been met with universal enthusiasm.[48] Among the obvious limitations are that they would be expensive. Even at a mere $10 per citizen, the vouchers would come to $2.2 billion if every eligible voter took advantage of the opportunity to use the full value of the voucher. The measure would require defining and registering eligible groups and candidates and would require a bureaucracy to administer and audit the program. Nevertheless, such a program would allow everyone, regardless of resources, to get into the political contributions game and, within limits, to register the intensity of their feelings by apportioning the total to different groups or candidates. Campaign vouchers would presumably result in an increase in citizen interest and knowledge. However, their most important consequence from the perspective of our concerns would be their impact in reducing inequality of political voice.[49]

A different kind of policy that equalizes political voice by placing a floor under participation involves making political activity mandatory rather than voluntary. To require attendance at meetings or rallies or contributions to a party is more the hallmark of an authoritarian than of a democratic system. However, in about thirty other nations, including eleven of the OECD countries, citizens are required to go to the polls at election time and may be fined if they do not.[50] Although there is evidence that countries that have introduced compulsory voting have seen reductions in inequalities in turnout

47. Ackerman and Ayres, in *Voting with Dollars*, pp. 26–30, also add a requirement that all contributions be anonymous, which reduces the threat of politicians' being "bought."

48. See, for example, Bradley Smith, "Some Problems with Taxpayer-Funded Political Campaigns," *University of Pennsylvania Law Review* 148 (1999): 591–628; David A. Strauss, "What's the Problem? Ackerman and Ayres on Campaign Finance Reform," *California Law Review* 91 (2003): 737; and Daniel H. Lowenstein, "Review: Voting with Votes," *Harvard Law Review* 116 (2003): 1971–1994.

49. Spencer Overton, "The Donor Class: Campaign Finance, Democracy, and Participation," *University of Pennsylvania Law Review* 153 (2004): 73–118.

50. See Sarah Birch, "Compulsory Electoral Participation and Political Legitimacy," paper delivered at the Annual Meeting of the American Political Science Association, Chicago, IL, September, 2007, and M. Gratschew, "Compulsory Voting," article published by the International Institute for Democracy and Electoral Assistance (IDEA), available at http://www.idea.int/vt/compulsory_voting.cfm#compulsory (accessed January 7, 2008).

among social groups, mandating turnout as a means of equalizing political voice is controversial among political scientists.[51] Besides, a proposal for policy making such a demand on citizens might be a tough sell in a nation uneasy with public mandates.

With regard to whether individualistic Americans would countenance being required to vote, we should note that there is a form of required civic involvement that is not usually included in discussions of political activity, jury service. A recent major study shows that, contrary to popular assumption, even though jury service is usually mandatory, those who serve on juries generally feel quite positive about the experience. Jury service seems to have an impact on political activity—increasing rates of turnout, especially for infrequent voters, and often other forms of involvement.[52]

Lowering Barriers to Activity

Another strategy for ameliorating inequalities of political voice involves lowering the barriers to participation. We have already discussed the extent to which the Internet has made it easier to take part, but there are also public policies—most commonly focused on voting—that facilitate activity. American electoral practices are notable for several reasons. Compared with that of other developed democracies, U.S. voter turnout is low, and voter participation is especially likely to be structured by education and income.[53] Further-

51. Arend Lijphart, in "Unequal Participation: Democracy's Unresolved Dilemma," *American Political Science Review* 91 (1997): 1–14, recommends mandatory voting as a means of equalizing turnout. Aina Gallego, in "Understanding Unequal Turnout: Education and Voting in Comparative Perspective," *Electoral Studies* 29 (2010): 239–247, notes that mandatory voting tends to reduce the inequality of voting by moving turnout so close to a universal level that there is no room for variation across SES groups. For an alternative view on compulsory voting, see, among others, Mark N. Franklin, "Electoral Engineering and Cross-National Turnout Differences: What Role for Compulsory Voting?" *British Journal of Political Science* 29 (1999): 205–216. Benjamin Highton and Raymond E. Wolfinger, in "The Political Implications of Higher Turnout," *British Journal of Political Science* 31 (2001): 179–192, argue that, because the differences between voters and nonvoters are fairly trivial, the consequences of requiring voters to go to the polls are overstated.

52. John Gastil, E. Pierre Deess, Philip J. Weiser, and Cindy Simmons, *The Jury and Democracy: How Jury Deliberation Promotes Civic Engagement and Political Participation* (Oxford, England: Oxford University Press, 2010), esp. chaps. 3 and 6.

53. On low voter turnout, see Lawrence LeDuc, Richard G. Niemi, and Pippa Norris, "Introduction: The Present and Future of Democratic Elections," in *Comparing Democracies: Elections and Voting in Global Perspective*, ed. Lawrence LeDuc, Richard G. Niemi, and Pippa Norris (Thousand Oaks, CA: Sage Publications, 1996), pp. 16–19, Table 1.3. See also David

more, like so many of the procedural arrangements discussed in this chapter, policies and practices around elections—such matters as registration, absentee voting, the management of voter rolls, the staffing of polling places, and balloting devices—vary widely across the U.S. states and localities. These local variations have implications for class-based inequalities in turnout. Poor communities are less likely to have well-trained poll workers, up-to-date equipment, and enough voting machines, with the result that lines are likely to be longer and the entire process is less likely to run smoothly.[54]

In considering the many proposals designed to lower barriers to turnout and make it easier to vote, we must not assume that they have the intended consequence of boosting turnout. Furthermore, we need to distinguish between the amount and the bias of activity. Even when procedural changes are successful in raising the level of electoral participation, they may not have the effect of equalizing political voice through voting.

In particular, the American system of leaving to the individual the responsibility for registering to vote is often cited as a factor that dampens turnout and increases the SES bias among voters. The requirement for registration is seen as posing a particular hurdle to the young, to the residentially mobile, and to those who have low levels of income and education and fewer skills or community ties.[55] Reforms designed to ease the registration process, such as

Hill, *American Voter Turnout: An Institutional Perspective* (Boulder, CO: Westview Press, 2006). On factors influencing turnout, see, in particular, G. Bingham Powell Jr., "American Voter Turnout in Comparative Perspective," *American Political Science Review* 80 (1986): 17–43.

54. See, for example, Henry Brady and Iris Hui, "Accuracy and Security in Voting Systems," in *Designing Democratic Government: Making institutions Work*, ed. Margaret Levi, James Johnson, Jack Knight, Susan Stokes (New York: Russell Sage Publications, 2008), ch.10. In the aftermath of the chaotic 2000 election, Congress passed the Help America Vote Act of 2002. Although its title might suggest that the objective of the legislation was to increase turnout, the bill was designed to establish standards for and to assist states and localities with the administration of federal elections. There seems to be real progress when it comes to the quality of voting machines, especially the replacement of most punch card and lever pull systems. However, according to Charles Stewart, "Despite the great deal of attention paid to voting reform from 2000 to 2004, and billions of dollars spent, there is surprisingly little systematic evidence of improvement in how elections are conducted in the United States." See "Measuring the Improvement (or Lack of Improvement) in Voting since 2000 in the U.S.," paper delivered at the Annual Meeting of the American Political Science Association, Washington, DC, September 2005), p. 1; revised for presentation at the Mobilizing Democracy Working Group Conference, Russell Sage Foundation, New York, January 20–21, 2006, available at http://web.mit.edu/cstewart/www/papers/measuring_2.pdf (accessed September 9, 2008).

55. See Raymond E. Wolfinger and Steven J. Rosenstone, *Who Votes?* (New Haven, CT: Yale University Press, 1980), chaps. 1–3; Peverill Squire, Raymond E. Wolfinger, and David P.

the provisions of the National Voter Registration Act of 1993—known as "Motor Voter"—have a mixed record of success. While mail-in registration seems to have no independent effect, permitting people to register to vote when they apply for a driver's license or vehicle registration seems to increase turnout somewhat, particularly among the young and residentially mobile.[56] In addition, postponing the closing date for registration or permitting election-day registration is also associated with higher rates of voting among the young and residentially mobile and may somewhat increase turnout rates among lower-income voters.[57] Michigan has a system that links the state's electronic databases. Registered voters who file a change of address within the state at the Department of Motor Vehicles are automatically reregistered to vote at their new residence.[58]

Reformers have offered various other proposals for increasing voter turnout by lowering the costs of voting, such as holding elections on weekends rather than on work days or making Election Day a national holiday, as it is in many other countries. Already in place in many states are arrangements that make it more convenient to vote: eased restrictions on absentee voting, often without a requirement for stating a reason; provisions for early voting at polling places; and, in Oregon, voting by mail. Empirical assessments of

Glass, "Residential Mobility and Voter Turnout," *American Political Science Review* 81 (1987): 45–65; and Frances Fox Piven and Richard A. Cloward, *Why Americans Still Don't Vote and Why Politicians Want It That Way* (Boston: Beacon Press, 2000). On reduced turnout among the residentially mobile in Canada, see Craig Leonard Brians, "Residential Mobility, Voter Registration, and Electoral Participation in Canada," *Political Research Quarterly* 50 (1997): 215–227. Brians finds that both reregistration requirements and the severance of social and community ties associated with a residential move play a role in decreasing voter turnout.

Benjamin Highton, in "Easy Registration and Voter Turnout," *Journal of Politics* 59 (1997): 565, finds that a requirement to register "does contribute to the upscale character of voters" but notes that there are also "substantial differences for which registration laws are not responsible."

56. Stephen Knack, "Does 'Motor-Voter' Work? Evidence from State-Level Data," *Journal of Politics* 57 (1995): 796–811; Staci L. Rhine, "An Analysis of the Impact of Registration Factors on Turnout in 1992," *Political Behavior* 18 (1996): 171–185; and Benjamin Highton and Raymond E. Wolfinger, "Estimating the Effects of the National Voter Registration Act of 1993," *Political Behavior* 20 (1998): 79–104.

57. Benjamin Highton, in "Registration and Turnout in the United States," *Perspectives on Politics* 2 (2004): 507–515, summarizes a great deal of literature. See also Stephen Knack and James White, "Election-Day Registration and Turnout Inequality," *Political Behavior* 22 (2000): 29–44. Rhine, in "The Impact of Registration Factors on Turnout," also finds that same-day voting registration is associated with increased voter turnout.

58. R. Michael Alvarez and Thad E. Hall, *Point, Click, and Vote: The Future of Internet Voting* (Washington, DC: Brookings Institution, 2004), p. 43.

reforms designed to lower the barriers to voting are not especially encouraging. Voting by mail seems to have the greatest success in actually increasing turnout in such invariably low-turnout elections as local elections and those on ballot propositions. Evidence for a positive impact on turnout in elections of greater visibility is more mixed.[59] Moreover, to the extent that these studies pay explicit attention to the matter at all, they do not find that greater turnout has the consequence of equalizing voter participation.[60]

At the same time that efforts have been made in the past two decades to ease access to the ballot, a concern about vote fraud has led to the enactment of other measures that have the possibility for the opposite effect. Especially controversial among these measures are mandates for frequent purging of nonvoters from the voting rolls and requirements that voters show photo ID at the polling place. With respect to the latter, political scientists are in agreement in finding very few cases of the particular form of vote fraud that voter ID laws seek to address: voter impersonation at the polls. Indiana, which has a strict voter ID law that was blessed by the Supreme Court in a 2007 case, has never had a single prosecution for that form of vote fraud. An extensive initiative to uncover and document vote fraud in Texas found only thirteen indictments for vote fraud, none of which would have been prevented by a requirement to show photo ID at the polls.[61] There is less agreement as to whether voter ID laws depress turnout.[62] Such measures designed to combat

59. John C. Fortier summarizes a number of studies in *Absentee and Early Voting: Trends, Promises, and Perils* (Washington, DC: American Enterprise Institute Press, 2006), chap. 3.

60. Adam J. Berinsky, in "The Perverse Consequences of Electoral Reform in the United States," *American Politics Research* 33 (2005): 471–491, summarizes a great deal of literature with the observation that (p. 471) "reforms designed to make it easier for registered voters to cast their ballots actually increase, rather than reduce, socioeconomic biases in the composition of the voting public." For similar conclusions with respect to voting by mail, see Jeffrey A. Karp and Susan A. Banducci, "Going Postal: How All-Mail Elections Influence Turnout," *Political Behavior* 22 (2000): 223–239; and Berinsky, Burns, and Traugott, "Who Votes by Mail?"; Grant W. Neeley and Lilliard E. Richardson Jr., in "Who Is Early Voting? An Individual Level Examination," *Social Science Journal* 38 (2001): 381–392, find (p. 381) that "some evidence suggests that early voting merely conveniences those who would have voted anyway." See also Jan E. Leighley and Jonathan Nagler, "Electoral Laws and Turnout, 1972–2008," paper delivered at the Fourth Annual Conference on Empirical Legal Studies, University of Southern California, Los Angeles, November 2009.

61. Davidson, "Historical Context of Voter Photo-ID Laws," pp. 94–95. To the limited extent that vote fraud compromises election integrity, absentee and mail-in votes pose more of a problem than does voter impersonation at the polls. However, Indiana's controversial law does not cover requests for an absentee ballot.

62. For literature reviews and contrasting empirical assessments, see the following articles contained in a symposium in *PS: Political Science and Politics* 46 (2009): 81–130: Richard

vote fraud—when taken together with the fact that, even when they increase turnout, attempts to lower barriers to voting so often have disappointing results with respect to reducing political inequalities—may imply that we have entered one of the periodic eras of contradictory trends with respect to equality of access to the franchise or perhaps even one of contraction rather than expansion.

Recruiting Activity

In Chapter 15 we demonstrated that one time-honored weapon in the arsenal of those who seek to expand participation, recruitment, does indeed catalyze activity. Political scientists emphasize the role of strategic elites in generating political participation.[63] In addition, Alan Gerber and Donald Green have conducted field experiments specifying what kinds of mobilization efforts yield results. For example, while telephone calls with a nonpartisan message have no impact, knocking on doors and delivering the same message person-ally can increase voter turnout substantially.[64] While our analysis in Chapter 15 makes clear that a great deal of political activity takes place in response to a request, it also demonstrates why it is critical to differentiate the level from the equality of participation. Taken together, efforts to recruit others to take part do produce more political activity, but processes of rational prospecting

---

Sobel, "Voter-ID Issues in Politics and Political Science"; Marjorie Randon Hershey, "What We Know about Voter-ID Laws, Registration, and Turnout"; Matt A Barreto, Stephen A. Nuño, and Gabriel R. Sanchez, "The Disproportionate Impact of Voter-ID Requirements on the Electorate—New Evidence from Indiana"; Timothy Vercellotti and David Andersen, "Voter-Identification Requirements and the Learning Curve"; Jason D. Mycoff, Michael W. Wagner, and David C. Wilson, "The Empirical Effects of Voter-ID Laws: Present or Absent?"; and Stephen Ansolabehere, "Effects of Identification Requirements on Voting: Evidence from the Experiences of Voters on Election Day."

63. See, in particular, Steven J. Rosenstone and John Mark Hansen, *Mobilization, Partici-pation, and Democracy in America* (New York: Macmillan, 1993), chap 6.

64. Alan S. Gerber and Donald P. Green, "The Effects of Canvassing, Direct Mail, and Telephone Contact on Voter Turnout: A Field Experiment," *American Political Science Review* 94 (2000): 653–663, and Donald P. Green and Alan S. Gerber, *Get Out the Vote: How to In-crease Voter Turnout* (Washington, DC: Brookings Institution, 2004). Subsequent experi-ments have demonstrated the power of social pressure, especially that of showing irregular voters a written record of their past turnout. See, among others, Alan S. Gerber, Donald P. Green, and Christopher W. Larimer, "Social Pressure and Voter Turnout: Evidence from a Large-Scale Field Experiment," *American Political Science Review* 102 (2008): 33–48, as well as the results reported in the articles in a special issue of *Political Behavior* 32 (2010): 331–430.

—in which those who seek to generate participation not only search for recruits who are likely to be active but also do so effectively by, for example, compelling letters or big checks—actually exacerbate inequalities of political voice.

Efforts to mobilize political activity traditionally rely not on tinkering with procedural arrangements but on the strength and effectiveness of the institutions that mediate between citizens and government—most importantly, political parties, organized interests, and social movements but also local newspapers.[65] Organizations on the left—socialist parties and unions—mobilize working-class citizens to levels above what they would have achieved based on their individual resources and motivation. Such organizations are weaker in the United States than elsewhere.[66]

Political scientists sometimes wax nostalgic about the era of strong urban party organizations at the end of the nineteenth century and argue that not only have contemporary political parties declined in strength but they have also abandoned any efforts to mobilize the poor.[67] There is no doubt that the political parties of the late nineteenth century were more successful in organizing working-class voters and bringing them to the polls—with the result that turnout of the eligible electorate was much less class stratified than it is today. Clearly, campaigns are run by candidates and their hired professionals rather than by parties, and for many reasons the urban machine is a thing of the past.

65. Local newspapers have traditionally played a role in explaining local issues to the public and in fostering turnout and other forms of local political participation. On the erosion of local newspapers, see, for example, David Folkenflik, "Imagining a City without its Daily Newspaper," National Public Radio (NPR), February 5, 2009, available at http://www.npr.org/templates/story/story.php?storyId=100256908, and David Folkenflik, "A Nonprofit Panacea for Newspapers?" NPR, February 6, 2009, available at: http://www.npr.org/templates/story/story.php?storyId=100310863 (both accessed November 29, 2010), and Paul Starr, "Goodbye to the Age of Newspapers (Hello to a New Era of Corruption)," *New Republic*, March 4, 2009, pp. 28–35. More generally, see Paul Starr, *The Creation of the Media: Political Origins of Modern Communications* (New York: Basic Books, 2004).

66. See Sidney Verba, Norman H. Nie, and Jae-on Kim, *Participation and Political Equality: A Seven-Nation Comparison* (New York: Cambridge University Press, 1978), chaps. 5–7, and Gallego, "Understanding Unequal Turnout." On the role of unions, see Richard Freeman, "What Do Unions Do to Voting?" NBER Working Paper, National Bureau of Economic Research, Cambridge, MA, 2003, and Jan Leighley "Unions, Voter Turnout, and Class Bias in the US Electorate, 1964–2004," *Journal of Politics* 69 (2007): 430–441.

67. See, for example, Benjamin Ginsberg and Martin Shefter, *Politics by Other Means: Politicians, Prosecutors, and the Press from Watergate to Whitewater*, revised and updated ed. (New York: W. W. Norton, 1999), pp. 44–46.

Nevertheless, the strong political parties that produced such high rates of turnout mobilized an eligible electorate that was white and male and were not notably anxious to enfranchise two large groups, African Americans and women.[68] Besides, over the past quarter century, the parties have become stronger not just in the legislatures but on the ground as well: more likely to have a local organization that engages in such electoral activities as canvassing and—as we saw in Chapter 15—more likely in recent years to contact voters to urge them to vote.[69] The national parties have devoted substantial resources to digitizing information about voters and to GOTV—get-out-the-vote—campaigns.[70] Furthermore, the Obama campaign drew on Obama's experience as a community organizer to build a massive ground organization.[71] Still, consistent with the principle that higher levels of participation do not necessarily reduce unequal political voice, our analysis has shown that both parties—including the Democrats, who are more reliant on the votes of those who are lower on the SES ladder—target their recruitment efforts at the affluent and well educated.

Moreover, although some organizations—for example, grassroots organizations with a strong local focus or religious institutions—can bring the politically quiescent into politics,[72] what we have learned about the overall

68. This bald statement oversimplifies the complicated relationships among the late nineteenth-century political parties, the post–Civil War disenfranchisement of blacks, and support for women's suffrage. According to Aileen S. Kraditor, in *The Ideas of the Woman Suffrage Movement, 1890–1920* (New York: Columbia University Press, 1965), chap. 8, the political parties rebuffed overtures from advocates of the enfranchisement of women, who, in turn, aligned with the antiparty spirit of their Progressive contemporaries. Furthermore, Alexander Keyssar, in *The Right to Vote*, demonstrates that the appeals of late nineteenth-century woman suffrage supporters were laced with racism (pp. 197–199), that the Democratic Party in Congress opposed federal efforts to protect black voters in the South (pp. 108–111), and that the North stood by quietly while African Americans were deprived of the franchise in the South, a movement with class as well as racial effect (pp. 113–116).

69. On canvassing, see Marjorie Randon Hershey, *Party Politics in America*, 14th ed. (New York: Longman, 2010), p. 55. On GOTV campaigns, see Paul R. Abramson, John H. Aldrich, and David W. Rohde, *Change and Continuity in the 2008 Elections* (Washington, DC: CQ Press, 2010), pp. 108–109.

70. William H. Flanigan and Nancy Zingale, *Political Behavior of the American Electorate*, 12th ed. (Washington, DC: CQ Press, 2010), pp. 50–52.

71. Christopher Arterton and William Greener, "Obama: Strategies and Tactics in the General Election," in *Campaigning for President 2008: Strategies and Tactics, New Voices and New Techniques*, ed. Dennis W. Johnson (New York: Routledge, 2009), pp. 183–184.

72. In a large body of literature, see, for example, Harry C. Boyte, *The Backyard Revolution: Understanding the New Citizen Movement* (Philadelphia: Temple University Press, 1980); Gary Delgado, *Organizing the Movement: the Roots and Growth of ACORN* (Philadelphia:

shape of the organized interest system suggests that mobilization efforts by organized interests would reinforce rather than transform the existing socio-economic bias in political activity. In particular, labor unions—which, across developed democracies, have traditionally been a force for mobilizing have-nots on the basis of their shared economic concerns—have become weaker as both a political and an economic force. Moreover, unions currently enroll a declining share of the private-sector workforce, and the unionized work-force has become, in relative terms, less blue collar and better educated as it has become more concentrated among public-sector workers. Without stronger unions and many more local grassroots groups, mobilization efforts in the current political configuration may increase the level but not the equality of political participation.

Developing Civic Capacity

We cannot conclude a discussion of the strategies for ameliorating inequali-ties of political voice without considering the need to develop individual civic capacity. In this chapter we have repeatedly made the point that the bar-riers on the path to participation loom larger for those of limited means and education. Sometimes we are able to specify concrete circumstances to explain why the hurdles seem differentially high. Producing proof of resi-dency is more difficult for the homeless or those who, through poverty, are forced to move frequently. Getting to town hall to register is more difficult for someone who has no car and is working two jobs. Writing a check in sup-port of a candidate is more difficult when there is not enough cash for the electricity bill. Squeezing in time to vote is more difficult for someone who is rushing from work to retrieve the baby from day care and confronts long lines at the polling place. In contrast, participation is easier when there are strong mobilizing institutions, parties, and organized interests to communi-cate information about political issues, to encourage and guide political involvement, and to offer services to facilitate activity.

Such circumstances go only so far in explaining the extent to which politi-cal voice is structured by SES, however. While the configuration of political institutions and arrangements has an impact on political inequalities, indi-viduals bring to their political activity different bundles of attributes—skills

---

Temple University Press, 1986); and Heidi J. Swarts, *Organizing Urban America: Secular and Faith-Based Progressive Movements* (Minneapolis: University of Minnesota Press, 2008).

and resources and such psychological orientations as political interest, knowledge, and efficacy—that lead them to want and to be able to take part. Without recognizing the extent to which inequalities of political voice are shaped by disparities in individual resources and motivations, no amount of procedural tinkering can fully confront their sources.

Addressing such individual differences would require a major public commitment—demanding both resources and patience and having no guarantee of positive outcome—for which Americans have shown little taste. As we made clear at the outset, the context for our inquiry into inequalities of political voice includes both the extent to which American ideological egalitarianism stops short of an embrace of economic redistribution and the growth of economic inequality over the past three decades. Improving educational outcomes, job prospects, housing alternatives, and health care for those at the very bottom are, to us, worthy goals in themselves quite apart from their impact on political inequalities, but such social engineering is difficult. In the era in which this book is being written, there seems to be little political will and no political constituency for making serious policy commitments to raise the educational and economic profile of those who have least.

In the absence of such a major social transformation, one much more limited strategy for developing the civic capacity of individuals focuses on civic instruction in the schools. Assessments of traditional civics classes find them to be widespread but not especially effective, even at imparting knowledge: despite the fact that three-quarters of all high school graduates in the mid-1990s had an American government course in grades 9–12. A 1998 study found that 35 percent of high school seniors were below even the most basic level of civics performance.[73] However, advocates for programs focusing on civic education and service-based learning emphasize the possibility that they can give a participatory lift to young people who might otherwise be inactive.[74]

---

73. On the prevalence of civics courses, see Richard G. Niemi and Julia Smith, "Enrollments in High School Government Classes: Are We Short-Changing Both Citizenship and Political Science Training?" *PS: Political Science and Politics* 34 (2001): 281–287. On the performance of students in such courses, see Robert L. Dudley and Alan R. Gitelson, "Civic Education, Civic Engagement, and Youth Civic Development," *PS: Political Science and Politics* 36 (2003): 263–267.

74. For a review of a variety of approaches to civic learning, see Peter Levine, *The Future of Democracy: Developing the Next Generation of American Citizens* (Medford, MA: Tufts University Press, 2007), chap. 7.

An extensive body of evaluative research indicates that, under certain conditions, civic education and service learning programs have the potential to reduce political inequality by endowing young people whose parents are not well educated and affluent with the skills, knowledge, and other resources they need to engage with politics.[75] The conditions that make such programs effective, however, are numerous and not easily met; both the design of the courses and the quality of the instruction matter for their success.[76]

If civic education is to have the desired impact on inequality, students must bring to civic education a basic level of cognitive ability and the learning tools and skills necessary to process and apply the civic information they learn. Children and teenagers from families that are the least active, who most need civic training to boost their participation, are the least likely to command the abilities needed to make it a useful and engaging learning experience. Moreover, such students are unlikely to attend resource-rich schools with the kinds of programs that studies suggest are the most effective.

Because resources are more readily available to those who need them least and least easily available to those who need them most, civic education and service learning pose a somewhat more complex version of the dilemma discussed with regard to several of the procedural changes we have reviewed. Under the right circumstances, these educational programs can operate to create civic capacity and to raise political engagement and participation, thus

75. For positive reports on various civic learning programs, see Shelley Billig, Sue Root, and Dan Jesse, "The Impact of Participation in Service-Learning on High School Students' Civic Engagement," Center for Information on Civic Learning and Engagement (CIRCLE) Working Paper 33, School of Public Policy, University of Maryland, College Park, 2005, http://www.civicyouth.org/PopUps/WorkingPapers/WP33Billig.pdf, p. 1; Alberto Dávila and Marie T. Mora, "An Assessment of Civic Engagement and Educational Attainment," CIRCLE fact sheet, School of Public Policy, University of Maryland, College Park, 2007, http://www.civicyouth.org/PopUps/FactSheets/FS_Mora.Davila.pdf; and Michael McDevitt and Spiro Kiousis, "Experiments in Political Socialization: Kids Voting USA as a Model for Civic Education Reform," CIRCLE Working Paper 49, School of Public Policy, University of Maryland, College Park, 2006, http://www.civicyouth.org/PopUps/WorkingPapers/WP49McDevitt.pdf, p. 2 (all accessed August 22, 2007).

More measured assessments can be found in Mary Kirlin, "Civic Skill Building: The Missing Component in Service Programs," *PS: Political Science and Politics* 35 (2002): 571, and Susan Hunter and Richard A. Brisbin Jr., "Civic Education and Political Science: A Survey of Practices," *PS: Political Science and Politics* 36 (2003): 759–763.

76. U.S. Agency for International Development (USAID) Office of Democracy and Governance, *Approaches to Civic Education: Lessons Learned*, USAID Technical Publication Series (Washington, DC: Office of Democracy and Governance, USAID, 2002), http://www.usaid.gov/our_work/democracy_and_governance/publications/pdfs/pnacp331.pdf (accessed August 22, 2007).

ameliorating one form of inequality of political voice, the skew on the basis of age, by bringing the young into politics. However, these optimum educational circumstances are less likely to be available to students from disadvantaged backgrounds. If those whose parents are well educated and affluent have differential access to well-designed programs of civic education—just as they have differential access to so many participatory resources—the result would be analogous to what we saw for online political participation: to raise the overall level of civic commitment and political activity of the young but not to reduce SES inequalities of political voice within the younger generation. In short, neither civic education nor service learning provides a silver bullet to solve the problem of political inequality.

Another approach is to foster the civic skills of adults. For example, the goal of the Right Question Project (RQP) is to help "people in low and moderate-income communities learn to advocate for themselves, participate in decisions that affect them and partner with service-providers and public officials" in such settings as "educational, health care, social service, community-based organizations and public agencies."[77] Although RQP indicates that its methods produce promising results, these kinds of efforts have been tried in very limited circumstances.

Political innovations on the local level also have a positive impact on political activity. For example, in Chicago neighborhood councils with local control over policing and public schools seem to have engaged and benefitted inner-city African American residents, although they seem not to have had the same positive effects for Spanish-speaking Latino immigrants.[78] Another study finds that city-supported neighborhood associations tend to "increase confidence in government and sense of community" and reports finding no evidence that the increased participation introduces racial or economic biases into the system.[79] Still, even this kind of intensive, local, city-supported participation did not seem to bring about fundamental change in the class bias of who participates.[80]

---

77. Right Question Project Web site, http://www.rightquestion.org/ (accessed on June 24, 2011).

78. See Archon Fung and Erik Olin Wright, *Deepening Democracy: Institutional Innovations in Empowered Community Governance* (New York: Verso Press, 2003), and Wesley G. Skogan, *Police and Community in Chicago: A Tale of Three Cities* (New York: Oxford University Press, 2006).

79. Jeffrey M. Berry, Kent E. Portney, and Ken Thompson, *The Rebirth of Urban Democracy* (Washington DC: Brookings Institution, 2003), p. 14.

80. Berry, Portney, and Thompson, *Rebirth of Urban Democracy*, pp. 284–285. See also Kaifeng Yang and Kathe Callahan "Citizen Involvement Efforts and Bureaucratic Respon-

Yet another possibility arises less commonly in discussions about how to foster civic capacity: the possibility created by the impact of the design and implementation of government policies in facilitating participation by different segments of the American citizenry. Recent studies suggest that the policy design of government benefit programs can have consequences for the propensity of beneficiaries to take part politically.[81] Policies that are universal rather than means tested and bureaucratic agencies that treat citizen-clients with respect and prompt service rather than with delays, negative assumptions, and invasions of privacy promote greater participation in politics.[82]

Conclusion

This review of policy innovations that might have the effect of ameliorating inequalities of political voice has drawn both on what is broadly known in political science about the process of making public policy and on our own analysis of the roots of political activity and the shape of the pressure system. Our discussion, which has been sobering, underlines why we have been reluctant in the past to rush headlong into recommendations for reform. Beyond the inertial effect of the policy status quo in a system that was crafted more than two centuries ago to place roadblocks in the path of policy change, the political obstacles to procedural reform are formidable—especially when the reform in question is expensive, requires action on the part of each of the states, threatens significant interests with stakes in current policies, or involves trade-offs with other cherished democratic values. Moreover, accomplishing the desired outcome is often difficult. Implementation may be lackadaisical. Determined stakeholders may find ways to exploit loopholes that subvert the original purpose. Even when implementation is vigorous and no one seeks to use details to undermine the achievement of the intended purposes, the results may not be as originally predicted. In short, procedural reforms often disappoint.

---

siveness: Participatory Values, Stakeholder Pressures, and Administrative Practicality," *Public Administration Review* 67 (2007): 249–264.

81. See, for example, Joe Soss, *Unwanted Claims: The Politics of Participation in the U.S. Welfare System* (Ann Arbor: University of Michigan Press, 2000); Andrea Campbell, *How Policies Make Citizens: Senior Political Activism and the American Welfare State* (Princeton, NJ: Princeton University Press, 2003); Suzanne Mettler, *Soldiers to Citizens: The G.I. Bill and the Making of the Greatest Generation* (Ithaca, NY: Cornell University Press, 2005); and Joe Soss, Jacob S. Hacker, and Suzanne Mettler, eds., *America: Democracy and Public Policy in an Age of Inequality* (New York: Russell Sage Foundation, 2007).

82. Campbell, in *How Policies Make Citizens*, uses Social Security as an example of the former in each case, and welfare as an example of the latter.

Nevertheless, our response to the question that animates this chapter, "What, if anything, should be done?" is "As long as we do not expect a full-scale transformation—a number if things." Short of a massive change in the configuration of the mediating institutions—parties and organized interests—that link ordinary citizens to public officials or a wholesale transformation of the American system of social stratification, we can subscribe to a number of much more limited reforms that hold the promise of having an impact in the desired direction on inequalities of political voice.

For example, it seems reasonable to make more serious efforts to ease registration requirements, for example, by linking various state-level electronic databases so that a change of residence noted by the agencies that collect taxes or register motor vehicles automatically updates a voter registration or by implementing more consistently the provisions of the National Voter Registration Act that mandate voter registration at public assistance agencies. Similarly, it should be possible for states to improve the administration of elections so that the voting experience—the length of the lines, the skill and training of the election workers, the quality and accuracy of the balloting devices—would be more positive and would not depend on the budget constraints of differing municipal budgets. We would also suggest a rethinking of the rules that constrain the lobbying by 501(c)3s—nonprofits to which contributions are privileged with tax deductibility.

With respect to campaign finance, the tide seems to be running in an inegalitarian direction. Still, we would urge consideration of citizen vouchers to allow all to make limited campaign donations and close scrutiny of the consequences of public funding schemes in the states that have enacted them. A properly structured system of public funding of campaigns seems to hold potential for reducing the inequalities of political voice. We would also suggest ongoing monitoring of the programs for civic education for youth and adults and service learning in the schools to ascertain what makes them work and efforts to make sure that such programs are available to the students who need them most.

In each case, there is reason to be cautious. Each of the proposed reforms runs into at least one of various daunting political realities: it would be expensive; it would require either changes in each of the states or a national policy that would raise questions about federalism; it would offend either a powerful stakeholder or another important democratic value. Overall, for each of the reforms we have discussed, there is a trade-off between political feasibility and consequences for inequalities of political voice: the changes that would have the greatest impact are the least likely to happen. A group of incremental changes, each one relatively contained, might have an impact on inequalities of political voice. After all, American history, which has been punctuated by periodic bursts of procedural reform, has probably not witnessed its last.

18

Conclusion: Equal Voice and the
Promise of American Democracy

Inside Job, Charles Ferguson's documentary about the 2008 economic crisis, includes the following interchange between Ferguson and Scott Talbott, the senior government relations specialist at the Financial Services Roundtable:

CHARLES FERGUSON: Do you think the financial services industry has excessive political influence in the United States?

SCOTT TALBOTT: No. I think that every person in, in the w—, in the country is represented here in Washington.

CHARLES FERGUSON: And you think that all segments of American society have equal and fair access to the system?

SCOTT TALBOTT: The, you can walk into any hearing room, uh, that you would like. Yes, I do.[1]

Talbott's replies to Ferguson are technically correct. If his claim that every person is represented in Washington means that every U.S. citizen is represented by two senators and a representative in the House—though not necessarily by the organized interest advocates ordinarily called "Washington representatives"—he is clearly on target. He is also right that any Hawaiian who has lost a house through mortgage foreclosure is permitted to listen—though not, unless previously invited, to speak—at a hearing on financial reform provided that he or she commands the resources to travel to Washington, DC, files through a metal detector, and finds an empty seat in the hearing room.

1. *Inside Job*, dir. Charles Ferguson (2010; Berkeley, CA: Sony Pictures Classics, 2011), DVD.

Still, everything in our long and complex analysis suggests that Talbott's affirmation that "all segments of American society have equal and fair access to the system" is, whether out of naïveté or disingenuousness, surely mistaken. Indeed, consistent with the evidence we have presented throughout this book, a study by Public Citizen of lobbying over financial regulation in the aftermath of the 2008 financial meltdown found, on the basis of lobbying registrations, that "lobbyists representing opponents of derivative reform have outnumbered pro-reform lobbyists by more than 11-to-1."[2] Of course, political voice is not the only factor shaping public outcomes. Policy makers have other sources of information about what is on citizens' minds—including, most prominently, the media and public opinion polls—in addition to what they learn through the medium of citizen voice expressed by individuals and organizations. Besides, policy outcomes are shaped by many forces other than the preferences of citizens.

In the case of financial regulation, reflecting a political configuration that included substantial Democratic majorities in both House and Senate and a Democratic president, the Dodd-Frank Wall Street Reform and Consumer Protection Act was passed and signed into law—in spite of the disproportionate organized interest firepower of the opposition. Nevertheless, in important ways the details of the final bill indicated that the arguments made by the opponents of financial reform had not been ignored. While they did not carry the day, they were much better off for having been present at the discussions. Furthermore, as is so often the case in political controversies, the story did not end with the signing of the legislation. As we conclude our project, the new regulatory agency created by Dodd-Frank is currently under siege by the financial services industry, which hopes that it will be as toothless as possible.

This book has treated in detail Ferguson's question about equal and fair access. Our subject has been equality of political voice in America: how the preferences and concerns of the public are conveyed to governing officials, where they come from, and how they are expressed by individuals and organizations. Some preferences and concerns receive louder and more sustained expression than others. Not only is the heavenly chorus of voices not inclusive of all but it is also not representative. As we have investigated various specific aspects of unequal political voice, a single theme has appeared and

2. Public Citizen, "Eleven to One," May 18, 2010, www.citizen.org (accessed January 28, 2011), p. 1.

reappeared with remarkable consistency: the power and durability of the links between inequalities of political voice and socio-economic status (SES).

That social class and political voice as expressed through the activity of individuals and organizations are closely connected is not news. However, we have extended and amplified our understanding of that association in multiple and novel ways. In particular, we have pushed the boundaries of what is known by considering political voice as expressed through both individual and organizational activity and by demonstrating how inequalities of political voice persist across time. More specifically, in Part I we introduced our subject by placing the study of the equality of political voice in the constitutional, cultural, and economic setting in which it is embedded: the historical debates about the role of equality in American democracy, the status of equality as a democratic value in the federal and in the state constitutions, the continuing ambivalence about equality in American political culture as evidenced by public opinion, and the context of growing economic inequality and weakening labor unions since the late 1970s. In Part II we dealt with the political voice of individuals, focusing on the extent of inequality; its persistence over time not only in the aggregate but in the ongoing participation of active individuals; its perpetuation across generations through the politically enabling impact of growing up in a politically rich home environment, and especially as a consequence of the intergenerational transmission of socio-economic status; the way that inequalities of political participation shift in predictable ways across the life cycle, with the elderly and especially young adults underrepresented in political activity; and the way that these processes operate to produce a circumstance such that the median participant—especially the median campaign donor—turns out to be substantially different from the median citizen.

In Part III we presented a parallel treatment of many of these issues with regard to political voice expressed through organized interests, demonstrating that the unheavenly chorus of the pressure system echoes the accent of individual participation, the extent to which the broad outlines of the distribution of organized interests have been consistent over time, and the way that various kinds of organized interest activity—including those in which money is the chief political resource—amplify the voices supporting some kinds of political interests. In Part IV we considered some ways in which the strong links between socio-economic status and political voice might be sundered—through processes of mobilization to politics, through political activity based in the Internet, and through political reform—and concluded that breaking these patterns would be extremely difficult.

Systematic Analysis and Ordinary Inequalities

Many of the matters we have considered are newsworthy. As citizens we are, like everyone else, fascinated by what attracts the public spotlight. As social scientists, however, we are interested to look beyond the widely reported cases at a broader picture of the disparities of representation in politics. We have adduced systematic evidence to illuminate what we sometimes call the "ordinary inequalities" that characterize the processes that produce political voice. By focusing on the everyday workings of the political and social processes in the United States, we have elaborated how the normal functioning of such basic social institutions as the family and the schools shape both who becomes active in politics and whose preferences and concerns are communicated to the government. Similarly, we have looked across the thousands of organized interests that are engaged in Washington politics on a day-to-day basis and asked about the kinds of interests they represent, the resources they command, and the relative weight of their efforts among the various activities undertaken by organized interests in the pursuit of political influence.

When we brought systematic data to matters that are sometimes fodder for exposés, we found, not unexpectedly, that what grabs attention is not necessarily typical. American political history has been punctuated by scandals involving bribery and other forms of cash-based political corruption. We have no way of ascertaining how much such corrupt activity goes undetected. A recent cartoon in which a lobbyist opens a briefcase and spills wads of cash across a desk while remarking, "What the hell, Senator—let's cut to the chase,"[3] suggests that Americans consider it to be common. Still, we believe but cannot substantiate that explicit quid pro quos of this kind are not the norm.

What we can substantiate is the way that the ordinary processes by which organizations come into being and are or are not mobilized into politics yields a pressure system in which the interests of organizations representing constituencies with political skills and deep pockets—especially business—weigh heavily and in which organizations representing the less advantaged and advocates for public goods figure much less importantly. Focusing on political scandal presumably overstates the extent of pay-to-play practices in the making of policy. However, it obscures what is learned from systematic examination of the ordinary politics of organized interest representation: the inequalities of political voice in a political domain in which representation of all potential interests is very uneven and in which resources facilitate the clear articulation of political points of view.

3. Lee Lorenz, *The New Yorker Cartoons of the Year* (New York: Condé Nast, 2010), p. 44.

When it comes to organized interests, systematic data demonstrate that the newsworthy exaggerates the extent of ordinary inequalities of political voice. In contrast, systematic data about the implications of the Internet for political participation demonstrate just the opposite. In authoritarian regimes, electronic media such as Facebook and Twitter have been utilized to bring together huge numbers of protesters, and in some notable cases ultimately to bring down deeply entrenched regimes. As we conclude our inquiry, the Occupy movement—which uses social media to generate publicity and to mobilize supporters—is making headlines in the United States. However, in contrast to such attention-grabbing examples, Internet-based citizen political participation in the United States has had the consequence not of revolutionizing political voice but of reproducing well-known class inequalities.

Similarly, the same pattern of ordinary inequalities emerged when we considered the day-to-day processes by which people are recruited by others to become active in politics. We noted that social movements, which are noisy and attention getting, have the capacity to mobilize marginalized publics—and especially to bring new issues—into politics and thus to ameliorate inequalities of political voice. However, when we examined the ordinary processes through which political participants are recruited, we found that those who ask their friends, workmates, or fellow members of organizations or religious congregations to become active act as rational prospectors.

Rational prospectors target potential activists who would be likely to assent to a request and who would be effective when they take part. The bottom line is that acts of political participation that take place in response to a request are especially likely to come from the affluent and well educated. Indeed, the highest SES quintile is responsible for 33 percent of the campaign dollars contributed spontaneously—compared to 60 percent of the campaign dollars contributed in response to a request. Thus, while the social movements that generate notice from the media and the public can mobilize new people and new issues into politics and therefore broaden the expression of political voice, ordinary processes of recruitment have the opposite impact—rendering the upper-class accent of the heavenly chorus even more pronounced.

This result illustrates another pattern that has recurred throughout our analysis: increasing political participation does not necessarily equalize participation. As we saw when we considered a variety of procedural reforms designed to raise the level of political participation, especially electoral turnout, increasing the level of political activity does not necessarily result in the diminution of participatory inequalities. As the chorus gets louder, its accent does not necessarily change.

The Power and Durability of Social Class in Shaping Political Voice

In the course of this inquiry we have used a number of methods and kinds of evidence to consider the puzzle of inequalities of political voice from a variety of perspectives. In placing unequal political voice in context, we have looked at historical debates, the federal and state constitutions, public opinion surveys, and economic data. We have reviewed cross-sectional evidence and evidence over time of inequalities of political voice among individuals and among organizations; among groups, across the life cycle, and between generations; in political participation as conventionally defined and in forms of involvement—for example, taking part in political discussions or engaging in what is sometimes called "creative participation"—that push the boundaries of conventional definitions of political activity; and in traditional political venues and on the Internet.

At the outset, we were concerned that the unheavenly chorus might sing multiple variations but have no theme; that our inquiry might consist of a collection of topics on political inequality but lack a coherent argument. We need not have worried. Over and over, our evidence has pointed to a single conclusion: the pervasiveness, power, and durability of the connection between socio-economic status and political voice. As we indicated in the introduction, inside this fox of a book beats the heart of a hedgehog.

Social Class and Group Differences in Political Voice

Political input through citizen voice is unrepresentative along many dimensions in addition to social class—among them, such politically relevant categories as age, gender, and race or ethnicity. As we have demonstrated, group differences in political participation—between men and women and among African Americans, Latinos, and non-Hispanic whites—are rooted in social class. That is, once disparities between groups defined in terms of socio-economic status are taken into account, group differences in political activity diminish, often to the point of statistical insignificance. That inequalities of political voice among groups that contend politically are associated with group differences in socio-economic status is helpful in understanding their origins. However, the story does not end there. For one thing, disparities among groups in socio-economic status are not mere accident but instead result from social and sometimes political processes that create and reinforce group differences in income and education. That is, such class differences among groups based on gender or on race or ethnicity have everything to do with those other social statuses.

Furthermore, that these group-based inequalities of political voice are connected to differences in social class does not obviate their political significance. Thus, whether the gaps in participation between women and men or among Anglo whites, blacks, and Latinos arise from disparities in education, income, or some other factor, public officials are hearing differentially from various groups—with potential consequences for equal political responsiveness. Besides, considering these groups separately—or groups based on other politically relevant distinctions such as party, region, or religion—we find within groups a strong relationship between social class and political voice, analogous to that for the population as a whole. Once again, the political preferences and concerns of collectivities are being filtered through the unrepresentative voices of their most advantaged members. And once again, the democratic principle of equal responsiveness is placed at risk.

Participatory differences among age groups constitute a special case. On one hand, unlike such social attributes as gender or race, age is not fixed. Therefore, age-related inequalities in participation—which cannot be fully explained by differences in education and income—even out over the life cycle. On the other hand, age groups differ in their experiences, needs for government assistance, and attitudes toward government policy, with the result that disparities in participation among age groups have consequences for equal consideration of interests.

ˎ Unequal Political Voice: Individuals

When it comes to the political participation of individuals, our findings reinforce previous research, including our own, that demonstrates the strong association between socio-economic status and political activity. Although we used a conventional understanding of political participation as involving the various acts that have the intent or effect of influencing government, we demonstrated the same link between political engagement and socioeconomic status for forms of involvement that do not fall under the umbrella of our definition—for example, discussing politics with others or engaging in "political consumerism," that is, buying or refusing to buy products with the objective of achieving a public good.

In exploring the way the political voice of individuals is unrepresentative, we presented evidence that casts a different light on a widely cited finding from the literature on voter turnout. That finding, which is confirmed in our data, holds that the uneven representation of various groups among voters may be of no consequence because voters and nonvoters are no different in their attitudes—at least as measured by the responses to questions on surveys. We expanded the inquiry beyond voting and beyond public opinion surveys to consider both more demanding forms of political participation that are richer in information and measures of politically relevant characteristics beyond the opinions registered in response to questions preselected by survey researchers. We showed that those who speak least loudly through individual participation are distinctive in many ways that are germane to politics. They are less likely to have health insurance and more likely to live in dilapidated dwellings and neighborhoods. They are more likely to have need for government assistance as measured by their poverty-level incomes, their reported need to cut back spending on such basics as food or to delay health care, or their reliance on means-tested government benefits. Furthermore, when those of limited education and income do take part in politics, their political activity is animated by a distinctive bundle of issue concerns, one that gives greater emphasis to matters of basic human need, and they are more likely than their more affluent and highly educated counterparts to deliver messages urging greater government efforts in alleviating economic need. Thus the ways in which participatory input from individuals is unrepresentative are not so easily dismissed as being without political consequence.

Unequal Political Voice on the Internet

We extended our understanding of individual-level inequalities of political voice in a new direction by considering the possibilities for political participation on the Internet. The Internet is having a major and constantly changing impact on the conduct of politics—offering new opportunities for political learning and discussion, the creation of links among like-minded individuals, and the attempt to influence political outcomes. Not only is the Internet transforming the ways that citizens can be engaged politically and mobilized to take political action but it also facilitates traditional forms of activity—by, for example, making it possible to send e-mails rather than "snail mail" to public officials or to make political contributions without resort to check, envelope, or stamp. Because the political capacities of the Internet are a work in progress, however, we must interpret with caution any conclusions drawn from the 2008 survey conducted in cooperation with the Pew Internet and American Life Project.

We were particularly interested in the relationship of age to political use of the Internet and the possibility that the Internet might ameliorate the traditional underrepresentation of the young among political activists. On one hand, the participatory deficit of the young that characterizes most forms of political activity does not appear for political participation on the Web. On the other hand, whatever relative boost they enjoy with respect to political participation on the Web derives from the fact that they are much more likely than their elders to be Internet users and not from any differential propensity to use the Internet for political purposes among those who use the Internet. Whether successive cohorts among the young will continue to act as pioneers in the rapidly evolving domain of the Web or whether the rapid diffusion of Internet literacy and connectivity will close the generation gap in Internet use is an open question.

When it comes to the matter of whether the Internet will reduce the social class structuring of political participation, we have limited reason for optimism. For those forms of political participation with an online counterpart to traditional offline activity, it seems unlikely that the Internet will level the political playing field. Just as it does offline, the strong association between social class and political participation obtains for political participation on the Internet. The socio-economic bias in Internet-based political activity derives from two sources. One is the digital divide: the fact that access to and the ability to use a computer and the Internet, although widespread, are not universal and that those who are disadvantaged when it comes to income and education are disproportionately likely to be on the wrong side of the digital divide. The other is the association between socio-economic status and using the Internet for political participation, even among those who are fully equipped with the needed hardware and computer skills. There is some indication that the brave new world of political social networking may be characterized by reduced levels of SES bias. However, when the Pew survey was conducted, social networking was dominated by the young. Among the under-thirtysomethings who were so much more likely to use social networking sites, the current students and, among nonstudents, those with college degrees were much more likely to engage in political social networking. In sum, high levels of education and income not only facilitate Internet access and use but foster political activity on the Internet—just as they have long been known to foster pre-Internet political activity.

Must It Be This Way? A Note on Religious Attendance

Is there something about activity per se that invites greater involvement by those who enjoy educational and economic advantage? Or is the connection between SES and activity unique to political participation? We have presented striking data about attendance at religious services showing that social class does not stratify all forms of voluntary activity. The rate of church attendance is fairly similar across all socio-economic levels, indicating that a steep socio-economic gradient is characteristic of political activity but not necessarily of activity in general. There is no iron law that voluntary involvements must be structured by class.

Unequal Voice through Organized Interests

Interest organizations serve as a major vehicle for the expression of citizen voice. We were not surprised that our findings about the interests represented by organizations reinforced what we learned about individual political voice. Although the range of organized interests active in Washington politics is astonishingly broad, it does not even approximate equal voice. No advanced musical training is needed to hear that the unheavenly chorus of the organized interests sings with the same upper-class accent as do politically active individuals.

When citizen political perspectives are represented by organizations rather by individuals, the already formidable problems in measuring departures from equal voice are compounded. As in the case of individual participation, a multidimensional issue space means that there is no way to determine what share of organized advocacy should be devoted to the representation of various points of view with respect to health care, crop supports for cotton, including intelligent design in high school biology curriculums, Middle East policy, affirmative action in public employment, abortion, immigration, and hundreds of other political issues.

Beyond that are special difficulties associated with the representation of interests by organizations. In contrast to the circumstance for individual-level participation where the baseline is the population, there is no natural baseline of organizations from which to measure over- and underrepresentation. Because any group of people with joint political concerns not only must have the necessary resources but also must overcome the free rider problem in order first to coalesce as a formal organization and then to take that organization into politics, the organizations that are active in politics represent only a small subset of the possibilities. There is thus no equivalent to a random sample of individuals, active and inactive, against which to compare the voice of the active organizations.

In addition, while individuals can be presumed to speak for themselves and to have equal weight as citizens, no such assumptions are possible when they are represented by organizations. Because organizations have vastly different numbers of members, there is no organizational equivalent of the democratic principle of one person, one vote. Besides, it is often difficult to determine for whom an organization speaks. In organizations composed of individual members, the members are unlikely to be uniform in their preferences and concerns; rather they are likely to be divided by generation, region, ideology, or any of a variety of other cleavages. Further complicating matters is the fact that the vast majority of organized interests in Washington politics are not voluntary associations of individuals but are instead either institutions such as corporations, museums, or hospitals or associations of such institutions. When an institution such as an art museum is politically active, it is not clear whose interests are being served—those of its management, board, staff, artists, donors, or visitors.

In spite of such representational complexities, when we placed the thousands of organizations active in Washington into a set of 96 categories, what we found was obviously far from a circumstance approximating equality of political voice. Both the free rider problem and the resource constraint problem have profound effects on whose voices are heard through the medium of collective representation. The interests of the advantaged, especially business, are well represented. In contrast, two kinds of interests receive much less extensive representation: broad public interests and the economically disadvantaged.

Compared to the number of people who presumably have an interest in such broad public interests as wilderness protection, low consumer prices, auto safety, access to firearms, or free speech, the number of organizations advocating for public goods is relatively small, accounting for less than 5 percent of the organizations listed in the 2001 *Washington Representatives* directory. In any political controversy, a public interest on one side may be opposed by a different public interest on the other: for example, clean water and economic development are both public goods, as are both national security and low taxes. Minimizing the delays in getting newly developed drugs to the people they can help is a public good, but so is ensuring that newly developed drugs are safe and effective. What this means is that, although in the aggregate the public interest community leans in a somewhat liberal direction, public goods favored by conservatives are also represented.

Organized Interest Representation: Advantaged and Disadvantaged

Just as they are in individual political participation, the economically disadvantaged are underrepresented in pressure politics. Organizations that advocate on behalf of the poor are relatively scarce, organizations of the poor themselves are extremely rare, and organizations of those who benefit from means-tested government programs acting on their own behalf are, quite simply, nonexistent.

Less frequently noted than the absence of organizations for the poor is the dearth of organizations advocating for the economic interests of those who are not affluent. Even those with ordinary jobs and middle-class incomes are vastly underrepresented. With respect to their nonoccupational economic interests, there are few, if any, organizations representing people who live in rental housing, who receive the Earned Income Tax Credit, whose jobs have been outsourced, or whose pensions are not vested.

With respect to occupational interests, labor unions and occupational associations that unite people on the basis of how they make their living constitute an important segment of the Washington pressure community. However, there is only a small number of unions, and their membership is declining. Other than unions, the relatively small number of associations that enroll nonprofessional and nonmanagerial workers tend to represent those in occupations that demand relatively high levels of skill and that confer relatively high levels of pay and status. Unless they are unionized, which is increasingly rare for private-sector workers, those who work in low-skill jobs have *no occupational associations at all* to represent their interests. In contrast, professionals and managers are quite well represented by occupational associations.

What is more, business is quite well represented among organizations in Washington politics. American corporations comprise by far the single largest category of organized interest; adding in the various other kinds of organizations that represent business interests—for example, trade associations and foreign corporations—a majority, 53 percent, of the all organized interests in Washington are associated with business.

In an exception to the overall pattern that characterizes interest representation in Washington, the very small number of organizations that represent people on the basis of some noneconomic identity—for example, race or ethnicity, nationality, age, sexual orientation, or gender—represent the less advantaged rather than the dominant groups. The small but diverse set of identity groups is unusual in being organized around the interests of marginal groups—for example, women, the elderly, gays and lesbians, Latinos, and especially Native Americans. Still, the mainstream organizations that advocate on the basis of a wide variety of interests other than shared identity —usually joint economic interests—hardly neglect the concerns and preferences of middle-aged white men.

Because the distribution of organized interests tilts so strongly away from the representation of public interests and the economically disadvantaged, we considered several additional sources of evidence to assess whether our categories somehow obscure ameliorating tendencies. Where possible, we located information about the universe of organizations in a particular category, whether or not political, and determined that organizations with more members and larger budgets are more likely to be active in politics than are the more modestly endowed organizations in the same category.

Using survey data we learned that, just as they are more likely to take part in politics, individuals who are higher on the SES scale are more likely to join organizations. Furthermore, once in an organization, they are more likely to be recruited to take some political action. Moreover, among organizational members, those higher on the socio-economic scale are more likely to be active in the organization, to have served on the board or as officers, to have expressed their views, and to perceive that their organization represents their interests.

Finally we examined organizations' Web sites to inquire whether the resource disadvantaged are gaining representation from other, perhaps more privileged, organizations in the pressure system. A detailed analysis of the possibilities for Web-based surrogate advocacy on behalf of various underrepresented constituencies suggests that, for a variety of reasons, any compensatory impact is very unlikely to be appreciable. Taken together, these disparate sources of additional evidence suggest that, if anything, the data about distribution of organizations into categories underestimate the upper-class accent of the organized interest chorus.

Political Voice through Organized Interest Activity

As is the case with individual participation, organizations can vary the volume of input regarding any form of political action, with the result that political voice is not necessarily proportional to the number of active organizations. We assembled data about several measures of organizational resources and activities: the number of in-house lobbyists on the payroll, the number of outside firms retained, the amount spent on lobbying, the number of congressional testimonies given, the number of briefs filed in Supreme Court cases, and contributions to political action committees (PACs). An analysis that covered several forms of organizational activity and numerous categories of organizations yielded dozens of microfindings about the techniques used by organizations to influence outcomes in Washington.

There are differences among forms of activity with respect to the tilt of the organized interest input. Because the initiative in lobbying lies with an organization itself, the distribution of lobbying expenditures is skewed especially sharply in the direction of well-heeled organizations. In contrast, because an organization testifies at a congressional hearing at the behest of congressional policy makers, the distribution of congressional testimonies is much less concentrated in the direction of the haves. The specialized nature of the issues that dominate the docket of the Supreme Court implies that certain kinds of organizations—in particular, state and local governments as well as identity groups and public interest groups—figure as important in the filing of amicus briefs with the Court.

Overall, however, the broad outlines reinforce the conclusions drawn from the distribution of political organizations about the upper-class accent of the organizations in the pressure system: organizations representing the advantaged, especially business, weigh heavily, especially when compared to organizations representing the disadvantaged—whether defined in terms of identity or economic wherewithal—and broad public interests.

Organizational Categories and Organizational Activity

Let us summarize very briefly a few of our results for some of the most significant organizational categories. There is no form of organized interest input for which activity on behalf of the poor—whether by organizations advocating for the poor or by organizations that provide social services—registers more than a trace. Such organizations account for 2 percent of the congressional testimonies and amicus briefs and less than 1 percent of the lobbying expenditures and PAC donations.

Because, other than unions, there are very few organizations representing the economic interests of nonprofessional, nonmanagerial workers and none at all representing the interests of unskilled workers, unions are responsible for just about all organized interest activity on behalf of workers other than professionals and managers. As individual organizations, unions are, on average, the most active kind of organization. However, because there are so few of them, they account for only 1 percent of the lobbying expenditures, 1 percent of the amicus briefs, and 3 percent of the congressional testimonies. Still, in a departure from the patterns we have described, union contributions form a significant share of PAC giving: 26 percent of donations to political action committees came from unions, and, most notably, 15 percent came from unions of blue-collar workers. It is ironic that PAC contributions—which are viewed with suspicion by advocates of political equality—are the mode of organized political input in which organizations representing the economic interests of nonelites weigh most heavily.

There is no way to specify what share of activity should represent public goods—which account for 11 percent of the congressional testimonies, 13 percent of the amicus briefs, 9 percent of PAC contributions, and, presumably reflecting the regulations affecting 501(c)3 organizations, a mere 2 percent of lobbying expenditures. However, it is worth noting that in no domain does activity by public interest organizations outweigh activity by organizations representing business. Furthermore, activity by conservative public interest organizations is a more substantial share of activity on behalf of diffuse public interests than is generally acknowledged.

Except when it comes to filing amicus briefs, where they are in second place to state and local governments, the various kinds of organizations representing business, taken together, are the modal kind of organization for each kind of activity. Most striking is the fact that business organizations are responsible for nearly three-fourths, 72 percent, of the lobbying expenditures. Even though unions are a significant source of PAC contributions, business organizations are responsible for nearly half, 48 percent, of the dollars donated to political action committees, additional evidence of the accent of the organized interest chorus.

Unequal Voice: Individuals and Organizations Together

An important contribution of this work is that we consider in tandem issues of equality of political voice with respect to both individuals and political organizations—and find many parallel results. Most important, the voices of those who are affluent and well educated sing loudly and clearly in both individual and organized interest activity. Whether the medium is individual or organizational activity, the preferences and concerns of the less advantaged receive less vigorous advocacy. Longitudinal data show that this stratification has been a feature of both individual participation and organized interest activity for decades—that is, as far back as we have systematic data to measure it. Furthermore, internal processes within membership associations of individuals reinforce this tendency. Not only is there class stratification in membership in organizations that take stands in politics, but high-SES organization members are more likely to hold leadership positions in political organizations. Echoing the processes of rational prospecting by which individuals mobilize one another to become involved politically, high-SES individuals in an organization are also more likely to have been asked to take some political action.

Our inquiry has uncovered an important distinction between individual and organizational political activity. Although we ordinarily combine educational attainment and family income into a single measure of socio-economic status, education is at the root of individual participation. Those who are well educated are more likely also to be politically interested, informed, and efficacious; to have the kinds of jobs that yield high incomes; and to have the kinds of involvements at work and in religious institutions and nonpolitical organizations that permit the development of civic skills and lead to requests for political activity. In sum, educational attainment is associated with nearly every other factor that fosters political activity among individuals.

In contrast, the critical resource for politically active organizations is money. An organization with a large budget will hire the expertise it needs—lobbyists, researchers, tax attorneys, public relations experts, and so on. Hiring high-priced talent helps to ensure political effectiveness. Hiring additional professionals allows an organization to multiply the volume of its political input substantially. In short, well-educated individuals are likely to have many other attributes that make them effective as activists. Affluent organizations can purchase those characteristics.

Dollar Politics and Unequal Political Voice

At numerous points on our journey we have pointed to the special challenge posed by forms of political voice that rely on money: how to reconcile inequalities of market resources with the desire to establish a level playing field for democracy. While all democracies face the dilemma of how much to regulate the free use of unequal resources in pursuit of political objectives, the

United States tends to allow more freedom in the legal use of market resources to influence political outcomes—especially and increasingly when it comes to campaign finance.

Of the various resources that individuals and organizations bring to political activity—among them time, political skills, allies, capable staffers, and an appealing message—money has some singular characteristics. Perhaps most significant, money is unusual in that it is simultaneously both a resource for political participation and a source of political contestation. Inequalities in income and wealth are much more likely to adhere to the boundaries of politically relevant categories—not only social class but also race or ethnicity and gender. Political issues that pit the interests of rich and poor (or middle income) against one another are common in American politics, but conflicts between the articulate and inarticulate or between the busy and the leisured are not.

In addition, among political resources, financial resources are particularly unevenly distributed. With respect to individuals, the Gini coefficient for dollars is much higher than for hours; that is, comparing the best and worst off with respect to money and spare time, the most affluent person is relatively much better off than the most leisured one. The various political resources differ in the extent to which they can be substituted for one another, but money is perhaps the most fungible—a characteristic that is especially important to political organizations that hire in-house staff or outside firms to assist in political advocacy.

These characteristics of money as a political resource yield a paradox for the forms of individual and collective political activity in which the expression of political voice is based on dollars. On one hand, political money has a special status among the resources that foster political activity as the one for which free use is regulated in terms of both the ways it can be used and the amounts that can be spent. Of course, as individuals we are permitted only one vote in each election. However, we can attend as many community meetings, march in as many protests, or give up as many weekends to work for a favored candidate as we wish. Not only are there no limits on our use of spare time for political participation, but there are also no restrictions on our ability to take full advantage of whatever skills we can muster for effective political action. However, when it comes to our bank accounts, we are not free in politics to spend as much as we wish in whatever ways we wish.

Nevertheless, our data have shown that, in spite of such restrictions, when the medium of participatory input is cash, the volume of political activity can be multiplied in a way not possible for other political acts. Even the most assiduous demonstrator can attend only so many protests, but the amounts legally given by heavy-hitter donors can be very, very substantial.

In addition, although numerous factors—for example, educational attainment, political interest, or requests for political action—predict undertaking political acts based on inputs of time, a single factor, family income, predicts not just the likelihood that an individual will make a political contribution but the size of that contribution. Hence, those major contributions originate with a very thin slice of affluent donors. We showed evidence about the high proportion of campaign contributions—especially of campaign contributions given in response to a request—that come from respondents in the top group in terms of family income. Moreover, at a more rarefied level, a recent study of campaign giving during the 2010 electoral cycle shows that, taken together, donors who contributed more than $10,000 to federal campaigns, a group representing less than one in ten thousand Americans, contributed just under a quarter—24.3 percent—of all contributions from individuals to candidates, parties, PACs, and independent expenditure groups. The members of this small group averaged $28,913 in donations, a figure that is higher than the median individual income for 2010.[4] Similarly, a listing of the organizations with which donors who have made $50,000 in campaign contributions over one or more election cycles are affiliated showed that 95 of the 98 individuals who had contributed such large sums had been associated with business-related entities.

When it comes to campaign finance, we need to add a caveat to our usual concern with the distribution of political activity rather than the level of political activity. We have reason to consider level as well. As the costs of running for office skyrocket, not only do candidates devote more and more time to raising money at the expense of focusing on making policy or meeting with constituents but they spend increasing amounts of time in the company of wealthy donors—with implications for equal political voice.[5] Furthermore, the high costs of campaigning may be linked to the recent increase in the width of the economic gulf that separates ordinary members of the public

4. Lee Drutman, "The Political One Percent of the One Percent," http://sunlightfoundation.com/blog/2011/12/13/the-political-one-percent-of-the-one-percent/ (accessed December 28, 2011).

5. See Mark Alexander, "*Citizens United* and Equality Forgotten," in *Money, Politics, and the Constitution: Beyond Citizens United*, ed. Monica Youn (New York: Century Foundation Press, 2011), pp. 160–163.

from members of the House and Senate, nearly half of whom were million-aires in November 2011.[6] The sharp climb in the cost of running a campaign means that public office may become relatively more attractive to those who have substantial assets that they can invest on their own behalf and to those who have wealthy friends willing to back their candidacies.[7] The bottom line is that congressional aspirants are less and less likely to be experiencing themselves—or to interact frequently with others who are experiencing—the buffeting of ordinary economic life, with potential consequences for their views about what government should or should not be doing.

Increasing the number of small political contributions is sometimes viewed as the way to overcome inequalities in political giving. To the extent that campaign contributions carry potential leverage, if an increased share of the campaign war chest derives from small contributions, inequalities of political voice will be ameliorated. In fact, data we presented showed that, as reported in the media, the possibility of making campaign contributions over the Internet increased the number of small donations to candidates in the 2008 elections. Still, our data also showed that small, Internet-based con-tributions come from the same kind of people who contribute offline, thus not broadening the characteristics of the donor base and reproducing the inequalities associated with offline giving.

Of the various ways that money can be converted into political voice, the public harbors particular concerns about campaign giving by political action committees. Because PAC donations arrive with a return address, PACs are widely viewed as raising the possibility of undue influence on electoral results or policy outcomes by "special interests" such as business and labor that have substantial war chests and recognized policy agendas. Lending credence to the stereotype is the fact that 85 percent of PAC donations come from a very limited set of organizations: corporations, trade and other business associa-tions, labor unions, and occupational associations. What is less widely recog-nized is that, when it comes to campaign giving, individual donations swamp the sums given by PACs, and when it comes to spending by organized inter-ests in politics, the aggregate sums devoted to lobbying dwarf PAC contribu-

6. Study conducted by the Center for Responsive Politics, reported in "Most Members of Congress Enjoy Robust Financial Status, Despite Nation's Sluggish Economic Recovery," http://www.opensecrets.org/news/2011/11/congress-enjoys-robust-financial-status.html (ac-cessed December 27, 2011).

7. Eric Lichtblau, "Economic Slide Took a Detour at Capitol Hill," New York Times, Decem-ber 27, 2011.

tions. Not only are PACs not the largest source of either campaign money or money spent on organized interest advocacy but PAC dollars give greater weight to the economic interests of ordinary people. Furthermore, the currently unfolding consequences of the decision in *Citizens United*, which gave corporations greater freedom in engaging unlimited independent spending during campaigns, may be tilting the balance of campaign finance further in the direction of corporate interests with deep pockets. Law professor Paul A. Freund's response to *Buckley* v. *Valeo* (1976), the decision that first interpreted campaign donations as a form of speech, seems germane in the aftermath of *Citizens United*: "They say that money talks. I thought that was the problem, not the solution."[8]

In contrast to voluntary individual political activity, the domain of organized interest advocacy is a professionalized sector in which financial resources permit the expansion of political activity and the purchase of skilled personnel. Individual political participation and organized interest activity have in common that the principal resources mobilized for the expression of political voice are time, money, and skills. However, individual participation differs from organized interest activity in that those who undertake individual participatory acts do so themselves. That is, while wealthy activists may dip deeply into their large bank accounts to fund favored candidates and causes, they do not ordinarily multiply their other activities by hiring mercenaries to attend demonstrations in their stead or contracting with a political Cyrano to compose especially articulate letters to public officials.

Political advocacy is very different through organized interests—a world in which activity is undertaken by professionals who are paid well, the contemporary version of the "expensive arguers" described by King Arthur in *The Once and Future King*.[9] Thus, in the domain of the Washington pressure community, a substantial share of an organization's budget is devoted to the purchase of the time and the often quite specific expertise of professional advocates. In short, in Washington pressure politics, money is time and skills. Spending on lobbying has grown rapidly in recent years, rising from $1.44 billion in 1998 to $3.47 billion in 2010.[10] This increase—which has been, in

8. Paul A. Freund, quoted in Anthony Lewis, *Freedom for the Thought That We Hate: A Biography of the First Amendment* (New York: Basic Books, 2007), p. 178.

9. See Chapter 10, "Do Organized Interests Influence Public Policy?"

10. Figures taken from calculations by the Center for Responsive Politics based on data from the Senate Office of Public Records, available at http://www.opensecrets.org/lobby/index.php (accessed February 5, 2011).

constant dollar terms, one of nearly 1.8 times the original amount—has outpaced any of such usual metrics of social change such as population or economic growth. In addition, between 1981 and 2006, the number of firms of
professionals listed in the *Washington Representatives* directory, most of them
law and public relations firms that engage in organized interest advocacy for
hire, multiplied more than fifteen times.

Data assembled as the result of the stricter reporting requirements imposed by the Lobbying Disclosure Act of 1995 show unambiguously that lobbying is an activity in which the heavenly chorus is especially unrepresentative.
Of the lobbying expenditures in 2000 and 2001, 1 percent came from labor
unions, 3 percent from groups organized around some noneconomic identity
such as race or religion, 2 percent from organizations representing broad public interests, and less than 1 percent from organizations that provide social services or advocate on behalf of the poor. In contrast, 72 percent came from
organizations representing business interests. The lobbying section of the
heavenly chorus contains many voices, but it clearly sings with an upper-crust
accent.

It seems that achieving political voice through any form of political activity in which the primary political resource is money illustrates the wisdom of
an observation from Sidney Verba's dad, Morris Verba: "Rich or poor, it's
good to have money."

Singing the Same Melody:
The Persistence of Unequal Political Voice

The other persistent theme of our inquiry has been persistence itself: the
durability over time, across generations, and through the life course of class-
based inequalities of political voice for both individuals and organized interests. At the beginning of Chapter 6 we discussed a number of trends with
possible consequences for inequalities of political voice. The obvious assumption is that soaring economic inequality, coupled with the attrition of union
membership and power, would exacerbate political inequality. However, we
suggested that several political theories that otherwise have little in common—
Downsian, Marxist, and pluralist—converge in predicting the opposite result.
In addition, both rising levels of educational attainment within the public
and the increasing institutional strength of the political parties and the greater
efforts they are making to mobilize voters would also have a contrary equal-

izing impact on unequal voice. Hence we brought no clear expectations to the matter of how inequalities of political voice would have changed in the new Gilded Age.

Time-series data from the American National Election Studies (ANES) containing information about various forms of election-related participation over a fifty-six-year period and from Roper Starch containing information about a set of electoral and nonelectoral political acts over a three-decade period made clear that what we have observed in cross-sectional data holds across time. The ongoing association between socio-economic status and political participation obtains, with varying degrees of strength, for all forms of political activity. Although all are stratified, voting is the least inegalitarian, campaign contributions the most, and other political acts fall in between. In each case, the lines tracing political participation over time for the five SES quintiles arrange themselves neatly from the highest to the lowest and rarely cross. In addition, the cross-sectional finding that attendance of religious services, unlike political participation, is not characterized by class stratification holds over the long run.

Contrary to the expectations of some observers of increasing levels of income inequality, the association between class and participation does not seem to have become more pronounced in recent decades. Indeed, with the possible exception that competitive presidential elections may ameliorate participatory inequalities, the peaks and valleys of participatory inequality do not seem to track trends in economic inequality or other obvious factors. As a matter of fact, the trajectories over time of relative inequality for different political acts do not move in sync. In short, what is most striking is not the inexplicable irregularities in the extent of participatory inequality across the decades but rather the remarkable persistence of that inequality—especially when viewed in contrast to the absence of stratification in religious service attendance.

From the perspective of the representation of politically relevant interests, it may not matter whether the enduring class differences in political participation reflect the continuing activity of the same kinds of people or the continuing activity of the same individuals. However, when we used three waves of ANES panel data to trace the participatory histories of individual respondents over a four-year period, we were struck by the extent to which individuals who are politically active—or inactive—at one point of time are likely to remain so. Interestingly, the Newtonian inertia of political activity and inactivity is roughly equivalent to that in the religious domain. Not unexpectedly, there is a habitual aspect to attendance of religious services. What is more surprising is that the tendency to take part politically—or not—is on a par with the tendency to attend religious services or to stay home. In addition, reinforcing our understanding of the power of the relationship of social class to political participation is the interaction between socio-economic status and the persistence of political activity. A political activist from the upper reaches of the socio-economic scale is more likely to remain active in the future than is an activist from lower on the SES ladder. Conversely, comparing two inactive individuals, one from a lower SES level is more likely to remain consistently out of politics than one from an upper-SES rung.

The Persistence of Political Participation across Generations

Not only do participatory inequalities persist, in the aggregate, over time, and not only do individuals tend to be politically active or inactive on an ongoing basis, but, in a serious challenge to the political equivalent of the American Dream of equality of opportunity, the propensity to take part politically is transmitted across generations. Students of political socialization long ago established the association between parents' socio-economic status and the likelihood that their offspring will be politically active as adults. The causal chain was presumed to include the following steps: parents who are well educated are likely to be politically interested and active and to talk about politics at home, and then, as adults, children who have been exposed to such political cues are likely to be politically interested and active themselves. Our data demonstrated that the transmission process by which the children of well-educated parents emulate their parents' example of political engagement indeed operates as posited. However, even more powerful than this political path is one that leads through socio-economic status. Well-educated parents tend to rear children who are themselves well educated and who, in turn, enjoy all the accompanying participatory benefits associated with high levels of educational attainment—for example, high incomes; opportunities to develop civic skills at work, in voluntary organizations, and in religious institutions; and such psychological orientations as political interest, information, and efficacy. There are thus powerful consequences for political participation from the processes that allow parents to hand down their class position to the next generation. When it comes to politics as well as economics, we are not equal at the starting line.

The Persistence of Organizational Voice

Data over a twenty-five year period about the kinds of organizations that are active in Washington tell a story about the persistence of organizational voice that is analogous to what we saw for individuals. As usual, when we dealt with data involving thousands of organizations placed into 96 categories, there were myriad subsidiary findings. The broad outlines, however, are unmistakable: between 1981 and 2006, the number of organizations in the pressure system increased substantially; the overall distribution of interests represented showed a great deal of continuity.

It would be erroneous to conclude from these trends—rising numbers of organizations and essential stability in the distribution—that the process is one in which, once in politics, organizations remain politically active for the duration and are joined by additional organizations that are mobilized into politics on a more or less permanent basis. Furthermore, it would be erroneous to conclude that the contours of the pressure community are shaped solely by the considerable difficulties entailed in founding a new organization and keeping it going. The barriers to organization are only the first hurdle. The second is the resource requirements for political activity. The result is that the aggregate growth in the number of active political organizations obscures considerable movement in and out of pressure politics by organized interests. Moreover, the two-step process of, first, organizational founding and, then, politicization implies that the universe of organizations includes many that are outside of politics. Still, analysis of the in-and-out patterns demonstrated that it is easier to bring an existing organization into politics than to get a new organization off the ground: of the organizations we could trace, a majority of those that were active in 2006 but not in 1981 were alive in 1981, just not involved in politics, rather than being new organizations founded in the interim.

In spite of the overall continuity in the distribution of kinds of organizations, variations in organizational growth rates work together to produce a circumstance such that the share of the kinds of organizations traditionally well represented in pressure politics—corporations, trade and other business associations, occupational associations of professionals and managers, unions, and the like—has diminished. However, this relative reconfiguration has not meant an upsurge in the share of the kinds of organizations that are traditionally underrepresented in pressure politics: organizations representing broad publics and the disadvantaged. Instead, there has been explosive growth in the representation of subnational governments, especially local governments, and such institutions as universities and hospitals. Taken together, the share of organizations in the pressure system accounted for by subnational governments and the health and educational sectors more than tripled from 1981 and 2006, at which point it accounted for more than a fifth of the organizations active in Washington. Besides, even though the growth rates for the categories of organizations representing business were relatively low over the period, in absolute terms, the number of *additional* business-related organizations was nearly twice the total obtained when all the unions, public interest groups, identity groups, and organizations representing the economically needy listed in 2006 were added together.

Of particular relevance to our concern with the representation of the less well off is the status of unions, the only category that did not register growth in absolute numbers over the quarter-century period. Several aspects of the history of unions have a bearing on our understanding of political voice. While the overall number of unions was flat, the number of unions representing blue-collar workers actually declined. Considering union membership rather than the number of unions, in a widely noted trend, the share of the workforce that is unionized and even the absolute number of union members have declined markedly. The erosion of union membership has taken place entirely among private-sector union members, who have traditionally been less well educated and less white collar than their public-sector counterparts, with the result that union members have, on average, moved up the socio-economic ladder in recent decades. What these changes have meant for individual-level participatory input is quite striking: a rough estimate showed that, in 2006, the share of individual participatory acts attributable to union members was less than half what it had been in 1967.

In sum, the organized interest chorus has enlarged and the particular singers have changed, but the mix of voices is quite similar.

Persistent Inequality: The Bottom Line

Although we have highlighted the increases in economic inequality that provide an important context for our inquiry into the extent of inequalities of political voice, our investigations have emphasized continuity rather than change and the extent to which political voice has been characterized by social class stratification rather than the exacerbation of that stratification. At least since there has been access to systematic data, regardless of whether we focus on individuals or on political organizations, the unheavenly chorus has been singing with an upper-class accent. In focusing on any perturbations in the level of inequality, we must not lose sight of the principal finding: that ongoing inequalities of political voice characterize American politics.

That said, it is worth pointing out that certain developments may be working together to produce greater inequality of political voice. The most obvious is the decline of unions, especially blue-collar unions of private-sector workers. Not only have unions lost clout as organized advocates for their members and for American workers in general, but also erosion in total union membership implies that fewer workforce members are exposed to the politicizing aspects of labor union membership—in particular, the cultivation of civic skills and exposure to requests for political action. Moreover, as campaign costs have skyrocketed, making political contributions has assumed greater relative importance within the participation of political activists, especially those at the very top of the of the social class ladder. In addition, as political activity among individuals has declined and the activity of organized interests has increased, the relative weight of the latter—a domain of political input in which market resources figure as especially important—has increased. Working together, these tendencies may be further tilting the level playing field of democracy. Still, what is remarkable about political voice in American democracy is how unequal it has been for so long.

Equal Political Voice and the Promise of American Democracy

During the debate in the House of Representatives over the Bill of Rights in 1789, Elbridge Gerry of Massachusetts underlined the importance of citizen voice in informing legislators of the opinions of the people:

> We cannot, I apprehend, be too well informed of the true state, condition, and sentiment of our constituents. . . . I hope we shall never shut our ears against that information which is to be derived from the petitions and instructions of our constituents. . . .
>
> I hope we shall never presume to think that all the wisdom of this country is concentred within the walls of this House. Men, unambitious of distinctions from their fellow-citizens, remain within their own domestic walk, unheard of and unseen, possessing all the advantages from a watchful observance of public men and public measures, whose voice, if we would descend to listen to it, would give us knowledge

superior to what could be acquired amidst the cares and bustles of public life; let us then adopt the amendment and encourage the diffident to enrich our stock of knowledge with the treasure of their remarks and observations.[11]

Gerry's bid to have a nonbinding right "to instruct their Representatives" included in what became the First Amendment was ultimately unsuccessful. James Madison argued in rejoinder that, if the intent was, as Gerry was advocating, to make the instructions nonbinding, protecting freedom of speech and the press rendered the clause unnecessary. If the clause were to be interpreted "to say that the people have a right to instruct their representatives in such a sense as that the delegates are obliged to conform to those instructions," great mischief might ensue.[12] Although Gerry failed in his object, there seems to have been no quarrel then—or now—with his understanding that democratic governance cannot take place outside of the people's right to make their wishes known or his emphasis on the need for all representatives to be "well informed of the true state, condition, and sentiment of our constituents."

We have accumulated a great deal of evidence showing that the information that public officials receive through the medium of individual and collective citizen political voice comes from a very selective set of sources. A recent and unremarkable exchange in the *New York Times* reminded us how important it is to hear multiple perspectives and the potential costs if one side speaks clearly and the other side is not heard from. An op-ed piece by food writer Mark Bittman, "A Food Manifesto for the Future," argued on grounds of the promotion of health, environmental preservation, the well-being of food workers, and the protection of animals for a series of policy changes in food production—among them outlawing concentrated animal feeding operations, encouraging sustainable animal husbandry, and educating Americans about the health and environmental benefits of plant-based diets.[13] Bittman's points seemed convincing until they were rebutted in a letter to the editor from Randy Spronk, the chairman of the Environment Com-

---

11. Elbridge Gerry, quoted in Robert A. Goldwin, *From Parchment to Power: How James Madison Used the Bill of Rights to Save the Constitution* (Washington, DC: American Enterprise Institute Press, 1997), pp. 116–117. The account of the fate of the amendment and Madison's rejoinder is taken from pp. 114–118.

12. James Madison, quoted in Goldwin, *From Parchment to Power*, p. 117.

13. Mark Bittman, "A Food Manifesto for the Future," *New York Times*, February 2, 2011.

mittee of the National Pork Producers Council, who argued that modern methods of raising livestock keep animals "safe and comfortable" and that "sustainable" methods would make meat affordable for "the wealthy, but not for a world population that is growing and demanding more protein."[14] Clearly, conscientious policy makers—who have, of course, other sources of information about the needs and preferences of the people other than citizen voice—would get very different impressions of the dimensions of the problem and the appropriateness of proposed solutions if they were exposed to only one of these two apparently sincere and serious advocates.

The inequalities of political voice we have documented so extensively threaten the democratic principle of equal responsiveness to all. We have discussed that, when it comes to economics, Americans believe in the American Dream: they are willing to countenance substantial inequalities of outcome as long as equality of opportunity obtains. However, they are less supportive of inequalities in the political realm of democracy, in which citizens are supposed to operate as equals. Our inquiry has underscored the multiple respects in which we are not equals when it comes to political input. Compounding the violation are the complicated processes by which inequalities of political voice are bequeathed from one generation to the next. On the playing field of democratic participation, we are not just unequal at the finish line. In what seems to be a double violation, we are not even on an equal footing at the starting line. To recognize the inequalities of political voice and, in Gerry's words, to "encourage the diffident to enrich our stock of knowledge"— that is, to listen more carefully to the accent of the unheavenly chorus and to take measures to include a more representative set of singers—would be a step toward delivering on the promise of American democracy.

14. Randy Spronk, "Safe Meat," *New York Times*, February 8, 2011.

APPENDIXES

APPENDIX A
EQUALITY AND THE STATE AND U.S. CONSTITUTIONS

Following are the provisions that bear on equality in the constitutions of the individual states.

Constitutional Provision	Alabama	Alaska	Arizona	Arkansas	California	Colorado	Connecticut	Delaware	Florida	Georgia	Hawaii	Idaho	Illinois	Indiana	Iowa	Kansas	Kentucky	Louisiana	Maine	Maryland	Massachusetts	Michigan
General Mention of Equality	X	X		X	X		X	X	X		X	X	X	X	X	X	X			X	X	
Equal Protection		X	X	X	X		X		X	X	X	X	X	X	X	X	X	X	X		X	X
Listed Categories of Nondiscrimination																						
Race		X		X	X		X		X		X	X					X				X	X
Color		X		X	X		X					X									X	X
Religion or Creed		X		X	X	X	X	X	X		X	X	X					X	X	X	X	X
Ancestry							X				X											
National / Ethnic Origin	X			X		X		X				X					X				X	X
Sex or "Little ERA"		X			X	X	X		X		X	X						X			X	X
Handicap / Disability							X		X				X					X			X	
Political Ideas																		X				
No Religious Tests	X			X	X	X		X		X			X	X	X					X	X	X
No Titles or Hereditary Privilege	X		X			X	X					X					X	X		X	X	X
Political Power Derives from the People	X	X	X	X	X	X	X	X	X	X	X	X	X	X	X	X	X	X	X	X	X	X
Citizen Right to Vote	X	X	X	X	X	X	X	X	X	X	X	X	X	X	X	X	X	X	X	X	X	X
Felony Disenfranchisement	X	X	X	X	X	X			X	X	X	X	X	X	X	X	X	X		X	X	X
Right to Petition	X	X	X	X	X	X	X	X	X	X	X	X	X	X	X	X	X	X	X	X	X	X
Right to Instruct Representatives					X				X			X	X	X	X	X					X	X
Direct Democracy: Initiative / Referendum		X	X	X	X	X			X			X	X					X		X	X	X
No Bribery	X				X	X	X	X	X			X	X	X			X	X		X	X	
Free Education				X	X	X	X	X	X	X		X	X	X			X			X		X

	Minnesota	Mississippi	Missouri	Montana	Nebraska	Nevada	New Hampshire	New Jersey	New Mexico	New York	North Carolina	North Dakota	Ohio	Oklahoma	Oregon	Pennsylvania	Rhode Island	South Carolina	South Dakota	Tennessee	Texas	Utah	Vermont	Virginia	Washington	West Virginia	Wisconsin	Wyoming	U.S.
		X	X	X	X	X	X	X		X	X	X		X	X				X		X		X	X		X	X	X	
			X	X			X		X	X	X	X				X	X	X	X	X		X	X		X				X
				X			X	X	X	X						X				X				X			X		
				X			X	X	X	X										X				X			X		
	X		X	X			X	X	X	X	X			X					X	X	X			X					
				X					X																				
					X	X														X		X							
				X			X		X							X	X			X	X			X	X		X		
																	X												
				X																									
				X			X		X		X	X				X	X	X		X	X	X			X	X	X	X	X
							X			X			X	X		X								X	X	X			X
	X	X	X	X	X	X	X	X	X	X	X	X	X	X	X	X	X	X	X	X	X	X	X	X	X	X	X	X	X
	X	X	X	X	X	X	X	X	X	X	X	X	X	X	X	X	X	X	X	X	X	X	X	X	X	X	X	X	X
	X	X	X	X	X	X				X			X	X	X		X	X	X	X	X	X	X		X	X	X	X	X
	X	X	X	X	X	X	X		X	X	X	X	X	X	X	X	X	X		X	X	X	X	X	X	X	X	X	X
							X	X		X			X		X					X		X		X					
		X	X	X	X	X				X			X	X	X	X				X		X			X			X	
		X						X		X	X		X			X				X	X	X		X		X	X		X
		X	X	X	X				X	X	X	X	X		X					X	X	X	X	X	X	X	X		X

APPENDIX B
THE PERSISTENCE OF POLITICAL
AND NONPOLITICAL ACTIVITY

In Table B.1 we study the question of the persistence of political and nonpolitical activity over time. This table includes data from every American National Election Studies (ANES) three-wave panel from 1956 through 2004. Each panel has covered a four-year period and three national elections—always one congressional election sandwiched between two presidential elections. These panels span almost fifty years, from 1956–1958–1960 through 1972–1974–1976 and 1992–1994–1996 up to 2000–2002–2004. There are many "holes" in the table because some activities were not completely covered by some surveys.

Each entry in the table is a measure of the strength of association between activity in one period and activity in the two-year period before it. For each three-wave panel we can calculate two of these measures. For example, for the 1972–1974–1976 panel we can calculate the association between activity in 1976 and 1974 and the association between activity in 1974 and 1972. The measure in the table is the autoregressive coefficient from a regression of the panel respondents' activity in one period on their activity two years earlier.[1] In every case, these coefficients are quite large and highly statistically significant (their standard errors are in parentheses). There is ample evidence for substantial persistence over time in voting, campaign activity, noncampaign activity, union membership, and religious service attendance.

What explains this persistence? There are three major types of explanations. One is preexisting, more or less fixed characteristics such as socio-economic status (SES) that are largely formed in one's youth and young adulthood. These

---

1. The table reports b in the regression equation: $Y_t = a + b\,Y_{t-1} + e_t$. If Y_t and Y_{t-1} have exactly the same variance, then b is not only the autoregressive parameter in a regression; it is also the autocorrelation. Most of these variables do have relatively stationary variances so that the entries in Table B.1 are roughly autocorrelations.

characteristics might also include "politicality" or "religiosity." A second type is life events—for example, getting a job, getting married, and having children—that lead to involvements in organizations where civic skills, social networks, and interest in the world are developed and nurtured. Finally, a third type is habituation, whereby engaging in an activity in the past leads to learning about it and to an ability, willingness, or desire to do it again.

Sorting out these factors requires a bit of statistical legerdemain. One approach would be to list every factor that might affect participation, to measure each and every one, and then to classify each one into the categories of fixed (or relatively fixed) characteristics, episodic life events, and past measures of activity. Then a regression of activity on all these factors would tell us which ones matter. Although we could theoretically do something like this, a brute force method is hard to carry out for two reasons. First, it would probably be impossible to list and measure each and every factor. Second, sorting out these factors would require the solution of some complicated statistical issues, which would necessitate a panel of respondents who have been observed repeatedly over a relatively long time (at least four years). Very few surveys have gone far enough in listing and measuring as many participatory factors as possible, so very few comprehensive data sets are available. Even when those conducting a survey have tried to make it comprehensive, important factors have surely been missed, and no survey, to our knowledge, has combined detailed measures of factors with a panel over time.[2] Here we try to get around the need to enumerate every factor by developing a very general framework for sorting out the three major causes of persistence. This framework makes it possible for us to use the quartet of four-year three-wave panels undertaken by the American National Election Studies.

One of the major causes of persistence of activity might be life events and experiences. These can be identified without having to name and measure every single possible one by assuming that life events occur at certain ages that can be represented by dummy variables for age groups. Another major cause of persistence might be habituation, which implies that activity during the last period ("lagged activity") should affect activity during this period, so we can test for habituation by including a measure of prior activity on the right-hand side of a regression equation.

That leaves us with relatively fixed characteristics as causes of persistence. Some of these, such as social class, can be enumerated and included in a regres-

---

2. The most detailed study of participation is probably the Citizen Participation Study (1990), which included an initial "screener" interview six months before a very detailed survey and then a subsequent third interview of selected respondents about four years later. This panel suffers from the fact that the first two waves were too close together to identify unique instances of political participation. In addition, the first wave did not have as much detailed information about factors causing participation as the second wave.

Table B.1 Persistence across Activities over Time: OLS Regressions

Regression of	Political Activities			Nonpolitical Activities	
	Voting	Campaign Activity	Noncampaign Activity	Union Membership	Religious Attendance
1956–1958–1960					
1960 Activity on 1958 Activity	.399			.794	.691
	(.021)			(.017)	(.023)
1958 Activity on 1956 Activity	.612			.797	.663
	(.029)			(.017)	(.023)
N = 1,024					
1972–1974–1976					
1976 Activity on 1974 Activity	.440	.494		.728	.776
	(.021)	(.028)		(.017)	(.019)
1974 Activity on 1972 Activity	.578	.489		.693	.759
	(.029)	(.031)		(.019)	(.019)
N = 1,091					

1992–1994–1996

1996 Activity on 1994 Activity	.457 (.032)	.633 (.037)	.777 (.028)
1994 Activity on 1992 Activity	.617 (.045)	.507 (.032)	.685 (.030)
N = 537			

2000–2002–2004

2004 Activity on 2002 Activity	.352 (.024)	.529 (.038)	.561 (.031)	.828 (.020)
2002 Activity on 2000 Activity	.650 (.036)	.397 (.034)	.569 (.032)	.814 (.020)
N = 748				

Source: American National Election Studies (1956–1958–1960, 1972–1974–1976, 1992–1994–1996, and 2000–2002–2004).

Notes: Campaign activity includes campaign work, making campaign contributions, attending campaign meetings, and trying to influence another voter; noncampaign political activity includes contacting political officials, protesting, doing informal community work, or attending a meeting on an issue facing one's community. Standard errors are in parentheses. Empty cells indicate no data available. See text for further explanation.

sion, but it seems unlikely that each and every one can be identified. This creates a thorny statistical problem. For any kind of reasonable theory of participation, the level of past participation that is included on the right-hand side of a regression to test for habituation must be explained by the same factors that explain current activity. As a result, unless the enumeration of fixed characteristics is complete and the dummy variables for age groups represent all of the possible life events, the lagged activity measure will inevitably proxy the factors left out and appear to be a significant predictor of current activity, even when it is not. Indeed the large coefficients on the lagged participation measures in Table B.1 are surely partly the result of having left out all fixed characteristics and all dummy variables for age groups. Thus including past participation in the equation not only tests for habituation but also includes a proxy, a Trojan horse, for all of the factors other than habituation that affect participation.

What can be done in this situation to distinguish the impact of habituation from that of life events and fixed characteristics? We must use some statistical tricks.[3] One trick is to subtract each person's level of activity during last period from his or her level of activity during the current period and to regress this on a similar variable constructed by subtracting the person's activity two periods ago from his or her activity during the last period. Each of these variables will get rid of *all* fixed effects,[4] because when we take the differences, those factors that are fixed for each individual will be subtracted out. To do this, we must have a three-wave panel so that there are just enough observations for each person in the sample to construct these variables. In addition, if we include dummy variables for age groups on the right-hand side of the equation, we will capture any changes that occur in each age group during the two-year period.

Unfortunately, this does not quite solve all the statistical problems. The differenced variables get rid of all fixed effects, so we are spared the difficult and probably impossible process of enumerating and measuring all of them, but the dependent variable comprises the difference between the person's current level of activity and his or her activity during the last period and the explanatory right-hand-side variable includes the difference between the person's

3. The best treatment of the statistical issues involved is Chapter 4, "Dynamic Models with Variable Intercepts," in Cheng Hsiao, *Analysis of Panel Data* (Cambridge, England: Cambridge University Press, 1986), pp. 71–96. See also Chapter 8, "Dynamic Panel Data Models," in Badi H. Baltagi, *Econometric Analysis of Panel Data* (New York: John Wiley and Sons, 1995), pp. 125–148.

4. If these are truly fixed effects, then they enter in exactly the same way into today's activity, the last period's activity, and activity from all previous periods. Hence the differences described in the text will "cancel" out these factors. In equations, if $Y_t = a + bY_{t-1} + cX + e_t$, where X is a "fixed characteristic" that has a constant impact (hence c stays the same from one time period to the next), $Y_t - Y_{t-1} = (a + bY_{t-1} + cX + e_t) - (a + bY_{t-2} + cX + e_{t-1}) = b(Y_{t-1} - Y_{t-2}) + (e_t - e_{t-1})$. The cX terms cancel out.

activity during the last period and the person's activity in the period before that. Consequently, the two variables have in common the last period's activity. A little algebra shows that these two differences must be negatively correlated with one another no matter what,[5] so a regression of the current difference (current activity minus last period's activity) on the lagged difference (the last period's activity minus activity during the period before that) inevitably and incorrectly yields a negative coefficient even though we would expect a positive coefficient when there is habituation. Another trick is needed, and in this case an "instrumental variable" must be produced that is correlated with the right-hand-side explanatory "lagged difference" but is not directly correlated with the left-hand-side dependent variable "current difference." Fortunately, activity from the first period of the panel has exactly the right properties.[6]

Table B.2 reports the results obtained from using this instrumental variables approach with the current difference regressed on the lagged difference and dummy variables for age groups. We have left out the coefficients on the age groups and just reported the coefficient that allows us to test for habituation. If this habituation coefficient is positive and statistically significant, then we have evidence for habituation. Negative values suggest that there is no habituation.[7] Only voting, union membership, and attendance at religious services have consistently positive habituation coefficients, at least a few of which are statistically significant, suggesting some kind of habituation. The habituation coefficient for noncampaign activity is not statistically significant, but it is positive, so the results neither clearly reject nor support habituation.

What about the impact of life events? The dummy variables for age groups do not reveal any clear-cut patterns for attendance at religious services, union membership, or campaign participation. There is some suggestion of a parabolic effect for noncampaign political participation, but there is strong and consistent evidence for a parabolic effect for voting. Figure B.1 summarizes these results.[8] Note that because the values reported in this figure are based on

5. If Y_t represents current activity, Y_{t-1} represents the last period's activity, and Y_{t-2} represents the activity of the period before that, then the two differenced variables are $Y_t - Y_{t-1}$ and $Y_{t-1} - Y_{t-2}$, so they must be negatively correlated with one another through Y_{t-1}.

6. Thus Y_{t-2} is clearly correlated with $Y_{t-1} - Y_{t-2}$ but it is not correlated with $(e_t - e_{t-1})$ as long as we assume that there is no autocorrelation in the error terms of the original equations.

7. Negative values could mean that the opposite of habituation—some form of "revulsion" —is occurring. This seems unlikely; the more plausible interpretation of negative values is that the instrumental variable has not worked very well.

8. These results are based on the coefficients in the regressions adjusted for the fact that turnout typically increases between a midterm and a presidential election. They represent the change over two years in turnout for each age group. For each age group, the plotted values are the cumulative effects calculated by summing the adjusted regression coefficients across all preceding age groups and the current age group.

Table B.2 Habituation among Activities over Time: Instrumental Variables Regression with Current Activity Difference Regressed on Lagged Activity Difference with Age Controls

Years	Political Activities			Nonpolitical Activities	
	Voting	Campaign Activity	Noncampaign Activity	Union Membership	Religious Attendance
1956–1958–1960					
Lagged Difference	.211			.451	.077
	(.089)			(.112)	(.080)
N = 1,024					
1972–1974–1976					
Lagged Difference	.121	–.101		.311	.366
	(.077)	(.043)		(.075)	(.093)
N = 1,091					
1992–1994–1996					
Lagged Difference	.189	.115		.101	
	(.133)	(.075)		(.099)	
N = 537					
2000–2002–2004					
Lagged Difference	.424	–.445	.072		.187
	(.142)	(.034)	(.087)		(.120)
N = 748					

Source: American National Election Studies (1956–1958–1960, 1972–1974–1976, 1992–1994–1996, and 2000–2002–2004).

Notes: Campaign activity includes campaign work, making campaign contributions, attending campaign meetings, and trying to influence another voter; noncampaign political activity includes contacting political officials, protesting, doing informal community work, or attending a meeting on an issue facing one's community. Standard errors are in parentheses. Empty cells indicate no data available. See text for further explanation.

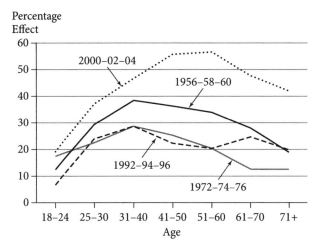

Figure B.1   Net Life-Cycle Effects for Voting from Three-Wave Panel Studies

Source: American National Election Studies Panels (1956–1958–1960, 1972–1974–1976, 1992–1994–1996, 2000–2002–2004).

the same people for each group, they are true life-cycle effects—cohort effects have been controlled[9]—and the results suggest that life events have a significant impact on voting turnout.

We can summarize these results as follows. There is substantial persistence in all forms of political participation. At least in the case of voting, some of this persistence is due to habituation and some to life events. These factors may also matter for noncampaign activity, although the evidence is weaker. For all forms of political participation, fixed characteristics such as SES are the most important reason for persistence, but for some forms of participation, life events and habituation also play a role by creating life cycle effects.

9. But they cannot distinguish between life-cycle and period effects. In this case, the most likely period effect is that there is some consistent age effect as we go from midterm to presidential elections. Perhaps, for example, the mobilization of young people is always better in a presidential election period than in a mid-term election period. Unfortunately, we would have to have a longer panel to rule out this possibility.

APPENDIX C
THE INTERGENERATIONAL TRANSMISSION
OF POLITICAL PARTICIPATION

For our analysis, the data we really need are longitudinal, with the same respondents tracked from their early years until they are mature adults active or inactive in politics. Our data are from a single point in time. In one sense, they represent longitudinal data. We ask respondents to report about earlier times, and we relate that information to their report of contemporaneous activity. If memories were perfect, such data would be longitudinal, but of course memories may not be accurate. Comparing the major retrospective measures, it seems that memories of parents' education are fairly accurate. Memories of political stimulation, however, might be less precise and, most significantly, more easily colored by the respondent's current situation. Respondents who are currently politically involved might be inclined to remember more politics in the family than actually had been the case. One must, therefore, be cautious.

We have some evidence to suggest that memories of parental education or of political stimulation are relatively undistorted. Data in Tables C.1 and C.2 support our belief that there is little backward distortion of memory in the light of current circumstances. Table C.1 shows the respondents' reports of their own education and political activity within several categories. As one can see from Table C.1, there are variations among our respondents in their current education or current involvement in politics. The variations we show in respondents' education are by race or ethnicity and gender. The variations in political involvement are by respondents' race or ethnicity, education, and gender. As one can see, minorities, people with less education, and women are less active in politics. And minorities and women have somewhat less education.

Table C.2 shows respondent reports about parental education and home stimulation at the time they were adolescents. The remembered circumstances for the several race or ethnic groups and the several educational groups show lower levels of political stimulation for the less advantaged categories. And for

Table C.1   Respondent's Current Education and Political Involvement

Mean Educational Level[a] by Race or Ethnicity and Gender

By Race or Ethnicity		By Gender	
Whites	0.41	Men	0.42
Blacks	0.34	Women	0.38
Latinos	0.29		

Mean Political Activity[b] by Race or Ethnicity, Education, and Gender

By Race or Ethnicity		By Education		By Gender	
Whites	0.41	Some high school	0.13	Men	0.42
Blacks	0.34	High school graduate	0.25	Women	0.38
Latinos	0.29	Some college	0.34		
		College graduate	0.44		

Source: Citizen Participation Study(1990).

[a] Educational level is measured on a scale that ranges from 0.0 to 1.0.
[b] Political activity is measured on a scale that ranges from 0.0 to 1.0.

race or ethnicity, the reports of parental education show lower levels among the disadvantaged groups. This is consistent with a causal connection between earlier patterns and respondents' current situation (because minorities and less well educated respondents are likely to have been raised in families with lower levels of education and political involvement). It could also be consistent with memories distorted by current circumstances. For our purposes, the contrast with the gender data is crucial. The women in our sample are somewhat less educated than the men and somewhat less active, but they were born randomly into families of varying education and political involvement. If memories are accurate, they should report levels similar to those of men in terms of parental education or political stimulation. If memories are distorted by current circumstances, they should report lower levels of parental education and stimulation. As one can see from Table C.2, the former situation holds.

Table C.2   Reports of Parental Education[a] and Exposure to Politics at Home by Respondent's Race or Ethnicity, Education, and Gender

Mean Reported Education of Parents[a]

By Respondent's Race or Ethnicity		By Respondent's Education		By Gender	
Whites	0.24	Some high school	0.10	Men	0.23
Blacks	0.18	High school graduate	0.18	Women	0.22
Latinos	0.13	Some college	0.24		
		College graduate	0.34		

Mean Reported Exposure to Politics at Home

By Respondent's Race or Ethnicity		By Respondent's Education		By Gender	
Whites	0.25	Some high school	0.19	Men	0.24
Blacks	0.23	High school graduate	0.20	Women	0.24
Latinos	0.18	Some college	0.27		
		College graduate	0.30		

Source: Citizen Participation Study (1990).

[a] Age-adjusted measure of parents' education.

APPENDIX D
AGE, PERIOD, AND COHORT EFFECTS

It is well known that because the *period* in which a survey is conducted (the year in which it is done) minus a person's *age* equals the year of his or her birth *cohort*, it is impossible to use calendar dates to separate out the impacts of events in a given period (e.g., a period of mass political mobilization), life cycle effects (e.g., involvement with a community) due to age, and generational effects (e.g., common socializing experiences) due to cohort. Hence some "identifying" assumption must be made. We assume that period effects can be neglected partly because we do not believe that they are typically very big, partly because we believe that they will "average out" over a long time period like that considered here, and partly out of necessity.

It is still impossible to separate out life-cycle and cohort effects with a single cross-sectional study because a middle-aged person in a survey might be highly active in politics due to a life cycle effect or due to membership in a cohort that became highly involved in politics. If we assume that period effects are constant, we can separate out life cycle and cohort effects by using a series of cross-sections over a long time period. Then we can see if the members of particular cohorts are always highly active or if their participation waxes and wanes over time—presumably due to life cycle effects.

We obtained data over time by using the American National Election Studies data from all surveys during presidential elections from 1952 to 2008. We took these data and "stacked" them on top of one another so that rows were cases for various years and columns were common variables such as whether or not the person voted or his or her age. We then ran regressions that had dummy variables both for age groups and for cohorts—thus controlling for cohort effects.[1] The implicit assumption is that we can ignore period effects.

1. The cohorts were all years up to 1916, 1920–1928, 1932–1944, 1948–1956, 1960–1964, 1968–1976, 1980–1988, and 1992–2008. The age groups were 18–24, 25–30, 31–40, 41–50, 51–60, 61–70, 71–80, and 81 and up.

619

For Figure 8.7 we ran separate regressions for each political activity (voting, writing a letter to an official, giving money to a candidate or campaign, working for a candidate or campaign, and going to a campaign meeting) on these age-group and cohort-group dummy variables. For Figure 8.8 we created a five-act scale that includes four of these five activities (all but writing a letter) and adds one other (talking to people about why they should vote). We regressed this scale on, first, just the age groups, then the age and cohort groups, and finally the age groups, cohort groups, and a large number of control variables, including dummy variables for gender, race (black, white, or other), marital status (married, never married, separated or divorced, or widowed), employment status and occupation if employed (professional or managerial, clerical or sales, laborer, farmer, homemaker, student, or other), education (up to eighth grade, some high school, high school graduate, education beyond high school but no college, some college, college degree, or advanced degree), union status for the household, and income quintile in the year the person was surveyed. We also added other variables such as caring which party won the election, interest in the election, following campaign news, efficacy (feeling as if one has a say in politics or believing the government cares), party identification, and partisan strength.

APPENDIX E
THE WASHINGTON REPRESENTATIVES DATABASE

This appendix contains information about the construction of the Washington Representatives database, the detailed categories used to classify organizations, and instructions given to the coders. The *Washington Representatives* directory is the most nearly comprehensive listing of politically active organizations in Washington. The 1991 General Accounting Office (GAO) report that was used as justification for the 1995 Lobbying Disclosure Act made the point that, of the 13,500 people named as lobbyists in the *Washington Representatives* directory, fewer than 4,000 were registered with Congress.[1] That the GAO relied on the directory for its evidence about lobbyists suggests its significance as a source of information.

According to an interview on November 10, 2003, with Valerie Sheridan, the editor of the *Washington Representatives* directory at Columbia Books, the directory includes all organizations that are active in Washington politics by virtue of either having an office in the D.C. area or hiring D.C.-area consultants or counsel to represent them. The out-of-town organization—a corporation in Dayton, union local in Seattle, or hospital in Tallahassee—that sends a vice president on a day trip to Washington to testify before a Senate committee is not listed.

To assemble its listings, Columbia Books sends a form annually to each currently listed organization in the book giving the current information and asking for an update. If the form is not returned, Columbia follows up with additional inquiries. Sheridan relies on congressional lobby registrations as the first source in listing organizations. She also reads several journals: *Congressional Quar-*

---

1. Jonathan D. Salant, "Senate Passes Tighter Rules on Registration, Disclosure," *Congressional Quarterly Weekly Report*, July 29, 1995, p. 2239.

terly, National Journal, Influence (which has an online newsletter, influenceonline
.com), *Legal Times,* and *Association Trends.* She uses her editorial judgment in
including organizations that are not registered with the House or Senate. Political action committees (PACs) are included if the organization (or its PAC) has
an office in the Washington area; PACs that are run out of the home office elsewhere are not included. The directory also lists registered foreign agents but
not organizations that file amicus briefs with the Supreme Court. Sheridan
used to contact several major executive branch agencies (e.g., the Federal Trade
Commission and Federal Maritime Commission and check their dockets. She
no longer does so because the effort did not yield enough additional listings.
Sheridan believes that organizations generally want to be listed in the directory
and often get in touch with Columbia Books to let them know about changes
in information.

It has been suggested that we should have used the *Encyclopedia of Associations* rather than the *Washington Representatives* directory. The *Encyclopedia* is an invaluable resource for those interested in voluntary associations. We
used it and its Web-based counterpart, Associations Unlimited, extensively in
assembling background information about the associations in the directories.
Nevertheless, it has two disadvantages for our purposes. First, a majority of
the organizations in the *Washington Representatives* directories are not associations at all, whether composed of institutional or individual members, but are
instead institutions of some kind. These institutions—corporations, universities, hospitals, and the like—are not listed in the *Encyclopedia of Associations.*
Furthermore, except when an organization category—for example, environmental organizations—is inherently political, it is impossible to discern whether an
organization is politically active. Because, as we shall see, many organizations
move in and out of politics, the failure to designate organizations as politically
active is a serious shortcoming for our purposes.

An important task was to place these political organizations—and the organizations not listed in the directories but active in politics—into categories. In
contrast to most studies of organized interests that rely on highly aggregated
categories, we deliberately proliferated the number of categories in order to
capture fine distinctions. Thus the interests of business are represented by several categories of organizations: corporations, both domestic and foreign; trade
and other business associations, again both domestic and foreign, which have
corporations as members; occupational associations of business executives and
professionals, such as human resources specialists, employed in corporate settings; and business-related research organizations.

In spite of the large number of categories, there were inevitably organizations that seemed to fit comfortably into more than one category. To accommodate such cases—for example, those of the National Medical Association
(NMA), Mothers against Drunk Driving, or the American Indian Higher Education Consortium—we permitted an organization to be coded into as many

as three categories. Thus the NMA, a membership group of African American physicians, was coded as both a professional association and an African American organization.

The categories in this classification scheme accommodate many distinctions. However, as might be expected, the boundaries between categories are sometimes imprecise. For example, it is not always possible to differentiate two kinds of business-related membership associations: trade associations, which bring together companies in the same industry on an ongoing basis to cooperate on multiple issues that confront the industry, and other business associations, a category that includes peak business associations like the National Association of Manufacturers as well as ad hoc coalitions and single-issue groups joining together firms from several industries.

To resolve ambiguities, we often dug deeply—considering mission statements, FAQs, organizational histories, and the composition of the board or the staff. As a result, we were able to find information about all but 164, or 1.4 percent, of the nearly 12,000 organizations in the 2001 directory. Still, the construction of this database required many judgment calls. Moreover, in spite of repeated efforts to clean the data base, the volume of the data coded implies that, inevitably, mistakes were made.

In large part the categorization of the organizations was the basis for ascertaining the membership status of organizations—that is, whether an organization was an association of individuals, an association of institutions, or something else. Categories containing the vast majority of organizations—for example, unions, professional associations, corporations, or trade associations—are defined by the character of their membership, if any. For categories—for example, "public interest"—that mixed membership associations, institutions, and associations of institutions, we coded the individual organizations one by one.

Before we replicated all the data analysis to make our archive file, we checked the entire database one final time and eliminated some duplications. The result of this process is that the total number of organizations in Chapters 11–14 may be slightly different from the figures contained in preliminary publications based on the Washington Representatives Study. While the total number of organizations decreased slightly, any changes in the distributions were minuscule, no more than one-tenth of a percent.

Categories for the Coding of Organizations Active in Washington

A. Don't know
B. Business organization
   1. Corporation
   2. U.S. subsidiary of a foreign corporation

    3. Cooperative

    4. Trade association

    5. Business coalition, consortium, or other business association

    6. Firm of professionals

C. Occupational association

    1. Association of business professionals, managers, executives, and administrators

    2. Association of public employees

    3. Professional association

    4. Other occupational association

    5. Association of administrators and managers of nonprofits

    6. Association of public employees—military

D. Union

    1. Blue-collar union—public employees

    2. White-collar union—public employees

    3. Blue-collar union—private sector

    4. White-collar union—private sector

    5. Public-sector union—mixed blue- and white-collar

    6. Private-sector union—mixed blue- and white-collar

    7. Peak union, union consortium, association of union executives, or other labor union

E. Farm

    1. Farm—commodity-specific

    2. Other farm

F. Education

    1. Students

    2. Educational institution—public

    3. Educational institution—private

    4. Educational institution—for-profit

    5. Educational institution—DK (don't know whether public or private)

    6. Other educational

G. Health

    1. Health institution

    2. Other health

H. U.S. government

    1. State government

    2. Local or county government (including departments and authorities)

    3. Government corporation or public–private partnership

    4. Consortium of governments

    5. Airport

    6. Other government

J. Foreign
  1. Foreign government (including embassies, ministries, and agencies)
  2. Foreign corporation
  3. Foreign business association or consortium
  4. Transnational public–private partnership
  5. Other foreign
  6. International organization
K. Public interest
  1. Consumer
  2. Environmental
  3. Wildlife and animals
  4. Single-issue (domestic) public interest group—liberal
  5. Single-issue (domestic) public interest group—conservative
  6. Single-issue (domestic) public interest group—other
  7. Multi-issue—liberal
  8. Multi-issue—conservative
  9. Civil liberties
  10. Citizenship empowerment (including voter education)
  11. Government reform
  12. International issues—liberal
  13. International issues—conservative
  14. International issues—other
  15. School choice
L. Electoral and partisan
  1. PAC or candidate organization
  2. Party or partisan organization
M. Veterans
  1. Veterans' association
  2. Members of the reserves
N. Civil rights, racial, religious, and nationality groups
  1. "Minorities"
  2. African Americans
  3. Latinos
  4. Asians
  5. Native Americans
  6. European ethnic groups
  7. Jewish
  8. Islamic or Arab nationality groups
  9. Other nationality groups
  10. "Christian"
  11. Protestant—mainline
  12. Protestant—evangelical

      13. Protestant—other or don't know what kind
      14. Catholic
      15. Other Christian
      16. Other religion
      17. Interfaith
      18. Islamic groups
O. Age
      1. Children or youth
      2. Elderly
P. Gender-specific
      1. Men
      2. Women
Q. Sexual orientation—lesbian, gay, bisexual, or transgender
R. Disabled and health advocacy
      1. Disabled
      2. Advocacy and research for a particular illness or disability
S. Group for social welfare or the poor
      1. Social welfare or poor
      2. Recipients of benefits (welfare, food stamps, unemployment benefits, housing)
      3. Providers of services (including disaster relief)
T. Recreational
U. Arts or cultural
V. Charity/philanthropy
W. Think tanks and other nonprofit policy research
      1. Think tank—liberal
      2. Think tank—conservative
      3. Business-affiliated research
      4. Other nonprofit research
X. Other

Codes for Categorizing Organized Interests

A. Don't know   101
B. Business organization
      1. Corporation   201

This category includes for-profit corporations including radio and television stations. Insurance companies in the health field present some ambiguities. If the company (for example, Aetna Inc.) is simply a processor of paper—collecting premiums, rationing health care, and paying benefits—it should be placed in this category. In contrast, if it actually delivers health care services, it is categorized as "other health organization." For-profit health care management systems that contract with hospitals, health maintenance organizations (HMOs), and physicians and manage the health care of large numbers of subscribers are classified as both "health institutions" and "corporations."

> Examples: Tyson Foods Inc.
> Microsoft Corp.

2. U.S. subsidiary of a foreign corporation   202

It will not always be possible to determine without further research whether a corporation is an American corporation, the American subsidiary of a foreign corporation, or a foreign corporation. If the corporation does not have its own office in Washington but only hires Washington-based counsel, the directory will list the location of the corporate headquarters. Use this to determine whether it is domestic or foreign. If this does not help, use what you know or any clues to help determine the category into which it falls. Sometimes there is actually prose. Corporations with "N.A." (North America) or "U.S.A." attached to their names are generally subsidiaries of foreign corporations. If you suspect that a corporation is an American subsidiary of a foreign corporation, place it in this category and mark it as "uncertain." We shall check later.

> Examples: Toyota Motor North America, U.S.A., Inc.
> BB Daimler-Benz Transportation, N.A.

3. Cooperative   203

> Examples: Basin Electric Power Cooperative
> Ocean Spray Cranberries

4. Trade association   204

The boundary between trade associations and other business associations is quite permeable. Both are membership associations whose constituent members are *firms*. In general, trade associations bring together companies in the same industry on an ongoing basis to cooperate on multiple issues that confront the industry. The "other business" category includes peak business associations like the National Association of Manufacturers as well as ad hoc coalitions and single-issue groups that may join together firms from several industries.

> Examples: National Frozen Pizza Institute
> The Fertilizer Institute

5. Business coalition, consortium, or other business association   205

> Examples: National Foreign Trade Council
> TVA Watch
> United States Council for International Business

6. Firm of professionals   206

This is another category with boundaries that are indistinct. There are a variety of firms that sell the services and expertise of partners or employees.

At one end of a continuum are the organizations in this category, which includes firms of various kinds of professionals—lawyers, engineers, architects, certified public accountants, and the like. At the other are firms—a real estate agency, a catering company, a stock brokerage firm, or a collection agency—whose employees (while they may, like barbers and realtors, be licensed) are not members of a profession requiring a recognized educational course and credentialing process. Several kinds of firms that sell expertise—in particular, firms of investment counselors and managers, advertising and public relations agencies, and computer and Web site experts—are on the border; we have determined, perhaps arbitrarily, that they should be coded as corporations. When in doubt, consult the listing from the *Statistical Abstract.* Consulting firms that do research for clients (including governments) belong here. Nonprofit think tanks that do not have clients are coded below.

> Examples: Skadden, Arps, Slate, Meagher, and Flom LLP
> Stone and Webster Engineering Corporation

C. Occupational association

The various categories of occupational associations in this section are all composed of individuals who share a common way of making a living. The overall rule is that if it is the *individual* who joins, it is coded here. If the employer (a firm, a government agency, etc.) is the member, it is coded elsewhere.

The boundaries among occupational categories are quite permeable. When an occupation is at the boundary between two categories, the classification in the *Statistical Abstract* is the authority—even when its categorizations might be open to question.

Occupational associations that bring together people who work in education, health, or agriculture (for example, the American Academy of Nurse Practitioners) will be coded in the single category of occupational association and not in "other education," "other health," or "other farm."

1. Association of business professionals, managers, executives,
   and administrators   301

This category brings together a variety of professionals, managers, executives, and administrators who work in the for-profit sector. Among them are managers and executives in a particular industry. This category also includes business professionals who work for someone else in the for-profit sector. If the occupation is one in which people set up shop for themselves or work in firms of similarly trained professionals, it is usually coded as a professional association or an "other occupational association."

Managers and administrators in the not-for-profit sector—for example, employees of museums or universities—are categorized elsewhere. While universities are very unlikely to be for-profit, the sector that specializes in the delivery of human services (hospitals, nursing homes, and day care centers) mixes for-profit and nonprofit institutions. Because we cannot discern whether we are dealing with for-profit or not-for-profit institutions, we shall code administrators and managers in this sector as working in nonprofits.

It may not be clear from the name of the organization whether it has individuals or firms as members, and thus whether it is an occupational association or a professional association. The organization's Web site might (or might not) help.

> Examples: American Society of Pension Actuaries
> Society of Consumer Affairs Professionals in Business
> Cable Television Administration and Marketing Society

2. Association of public employees   302

Associations of nonunion civilian government employees are coded here. Public employee unions and associations of members of the military are coded below.

> Examples: National Federation of Federal Employees
> National Association of Medicaid Directors

3. Professional association   303

It is not always easy to discriminate between professional associations and other occupational associations. In general, in order to be a professional association, the occupation in question must be one in which training requires a recognized educational course and at least a B.A. Nutritionists, social workers, and pharmacists are professionals. Nurses' aides are not. When in doubt, consult the listing from the *Statistical Abstract,* which, for example, lists athletes as professionals.

Unless they are unions, associations of health and educational professionals are coded here, not under "other health" or "other educational."

> Examples: American Society of Civil Engineers
> American Speech, Language, and Hearing Association
> American Academy of Family Physicians
> National Association of Biology Teachers

4. Other occupational association   304

> Examples: National Association of Executive Secretaries and
> Administrative Assistants
> National Association of Realtors
> National Association of Health Underwriters

5. Association of administrators and managers of nonprofits   305

> Examples: Association of Physical Plant Administrators of
> Universities and Colleges
> National Association of College and University
> Business Officers

Foundation of the American College of Nursing
Home Administrators

6. Association of public employees—military   306

Associations of members of the armed services and the national guard—even those like physicians and lawyers in the military—are coded here. Veterans' organizations and associations of reservists are coded elsewhere.

Examples: National Military Intelligence Association
Non-Commissioned Officers Association of the U.S.A.
Pennsylvania National Guard Association
Association of Military Surgeons of the U.S.

D. Union

Certain unions bring together members of occupations that would be considered professions (e.g., teaching), as defined above, or that are quite well paid (e.g., the Air Line Pilots Association). For our purposes, what distinguishes a union is that it *bargains collectively* with employers on behalf of its members.

In a manner analogous to occupational associations, unions that bring together people who work in education or health (for example, the National Education Association) will be considered under the single category "union" and not under "other education" or "other health."

1. Blue-collar union—public employees   401

Examples: National Association of Letter Carriers of the U.S.A.
International Association of Fire Fighters

2. White-collar union—public employees   402

Examples: American Federation of Teachers
National Air Traffic Controllers Association

3. Blue-collar union—private-sector employees   403

Examples: Int'l Brotherhood of Electrical Workers
United Mine Workers

4. White-collar union—private-sector employees   404

Examples: Association of Flight Attendants
Retail, Wholesale, and Department Store Workers Union

5. Public-sector union—mixed blue- and white-collar   405

Examples: American Federation of Government Employees
American Postal Workers Union

6. Private-sector union—mixed blue- and white-collar   406

Example: United Electrical, Radio, and Machine Workers

7. Peak union, union consortium, association of union executives, or other labor union   407

    Examples: AFL-CIO Maritime Trades Department
                 National Federation of Independent Unions

E. Farm
  1. Farm—commodity-specific   501

Agricultural organizations that are commodity specific often include interested parties (for example, processors or farm equipment manufacturers) in addition to producers. Even so, consider them commodity-specific farm organizations. Agricultural cooperatives are coded as cooperatives (203). Other industries that involve the harvesting of living things (e.g., fishing or lumbering) are also coded here.

    Examples: National Pork Producers Association
                 National Potato Council

  2. Other farm   502

    Examples: American Farm Bureau Federation
                 Agribusiness Council

F. Education
  1. Students   601

    Example: United States Students Association

  2. Educational institution—public   602

Local school districts and their boards of education are not categorized here. They are considered local governments (802).

    Examples: University of California at Riverside
                 Alabama A&M University

  3. Educational institution—private   603

Religiously affiliated or single-sex institutions are coded here as educational institutions and are not given a second categorization that would specify their identity group affiliation.

    Examples: University of Notre Dame
                 Boston College

  4. Educational institution—for-profit   604

    Example: DeVry Inc.

  5. Educational institution—DK (don't know whether public or private)   605

Examples: Philadelphia University
New Jersey Institute of Technology

6. Other educational   606

Examples: National Foundation for the Improvement
of Education
National Association of Independent Colleges
and Universities

G. Health
1. Health institution   701

This category includes a variety of health care delivery institutions, including not only hospitals but also nursing homes and rehabilitation centers. Medical schools should be classified as both educational and health institutions.
For-profit health care management systems that contract with hospitals, HMOs,
and physicians and manage the health care of large numbers of subscribers are
classified as both health institutions and corporations.

Examples: Partners Healthcare System Inc.
Joslin Diabetes Center
St. Mary's Hospital
Blood Center of Southeastern Wisconsin

2. Other health   702

Examples: National Association of Public Hospitals and
Health Systems
Academic Health Center Coalition

H. U.S. government
1. State government (including departments and authorities)   801

Examples: Washington Office of the State of Florida
Association of California Water Agencies

2. Local or county government (including departments
and authorities)   802

Examples: St. Louis / Lake Counties Regional Rail Authority
City of Denton, Texas
Riverside Unified School District

3. Government corporation or public–private partnership   803

This category includes a variety of kinds of government corporations and
public–private partnerships. There are a number of councils and alliances that
bring together representatives of government, industry, universities, and so on
to discuss, conduct research, and advocate with respect to particular public pol-

icy problems. Among the common topics are regional economic development, transportation, and environmental preservation. When the subject is education, this kind of council is coded as Other Educational (606). When the subject is health, this kind of council is coded as "other health" (702). Community development corporations are also coded here.

> Examples: Minnesota Transportation Alliance
> Corporation for Public Broadcasting

4. Consortium of governments   804

> Examples: National Association of Flood and Stormwater
> Management Agencies
> National League of Cities

5. Airport   805

> Examples: Akron–Canton Airport
> Denver Airport

6. Other government   806

J. Foreign organization
1. Foreign government (including embassies, ministries, and agencies)   1001

> Examples: Embassy of the Republic of Azerbaijan
> Gibraltar Information Bureau

2. Foreign corporation   1002

> Examples: AeroRepublica, S.A.
> Ajinomoto Company Inc.

3. Foreign business association or consortium   1003

This category also includes federations of agricultural exporters and federations of industries in more than one country.

> Examples: Association of Foreign Investors in U.S. Real Estate
> Association of Chocolate, Biscuit, and Confectionery
> Industries of the European Union

4. Transnational public–private partnership   1004

> Example: INTELSAT

5. Other foreign   1005

This catch-all category includes, among other things, foreign nongovernmental organizations (NGOs) and political parties in other countries. International NGOs that engage in relief efforts abroad or provide development assistance abroad are also coded here. (To determine whether such an organization is American or international, check where its offices are located and who is on its board.)

Examples: Lao Progressive Institute
            Luso American Foundation

6. International organization   1006

This category includes international organizations and alliances (and their agencies) in which national governments are members.

Examples: Group of 20
            World Health Organization

K. Public interest

These are advocacy organizations that seek public goods. Whether a policy objective is a public good is a complicated business and usually depends on the nature of the membership. In the first example below, an organization that seeks better rail transportation is a public interest organization if its members are rail passengers but not if its members are engineers or railroad executives. If the members or supporters of an organization are in a position to benefit selectively from the realization of its policy goals, it is *not* a public interest organization.

1. Consumer   1101

Examples: National Association of Rail Passengers
            American Consumers for Affordable Homes

2. Environmental   1102

Whether they are polluters seeking relief from federal regulation or manufacturers of environmentally friendly home cleaning products, corporations often seek to wrap themselves in the mantle of environmentalism. However, they are not public interest groups. This category contains public interest organizations only. Thus organizations listed here must be composed of members with no selective interest in environmental policy.

Examples: Friends of the Earth
            Natural Resources Defense Council

3. Wildlife and animals   1103

This category includes several kinds of organizations that are concerned about the well-being of animals—not only wildlife but also laboratory animals, pets, and farm animals.

Examples: Ducks Unlimited
            International Fund for Animal Welfare

4. Single-issue (domestic) public interest group—liberal   1104

    Examples: National Prison Project
                  National Abortion and Reproductive Rights
                      Action League

5. Single-issue (domestic) public interest group—conservative   1105

    Examples: Accuracy in Academia
                  National Right to Work Committee

6. Single-issue (domestic) public interest group—other   1106

If it is not clear where the position espoused by a single-issue public interest organization falls on a left–right continuum, list it here and we can check again later.

    Examples: National Whistleblower Center
                  National Fire Protection Association

7. Multi-issue—liberal   1108

    Example: Americans for Democratic Action

8. Multi-issue—conservative   1109

    Examples: American Conservative Union
                  Landmark Legal Foundation for Civil Rights

9. Civil liberties   1110

    Examples: American Civil Liberties Union
                  Free Speech Coalition

10. Citizenship empowerment (including voter education)   1111

Organizations that focus on classroom teaching about government for the young are categorized as "other educational" (606). Organizations that focus on the textbook civic education of adults or hands-on political learning for either adults or the young are coded here.

    Examples: Close Up Foundation
                  Committee for Citizen Awareness

11. Government reform   1112

Organizations concerned about governmental reform (for example, campaign finance reform, term limits, and elimination of government waste and corruption) are coded here. Organizations concerned about reform of policy (for example, trade, tax, or environmental policy) are coded elsewhere.

    Examples: OMB Watch
                  Common Cause

12. International issues—liberal   1113

There are three categories of U.S. organizations that focus on country-specific issues or on international relations more generally. When the emphasis is on peace and disarmament or on human rights, they are coded here.

> Examples: Human Rights Watch
> Fund for Peace

13. International issues—conservative   1114

Organizations are coded here when the emphasis, in contrast, is on national security and defensive strength.

> Examples: American Security Council
> Free the Eagle

14. International issues—other   1115

Most organizations that focus on international matters do not have an obvious liberal or conservative tilt. American organizations that engage in relief efforts abroad or provide development assistance abroad are coded here, as are most organizations that focus on political conflicts in a particular locale abroad. Some of the latter organize a diaspora group concerned about the homeland—in which case they are also coded as an ethnic or nationality group.

15. School choice   1116

Whether subsidized by parent members, outside benefactors, or conservative foundations, organizations that promote school choice—including vouchers and charter schools—are coded here. Such organizations may also give scholarships to help needy children attend schools other than their local public schools.

L. Electoral and partisan
1. PAC or candidate organization   1201

The PACs listed here are essentially electoral organizations, which, while they may be ideological or affiliated with a particular politician, are not simply the political giving arm of an organization that could be classified elsewhere. PACs should ordinarily be classified in the same category as the organization or institution with which they are affiliated.

> Examples: Straight Talk America
> National Committee for an Effective Congress

2. Party or partisan organization   1202

> Examples: National Republican Senatorial Committee
> Democratic Governors Association

M. Veterans
    1. Veterans' association   1301

        Examples: American Legion
                     Vietnam Veterans of America

    2. Members of the reserves   1302

        Examples: Senior Army Reserve Commanders Association
                     Marine Corps Reserve Officers Association

N. Civil rights, racial, religious, or nationality group
    1. "Minorities"   1401

Organizations (for example, the Minority Business Enterprise Legal Defense and Education Fund) that refer to "minorities" rather than to members of a particular racial or ethnic group are coded here. Many of these organizations fit into more than one category.

    2. African Americans   1402

        Examples: National Association for the Advancement
                       of Colored People
                     National Urban League

    3. Latinos   1403

Included in this category are organizations that bring together various Hispanic or Latino groups as well as those that are specific to one nationality group (for example, Mexican Americans, Puerto Ricans, or Cubans).

        Examples: National Puerto Rican Coalition
                     Mexican-American Legal Defense and Educational Fund
                     National Alliance for Hispanic Health

    4. Asians   1404

        Examples: Japanese American Citizens League
                     Organization of Chinese Americans

    5. Native Americans   1405

        Examples: Tunica Biloxi Indians of Louisiana
                     Blackfeet Tribe of Montana

    6. European ethnic groups   1406

        Examples: National Federation of Croatian Americans
                     United Hellenic American Congress

    7. Jewish   1407

        Examples: American Jewish Committee
                     B'nai B'rith International

8. Islamic or Arab groups   1408

    Examples: American–Arab Anti-Discrimination Committee
                 Arab American Institute

9. Other nationality groups   1409

10. "Christian"   1410

    Examples: Traditional Values Coalition
                 Christian Coalition

11. Protestant—mainline   1411

There is dispute as to exactly how to differentiate mainline from evangelical Protestants. Our rule of thumb is to consider as mainline all Protestant denominations in the National Council of Churches. By this definition, all Methodist, Lutheran (including Missouri Synod), Presbyterian, Episcopalian, Congregationalist (United Church of Christ), and Quaker organizations are categorized as mainline Protestant, as are the American Baptist Association, the American Baptist Church, the National Baptist Convention of America, and the National Baptist Convention, U.S.A. Other Baptists, including the nation's largest Protestant denomination, the Southern Baptist Convention, are considered to be evangelical Protestants, as are those who named a variety of evangelical and Pentecostal groups—for example, the Assemblies of God, Church of Christ, Church of the Nazarene, and the Pentecostal Church. If in doubt, place in one of the "don't know" or "other" categories.

    Examples: Progressive National Baptist Convention
                 United Church of Christ Justice and Witness Ministry

12. Protestant—evangelical   1412

The National Association of Evangelicals and its constituent denominations are coded here, as well as the Baptist, evangelical, and Pentecostal denominations discussed above.

13. Protestant—other or don't know what kind   1413

    Example: Church of the Brethren Washington Office

14. Catholic   1414

    Example: U.S. Catholic Conference

15. Other Christian   1415

    Example: Church of Jesus Christ of Latter-Day Saints

16. Other religion   1416

17. Interfaith   1417

    Example: National Conference of Christians and Jews

O. Age

    1. Children or youth   1501

This category includes not only advocates for children but youth organizations. Medical organizations focusing on pediatric issues or diseases specific to the young (for example, the Juvenile Diabetes Foundation or the Shriners Hospitals for Children) should be categorized as health organizations and should not be listed here.

    Examples: National 4-H Council
                     Children's Defense Fund

    2. Elderly   1502

    Examples: United Seniors Association
                     TREA Senior Citizens League

P. Gender-specific

This category brings into relief a difficulty that runs through many of the categories in this classificatory scheme: are we interested in the membership of an organization or in its goals? When it comes to gender classifications, we shall code here any organization that focuses on advocacy for men's or, more often, women's distinctive experiences, needs, and problems. Examples of men's organizations that do so are the Promise Keepers, which is not listed in the directory, and advocates for the rights of divorced fathers.

Many organizations (for example, the Disabled American Veterans or the American Dental Hygienists' Association) that do not focus on such gender-specific advocacy are essentially single sex in their membership. However, unless the organization self-consciously excludes members of one sex, it should not be coded here. (The Knights of Columbus, which is not in the directory, excludes women; Hadassah, which is, excludes men. The Lutheran Brotherhood, the Sons of Italy, and B'nai B'rith may once have excluded women but do not now.)

    1. Men   1601
    2. Women   1602

    Examples: National Women's Political Caucus
                     Feminist Majority

Q. Sexual orientation group—lesbian, gay, bisexual, or transgender
   (LGBT)   1701

LGBT organizations and other organizations concerned with sexual orientation or freedom are coded here.

    Examples: National Gay and Lesbian Task Force
                     Human Rights Campaign Fund

R. Disabled and health advocacy

   1. Disabled   1801

      Examples: National Rehabilitation Information Center
                      Christopher Reeve Paralysis Foundation

   2. Advocacy and research for a particular illness or disability   1802

      Examples: National Psoriasis Foundation
                      Parkinson's Disease Foundation
                      National Association for the Deaf
                      National Federation for the Blind

S. Social welfare/poor

   1. Social welfare or poor   1901

These organizations advocate on behalf of the poor in the United States or in favor of more comprehensive guarantees with respect to basic human needs in American politics. They may also attempt to organize the poor. Many organizations not only engage in advocacy but also provide direct services. In placing an organization into one of the two categories (1901 or 1903), consider the overall balance in organizational activities.

      Examples: National Alliance to End Homelessness
                      Food Research and Action Center
                      ACORN

   2. Recipients of benefits (welfare, food stamps, unemployment, housing)   1902

Included in this category are any organizations, if there are any, that bring together recipients of social welfare benefits (jobless workers, public housing residents, and the like) advocating *on their own behalf.* The now defunct National Welfare Rights Organization would have fallen into this category.

   3. Providers of services (including disaster relief)   1903

These organizations provide direct services to those in need in the United States. Included here as well are organizations that bring together such agencies (in essence, trade associations of nonprofits that deliver direct services to the economically needy) and provide technical assistance, organizational support, or opportunities for mutual consultation.

      Examples: Indianapolis Neighborhood Housing Partnership
                      Goodwill Industries
                      Metropolitan Family Services

T. Recreational   2001

Organizations that bring together people who enjoy a particular activity or form of recreation belong here. However, if all or most the members make a living by providing opportunities to enjoy the activity or by teaching the activity, the organization should be coded elsewhere.

Examples: American Kennel Club
International Traditional Karate Federation

U. Arts/cultural   2101

This category includes not-for-profit zoos, museums of all kinds, and public radio and television stations, as well as arts and cultural institutions and associations.

Examples: New England Aquarium
American Association of Museums
American Arts Alliance

V. Charity/philanthropy   2201

This category brings together several kinds of organizations. Among them are foundations and other charitable consortia (for example, the United Jewish Communities, which is the successor to the Combined Jewish Appeal) that make grants or contributions to direct-service providers. In addition, organizations that seek to encourage volunteering or philanthropy, that study philanthropy, or that advocate on behalf of philanthropy before the government are coded here. Service providers are coded elsewhere (1903). By the way, although it would seem to be the Catholic analogue of the United Jewish Communities, Catholic Charities is coded as a 1903 (as well, of course, as a 1414) because it is a provider of direct services.

Examples: Points of Light Foundation
Ford Foundation
Philanthropy Roundtable
Council on Foundations

W. Think tanks and other nonprofit policy research
1. Think tank—liberal   2301

Examples: Progressive Policy Institute
Urban Institute

2. Think tank—conservative   2302

Examples: Cato Institute
National Center for Public Policy Research

3. Business-affiliated research   2303

Companies and trade and other business associations frequently set up nonprofit research entities. Business-sponsored nonprofit research enterprises and think tanks belong in this category.

Examples: American Cocoa Research Institute
            Insurance Information Institute

4. Other nonprofit research   2304

Examples: Institute for Alternative Futures
            Urban Land Institute

X. Other   2401

Sometimes it is clear what an organization is, but the available categories do not accommodate it easily. Organizations with hybrid clienteles or goals are especially likely to be difficult to categorize. Organizations that just do not fit anywhere belong in this category. In coding PACs, third parties (the Green Party, Reform Party, and Libertarian Party) are categorized here.

Examples: National Geographic Society
            Aircraft Owners and Pilots Association

Instructions for Coding Organizations

Coding the organizations that are active in Washington politics poses several difficulties. These guidelines are designed to help with the thousands of discretionary decisions that have to be made.

Code each organization with a three- or four-digit code.

If neither the name of the organization nor any attached information makes clear what it is, you can usually find out enough to make a reasonable categorization by looking on the Web. (Use Google—entering the organization name in quotation marks—to find the Web site. The necessary information can usually be located on the home page or under "About Us" or "FAQs.") If you cannot find any information on the Web (or if it is not clear which of many organizations with the same name—for example, the "Clean Water Coalition"—is being referenced), place it in the "don't know" category for further research. After you have finished coding all the organizations in your batch, you can return to these organizations and use print sources to research them. If necessary, we can phone them.

If you think you have the right category (or categories) for an organization but are not really sure, place a "U" in the "Uncertainty" column and we can discuss it or do more research later.

The boundaries between the various categories are sometimes indistinct. Suggestions follow about how to distinguish between particular sets of categories. Sometimes you will need additional information (for example, whether the organization is composed of individual employees or firms) in order to choose between adjacent categories. You can usually find the relevant information on the organization's Web site.

This scheme permits the coding of organizations into as many as three categories. It is not always clear whether an organization belongs in a single category or more than one. You may be required to make a subjective judgment as to whether one aspect of an organization clearly outweighs the others or whether they are more or less equal. For example, professional associations like the American Political Science Association (APSA), the learned society for political scientists, often make provision for institutional memberships. Both the Harvard Government Department and the Boston College Department of Political Science are institutional members of the APSA. Nonetheless, the APSA's membership and activities are clearly weighted in the direction of individual political scientists, and providing assistance to institutional members is a very secondary part of what the APSA does. Hence, the APSA would be placed in the single category of professional association (303). Perhaps the kind of organization that most frequently requires placement in more than one category is an organization that joins a common occupation or policy goal with some kind of shared identity (race, religion, gender, etc.). Examples include the National Medical Association (African American physicians), Mothers against Drunk Driving, or the American Indian Higher Education Consortium.

Additional Suggestions for Coding Organizations

1. Check the entry in the *Washington Representatives* directory, which may give the information needed to code the organization. If not, it may indicate a Web site or, for later use, a phone number.

2. Using a search engine like Google, find any information about the organization on the Web. If the organization has a Web site, the necessary information can usually be located on the home page or under "About Us" or "FAQs." If there are ambiguities, see what can be learned from the information about membership categories, lists of members, or the names and institutional affiliations of board or staff members. If there is no Web site, you may be able to learn about the organization from other materials on the Web.

3. Consult Associations Unlimited online or the *Encyclopedia of Associations* in hard copy.

4. Check the electronic archives (for appropriate dates) of publications like *Congressional Quarterly,* the *National Journal,* the *New York Times,* the *Washington Post,* and the *Wall Street Journal.* Do a search on Lexis-Nexis. Check the Supreme Court briefs on Lexis-Nexis.

5. Check any other relevant Web sites—for example, the FEC PACronyms file; guidestar.org, which lists nonprofits; or influence.biz.

6. If the directory lists a location, use infousa.com to search for the organization.

7. Check the hard copies of the various editions of the *Almanac of Federal PACs,* which can be found at the Kennedy School.

8. If there is a phone number, use a search engine to search on the phone number. Use infousa.com to do a backward lookup to see whether the organization can be located. Call the organization.

9. For organizations in the 1981 or 1991 directory, consult bound copies of the *Encyclopedia of Associations* for 1980–1982 or 1990–1992.

10. Make a list of the cases in which there are two or three entities with the same name. We can call Valerie Sheridan at Columbia Books and ask her which one was referenced in the listing.

11. If no other information is available and the organization is listed in the 1981 directory, use the 1981 code from the archives of the Organized Interests project. If no categorization was made then (DK), classify the organization as 101 (don't know) and give up.

12. If no information is available and the organization is not listed in the 1981 directory, classify it as 101 (don't know) and give up.

APPENDIX F
ADDITIONAL TABLES

Table F.1 Organizations Representing State and Local Governments[a]

State	Distribution of Organizations[b] (Percent)	Distribution of Population (Percent)	Representation Ratio[c]
Alabama	1.4%	1.6%	0.9
Alaska	2.8	0.2	12.7
Arizona	2.3	1.9	1.2
Arkansas	0.1	0.9	0.1
California	26.8	12.1	2.2
Colorado	2.0	1.6	1.3
Connecticut	1.0	1.2	0.9
Delaware	0.2	0.3	0.8
Florida	6.3	5.7	1.1
Georgia	1.0	3.0	0.4
Hawaii	0.3	0.4	0.8
Idaho	0.2	0.5	0.5
Illinois	3.0	4.4	0.7
Indiana	2.2	2.2	1.0
Iowa	1.3	1.0	1.2
Kansas	0.2	0.9	0.2
Kentucky	0.0	1.4	0.0
Louisiana	3.2	1.6	2.1
Maine	0.0	0.5	0.0
Maryland	1.4	1.9	0.7

continued

Table F.1   Continued

State	Distribution of Organizations[b] (Percent)	Distribution of Population (Percent)	Representation Ratio[c]
Massachusetts	1.7%	2.2%	0.7
Michigan	2.2	3.5	0.6
Minnesota	2.0	1.8	1.1
Mississippi	1.4	2.0	0.7
Missouri	0.6	1.0	0.6
Montana	0.5	0.3	1.4
Nebraska	0.5	0.6	0.8
Nevada	2.3	0.7	3.1
New Hampshire	0.0	0.4	0.0
New Jersey	1.7	3.0	0.6
New Mexico	1.1	0.6	1.7
New York	5.0	6.7	0.7
North Carolina	1.3	2.9	0.4
North Dakota	0.5	0.2	2.1
Ohio	1.7	4.0	0.4
Oklahoma	1.0	1.2	0.8
Oregon	2.9	1.2	2.4
Pennsylvania	1.6	4.3	0.4
Rhode Island	0.3	0.4	0.9
South Carolina	0.9	1.4	0.6
South Dakota	0.3	0.3	1.3
Tennessee	0.9	2.0	0.5
Texas	5.0	7.5	0.7
Utah	1.5	0.8	1.9
Vermont	0.0	0.2	0.0
Virginia	2.2	2.5	0.9
Washington	3.8	2.1	1.8
West Virginia	0.5	0.6	0.7
Wisconsin	0.7	1.9	0.4
Wyoming	0.2	0.2	1.3
	100.0%	100.0%	

Source: *Washington Representatives* directory (2001).

[a] The table includes organizations listed in the 2001 *Washington Representatives* directory.
[b] Distribution of organizations representing state and local governments.
[c] Ratio of the share of organizations to the share of the population.

Table F.2   Do Mixed-Category Organizations Change the
Distribution of Organizations in Washington Politics?[a]

Categories of Organized Interests	Percentage of All Organizations	Percentage of Organizations in a Single Category
Corporations[b]	34.9%	36.4%
Trade and Other Business Associations	13.2	13.7
Occupational Associations	6.8	6.8
Unions	1.0	0.9
Education	4.2	4.0
Health	3.5	3.2
Social Welfare or Poor	0.8	0.6
Public Interest	4.6	4.3
Identity Groups[c]	3.8	2.5
State and Local Governments	10.4	10.9
Foreign	7.8	8.1
Other	7.7	7.2
Unknown	1.4	1.5
Total	100.1%	100.0%
N	11,651	11,096

Source: Washington Representatives Study (2001).

[a] Distribution of organizations listed in the 2001 *Washington Representatives* directory.
[b] Includes U.S. corporations, U.S. subsidiaries of foreign corporations, and for-profit firms of professionals such as law and consulting firms.
[c] Includes organizations representing racial, ethnic, or religious groups; the elderly; women; or lesbian, gay, bisexual, or transgender sexual orientation.

Table F.3   Mobilization into the Pressure System:
1981 Status of Organizations Listed in the 2006
Washington Representatives Directory but Not in 1981

Categories of Organized Interests	Not Yet Founded	In Existence but Not in Politics		
Trade and Other Business Associations	55%	45	= 100%	(904)
Occupational Associations	33%	67	= 100%	(433)
Unions	20%	80	= 100%	(45)
Education	18%	82	= 100%	(672)
Health	31%	69	= 100%	(516)
Public Interest	64%	36	= 100%	(444)
Identity Groups	32%	68	= 100%	(398)
Social Welfare or Poor	54%	46	= 100%	(104)
State and Local Governments	18%	82	= 100%	(1,293)
Foreign	38%	62	= 100%	(322)
Other	46%	54	= 100%	(995)
Don't Know	64%	36	= 100%	(31)
Total	36%	64	= 100%	(6,157)

Source: *Washington Representatives* directories for 1981 and 2006.

APPENDIX G
DO ONLINE AND OFFLINE POLITICAL ACTIVISTS
DIFFER FROM ONE ANOTHER?

We have shown that offline and online participant publics do not appear appreciably different with respect to socio-economic status (SES). In contrast, the data suggest that the age profile of political participation on the Web differs from the age profile of offline activity.

Standard statistical "F-tests" provide one way to confirm whether there is indeed such a difference between age and SES with respect to the way they are associated with political participation on and off the Internet. F-tests are used in a variety of ways to test for whether there is structural homogeneity or heterogeneity across a series of years in time-series data or a set of groups in cross-sectional data. For example, in studying the relationship between voting and economic conditions, F-tests can be used to see if there are "regime changes"—that is, if the structural relationship (the coefficients of a regression) is the same for one set of years (say, the years before a recession) and another set of years (after the recession). The method can also be used to see if subsets of the coefficients stay the same while others change.

Our case is somewhat unusual in that we have two different dependent variables for the same set of people. We have a five-act measure of participation off the Web and a comparable five-act measure of participation on the Web. But we can "stack" the data so that all the independent variables are repeated for everyone (thus doubling the size of the data set) and use the off-Web participation variable for the first half of the data and the on-Web participation variable for the second half. Then we can see if there is "structural change" between the two data sets. In our case, this means we are asking whether the coefficients on the independent variables are different for offline political participation than for online participation. In every case, we allow offline and online political participation to differ by a constant, but we constrain some or all of the other independent variables to have the same coefficient for offline as for online participation.

The resultant regression results should not be interpreted as causal stories about the relationship between some independent variables and political participation. Rather they should be seen as multivariate descriptions of the correlates of participation for those participating via the Web versus those participating off the Web, and therefore of the demographic characteristics of the two overlapping sets of political activists.

The regressions were done for the whole sample, for those using the Internet, and for those with high-speed Internet.[1] In each case, three different sets of regressions were run:

- *Highly constrained:* one set compared two separate regressions for on-Web acts and off-Web-acts with one regression in which all coefficients for the variables above were constrained to be equal to one another. Our presumption was that we would reject the constraints.

- *Only socio-economic variables constrained:* another set compared two separate regressions for on-Web acts and off-Web acts with a regression in which some but not all coefficients for the variables above were constrained to be equal to one another. In this regression only the coefficients for education and income were constrained. We thought that we would accept these constraints.

- *Socio-economic plus age variables constrained:* a third set compared a regression with constraints on just the income and education variables (the unconstrained equation in this case) with a more constrained regression with constraints on income, education, and age. We thought that we would reject the constraints on age, at least for the whole sample.

Table G.1 summarizes the results of the *F*-tests. As expected, we essentially rejected the notion that a fully constrained model made sense—see rows A, D,

---

1. We employed the following variables in the regressions: education (seven categories—none or grades 1–8, some high school, high school graduate, technical trade or vocational school after high school, some college, college graduate, postgraduate education); income (nine categories—less than $10,000; $10,000–20,000; $20,000–30,000; $30,000–40,000; $40,000–50,000; $50,000–75,000; $75,000–100,000; $100,000–150,000; $150,000 or more); male; female; urban; suburban; rural; religious attendance (five categories indicating the number of times the respondent attends church per year); African American; Latino; all other; and age in seven dummy variable categories (18–25, 26–30, 31–40, 41–50, 51–60, 61–75, 76 and up).

Table G.1 SES and Age Differences in Online and Offline Political Activists: Results of *F*-Tests for Five-Act Measures of Online and Offline Activity

Sample	Equation	*F*-Test Value	Critical Point for .10/.05/.01 Level[a]	Conclusion
All Respondents (3,532)				
A	Null: Fully constrained[b] Alt: Unconstrained	2.450	1.49/1.67/2.04	Rejection: Far too constrained
B	Null: Education and income constrained Alt: Unconstrained	0.706	2.30/3.00/4.61	No rejection: Constraints are acceptable
C	Null: Education, income, and age constrained Alt: Education and income only constrained	2.693	1.77/2.10/2.80	Partial rejection: Additional constraints on age rejected at .05 level
All Web Users (2,816)				
D	Null: Fully constrained[b] Alt: Unconstrained	1.717	1.49/1.67/2.04	Partial rejection: Far too constrained at .05 level

continued

Table G.1 Continued

Sample	Equation	F-Test Value	Critical Point for .10/.05/.01 Level[a]	Conclusion
E	Null: Education and income constrained Alt: Unconstrained	0.803	2.30/3.00/4.61	No rejection: Constraints are acceptable
F	Null: Education, income, and age constrained Alt: Education and income only constrained	1.700	1.77/2.10/2.80	No rejection: Additional constraints on age acceptable
All High-Speed Web Users (2,148)				
G	Null: Fully constrained[b] Alt: Unconstrained	2.461	1.49/1.67/2.04	Rejection: Far too constrained
H	Null: Education and income constrained Alt: Unconstrained	0.908	2.30/3.00/4.61	Acceptance: None of these factors vary
I	Null: Education, income, and age constrained Alt: Education and income only constrained	1.203	1.77/2.10/2.80	No rejection: Additional constraints on age acceptable

Source: Pew Internet and American Life Survey (2008).

[a] Note that F-level values are the same for all three samples because the sample sizes are essentially infinity for an F-test table.
[b] Except for constant allowing for variation in the level of participation.

and G, where the F-values always reject the full constrained model at least at the .05 level and in two cases at the .01 level as well. And, as anticipated, we never rejected the notion that income and education should be constrained across off-Web and on-Web activity (see rows B, E, and H). The F-values are never even significant at the .10 level—indeed their probability values are around .50, which suggests that the constraints on income and education make a great deal of sense.

Finally we tested to see whether it made any sense to impose additional constraints on age. The F-test rejects (at the .05 and almost at the .01 level) any such constraints on age. This is not surprising, because we know from our figures and tables that the age profile of those participating in politics over the Internet is much different from the age profile of those participating in politics using conventional modes. But, as we narrow the sample to include only Web users and then only high-speed Internet users, the constraints on age are not rejected. This suggests that age affects access to the Internet (and thus political participation based on the Internet), but once someone has access to the Internet, there is no difference in how age affects offline or online political activity.

Probably the most important comparisons are among those who use the Internet or e-mail at least occasionally and those who have high-speed Web access at home, because in these two cases we have "controlled" for Web use. When we consider all respondents regardless of Web access, we are probably confusing two processes: the impact of the factors related to Web access and the impact of the factors related to political participation. For these comparisons focusing on those who use the Internet and those who have broadband access, we find that income, education, and age all have similar relationships with offline and online political participation. The bottom line is that income and education appear to have the same stratificational impact for online acts as for offline acts, and there is no evidence that the relationship between Web-based participation, on the one hand, and education or income, on the other, is different from the relationship between offline political participation and these SES factors. In contrast, when it comes to age, the nature of the relationship depends on whether the political activity is Internet-based or engaged in offline. However, this finding no longer holds once we consider Web users or those who have high-speed Internet access. Thus the extent to which the young are less underrepresented with respect to political participation via the Internet is related to their greater likelihood to be Web users rather than to any enhanced propensity to use the Internet politically once on the Web.

INDEX

AARP (formerly American Association of Retired Persons), 131, 145, 272, 333, 410, 523–524, 526
abortion, 243, 246
Abramowitz, Alan I., 252n38, 253n41
Abrams, Samuel J., 236n10, 252nn38–39, 253n41
Abramson, Paul R., 152n10, 566n69
Achen, Christopher H., 141n26, 469n27
Ackerman, Bruce, 558n46, 559nn47–48
Acs, Gregory, 82n37
Adamany, David W., 558n46
Adams, James Truslow, 80–81
Adams, John, 38
Addison, Tony, 234n3, 236n9
African Americans: disenfranchisement and, 16, 40–41, 554, 556; educational inequality and, 137, 580, 617; identity group organizations and, 333–335, 390; income inequality and, 76, 137, 580; intergenerational transmission of inequality and, 192–196; lobbying efforts and, 404, 410–411, 433; political participation and, 137–139,

222, 224, 231, 579; political recruitment and, 471–472, 480–481; surrogate advocacy and, 386–390; unequal political voice and, 23–24, 137–138, 219; views of equality and, 55
age: campaign contributions and, 218, 226–229, 576; campaign meeting attendance and, 226–229; campaign work and, 217–218, 226–229; civic skills and, 212, 214, 219, 221–222, 224; contacting government officials and, 218, 226–228; Internet and, 203, 486, 493, 498–502, 505–506, 508–509, 511–512, 514, 531–533, 582; opinion about educational funding and, 207–209; opinion about gay rights and, 205–207; opinion about sex on television and, 205–206; opinion about Social Security and, 207–208; partisanship and, 213, 222, 228–229; persuading other voters and, 228–229; political voice and, 23, 576, 580; protests and, 217–218, 227; psychological engagement with politics and,